God's Grace Inscribed on the Human Heart

Essays in Honour of
James R. Harrison

Edited by Peter G. Bolt and Sehyun Kim

SCD Press
2022

God's Grace Inscribed on the Human Heart
Essays in Honour of James R. Harrison
(Early Christian Studies, 23)
Edited by Peter G. Bolt and Sehyun Kim
© 2022, SCD Press and authors

SCD Press
PO Box 1882
Macquarie Centre NSW 2113
Australia
scdpress@scd.edu.au

All rights reserved. No part of this book may be reproduced or transmitted in any form or by any means, electronic or mechanical, including photocopying, recording or by any information and storage system without permission in writing from the publishers.

ISBN-13: 978-1-925730-33-3 (paperback)
ISBN-13: 978-1-925730-34-0 (ebook)

Layout and design by: Lankshear Design Pty Ltd
Printed and bound by: Ingram Spark

God's Grace Inscribed on the Human Heart

Essays in Honour of
James R. Harrison

Edited by Peter G. Bolt and Sehyun Kim

SCD Press
2022

Early Christian Studies 23

SCD Press Editorial Board

Professor Stephen Smith

Professor James R. Harrison

Professor Peter G. Bolt

Additional Series Editors

Professor Pauline Allen (Australian Catholic University)

Professor Wendy Mayer (Australian Lutheran College)

Professor Bronwen Neil (Macquarie University)

Early Christian Studies

1. Jan Harm Barkhuizen, *Proclus Bishop of Constantinople. Homilies on the Life of Christ* (2001).
2. Robert C. Hill, *Theodoret of Cyrus. Commentary on the Song of Songs* (2001).
3. Johan Ferreira, *The Hymn of the Pearl* (2002).
4. Alistair Stewart-Sykes, *The Life of Polycarp. An anonymous vita from third-century Smyrna* (2002).
5. Daniel Van Slyke, *Quodvultdeus of Carthage. The Apocalyptic Theology of a Roman African in Exile* (2003).
6. Bronwen Neil & Pauline Allen, *The Life of Maximus the Confessor. Recension 3* (2003).
7. George Kalantzis, *Theodore of Mopsuestia. Commentary on the Gospel of John* (2004).
8. Rudolf Brändle, *John Chrysostom. Bishop – Reformer – Martyr* (2004).
9. J. Mark Armitage, *A Twofold Solidarity. Leo the Great's Theology of Redemption* (2005).
10. Alistair Stewart-Sykes, *The Apostolic Church Order. The Greek Text with Introduction, Translation and Annotation* (2006, 2021).
11. Geoffrey D. Dunn, *Cyprian and the Bishops of Rome: Questions of Papal Primacy in the Early Church* (2007, 2018).
12. Pauline Allen, Majella Franzmann, & Rick Strelan (eds.), *"I Sowed Fruits into Hearts" (Odes Sol. 17:13). Festschrift for Professor Michael Lattke* (2007).
13. David Luckensmeyer & Pauline Allen (eds.), *Studies of Religion and Politics in the Early Christian Centuries* (2010).
14. Oliver Herbel, *Sarapion of Thmuis: Against the Manicheans and Pastoral Letters* (2011).

15. Raymond Laird, *Mindset, Moral Choice and Sin in the Anthropology of John Chrysostom* (2012, 2017).
16. Alexander L. Abecina, *Time and Sacramentality in Gregory of Nyssa's Contra Eunomium* (2013).
17. Johan Ferreira, *Early Chinese Christianity: The Tang Christian Monument and Other Documents* (2014).
18. Wendy Mayer & Ian J. Elmer (eds.), *Men and Women in the Early Christian Centuries* (2014).
19. Silouan Fotineas, *The Letters of Bishop Basil of Caesarea: Instruments of Communion* (2018).
20. Andrey Romanov, *One God as One God and One Lord. The Lordship of Jesus Christ as a Hermeneutical Key to Paul's Christology in 1 Corinthians (with a special focus on 1 Cor 8:6)* (2021).
21. Hyueng Guen Choi, *Charity and the Letters of Barsanuphius and John of Gaza* (2020).
22. Alistair C. Stewart, *The Canons of Hippolytus. An English version, with introduction and annotation and an accompanying Arabic Text* (2021).
23. Peter G. Bolt and Sehyun Kim (eds.), *God's Grace Inscribed on the Human Heart. Essays in Honour of James R. Harrison.* (2022).

Contributors

Peter Arzt-Grabner, Professor of Papyrology, Dept of Biblical Studies and Ecclesiastical History, University of Salzburg, Austria. He is main editor of the series 'Papyrologische Kommentare zum Neuen Testament', in which he has also authored vol. 1, *Philemon* (2003), and vol. 4, *2. Korinther* (2014).

Richard S. Ascough is Professor of New Testament in the School of Religion at Queen's University in Kingston, Canada. He has written extensively on the formation of Christ groups and Graeco-Roman religious culture, having published more than fifty articles and essays along with thirteen books, including *1 and 2 Thessalonians: Encountering the Christ Group at Thessalonike* (2014) and *Early Christ Groups and Greco-Roman Associations: Organizational Models and Social Practices* (2022).

Paul Barnett has combined pastoral with academic ministries, having served in three congregations and lectured at Moore College, Regent College and Macquarie and Sydney Universities. He has written on New Testament history and texts.

Stephen C. Barton is an Honorary Fellow of the Department of Theology and Religion, Durham University and Honorary Research Fellow of the Department of Religions and Theology, Manchester University. He studied in the School of History at Macquarie University, Sydney, the Department of Religious Studies at Lancaster University, UK, and King's College London where he gained his doctorate in New Testament Studies. He was Tutor in Biblical Studies at Salisbury and Wells Theological College between 1984 and 1988. From 1988 to 2010, he was Lecturer (and subsequently Reader) in New Testament in the Department of Theology and Religion at Durham University. His publications include *The Spirituality of the Gospels* (London: SPCK, 1992); *Discipleship and Family Ties in Mark and Matthew* (Cambridge: CUP, 1994); *Invitation to the Bible*

(London: SPCK, 1997); and *Life Together. Family, Sexuality and Community in the New Testament and Today* (Edinburgh: T&T Clark, 2001). Volumes he has edited include, *The Family in Theological Perspective* (Edinburgh: T&T Clark, 1996); *Holiness Past and Present* (Edinburgh: T&T Clark, 2003); *The Cambridge Companion to the Gospels* (Cambridge: CUP, 2006; second edition, with Todd Brewer, 2021); and, with David Wilkinson, *Reading Genesis After Darwin* (New York: OUP, 2009). Currently, he is co-editing, with Andrew Byers, a multi-authored collection of essays, *One God, One People: Oneness, Unity and Christian Origins* (Atlanta: SBL Press, forthcoming).

Bradley J. Bitner (PhD, Macquarie University) is Associate Professor of New Testament at Westminster Seminary California.

Darrell L. Bock is Senior Research Professor of New Testament Studies at Dallas Theological Seminary in Dallas, Texas. He also serves as Executive Director of Cultural Engagement for the Seminary's Center for Christian Leadership. His special fields of study involve hermeneutics, the use of the Old Testament in the New, Luke-Acts, the historical Jesus, Gospel studies and the integration of theology and culture. He has served on the board of Chosen People Ministries for over a decade and also serves on the board at Wheaton College. He is a graduate of the University of Texas (B.A.), Dallas Theological Seminary (Th.M.), and the University of Aberdeen (Ph.D.). He has had four annual stints of postdoctoral study at the University of Tübingen, the second through fourth as an Alexander von Humboldt scholar (1989-90, 1995-96, 2004-05, 2010-2011). He also serves as elder emeritus at Trinity Fellowship Church in Richardson, Texas, is a writer for *Christianity Today*, served as President of the Evangelical Theological Society for the year 2000-2001, and has authored over forty books, including a New York Times Best Seller in non-fiction and award winning commentaries on Luke and Ephesians. He is married to Sally and has three married children (two daughters and a son), three grandsons and two granddaughters.

Peter G. Bolt is the Director of Academic Strategy at Sydney College of Divinity, the Director of the Centre for Gospels and Acts Research, and the editor of the *Journal of Gospel and Acts Research*. His publications on the Gospels include *Jesus' Defeat of Death. Persuading Mark's Early Readers* (2003), *The Cross from a Distance. Atonement in Mark's Gospel* (2004), *Matthew: A Great Light Dawns* (2014), and *The Narrative Integrity of Mark 13:24–27* (2021).

Cilliers Breytenbach, Dr. theol. (Munich 1983), Dr. theol. habil. (Munich 1986), Professor for New Testament in Berlin (1990–2019), Professor Extraordinary for New Testament and for Ancient Studies at Stellenbosch University (since 2003), co-founding director of the *Berlin Graduate School of Ancient Studies* (2010–2020). Author of *Grace, Reconciliation and Concord* (Leiden 2010), *The Gospel of Mark as Episodic Narrative* (Leiden 2021), Co-author of *Early Christianity in Lycaonia* (Leiden 2018), and *Early Christianity in Athens and Attica* (Leiden 2022).

Alan H. Cadwallader is a Research Professor at the Australian Centre for Christianity and Culture at Charles Sturt University in Canberra. Recent monographs have been *Beyond the Word of a Woman* (ATF, 2008), *Fragments of Colossae* (ATF, 2015), *The Politics of the Revised Version* (T&T Clark, 2019). He has edited a number of volumes on the interface of early Christianity, ancient culture, and contemporary issues: *Colossae in Space and Time* (V & R, 2011), *Pieces of Ease and Grace* (ATF, 2013), *Where the Wild Ox Roams* (Sheffield Phoenix, 2013), and *Stones, Bones and the Sacred* (SBL, 2016). He is currently completing an Earth Bible commentary on Mark's Gospel and a new monograph on Colossae and the letters to the Colossians and Philemon.

Constantine R. Campbell (PhD, Macquarie) is Professor and Associate Research Director at Sydney College of Divinity. He is the author of several monographs on the apostle Paul and on Ancient Greek.

Doru Costache is Associate Professor in Patristic Studies with the Sydney College of Divinity, currently lecturing for two SCD colleges, Nisibis and St Cyril's. He also is Honorary Associate of Department of Studies in Religion at the University of Sydney, as well as Selby Old Fellow in Religious History of the Orthodox Christian Faith at the University of Sydney's Fisher Library (2021–2022). Moreover, he is the ISCAST Research Director and a member of the International Association of Patristic Studies and of the North American Patristics Society. Author of *Humankind and the Cosmos: Early Christian Representations* (Brill, 2021) and co-author of *Dreams, Virtue and Divine Knowledge in Early Christian Egypt* (Cambridge, 2019).

John A. Davies is an Honorary Research Associate of the Sydney College of Divinity and Principal Emeritus of Christ College, Sydney, where he taught biblical studies. He holds the degrees of MA (Hons) and PhD from the University of Sydney and MDiv from Westminster Theological Seminary, Philadelphia. His publications include *A Royal Priesthood* (2004), *A Study Commentary on 1 King*s (2012), *Unless Someone Shows Me* (2015), *Lift Up Your Heads* (2018), and *Heaven— Ain't Goin' There: A Down-to-Earth Look at Eternal Life* (2019).

Kathy Ehrensperger is Research Professor of New Testament in Jewish Perspective at the Abraham Geiger Kolleg, University of Potsdam. Among her publications are *Paul and the Dynamics of Power* (2008), *Paul at the Crossroads of Cultures* (2013), *Searching Paul. Conversations with the Jewish Apostle to the Nations* (2019), *Gender and Second Temple Judaism* (2020, ed. with Shayna Sheinfeld), as well as numerous articles in edited volumes and journals. She is the Executive Editor of the *Encyclopedia of Jewish-Christian Relations*.

Joseph D. Fantin is professor of New Testament at Dallas Theological Seminary where he has taught since 2003. He has published monographs on Greek Grammar and Roman Imperial ideology and Paul. His research interests include the first-century world, Greek language and linguistics, exegetical method, and exegesis of the Gospel of John and Hebrews.

Louise A. Gosbell is Principal and Lecturer in New Testament at Mary Andrews College in Sydney. Louise completed her PhD at Macquarie University in 2015. Louise's PhD thesis, '"The Poor, the Crippled, the Blind, and the Lame": Physical and Sensory Disability in the Gospels of the New Testament' was published with Mohr Siebeck in 2018. Louise continues to publish in the overlap of disability and biblical studies as well as sensory studies and the New Testament. Louise has forthcoming entries on disability in the *Dictionary of Paul and His Letters*, the *Routledge Handbook of Marginalization and the Bible*, as well as the *Routledge Handbook of Interdisciplinary Approaches to Biblical Studies*.

Edwin A. Judge is Emeritus Professor of History at Macquarie University, being a classics graduate from both New Zealand and Cambridge. A social study of the early christian groups won him the Hulsean prize at Cambridge and a Doctorate of Letters at New Zealand. At Berkeley, California, he held a chair jointly in Classics and History.

Rosalinde Kearsley is currently an Honorary Senior Research Fellow in the Department of History and Archaeology at Macquarie University following over thirty years as a member of academic staff in the Department of Ancient History. Much of her research has focused on the Graeco-Roman cities in Asia Minor and the cultural context of early church groups there.

Sehyun Kim (PhD, Sheffield), Lecturer of Sydney College of Divinity Korean School of Theology since 2016, and recently appointed Principal. His PhD thesis, *The Kingship of Jesus in the Gospel of John* was published with Pickwick in 2018. His research interests include New Testament Christology, Greek language, and critical theories and New Testament exegesis.

John S. Kloppenborg holds the rank of University Professor at the University of Toronto and is a fellow of the Royal Society of Canada. He has published widely in the field of synoptic studies, social history of Mediterranean antiquity, and the letter of James. His most recent publications are *James* (New Testament Guides, 2022), *Christ's Associations: Connecting and Belonging in the Ancient City* (2019), Vols. I and III of *Greco-Roman Associations: Texts, Translations, and Commentary* (with R. Ascough, 2011, 2020) and *Q, The Earliest Gospel: An Introduction to the Original Sayings and Stories of Jesus* (2008).

Peter Lampe Prof. Dr. theol. Dr. habil., Chair of New Testament Theology/History of Early Christianity at the University of Heidelberg, Germany, since 1999; Hon. Prof. at the Universiteit van die Vrystaat, South Africa; previously professorial chairs at the University of Kiel, Germany (1992–1999, also dean), and Union Theol. Seminary in Virginia (1987–1992). Some of the fields of research: Social History of Early Christianity, Early Christian archaeology (field project in Phrygia), (socio-) psychological interpretation of early Christian texts, research on emotions in both ancient texts and reader responses (also empirically). Pauline Studies, Montanism.

Stephen Llewelyn is a retired teacher from the former Ancient History Department, Macquarie University, where he taught Hebrew Language and the History of Ancient Israel. He was also the editor of the series *New Documents Illustrating Early Christianity*, volumes 6–10. In the latter part of his career and now in retirement he has shown a strong interest in encouraging younger scholars to advance their research skills and profiles.

Harry O. Maier is Professor of New Testament and Early Christian Studies at Vancouver School of Theology, Canada and a Fellow of the Max Weber Center for Advanced Cultural and Social Studies at the University of Erfurt. Amongst many other works, he has published *New Testament Christianity in the Roman Empire* (2018), *Picturing Paul in Empire: Imperial Image, Text, and Persuasion in Colossians, Ephesians, and the Pastoral Epistles* (2013), and most recently, *Experiencing the Shepherd of Hermas,* coedited with Angela Kim Harkins (2022).

Peter Oakes is Rylands Professor of Biblical Criticism and Exegesis at the University of Manchester, where he has taught since 1997. His publications include *Philippians: From People to Letter* (SNTSMS; Cambridge: CUP, 2001); *Reading Romans in Pompeii: Paul's Letter at Ground Level* (Minneapolis: Fortress/London: SPCK, 2009); *Galatians* (Paideia Commentaries; Grand Rapids: Baker Academic, 2015); *Empire, Economics, and the New Testament* (Grand Rapids: Eerdmans, 2020); and, with Andrew K. Boakye, *Rethinking Galatians: Paul's Vision of Oneness in the Living Christ* (London: Bloomsbury T&T Clark, 2021).

Julien M. Ogereau (PhD, 2014) studied Theology, New Testament, and Early Christian Studies at the Sydney College of Divinity and Macquarie University, Sydney. He was a research associate with the Excellence Cluster 264 Topoi at Humboldt-Universität zu Berlin from 2014 to 2016, a LMUexcellent Research Fellow at Ludwig-Maximilians-Universität München from 2017 to 2018, and has been a Senior Researcher at the University of Vienna since 2019. His publications include *Paul's Koinonia with the Philippians* (Mohr Siebeck, 2014), *Authority and Identity in Emerging Christianities in Asia Minor and Greece* co-edited with C. Breytenbach (Brill, 2018), and *Early Christianity in Macedonia* (Brill, forthcoming).

Neil Ormerod works in the Research Office of the Sydney College of Divinity in the area of research quality. Previously he was Professor of Theology at Australian Catholic University for fourteen years. He has published fourteen books and over ninety articles in theological journals, including *Theological Studies, Irish Theological Quarterly, Gregorianum* and *Louvain Studies*. His research interests include the doctrine of the Trinity, Christology and Ecclesiology. He is recognised internationally for his expertise in the thought of Bernard Lonergan.

Mark Reasoner received his BA degree from Bethel College in St. Paul, Minnesota; MDiv and MA in New Testament degrees from Trinity Evangelical Divinity School; and PhD in New Testament and Early Christian Literature from the University of Chicago. He taught at his alma mater, now called Bethel University, for about twenty years, and then since 2010 has taught at Marian University in Indianapolis, Indiana, where he is Professor of Biblical Theology. His friendship with Jim Harrison began in November of 2004 when they met at the SBL meeting in San Antonio, Texas.

E. Randolph Richards is the Research Professor of New Testament at Palm Beach Atlantic University, having previously served there as dean and then provost. He has written, co-written or edited over a dozen books and dozens of articles, including *The Secretary in the Letters of Paul* (WUNT) and *Misreading Scripture with Western Eyes* (IVP). Among his current projects, he is co-editing with Jim Harrison, *Inscriptions, Graffiti, Documentary Papyri* (ALNTS 10) and is writing two volumes on *John* (Word Biblical Commentary).

William Robinson is an independent researcher based in London.

Guy MacLean Rogers studied Classics and Ancient History at the University of Pennsylvania and University College London. He received his PhD in Classics from Princeton University. He has taught Ancient History at Wellesley College since 1985, where he was Chairman of the Department of History from 1997–2001. In 1997 he was a Visiting Fellow of All Souls College Oxford and in 2003 he received the Perennial Wisdom Medal of the Monuments Conservancy of New York City. His most recent book, *For the Freedom of Zion: The Great Revolt of Jews Against Romans, 66–74 CE* was published by Yale University Press in 2022.

Benjamin Schliesser is Associate Professor for the Literature and Theology of the New Testament at the Theological Faculty of the University of Bern, Switzerland.

Isaac T. Soon is Assistant Professor of Religious Studies (New Testament) at Crandall University. He has degrees from the University of Oxford and Durham University. His first monograph entitled A Disabled Apostle is forthcoming with Oxford University Press.

Mark Stephens joined the faculty at Sydney Missionary and Bible College in 2021 as lecturer in New Testament. His primary areas of teaching include the Gospels, Pauline Theology, and the book of Revelation. Before coming to SMBC, Mark spent over a decade lecturing in theology and integrative studies at Excelsia College, Sydney, before a two-year stint serving as a Senior Research Fellow at the Centre for Public Christianity. His doctoral studies focused on the theme of new creation within the book of Revelation, and his thesis, *Annihilation or Renewal? The Meaning and Function of New Creation in the Book of Revelation*, was published by Mohr Siebeck (2011).

Michael Trainor is senior lecturer in biblical studies with the Australian Catholic University and parish priest of the Adelaide western suburb parish of Lockleys in the Archdiocese of Adelaide, South Australia. He holds an MA in biblical literature and languages (Chicago), MEd (Boston) and DTheol (Melbourne). His area of specialisation is the study of the New Testament and its relevance for our contemporary world, ecology, and pastoral life. His latest books include *About Earth's Children: An Ecological Listening to the Acts of the Apostles* (Bloomsbury/T.&T.Clark, 2020), *About Earth's Child: An Ecological Listening to the Gospel of Luke* (Sheffield, 2012), *The Body of Jesus and Sexual Abuse: How the Gospel Passion Narratives inform a Pastoral Response* (Wipf & Stock, 2015), and *Owning and Consuming: Neo-Liberalism and the Biblical Voice* (Routledge, 2018—co-authored with Prof Paul Babie of Adelaide University Law School). Michael is also a contributor to *Enabling Dialogue about the Land: A Resource Book for Jews and Christians* (Paulist, 2021).

Paul Trebilco is Professor of New Testament Studies and Head of the Theology Programme, University of Otago, Dunedin, New Zealand. He is the author of *Jewish Communities in Asia Minor* (1991), *The Early Christians in Ephesus from Paul to Ignatius* (2004), *Self-designations and Group Identity in the New Testament* (2012), and *Outsider Designations and Boundary Construction in the New Testament: Early Christian Communities and the Formation of Group Identity* (2017).

Samuel Vollenweider is Emeritus Professor of New Testament Studies in Zurich (Switzerland). His research interests encompass the area of antiquity and Christianity, the reception history of the Bible, and the relations between science and cultural disciplines. His recent publications include studies on Paul and on Early Christian theology: *Horizonte neutestamentlicher Christologie* (Tübingen: Mohr Siebeck, 2003); *Antike und Urchristentum. Studien zur neutestamentlichen Theologie in ihren Kontexten und Rezeptionen* (Tübingen: Mohr Siebeck, 2020).

L. L. Welborn is Professor of New Testament and Early Christianity at Fordham University. He is the author of *Politics and Rhetoric in the Corinthian Epistles* (1997), *Paul, the Fool of Christ* (2005), *An End to Enmity: Paul and the 'Wrongdoer' of Second Corinthians* (2011), and *The Young Against the Old: Generational Conflict in First Clement* (2018). He is editor of the book series *Synkrisis: Comparative Approaches to Early Christianity in Greco-Roman Culture* (Yale University Press).

Preface

This volume was presented to James R. Harrison on 28 September 2022, five weeks prior to his seventieth birthday and on the eve of his impending retirement as Research Director of the Sydney College of Divinity.

James R. Harrison has been Professor of Biblical Studies and the Research Director at the Sydney College of Divinity, Australia, since 2013. Formerly he was the Head of Theology at Wesley Institute, Drummoyne, from 2002–2012, having taught there as a senior lecturer from 1998. Prior to his appointment at Wesley Institute, he was the Director of the School of Christian Studies at Robert Menzies College, Macquarie University, 2000–2001.

After gaining a Bachelor of Arts and a Diploma of Education from Macquarie University (1976), Jim began his professional career as a high school history teacher in both city and country. His thesis on *The Role of Joel's Prophecy in Luke-Acts in Its Graeco-Roman Religious Context* earned him a Master of Arts from Macquarie University (1990), and his thesis on *Paul's Language of Grace* (*charis*) *in Its Graeco-Roman Context* then not only gave him a Macquarie University PhD (1997), but after it was published (2003), an award winning book (2005). Apparently always writing and editing, with plenty more to follow, Jim's extensive output is characteristically grounded in the primary source analysis, and particularly the inscriptional evidence, for which he has become well-known.

When we issued invitations to contribute to this celebratory volume, we were overwhelmed with the enthusiastic responses we received. Not only were Jim's friends and colleagues over the years willing to offer quality essays, but their many comments showed their high regard for Jim's work as well as great warmth towards him personally.

It has been a delight to be able to work on this volume. Those who know his humility (or his work!) know that Jim has no desire to be elevated as some great man to a scholarly celebrity circuit, nor to boast about his many achievements. Fittingly, his academic work began with a study of God's grace. His life adds its further testimony to the work of Christ in our midst. There is much that can be said about what was inscribed in stone in the ancient world, and still more to say after Jim's contributions! But the apostolic gospel inscribes a different kind of commendation.

> Are we beginning to commend ourselves again? Or do we need, like some, letters of recommendation to you or from you? You yourselves are our letter, written on our hearts, known and read by everyone. You show that you are Christ's letter, delivered by us, not written with ink but with the Spirit of the living God—not on tablets of stone but on tablets of human hearts. (2 Cor. 3:1–3).

Peter G. Bolt
Sehyun Kim

Contents

GRACE BEHIND PAUL 1

John A. Davies	The A to Z of God's Grace Inscribed on the Human Heart: Psalm 119	3
Stephen Llewelyn and William Robinson	The Salt Parable (Mark 9:50, Par. Matthew 5:13 and Luke 14:34–35)	19
Mark Stephens	Jesus and the Possibilities of Humour	45
Doru Costache	Burning Hearts. Emmaus as Realised Eschatology in the *Philokalic* Tradition	61
Peter G. Bolt	The Doctor, the High Priest, the Aristocrat, and the Apostle	79
Darrell L. Bock	A Note Tracing a Theme: John 6:45 and Being Taught by God	109

GRACE THROUGH PAUL 117

E. Randolph Richards	Greek Shorthand in the Time of the New Testament	119
Michael Trainor	The Jews of Ancient Rome: Their Burial Inscriptions and Implications for Paul's Letter to the Romans	143
Paul Trebilco	The Human Heart, the Centre of a Person, and the Holy Spirit (Galatians 4:6; Romans 5:5; and 2 Corinthians 1:22)	155
Mark Reasoner	Reading Romans 9 on Election with the Rabbis and the Greek Fathers	171

Benjamin Schliesser	Can Faith Be Measured? Paul's Phrase 'The Measure of Faith' Reconsidered (Rom. 12:3)	189
Richard S. Ascough	Paul in Illyricum	211
John S. Kloppenborg	Intimations of Democracy in Early Christ Groups	227
L. L. Welborn	The Materiality of Grace: Paul's Collection for the Poor	241
Louise A. Gosbell	Charis, Charisms and the 'Greater Gifts' in 1 Corinthians 12	271
Stephen C. Barton	'But by the Grace of God I Am What I Am' (1 Corinthians 15:10a): Pauline Identity in Theological Perspective	293
Bradley J. Bitner	Grace, Gratitude, and Glory In 2 Corinthians 4:15	309
Paul Barnett	Ephesian Mysteries	331
Joseph D. Fantin	Adoption into the Family of God: Ephesians 1:5 in Light of Roman Adoption	341
Constantine R. Campbell	Grace and Faith in Ephesians 2:8–10: Engaging Barclay and Bates	371
Peter Oakes	The Value of the Local	387
Samuel Vollenweider	Christ and Alexander the Great. Philippians 2 Compared with Plutarch's Tractate *De Alexandri Magni Fortuna Aut Virtute*	399
Kathy Ehrensperger	'Become Fellow-Imitators together with Me' (Phil 3:17): Embodying Christ in the Face of Enemies of the Cross	421

| Alan H. Cadwallader | Greetings in Stone: Shifting the Accent from Papyri to Epigraphy in Colossians 4:15–17 | 441 |
| Julien M. Ogereau | Πίστις, Ἀγάπη, and Ἐλπίς in 1 Thessalonians: New Insights from Old Stones | 467 |

Grace After Paul ... 485

Cilliers Breytenbach	Virtues in New Testament Letters and Corresponding Names on Early Christian Sepulchral Epitaphs in *ICG*	487
Rosalinde Kearsley	Antioch, Rome, and 1 Peter	505
Guy MacLean Rogers	Alexander and the High Priest	531
Harry O. Maier	Reading the *Shepherd Of Hermas* with Roman Eyes: Urbanity, Self, and Emergent Neighbourhood Religion in the Imperial Capital	543
Peter Arzt-Grabner	The Literal Meaning of the Most Common Epistolary Greeting— and How Seriously We Should Take It	561
Peter Lampe	Christian Women in Oxyrhynchus and Environs (2nd–6th Century C.E.)	577
Isaac T. Soon	Raised in Pieces: Resurrection and Disability in the Ezekiel Cycle of the Dura-Europos Synagogue	611
Neil Ormerod	The Language of Grace	627
Edwin A. Judge	On Finding One's Way in Ancient History	639

Publications of James R. Harrison ... 657

GRACE BEHIND PAUL

The A to Z of God's Grace Inscribed on the Human Heart:
Psalm 119

John A. Davies

'Grant what you command, and command what you will.'
— Saint Augustine

Abstract

The longest Psalm, with its echoes of Israel's Compassion Creed, is a celebration of God's grace bestowed in his revelation of himself, his will for humanity, and his empowerment of his people to live in harmony with his purposes.

It is a pleasure to offer this paper to Prof. James Harrison who has done much to enrich our understanding of grace.

The expansive Psalm 119 is rarely read in its entirety, at least in a public context. It is something to be dipped into for scattered gems about God's word. Yet we may be losing something of its force when we treat it as a catena of isolated thoughts, randomly strung together. Structured as an acrostic poem with each group of eight verses beginning with the same letter of the Hebrew alphabet,[1] it boldly proclaims its comprehensive scope on that which it declares. While we would be

---

1   The choice of an eight-verse stanza for each letter may have been suggested by the eight words used for 'law, commandment' repeated throughout (see below), though the creative writer does not mechanically use all eight in every stanza.

disappointed if we tried to treat it as a sustained theological argument, as, say, Paul's letter to the Romans, there is a great deal we can learn if we view it as a kaleidoscope of what a pious Israelite believed about their God and their relationship with him.[2] While there are points of tension within the poem, it may be these very tensions that lie at the heart of Israelite religion.

But why the 'A to Z of God's *grace*'? At a casual glance, the poem may not seem to say much about grace. Within its 176 verses, there is no instance of the word sometimes translated 'grace' or 'favour' (*ḥen*), which in fact is only found twice in the Psalter, and then only once with reference to the grace God bestows (Ps. 84:11 [Heb. 12]). The cognate verb *ḥanan* 'be gracious, show favour' is found three times in Ps. 119 (vv. 29,58,132), each time as a request of the psalmist for divine grace. Once it is paired with the appeal, 'I implore your favor with all my heart' (v. 58),[3] where 'implore your favor' (*ḥilliti paneka*) is literally 'entreat your face', the action of a suppliant. The psalmist brings his 'supplication' (v. 170) before YHWH where the word for supplication (*teḥinnah*, related to *ḥanan*) means an appeal for grace. Of the three requests for grace with the verb *ḥanan*, the first (v. 29) is the most striking and perhaps the most easily overlooked because in translations the grace element is sometimes relegated to adverbial status modifying another verb. NRSV reads 'graciously teach me (*ḥonneni*) your law'.[4] While *ḥanan* normally takes a personal object ('be gracious to someone'), it is construed here unusually with a double object (personal and impersonal) as in Genesis 33:5 where Jacob tells Esau of 'the children whom God has graciously given (*ḥanan*) your servant'. YHWH's law is given as a manifestation of his grace. *The Message* comes close to capturing it with 'grace me with your clear revelation'. It is not that the psalmist lacks access to YHWH's revelation. He has much to say about

---

2 For the intricate structure and careful artistry of the poetry, and major studies on the psalm generally, see Soll, *Psalm 119*; Freedman, *Psalm 119*; Reynolds, *Torah*.
3 Unless otherwise stated, Bible quotations are from the NRSV.
4 The Syriac version, perhaps feeling awkward about this use of *ḥanan*, rendered it 'teach me' which may have influenced English translations which inject the notion of teaching (NIV, NRSV).

it and gives every indication he is familiar with it.⁵ Rather, as the parallel colon suggests, 'Put false ways far from me', his request is for Yhwh to grant him the ability to take this revelation to heart and have it shape his life, 'the grace of living by your law' (REB). To have his message internalised, for it to be part of one's fabric, such that the one who has the law is an embodiment of its teaching, is the great blessing God's people enjoy.

The psalm is sometimes classified as a torah psalm (cf. Psalms 1, 19) or more generally as a wisdom psalm,⁶ though it also contains elements of praise, lament, and supplication. It begins in a similar vein to another torah / wisdom psalm, Psalm 1: 'Happy are those whose way is blameless, who walk in the law of the Lord' (Ps. 119:1). For some theological traditions this immediately raises the issue: Is this an empty set? Has the psalmist depicted an unrealisable ideal? Are there in fact any who are 'blameless'? Well, this psalmist for one. He has 'an upright heart' (v. 7); he has 'chosen the way of faithfulness' (v. 30); he clings to and keeps Yhwh's decrees (vv. 22,31,129,157,167,168); he has 'done what is just and right' (v. 121). He runs 'the way of your commandments' (v. 32); he commits to 'keep your law continually' (v. 44); he claims not to 'turn away from your law' (v. 51); he has 'kept your precepts' (v. 56) and 'your word' (v. 67); he does 'not forget your law' (v. 153). A sustained section (*mem*, 97–104), declares his unswerving commitment to observing Yhwh's instruction. He loves Yhwh's law and meditates on it (or recites it) constantly (v. 97; cf. vv. 15,27). He not only understands it better than his venerable teachers (vv. 99,100), but he avoids evil in all its forms and keeps Yhwh's precepts (vv. 100–102).

Such adherence to Yhwh's instruction as the psalmist commends is no restrictive imposition. Rather it broadens one's understanding and gives liberty (vv. 32,45,96). Yhwh's commands are a blessing to be treasured (vv. 11,162). No mere outward performance of duty is in

---

5   I am following convention in using 'he' for the implied author of the psalm and this is suggested by the references to 'your servant' and perhaps the youth of v. 9. The writer has adopted a persona, such that while the poem is not necessarily autobiographical of the real author, it reflects the typical attitude of the pious living in trying times.
6   See Perdue, *Wisdom*, 305; Allen, *Psalms*, 139; deClaissé-Walford, *Psalms*, 870.

view, but a totally willing commitment: 'Happy are those who keep his decrees, who seek him with their whole heart' (v. 2). The psalmist claims that his own observance is 'with my whole heart' (v. 69), that his heart is 'upright' (v. 7). Yhwh's commandments are the object of his admiration and longing (vv. 6,15,18,20,40,131). He has confidence in Yhwh's revelation (vv. 42,66). Using a range of vocabulary, he declares Yhwh's disclosure of his will a constant joy and delight (vv. 14,16,24, 35,47,70,74,77,92,102,111,143,162,174).[7] He loves the commandments 'more than gold' (v. 127; cf. vv. 47,48,72,97,113,119,159,163) and reaches a superlative note: 'My soul keeps your decrees; I love them exceedingly' (v. 167). Yhwh's words are 'sweeter than honey to my mouth', informing the psalmist's worldview and values system (vv. 103–104). Conversely, he is emotionally affected because of those who forsake Yhwh's law. His 'eyes shed streams of tears because your law is not kept' (v. 136; cf. vv. 53,139). He will not be ashamed to speak of Yhwh's decrees before kings (v. 46). They are cause for bursting into song giving praise to Yhwh (vv. 7,13,54), even getting him out of bed in the middle of the night to do so (vv. 62,148,172). For this psalmist there is clearly a strong affective element to his commitment.

That with which the psalmist has been 'graced' is Yhwh's law, or more broadly, his instruction (*torah*, v. 29). This word occurs 25 times throughout the psalm (vv. 1,18,29,34,44,51,53,55,61,70,72,77,85, 92,97,109,113,126,136,142,150,153,163,165,174). *Torah* is connected with a verb *yarah* 'show, teach' (used in vv. 33,102 of Yhwh's instruction of the psalmist) and while it often includes the idea of prescriptive commands, *torah* may encompass any form of teaching. Throughout the psalm, it seems to carry the sense of an 'instruction manual' for life, which, as well as commands, includes encouragements, models, and advice for living as a creature of God (v. 73) in the world he has made and controls by his word (vv. 89–91).[8]

---

7 Burt, 'Your Torah', notes the emphasis on 'delight' as a key theme of the poem.
8 To this, Dahood would add v. 57, understanding ḥ-l-q-y as vocative 'My Creator': Dahood, *Psalms III*, 180. For the interpretation of Yhwh's 'word' exercising governance, see Booij, 'Psalm 119, 89–91'. Further, v. 4 may be translated, 'You have commanded your precepts to keep diligent watch'. While generally translated as a passive, 'to be kept', the verb, as it stands in MT is active.

The psalmist also uses as a close synonym the more general word *dabar* (24 times), often translated 'word', but meaning any item of communication. Sometimes it bears the nuance 'promise', the source of hope for the psalmist (vv. 25,28,49,65,74,81,107,114,147). At other times the context suggests it is used (in the singular or plural) for a body of commandments to be kept (vv. 9,16,17,43,57,101,105,130,13 9,160,161,169). When the psalmist has an 'answer' (*dabar*, v. 42) for his taunter, because of his trust in YHWH's 'word' (*dabar*), it could be any aspect of God's revelation that meets the occasion.

Similarly the word *'imrah* 'utterance, saying' (19 times) is sometimes used in the sense of promise: 'Confirm to your servant your promise, which is for those who fear you' (v. 38; cf. vv. 41,50,58,76,82, 116,123,140,148,154,170,172). More rarely, *'imrah* has the sense of 'command': 'I look at the faithless with disgust, because they do not keep your commands (*'imrateka*)' (v. 158; cf. v. 67).[9] Several times the psalmist speaks of how he values YHWH's speech where it is not easy to tell if he has either nuance (or some other) particularly in mind: 'How sweet are your words (*'imrateka*) to my taste' (v. 103; cf. vv. 11,162).

Other words for God's valued revelation refer more explicitly to prescriptive speech. They include YHWH's ordinances (*mišpaṭim*, 23 times: vv. 7,13,20,30,39,43,52,62,102,106,108,160,164,175); his decrees (*'ed(ev)ot*, 23 times: vv. 2,14,22,24,31,36,46,59,79,88,95,99,111,119, 125,129,138,144,146,152,157,167,168);[10] his commandments (*miṣvot*, 22 times: vv. 6,10,19,21,32,35,47,48,60,66,73,86,96,98,115,127,131, 143,151,166,172,176); his statutes (*ḥuqqim, ḥuqqot*, 22 times: vv. 5,8, 12,16,23,26,33,48,54,64,68,71,80,83,112,117,118,124,135,145,155, 171); and his precepts (*piqqudim*, 21 times: vv. 4,15,27,40,45,56,63, 69,78,87,93,94,100,104,110,128,134,141,159,168,173).

While these words have a range of nuances, the psalmist does not seem to be differentiating them. These near synonyms are used more for stylistic variation and for indicating the all-encompassing nature of

---

9   LXX has plural τὰ λόγια 'the utterances' for MT singular *'imratka*.
10 The MT singular *'edut* at v. 88 is probably to be read as a plural *'ed(ev)ot* with Qumran, LXX and Vulgate, as all the other occurrences of this word in the psalm.

Yhwh's self-disclosure.[11] These words are not infrequently found elsewhere in groups of three (not always the same three), or even four, particularly in Deuteronomy and literature usually felt to have an affinity with that book, as a way of reinforcing the comprehensive character of God's revelation of his will: 'These are the decrees and the statutes and ordinances that Moses spoke to the Israelites when they had come out of Egypt' (Deut. 4:45; cf. Deut. 6:17,20; 11:1; 30:16; 1 Kgs 2:3; 2 Kgs 23:3; 1 Chr. 29:19; 2 Chr. 34:31; Neh. 9:34; Jer. 44:23). If, as seems likely, Psalm 119 is a composition emanating from the pious scribal circles of the Persian period, then a written form of God's law will be in mind (and this may be implied by v. 148). So at least a strong element of the grace the psalmist rejoices in is the prescriptive component of revelation. God both informs and tutors his people how to live in his world.

Two further words the psalmist uses are 'way' (*derek*) and 'path' (*'oraḥ*). These too can refer to Yhwh's standards (vv. 3,14,15,27, 33,37,59) with which there ought to be an alignment in human conduct, 'the way of faithfulness' (v. 30). The psalmist desires metaphorically to walk, or run, along this track (vv. 1,5,9,14,26,27,32,33,35). But God's 'ways' may refer at times more broadly to how God himself chooses to operate in his world in conformity with his nature. In the aftermath of the golden calf episode, Moses appeals to God, 'show me your ways (*derakeka*), so that I may know you and find favor (*ḥen*) in your sight' (Exod. 33:13). It is a request for insight into God's essential character (LXX has 'show me yourself'). How will he respond to the apostasy? It is answered by Yhwh's self-declaration in the Compassion Creed: 'the Lord, the Lord a God merciful and gracious, slow to anger, and abounding in steadfast love (*ḥesed*) and faithfulness (*'emet*)', (Exod. 34:6; repeated with minor variations at Num. 14:18; Neh. 9:17; Ps. 86:15; 103:8; 145:8; Joel 2:13; Jonah 4:2). When this declaration is recalled by the psalmist of Psalm 103 (v. 8) it is similarly introduced by the words: 'He made known his ways (*derakav*) to Moses, his acts to

---

11 Burt notes the interchangeability of most of the verbs ('observed', 'guarded', 'loved', 'delighted in', etc.) with the eight near-synonyms, suggesting the poet is not differentiating the various words for law: Burt, 'Your Torah', 690-91.

the people of Israel' (v. 7). Another psalmist requests, 'Make me to know your ways (*derakeka*), O LORD; teach me your paths (*'oreḥoteka*)' (Ps. 25:4), and is able to affirm, 'All the paths of the LORD are steadfast love (*ḥesed*) and faithfulness (*'emet*), for those who keep his covenant and his decrees' (Ps. 25:10). Since he is a diligent student of Scripture, for the psalmist of Psalm 119 to fix his eyes on YHWH's 'ways' (v. 15) may include the idea of marvelling at God's compassionate nature.

Why should YHWH's law and his ways be so vital to the psalmist? It is because it is through faithful obedience that the relationship with YHWH is sustained. In this psalmist's theology, it is only by looking to YHWH's revelation, walking in his ways, and holding to his precepts that one may come to experience true life, and such life is a constant preoccupation of the psalmist. He may speak of experiencing this life now, as a result of having YHWH's precepts: 'I will never forget your precepts, for by them you have given me life' (v. 93). More commonly, he appeals for such life to be his on the basis of YHWH's promises, his righteousness, his steadfast love (vv. 17,40,50,77,88,107,116,144,149, 154). Likewise 'salvation' or 'deliverance' is a prospect more anticipated than currently experienced, where again a causal link may be expressed with the psalmist's commitment to YHWH's law: 'I am yours; save me, for I have sought your precepts' (v. 94; cf. vv. 117,123,146,166,174).

As well as the constant references to keeping YHWH's decrees and the like, those who share the psalmist's passion can be described as those who fear YHWH (vv. 38,63,74,79), and, lest we be tempted to reduce this fear to an insipid respect, the psalmist declares, 'My flesh trembles for fear of you, and I am afraid of your judgments' (v. 120).

This psalmist loves YHWH's 'name', that is, his revealed character, another way of saying he loves YHWH (v. 132). He is among those who 'seek him with their whole heart' (vv. 2,10). So at the core of all the psalmist says about God's law is the gracious relationship with him to which the psalmist makes abundant reference, echoing various aspects of covenantal language: 'The LORD is my portion' (v. 57; cf. Deut. 32:9; Zech. 2:12 [Heb. 16]); or he is simply 'my God' (v. 115; cf. Exod. 6:7). Apart from this one usage of 'God' (*elohim*, required because YHWH cannot take a possessive suffix), all other references to deity in the psalm (24) are with his name YHWH, the name revealed to Moses and expounded in the Compassion Creed (see above).[12] The psalmist repeatedly declares himself to be 'your servant' (vv. 17,23,38,49,65,76, 84,122,124,125,135,140,176) or simply 'yours' (v. 94). His God is relationally 'near' the psalmist (v. 151; cf. Lev. 10:3; Deut. 4:7). The 'good' (*tob*, v. 65) that God has done is a word rich in covenantal associations. In revealing himself to Moses, God promised, 'I will make all my goodness (*tob*) pass before you, and will proclaim before you the name, "The LORD"; and I will be gracious to whom I will be gracious, and will show mercy on whom I will show mercy' (Exod. 33:19).

But does all this mean that the psalmist considers himself to have 'arrived'? Is he sinlessly perfect? Is there no need for repentance, for further growth in understanding, for renewed efforts at obedience? The answer is decidedly 'No!' to all of these questions. The psalmist is using the language of covenant faithfulness. He is a member of the community of the redeemed (v. 154). He is like blameless Job (Job 1:1). He is like Abraham for whom the covenant promises were confirmed, 'because you have obeyed my voice' (Gen. 22:18; cf. Gen. 26:5). He is like David, 'who kept my commandments and followed me with all his heart, doing only that which was right in my sight' (1 Kgs 14:8). Despite their not insignificant faults and failures, these men placed their trust in God, relied on his grace and forgiveness, and endeavoured to live lives pleasing to him.

Our psalmist confesses his past shortcomings. In v. 67 he declares, 'Before I was afflicted I went astray', and in the closing verse he reminds us, 'I have gone astray like a lost sheep' (v. 176). His lament, 'How can a youth purify his way to keep it according to your word?' (v. 9) is a recognition of the struggle of the pious against sin, and tantamount to an appeal for assistance.[13] It requires YHWH's intervention to keep him from straying (v. 10). He prays, 'Let your mercy come to me, that I may live' (v. 77; cf. v. 156). He needs YHWH to instruct him, repeatedly

---

12 The etymology of the tetragrammaton, though much discussed, is beside the point. Rather the focus is on what YHWH, having said that he would be who he chose to be (Exod. 3:14), and would exercise his grace as he saw fit (Exod. 33:19), now reveals as his nature and his intentions towards Israel.

13 The translation, and the point made, are those of Soll, 'Question'. For a response, see Reynolds, 'Answer'.

calling on him to 'teach me (*lammedeni*) your statutes' (vv. 12,26,64,68, 124; cf. vv. 66,108,135,171). Likewise, with the verb related to *torah*, he appeals: 'Teach me (*horeni*), O LORD, the way of your statutes, and I will observe it to the end' (v. 33; cf. v. 102). He continues to learn (*lamad*), in part prompted by his life's experiences: 'It is good for me that I was humbled, so that I might learn your statutes' (v. 71; cf. vv. 7, 67,73). He desires not mere formal knowledge of God's expectations, but insight into their rationale, 'Make me understand the way of your precepts' (v. 27; cf. vv. 34,73,125,130,144,169).

The psalmist relies on YHWH's generosity to enable him to live in obedience: 'Deal bountifully with your servant, so that I may live and observe your word' (v. 17; cf. Ps. 13:6). The word 'deal bountifully' (*gamal*) is elsewhere associated with God's lavish grace at the time of the exodus (Isa. 63:7). The psalmist keenly feels the need for perseverance: 'O that my ways may be steadfast in keeping your statutes!' (v. 5). The wish interjection 'O that' (cf. 2 Kgs 5:3) in the context of an address to God is effectively a prayer that God might enable this. While he can say, 'I incline my heart to perform your statutes forever, to the end' (v. 112), it is because, using the causative stem of the same verb, he has already called upon YHWH to give effect to this, 'Turn my heart to your decrees, and not to selfish gain' (v. 36; cf. vv. 35,37), and further, 'May my heart be blameless in your statutes, so that I may not be put to shame' (v. 80). For all this, he needs, and pleads for, God's constant enabling presence (v. 8).

The word that perhaps comes closer than any other single word to expressing the essential character of YHWH is that he is a God who exercises *hesed*. There is much discussion on the meaning of this word which NRSV translates 'steadfast love'.[14] The main issue is whether it refers to the fulfilment of a commitment within an existing relationship or whether it can refer to a kindness or favour spontaneously exercised. Either way, our psalmist is keenly aware of how dependent he is on YHWH's *hesed*, appealing for its continued exercise on his behalf:

---

14 Glueck, *Hesed*; Sakenfeld, *Meaning of Hesed*; Andersen, 'Yahweh'; Clark, *The Word 'Hesed'*; Zobel, 'Ḥeseḏ'; Routledge, 'Ḥesed'.

'Deal with your servant according to your steadfast love' (v. 124; cf. vv. 41,64,76,88,149,159). This sevenfold use of *ḥesed* may not be accidental, as the scribes of this period were prone to work their keywords into a text seven times (or a multiple of seven).[15]

With a jussive verb, the psalmist prays, 'Let your steadfast love come to me, O LORD' (v. 41), and *ḥesed* is expounded in terms of 'salvation'. That is, YHWH must intervene with aid, if, as the *vav* section (vv. 41–48) goes on to say, the psalmist is to 'keep your law continually, forever and ever' (v. 44). The parallel (negative) jussive expression of verse 43, 'Do not take the word of truth utterly out of my mouth', uses the word *'emet* 'truth, faithfulness' often paired with *ḥesed* in the expression 'steadfast love and faithfulness' as a hendiadys for YHWH's consistent compassionate nature. It is probably here a deliberate echo of its use in the Compassion Creed (Exod. 34:6–7), given in the context of the flagrant breach of God's law in the worship of the golden calf. The psalmist appropriates words from that Creed, when YHWH revealed himself to be 'merciful and gracious', and now takes that 'promise' as applying to himself. Again in verse 64 he links YHWH's 'steadfast love', which fills the earth, with learning to live out his statutes. It is not that he looks for a separate reward for observing YHWH's statutes. To be taught them by YHWH is itself a manifestation of that steadfast love, and the 'end' (*'eqeb*) or 'reward' (REB) of such instruction is the delight of observing them (v. 33; cf. v. 112).

The psalmist appeals, 'Let your steadfast love become my comfort according to your promise to your servant' (v. 76; cf. vv. 52,82). The word for 'become my comfort' (*lenaḥameni*) is used for God's relenting from deserved punishment, a manifestation of his grace in two of the iterations of the Compassion Creed: 'abounding in steadfast love, and relents from punishing' (Joel 2:13; Jonah 4:2). It is also the word that announces the end of the suffering of exile in Isaiah: 'Comfort, O

---

15 Compare, for example, the sevenfold repetition of Qohelet's *carpe diem* theme (Eccl. 2:24; 3:12–13,22; 5:18–20; 8:15; 9:7–10; 11:7–10), or Jonah's fourteen 'big' things (Jonah 1:2,4 [X2],10,12,16,17; 3:2,3,5,7; 4:1,6,11) or the 21 occurrences of the theme-word *ga'al* 'redeem' in Ruth (2:20; 3:9,12 [X2]; 3:13 [X4]; 4:1,3,4 [X5],6 [X4],8,14). See Gordis, 'The Heptad'; Davies, 'Heptadic Verbal Patterns'.

comfort my people, says your God' (Isa. 40:1).

Several times Yhwh's *ḥesed* is bound up with the blessing of 'life' (vv. 88,149,159). As noted above, life is also the result of faithful obedience, as well as leading to the privilege of further engagement with Yhwh's law (vv. 37,40,50,88,93,109,159). It is then a manifestation of Yhwh's steadfast love that he grants his law and the heart to observe it as the way to life (see also Isa. 55:3; Ps. 23:6; 42:8 [Heb. 9]; 103:4; Job 10:12).

The notion of observing God's law as the means to life and blessing in fellowship with God is of course central to Israel's faith. Moses summed up his parting message to Israel as they were poised to enter the land: 'If you obey the commandments of the Lord your God that I am commanding you today, by loving the Lord your God, walking in his ways, and observing his commandments, decrees, and ordinances, then you shall live and become numerous, and the Lord your God will bless you in the land that you are entering to possess' (Deut. 30:16). Yet it became painfully and repeatedly evident that God's people collectively failed to meet this expectation. This gave rise to the prophetic hope that God would, after a time of discipline, forgive his people and renew their obedience by granting his spirit, placing his words in their mouths, circumcising their hearts, writing his law on their hearts, or granting a new heart (Deut. 30:1-14; Isa. 59:21; Jer. 31:31-34; Ezek. 36:26).[16]

While for the nation as a corporate entity such forgiveness and renewal was an eschatological expectation,[17] it was always open to any individual to appeal for such grace and so to live in faithfulness. It is David's prayer for Solomon: 'Grant to my son Solomon that with single mind he may keep your commandments, your decrees, and your statutes, performing all of them' (1 Chr. 29:19), where 'single mind' (*lebab šalem*) might also be rendered 'wholly devoted heart'. Solomon himself prays for his people that God might 'incline our hearts to him,

---

16 For the work of the Spirit in the heart, see Coxhead, 'Cardionomographic Work'.
17 For the eschatological dimension of Deut. 30, see Coxhead, 'Deuteronomy 30:11-14'; Meade, 'Circumcision'.

to walk in all his ways, and to keep his commandments, his statutes, and his ordinances, which he commanded our ancestors' (1 Kgs 8:58). A penitent psalmist appeals, 'Have mercy on me, O God, according to your steadfast love' (Ps. 51:1 [Heb. 3]) and follows this up with a request for inner transformation, 'You desire truth in the inward being; therefore teach me wisdom in my secret heart' (v. 6 [Heb. 8]). Our psalmist of Psalm 119 writes very much in this tradition.

For all his upright behaviour, the psalmist does not lead a trouble-free life. He lives as an alien in the land (v. 19), suffering 'scorn and contempt' (v. 22) and plots of various kinds against him (vv. 23,61, 78,85,95), knows grief (v. 28), fears disgrace (v. 39) and mockery (vv. 42,51), suffers calumny (v. 69) and persecution (vv. 84,86,150,157, 161). All of this adds to the urgency as the psalmist appeals for YHWH's intervention to deal with 'the wicked', 'the insolent', 'the arrogant', or the 'enemies' who oppose him (vv. 21,53,84,98,119,139). Of greater concern to the psalmist, however, is the opposition of this group to YHWH's law (vv. 21,53,85,126), and, as demonstrated by Botha, this functions as a foil for the attitude of the pious.[18]

Much of what the psalmist has to say relates to the individual experience of faith (most of the verbs and pronouns are singular). He has personally appropriated the promises and embraced the lifestyle enjoined upon Israel. Yet he is conscious that he is part of a community of those of like mind, introducing his appropriation of Israel's traditions of law and wisdom with macarisms of general application, 'Happy are those ...' (vv. 1–3; cf. Ps. 1:1–3; 32:1,2; 112:1; 128:1; Matt. 5:3–12; Luke 11:28; John 13:17; Jas 1:25; Rev. 22:14).[19] He does not lose sight of this community setting, observing, 'I am a companion of all who fear you, of those who keep your precepts' (v. 63; cf. vv. 74,79,132). These 176 verses are not the words of a super-saint. The poet has written in the conventional language of covenant righteousness, the normal experience of the faithful remnant of the people of God who know they are dependent on the grace, the mercy, the forgiveness, and the

---

18 Botha, 'Function'.
19 Lipinski, 'Macarismes'.

enabling of God every step in the way of covenant faithfulness. Does grace lead to obedience, or does obedience lead to grace? There are suggestions of both in this psalm and the psalmist seems content to live with any apparent tension. He similarly does not seem troubled by the fact that there are those under God's judgement and curse (vv. 21,84), yet God's steadfast love is universal (v. 64).

There is more of grace in this psalm than may first meet the eye. It is suffused with grace from beginning to end, with resonances with Israel's foundational credal statement about the grace of God. Our psalmist is not guilty of a tendency to self-righteousness,[20] and knows nothing of a law–grace antithesis. Rather, he delights in the grace of the law.

John A. Davies
Sydney College of Divinity

---

20 The evaluation, e.g., of Weiser, *Psalms*, 741.

Bibliography

Allen, L.   *Psalms 101–150* (WBC; Waco TX: Word, 1987).

Andersen, F. I.   'Yahweh, the Kind and Sensitive God', in P. T. O'Brien, and D. G. Peterson (eds.), *God Who Is Rich in Mercy: Essays Presented to D. B. Knox* (Homebush: Lancer, 1986), 41–88.

Booij, T.   'Psalm 119, 89–91', *Bib* 79 (1998), 539–41.

Botha, P. J.   'The Function of the Polarity between the Pious and the Enemies in Psalm 119', *Old Testament Essays* 5 (1992), 252–63.

Burt, S.   '"Your Torah Is My Delight": Repetition and the Poetics of Immanence in Psalm 119', *JBL* 137 (2018), 685–700.

Clark, G. R.   *The Word 'Hesed' in the Hebrew Bible* (Sheffield: JSOT Press, 1991).

Coxhead, S. R.   'Deuteronomy 30:11–14 as a Prophecy of the New Covenant in Christ', *WTJ* 68 (2006), 305–20.

Coxhead, S. R.   'The Cardionomographic Work of the Spirit in the Old Testament', *WTJ* 79 (2017), 77–95.

Dahood, M.   *Psalms III: 101–150* (AB; Garden City, NY: Doubleday, 1970).

Davies, J. A.   'Heptadic Verbal Patterns in the Solomon Narrative of 1 Kings 1–11', *Tyndale Bulletin* 63 (2012), 21–34.

deClaissé-Walford, N., R,. A. Jacobson, and B. L. Tanner   *The Book of Psalms* (NICOT; Grand Rapids, MI: Eerdmans, 2014).

Freedman, D. N.   *Psalm 119: The Exaltation of Torah* (Biblical and Judaic Studies from the University of California, San Diego 6; Winona Lake, IN: Eisenbrauns, 1999).

Glueck, N.   *Hesed in the Bible* (Eugene, OR: Wipf and Stock, 1967).

Gordis, R.   'The Heptad as an Element of Biblical and Rabbinic Style', *JBL* 62 (1943), 17–26.

Lipinski, E.   'Macarismes et psaumes de congratulation', *RB* 75 (1968), 321–67.

Meade, J.   'Circumcision of the Heart in Leviticus and Deuteronomy: Divine Means for Resolving Curse and Bringing Blessing', *The Southern Baptist Journal of Theology* 18 (2014), 59–85.

Perdue, L.	*Wisdom and Cult* (SBLDS 30; Missoula, MT: Scholars, 1977).
Reynolds, K.	'The Answer of Psalm cxix 9', *VT* 58 (2008), 265–69.
Reynolds, K.	*Torah as Teacher: The Exemplary Torah Student in Psalm 119* (VT Supplement 137; Leiden: Brill, 2010).
Routledge, R.	'Ḥesed as Obligation: A Re-Examination', *Tyndale Bulletin* 46 (1995), 179–96.
Sakenfeld, K. D.	*The Meaning of Hesed in the Hebrew Bible: A New Inquiry* (HSM 17; Missoula, MT: Scholars, 1978).
Soll, W. M.	'The Question of Psalm 119:9', *JBL* 106 (1987), 687–88.
Soll, W. M.	*Psalm 119: Matrix, Form, and Setting* (CBQMS 23; Washington, DC: Catholic University of America Press, 1991).
Weiser, A.	*The Psalms: A Commentary* (London: SCM, 1962).
Zobel, H.-J.	'Ḥeseḏ', in G. J. Botterweck, H. Ringgren, and H. Fabry (eds.), *Theological Dictionary of the Old Testament* (vol. 5; rev. ed.; Grand Rapids, MI: Eerdmans, 1986): 44–64.

The Salt Parable
(Mark 9:50, Par. Matthew 5:13 and Luke 14:34–35)

Stephen Llewelyn and William Robinson

καλὸν τὸ ἅλας· ἐὰν δὲ τὸ ἅλας ἄναλον γένηται, ἐν τίνι αὐτὸ ἀρτύσετε; ἔχετε ἐν ἑαυτοῖς ἅλα, καὶ εἰρηνεύετε ἐν ἀλλήλοις. Mark 9:50

Καλὸν οὖν τὸ ἅλας· ἐὰν δὲ καὶ τὸ ἅλας μωρανθῇ, ἐν τίνι ἀρτυθήσεται; οὔτε εἰς γῆν οὔτε εἰς κοπρίαν εὔθετόν ἐστιν· ἔξω βάλλουσιν αὐτό. Luke 14:34–35

Ὑμεῖς ἐστε τὸ ἅλας τῆς γῆς· ἐὰν δὲ τὸ ἅλας μωρανθῇ, ἐν τίνι ἁλισθήσεται; εἰς οὐδὲν ἰσχύει ἔτι εἰ μὴ βληθὲν ἔξω καταπατεῖσθαι ὑπὸ τῶν ἀνθρώπων. Matt 5:13[1]

Abstract

The salt parable is structured as a counterfactual conditional that asked of its original hearers a question. When first uttered, co-text and context would have given clues to the issue that prompted the question and its corresponding answer. Mark, Matthew and Luke lacked such clues but used their narratives to provide to its new hearers an insight into its meaning; they differ, however, as to whether salt is used as a metaphor for the disciple (Matthew and Luke) or a quality possessed by the disciple (Mark). The curious use of μωρανθῇ in Q has contributed to this difference and shows, it is argued, that the translator (?) had sought to provide a clue as to the target domain of the salt parable.

---

1 On the text-critical variants in Mark 9:50, Luke 14:34–35 and Matt. 5:13 see Lattke, 'Salz', 46–48.

Introduction

In reading the salt parable across the synoptic gospels, one is presented with a number of questions: (1) How are the differences between Mark and Q to be explained? (2) How does one account for the nonsensical proposition that salt can lose its saltiness? and (3) What effect does each evangelist's use of the parable have on its meaning? Each of these questions will be addressed in turn in the following discussion. The two-document hypothesis will be assumed and the salt parable will be interpreted as an extended or narrated metaphor using:

> 1. The Cognitive Theory of Metaphor[2] according to which *saltless salt* is defined as the source domain and the target domain remains to be determined; and

> 2. Relevance Theory[3] that assumes that language, as an encoded text, is ambiguous and its meaning is to be inferred either from an utterance's co-text (its linguistic environment) and/or context (its historico-social environment).[4]

In using these theories one must be conscious of the fact that the metaphor here is narrated. As a parable, it had a surface reference (= source domain) concerned with salt, the loss of saltiness and taste, but it also had another reference (= target domain) that was to be inferred by its audience. There were also mappings between the elements and their relationships in these two domains. It will be argued here that, as an utterance of Jesus, the parable would have had both co-text and context and thereby the audience was able to infer how it was to be applied and thus its meaning; however, as a repeated utterance in its transmission among early believers, the co-text and context had changed. The

---

2   See Lakoff and Johnson, *Metaphors*; Kövecses, *Metaphor*; and Kövecses, *Where Metaphors Come From*.
3   See Sperber and Wilson, *Relevance*; Carston, 'Truth-Conditional Content', 65–100; Wilson and Carston, 'Metaphor', 404–33; Sperber and Wilson, 'A Deflationary Account', 84–105; Allott, 'Relevance Theory', 61–84; Carston and Wearing, 'Hyperbolic Language', 79–92.
4   In the idiom of Relevance Theory, an encoded text has numerous explicatures that the implicatures of co-textual/contextual factors can be used to disambiguate.

tradition sought other ways to indicate the parable's application (target domain) on the occasion of its repetition. Thus, Mark used its location in his Gospel (co-text) and the encoded text that followed it (ἔχετε ἐν ἑαυτοῖς ἅλα, καὶ εἰρηνεύετε ἐν ἀλλήλοις) to indicate a meaning; Q used whatever co-textual and contextual factors it had to hand, but more significantly the choice of μωρανθῇ to indicate that the target domain concerned a particular human characteristic. In doing so, Q has allowed a mapping to the target domain to intrude into the telling of the parable.[5] In using Q, both Matthew and Luke recognised this target domain and, like Mark, named its owner as 'disciple'. This is most clearly indicated by Matthew when he introduces the parable with the words: Ὑμεῖς ἐστε τὸ ἅλας τῆς γῆς.

1. Accounting for differences between Mark and Q

Mark 9:50 and Q overlap in their use of the salt parable. Since both Matthew and Luke show significant agreement[6] against Mark (i.e. both agree in reading μωρανθῇ—*becomes foolish* instead of Mark's ἄναλον γένηται—*becomes saltless*) and record it in a different co-text (i.e. Matthew in the Sermon on the Mount, and Luke, as with much other Q material, after Jesus turns to go to Jerusalem), their versions of the salt parable have been assigned to the sayings source Q. Hoffmann and Heil postulate that Q 14:34–35 read: [34][[Καλὸν]] τὸ ἅλας· ἐὰν δὲ τὸ ἅλας μωρανθῇ, ἐν τίνι [[ἀρτυ]]θήσεται;[35] οὔτε εἰς γῆν οὔτε εἰς κοπρίαν [[εὔθετόν ἐστιν]], ἔξω βάλλουσιν αὐτό.[7]

---

5   If 'salt that becomes saltless' is a word of nonsense, as the Babylonian Talmud (see below) terms it, one is also tempted to see in the use of μωρανθῇ a further intrusion into the world of the parable from outside it.
6   One must hasten to add that Matthew and Luke are in other ways quite divergent from each other. Three possibilities present themselves: (a) that they have derived the saying from different sources, perhaps Q and another; (b) that Q itself existed in different versions; and (c) both Matthew and Luke freely redacted it to express their interpretations of it. The latter possibility is preferred here. Fitzmyer, *Luke X–XXIV*, 1067, adopts this latter possibility in arguing that Luke has made his reiteration of the parable to conform in part with that in Mark. Cf. also Hans Klein, *Das Lukasevangelium*, 514, 'Lk hat das Q-Wort mit Mk 9,50 zusammengearbeitet'.
7   Hoffmann and Heil, *Die Spruchquelle Q*, 100.

The use of μωρανθῇ by Q is unusual. The lexicons show 'be foolish' or the causal 'make foolish' as its primary meanings. LSJ adds 'become insipid' as a meaning for the passive causal sense but cites in evidence only Matthew 5:13. In other words, there is no evidence for the verb's meaning 'become insipid' other than the salt saying itself.[8] However, in support for this meaning, appeal is made to the cognate adjective μωρός (dull, stupid), which on occasion by metonymic extension displays the meaning 'insipid, flat, unsavoury'.[9] The references in LSJ are: *Comica adespota* 596 citing Photius – μῶρον: *Attic writers use a penultimate circumflex. And so they speak of dull* (ἀμβλύ) *and unsalted* (ἄναλον) *food as in 'to be altogether neither salty* (ἀλμυρόν) *nor insipid* (μῶρον)'; Diocles, frag. 138 – *it is necessary to boil those (foods) that are moist and unsavoury* (μωρά) *with vinegar*; and Dioscorides 4.19 – *roots (of epimedion) are delicate, black, heavily scented and to one tasting (them)* μωραί. But an occasional meaning in a cognate adjective does not prove that the verb possessed a similar encoded meaning. Moreover, the adjective μωρός is attested with the meaning 'insipid/flat/unsavoury' when used to modify an object, but no similar usage is attested for the cognate verb μωραίνω; indeed, insofar as the verb speaks of foolishness, that property can only properly be used in reference to a 'human characteristic'.[10]

An alternative explanation is sought in the languages spoken by Jesus. Lightfoot[11] noted that in Hebrew (and presumably also in Aramaic) the word תפל can mean both 'lose savour' or 'be foolish', and therefore that its two senses may lie behind the translation by ἄναλον γένηται in Mark and μωρανθῇ in Q. His insight has been taken up by others. Matthew Black[12] views Mark as a literal translation and Q as an

---

8 See Vattamány, 'Kann das Salz verderben?', 144, on the problematic meaning of μωραίνω.
9 See François Bovon, *Lukas*, 547.
10 Nauck, 'Salt', 175.
11 Lightfoot, *Horae Hebraicae*, 152–3. Lightfoot cites in evidence: (a) Job 6:6 for 'unsavoury'; and (b) Lam. 2:14 and Jon. 1:22 for 'foolish' based on the LXX's translation by ἀφροσύνη.
12 Black, *Aramaic Approach*, 166.

interpretation of תפל;[13] he further suggests that the likelihood of this explanation for the difference between Mark and Q is further confirmed by a word-play in Aramaic between תפל and תבל (salted/seasoned).[14] He renders the saying back into Aramaic: אן תפל מלח במא תבלונה—*If salt loses its savour, with what do they season it?* Joachim Jeremias[15] sees Mark as the literal translation but believes that Matthew and Luke have 'anticipated the interpretation of the saying as referring to the foolish disciples, or foolish Israel'. More probably the difference arises from Q's translational policy to render the target domain of the salt parable (a human characteristic) rather than its source domain (saltless salt).[16]

Excursus

Gyula Vattamány has proposed another solution. He argues that: (a) b. Bek 8b cites the salt parable as it was originally spoken by Jesus: מילחא כי סריא במאי מלחי לה; (b) the parable was at first correctly translated into Greek by ἐὰν δὲ τὸ ἅλας μαρανθῇ (waste away, disappear, die away), ἐν τίνι ἁλισθήσεται; (c) μαρανθῇ was soon corrupted to μωρανθῇ; and (d) the parable by its use of סרי (decay, be spoiled, smell offensively) originally spoke of the preserving quality of salt. His argument is based on a number of problematic assumptions: (i) that b. Bekh. 8b cites Jesus' salt parable in a context of Jewish-Christian polemic.[17] In b. Bekh. 8b *the mule that gives birth* is a Jewish slur against the virgin birth and *the salt that becomes insipid* is a counter slur against

---

13 Krämer, 'das Salz', 133–57, appears correct in seeing μωρανθῇ rather than ἄναλον γένηται as the literal meaning, i.e. it is used of the target domain of the metaphor.
14 According to Sifre Deut. 37.7, the land of Israel is called תבל because it contains תבלין (seasoning) which in turn is taken to be a reference to Torah. In reference to Deut. 1:1 'between Paran and Tofel', Sifre Deut. 1.14 puns on the place name Tofel (תופל) declaring them 'words of foolishness (דברי תפלות) which they foolishly spoke concerning the Manna'.
15 Jeremias, *Parables*, 168. So also Fitzmyer, *Luke X–XXIV*, 1069.
16 Cf. Gundry, *Matthew*, 76: 'To call μωρανθῇ a mistranslation is to overlook the possibility of an accepted carry-over from the Semitic verb to the Greek verb. The utter nonsense of "the salt becomes foolish" makes a mistake unlikely.'
17 On the questionable nature of Vattamány's contextualisation of b. Bekh 8b see Nauck, 'Salt', 174–75.

Judaism and its covenant of salt, i.e. eternal covenant. But a polemical context is only one possible *Sitz im Leben* placed on the text; more particularly the nature of the charge against Judaism is rather attenuated and otherwise unsupported, especially when it draws in the expression 'covenant of salt'. We also hasten to note that the allusion to Leviticus 2:13 is not found in Matthew, whose text Vattamány cites but in Mark, and there it is not a *covenant of salt* but *salt of the covenant*, an interpretation of the use of salt in the performance of the cult; (ii) that the Syrian tradition (Ignatius of Antioch, *Ep. ad Magn.* 10.2 and Ephraem Syrus, *Encomium in Petrum*) somehow retained knowledge of the correct sense of the salt parable. Verbal divergence makes it unlikely that Ignatius even cites the salt parable, and the allusion by Ephraem Syrus to the salt parable does not prove his awareness of a version that used סריא. His use of the word μαρανθῇ may be secondary, e.g. as a play on μωρανθῇ or as his attempt to explain a difficult text. In other words, the maxim *lectio difficilior potior* is ignored. It is easier to understand the reading μαρανθῇ as an attempt to solve the harder reading;[18] (iii) that only Matthew's version is considered. In Luke and Mark it is the taste of salt, not its preservative value, that is in view; and (iv) that the argument equates the meanings of סרי and μαραίνω when those terms show various meanings which can only be construed as overlapping in a context that requires an extension to one or other of those meanings. For example, 'decay' and 'waste away' might be construed in a given context as having the same extended meaning but this disregards the meaning of each in its lexicon (decay, be spoiled, smell offensively *vs* waste away, disappear, die away). Meaning is further complicated in the salt parable because of the overriding presence of metaphor.

Whether one approaches the interpretation of the term in Greek

---

18 Lattke, 'Salz', 47, notes the textual variant μαρανθῇ in a number minuscules (56, 15th century and a few others) and believes that it represents a later attempt to bring the metaphorical back to reality. I would argue that the variant μαρανθῇ is an attempt to restore the surface meaning of the text (i.e. the meaning at the level of the source domain in the metaphor of salt). Either way, Vattamány's argument that sees in the Vulgate's use of *evanesco* (disappear, pass away) a support for an original reading of μαραίνω is questionable by the same criterion.

or Aramaic, a residual problem persists. Given the possible meanings of μωρανθῇ/תפל, a hearer would still need to be able to disambiguate them and to assign the meaning that makes optimal sense. In other words, a hearer would need co-text and/or context to infer meaning. As spoken by Jesus, the salt parable would have had both co-text (i.e. what is said before and after it) and context (i.e. its social, cultural, and physical setting) to help the hearer infer a best-fit meaning. However, if one were to assume that Q (and presumably also the tradition used by Mark) recorded the salt parable as part of a loose collection of co-textually and contextually isolated sayings, a problem with disambiguating meanings arises. But to understand Q, or for that matter any 'implicit similitude',[19] in this way is to apply a model of transmission derived from the age of the printed text. Rather Q should be viewed as an *aide-mémoire*, an encoded text which was both situated and performed, perhaps in part, as the occasion required.[20] Thereby an audience was enabled to determine its target domain and thereby to recognise its meanings. With regard to the term's translation:

> a) Mark or his source offers the meaning (תפל > ἄναλον γένηται) that the expression's encoded text (the concepts of salt and savour) suggests; its metaphorical referent is later indicated and then specified in the second half of the verse. *Have salt in yourselves* signals that 'salt' is a metaphor; *and be at peace with one another* points to the target domain of that metaphor; but

---

19 Cf. Fitzmyer, *Luke X–XXIV*, 1068: 'Form-critically considered, the sayings about salt are an implicit similitude, metaphorical sayings which have become a popular proverb (HST 168), devoid of any explicit comparison. They even sound like a proverb of secular wisdom. However, they have an application, not from their own wording, but from the context in which they are used.' Cf. Zahn, *Matthäus*, 198–99, for a similar sentiment on Matt. 5:13.

20 It will be noted with Betz, *Sermon*, 157, that each iteration of the parable assumes that 'the image of salt was already known [...] as denoting discipleship'. As such, the hearer connects 'salt' and 'disciple' and infers by implication that 'disciple', rather than the nonsensical 'salt', is the subject of the verb μωρανθῇ. Moreover, if one concludes that the salt parable was an isolated *logion*, as, for example, both Nauck, 'Salt', 174, and Strecker, *Die Bergpredigt*, 51, do, it does not follow that it was without co-text or context in its performative reception by each evangelist.

b) Q offers a translation where the target domain of the metaphor is already indicated in the wording of the utterance (תפל > μωρανθῇ). Presumably the co-text and/or context of the utterance's performance would have also indicated as much. We will return to that meaning when we discuss Luke's and Matthew's recording of the salt parable.

2. Accounting for the nonsensical nature of the salt saying

In the Talmud (b. Bekh. 8b) the sages of Athens are reported to ask for מילי דבדיאי, i.e. words of nonsense or fictions (בדיאי), and Rabbi Yehoshua tells them of a mule that gave birth. Recognising the impossibility they ask, 'But the mule does she give birth?', to which Rabbi Yehoshua replies, 'Here are words of nonsense.' Not to be outdone, the sages then ask, 'Salt when it is spoiled, with what is it salted?' (מילחא כי סריא במאי מלחי לה). Rabbi Yehoshua picks up the thread of his previous example of nonsense and answers, 'With the placenta of the mule.' In turn the sages question whether the mule has a placenta to which the rabbi replies, 'And salt, does it spoil?' (ומילחא מי סרי). Clearly, that salt can spoil or lose its saltiness is considered in the tradition to be a nonsense. Like the offspring of a mule, it is implied to be an impossible event; to assume otherwise is to entertain a counterfactual proposition. On the basis of the similarity between Matthew 5:13 (par. Mark 9:50 and Luke 14:34–35) and b. Bekh. 8b, Black suggests that it was a 'well-known saying, perhaps even a popular proverb' but questions whether this can explain the language and variants in the Gospels.[21] Be that as it may, Matthew's joining of the salt parable to two either impossible or improbable actions (i.e. hiding a city on a hill and putting a lamp under a bushel basket, vv. 14–15) suggests that he was aware of the parable's improbability.

It has long concerned readers of the Gospel that the salt parable makes little sense, for the simple reason that, as the rabbis realised, it is

---

21 See Black, *An Aramaic Approach to the Gospels and Acts*, 166.

physically impossible for salt to lose its saltiness.[22] It is for that reason that it should be construed as a counterfactual conditional or in the idiom of the Talmud 'a word of nonsense'.[23] Gilles Fauconnier and Mark Turner[24] make the case for the fundamental importance of counterfactuals in human thought. As such, a counterfactual conditional, as a forced incompatibility, permits comparisons between divergent mental spaces that can result in a global insight. It is really saying, 'Just imagine if salt lost its saltiness, what would you do with it?' Furthermore, in the case of the salt parable, the *apodosis* of the counterfactual conditional is a rhetorical question to which the hearer knows the answer. If something has lost that property for which it is used, then it is useless and to be disposed of. The source domain consists of such elements as salt, saltlessness, and taste, and the possible relationships that pertain between them, and these are selectively projected or mapped onto the target domain in order to give insight into that target domain.[25] Whether we assume that the saying was an *ipsissimum verbum*, as implied by certain felicitous features of its translation back into Hebrew/Aramaic, or was created in the early tradition of believ-

---

22 The puzzlement of exegetes appears to derive from a desire to provide all parables with a concrete *Sitz im Leben*. See, for example, Schlatter, *Matthäus*, 147, and Zahn, *Matthäus*, 201–202 n.55. The fear is that admitting the fantastic or, as I contend, the counterfactual, opens the door to allegory. As a result, there is an attempt to explain the protasis of the salt parable by, for example, the impure nature of salt mined from the Dead Sea or Syrian desserts. But this is unnecessary.
23 See also Georg Strecker, *Die Bergpredigt*, 52, and Bovon, *Lukas*, 546. Luz, *Matthew 1–7*, 206, raises the possibility that the salt parable refers to an 'impossible situation' and in support refers to b. Bekh. 8b. He dismisses the possibility, arguing that a hearer must be able to agree with the image but that there is no situation under which salt would be thrown out. His argument is a *non sequitur*.
24 Fauconnier and Turner, *Way*.
25 In terms of Conceptual Blending Theory the same process would be understood as two mental spaces, i.e. 'small conceptual packets constructed as we think and talk, for purposes of local understanding and action', that are blended in order to give feedback concerning one of those mental spaces. In the words of Fauconnier and Turner: 'We do not establish mental spaces, connections between them, and blended spaces for no reason. We do this because it gives us global insight, human-scale understanding, and new meaning' (*Way*, 92).

ers, the co-text and context of its utterance remains opaque to us.[26] We can, however, be on a surer footing when we consider the saying within its Gospel setting.

3. Explaining how each evangelist uses the saying
(i) Mark
It has been previously argued that the salt parable in Mark forms the final verse in an extended section (Mark 9:30–50) that begins with the second passion prediction (vv. 30–32) and continuously treats the theme of discipleship.[27] Within the section there are two pericopes:

> (a) verses 33–37—after learning that the disciples had been arguing among themselves concerning their importance, Jesus inverts the social order (*first must be last*, v. 35) and taking a child teaches them: *Whoever receives one such child in my name* (ἐπὶ τῷ ὀνόματί μου) *receives me*; and

> (b) verses 38–41—after hearing that the disciples had stopped someone from casting out demons in Jesus' name (ἐν τῷ ὀνόματί σου), Jesus rebukes his disciples and declares the other person also a follower (i.e. he will not speak evil of Jesus, is 'for us' and will receive his reward), contrary to what the disciples thought (ὅτι οὐκ ἠκολούθει ἡμῖν, v. 38). Read in light of the previous teaching about receiving a child, the disciples, by hindering that person, have failed to *receive one such child* and in consequence have also failed to receive Jesus.

The two pericopes demonstrate how the twelve have now failed to understand what it means to follow Jesus, just as they had previously failed to understand Jesus' passion prediction (v.32). Verse 42 now acts as a bridge between verses 38–41 and the teachings that follow. It looks back to the failure of the disciples to receive the person cast-

---

26 That said, in Q the glossing of תפל with μωρανθῇ is suggestive that the saying was applied to foolish persons.
27 Llewelyn and Robinson, 'Questions', 425–51.

ing out demons (*you put a stumbling-block before one of these little ones who believe in me*, v. 42) and anticipates the theme of stumbling and its punishment found in verses 43–50.

Verses 42–50 are linked by a sequence of overlapping catchwords that at first sight appear to prefer word repetition over the coherence of the argument:[28]

> Mark 9:42–47 associates 'stumble', 'Gehenna', and 'fire', in the first instance when one causes another to stumble (v. 42) and in the second, if it is self-inflicted (vv. 43–47). 'Stumbling' is what the disciples are later described as doing after Jesus' arrest (14:27–29) and it is a risk faced more generally by any believer;

> Mark 9:48 (citing Isa. 66:24) picks up the description of Gehenna in verse 43 to offer scriptural warrant to it as a place of unquenchable 'fire'. However, in using this quotation he has left the pronoun αὐτῶν without an antecedent when in Isaiah it referred to 'the corpses of the people who rebel against me';

> Mark 9:49 (πᾶς γὰρ πυρὶ ἁλισθήσεται—*for everyone will be salted with fire*) is assumed to be an allusion to the salting of sacrificial offerings in Leviticus 2:13, but Mark's rewording of it is significant in three ways: (a) whereas both the MT and LXX refer to the salting (i.e. seasoning)[29] of the sacrificial meal-offering with salt (וכל קרבן מנחתך במלח תמלח —καὶ πᾶν δῶρον θυσίας ὑμῶν ἁλὶ ἁλισθήσεται), in Mark it is now the fire that seasons rather than the salt; (b) any reference to the offering is omitted; and (c) the neuter univer-

---

28 So Lattke, 'Salz', 45. Krämer, 'Salz', 149, notes that the use of catchwords as a mnemonic device does not rule out a paraenetic connectedness in Mark.
29 Given that v. 50 specifically focuses on salt, ἁλισθήσεται in v. 49 is best glossed with 'be salted', (e.g. RSVA); however, it, no doubt, connotes the seasoning property of salt rather than its preservative property. In this regard we note that Lev. 2:13 goes on to speak of the salt of the covenant (מלח ברית) and not an everlasting covenant, i.e. a covenant of salt (ברית מלח), Num. 18:19, 2 Chron. 13:5). Contra Fitzmyer, *Luke X–XXIV*, 1068, 'salt' in this last expression is used metonymically (agent/cause for effect) and thus figuratively.

sal πᾶν is changed to the masculine universal πᾶς. As a result of (b) and (c), πᾶς, now left without a noun to modify, finds its antecedent in the ill-defined 'them' of the preceding verse. Assuming that Mark together with his audience recognised its citation of Isaiah 66:24, πᾶς would be understood as 'everyone (who rebels against the Lord)'. As to (a), the implication of the change from 'salt' to 'fire' is that fire is to function like salt as a seasoning agent. But it is not immediately obvious what this can mean, when, on the one hand, salt is good (v. 50) and, on the other hand, fire is the descriptor of Gehenna (vv. 43–48). So why the change? First, in terms of forming a formal bridge between the catchwords of 'fire' (vv. 43–48) and 'salt' (v. 50) the solution is neatly achieved by the substitution of πυρὶ (Mark 9:49) for ἁλὶ (Lev. 2:13). The resulting expression πυρὶ ἁλισθήσεται now looks back (πυρὶ to vv. 43-48) and forward (ἁλισθήσεται to v. 50). Second and more importantly, as πᾶς in verse 49 finds its antecedent in Isaiah 66:24, so also does 'fire' derive its connotation from Isaiah 66:24 and that chapter more generally. Here, fire acts as the instrument of God's contention with or judgement of his enemies. The net result is that the words πᾶς γὰρ πυρί evoke the image of judgement, πᾶς and πυρί by recalling Isaiah 66 and the logical conjunction γάρ by recalling the threat of Gehenna (vv. 43–48). In turn the image of judgement evoked by the opening words supplies the target domain for the metaphor in ἁλισθήσεται, namely that to be salted is to be judged. The original sense of Leviticus 2:13 has been subverted in its Markan rendition. For Mark, then, every rebellious person will be judged by fire; and

Mark 9:50a and 50b convey the salt saying as understood by Mark or his tradition, *Salt is good. If salt has lost its saltiness, how can you season it?* One notes that contrary to Q, Mark uses an active second person verb (ἀρτύσετε), unlike Luke and Matthew who use a passive (ἀρτυθήσεται/ ἁλισθήσεται). The focus is therefore on the addressees and what they will do with the salt; the second person address is then continued over into verse 50c. Salt is not a metaphor for the disciple but a quality that they should display. 'Salt', like 'to be salted' in the previous verse, is deployed as a metaphor; however, now the target domain of that metaphor has changed to a quality that a disciple should have (ἔχετε ἐν ἑαυτοῖς ἅλα). In other words, there is a built-in tension in the juxtaposition of the two metaphors with the same source domain of salt, but different target domains. Mark seeks to transition between them by signalling that change with his insertion of 'Salt is good'. In so doing, he points his audience to the value of salt. As salt has a number of uses (i.e. as a preservative, as a seasoning/condiment, and in sacrifices) the nature of its value is specified by the verb (ἀρτύσετε) in the question that follows, *how can you season it?* The question, as we have already noted, is constructed as part of a counterfactual conditional, i.e. if one assumes that salt could lose its saltiness, it can no longer be considered salt. It is useless and by inference to be discarded. Herein lies the conceptual nexus between verse 50 and the teaching that preceded it; a disciple who loses his/her saltiness faces the dire fate of Gehenna and its unquenchable fire.

Mark 9:50c continues: ἔχετε ἐν ἑαυτοῖς ἅλα which is best understood as an imperative. The command speaks of salt as a quality that resides in a community (note the change to the second person plural). At the same time, it signals that salt is used metaphorically for a valued quality that a member of a community can possess but also lose. However, if the verse ended here, there would not be enough information to assign a meaning to the saying. Therefore, Mark adds the further imperative εἰρηνεύετε ἐν ἀλλήλοις. Salt is to be understood by the Markan audience as a metaphor for peace.[30] Peace is like the seasoning quality of

---

30 Nauck, 'Salt', 165–178, relies on the assumption that the rabbinical teaching, 'The ways of the students of wise persons: (he is) kind and humble of spirit, industrious (זריז) and salted (ממולח), suffering insult and loved by everyone', was known to Mark 9:50 and Col. 4:6. For Nauck the fact that Mark refers the term 'salt' to the disciples and goes on to speak of being at peace with one another ('suffering insult and loved by everyone'), is more than coincidental. Both Mark and rabbinical teaching use the metaphor of salt, he argues, for wisdom.

salt[31] in the community, but once it is lost the harmony of that community cannot be restored. In interpreting the salt saying in this manner, Mark may well be recalling the earlier failure of the disciples in verses 33–37 (disputing who of them is the greatest) and verses 38–41 (hindering another from casting out demons in Jesus' name).[32]

(ii) Luke 14:25–35

Luke 14:34–35 offers an interesting example of the roles that co-text and context play both in terms of the earlier transmission of the Jesus tradition and the evangelist's constrained reiteration of its encoded text but freedom in the interpretative arrangement of materials (i.e. co-text). As Joseph Fitzmyer[33] notes, the pericope beginning at 14:25 draws the hearers' attention to Jesus' journey to Jerusalem, and the teaching of verses 25–35, as a whole, contrasts the invitation to guests both 'far and wide' in the preceding Parable of the Great Dinner (14:15–24) with the stringent demands of discipleship (14:25–35).

---

31 One is tempted to see in the metaphorical use of salt a mapping between its capacity as a preservative and the peace as the preservative of community. However, the use of ἀρτύσετε makes this unlikely. See Luz, *Matthew 1–7*, 206.
32 Krämer, 'Salz', 136–37, noted a certain tension between v. 30b (salt is endangered) and v. 30c (salt is not endangered but those who don't have it in them), not to mention v. 49 as well. See Lattke, 'Salz', 48–53, on the various interpretations of 'salt' in Mark 9:50c. Many see 'salt' (9:50cα) as a reference either to 'the teaching/torah of Jesus' or to 'wisdom/prudence', and in 'have peace' (Mark 9:50cβ) a reference to the earlier disputes and failures of the disciples. Lattke's focus is on the two-part composition of v. 50c. He notes that, as per BDF §287 on Mark 9:50c, the reflexive pronoun (ἑαυτοῖς) can be used for the reciprocal pronoun (ἀλλήλοις). Verse 50c is thus seen to have two parallel members, where the concepts of 'salt' and 'peace' stand in parallel. The meaning of the terms is then determined with particular reference to Philo, *De Iosepho* 210, where 'salt and table' are described as symbols of genuine friendship (σύμβολα γνησίου φιλίας). The argument, however, is only plausible if one assumes: (a) that v. 50c was an independent *logion* that has no connection with what precedes it (v. 50ab) other than the connection of a shared catchword; (b) that there was at the point of its formulation a co-text or context that was sufficient to disambiguate the multiple senses in which 'salt' can be construed; (c) that 'salt' alone, i.e. without 'and table', was sufficient to evoke the concept of friendship. But the use of 'table' seems to give direction as to the meaning of salt even in a context of banqueting; and (d) that there is little difference between friendship and peace.
33 Fitzmyer, *Luke X–XXIV*, 1060.

The salt parable forms the final verses of a conceptually structured unit (vv. 25–35) concerned with the need to count the cost of discipleship. In summary, it is the person who does not plan ahead and count the cost of his undertaking who is like salt that has become foolish. The pericope is constructed as follows:

> Luke 14:25 names the audience as being a large crowd of unnamed persons who were following Jesus and to whom he turns to address the teaching in vv. 26–35;

> Luke 14:26-27 uses both domain-preserving (v. 25) and domain-switching hyperbole[34] (v. 26) to stress the cost of discipleship;[35] one must be ready to *hate father and mother, wife and children, brothers and sisters, yes, and even life itself* (v. 25) and to *carry the cross and follow* (v. 26). The statement of cost is followed by two examples (vv. 28–30 and vv. 31–32) of foolish persons who failed to count that cost before starting their endeavours;

> Luke 14:28-30 engages the audience by asking *which of you, intending to build a tower, does not first sit down and estimate the cost, to see whether he has enough to complete it?* In failing to count the cost and to complete the tower, the builder is then subjected to public ridicule (ἐμπαίζειν, v. 29), *This fellow began to build and was not able to finish.* BAGD (s.v. ἐμπαίζω) gives two meanings for ἐμπαίζειν: (a) *ridicule, make fun of, mock*; and (b) *deceive, trick, make a fool of.* The usage here primes the hearer to construe 'salt becomes foolish' as a metaphor for an individual who manifests the human characteristic of foolishness;

---

34 On the distinction between domain-preserving and domain-switching hyperbole see Claridge, *Hyperbole*, 41. Claridge distinguishes between domain-preserving (basic hyperbole involving amplifying synonyms 'beyond the limits of credibility', e.g. 'freezing' for 'cold', 'always' for 'often') and domain-switching (composite or metaphorical hyperbole, e.g. 'petrified' for 'unable to move or speak', 'asking for his head' for 'blaming him'), with the latter type often being phrasal in nature. On the application of these definitions to Luke 14:26 see Llewelyn and Robinson, 'Hyperbole'.

35 By understanding vv. 26–27 as giving expression to the cost of discipleship, one removes any possible perceived tension (*pace* Klein, *Das Lukasevangelium*, 512) between them and vv. 28–32.

Luke 14:31–32 reiterates the theme of the previous verses but with a new example, namely of a king who intends to wage war but must first calculate the relative strengths of the opposing armies. Implicit in this parable is also the public humiliation that a foolish king might suffer, especially if taken alive.[36] Both the example of the builder and the king are special Lukan material without parallel in the other synoptics;

Luke 14:33 draws the conclusion[37] from the two previous examples (note the logical conjunction, οὕτως οὖν) and relates its message back to verses 26–27 by repeating οὐ δύναται εἶναί μου μαθητής.[38] However, whilst the previous verses had singled out loss of family and personal suffering, verse 33 converts the currency to one of property (τοῖς ἑαυτοῦ ὑπάρχουσιν) and states the demand without any apparent expressive force. However, in drawing its conclusion the message is now personalised; for whereas verses 27–28 speak impersonally (note τις ... ὅστις) of the cost of discipleship, verse 33 is addressed directly to the audience (πᾶς ἐξ ὑμῶν) and references the opening question of the previous examples (τίς γὰρ ἐξ ὑμῶν, v. 29). Even so, as Bovon[39] points out, verse 33 shifts the focus from counting the cost to the cost itself. But as we will see, this shift is only temporary; and

Luke 14:34–35a penultimately concludes the teaching on the cost of discipleship with a warning: *Salt is good; but if salt has lost its taste* (μωρανθῇ, lit. *has become foolish*), *how*

---

36 Pace Klein, *Das Lukasevangelium*, 513-14.
37 Bovon, *Lukas*, 529, sees v. 33 as Luke's filling a gap and giving expression to the previous parables' application, which they otherwise lacked.
38 Bovon, *Lukas*, 530-31, sees v. 33 as modelled on vv. 26-27. Cf. also Fitzmyer, *Luke X–XXIV*, 1061, who sees the verse as a piece of Lukan redaction 'to add a further condition of discipleship, his favourite idea of disposing of material possessions. He makes the verse end with a refrain of vv. 26 and 27.'
39 Bovon, *Lukas*, 543.

can its saltiness be restored? It is fit neither for the soil[40] *nor for the manure heap; they throw it away.* Just as verse 33 was linked to the verses that preceded it by means of the logical conjunction οὖν, so also are verses 34–35a linked to verse 33 by that same conjunction. Verse 33 stated the cost demanded of a disciple, verses 34–35a state the consequence of failure when one has acted foolishly and not calculated beforehand the cost of discipleship.[41] For the salt parable to work, one does not need μωρανθῇ to have the encoded meaning 'to become insipid' but only that the hearer would recognise a pun on μωρός which can, though infrequently, mean insipid. In terms of the metaphor here, there are in the parable mappings between the source domain of 'salt' and its target domain of 'the disciple/follower'. Just as salt is good (i.e. useful), so also is discipleship. But there is also a mapping between salt that has become insipid (μωρός), and the disciple that has become foolish (μωρανθῇ). As pointed out above, the verb μωρανθῇ attributes to its subject a 'human characteristic', and as such the parable has taken into its wording the aim or object of the metaphor. In other words, the target domain of the parable has become part of the parable. The warning in verses 34–35a is not, as Klostermann assumes, based on a mapping between the usefulness of salt and 'a disciple […] who is determined to make every sacrifice

---

40 The form of the saying 'it is fit neither for x nor for y' can be read to imply an asymmetry between x and y, which is just not present in γῇ and κοπρία. Perles, 'Zwei Übersetzungsfehler', 96, restored that asymmetry arguing that γῇ is a mistranslation of the Aramaic homonym תבל (= world or seasoning). In other words, the sentence spoke of the salt being fit neither for seasoning nor for dung. Alternatively, Fitzmyer, *Luke X–XXIV*, 1069-70, views the two parts of the expression in terms of symmetry and translates it accordingly: *fit neither for the ground nor for the dung-heap*.
41 *Pace* Krämer, 'Salz', 137, and Lattke, 'Salz', 45, who see no connection between the salt parable and its co-texts. Form-critically they must be recognised as separate units of tradition but they have been brought together cleverly by the redactor.

for the sake of Jesus'.[42] It is rather based in the pun on salt that has become tasteless and the foolish disciple who has not counted the cost beforehand. The parable gives global insight into the worthless nature of ill-considered discipleship; it is as if salt had become unsalty.[43]

Luke 14:35b (*Let anyone with ears to hear listen!*) is a literary device both to end the teaching on discipleship and to emphasise its importance.

(iii) Matthew 5:13

Matthew differs from both Mark and Luke in his placement of the parable. It is now found towards the beginning of the Sermon on the Mount immediately following the beatitudes. As Allison[44] comments, verses 13–16 act as a unit of transition between the beatitudes ('the life of the blessed future') and 'the demands of the present' (5:17—7:23). The sermon is ostensibly delivered to the disciples as opposed to the crowd whom Jesus had left to ascend the mountain (Matt. 5:1). The nominal addressees of each blessing are named in the third person (vv. 3–10), i.e. 'the poor in spirit' (v. 3), 'those who mourn' (v. 4)

---

42 Klostermann, *Das Lukasevangelium*, 517. Similarly, Fitzmyer, *Luke X-XXIV*, 1068, 'Salt expresses the willingness of the disciple to offer himself/herself in allegiance to Jesus. Just as salt can lose its saltiness, so too can the allegiance deteriorate'; Reich, *Figuring Jesus*, 91, when he states 'refusing to renounce one's possessions would equal losing one's saltiness', interprets the metaphor of salt as if it were a comment of the previous verse alone; Bovon, *Lukas*, 545–46, who sees the issue in vv. 34–35 as not that of becoming but remaining a disciple. It has a long view of discipleship in mind. For him the mapping is between 'lost its savour' and 'ceasing to be a disciple'. But as Rienecker, *Lukas*, 357, observes, vv. 25–35 are uttered 'in order to protect the masses from folly and delusion'. And on vv. 34–35, in particular, 'the saying here forms the cornerstone of the warning against ill-considered enthusiasm' (360). Reineker wrongly supposes that it is the preservative quality that is in view in the salt parable, when the parable itself stresses its seasoning quality.
43 Krämer, 'Salz', 150–51, et al., see the message as one delivered to the faithful to remain faithful. This view may be true of the parable's meaning devoid of its Lukan co-text; however, this co-text indicates that the author and his audience should understand it in terms of the Christian mission and the message communicated to intending believers.
44 Allison, *Sermon*, 30–31.

etc., but as the blessings continue the hearer senses that each quality engendered in the blessing is a quality demanded of a disciple, e.g. 'those who hunger and thirst for righteousness' (v. 6), 'the pure in heart' (v. 8), and 'those who are persecuted for righteousness' sake' (v. 10). The final beatitude makes that inference explicit by the change to the second person plural: *Blessed are you when people revile you and persecute you and utter all kinds of evil against you falsely on my account. Rejoice and be glad, for your reward is great in heaven, for in the same way they persecuted the prophets who were before you.* The second person is marked 7 times, by both verb and pronoun, in these two verses, and, as Theodor Zahn[45] points out, the disciples' suffering in verses 11–12 occurs because of their relationship to Jesus (ἕνεκεν ἐμοῦ) rather than because of righteousness. The relationship between Jesus and his disciples is made explicit.

Both Mark and Luke introduce the salt parable with the words, *Salt is good*, and in so doing, the meaning of the parable, i.e. its target domain, is not immediately clear. Matthew, however, makes the target domain transparent at the outset when he states: *You are the salt of the earth* (v. 13) [...] *You are the light of the world* (v. 14). By the redactional addition of these words,[46] the meaning of the salt and light parables is made clear; in terms of the salt metaphor there are mappings: (a) between salt and disciple; (b) between the quality of salt (i.e. its saltiness) and the qualities of discipleship as listed in the preceding beatitudes (5:3-12) and referenced in the paraenesis that follows (Matt. 5:17—7:23);[47] and (c) between the loci of their applications

---

45 Zahn, *Matthäus*, 195.
46 Matt. 5:13a, 14 and 16 are special Matthean material without parallels in the other Gospels. See Lattke, 'Salz', 45.
47 Strecker, *Die Bergpredigt*, 54–55, notes the v. 16 is not only the highpoint of vv. 13-15 but also of the preceding beatitudes (vv. 3-12). As such, it underlines in the expression τὰ καλὰ ἔργα the paraenetic aim of the Sermon as a whole. In Strecker's analysis of the Sermon on the Mount (p. 12), vv. 13-16 form the end of what was the prelude to that sermon. Cf. also Luz, *Matthew 1-7*, 205, and Betz, *Sermon*, 155–56 and 158, who notes that vv. 13-16 act as a commissioning of that audience where the verses 'formulate programmatically what the community, for which the Sermon on the Mount was composed, regarded as their role and task in the world'. Betz (155) also notes in the beatitudes the changing gaze of the hearer between earth and heaven and sees the same principle at work between vv. 11-12 (focus on heaven) and 13-16 (focus on 'daily life down here').

(food is mapped onto γῆ par. κόσμος in v. 14, where both terms are used metonymically for their inhabitants).[48] The emphatic placement of ὑμεῖς at the beginning of verses 13 and 14 picks up its usage in verses 11–12, and the redactional unit (vv. 13–16) as a whole acts as a form of commissioning that is programmatic for the instructions that follow.[49] Importantly, also, one notes the addition of a reference to the ἀνὴρ μωρός in verse 26 (*everyone who hears these words of mine and does not act on them will be like a foolish man who built his house on sand*) in Matthew's version of the Q saying (Q 6:49) which rounds off the Sermon on the Mount. In other words, the Sermon is book-ended with threatening warnings against foolishness[50] which in turn appears to be reflected in Matthew's wider concern over 'stumbling'. But how was Matthew led to this interpretation? In the first place, both Matthew and Luke interpret the salt with regard to the disciple, which may imply that the communication of Q entailed the metaphorical identification of disciple with salt. Secondly, both Matthew and Luke use the verb μωρανθῇ (*become foolish*) that has as its implied subject a person. Thirdly, and as has already been pointed out above, by the use of μωρανθῇ the interpretation of the metaphor had already intruded into the telling of the parable. The verb signals to its audience that salt represents persons with whom Jesus, as the parable's speaker, converses.

Matthew 5:13 is then followed by the two parables concerned with 'seeing', i.e. the city on the hill that cannot be hidden (v. 14b) and the lamp placed on the lampstand that gives light to all in the

---

48   Strecker, *Die Bergpredigt*, 52: Das Wort γῆ ('Erde') hat die Bedeutung von κόσμος ('Menschenwelt'; so auch 18,7; vgl. Gen 11,1 LXX); see also Betz, *Sermon*, 163, and Gundry, *Matthew*, 75. Due to the absence of ἀρτύσετε/ἀρτυθήσεται in Matthew's version of the salt parable, it is possible to argue, as both Zahn, *Matthäus*, 200, and Krämer, 'Salz', 134–35, do, that both functions of salt (i.e. as seasoning and as preservative) are in mind here. Evans, *Matthew*, 111, contemplates in Matthew's version the purifying/preserving capacity of salt.
49   Strecker, *Die Bergpredigt*, 51, observes Matthew's introduction of the second person into his rewording of vv. 13–16 (cf. Mark 9:50 and Luke 14:34–35) and notes its bridging function between what has gone before and what will follow in his text.
50   Also Matt. 5:22 also warns against calling a brother *fool*—μωρέ.

house (v. 15).⁵¹ The parables are contextualised by Matthean redactions:⁵² (a) by paralleling verse 14a (ὑμεῖς ἐστε τὸ φῶς τοῦ κόσμου) to verse 13 (ὑμεῖς ἐστε τὸ ἅλας τῆς γῆς); and (b) by the addition of verse 16: *In the same way, let your light shine before others, so that they may see* (ἴδωσιν) *your good works* [...]. Thus, the two human sensory perceptions of taste (v. 13) and sight (vv. 14–16) are aligned and are to be interpreted reciprocally. In other words, just as salt imparts its saltiness to food, so also light illuminates its surrounds.⁵³ The disciples are both the salt of the earth and light of the world.⁵⁴

Conclusion

For Mark, peace, as the metaphorical referent of salt, is the quality that Jesus' followers are commanded to have in themselves (ἔχετε ἐν ἑαυτοῖς ἅλα, καὶ εἰρηνεύετε ἐν ἀλλήλοις). It is a quality that, once lost (ἐὰν δὲ τὸ ἅλας ἄναλον γένηται), the followers are unable to regain, as the rhetorical question (ἐν τίνι αὐτὸ ἀρτύσετε) assumes. As such, there is no expressed threat against 'the salt', as is found in both Luke and Matthew. For both Luke and Matthew, Jesus' followers themselves are the referent of salt. With a play on the expression μωρὸς ἅλς (insipid/tasteless salt), Jesus' followers are warned against becoming saltless/foolish (ἐὰν δὲ [καὶ] τὸ ἅλας μωρανθῇ), for what is lost thereby renders them unable to be restored (ἐν τίνι ἀρτυθήσεται/ἁλισθήσεται). Thus both Luke and Matthew conclude their parable with the threat of exclusion. However, they emphasise different aspects of what being

---

51 Against the suggested artificiality of the connection of the two parables, one notes their connection in Mark 4:21-22. Mark 4:21 parallels Matt. 5:15, and Mark 4:22 that plays on the theme of the inevitability of what was hidden (κρυπτόν, ἀπόκρυφον) being revealed (φανερωθῇ, ἔλθῃ εἰς φανερόν) parallels the theme of Matt. 5:14 that speaks of the impossibility of hiding a city on a hill.
52 See Krämer, 'Salz', 143-47, who attempts to explain the redactional developments in Matt. 5:14-16, in particular against the three other versions of the 'lamp' saying, i.e. Matt. 5:15 par. Mark 4:32, Luke 8:16 and 11:33.
53 Schlatter, *Matthäus*, 146.
54 At the level of *ipsissima verba* some see vv. 13 and 15 as polemic against either the leaders of Israel or Israel itself and their/its failure to accept Jesus' teaching; see, for example, Jeremias, *The Parables of Jesus*, 41-42 and 168, and Krämer, 'Salz', 139 and 148. However, within early Christian transmission, it is argued, the audience of the parables (i.e. their target domains) has been changed.

saltless salt means. Luke, by placing the parable in the teaching of Luke 14:25–35, speaks of the disciple who is foolish in not counting the cost of discipleship. Matthew, by placing it after the beatitudes (Matt. 5:3–12) but before the commands imposed in the Sermon (Matt. 5:17—7:23), speaks of the disciple who is foolish in hearing Jesus' commands and not doing them (Matt. 7:26).

Stephen Llwelyn
now retired from Macquarie University

William Robinson
Independent researcher

Bibliography

Allison, D. C.	*The Sermon on the Mount. Inspiring the Moral Imagination* (New York, NY: Herder & Herder, 1999).
Allott, N.	'Relevance Theory', in A. Capone, F. Lo Piparo, and M. Carapezza (eds.), *Perspectives on Linguistic Pragmatics* (Heidelberg: Springer, 2013), 61–84.
Betz, H. D.	*The Sermon on the Mount* (Hermeneia; Minneapolis, MN: Fortress, 1995).
Black, M.	*An Aramaic Approach to the Gospels and Acts* (Oxford: Oxford University Press, 1967).
Bovon, F.	*Das Evangelium nach Lukas, 2, Lk 9,51—14,35* (Zürich: Benziger, 1996).
Claridge, C.	*Hyperbole in English. A Corpus-based Study of Exaggeration* (Cambridge: CUP, 2011).
Carston, R.	'Truth-Conditional Content and Conversational Implicature', in C. Bianchi (ed.), *The Semantics/Pragmatics Distinction* (Stanford: CSLI, 2004), 65–100.
Carston, R. and C. Wearing	'Hyperbolic Language and its Relation to Metaphor and Irony', *Journal of Pragmatics* 79 (2015), 79–92.
Evans, C. A.	*Matthew* (New York, NY: Cambridge University Press, 2012).
Fauconnier, G. and M. Turner	*The Way We Think: Conceptual Blending and the Mind's Hidden Complexities* (New York, NY: Basic Books, 2002).
Fitzmyer, J.	*The Gospel according to Luke X–XXIV* (Anchor Bible 28a; New York, NY: Doubleday, 1985).
Gundry, R. H.	*Matthew. A Commentary on His Literary and Theological Art* (Grand Rapids, MI: Eerdmans, 1982).
Jeremias, J.	*The Parables of Jesus* (London: SCM, 1969).
Hoffmann, P. and C. Heil	*Die Spruchquelle Q* (Darmstadt: Wissenschaftliche Buchgesellschaft, 2002).
Klein, H.	*Das Lukasevangelium* (Göttingen: Vandenhoeck and Ruprecht, 2006).

Klostermann, E.   *Das Lukasevangelium* (Tübingen: Mohr, 1919).

Kövecses, Z.   *Metaphor: A Practical Introduction* (Oxford: Oxford University Press, 2002).

Kövecses, Z.   *Where Metaphors Come From: Reconsidering Context in Metaphor* (Oxford: Oxford University Press, 2015).

Krämer, M.   'Ihr seid das Salz der Erde', *MüTZ* 28 (1997), 133–57.

Lakoff. G and Mark Johnson   *Metaphors We Live By* (Chicago: University of Chicago Press, 1980).

Lattke, M.   'Salz der Freundschaft in Mk 9,50c', *ZNTW* 75.1 (1984), 44–59.

Lightfoot, J. B.   *Horae Hebraicae et Talmudicae*, vol. 3 (Oxford: Oxford University Press, 1859).

Llewelyn, S. and W. Robinson   'Hyperbole and the Cost of Discipleship: A Case Study of Luke 14:26', *HTR* (forthcoming).

Llewelyn, S. and W. Robinson   '"If Your Hand Causes You to Stumble, Cut It Off." Questions over the Figurative Nature of Mark 9:43–47 and Its Synoptic Parallels', *NovT* 63 (2021), 425–51.

Luz, U.   *Matthew 1–7. A Commentary* (Hermeneia; Minneapolis, MN: Fortress, 2007).

Nauck, W.   'Salt as a Metaphor in Instructions for Discipleship', *Studia Theologica* 6.2 (1952), 165–78.

Perles, F.   'Zwei Übersetzungsfehler im Text der Evangelien', *ZNTW* 19 (1920), 96.

Reich, K. A.   *Figuring Jesus. The Power of Rhetorical Figures of Speech in the Gospel of Luke* (Leiden: Brill, 2011).

Rienecker, F.   *Das Evangelium des Lukas* (Wuppertal: Brockhaus, 1959).

Schlatter, A.   *Der Evangelist Matthäus* (Stuttgart: Calwer, 1982).

Sperber, D. and D. Wilson   'A Deflationary Account of Metaphors', in R. W. Gibbs (ed.), *The Cambridge Handbook of Metaphor and Thought* (Cambridge: Cambridge University Press, 2008), 84–105.

Sperber, D. and D. Wilson   *Relevance: Communication and Cognition* (Oxford: Blackwell, 1995).

Strecker, G.   *Die Bergpredigt. Ein exegetischer Kommentar* (Göttingen: Vandenhoeck & Ruprecht, 1985).

Vattamány, G.   'Kann das Salz verderben? Philologische Erwägungen zum Salz-Gleichnis Jesu', *NTS* 59 (2013), 142–49.

Wilson, D. and R. Carston   'Metaphor, Relevance and the "Emergent Property"', *Mind & Language* 21.3 (2006), 404–33.

Zahn, T.   *Das Evangelium des Matthäus* (Wuppertal: Brockhaus, 1984).

Jesus and the Possibilities of Humour

Mark Stephens

Abstract

It has been a matter of some debate whether Jesus can be regarded as funny or humorous. A traditional answer throughout church history, and reaffirmed by some modern psychologists, is that humour and the divine make uncomfortable bedfellows. But a more nuanced answer might be possible. Contemporary theories of humour, such as theories of superiority, incongruity, and relief, provide some insight. But a pragmatic approach to humour suggests that even if a grand theory escapes, humour offers possibilities for personal and spiritual formation.

Throughout the last century, biblical scholars have pointed to various features of Jesus' ministry which could rightly be construed as comedic or funny. But this humour serves Jesus' broader message of the in-breaking kingdom of God, which surprises people with its calls for honest repentance, and the hospitable welcome offered to the undeserving. This kind of humour, in which comedy is deployed to promote reflection and renewal of faith, suggests that one may even laugh about the Christian life, not because the Christian life is a joke, but because our performance of the faith is, at times, laughable.

Introduction

In 1990 the avant-garde rock band King Missile produced a spoken word piece called 'Jesus Was Way Cool'. Amongst the many reasons enumerated for Jesus' being cool was that 'Jesus could have been funnier than any comedian you can think of'.[1] In their own way, King Missile captures a sentiment many wish to be true. Jesus must have been a funny guy. Yet this sentiment stands in stark contrast to centuries-long portrayals of Jesus as a figure of the utmost seriousness, and the evidence of repeated injunctions in church tradition that laughter was best avoided in the pursuit of godliness.

What are the possibilities that Jesus was funny or humorous? And what might the possibilities be for a 'Jesus-shaped' humour in the Christian life? To even attempt answering this requires insight both modern and ancient. From our modern context, we must consider how humour is conceptualised, and explore its perceived relationship with religion. From the ancient context, we need to examine the teaching of Jesus within first-century context, opening ourselves to the possibilities of humour within the Gospels. Finally, we can then suggest how humour might fit within Jesus' broader teaching and how it could be applied in the contemporary practice of faith.

The View from Modernity

The American humorist E. B. White once famously quipped: 'Humor can be dissected as a frog can, but the thing dies in the process and the innards are discouraging to any but the purely scientific mind'.[2] Despite such concerns, the modern field of 'Humour Studies' has attempted to generate theoretical frameworks to delineate the essence of comedy. For our purposes, the three most common theories can be briefly engaged: the Superiority Theory, the Incongruity Theory and the Relief Theory.

The Superiority Theory argues that laughter results from feelings of superiority with regard to another person or group.[3] To quote Thomas Hobbes, the laugher experiences 'sudden glory arising from some conception of eminency in ourselves, by comparison with the

---

1   Missile, 'Jesus Was Way Cool'. I gratefully acknowledge that my thoughts on the topic of this essay were helpfully shaped by a former student and colleague, Rebecca Kellahan, who delivered a brilliant conference paper on Australian comedy in 2018.
2   E. B. White, as cited in Lindvall, 'Freud', 1.
3   Morreall, *Taking Laughter*, 5.

infirmity of others'.[4] Such feelings of superiority easily lend themselves to humour being anti-social, even to the point of being an expression of aggression and hostility. In its harsher forms humour fosters emotional distance from the 'other' and causes social harm and damage.[5] But there are ways of conceptualising 'superiority' that foster social good rather than harm. This is where comedy might be used to dampen vice, insofar as mockery or ridicule or satire undercuts the attractional pull of certain vicious behaviours or attitudes.[6]

The Incongruity Theory proposes that humour results from occurrences that 'violat[e] our normal mental patterns and normal expectations'.[7] Here the focus is on what is unexpected, illogical, or out of place.[8] Perhaps here the ancient orator Cicero captured things best when he states: 'The most common kind of joke is that in which we expect one thing and another is said; here our own disappointed expectation makes us laugh'.[9] In terms of a Christian application of incongruity theory, one example might be the work of C. S. Lewis. Lewis regarded laughter as intrinsically human, and in part arising from the incongruity of our created nature, being a mixture 'of dust and divine breath'.[10] However much theories of incongruity seem intuitively plausible, they also have some potential flaws. Chief among them is the question of why we *enjoy* incongruity. In many cases the presence of incongruity does not inspire laughter, but rather provokes in us a desire for explanation. Therefore, delineating which incongruities we find humourous, and why, remains an important topic for discussion.

A third theory is known as the Relief Theory. Relief Theory focuses on laughter as an embodied phenomenon, in which there is a release of accumulated tension. The precise details of how such tension

---

4   Thomas Hobbes as cited in McIntyre, 'God's Comics', 54.
5   Morreall, *Comic Relief*, 4–8.
6   See the words of Philip Sidney in his *Defense of Poesie*: 'Comedy is an imitation of the common errors of our life, which he [the dramatist] representeth in the most ridiculous and scornful sort that may be, so as it is impossible that any beholder can be content to be such a one' (as cited in Morreall, *Comic Relief*, 8).
7   Morreall, *Comic Relief*, 11.
8   McIntyre, 'God's Comics', 57–61.
9   Cicero, as cited in Morreall, *Comic Relief*, 11.
10 Lewis as cited in Lindvall, 'Freud', 4.

is formed, and released, are often grounded in particular theological and philosophical anthropologies. Some, such as Herbert Spencer, paired relief theory with incongruity, insofar as laughter allows the release of nervous energy which is built up through our expectations. Others, such as Sigmund Freud, tied 'Relief Theory' to the repression of thoughts deemed socially inappropriate.[11] Inasmuch as religion is often cited as a constitutive source of taboos, Relief Theory could provide some insight into the topic of religion and humour.[12]

In John Moreall's comprehensive survey of the philosophy of humour, he concludes by moving away from pure theory as summarised above, to instead examine the sapiential functions of humour. Speaking empirically, Morreall concludes that 'comedy fosters wisdom'.[13] As exemplars, Morreall points to humour's capacity to create honesty about weaknesses, to think critically about authorities and institutions, to forestall anger and resentment, to see problems in a new light, and to promote community. This kind of pragmatic account of humour and its functions indicates that even if a grand theory escapes us, the tangible benefits seem clearly evident.[14]

The 'Modern' Relationship Between Humour and Religion

A second modern consideration is the perceived disconnect between humour and religion. Throughout history, Christians have repeatedly expressed antipathy towards comedy. Church fathers like Clement of Alexan-dria, Basil of Caesarea, and John Chrysostom all saw laughter as corrosive of the solemnity and self-mastery that should mark a true Christian.[15] Indeed, the Benedictine tradition forbade 'speech

---

11 For both Freud and Spencer see Morreall, *Comic Relief*, 16–23; see also McIntyre, 'God's Comics', 57.
12 Cf. the suggestions of Samuel Joeckel with regard to various festivals in the medieval church calendar which provided 'interludes of humor occasioned by the momentary relaxation of dogma ... Laughter in such a context is a safety valve' ('Funny as Hell', 417).
13 Morreall, *Comic Relief*, 142.
14 Morreall, *Comic Relief*, 142–45.
15 For various brief accounts of historic Christian antipathy from the patristic period onwards, see Reyburn, 'Laughter', 20–1; Joeckel, 'Funny as Hell', 415–16; Morreall, *Comic Relief*, 5.

provoking laughter'.[16] To this historic sense of conflict between Christ and comedy has been added the modern perspective of personality psychology. Vassilis Saroglou has repeatedly argued that religious belief is negatively correlated with the capacity for humour because religious belief stresses certainty and dogmatism, which creates inherent resistance to the paradoxes and ambiguity of comedy.[17]

To be sure, the twentieth century has witnessed a reappraisal of the potential value of comedy, both at the academic and popular levels. In terms of academia, G. K. Chesterton,[18] C. S. Lewis,[19] Elton Trueblood,[20] Douglas Wilson,[21] and Terry Lindvall[22] have all attempted to both analyse and legitimate the place of humour in the Christian life. In addition, within contemporary evangelicalism, humour has become something of a staple within evangelical preaching, so much so that specialist resources are produced to this end.[23] Furthermore, within the United States, and to a lesser degree the UK, we have seen the emergence of professional Christian comedians, and the development of a broader genre of 'clean' comedy.[24]

Accordingly, the view from modernity communicates both possibility and tension. There seems to be an awareness that humour is an inextricable part of what it means to be human,[25] coupled with an anxiety towards the profound threats and dangers that comedy inherently presents.[26]

---

16 '[o]f speech provoking laughter ... we condemn everywhere to eternal exclusion; and for such speech we do not permit the disciple to open his lips' (as cited in Joeckel, 'Funny as Hell', 416).
17 Vassilis Saroglou, 'Sense of Humor', 205–206.
18 Reyburn, 'Laughter', 18–51.
19 Lewis, *The Screwtape Letters*.
20 Trueblood, *The Humor of Christ*.
21 Wilson, *A Serrated Edge*.
22 Lindvall, *Surprised by Laughter*; *God Mocks*.
23 Rowell and Steffen (eds.), *Humor*.
24 McIntyre, 'God's Comics', *passim*.
25 Cf. Conrad Hyers comment: 'Yet what does the full humanity of Jesus mean if it does not include the freedom of laughter and humor' (*The Comic Vision*, 16).
26 Cf. McIntyre, 'God's Comics', chapter 3, entitled 'Addressing the Challenge of Humour'.

The Humour of Jesus

We now turn to the possibility of humour in the life and teaching of Jesus. Professor Jim Harrison has himself surveyed the possibility of humour in the letters of Paul.[27] His impressive overview of the form and function of comedy within the Graeco-Roman world uncovers the ways Paul carefully appropriated ancient forms of parody and satire to critique his opponents, but also the ways Paul turned parody against himself as a servant of Christ. Harrison shows that Paul's use of humour was never an end in itself, but rather served the noble purpose of '[establishing] communities of faith to grow in Christ together.'[28]

A similar kind of nuance is required in evaluating the possibilities of humour in the Jesus tradition. In terms of the Gospels, the initial returns seem both hopeful *and* ambiguous. In the 1960s the Quaker theologian D. Elton Trueblood briefly surveyed the humour of Jesus through categories like hyperbole, paradox, wit, and irony.[29] More recently the communications scholar Terry Lindvall has examined Jesus through the lens of prophetic satire, placing him within a broader tradition stretching back to the Hebrew prophets. Lindvall opens his chapter on the New Testament as follows:

> In the Gospels, Jesus took on legalistic Pharisees, politically compromised Sadducees, and others, with vim and vigor and no slight bit of satire. With playful exaggeration, Jesus pulled the rug out from under the religious leaders.[30]

Within the storied world of Jesus' parables, it is possible to discern traces of the comic. Trueblood points to the presence of the deliberately preposterous, such as the absurd amounts of indebtedness in the parable of the unforgiving servant (Matthew 18:23–35).[31] Pursuing a

---

27 Harrison, '"Laughter"', 209–40.
28 Harrison, '"Laughter"', 239.
29 Trueblood, *Humor of Christ*, 39–49, 53–67.
30 Lindvall, *God Mocks*, 28.
31 Trueblood, *Humour of Christ*, 48–49. Cf. Klyne Snodgrass' comment: 'Depending on which metal was used, a talent was the equivalent of about 6000 denarii, which would make the first servant's debt 60,000,000 denarii, and at one denarius a day (as in Matt 20:2) would require a day laborer over 164,000 years to repay!' (*Stories with Intent*, 66).

different apparaoch, J. Andrew Doole contends that Luke is the funniest of the evangelists, a judgement which comports well with the way story-parables are such a feature of the Lukan portrait. Doole points to examples such as the parable of the widow and the judge, where the supposedly powerful unjust magistrate fears getting a punch in the face (ὑπωπιάζῃ) from the lowly widow (Luke 18:1–18).[32] Or take the comic exaggerations present in the parable of the dishonest steward (Luke 16:1–8), a series of hyperboles which has continued to baffle interpreters ever since.[33] Finally, Doole points to comic features throughout the whole series of 'lost' parables in Luke 15, such as the strange behaviour of shepherds who abandon ninety-nine sheep in order to find one, or the woman who finds a lost coin and then throws a party.[34]

If we move our attention briefly to Matthew, there appears to be comic potential through wordplay in the teaching of Jesus. For example, the saying in Matthew 23:24, 'You strain out a gnat while swallowing a camel', appears to be a prophetic pun, employing an Aramaic wordplay between the word 'gnat' (*qalma*) and 'camel' (*kamla*).[35] The resulting image is of a 'Pharisee bent over a drink or a pot of soup, straining to get the tiny speck, that nagging gnat out, while a camel's front legs and head are sticking out of his mouth!'[36]

Although the above survey is brief, and to some degree speculative, there is something to suggest the presence of humour in the life and ministry of Jesus. The suggestion of Lindvall that Jesus continues the tradition of Hebraic satire is worth acknowledging.[37] But that satire is purposeful and directed. It has a strategy and a *telos*. To quote Lindvall: 'In the Gospels, satire works as a refining fire that often punishes, but also seeks to purify.'[38]

---

32   Doole, 'Observational Comedy', 183.
33   King, 'A Funny Thing', 18–25.
34   Doole, 'Observational Comedy', 190–96.
35   Keener, *Matthew*, 552.
36   This quote is taken from the NT scholar George Guthrie, speaking to his college magazine, *The Regent World* ('Seven Scholars').
37   Lindvall, *God Mocks*, 28–30.
38   Lindvall, *God Mocks*, 28.

The Humour of Jesus in Film Reception

As a brief aside from the biblical text, we might also consider the genre of Jesus films as meaningful receptions of the Gospel tradition, to examine the degree to which they see the possibility of humour and laughter in the Gospels. A commonplace portrait of the filmic Jesus is portray him as serene, impassive, serious, and dignified, such as we see in *King of Kings* or *The Greatest Story Ever Told*.[39] But from the 1970s onwards, the possibilities of joy and laughter were more richly explored through movies such as Jon-Michael Tebelak's *Godspell* (in which Jesus is portrayed in the garb of a clown), and *The Visual Bible: Gospel According to Matthew*, where the lead actor, Bruce Marchiano, came to be labelled 'The Smiling Jesus', presumably because such phenomena felt so new to many viewers.[40]

The Possibilities of Humour in the Life of Christ

From the limited evidence we possess, it is conceivable and comprehensible that the life and teaching of Jesus possesses traces of humour. Yet the specifics of Jesus' humour remain the subject of speculation. Whatever we purport to find, suggestions of humour must be situated within the context Jesus' broader mission and ministry. The message of Jesus, particularly as captured within the Synoptics, is configured around the urgent need of response to the in-breaking of the reign of God.[41] Such a message is serious (Mark 9:47), demanding repentance (Mark 1:15), and expecting a greater and intensified righteousness (Matt. 5:20). That righteousness finds concrete expression in individual and communal praxis. It is a vision focused on both holiness and hospitality, oriented in love towards God and love towards others (Matt. 22:34–40//Mark 12:28–31).[42]

These summary insights provide a framework for understanding the possibilities of humour, wit, and satire in the ministry of Jesus.

---

39 Lang, *Bible*, 177.
40 Bruce Marchiano, *Footsteps*, 76–88.
41 McKnight, 'Ethics of Jesus', 243.
42 Neufeld, *Recovering Jesus*, 227.

Contra King Missile, Jesus was not necessarily funnier than any comedian. The theology of incarnation does not demand such facile characterisations. But we can ask how the possibility of humour contributes to Jesus' proclamation of repentance, the way satire could inform his prophetic challenge to the powers of his day, or the way playful exaggeration promotes humble self-reflection and a surrendering to God's reign.[43] As a reflective activity, reading the practice of humour through the lens of the Sermon on the Mount could prove a most interesting exercise. Amongst other things, the humour that Jesus endorses lifts up the poor in spirit, the mourners, it encourages a thirst for righteousness, and for engaging the task of peacemaking. Given the way contemporary humour often performs humour as a means of retaliation and insult, the words of the Sermon on the Mount constitute a profound reconfiguring of what it means to be funny.

The Possibility of Humour about the Christian Life

Despite feelings of tension and difficulty, humour seems an inevitable and essential part of human existence. Sociologists point to the way humour functions as a kind of social glue, insofar as it creates solidarity within groups.[44] This potential for humour to both include and exclude frames the horizons of possibility for how humour might be employed in Christian community. For example, Rick Moore's comparative survey of humour amongst a sample of Christians and atheists managed to identify that the Christian group nurtured a self-identity of 'broken individuals striving to emulate Jesus Christ'.[45] Emerging out of such a self-concept was the practice of humour where jokes and ridicule were gently directed within rather than without.[46] In Professor Harrison's own survey of humour in Paul, he identified how the apostle directed his 'sharp rhetorical thrusts' mainly for 'insiders' needing correction

---

43 As one comedic example, I can remember during my teenage years hearing the track 'Log Eye,' by the Christian comedian Paul Aldrich. It can be found online here https://www.youtube.com/watch?v=b2pXsUeEpDU
44 Moore, 'Sardonic Atheists', 447–65.
45 Moore, 'Sardonic Atheists', 453.
46 Moore, 'Sardonic Atheists', 452–53.

and reintegration. Furthermore, he even directed satire against *himself* as a means of rebuke aiming at spiritual formation.[47] At least some of these insights can also be found within the life and teaching of Jesus, whose comedic practices worked comfortably within a ministry of hospitality towards the stranger and the sinner.

Yet the possibility of humour remains vexed because of the ways that comic mockery, ridicule, and insult are often deployed *against* the disciple of Jesus. The Gospels are aware of this possibility (cf. Matt. 5:11//Luke 6:22), as are a number of other early Christian writings (Heb. 10:33; 1 Peter 3:9; 4:14). The painful experience of being shamed and marginalised, in part through the use of humour,[48] has been a persistent experience of Christians throughout the ages. This raises a further question: is it possible to usefully mock the Christian life?

A classic instantiation of this question surrounds the Monty Python film, *Life of Brian*. Upon its release in 1979, it was branded offensive, sacrilegious, and something more befitting Judas than Jesus.[49] Yet in the ensuing decades, the film has become much loved among many biblical scholars, prompting academic articles and even entire academic conferences.[50] It is possible to regard the *Life of Brian* as a denigration of Christ, as the journalist Malcolm Muggeridge did upon

---

47 Cf. Professor Harrison's comments on the praxis of Paul: 'Paul reserves his sharp rhetorical thrusts of humour only for "insiders" within the Body of Christ who needed spiritual correction and reintegration within its fellowship and ministries. [...] Paul directed satire against himself in defiance of the contemporary canons of comedy in the hope that through his self derision his opponents within the Body of Christ would be shamed into returning to the gospel of Christ the crucified Lord. But for Paul, as far as the unbelieving world outside is concerned, gracious and persuasive speech rather than satirical attack is the strategy for moving "outsiders" towards becoming "insiders" in the Body of Christ' ('"Laughter"', 238).
48 Cf. the famous Alexamenos graffiti discovered in the 19th century. See Siker, 'Alexamenos'.
49 For a local account, see Egan, '"Film"', 152–71. The reference to Judas is drawn from the reflections of the Bishop Mervyn Stockwood, who in an infamous BBC debate about the film stated: 'You'll get your thirty pieces of silver!' (See Richard Burridge, 'The Church of England's *Life of Python*', 26).
50 See Taylor, *Jesus and Brian* as the classic example. For an earlier instance, see Davies, 'Life of Brian Research', 400–14.

its initial release.[51] But further reflection suggests that the central point of the film is that it isn't about Jesus at all (who appears only tangentially). Instead, *Life of Brian* follows the story of Brian Cohen, who is born at the same time as Jesus, and who is mistaken for the Messiah throughout. The story that ensues is merciless in its satire. Yet here is precisely where nuance is required. If the film were directly about Jesus, a possibility the Python troupe originally considered,[52] then the film would be an experience of shameful mockery and insult. But the clever conceit of making the film about Brian enables the Pythons to target something else altogether: mindless religious belief. In a now-famous panel discussion on the BBC, John Cleese remarked that the point of the film was: 'Make up your own mind, don't let other people tell you.'[53] Anthony Ashley Cooper, the third early of Shaftesbury, famously regarded ridicule as the test of truth.[54] Read with patience and charity, *Life of Brian* ironically affirms the maturation of faith, insofar as it encourages the movement from a conventional to a reflective faith.[55] It stands as a lived example that even the non-believing can craft humour about the Christian life in ways that might strengthen, rather than diminish, the practice of faith.

Conclusion

Humour is a deeply human practice, which opens up possibilities for physical and mental relief, the potential for subversive truth-telling, and the ever-present prospect of being surprised by joy. While it is not the centrepiece of his ministry, it seems legitimate to construe Jesus as employing forms of comedy as part of his rhetoric. Yet humour is never an end in itself—it serves the broader vision of the kingdom of

---

51 Burridge, 'The Church of England's *Life of Python*', 24–36.
52 The title *Jesus Christ: Lust for Glory* was originally tossed around. See Burridge, 'The Church of England's *Life of Python*', 30.
53 The debate can be viewed in full at https://www.youtube.com/watch?v=ZYMpObbt2rs
54 Amir, *Humor*, 69–70.
55 Here I draw on the faith development language of James Fowler, as refracted through Demarest, 'Reflections', 153.

God where sinners repent, the undeserving are showered with grace, the broken are made whole, and the poor are lifted up. It is an honour to offer this short article in honour of Professor Jim Harrison, a man of sharp wit and humour, but one who wields his comedy for the sake of the gospel, and in imitation of his joyous Lord.

Mark Stephens
Sydney Missionary and Bible College

Bibliography

Amir, L. B.	*Humor and the Good Life in Modern Philosophy: Shaftesbury, Hamann, Kierkegaard* (Albany, NY: SUNY Press, 2014).
Burridge, R.	'The Church of England's *Life of Python* – or "What the Bishop Saw"', in J. E. Taylor (ed.), *Jesus and Brian: Exploring the Historical Jesus and his Times via Monty Python's Life of Brian* (London: Bloomsbury, 2015), 19–42.
Davies, P. R.	'Life of Brian Research', in J. C. Exum and S. D. Moore (eds.), *Biblical Studies, Cultural Studies: The Third Sheffield Colloquium* (Sheffield: Sheffield Academic Press, 1998), 400–14.
Demarest, B.	'Reflections on Developmental Spirituality: Journey Paradigms and Stages', *Journal of Spiritual Formation & Soul Care* 1 (2008), 149–67.
Doole, J. A.	'Observational Comedy in Luke 15', *Neotestamentica* 50 (2016), 181–210.
Egan, K.	'"The Film That's Banned in Harrogate": Monthy Python's Life of Brian (1979), Local Censorship, Comedy, and Local Resistance', *Historical Journal of Film, Radio, and Television* 41 (2021), 152–71.
Harrison, J. R.	'"Laughter is the Best Medicine": St. Paul, Well-Being and Roman Humour' in D. Costache, D. Cronshaw, and J. R. Harrison (eds.), *Well-Being, Personal Wholeness and the Social Fabric* (Newcastle upon Tyne: Cambridge Scholars, 2017), 209–40.
Hyers, C.	*The Comic Vision and the Christian Faith: A Celebration of Life and Laughter* (New York, NY: Pilgrim, 1981).
Joeckel, S.	'Funny as Hell: Christianity and Humor Reconsidered', *Humor* 21 (2008), 415–33.
Keener, C. S.	*The Gospel of Matthew: A Socio-Rhetorical Commentary* (Grand Rapids, MI: Eerdmans, 2009).
King, F. J.	'A Funny Thing Happened on the Way to the Parable: The Steward, Tricksters, and (Non)sense in Luke 16:1–8', *Biblical Theology Bulletin* 48 (2018), 18–25.
King Missile	'Jesus Was Way Cool', *Instinct Records* (2004) <https://open.spotify.com/track/0Tos24ah4Q1OSe1qBH9TBW?si=-10d515126a7c4ebb> [Accessed February 4, 2022].

Lang, J. S.	*The Bible on the Big Screen: A Guide from Silent Films to Today's Movies* (Grand Rapids, MI: Baker, 2007).
Lewis, C. S.	*The Screwtape Letters* (New York, NY: MacMillan, 1941).
Lindvall, T.	'Freud and Lewis on Jokes, Humor and Laughter: A Preliminary Study', *CSL: The Bulletin of the New York C. S. Lewis Society* 42 (2011), 1–10, 12–15.
Lindvall, T.	*God Mocks: A History of Religious Satire from the Hebrew Prophets to Stephen Colbert* (New York, NY: NYU Press, 2015).
Lindvall, T.	*Surprised by Laughter: The Comic World of C.S. Lewis* (Nashville, TN: Thomas Nelson, 2012).
Marchiano, B.	*In the Footsteps of Jesus: One Man's Journey Through the Life of Christ* (Eugene, OR: Harvest House, 1997).
McIntyre, E.	'God's Comics: Religious Humour in Contemporary Evangelical Christian and Mormon Comedy' (Unpublished PhD dissertation, University of Sydney, Faculty of Arts and Social Sciences, 2014).
McKnight, S.	'Ethics of Jesus', in J. B. Green, J. K. Brown, and N. Perrin (eds.), *Dictionary of Jesus and the Gospels* (2nd edn; Downers Grove, IL: InterVarsity, 2013), 242–51.
Moore, R.	'Sardonic Atheists and Silly Evangelicals: The Relationship between Self-Concept and Humor Style', *Qualitative Sociology* 40 (2017), 447–65.
Morreall, J.	*Comic Relief: A Comprehensive Philosophy of Humour* (Chichester: Wiley-Blackwell, 2009).
Morreall, J.	*Taking Laughter Seriously* (Albany, NY: SUNY Press, 1983).
Neufeld, T. R. Y.	*Recovering Jesus: The Witness of the New Testament* (Grand Rapids, MI: Baker, 2007).
Regent College	'Seven Scholars Share Their Favourite Moments of Biblical Humour', <https://world.regent-college.edu/leading-ideas/biblical-humour> [Accessed on Friday 4 Feb 2022]
Reyburn, D. B.	'Laughter and the Between: G.K. Chesterton and the Reconciliation of Theology and Hilarity', *Radical Orthodoxy: Theology, Philosophy, Politics* 3 (2015), 18–51.
Rowell, E. K. and B. L. Steffen (eds.)	*Humor for Preaching and Teaching: From Leadership Journal and Christian Reader* (Grand Rapids, MI: Baker Books, 1998).

Saroglou, V.	'Religion and Sense of Humour: An A Priori Incompatibility? Theoretical Considerations from a Psychological Perspective', *Humor* 15 (2002), 191–214.
Siker, J. S.	'Alexamenos (inscription)', in R. S. Bagnall, K. Brodersen, C. B. Champion, A. Erskine, and S. R. Huebner (eds.), *The Encyclopedia of Ancient History* (Malden: Wiley-Blackwell, 2013), <https://doi-org.ezproxy.library.sydney.edu.au/10.1002/9781444338386.wbeah30596>.
Snodgrass, K. R.	*Stories with Intent: A Comprehensive Guide to the Parables of Jesus* (Grand Rapids, MI: Eerdmans, 2008).
Taylor, J. E.	*Jesus and Brian: Exploring the Historical Jesus and his Times via Monty Python's Life of Brian* (London: Bloomsbury, 2015).
Trueblood, E.	*The Humor of Christ* (New York, NY: Harper & Row, 1964).
Wilson, D.	*A Serrated Edge: A Brief Defense of Biblical Satire and Trinitarian Skylarking* (Moscow: Canon, 2003).

Burning Hearts
Emmaus as Realised Eschatology in the *Philokalic* Tradition

Doru Costache

the new age of grace and the new creation had already begun
James R. Harrison

Abstract

For the *philokalic* tradition the burning hearts at Luke 24:32 are a charismatic experience of the divine presence that can best be understood as realised, or inaugurated, eschatology. To make this assertion intelligible, first I introduce *philokalic* literature as a body of Byzantine writings that map spiritual experiences. Second, I provide a rough inventory of textual occurrences of warm, or burning, hearts in the eighteenth-century Athonite *Philokalia*. Third, I exemplify this experience as a charism, or sacrament, of the divine presence by adducing hagiographical witnesses, especially the sixth-century *Life of St Mary of Egypt*. Finally, I interpret the Emmaus narrative as denoting a charismatic experience of the *philokalic* sort, representative for realised, or inaugurated, eschatology. As critical keys, I draw upon Bucur's analysis of patristic reception of the Emmaus narrative, Florovsky's take on eschatology, and Harrison's views of the Pauline age of grace.

In his recent book, *Scripture Re-envisioned*, Bogdan Bucur deploys the Emmaus narrative in Luke 24:13–35 as a 'pattern of biblical exegesis' and a 'methodological prolegomenon' for examining biblical theophanies.[1] For him, this scriptural story represents a key to interpreting

---

1   Bucur, *Scripture Re-envisioned*, 4. The relevant chapter is found at 6–41. See also my review of this book in *Journal of Religious History* 45:3 (2021), 509–11.

other narratives, such as the many Old Testament references to the glorified Messiah.[2] But more relevant to my purposes is Bucur's detailed analysis of the burning hearts of the two disciples (Luke 24:32),[3] where he also discusses scriptural antecedents of this image and its recurrence within the patristic tradition.[4] He examines various scriptural connections of this phrase, indeed, especially theophanies such as the burning bush and the Sinai narrative in Exodus. Interestingly, Bucur does not clarify whether the burning hearts signify a genuine experience or a metaphorical sign of the Lord's presence. If I read his analysis correctly, he seems to understand it as a literary trope that corresponds to other scriptural and patristic devices meant to indicate the divine presence—all of which proposing luminous imagery—not as an actual experience.[5]

While I have no intention to deny the manifold literary connections of the burning hearts at Luke 24, as Bucur outlines them, in this paper I set out to show that his reading—as a metaphorical trope—is not the only possible approach. For example, for the *philokalic* literature the phrase under consideration signifies a charismatic way of experiencing the divine presence that can best be understood as realised or inaugurated eschatology, or eschatology experienced in the here and now. True, this understanding has profound scriptural roots. As James Harrison aptly points out, 'for Paul, the new age of grace and the new creation had already begun and were currently experienced in the body of Christ'.[6] No surprise there, then, as Paul's wisdom is a primary source

---

2   For a review of this messianic material, see *Scripture Re-envisioned* 12–18. The narratives of interest are located in Genesis 18, Exodus 3 and 33, Psalms 98–99 and 131–132, Isaiah 6, Habakkuk 3:2 (LXX), and Daniel 3 and 7.
3   Bucur, *Scripture Re-envisioned*, 29–34.
4   Bucur, *Scripture Re-envisioned*, 35–41.
5   If that were the case, Bucur's views would correspond to Giulea's conclusions based on a range of sources. See Giulea, 'Heavenly Fire', 252–72. In turn, Giulea's analysis finds a clear echo in the approach of Biriukov, 'Neilos Kabasilas', 373–91.
6   Harrison, 'Paul', 83. See also Harrison, *Paul's Language*, 226–33.

of *philokalic* spirituality.⁷ In addition, the realistic take on the narrative corresponds to the standard view of the Orthodox tradition, where, as the Byzantine liturgy attributed to John Chrysostom has it, 'you (that is, God) brought us up to heaven and bestowed on us your kingdom to come'.⁸ Future glory is the content of the Christian experience on this side of eternity.

In a narrow sense, the word *philokalic* designates a Byzantine corpus of writings on holiness and the spiritual life, spanning a millennium, and more broadly the quest for such a way of life.⁹ To make intelligible my assertion about the *philokalic* view of the burning hearts as a charismatic experience, first I introduce the literary corpus under consideration. Second, I produce a partial inventory of textual occurrences in the eighteenth-century *Philokalia* compiled at Mount Athos, which document an understanding of this phrase, literally, as indicating a charismatic experience, illustrating the point by analysing a couple of relevant passages. Third, I exemplify this charismatic way of experiencing the divine presence by quick glances at the sixth-century *Life of St Mary of Egypt* and other hagiographical sources. Finally, in the light of this evidence I propose a view of the Emmaus narrative as denoting a charismatic experience of the *philokalic* sort, and as illustrating what modern theologians call realised, or inaugurated, eschatology. In so doing, rather than parting ways with Bucur's views, I corroborate his interpretation of the Emmaus story as showcasing the mystery of the glorified Messiah *truly* present in the midst of his disciples.

---

7   The towering figure of Paul permeates the *Philokalia*. By my rough word-count, he is mentioned by name 377 times (41 in vol. 1; 51 in vol. 2; 144 in vol. 3; 87 in vol. 4; 54 in vol. 5). See *The Philokalia*, four vols, trans. Palmer, Sherrard, and Ware (the fifth volume was published much later, unprofessionally; Kottayam: R. I. C. Foundation, 2017).

8   ἡμᾶς εἰς τὸν οὐρανὸν ἀνήγαγες καὶ τὴν βασιλείαν σου ἐχαρίσω τὴν μέλλουσαν. *Divine Liturgy*, 70–71. Apart from this one, all translations from the original Greek belong to me.

9   Several *philokalic* collections are known. See McGuckin, '*Philokalia*', 35–49; McGuckin, '*Philokalic* Tradition', 5–11; Ware, 'St. Nikodimos and the *Philokalia*', 9–35. The most celebrated of these collections is that of Mount Athos, originally published in 1782, in two volumes, available in English in five volumes (translated from the third edition, 1957–1963). For the spiritual nature of the *philokalic* quest, see Louth, 'The Theology of the *Philokalia*', 351–61.

1. Introducing the *Philokalic* Tradition

Now, what is, more specifically, the *philokalic* tradition? Before anything, I consider the lexical family of this technical term. The dictionaries give the verb φιλοκαλέω, which they render as to cultivate a taste for the beautiful, to be enthusiastic about the beautiful or the good, to study, elaborate, and to put things in good order. In turn, the noun φιλοκαλία means love for the beautiful, love of cleanliness, calculation, working out a problem, care, and attention.[10] The early Christian authors used *philokalic* either in an ethical sense or as referring to scholarly endeavours, including diligence in study and gathering useful information. Thus, Clement of Alexandria (d. c. 215) contrasted the saints' 'true love for the beautiful' (ἀληθοῦς φιλοκαλίας) and the 'voluptuous and ignoble life' of the crowds (*The Educator* 3.7.37.1).[11] In turn, Athanasius of Alexandria (d. 373) praised an interlocutor who 'diligently' (φιλοκάλως) desired to understand the fundamentals of the faith (*Against the Gentiles* 1.1–2). Finally, two younger contemporaries of Athanasius, Basil of Caesarea (d. 379) and Gregory the Theologian (d. c. 389), took the term to mean the activity of selecting worthwhile thoughts from the writings of others, for example 'the *philokalia* of Origen' ('Ὠριγένους φιλοκαλίας; *Letter to Theodore of Tyana* 4.6–7).[12]

It is these three meanings—that is, ethical values, search for understanding, and collection of noteworthy texts—that later writers associated with the *philokalic* quest. Efforts to map the history of this quest have been already undertaken.[13] Nevertheless, what we know best is one of its eighteenth-century outcomes, the Athonite *Philokalia* compiled by Macarius of Corinth (d. 1805) and Nicodemus of the Holy Mountain (d. 1809), especially due to its modern translations.[14] This collection, first printed in 1782, largely based on manuscripts found in

---

10 For details, see McGuckin, 'Philokalia', 36–37; McGuckin, 'Philokalic Tradition', 2–3.
11 Mondésert, *Clément*.
12 Text in Harl and de Lange, *Origène*.
13 Harmless, 'Monasticism', 493–517; Louth, 'The literature', 373–81; McGuckin, 'Philokalia', 37–48.
14 Deseille, *La spiritualité orthodoxe*, 230–69; Ware, 'St. Nikodimos and the Philokalia', 18–32.

the monasteries of Mount Athos, covers a thousand years of spiritual literature, from the fourth to the fifteenth century. In geographical progression, moving northwards, this literature originates in centres from Egypt, Sinai, Palestine, Syria, Greece, Athos, and Constantinople. Initially, the impact of the Athonite edition was limited, given that it presents the works in their original languages—late antique Greek and its Byzantine iteration—at that time mastered only by very few people. Much more impactful have been the 1779 Slavonic translation of Paisij Velichkovsky (d. 1794), *Dobrotulubiye*, soon enough rendered into Russian,[15] and the Romanian translation of Monk Rafael, of 1769, the *Philokalia of Dragomirna*, the latter both continuing and catalysing an already rich local *philokalic* tradition.[16] What matters is that the early modern *philokalic* quest caused positive ripples throughout the Orthodox world and beyond it.[17]

A quick look at the title of the Athonite *Philokalia* of 1782 will suffice to explain this success. It reads as follows:

> *The Philokalia* of the holy ones (who are) sober (watchful/vigilant), collected from our holy and God-bearing fathers, on how the mind is purified, enlightened, and perfected by way of praxis and contemplation, which pertain to ethical philosophy (Φιλοκαλία τῶν ἱερῶν νηπτικῶν συνερανισθεῖσα παρὰ τῶν ἁγίων καὶ θεοφόρων πατέρων ἡμῶν ἐν ᾗ διὰ τῆς κατὰ τὴν πρᾶξιν καὶ θεωρίαν ἠθικῆς φιλοσοφίας ὁ νοῦς καθαίρεται, φωτίζεται, καὶ τελειοῦται).

---

15 McGuckin, 'Philokalia', 39–43; McGuckin, 'Life and Mission', 157–73.
16 This work is preserved in the Library of the Romanian Academy as Ms. rom. 2597. It has also become available in digital format at https://medievalia.com.ro/manuscrise/item/ms-rom-2597. For references to this manuscript, see Costache, 'Orthodox Gnosis', 431; McGuckin, 'Philokalia', 42; McGuckin, 'Life and Mission', 165. While not much is known by the Anglophone reader about this first-ever translation of *philokalic* writings into a modern language, i.e. Romanian, several studies in Romanian mention it. For a detailed description of this manuscript, see Zaharia, 'Biserica ortodoxă română', 50–54.
17 Costache, 'Orthodox Gnosis', 431–434; Louth, *Modern Orthodox Thinkers*, 1–12, 341–48; McGuckin, 'Christian Spirituality', 102–103; McGuckin, 'Life and Mission', 168–71.

This lengthy title captures the idea of a philosophical kind of quest for spiritual wisdom—in the sense of philosophy as a way of life[18]—and the traditional—or patristic—anchoring of this effort,[19] as well as the perspective of a transformative process leading to holiness. The literature on this curriculum of holy life, having its roots in the Platonic tradition mediated by a plethora of early Christian authors, is immense.[20] The aftermaths of the eighteenth-century *philokalic* movement show that it has not lost its appeal to modern seekers either.[21] It is against this backdrop that I must now turn to the burning hearts of the *Philokalia*.

2. Charismatic Experiences in the *Philokalia*

I do not intend either to offer a comprehensive list of relevant passages or to discuss all of the selected texts in great detail. My goal is to establish, by several illustrations, the *philokalic* representation of the burning hearts as a charism that signals God's presence. Such an undertaking is demanded by the curious lack of interest of scholars of the *Philokalia* in the reality of this charism, beyond the known literary tropes.[22] In what follows, specifically, I consider the relevant texts as they are found, according to the order of the Athonite collection.

The first allusion to this charismatic experience appears in Isaiah the Solitary (d. c. 491), who refers to expecting God to arrive 'with

---

18   This, overall, was the perception of the early Christians about their experience. See Costache, 'The Teacher and His School', 227–51 (end the sources quoted therein). At pp. 243–245, I discuss the relevant views of a *philokalic* author, Neilus the Ascetic (d. c. 430).
19   The same idea of relying upon patristic sources in order to articulate the spiritual discourse appears in yet another *philokalic* author, Maximus the Confessor (d. 662). See Costache, 'Asceticism', 136–37.
20   Here are a few sources, but see also the bibliography they include. Bucur, 'Hierarchy', 2–45; Costache, 'Christian Gnosis', 260–61, 262–65; Costache, 'Being', 57–62, 66–71, 73–84; DeConick, 'Traumatic Mysteries', 23–26; Louth, *The Origins*, 56–60, 97–110; Niculescu, 'Spiritual Leavening', 465–68.
21   McGuckin, '*Philokalia*', 42; McGuckin, '*Philokalic* Tradition', 7, 12–17; Russell, *The Doctrine of Deification*, 310–20; Ware, 'St. Nikodimos and the *Philokalia*', 33–35.
22   See, for example, Gillet, *The Jesus Prayer*, 56, 63, 78, 82, 95, who mentions it without bothering to note its strange frequency in *philokalic* and non-*philokalic* sources. See also Cunningham, 'The Jesus Prayer', 199; Toti, 'The Hesychast Method', 18–19.

sweetness of heart' (ἐν ἡδύτητι καρδίας; *On Guarding the Intellect*, 13).[23] This phrase might not explicitly mention warmth or fire, but the notion of the heart's sweetness, elsewhere called joy, usually signals that very experience. Thus, Diadochus of Photiki (d. c. 486) points out that, even though sometimes it experiences a waning of the inner fire, the spiritually awakened person quickly 'revives the fire within it (ἀναζωπυροῦσα) by the warmth of the love of God (τῇ θέρμῃ τῆς ἀγαπῆς τοῦ Θεοῦ)'; as a result, the person turns towards the neighbour 'with great joy' (μετὰ πολλῆς χαρᾶς; *On Spiritual Knowledge*, 15).[24] Divine warmth and joy appear together here. It is true that the heart is missing, but the point about love presupposes it. That said, Diadochus has much more to say about the charism under consideration. According to him, the heart, or soul, registers the divine presence in stages. Here is what he has to say at some point:

> When the soul has reached awareness of itself (ἐν τῇ ἑαυτῆς ἐπιγνώσει), it produces from within a certain warmth and God-loving reverence (θέρμην τινὰ καὶ θεοφιλῆ αἰδῶ). When (this feeling) is not disturbed by worldly cares, it gives birth to a certain yearning for peace (ἔρωτά τινα ἀποτίκτει ἐν τῇ εἰρήνῃ) that, accordingly (συμμέτρως), searches out the God of peace. But it [namely, this blessed state] quickly dissipates [...]. In turn, the warmth (θέρμη) the Most-Holy Spirit brings to the heart (τῇ καρδίᾳ) is both wholly peaceful and lasting (εἰρηνική ἐστιν ὅλη καὶ ἀνένδοτος). It stirs in all the parts of the soul a longing for God. It is not fanned by anything exterior to the heart, but rather brings delight and joy to the whole person by itself, with a kind of endless love. And so, while we become aware of the first [kind of warmth], we should pursue the second one (*On Spiritual Knowledge* 74).[25]

According to this excerpt, the charismatic experience progresses in two stages, from a natural warmth to a supernatural one, for want of better

---

23 Φιλοκαλία, 1:35.
24 Φιλοκαλία, 1:208.
25 Φιλοκαλία, 1:224.

words. What facilitates the first stage is the person's own effort—very likely consisting in ascetic purification and prayerful contemplation, by which the mind is quieted[26]—which leads to what Diadochus calls the soul's 'awareness of itself' (see ἐν τῇ ἑαυτῆς ἐπιγνώσει). Here, as in many other patristic contexts, soul or heart—sometimes the mindful soul[27]—signifies what we, in modern times, would call person.[28] The person's clear, knowing, stilled, and focused mind is what facilitates this strange experience. During this phase, 'a certain warmth' (θέρμην τινά) comforts the recipients, enticing them to seek further closeness with the Lord and to attain peace. Diadochus refers to this feeling without bothering to describe or to explain it. He takes for granted that the readers would know what it means, especially readers who experience it, too. For the readers unaware of this experience, he only qualifies the feeling of warmth by τινά: a certain/sort of/kind of pleasant fire or warmth. This feeling seems to be identical to what Isaiah calls the 'sweetness of heart'.

Either way, the heart's warmth is something that can truly be felt—it registers physiologically, as it were—but we should not expect it to correspond to anything we usually feel in terms of, say, pain or pleasure. By the way, when I have become aware of this experience, repeatedly mentioned in the *philokalic* literature, I asked a cardiologist about it, and he dryly remarked that the heart's nervous system is not equipped to feel anything. The overwhelming evidence within the *Philokalia* and elsewhere nevertheless points to something truly occurring,[29] even though this experience eludes modern measuring devices.[30] That said, neither the warmth nor the peace experienced at this stage—both marking a measure of success in the quest for holiness—are per-

---

26 See Chryssavgis, 'Solitude', 262-76.
27 For example, Athanasius of Alexandria refers interchangeably to 'soul', 'mind', and the 'mindful soul' in *Against the Gentiles* 30.13-25; 33.40-43.
28 See Lossky, *Mystical Theology*, 120-21, 123-24, 127. For the overlapping of soul and heart in patristic sources, see also Costache, 'Adam's Holiness', 331-32, 338.
29 For a survey of relevant sources outside the *philokalic* tradition, see Harvey, 'Sensing More', 97-106.
30 Of late, I have become increasingly interested in this matter. See, for example, my *Humankind*, 47-48, 256-57; 'Orthodox Gnosis', 427.

manent and stable. Elsewhere, Diadochus says that they who merely begin to experience the 'spiritual energy' (πνευματικὴ ἐνέργεια) have their hearts only 'partially (μερικῶς) warmed up by the holy grace'; through an analogy, they are like the persons who, in winter, face east at sunrise and enjoy a bit of warmth on their cheeks, while their back remains cold (*On Spiritual Knowledge* 88).[31] It is only when the recipients advance to the next, supernatural phase that their hearts receive the Spirit's own gift, experiencing enduring warmth (θέρμη) and peace in its presence.

This twofold process seems to amount to the person's advancement towards compatibility with the Spirit, as denoted by the adverb συμμέτρως, which I have translated by 'accordingly', but which suggests proportionality, thus a *tantum quantum* principle—not unlike what Harrison has discovered in Paul's theology of grace.[32] Thus, only by achieving a measure of peace—or equanimity, serenity—undoubtedly by way of the ascetic and contemplative reorientation of the 'passions',[33] can the person strive to meet the 'God of peace', the transcendent source of true peace. It is progress in the virtuous life, the life of holiness, that brings us increasingly closer to the Holy Spirit, who is the fulness of holiness. And the holy warmth of the first stage, as feeble and as impermanent as it might be, marks our preparedness for a truer and a fuller experience. The steps of progress (ἐπεκτάσεις) of patristic literature—understood as cognitive leaps conditioned by ascetic purification[34]—are here rendered as existential states whose measure is given by the intensity of the fire felt inside, within our physiologically insensitive hearts.

In short, Diadochus refers to the soul's or the mind's achievement marked by its own warmth—natural, as it were, but without a doubt

---

31 Φιλοκαλία, 1:230. See Williams, 'The Theological World', 106.
32 Harrison, 'Paul', 91; Harrison, *Paul's Language*, 110-14, 247-48.
33 See Blowers, 'Hope', 216-29.
34 For an analysis of the concept of ἐπέκτασις in the thinking of an indirect contributor the *philokalic* tradition, Gregory of Nyssa, see Daniélou, *Platonisme*, 291-307. Gregory is an indirect contributor in that his works are not included in the Athonite collection, but he is a contributor nonetheless, in that his views influenced major *philokalic* authors such as Maximus.

ascetically and prayerfully catalysed—with the climax of this experience being a Spirit-induced, supernatural or gracious warmth, characterised by peace and permanence (εἰρηνική ἐστιν ὅλη καὶ ἀνένδοτος). Even the first phase of this experience entails certain physiological changes, as the heart naturally has no feelings, but transformation increases exponentially with the person advancing in virtue. The advanced person, who 'makes progress in keeping the commandments and calls ceaselessly (ἀπαύστως) upon the Lord Jesus' (*On Spiritual Knowledge* 85),[35] experiences fundamental changes, of a biological and a cognitive nature. For such a person,

> the fire of the holy grace (τὸ πῦρ τῆς ἁγίας χάριτος) spreads even to the heart's external organs of perception (τὰ ἐξώτερα αἰσθητήρια τῆς καρδίας) [...]. When the struggling persons have finally acquired all the virtues (πάσας τὰς ἀρετάς) [...] then some kind of deeper sense-perception (βαθυτέρα τινὶ αἴσθησις) illumines their whole being (πᾶσαν φύσιν), warming (περιθάλπουσα) it with great love of God.[36]

No wonder Evagrius the Solitary (d. 399), elsewhere in the *Philokalia*, could assert that persons who reach this state, resembling Cleopas of Luke 24, 'bring (to God) a heart burning (καρδίαν καιομένην) with the mysteries' of spiritual experience (*On Discernment*, 7).[37] Norman Russel summarises this charismatic experience as a threefold progression, from the initial warming heart to the fiery stage to the whole being permeated by divine fire.[38]

Overall, the experiences captured by the authors mentioned above are either their own or belong to ascetics known to them. And while *philokalic* authors resisted the temptation of saying plainly that they lived such things themselves, the details they provided and the consistency of their descriptions lead to the conclusion that such occurrences

---

35 Φιλοκαλία, 1:229.
36 Diadochus' *On Spiritual Knowledge* 85, Φιλοκαλία, 1:229. Cf. John of Karpathos, *Texts for the Monks in India* 96, in Φιλοκαλία, 1:257.
37 Φιλοκαλία, 1:49.
38 Russell, *The Doctrine of Deification*, 246–47.

are real. Abundant internal and external evidence confirms it. Regarding internal sources, the transformative and deifying experience of the burning hearts can be found throughout the *Philokalia*.[39] Below I briefly review several examples from the second kind of sources.

3. Other Witnesses

The examples discussed above, which evidence the charismatic understanding of the burning hearts in *philokalic* literature, are not isolated cases. And while other charisms are better represented in related sources, insofar as they are much more common, the warming of hearts is not unheard of either. I conclude my survey by adducing other accounts, but focusing on *Life of St Mary of Egypt*.

It is assumed that Mary of Egypt, formerly an eccentric prostitute who did not seek money, lived in the sixth century, but her identity cannot be established with absolute certainty.[40] Upon her conversion under the guidance of the Lord's Virgin Mother, that is, when a 'saving word' (λόγος σωτήριος) touched, or lit up, the 'eyes of the heart' (τῶν

---

39 θέρμη τοῦ πόθου ('warmth of desire'; Abba Philemon, *Discourse*, in Φιλοκαλία, 1:487); ἐθερμάνθη ἡ καρδία μου ('my heart warmed up'); Ilias the Presbyter, *Gnomic Anthology* 94, in Φιλοκαλία, 1:544); καρδιακήτις θέρμη ('hearty warmth'; Theophanes the Monk, *The Ladder of Divine Graces* 2, in Φιλοκαλία, 1:549); (grace wakes up the heart and) θερμαίνοντος τὰς [...] δυνάμεις ἡμῶν ('warms up our aptitudes'; Nikitas Stithatos, *Practical Chapters* 1.9, in Φιλοκαλία, 2:787); (the energy of prayer) ἐν τῇ καρδίᾳ ἐνεργοῦσαν ἔχειν [...] θερμαίνουσαν τὸν νοῦν καὶ εὐφραίνουσαν ('has the heart energised, and the mind warmed up and full of gladness'; Gregory of Sinai, *On the Signs of Grace and Delusion* 3, in Φιλοκαλία, 2:909); (the energy of grace is) δύναμις τοῦ πυρὸς τοῦ πνεύματος [...] καρδιακῶς κινουμένη [...] καὶ θερμαίνουσα τὴν ψυχήν ('the power of the spirit's fire that moves within the heart and warms up the soul'; Gregory of Sinai, *On the Signs of Grace and Delusion* 9, in Φιλοκαλία, 2:910); ἐνέργεια γίνεται ἐν καρδίᾳ [...] τῆς θείας θέρμης ἀναφανείσης ('at the occurrence of the divine warmth, energy fills the heart'; Gregory of Sinai, *On Serenity and Two Kinds of Prayer* 1, in Φιλοκαλία, 2:911) etc.

40 For details of her identity and various biographies, see Gunderson and Huehnergard, 'An Ethiopic Version', 152-57; Kouli, 'Introduction', 65-69; Mena, *Place and Identity*, 85-114. None of these sources discusses Mary's charismatic experiences. For a recent translation of the main hagiography, see *Life of St Mary of Egypt*, trans. M. Kouli, in *Holy Women*, 70-93.

ὀφθαλμῶν τῆς καρδίας; *Life of St Mary of Egypt*, 23),[41] Mary felt within her 'the fire of faith' (τὸ τῆς πίστεως ἔμπυρον), which she received 'like a kind of assurance' (ὥσπερ τινὰ πληροφορίαν) regarding her salvation (*Life of St Mary of Egypt*, 24).[42] We notice, here, the internalisation of the charismatic fire we encountered throughout the *Philokalia*, together with the indefinite pronoun τινά, denoting the strangeness of the experience. Afterwards, spending decades in the wilderness of Jordan as a hermit, Mary was constantly comforted by the sight of a 'sweet light' (τὸ φῶς [...] τὸ γλυκύ) that 'shone everywhere around' (πάντοθεν περιαστράπτον) her (*Life of St Mary of Egypt*, 28–29).[43] Apart from the synaesthetic sense of tasting the supernal light, what she experienced corresponds to Isaiah the Solitary's 'sweetness of heart'. We are on familiar grounds. Other early Christian and Byzantine hagiographies contain more references of this sort,[44] all of which document the reality of the charism under consideration. Later saintly witnesses of this experience, such as Theodora of Sihla (d. c. 1700), Seraphim of Sarov (d. 1833), and Silouan the Athonite (d. 1938), confirm Mary's perception of the same heartfelt warmth become perceptible around them.[45]

Against this backdrop, the burning hearts of the two disciples in the Lord's presence (Luke 24:32) should not be taken as a peculiar way of describing emotion, a literary trope, or an empty metaphor. As evidenced by the *Philokalia* and further hagiographical material, the burning hearts are a genuine experience, a supernaturally induced response of human nature in God's presence; a sacrament of the presence, as it were. Regardless of how this experience is worded—as sweet light, warmth, or fire—something does happen within the human

---

41 *Patrologia Graeca* (hereafter, PG) 87.3713B.
42 PG 87.3713D.
43 PG 87.3717B.
44 *Life of St Matrona of Perge* 39, 40; *Life of St Theodora of Thessaloniki*, 32. For English translations of these hagiographies, see *Holy Women of Byzantium*, 18–64, 164–217. See also the cases discussed in Costache, 'Adam's Holiness', 337–40.
45 See Costache, 'Orthodox Gnosis', 431, 433; Gallaher, 'Pneumatology', 513–16; Sophrony, *Saint Silouan*.

heart, in the person's inner temple, to then envelop other parts of the body, and the body in its entirety, as well as becoming manifest around the saints, impacting the environment. Especially the accounts on Mary of Egypt and Seraphim of Sarov are illustrative of the latter aspect, but so are, too, various other stories.[46] It is true that this experience pertains to the glory of the age to come, but, to paraphrase George Florovsky, for the saints realised or inaugurated eschatology is no longer a way of thinking about things; it is a way of experiencing reality in the here and now.[47] I have shown elsewhere that it is only in the light of the saints' experiences that we can truly grasp the meaning of certain scriptural narratives.[48]

As with my earlier reference to the liturgy, this sense of celebrating the Lord's presence in the here and now finds its perfect expression in the Byzantine ritual of the 'kiss of peace', consistently accompanied by the exclamation 'Christ in our midst!'[49] This is *parousia* as presence, as a *fait accompli*. This understanding corresponds to the message of my motto—'the new age of grace and the new creation had already begun'—inspired by Jim Harrison's insightful analysis of Pauline eschatology. Against this backdrop, my conclusion is that Luke's burning hearts refer to a real, charismatic form of experiencing God's presence, even the glorified Messiah of the Hebrew Scriptures, in the Holy Spirit, not merely a literary trope.

Doru Costache
Department of Studies in Religion, University of Sydney

---

46 See Costache, *Humankind and the Cosmos*, 46-48; Costache, 'John Moschus', 21-34.
47 Florovsky, *Christianity*, 58, 61, 65, 129; Florovsky, *Aspects*, 63-78.
48 Costache, 'Adam's Holiness', 330-31, 334-36; *Humankind and the Cosmos*, 150, 172-78.
49 ὁ Χριστὸς ἐν τῷ μέσῳ ἡμῶν. *The Divine Liturgy*, 64.

Bibliography

Biriukov, D. — 'Neilos Kabasilas's *Rule of Theology* and the Distinction between the Light and Warmth of Fire in Neilos Kabasilas and Gregory Palamas', *Scrinium* 14 (2018), 373-91.

Blowers, P. — 'Hope for the Passible Self: The Use and Transformation of the Human Passions in the Fathers of the *Philokalia*', in B. Bingaman and B. Nassif (eds.), *The Philokalia: A Classic Text of Orthodox Spirituality* (Oxford University Press, 2012), 216-29.

Bucur, B. G. — *Scripture Re-envisioned: Christophanic Exegesis and the Making of a Christian Bible* (The Bible in Ancient Christianity 13; Leiden and Boston: Brill, 2019).

Bucur, B. G. — 'Hierarchy, Eldership, Isangelia: Clement of Alexandria and the Ascetic Tradition', in D. Costache, P. Kariatlis, and M. Baghos (eds.), *Alexandrian Legacy: A Critical Appraisal* (Newcastle upon Tyne: Cambridge Scholars, 2015), 2-45.

Chryssavgis, J. — 'Solitude, Silence, and Stillness: Light from the Palestinian Desert', in B. Bingaman and B. Nassif (eds.), *The Philokalia: A Classic Text of Orthodox Spirituality* (Oxford: Oxford University Press, 2012), 262-76.

Costache, D. — 'Adam's Holiness in the Alexandrine and Athonite Traditions', in D. Costache, P. Kariatlis, and M. Baghos (eds), *Alexandrian Legacy: A Critical Appraisal* (Newcastle upon Tyne: Cambridge Scholars, 2015), 322-68.

Costache, D. — 'Asceticism, Well-Being, and Compassion in Maximus the Confessor,' in P. G. Bolt and J. R. Harrison (eds.), *Justice, Mercy, and Well-Being: Interdisciplinary Perspectives* (Eugene, OR: Pickwick, 2020), 134-47.

Costache, D. — 'Being, Well-being, Being for Ever: Creation's Existential Trajectory in Patristic Tradition', in D. Costache, D. Cronshaw, and J. Harrison (eds.), *Well-being, Personal Wholeness and the Social Fabric* (Newcastle upon Tyne: Cambridge Scholars, 2017), 55-87.

Costache, D. — 'Byzantine and Modern Orthodox Gnosis: from the Eleventh to the Twenty-First century', in G. W. Trompf, G. B. Mikkelsen, and J. Johnston (eds.), *The Gnostic World*

	(Routledge Worlds; London and New York, NY: Routledge, 2019), 426–35.
Costache, D.	'Christian Gnosis: From Clement the Alexandrian to John Damascene', in G. W. Trompf, G. B. Mikkelsen, and J. Johnston (eds.), *The Gnostic World* (Routledge Worlds; London and New York, NY: Routledge, 2019), 259–70.
Costache, D.	*Humankind and the Cosmos: Early Christian Representations* (Supplements to Vigiliae Christianae 170; Leiden and Boston: Brill, 2021).
Costache, D.	'John Moschus on Asceticism and the Environment', *Colloquium* 48:1 (2016), 21–34.
Costache, D.	'The Teacher and His School: Philosophical Representations of Jesus and Christianity', in P. G. Bolt and J. R. Harrison (eds.), *The Impact of Jesus of Nazareth: Historical, Theological, and Pastoral Perspectives*, vol. 2: *Social and Pastoral Studies* (CGAR Series 2; Macquarie Park: SCD Press, 2021), 227–51.
Cunningham, M. B.	'The Place of the Jesus Prayer in the *Philokalia*', in in B. Bingaman and B. Nassif (eds.), *The Philokalia: A Classic Text of Orthodox Spirituality* (Oxford: Oxford University Press, 2012), 195–202.
Daniélou, J.	*Platonisme et Théologie Mystique: Essai sur la Doctrine Spirituelle de Saint Grégoire de Nysse* (Aubier: Montaigne, 1944).
DeConick, A. D.	'Traumatic Mysteries: Pathways of Mysticism among the Early Christians', in A. A. Orlov (ed.), *Jewish Roots of Eastern Christian Mysticism: Studies in Honor of Alexander Golitzin* (Supplements to Vigiliae Christianae 160; Leiden and Boston: Brill, 2020), 11–51.
Deseille, P.	*La spiritualité orthodoxe et la Philocalie* (Paris: Albin Michel, 2003).
Florovsky, G.	*Aspects of Church History* (Collected Works 4; Belmont, MA: Nordland, 1974).
Florovsky, G.	*Christianity and Culture* (Collected Works 2; Belmont, MA: Nordland, 1974).
Gallaher, B.	'Pneumatology', in E. Howells and M. A. McIntosh (eds.), *The Oxford Handbook of Mystical Theology* (Oxford: Oxford University Press, 2020), 507–28.

Gillet, L.   *The Jesus Prayer* (revised edn; Crestwood, NY: St Vladimir's Seminary Press, 1987).

Giulea, D. A.   'The Heavenly Fire Working the Earth of the Heart: Origen, Antony, Pseudo-Macarius, and the Internalisation of the Image of Divine Fire', *Scrinium* 5 (2009), 252–72.

Gunderson, J. and J. Huehnergard   'An Ethiopic Version of the Life of St Mary of Egypt', *Vostok* 3 (2019), 151–79.

Harl, M. and N. de Lange (eds.)   *Origène: Philocalie, 1–20 et Lettre à Africanus* (Sources chrétiennes 302; Paris: Cerf, 1983).

Harmless, J. W.   'Monasticism', in S. Ashbrook Harvey and D. G. Hunter (eds.), *The Oxford Handbook of Early Christian Studies* (Oxford: Oxford University Press, 2008), 493–517.

Harrison, J. R.   'Paul, Eschatology and the Augustan Age of Grace', *Tyndale Bulletin* 50.1 (1999), 79–91.

Harrison, J. R.   *Paul's Language of Grace in Its Graeco-Roman Context* (Wissenschaftliche Untersuchungen zum Neuen Testament 172; Tübingen: Mohr Siebeck, 2003).

Harvey, S.   'Sensing More in Ancient Religion', *Svensk Teologisk Kvartalskrift* 89 (2013), 97–106.

Kouli, M.   'Life of St Mary of Egypt: Introduction', in A. M. Talbot (ed.), *Holy Women of Byzantium: Ten Saints' Lives in English Translation* (Washington, DC: Dumbarton Oaks Research Library and Collection, 1996), 65–69.

Lossky, V.   *The Mystical Theology of the Eastern Church* (Crestwood, NY: St Vladimir's Seminary Press, 2002).

Louth, A.   *Modern Orthodox Thinkers: From the* Philokalia *to the Present* (London: SPCK, 2015).

Louth, A.   'The literature of the monastic movement', in F. Young, L. Ayres, and A. Louth (eds), *The Cambridge History of Early Christian Literature* (Cambridge: Cambridge University Press, 2004), 373–81.

Louth, A.   *The Origins of the Christian Mystical Tradition: From Plato to Denys* (2nd edn; Oxford: Oxford University Press, 2007).

Louth, A.   'The Theology of the *Philokalia*', in J. Behr, A. Louth, and D. Conomos (eds.), *Abba: The Tradition of Orthodoxy in the West* (Crestwood, NY: St Vladimir's Seminary Press, 2003), 351–61.

McGuckin, J. A.   'Christian Spirituality in Byzantium and the East (600–1700)', in Arthur Holder (ed.), *The Blackwell Companion to Christian Spirituality* (Chichester: Blackwell, 2005), 90–105.

McGuckin, J. A.   'How the Philokalic Tradition Came to Modern America—And what America Made of It' (Orthodoxy in America Series; New York: Fordham University, 2012), 1–20.

McGuckin, J. A.   'The Life and Mission of St. Paisius Velichkovsky (1722–1794): An Early Modern Master of the Orthodox Spiritual Life', *Spiritus* 9 (2009), 157–73.

McGuckin, J. A.   'The Making of the *Philokalia*: A Tale of Monks and Manuscripts', in B. Bingaman and B. Nassif (eds.), *The Philokalia: A Classic Text of Orthodox Spirituality* (Oxford: Oxford University Press, 2012), 35–49.

Mena, P. A.   *Place and Identity in the Lives of Antony, Paul, and Mary of Egypt: Desert as Borderland* (Religion and Spatial Studies; Cham: Palgrave Macmillan, 2019).

Mondésert, C. (ed.)   *Clément d'Alexandrie: Le Pédagogue—Livre III* (Sources chrétiennes 158; Paris: Cerf, 1970).

Niculescu, M. V.   'Spiritual Leavening: The Communication and Reception of the Good News in Origen's Biblical Exegesis and Transformative Pedagogy', *Journal of Early Christian Studies* 15.4 (2007), 447–81.

Palmer, G. E. H., P. Sherrard, and K. Ware (trans.)   *The Philokalia: The Complete Text Compiled by St Nikodimos of the Holy Mountain and St Makarios of Corinth* (4 vols; London and Boston: Faber & Faber, 1994).

Russell, N.   *The Doctrine of Deification in the Greek Patristic Tradition* (Oxford Early Christian Studies; New York, NY: Oxford University Press, 2004).

Sophrony, A.   *Saint Silouan the Athonite* (New York, NY: St Vladimir's Seminary Press, 1991).

The Divine Liturgy of Our Father among the Saints John Chrysostom (bilingual edn; Sydney: St Andrew's Orthodox Press, 2005).

Thomson, R. W. (ed.)   *Athanasius: Contra Gentes and De Incarnatione* (Oxford Early Christian Texts; Oxford: Clarendon, 1971).

Toti, M.	'The Hesychast Method of Prayer: Its Anthropological and Symbolic Significance', *International Journal for the Study of the Christian Church* 8:1 (2008), 17–32.
Ware, K.	'St. Nikodimos and the *Philokalia*', in B. Bingaman and B. Nassif (eds.), *The Philokalia: A Classic Text of Orthodox Spirituality* (Oxford: Oxford University Press, 2012), 9–35.
Williams, R.	'The Theological World of the *Philokalia*', in B. Bingaman and B. Nassif (eds), *The Philokalia: A Classic Text of Orthodox Spirituality* (Oxford: Oxford University Press, 2012), 102–21.
Zaharia, C.	'Biserica ortodoxă română şi traducerile filocalice şi patristice în limbile moderne,' in D. Zamfirescu (ed.), *Paisianismul: Un moment românesc în istoria spiritualităţii europene* (Bucureşti: Roza Vânturilor, 1996), 46–64.

The Doctor, the High Priest, the Aristocrat, and the Apostle

Peter G. Bolt

Abstract

In the New Testament, Luke is associated with Theophilus, Joanna, and Paul. Following up suggestions about the identification of Luke, Theophilus, and Joanna, often long-made but just as often ignored, opens up some intriguing possibilities for relationships within the earliest Christian missionary movement.

1. Introduction

Theophilus and Joanna are both briefly but prominently mentioned in the writings of Luke, the long-term companion of Paul. Just like Ellis was sure that 'a clarification of [Paul's associates'] role may serve to illuminate the structure of the early Christian mission,'[1] the clarification of Paul's relationship to Luke and his two friends also promises to throw light on the earliest days of that mission.[2]

In method, this exploration draws together a number of suggestions—mostly previously advanced and known for a long time—in order

---

1 Ellis, 'Paul and his Coworkers', 3.
2 In bringing together Paul and Luke, serving together in the gospel of God's grace, the essay touches upon some of Jim Harrison's major interests. We first met in the early 90s as graduate students at Macquarie University and committee members of the Society for the Study of Early Christianity. In 'these latter days', it is my privilege to count Jim as a friend and my delight to serve with him as a colleague at the Sydney College of Divinity and a co-worker in Christ's mission of grace. With apologies to my fellow-contributors, the length of this essay perhaps expresses the 'editor's indulgence' often displayed in the mutual inability to keep to word limits as Jim and I contribute to our various co-edited works!

to propose a hypothesis that might be tested by its results.[3] As I have argued already in a similar (and overlapping) study, these suggestions:

> seek to integrate the broader available data on the assumption of the coherence of the early Christian movement, especially in view of the fact that it originated with a small group of people which then expanded its membership through natural networks. Because the rationalistic criticism that has plagued New Testament studies for centuries has maximised diversity and demanded certainty, it has often too quickly dismissed such possibilities as 'conjecture', or even 'speculation', as if coherence is not a necessary and natural part of a burgeoning movement and conjecture is not a fundamental and necessary part of empirical historical inquiry. The principle of 'realistic coherence' allows for historical possibilities to be tabled and duly considered, as the empirical data are brought together.[4]

2. The Doctor: Luke

Through his famous 'we-passages' (11:28 D; 16:10–17; 20:5–21:18; 27:1–28:16), the author of the Book of Acts subtly revealed that he was a close companion of the apostle Paul.[5] Along with other similarities, the fact that both the Third Gospel and Acts were addressed to the same Theophilus (Luke 1:3; Acts 1:1), indicates that both volumes

---

[3] This method is the same as that followed in 'Untangling the Pauline Handshakes', in which I noted (p.392 n.2) a methodological similarity with Robinson, *Redating*, 207, who 'seeks not a conclusive demonstration but a hypothesis that gives the most reasonable explanation for the largest amount of the data', to 'allow it to be tested by the results it yields' (pp.33, 207). Rather than seeking the supposed 'certainty' of foundational truths upon which an edifice can then be constructed, this method examines multiple interlocking elements that may mutually reinforce the truth of a complex historical reality as it emerges from their re-sifting.
[4] Bolt, 'Untangling the Pauline Handshakes', 416.
[5] For the historical authenticity of the we-passages based upon chronological and topographical detail, see Riesner, *Paul's Early Period*, 321–26.

were penned by the same person.⁶ This author is traditionally and solidly identified as Λουκᾶς, the companion of the Apostle Paul (Col. 4:14; Phlm. 24; 2 Tim. 4:11).⁷ In a solitary brief description of this man, Paul calls him 'the [my?] beloved physician' (ἰατρὸς ὁ ἀγαπητός) (Col. 4:14). Thus, the Book of Acts and Paul's own letters together testify to the long-term and warm personal relationship between these two men, serving together as co-workers engaged in the earliest days of Christ's mission to the nations.

Luke is the last named of six men sending greetings to the Colossians (Col. 4:10–14). After mentioning Aristarchus, Mark, and Jesus-Justus, Paul notes οἱ ὄντες ἐκ περιτομῆς, οὗτοι μόνοι συνεργοὶ εἰς τὴν βασιλείαν τοῦ θεοῦ. If ἐκ περιτομῆς 'from [the] circumcision' is interpreted as designating the first three men Jews, the second three—excluded from this description by οὗτοι μόνοι 'these only'—must be Gentiles. On this reading, Λουκᾶς thereby becomes the only gentile contributor to the New Testament, and, given the length of Luke-Acts, a major one.

Despite the strength and frequency with which this conclusion is drawn, however, this is not the best reading either of this passage or of Luke's cultural background. Timothy, declared to be the co-author of the letter (1:1), was a Jew because he had a Jewish mother, and he was also circumcised (Acts 16:1–3). The fact that he, too, is excluded by the expression οἱ ὄντες ἐκ περιτομῆς, οὗτοι μόνοι […], should not be trivialized by weak explanations.⁸ The expression most likely refers to those from Jewish stock who originate in Jerusalem, that is, the group who were also known as the 'Hebrews', distinguished from those

---

6   This long-standing view has been reassessed by Walters, *Assumed Authorial Unity*, but this is not the place for a detailed interaction.
7   Antimarcionite Prologue; Iren 3.1.1; 3.14.1. Ellis, *Luke*, 2, 37–38. See the title for the Gospel in early manuscripts, demonstrably established by A.D. 140–150, but almost certainly there from the beginning; so Ellis, *Luke*, 40, 41; and see Hengel, 'Titles'; *Four Gospels*, 48–56. This essay considers Paul's authorship of Colossians well-founded.
8   E.g. because 'Paul was responsible for his circumcision' (Barth and Blanke, *Colossians*, 481); because he refers 'to those presently with him' (!) (Lohse, *Colossians*, 172); or because Timothy's co-authorship made it inappropriate to send separate greetings (Bruce, *Colossians*, 180 n.51).

known as 'Hellenists' on the grounds of their mother-tongues (Acts 6:1–6; cf. 9:29; 11:19–20 B D² E Ψ et al.).[9] Whereas in Rom. 4:12 Paul appears to use the expression derivatively to refer to Jews in general, in Acts 10:45, 11:2 'it alludes to a dispute not betweeen jewish and gentile Christians but between two groups in the Jerusalem church'.[10] Well aware of the need for good relations with other Jerusalemite Jews, who were particularly concerned about the new Christian movement's relationship to the Law (cf. Acts 21:20), Christians 'from the circumcision' maintained a concern for Jewish customs as much as the gospel of Christ permitted. However, at the point that this concern threatened to undermine that gospel for the Gentiles, they were in danger of becoming its opponents (Gal. 2:12; Titus 1:10).[11] In Colossians 4, Luke is excluded from this group, not because he is a Gentile, but because, like Timothy, he is a Hellenistic Jew from

---

9   Cf. Trypho's self-designation, Ἑβραῖος ἐκ περιτομῆς (Justin, *Dialogue with Trypho* 1,3) and its use in Eusebius, *H.E.* III, 35; IV, 5,2–4; 6,4 (citing Hegesippus?) 'for Hebrew believers (ἐξ Ἑβραίων πιστῶν), i.e., orthodox jewish Christians in the Jerusalem church during A.D. 70–135'; Ellis, '"Those of the Circumcision"', 389. Although labelled by linguistic terms distinguishing those who spoke only Greek from those who also spoke a Semitic language (Peshitta on Acts 9:29; Chrysostom, *Hom.* 4 [Acts 6:1]; 21 [Acts 9:29]; 25 [Acts 11:21]; Moule, 'Once More'), as part of their 'wider connotations' (Moule, 'Once More', 100) the two groups also expressed the Diasporan / Palestinian cultural distinction. It is also significant to note that Moule speaks of the distinction between the two groups 'with reference to a situation in Jerusalem' (p.102).

    For the connection with Jerusalem, note the presence of synagogues 'of the Hebrews' amongst Greek-speaking Jews (Ellis, '"Those of the Circumcision"', 391 n.5 for literature; 396. The superiority of 'the Hebrews' of 2 Cor. 11:22 and those presupposed in Phil. 3:5 is also to be explained in terms of their claimed connections with Jerusalem (pp.392–393).

    For a sample of the discussion of the Hebrews/Hellenists, see Moule, 'Once More'; and Hengel, 'Between Jesus and Paul'. For the significance of Jewish Christians in earliest Christianity, traced through the expression 'the saints', see Robinson, '"To submit"'; 'Who were "the saints"?'; 'We are the circumcision'. Robinson's conclusions can be strengthened by greater attention to the connections of 'the saints' to the Jerusalem church (but cf. pp.160, 161).
10 Ellis, '"Those of the Circumcision"', 390.
11 Ellis, '"Those of the Circumcision"', 390. The recipients of the letter to the Hebrews probably also belong to this group (p.399, building upon W. Manson). Contra Moule, 'Once More', 101.

the diaspora.¹² As Paul sends greetings from his co-workers, he divides them into two groups, matching the twin-focused mission in which they were all engaged (cf. Gal. 2:9).¹³

With Luke's Jewish background no longer obscured, Paul's 'beloved physician' would come into even clearer view if he could be identified with the persons or person named Lucius, mentioned twice in the New Testament in clear association with Paul (Acts 13:1; Rom. 16:21). A major argument raised against identifying the Luke of Paul's later letters and of the Gospel with Lucius is that Λουκᾶς could be an abbreviation of Lucanus, or Lucilius, or Lucianus, but not Lucius (Λούκιος). But this etymological prohibition was 'answered with certainty' long ago.¹⁴ Two decades after being disputed by comparative linguist Wilhelm Schulze, who argued that Λουκᾶς was the shortened form of Λούκιος,¹⁵ it was also empirically refuted. Inscriptional attestations of Λουκᾶς are not numerous,¹⁶ but amongst the votive inscriptions in a sanctuary of Men Ascaënus in Pisidian Antioch is found the name Λουκᾶς Τίλλιος Κρίτων, the threefold sequence making it 'probable that the man's name was really Latin, Lucius Tillius Crito'.¹⁷ Two others noted by Sir William Ramsay provided even more definitive evidence.¹⁸

Fig 78: [SEG 6:558]

Μηνὶ | εὐχή[ν]. | Γάμος Ἀβασκά[ντ-] | ου μὲ γυν[αικός,] | Λούκιος υἱός, | Πουμπούλιος | υἱός

---

12 Even by 1996, Allen, 'Lukan Authorship', 4, could declare that 'there is no consensus that Luke was a Gentile', briefly arguing a case for his Jewishness (pp.16-17) and listing in support (p.17 n.18) Clarke, Reicke, Schlatter, Easton, Ellis, Drury, Juel. For a collection of viewpoints on either side of the debate, see Tyson, *Luke-Acts and the Jewish People*. Ellis, *Luke*, 52-53.
13 Ellis, '"Those of the Circumcision"', 395-97.
14 Deissmann, 'Appendix IV', 435.
15 Schulze, *Graeca Latina*, 12. For Schulze, see Fraenkel, 'Wilhelm Schulze'.
16 Deissmann, 'Appendix IV', 435 n.3 calls attention to the four inscriptions he knew: from Egypt: CIG III 4759 [=Lepsius, Monum. Aegypt. Inscr. No. 114] Λουκᾶς (on the Memnon colossus); CIG III Add. 4700 k Λουκᾶς (on a claw of the Great Sphinx; CIL VI 17685 C. Iulius Lucas (a marble tablet, now at Rome). A search of the PHI database reveals 27 occurrences.
17 Deissmann, 'Appendix IV', 435.
18 Ramsay, *The Bearing*, 370-84. Ramsay's figures 78 and 79 are reproduced here from Deissmann, 'Appendix IV', 436.

A vow to Men. Gamus the son of Abascantus (together with) my wife, son Lucius, son Pumpulius (=Pompilius).

Fig 79: [SEG 6:559]

Μηνὶ εὐχήν. | Γάμος Ἀβασκάντου | υὸς [sic] καὶ Λουκᾶς καὶ | Πουμπούμλιος [sic] | καὶ Εὔδοξος.

A vow to Men. Gamus the son of Abascantus (together with) sons Lucius and Pumpulius (=Pompilius) and Eudoxus.

Deissmann comments:

> The Lucius of the first inscription is called *Lucas* in the second: here we have the most authentic soution of the name-problem. There is no need to prove other instances of the normal form of a name alternating with the pet name in the same family.[19]

With Λουκᾶς freed up to be both a Hellenistic Jew and a.k.a. Λούκιος, Lucius of Cyrene (Acts 13:1) is a very good candidate for being the author of Luke-Acts,[20] modestly inserting his name into the account (cf. Matt. 9:9; Mark 14:51–52; John 13:23; 19:26; 20:2; 21:7; 21:20; 2 Cor. 12:2) and thus briefly supplying his credentials to undergird his

---

19 Deissmann, 'Appendix IV', 436. Far from remaining obscure, this evidence then found its way into the standard lexicon, *BDAG*, to illustrate Λουκᾶς as 'an affectionate or pet name for Lucius'.
20 The identification was made by Ephraem Syrus, *Latin Prophetiae ex omnibus libris collectae*. Published in 1921, Ephraem's reading was not available to Cadbury when he claimed there was no early identification of Luke and Lucius of Cyrene ('The Tradition', 247). However, after becoming aware of the Armenian commentary of Ephrem Syrus, he drew attention to the comment on Acts 12:25–13:1 ('Lucius', 494): 'But Saul and Barnabas, who carried food for the saints in Jerusalem, returned with John who was called Mark and so did Luke of Cyrene. But both these are evangelists and wrote before the discipleship of Paul, and therefore he used to repeat everywhere from their gospel'. He also noted that the western reading of Acts 11:27 known from the Latin MS of the 9th c. Codex 133 also offers evidence that Luke was identified with Lucius of Cyrene (p.492).

eyewitness accounts to follow later in the 'we-passages'.[21] He was evidently one of the 'men of Cyrene' who arrived from Jerusalem after being scattered by the post-Stephen persecution and who began to take the gospel beyond Jewish circles to the Greeks (Acts 11:19–21).[22] Simon Niger (Acts 13:1) could have been another, if he can be identified with Simon of Cyrene,[23] whose family became well-known to the earliest Christian movement (Luke 23:26; Mark 15:21; Rom. 16:13), with both men most likely former members of Hellenistic synagogues, which, like that of the Freedmen, could not stand up to the Spirit-wisdom of Stephen's preaching (Acts 6:9–10).[24] If Luke's medical training was in Cyrene, a great intellectual centre, then he was amongst the physicians who were reputed to be, according to Herodotus, second only to those of Croton (3.131), numbering amongst them the likes of Eratosthenes, Aristippus, and Callimachus.[25]

Similarly, with Doctor Luke a Hellenistic Jew and Λουκᾶς / Λούκιος being 'alternative forms of the same name', this 'leaves open the possibility that Luke is the Lucius (Paul's cousin?) mentioned in Rom. 16:21'.[26] This identification is as old as Origen (mentioned in In Rom. Comm. 10, 39) and consistent with Pseudo-Dorotheus calling this Lucius Λουκᾶς.[27] Lucius is Jewish, because he is one of six amongst the

---

21 Cf. Bultmann's suspicion that another 'we' passage is behind 13:1, as noted by Ellis, *Luke*, 53.
22 Ἕλληνας (𝔓⁷⁴ ℵ² A D* arm slav) is the better reading (Moule, 'Once More', 100), although Ἑλληνιστάς (B D² E Ψ et al) is also true to the historical mission strategy.
23 Ford, 'St Luke and Lucius', 219.
24 Ford, 'St Luke and Lucius', 220, suggesting he may have been converted under the influence of Stephen's words and martyrdom.
25 Gemmill, 'Study of Ancient Cyrene', 422. Their success may have been at least partly related to expertise in the use of silphium, used for a vast range of conditions and for which Cyrene was famous. For the history and medicinal usage of this plant, see Gemmill, 'Silphium'; Totelin, 'When foods become remedies', 32–34.
26 Ellis, *Luke*, 53. Sanday and Headlam, *Romans*, 432, identified this Lucius with Lucius of Cyrene and Luke, only to be summarily dismissed by Cranfield, *Romans* 2, 805.
27 Deissmann, 'Appendix IV', 437–38. Taking Romans 16 to be 'a little letter to the Ephesians', Deissmann noted that it and Acts 20:4 reveal the names of Paul's comrades at Corinth. Since according to his 'we' (Acts 20:5), Luke (Λουκᾶς) was amongst that number, he should be identified with the Lucius (Λούκιος) of Rom. 16:21.

greetings whom Paul describes as συγγενεῖς μου (cf. Jason and Sosipater, v.21; Herodion, v.11; and Andronicus and Junia, v.7). Given Paul's use of this expression in his impossible wish to be cursed 'on behalf of my brethren, my kinsfolk according to the flesh' (Rom. 9:3, ὑπὲρ τῶν ἀδελφῶν μου τῶν συγγενῶν μου κατὰ σάρκα), translations and commentators commonly assume that in the final greetings it indicates 'fellow Jews' rather than relatives—despite acknowledging that this is unusual and that there are other Jews in his greetings that are not accorded this description (16:3,6,13).[28] However, despite the frequency of this preference for the metaphorical, in keeping with both wider and New Testament (cf. Mark 6:4; Luke 1:58; 2:44; 14:12; 21:16; John 18:26; Acts 10:24) usage, this expression ought to be consistently translated concretely as 'my kin, my relatives',[29] with the recognition that in his impassioned cry (Rom. 9:3) Paul poignantly refers to his actual kin, not by way of a simple metaphor, but as hyperbolic metonymy for the sake of heightened rhetorical force.

Following regular relational dynamics, the gospel spreads along already established human networks with the consequence that the resultant movement is riddled with friends and relatives. This was clearly the case for both Jesus' own circle of disciples and the earliest Christian movement. Rather than providing a snapshot of the Roman church(es) to whom the letter was written, I have elsewhere argued that Romans 16:1–16a is best taken as a snapshot of the mission team arriving with Phoebe who carried the letter.[30] This slice-of-life shows that this significant mission team included a number of persons related to each other (vv.3,7,10b,11,12a,13,15), and, whether at the mission's

---

28 E.g. Bauckham, 'Joanna', 170.
29 LSJ: congenital, inborn; II of the same kin, descent; b. subst. kinsman, relative. This is the rendering of the classic English translations ('kinsmen': AV, RV, ASV, NASB, ESV; 'relatives': NRSV), rather than that of the more recent ('fellow Jews': NIV; 'fellow countrymen': HCSB; 'compatriots': NET).
30 See Bolt, 'Untangling the Pauline Handshakes'. As such, it also provides the evidence found lacking by Ellis, '"Those of the Circumcision"', 396, 'that travelling missionaries deliberately organized as Hebrew/Hellenist teams', for when the personnel are carefully noted, representatives of both 'Hebraic' and 'Hellenistic' origin are now together in Rome, poised for their parallel work amongst the churches of Rome.

sent or sending end, six of Paul's own relatives, one of whom was the beloved physician Luke—still Jewish, but referred to appropriately by the Roman form of his name, Lucius.

3. The High Priest: Theophilus

The suggestion that Luke wrote his two-volumes to Theophilus the High Priest as an apologia for the Jesus movement and for earliest Christianity (especially Paul) respectively was first made by Theodore Hase in 1721.[31] However, it has only attracted occasional attention since that time,[32] largely because of the assumption that Theophilus was a prominent Gentile representing Luke's purportedly gentile audience.

The papyrological evidence shows that 'the name Theophilos is frequently attested in papyri from III BC–VII/VIII,'[33] and even in samples in which it refers most often to those of freed or servile status, the name

---

31 Hase, "IV. ad praecedentem de THEOPHILO". Hase's article is usually referred to only vaguely (e.g. Anderson, *Who are Johanna and Theophilus?* [loc. 556–59]: 'some time prior to 1802'), being accessed only through its citation by Michaelis, 'Of the person of Theophilus', who misattributed it to *Bibliotheca Bremensis* Class. 4, Fasc. 3 (https://babel.hathitrust.org/cgi/pt?id=ucm.53243 60556;view=1up;seq=30). The articles Michaelis refers to are Heumann, 'III. Dissertatio de THEOPHILO', and Hase, 'IV. ad praecedentem de THEOPHILO', both found in *Bibliotheca Historico-Philogico-Theologica* Class. 4, Fasc. 3 (1721).

32 E.g. Michaelis, 'Of the person of Theophilus', 238: 'The arguments advanced [by Hase] in favour of this opinion are so strong, as to render it more probable than any other'; Anderson, 'Theophilus' and *Who are Johanna and Theophilus?*, who notes the analogy with Justin Martyr addressing his *Apology* to the Roman emperor, and MMT to the High Priest (p.198 and loc. 515); Allen, *Lukan Authorship*, 327; Newman, *Luke*, 33–36.

33 Horsley, *NewDocs* 3, #9, 38, discussing a dated inscription from Lydia, A.D. 96/97, referring to a Theophilos married to Tryphosa. In Fraser and Matthews, *Lexicon*, Anderson, *Who are Johanna and Theophilus?*, loc. 423, notes 529 instances outside Palestine from earliest writings to 6th c. A.D. (0.21% of names in the database).

is attested for some of high social standing.³⁴ That Luke's Theophilus is not of servile status is clearly indicated by him being addressed as κράτιστε, 'O most excellent one', the address used for procurators Felix and Festus later in the Acts account (23:26; 24:3; 26:25). In wider usage this address was used for others of rank,³⁵ and οἱ κράτιστοι was used for 'the aristocracy' (Xen, *HG* 7.1.42). Thus Luke's two volumes were addressed to someone from a family 'of considerable status'.³⁶

Theophilus as a Jewish name was far less frequent. In the period 330 B.C. to A.D. 200, seven Jews from the Western Diaspora were known by the name and none from the Eastern Diaspora.³⁷ Of the three from Palestine known from other literary sources,³⁸ with the

---

34 Horsley, *NewDocs* 3, #9, 38, notes that of the 33/66 examples known from Rome (Solin, *GPR* 1.81–82), 'one is of senatorial standing (IV²), and one other is free-born (I A.D.); the remainder are freed or of servile status'. Horsley recalls *NewDocs* 2, #18, 'a posthumous honorific inscription for Theophilos son of Thynites, clearly a man of some position at Iulia Gordos (75/76)'. At *NewDocs* 4 #94, 178, despite Theophilos being listed on 'Reilly's catalogue of 3,250 slave names derived from manumission texts from Greece and the Aegean islands from V B.C. to III A.D.' (1453–55, 1468), Horsley warns against assuming all these names were customary slave names, as the presence of Scipio (Reilly, 2503) shows.

35 LSJ: esp. = Lat. *egregius*, ὁ κ. ἡγεμών *P.Fay*. p.33 (I A.D.); ὁ κ. ἐπίτροπος BGU 891 (II A.D.); ἡ κ., of a woman of the *equester ordo*, IG 14. [p. 992] 1346; also, = Lat. *clarissimus*, of Senators, ὁ κ. ἀνθύπατος ib. 9(1).61; ὁ κ. συγκλητικός *IGRom*. 3.581, etc.; ἡ κ. βουλή *P.Oxy*. 2108.6 (III A.D.).

36 Cf. *NewDocs* 3, #2, p.11, where the term in *P.Oxy*. 3313 is taken to indicate a 'family of the recipient of this letter as one of considerable status'.

37 Ilan, *Lexicon* vol. 3 [Western Diaspora], 306–308: of 18 listings total, 7 are dated 2nd c. CE and earlier: 1. the historian, ?Jew, P: -, CA 1.216 [pre-100 BCE]; 3. Son of Dositheus (7), thief of the epigone, P: Egypt, Jew (see n.9), CPJ 21 [210 BCE]; 4. Ostracon, CPJ 226, Jew, P: Egypt [115/6 CE]; 5. Father of Dositheus (36), Jew (see n.14), P: Egypt, CPR 18.8 [232 BCE]; 6. Σαμαρειας 'Of Samaria', P: Egypt, P.Petrie 2.28, 3.66 [3rd–1st BCE]; 9. Father of Abraham (12), Jew (see n.25), P: Egypt, P.Vindob. Tendern 15 [1st–2nd CE]; 15. Valerius (8), aged 39, Jew, epitaph, P: Cyrenaica [pre 117 CE]; 16. Father of Zenodorus (1), P: Cyrenaica, CJZC 72 [55/56 CE]; On the possibility of this name being jewish, see introduction 1.2.3.1, 'however, it was certainly not exclusively jewish, see introduction 1.2.4' (p.307). Ilan, *Lexicon* Vol. 4 [Eastern Diaspora] has no listings.

38 Ilan, *Lexicon* Vol. 1 [Palestine], 287–88, has three listings: Arist 49 [3rd c. BCE], of the LXX translators, 'fictitious', תאופילוס 'So according to Epiphanius, in the Syriac script (Wendland, *Aristeae*, 143), see Introduction 2.8.3' ; AJ 17:78 Mattathias' father [4 BCE]; High Priest, Hanan's son, Mattathias' father [37 CE]; Ossuary: Barag and Flusser; AJ 18.123; CJO no 871 [37 CE].

(probably fictitious) third century B.C. Septuagint translator (*Aristeas* 49) and the father of the Jerusalem-born high priest Matthias, Herod's replacement for Simon Boethus in A.D. 6 (*Ant.* 17.78) both being too early, the only possible known candidate for Luke's addressee was the High Priest Theophilus, son of Annas, and thus a member of the Jerusalem aristocracy warranting the epithet κράτιστε.[39] Previously known only from Josephus (*Ant.* 18.123–124),[40] the existence of this high priest was confirmed in the summer of 1983 by the discovery of his name on the ossuary of his granddaughter,[41] which reads:

> Yehoḥanah
> Yehoḥanah the daughter of Yehoḥanan
> Son of Theophilus the High Priest

Theophilus was one of the five sons of Annas to hold the priesthood (*Ant.* 20.198) and, with Caiaphas being a son-in-law of Annas (John 18:13), he was therefore a part of the dynasty that dominated the high-priesthood across the first century. This high priestly family is well known to the New Testament through Annas, Caiaphas (Caiaphas alone: Matt. 26:3, 57; John 11:49; 18:28; Caiaphas and Annas: Luke 3:2; John 18:13–14, 24; Acts 4:6), Jonathan (probably the John of Acts 4:6, see D it[(d), (gig), (p)] vg[ms] Jerome),[42] and Ananias (Acts 23:2).

As High Priest, Theophilus reigned over a particularly turbulent period of Jewish history. With his reign matching that of Caligula in Rome (A.D. 37–41), Theophilus held office in A.D. 39, when Antipas was sent into exile as a result of Herodias's lusting after the title 'king' for her husband after it was awarded to her brother Agrippa (*Ant.*

---

39 Kokkinos, *Herodian Dynasty*, 384, reconstructs a possible genealogical connection between the latter two, although Ilan doubts any relation.
40 Barag and Flusser, 'Ossuary', 43 n.20, also note that he appears on a medieval list of high priests.
41 Israel Department of Antiquities and Museums, No. 84-503, reported to have been found at the village Ḥızma, 7 km NNE of Jerusalem. See Barag and Flusser, 'Ossuary'. For a discussion of this ossuary (pp.108–109) in the context of other priestly ossuaries, see Evans, *Jesus and the Ossuaries*, 104–112.
42 Barag and Flusser, 'Ossuary', 42–43. Hengel and Schwemer, *Paul Between Damascus and Antioch*, 250 n.1309, mistakenly identify the Jonathan of Acts 4:6 with the Jonathan, son of Theophilus, on the ossuary.

18.240–255); and in A.D. 40 during the major crisis provoked by the unhinged (*Ant.* 18.256) emperor's plans to erect a statue of himself in the Jerusalem temple (Philo, *Leg.* 207–60; Josephus, *War* 2.184–203; *Ant.* 18.261–88), although the accounts do not show him taking any leadership in resisting the assault on his people.[43] Alongside the external threat from Rome in a period of widespread turbulence for the Jews (see Philo, *ad Flacc.*, and *Leg.*), he also presided over Judaism's internal problems that followed the death of Jesus of Nazareth, caused by the claim of the earliest Christian movement that Jesus had risen from the dead. As this new movement made great advances in Jerusalem, even amongst the priests (Acts 6:7), the preaching of Stephen stirred up the Hellenistic synagogues and the situation reached a flashpoint when Stephen was stoned to death (Acts 6:8–7:53). This cannot be written off as mob violence, for Stephen was heard before the Sanhedrin and his death was swiftly followed by a systematic persecution, possibly against only those known as the Hellenists,[44] but more probably against the Jerusalem church as a whole (in view of Acts 8:1, where the Galilean apostles went untouched;[45] and also Gal. 1:13; Phil. 3:6[46]). This persecution was led by a young Pharisee named Saul, backed by the authority of the high priest (Acts 8:3; 9:1–2,13–14,21; 22:4–5,19–20; 26:9–11; Gal 1:13–14,22–23).

This high priest may have been Jonathan, taking advantage of the interregnum between prefects and the absence of the Roman legate to Syria, Vitellius.[47] But rather than Jonathan being solely responsible for this 'bloody persecution,'[48] it seems more likely that he was merely con-

---

43 As noted by Smallwood, 'High Priests', 23, and accepted by VanderKam, *From Joshua to Caiaphas*, 440 n.118 and Horsley, 'High Priests', 38.
44 Gaechter, 'Hatred', 17–21.
45 Moule, 'Once More', 101.
46 Barnett, *Jesus*, 222.
47 When Vitellius visited Jerusalem in mid-December A.D. 36 to mid-January A.D. 37 (Smallwood, 'High Priests and Politics', 22; see also her 'Date of the Dismissal'), he dismissed Pontius Pilate and replaced Caiaphas with Jonathan, before going to the Euphrates for negotiations with the Parthian king Artabanus, accompanied by Herod Antipas (*Ant.* 18.96–105).
48 Gaechter, 'Hatred', 20–21, who locates Stephen's death between Tabernacles A.D. 36 and Passover A.D. 37 and the persecution in the reign of Jonathan (pp.16–17).

tinuing what Caiaphas had initiated, under the acquiescence of Pilate.[49] Either way, Theophilus was appointed in the aftermath, presumably 'to restore [Rome's] troubled peace, or to prevent further disturbances'[50] (cf. John 11:47-53).[51]

Late in A.D. 36, the Nabatean king Aretas IV had destroyed Herod Antipas's army in an attack (at least partly) fuelled by Herod's famous divorce of his daughter Phasaelis[52]—the destruction being taken by some Jews as God's punishment because Antipas had killed John the Baptist (*Ant.* 18.116-19). In the spring of A.D. 37, marching under orders to retaliate on behalf of Rome's friend Antipas, Vitellius left his army on the Great Plain after the principal men of Judea persuaded him not to march his army through their region. Along with Antipas and his friends, Vitellius visited Jerusalem 'to offer sacrifice to God, an ancient festival of the Jews being then just approaching' (*Ant.* 18.120-22). During this three-day visit (*Ant.* 18.123), Vitellius replaced Jonathan with his brother Theophilus. On the fourth day, he received letters informing him of the death of Tiberius (*Ant.* 18.124). Since Tiberius died on 16 March A.D. 37 (Tac., *Ann.* 6.50; Suet., *Tib.* 73), Theophilus's high priesthood commenced during the Passover season of that year.[53] His term came to an end in A.D. 41, when Agrippa I

---

49   Although this essay is not the place to solve the difficult questions of chronology surrounding the events underlying Acts, including the date of the crucifixion, it should be noted that the martyrdom of Stephen and the related persecution have been variously dated to A.D. 31/32, 34/35, and 36/37; see Riesner, *Paul's Early Period*, Ch. 4.
50   Gaechter, 'Hatred', 22. This was 'a necessary step because Judea was to be the rear in his expedition against the Nabateans'. Gaechter (pp.22-23) estimates that the scattering of Hellenistic Christians from Jerusalem involved 'maybe three or four thousand' people, with a considerable impact upon the city; and suggests that this would be enough for the Pharisaic party (opposed to the Sadducean high priests), 'to invite Vitellius to depose Jonathan'.
51   For the role in keeping peace with Rome, see Horsley, 'High Priests', 32, 35-37.
52   Kokkinos, *Herodian Dynasty*, 230-33.
53   In A.D. 37, Nisan 15 fell on Thursday 19 March; Midrash.org/calendar. Kokkinos, 'Crucifixion', 147, puts it in April.

arrived as king of Judea (*Ant.* 19.297).⁵⁴

Acts does not mention Theophilus, either by name or title, and quickly passes over the years of his tenure. Although fixing the chronology of the underlying history is difficult,⁵⁵ to roughly correlate this period with the events depicted in the narrative, Theophilus was appointed in the aftermath of the first great persecution of the earliest Christian movement which resulted in the conversion of its chief persecutor (6:8–9:30), and dismissed on the eve of the second, when Agrippa targeted the leadership of the Jerusalem church (Acts 12:1–19), as part of his strategy to win the Jews of the city by appearing to be a champion of Judaism.⁵⁶ The change of regime from that of Caiaphas-Jonathan is presumably reflected in the scattered Jerusalem Church enjoying a time of peace (9:31), permitting Peter to engage in some significant ministry on the coastal plain, which demonstrated the divine intention that the gospel should also move into gentile territory (Acts 10–11; cf. 15:6–11,13–18). This fuels Gaechter's observation that Theophilus and his son Matthias (A.D. 65–67; *Ant.* 20.223),⁵⁷ were the only two high priests of the Annas family who did not preside over a persecution of the Jesus movement.⁵⁸ It does not seem sufficient to argue that Theophilus curbed a hatred for the Jesus movement he shared with the rest of the house of Annas only because of the external restraints imposed by Rome. Caligula showed his own hostility

---

54   Barag and Flusser, 'Ossuary', 40. It is generally agreed that Agrippa I removed Theophilus after he arrived to take control of Judea in A.D. 41. Steinmann, *From Abraham to Paul*, 328, argues that it was in the summer. Although Schwartz, *Agrippa I*, 11–14, argues for the dismissal in A.D. 38, VanderKam, *From Joshua to Caiaphas*, 440–443, refutes Schwartz's arguments.

55   Cf. Riesner, *Paul's Early Period*, 319, who notes that from Paul's conversion, which is connected with Stephen's martyrdom, to the Apostolic council, 'no single date can stand on its own. Only a multifaceted correlation of variously reliable data can lead to a relatively satisfactory result'.

56   According to Gaechter, 'Hatred', 26–27, that Agrippa I initially sought to replace Theophilus with Jonathan, indicates his desire to gain support of the Sadducees and the Jews in opposition to the Jesus movement. Even when his brother Matthias was installed instead, the persecution was reignited, and, this time, it was not only against the Hellenists.

57   Matthias was Israel's last legitimate high priest, followed only by Phannias, who was appointed by the zealots and not of high priestly descent (*War* 4.153–56).

58   Gaechter, 'Hatred', 33–34.

towards Judaism with his plans to erect the statue of himself in the temple, and he was the one who appointed Agrippa I. The fact that the new king of Judea dismissed Theophilus, in order to re-open the attack on the Jerusalem church, strongly suggests that there were known reasons for Theophilus's preferring peace to persecution.[59] If so, then it would make sense for Luke, the Hellenistic Jew turned Christian apologist, to address his work to Theophilus so that 'his excellency' might favour the Christian mission by applying his influence within the Jewish corridors of power that were also well-connected to those of Rome. But as well as this being shrewd politics, perhaps Luke also knew that Theophilus already had some connections with the Christian movement that were of a much more personal nature.

4. The Aristocrat: Joanna

Luke introduces Joanna as one of the women healed by Jesus in Galilee, who subsequently provided for his band of disciples out of their own means (Luke 8:1–3).[60] Whereas Mary Magdalene was specifically said to be delivered of demons, Joanna and Susanna were probably amongst those healed of other afflictions, and these three named women were part of a larger company ('many others'). In Luke's final chapter, Joanna is in Jerusalem, supporting the women who had discovered Jesus' tomb empty as they reported it to the disciples (Luke 24:10–11).[61] With her naming both before and after his 'travel narrative', it is likely that

---

59 For Matthias, Gaechter, 'Hatred', 34, suggests that there were 'hardly any Christians left', and he implies that Theophilus felt the restraint of Rome. If the arguments of this essay are correct, then Theophilus's links to Herod Antipas (through Joanna), may have also played a role in his dismissal, because of Agrippa's personal animosity towards Antipas his brother-in-law.
60 According to Ilan, 'Attraction', the women who supported, respectively, Pharisaism, the community at Qumran, and the Jesus movement, did so because of the 'oppositional stance' of these movements.
61 Despite the frequency with which Joanna is said to have been at the empty tomb, Luke is explicit only about her presence at the report-back (24:10). I suggest that, Mary Magdalene having left on their arrival, the two women who had discovered the tomb to be empty then collected Joanna from her Jerusalem residence on their way to report to the disciples. See further, Bolt, 'What Actually Happened?'.

Joanna was one of Luke's eyewitness sources,[62] especially for this portion of Jesus' ministry, and for his clear interest in Antipas (Luke 3:19; 8:3; 9:7,9; 13:1–3,31–32; 23:7–15; Acts 4:27; 13:1).[63]

On the other hand, Joanna would have also been a source of information about the Jesus movement for the tetrarch, directly or indirectly.[64] Despite the clear hint that she was a woman of (independent) means (ἐκ τῶν ὑπαρχόντων αὐταῖς), Luke also reports that Joanna was 'the wife of Chuza, the manager of Herod's household' (8:3).[65] Luke thus deliberately places her amongst a small but significant group of known Herodians in the earliest Christian movement. Manaen, σύντροφος of Antipas—perhaps the 'foster-brother', but certainly 'a trusted member of the king's inner circle of court'[66]—was associated with both Lucius/Luke and Paul (Acts 13:1),[67] as was Herodion by kin (Rom. 16:11).[68] Whereas contributing to the common pool of support

---

62 Ford, 'St Luke and Lucius', 219 (citing Holdsworth, Sanday); Bauckham, 'Joanna', 112–13, 186–94.
63 See Bauckham, 'Joanna', 189; Anderson, 'Theophilus', 205.
64 Bauckham, 'Joanna', 189. Anderson, *Who are Johanna and Theophilus?* (loc. 757–58, 761–64). Even if her information was limited to his knowledge of her own healing, this would have been nevertheless of great significance (cf. Luke 23:8).
65 For a discussion of the possibilities for her disposable income, see Bauckham, 'Joanna', 113–34. Although her independent means may have come through being widowed (a possibility discussed and kept open by Bauckham, pp.117, 130–31, 134–35), since Luke speaks of her as Chuza's wife (γυνή) not widow (χήρα), and without any indication of this relationship being in the past, he appears to be describing her current marital status. Being distinguished by association with a husband is exceptional for Luke (p.119), and unusual for the Gospels generally (cf. Mary wife of Clopas). Still married, Joanna's independent and disposable means would have been gained only through inheritance or deed of gift (pp.133, 121–27).
66 Bauckham, 'Joanna', 138, noting that he is 'almost certainly the same person' referred to by Papias as Manaim (Μαναιμ), whose mother was raised from the dead (Pap. 5.7), cf. p.196.
67 An erroneous translation in Bolt, 'Untangling', 417, implied that Paul was also brought up with Antipas. However, the syntax is against Saul also being a foster-brother of Manaen, for, despite one 12th c. MS (618) reading the genitive, Σαῦλος is the nominative, which co-ordinates with Μαναήν, not Ἡρώδου, and simply refers to both men being in the Antiochene congregation without comment about any former connection.
68 Herodion may also have been 'a former courtier of the tetrarch'; Bauckham, 'Joanna', 138 n.110.

doesn't necessarily make Joanna wealthy, her Herodian connections open up the possibility that she contributed 'the lion's share', not as a patron/benefactor in the usual sense, but as part of her paradoxical (cf. Luke 22:27) Christian service, which followed the costly conversion precipitated by her own healing[69] (in the context of other remarkable healings).[70] In any case, her marriage to Chuza and yet her freedom to travel without her husband indicates that she belonged to (Romanised) aristocratic circles.[71]

Following Bauckham, it is probable that Joanna was the same person as Junia (Rom. 16:7), a member of Paul's mission team being introduced to the churches at Rome with the Latin name by which she was known within Herodian circles.[72] On this view, Andronicus could be the Latin name adopted by the Nabataean Chuza in those same circles.[73] That this couple was in Christ before Paul is easily explained from Joanna's long-term association with Jesus (Luke 8:1–3; 24:10), and consistent with Luke assuming they are both well known to his readers.[74] Although the specific details are irrecoverable, that these two can be named as Paul's fellow prisoners-of-war (συναιχμαλώτους μου; cf. Col. 4:10; Phlm. 23) —despite previous associations with such a proven enemy of the Jesus

---

69 Bauckham, 'Joanna', 161, 162–65.
70 Cf. the many other women (Luke 8:1–3), Manaen's mother (see n.66), and the royal official (βασιλικός) of John 4:46, who may have been Chuza himself (see Bauckham, 'Joanna', 137–38).
71 Bauckham, 'Joanna', 116, 118, 145.
72 For the discussion, see Bauckham, 'Joanna', 165–86. My view that Romans 16 is the introduction of Paul's mission team is not shared by Bauckham. For the rarity of Latin names amongst Jews, but their prevalence amongst the aristocrats associated with Antipas at Tiberias, see pp.139–43, 182, 184–85, and Bauckham, 'Paul and Other Jews'.
73 See Bauckham, 'Joanna', 186, allowing also for the possibility that Chuza had died and Andronicus was Junia's second husband (p.198).
74 Bauckham, 'Joanna', 119, notes that it cannot be ruled out that Chuza was also a disciple known to the early Christian communities. Alongside Bauckham's treatment, Ilan, 'Attraction', 23, also notes that Joanna was one of the 'real women who played an active role in founding the Christian movement after Jesus' death'.

movement as Antipas—enhances their gospel credibility.[75]

With Bauckham again, it is difficult to imagine two women named Joanna/Junia both being 'prominent among the apostles'.[76] This expression has generated debate over whether or not Junia was counted as an apostle,[77] despite the recognition that she would not be an apostle as understood by Luke.[78] But it is clear that a person could be prominent in apostolic circles without being specifically commissioned as an apostle (e.g. Barnabas). Joanna's prominence is easily explained from her associations with Jesus from the early days in Galilee and with the women who reported the empty tomb,[79] and, exactly because of those credentials, her ongoing role in the Christian mission. Given the limited size of both Herodian and Lukan relational networks, it is highly likely that Joanna was also known to the apostle. But the connection was more than casual, for since Andronicus/Chuza was Nabataean, when Paul specifically numbers this couple amongst his own relatives, the blood-relation would be through the aristocrat Junia/Joanna.

But what were her aristocratic roots exactly? Chuza was a Nabataean,[80] and, as with Antipas's marriage to the daughter of King Aretas IV, Chuza's marriage to the Jewish Joanna was no doubt part of some political alliance.[81] Following the norm in Herodian circles,

---

75   Perhaps the best suggestion to explain the term in keeping with its usage for both Aristarchus and Epaphras would be not only that Joanna and Chuza openly and voluntarily took their turn sharing Paul's imprisonment (cf. Bauckham, 'Joanna', 171), but also that this was while he was imprisoned in Caesarea (ca. A.D. 58–60); cf. Reicke, 'Caesarea', 'Historical Setting', 435–38. A more radical suggestion would be that the couple were amongst those arrested by Saul in the original persecution, in which case Paul's description 'my fellow prisoners' would be strongly ironic.
76   Bauckham, 'Joanna', 184.
77   Bauckham, 'Joanna', 172–80.
78   Bauckham, 'Joanna', 188.
79   If Mary (Rom. 16:6) is the wife of Cleopas (see Bauckham, 'Mary of Clopas'), then their association continued as co-members of the mission team to Rome (Bolt, 'Untangling', 394–95).
80   Bauckham, 'Joanna', 150–61, for discussion of the 5 or 6 occurrences of the name outside Luke, 4 of which are reliable (p.157).
81   Anderson, *Who are Johanna and Theophilus?* (loc. 778–89). Antipas was himself part Nabataean and had other Nabataean courtiers; Bauckham, 'Joanna', 155, 156.

Chuza would have converted to Judaism prior to the marriage.[82] Since Chuza was 'a very high ranking official at Herod's court' and most likely 'in charge of Antipas's property and revenues generally',[83] Joanna would also have been from an aristocratic Jewish family, as also indicated by her holding her own property 'in title'.[84] However, as with Chuza himself, that she ended up in the court at Tiberias does not mean that her aristocratic family of origin was Galilean.[85]

To raise another aristocratic possibility, was Joanna/Junia the same person as Yehoḥanah of the ossuary?[86] Apart from Yehoḥanah's descent through Yehoḥanan from Theophilus the high priest, little else can be known from the ossuary itself, except that she died sometime after A.D. 37 (when Theophilus became high priest) and she was not buried in her family tomb 'for reasons which elude us'.[87]

Ossuaries of individuals from the Herodian period known from other sources are very rare.[88] Although Joanna is the fifth most common of the 247 named Jewish females from 330 BCE – 200 CE, it

---

82 Bauckham, 'Joanna', 158–61, Kokkinos, *Herodian Dynasty*, 229–32.
83 Bauckham, 'Joanna', 136, 137, and 135–50, for the significant role of the ἐπίτροπος, especially of a king. As such, Chuza would be significantly wealthy, a member of the court and resident (p.141) at Tiberias, and a landowner in his own right.
84 Anderson, *Who are Johanna and Theophilus?* (loc. 715-21). He uses this expression to draw out the genitive (αὐτῶν) of Codex Beza (05 D), which is also found in the ℵ* (and 2, 579), but the dative (αὐτοῖς) can also imply possession. Bauckham's arguments adequately refute the attempt by Corley, *Private Women*, 111 n.13, to make Chuza a slave or a freedman, depriving Joanna of any aristocratic status; Bauckham, 'Joanna', 161. Note also the comment by Ilan, 'Attraction', 23, that Joanna 'as the wife of Chuza, Herod Antipas's treasurer, is obviously an aristocrat'.
85 Contra Bauckham, 'Joanna', 142, 144, 195.
86 Barag and Flusser, 'Ossuary'. For the identification, Anderson, *Who are Johanna and Theophilus?*, Ch.2; Allen, *Lukan Authorship*, 330–31; Bolt, 'What Actually Happened?', 94–96; 'Untangling', 417–18.
87 Barag and Flusser, 'Ossuary', 41, 44, who also argue that she was unmarried, due to being related not to a husband but to her father. However, there may be other reasons for this.
88 Barag and Flusser, 'Ossuary', 44 and n.23, mentioning only *CIJ* no. 1256 and the sarcophagus of Helena, Queen of Adiabene, discovered in the Tomb of the Kings.

nevertheless represents only 3.24% of the total.[89] Statistically, the very rarity of the name in collocation with the equally rare (within Palestinian Judaism) Theophilus increases the likelihood that the Joanna of Luke-Acts should be identified with Yehoḥanah,[90] and, of course, this likelihood increases exponentially with the likelihood that Luke's Theophilus was the high priest. The ossuary raises the intriguing possibility that, as part of the turmoil in which Theophilus entered into the high priesthood, matters were further complicated by the fact that his own granddaughter, who had been politically married into Antipas's circles, had become entangled in the John-Jesus movement, and was now known to be ardently supporting the testimony that Jesus was Messiah, because he had risen from the dead. Knowing these connections, her co-worker Luke first supplied her still influential grandfather with an orderly account about Jesus, and then with an apologia for their mutual blood-relative, Saul/Paul.

5. The Apostle: Paul

If these suggestions about Luke, Theophilus, and Joanna give us access to the first-century realities, then together they not only add to the biography of the apostle Paul, but also illuminate some significant aspects of the early Christian mission.

Born in Tarsus, Cilicia (Acts 22:3), holding its citizenry (21:39; 22:28), and with continuing associations (Acts 9:30; 11:25), Saul was known as a Tarsean (Acts 9:11). However, according to his own insistence, Paul was also 'from the circumcision', that is, a 'Hebrew' from a

---

89 This figure comes from Anderson, *Who are Johanna and Theophilus?* (loc. 639), drawing upon Ilan, 'Notes'. Ilan, *Lexicon* 1 [Palestine], 420-21, including Luke 8:3 (1), lists 12 occurrences, with one (9) dated 257 BCE; 7 (2,3,4,5,6,7,8) pre-70 CE; 3 (10, 11, 12) pre-135 CE. Bauckham, 'Joanna', 143, including Luke's Joanna, refers to 'six or seven Palestinian Jewish women who bore that name' and elsewhere 'only two examples from Egypt'.
90 Anderson, *Who are Joanna and Theophilus?*, loc 695, noting Milik's similar argument from collocation of names to argue that the ossuary of 'Alexander son of Simon of Cyrene' belongs to the family of the man who carried Jesus' cross. On the same set of ossuaries, Evans, *Ossuaries*, 339, finds this 'very interesting constellation' suggestive, as do both Hengel, *The 'Hellenization' of Judaea*, 67 n.39 and van der Horst, *Ancient Jewish Epitaphs*, 140-41.

Hebrew family from Jerusalem (2 Cor. 11:22; Phil 3:5), where, despite being born in Tarsus, he was himself brought up and educated under Gamaliel (Acts 22:3; cf. 5:34).

Gauging from such factors as his father's ability to purchase citizenship,[91] his Jerusalem education, his tent-making trade (Acts 18:3), his ability to self-support (1 Cor. 9:1–18), and the expectation of Felix that he might give him a bribe (Acts 24:26), Paul's family were wealthy and known for it. At the time of Felix, Paul's nephew was resident in Jerusalem with sufficient connections amongst Paul's Jewish opponents to discover their plot against the apostle's life (Acts 23:16). Paul's sister may have also lived in the city,[92] but since the 'young man' (νεανίας: 23:17; cf. 7:58; 20:9; νεανίσκος: 23:18,22) was likely just twenty,[93] by coming to Jerusalem to be educated he may have been fol-

---

91 Bruce, *Acts*, 432 and n.40.
92 Peterson, *Acts*, 621.
93 That the nephew was 'quite young' is entailed neither by the commander taking him by the hand (v.19; Marshall, *Acts*, 388; Peterson, *Acts*, 621 n.48), nor by the use of the diminutive νεανίσκος (vv.18,22), which, besides being more frequent in later Greek (LSJ), could be either affectionate or contemptuous in this context (cf. Goodwin, *Greek Grammar*, §§844–845). Polhill, *Acts*, 473, is closer with 'perhaps in his late teens', but, despite both forms indicating a stage of life rather than a precise age, usage points to the early twenties. Pythagoras (D.L. 8.10) used the two forms for the two successive middle periods of the four quarters of a man's life: 'twenty years a boy, twenty years a youth, twenty years a young man, twenty years an old man' (παῖς εἴκοσι ἔτεα, νεηνίσκος εἴκοσι, νεηνίης εἴκοσι, γέρων εἴκοσι). While asserting that a man was in the prime of life at thirty, Plato spoke of three stages: 'in both boy and (stages of) youthfulness, and in man' (ἔν τε παισὶ καὶ νεανίσκοις καὶ ἐν ἀνδράσι, Pl., Resp. 413e). Since the same person could be called both νεανίσκος and μειράκιον (Antipho 3.4.6 and 8; Xen., *Mem.* 2.2.1 cf. Pl., *Ap.* 34d), the latter term assists with greater specificity (LSJ), but they are nevertheless not overlapping. Epictetus associates μειράκιον with the middle stage of education. Between a boy (παῖς) checking his work, and a young man (νεανίσκος) beginning to take part in politics and to plead cases, the 'youth' (μειράκιον) 'attended the lectures of the rhetoricians' and practised the art (Arr., *Epict.* 3.9.8–9). Having used both terms, Lucian explicitly stated that the young man concerned was 'roughly about twenty' (Luc., *DMort.* 9:4 [LCL Macleod: 19 (9).4] σχεδὸν ἀμφὶ τὰ εἴκοσι). Even more precisely, when Brutus became consul he was 'a mere youth, being in his twentieth year' (LCL), or, perhaps better, 'not still being altogether a youth, but registered [as being in his] twentieth year' (Plut., *Brut.* 27.2; οὔπω πάνυ μειράκιον ὤν, ἀλλ' εἰκοστὸν ἄγων ἔτος), which would indicate that he was no longer a teen, but not yet 21.

lowing in the steps of his uncle.[94] Since the nephew would have only ever known Paul as a Christian,[95] his loyalty suggests that elements of Paul's family had at least come to terms with his conversion and leadership in the Christian mission, or even that they were associated with it themselves.

In fact, if the language of 'kin' is left to its natural sense, the greetings of Romans 16 name three of Paul's relatives who were part of Paul's vanguard mission team sent to Rome, and three who remained with him on its sending. The first group consists of three former associates of Herod Antipas: Herodion (v.11), and Andronicus/Chuza and Junia/Joanna (v.11)—with the blood-relation being through Junia, who could provide eyewitness testimony back to the early days of Jesus in Galilee (Luke 8:1; 24:10). With Jason and Sosipater, the second group also includes Lucius (v.21), originally from Cyrene and a Hellenist synagogue in Jerusalem, before becoming part of the Jerusalem church, and, after its dispersal, instrumental in the early mission in Antioch (Acts 11:19-21; 13:1). Called 'the beloved physician' (Col. 4:14), this relative of Paul was thoroughly engaged with the apostle and Joanna in the Christian mission, and became renowned for his two-volume work written to Theophilus.

If this Theophilus was the high priest by that name, Luke's Joanna may well have been his granddaughter and so a niece of Jonathan and grandniece of Caiaphas. Paul's kinship with Junia/Joanna would then indicate that Saul was part of the relational network of the powerful dynasty of Annas, and the zeal that made him stand out from his contemporaries, through fiercely persecuting the Jerusalem church when just a young man in his twenties (7:58) is consistent with the long-standing hatred of that dynasty towards Jesus and his movement (Gal. 1:14; Phil. 3:6; Acts 22:3; cf. Acts 5:17).[96] With Saul authorised by Caiaphas and Jonathan his immediate predecessors in office,

---

94 Bruce, *Acts*, 432.
95 This would be so whether Saul's conversion was 31/32 or 33/34, and whether Felix left office in A.D. 55 or 59/60 (cf. Riesner, *Paul's Early Period*, 64-71, 219-24; Barnett, *Jesus*, 21, 341).
96 See Gaechter, 'Hatred'.

Theophilus would have most likely known Saul in person, a rising star amongst his younger relatives, but, if not, certainly by reputation. One way or another, he would have felt the shock of Saul's 'defection' at the time, and been deeply aware of the personal factors that were part of the internal divisions of the Jews that he was appointed to solve.

For his surprises had begun several years before he took office, when his own granddaughter, despite her aristocratic family and her connections with Herodian circles by marriage, had been publicly associated first with Jesus and then with the Christian movement. This personal connection was no doubt a part of his preference for peace rather than persecution. Likewise, Joanna's association with Luke would explain why this Hellenistic Jewish doctor hailing from Cyrene, who also inhabited Theophilus's wider relational network, wrote two apologies for his instruction. The first (perhaps from Caesarea) set out the facts about Jesus, utilising the testimony of the high priest's own granddaughter. The second (from Rome) gave an apology for Paul by setting out the facts about his role in the Christian mission, the survival of which spoke, according to Paul's teacher Gamaliel (Acts 5:34; 22:3), of divine blessing. Theophilus would have been well aware that, once again, his granddaughter had a key role in the divinely-wrought success of that movement, with its roots firmly in Jerusalem, but now expanding across the ancient world, even to the ends of the earth (Acts 1:8).

Considering the impact of Jesus both on himself and within his family, as represented by the doctor, the aristocrat, and the high priest, the apostle who styled himself 'the first of sinners' (1 Tim. 1:15) could only appreciate more firmly the grace of God, which had formed him to be the apostle of the risen Christ (1 Cor. 15:10) in his gracious conquest of the nations (Titus 2:11; 1 Cor. 15:25–28,58; cf. Acts 4:23–30).

Peter G. Bolt
Sydney College of Divinity

Bibliography

Allen, D. L. — 'The Lukan Authorship of Hebrews: A Proposal', *J. Translation and Textlinguistics* 8 (1996), 1–22.

Allen, D. L. — *Lukan Authorship of Hebrews* (Nashville: B&H, 2010).

Anderson, R. H. — *Who are Johanna and Theophilus? The Irony of the Intended Audience of the Gospel of Luke* (Wallingford, PA: R. H. Anderson, 2011). Kindle edition.

Anderson, R. H. — 'Theophilus: A Proposal', *EQ* 69.3 (1997), 195–215.

Barag, D. and D. Flusser — 'The Ossuary of Yehoḥanah Granddaughter of the High Priest Theophilus', *Israel Exploration Journal* 36.1/2 (1986), 39–44.

Barnett, P. W. — *Jesus and the Rise of Early Christianity. A History of New Testament Times* (Downers Grove, IL: IVP, 1999).

Barth, M., and H. Blanke — *Colossians* (AYB; New Haven, CT: Yale University Press, 1974).

Bauckham, R. — 'Joanna the Apostle', *Gospel Women. Studies of the Named Women in the Gospels* (Grand Rapids, MI: Eerdmans, 2002), 109–202.

Bauckham, R. — 'Mary of Clopas', *Gospel Women. Studies of the Named Women in the Gospels* (Grand Rapids, MI: Eerdmans, 2002), 203–23.

Bauckham, R. — 'Paul and Other Jews with Latin Names in the New Testament', *The Jewish World around the New Testament* (Grand Rapids, MI: Baker Academic, 2008), 371–420.

Bolt, P. G. — 'Untangling the Pauline Handshakes: Who is Greeting Whom in Romans 16?', in P. G. Bolt and J. R. Harrison (eds.), *Romans and the Legacy of Paul. Social, Theological, and Pastoral Perspectives* (Macquarie Park, NSW: SCD Press, 2019), 391–427.

Bolt, P. G. — 'What Actually Happened on Resurrection Morning? A Clear and Simple Account', *JGAR* 2 (2018), 86–100.

Bruce, F. F. — *The Book of Acts* (NICNT; Grand Rapids, MI: Eerdmans, 1988).

Bruce, F. F. — *The Epistles to the Colossians, to Philemon, and to the Ephesians* (NICNT; Grand Rapids, MI: Eerdmans, 1984).

Cadbury, H. J.	'Lucius of Cyrene', in F. J. Foakes-Jackson and K. Lake (eds.), *The Beginnings of Christianity. Part 1: The Acts of the Apostles*. Vol. 5: *Additional Notes* (London: Macmillan, 1933), 489–95.
Cadbury, H. J.	'The Tradition', in F. J. Foakes-Jackson and K. Lake (eds.), *The Beginnings of Christianity. Part 1: The Acts of the Apostles*. Vol. 2: *Prolegomena II: Criticism* (London: Macmillan, 1922), 209–64.
Corley, K. E.	*Private Women, Public Meals. Social Conflict in the Synoptic Tradition* (Peabody, MA: Hendrickson, 1993).
Cranfield, C. E. B.	*A Critical and Exegetical Commentary on the Epistle to the Romans* (ICC; 2 vols.; Edinburgh: T&T Clark, 1985).
Deissmann, A.	'Appendix IV: Lucius—Luke', *Light from the Ancient East. The New Testament illustrated by recently discovered texts of the Graeco-Roman world* (L. R. M. Strachan, transl.; Peabody, MA: Hendrickson, 1995, 4th edition), 435–38. Previously published: New York, NY: George H. Doran, 1927 [German: 1922]. The essay is slightly altered from its first publication in *Festgabe für A. von Harnack* (Tübingen, 1921), 117–120. Archive.org.
Ellis, E. E.	'Paul and his Co-Workers', in E. E. Ellis, *Prophecy and Hermeneutics in Early Christianity. New Testament Essays* (WUNT 18; Tübingen: Mohr Siebeck, 1978; reprinted: Grand Rapids, MI: Eerdmans, 1980), 3–22.
Ellis, E. E.	*The Gospel of Luke* (NCB; Grand Rapids, MI and London: Eerdmans, and Marshall, Morgan & Scott, 1974 revised [1966]).
Ellis, E. E.	'"Those of the Circumcision" and the early Christian mission', *Studia Evangelica* 4 (1968), 390–99.
Evans, C. A.	*Jesus and the Ossuaries* (Waco, TX: Baylor University Press, 2003).
Ford, R. C.	'St. Luke and Lucius of Cyrene', *ExpT* 32.5 (1921), 219–20.
Fraenkel, E.	'Wilhelm Schulze', *Classical Review* 49.6 (1935), 217–19.
Fraser, P. M., and E. Matthews	*Lexicon of Greek Personal Names* (Oxford: Clarendon; New York, NY: Oxford University Press, 1987–2005).

Gaechter, P.   'The Hatred of the House of Annas', *Theological Studies* 8.1 (1947), 3–34.

Gemmill, C. L.   'Study of Ancient Cyrene as a Medical Center', *BioScience* 15.6 (1965), 422.

Gemmill, C. L.   'Silphium', *Bulletin of the History of Medicine* 40.4 (1966), 295–313.

Goodwin, W. W.   *A Greek Grammar* (London: St Martin's Press, 1879, new 1894, repr. 1987).

Hase, T.   'IV. Theodori Hasaei ad praecedentem de THEOPHILO dissertationem sicilimentum', *Bibliotheca Historico-Philogico-Theologica* Class. 4, Fasc. 3 (1721), 506–30. https://babel.hathitrust.org/cgi/pt?id=ucm.5324360082.

Hengel, M.   *The Four Gospels and the One Gospel of Jesus Christ. An Investigation of the Collection and Origin of the Canonical Gospels* (John Bowden, transl.; London: SCM, 2000).

Hengel, M.   *The 'Hellenization' of Judaea in the First Century after Christ* (London & Philadelphia, PA: SCM & Trinity, 1989).

Hengel, M.   'The Titles of the Gospels and the Gospel of Mark', *Studies in the Gospel of Mark* (John Bowden, transl.; London: SCM, 1985 [German: 1984], Ch.3.

Hengel, M.   'Between Jesus and Paul. The "Hellenists", the "Seven" and Stephen (Acts 6:1–15; 7:54—8:3 [1975]', *Between Jesus and Paul. Studies in the Earliest History of Christianity* (John Bowden, transl.; London: SCM, 1983; Repr. Eugene, OR: Wipf and Stock, 2003), 1–29.

Hengel, M., and A. M. Schwemer   *Paul Between Damascus and Antioch. The Unknown Years* (J. Bowden, transl.; London & Louisville, KY: SCM & Westminster John Knox, 1997).

Horsley, G. R. H. (ed.)   *New Documents Illustrating Early Christianity*, 4. *A Review of the Greek Inscriptions and Papyri published in 1979* (Macquarie University: Ancient History Documentary Research Centre, 1987).

Horsley, G. R. H. (ed.)   *New Documents Illustrating Early Christianity*, 3. *A Review of the Greek Inscriptions and Papyri published in 1978* (Macquarie University: Ancient History Documentary Research Centre, 1983).

Horsley, G. R. H. (ed.)   *New Documents Illustrating Early Christianity*, 2. *A Review of the Greek Inscriptions and Papyri published in 1977* (Macquarie University: Ancient History Documentary Research Centre, 1982).

Horsley, R. A.   'High Priests and the Politics of Roman Palestine. A Contextual Analysis of the Evidence in Josephus', *JSJ* 17.1 (1986), 23–55.

Ilan, T., and K. Hünefeld   *Lexicon of Jewish Names in Late Antiquity.* Part IV: *The Eastern Diaspora 330 BCE–650 CE* (Texts & Studies in Ancient Judaism 141; Tübingen: Mohr Siebeck, 2011).

Ilan, T., and T. Ziem   *Lexicon of Jewish Names in Late Antiquity.* Part III: *The Western Diaspora 330 BCE–650 CE* (Texts & Studies in Ancient Judaism 126; Tübingen: Mohr Siebeck, 2008).

Ilan, T.   *Lexicon of Jewish Names in Late Antiquity.* Part I: *Palestine 330 BCE–200 CE* (Texts & Studies in Ancient Judaism 91; Tübingen: Mohr Siebeck, 2002).

Ilan, T.   'The Attraction of Aristocratic Women to Pharisaism During the Second Temple Period', *HTR* 88 (1995), 1–33.

Ilan, T.   'Notes on the Distribution of Jewish Women's Names in Palestine in the Second Temple and Mishnaic Periods', *JJS* 40 (1989), 186–200.

Kokkinos, N.   *The Herodian Dynasty. Origins, Role in Society and Eclipse* (London: Spink, 2010 [Reprint and expansion of original: 1998]).

Kokkinos, N.   'Crucifixion in A.D. 36: The Keystone for Dating the Birth of Jesus', in J. Vardaman and E. M. Yamauchi (eds.), *Chronos, Kairos, Christos. Nativity and Chronological Studies Presented to Jack Finegan* (Winona Lake, IN: Eisenbrauns, 1989), 133–63.

Lohse, E.   *Colossians and Philemon: A Commentary on the Epistles to the Colossians and to Philemon* (Hermeneia; Minneapolis, MN: Fortress, 1971).

Marshall, I. H.   *Acts: An Introduction and Commentary* (TNTC; Downers Grove, IL: InterVarsity, 1980). Accordance Edition.

Michaelis, J. D.   'Of the person of Theophilus', *Introduction to the New Testament* (H. Marsh, transl. and augmented; London: Rivington, ⁴1823), Volume 3, Part 1, 236–41. Google Books.

Midrash.org   Midrash.org/calendar

Moule, C. F. D.	'Once More, Who Were the Hellenists?', *ExpT* 70.4 (1959), 100–102.
Newman, W. C.	*Luke, John and Acts: Background, Outline and Commentary* (Tacoma, WA: Newman International, 2006, expanded 2009).
Peterson, D.	*The Acts of the Apostles* (PNTC; Grand Rapids, MI: Eerdmans, 2009). Accordance Edition.
Polhill, J. B.	*Acts* (NAC 26; Nashville, TN: Broadman and Holman, 1992). Accordance Edition.
Ramsay, W. M.	*The Bearing of Recent Discoveries on the Trustworthiness of the New Testament* (London: Hodder & Stoughton, 1915), 370–84.
Reicke, B.	'Caesarea, Rome, and the Captivity Epistles', W. W. Gasque and R. P. Martin (eds.), *Apostolic History and the Gospel. Biblical and Historical Essays Presented to F. F. Bruce* (Exeter: Paternoster, 1970), 277–86.
Reicke, B.	'The Historical Setting of Colossians', *RevExp* 70.4 (1973), 429–38.
Riesner, R.	*Paul's Early Period. Chronology, Mission Strategy, Theology* (D. Stott, transl.; Grand Rapids, MI and Cambridge, UK: 1998 [German: 1994]).
Robinson, D. W. B.	'"To submit to the judgement of the saints"', 'Who were "the saints"?', '"We are the circumcision"', in P. G. Bolt and M. D. Thompson (eds.), *Donald Robinson. Selected Works.* Vol. 1: *Assembling God's People* (Camperdown, NSW: Australian Church Record/ Moore College, 2008), 152–59, 160–69, 170–78.
Robinson, J. A. T.	*Redating the New Testament* (London: SCM, 1976; Eugene, OR: Wipf & Stock, 2000).
Sanday, W. and A. C. Headlam	*A Critical Exegetical Commentary on the Epistle to the Romans* (ICC; 5th ed.; Edinburgh: T&T Clark, 1908).
Schulze, W.	*Graeca Latina* (Göttingen: Officina Academica Dieterichiana, 1901 [1891]). Republished in W. Schulze, *Orthographica et Graeca Latin* (E. Fraenkel, ed.; Rome: Edizioni di Storia e Letteratura, 1958).

Schwartz, D. R. *Agrippa I: The Last King of Judea* (Tübingen: Mohr Siebeck, 1990).

Smallwood, E. M. 'High Priests and Politics in Roman Palestine', *JTS* 13.1 (1962), 14–34.

Smallwood, E. M. 'The Date of the Dismissal of Pontius Pilate from Judaea', *JJS* 5 (1954), 12–21.

Solin, H. *Die griechischen Personennamen in Rom. Ein Namenbuch* (3 vols; Berlin: De Gruyter, 1982). [=GPR]

Steinmann, A. E. *From Abraham to Paul. A Biblical Chronology* (St Louis, MO: Concordia, 2011).

Totelin, L. 'When foods become remedies in ancient Greece: The curious case of garlic and other substances', *J.Ethnopharmacol.* 167 (2015), 30–37. https://www.ncbi.nlm.nih.gov/pmc/articles/PMC4469375/.

Tyson, J. B. *Luke-Acts and the Jewish People: Eight Critical Perspectives* (Minneapolis, MN: Augsburg, 1988).

VanderKam, J. C. *From Joshua to Caiaphas: High Priests after the Exile* (Minneapolis, MN & Assen: Fortress & Van Gorcum, 2004).

van der Horst, P. W. *Ancient Jewish Epitaphs: An Introductory Survey of a Millennium of Jewish Funerary Epigraphy (300 BCE –700 CE)* (Kampen: Kok Pharos, 1991).

Walters, P. *The Assumed Authorial Unity of Luke and Acts. A Reassessment of the Evidence* (SNTSMS 145; Cambridge: Cambridge University Press, 2009).

A Note Tracing a Theme:
John 6:45 and Being Taught by God

Darrell L. Bock

Abstract

The essay traces the potential conceptual background to an allusion to Isaiah 54:13 in John 6:45. Backgrounds in its original context and in later Jewish usage of the texts are considered, as well as where these related texts reappear in the New Testament. The texts include Joel 3:16–17, Jeremiah 33:31–34, Ezekiel 36:22–31, and Isaiah 8:14–16. This seemingly quickly noted allusion to being taught by God may have much more background behind it than has been previously observed. The evocation of the New Covenant and themes tied to it reflect core New Testament ideas drawn from Jewish eschatological hope.

Introduction

One of the things Jim Harrison is known for is tracing themes. Usually they come out of the Graeco-Roman world. I am going to trace a theme that comes from the Jewish world. There is an irony to the theme I will trace given this is a textual note for an academic audience, where being taught by people sharing expertise is the goal. The theme is about being taught by no one else but God. The remark appears in John 6:45. It shows up in a discourse where Jesus claims to be the bread of life. The theme is introduced by what seems to be almost a side remark: 'It is written in the prophets, "And they shall all be taught by God". Everyone who has heard and learned from the Father comes to me'. (NRSV)

Isaiah 54:13

The generic introductory formula does not specify the citation. It simply appeals to the prophets as a group. However, most recognise it to be connected to Isaiah 54:13 and its promise of direct teaching from God.[1] It is probably best described as a paraphrase of that verse, but it also introduces a theme found in the prophets at large. Isaiah 54:13 reads, 'All your children shall be taught by the Lord'. It comes in a context where God is promising a restoration to his people that includes building a house made of precious stones where they will reside. The result will be a place where oppression, fear, and terror are not present. Those who store up strife shall fall. No weapon fashioned against God's own will prosper. This is the heritage of the Lord's servants as they gain vindication from God (Isa. 54:14–17). What is being described is a place of peace, a classic description of salvation in terms common to the Hebrew Scripture. Framing the citation of Isaiah 54 in terms of the prophets as a whole makes sense when the context is seen in this light.

The theme is common to the Hebrew Scripture and it is also tied to other ideas associated with the ancient hope of salvation. Plummer asks us to compare the use of Isaiah 54 with other texts: Joel 3:16–17 and Jeremiah 31:33–34.[2]

Joel 3:16–17

Joel 3:16–17 has the Lord roaring from Zion as he is a refuge for his people with Jerusalem as a holy place which strangers never pass through again. Context here is also important. Earlier in Joel 2:28–3:5, there is a promise of pouring out God's Spirit on all of his people, a text that shows up as prominent in Peter's speech at Pentecost in Acts 2. Judgement and restoration come to God's people and the nations opposed to them as God moves to restore peace for his people.

At Qumran, the Spirit is said to enable discernment in the eschatological community (1QH^a 15.6–10; 1QS 4.2–4 = Treatise of the Two

---

1   Westcott, *The Gospel according to St. John*, 105.
2   Plummer, *The Gospel according to St. John*, 159.

Spirits).³ This also fits to a degree with Jewish expectation at least as expressed in later Jewish texts. In these texts, God's presence is said to rest on his people and guide them. Numbers Rabbah 15.25 says, 'in the world to come all Israel will be made prophets'. This is said in contrast to the few, like Moses and Joshua who had the Spirt in the past. Midrash Rabbah on Psalm 14:6 ties Joel 3 to Numbers 11:29 as it speaks of instruction. In fact, Ezekiel 36:26 and Joel 3:1 appear side by side.⁴ Deuteronomy Rabbah 6.14 (203ᵈ) ties this blessing to the future time when the evil inclination is removed with Ezekiel 36:26 and Isaiah 54:13(!).⁵

Jeremiah 31:33–34

Jeremiah 31:33–34 is also a significant text as it is part of Jeremiah's declaration about a New Covenant. It reads,

> But this is the covenant I will make with the house of Israel after those days, says the LORD: I will put my law within them, and I will write it on their hearts; and I will be their God, and they shall be my people. No longer shall they teach one another, or say to each other, 'Know the LORD', for they all shall know me, from the least of them to the greatest says the LORD; for I will forgive their iniquity and remember their sin no more.

There are two elements to this verse that are important and connected conceptually to John 6. First, is the internal nature of this work that parallels the ingesting of Jesus as the bread of life that the John 6 dis-

---

3 Bock, *Acts*, 112; Keener, *Acts*, 1:876 n.153.
4 Braude, *Midrash*, 186. For more on Ezekiel 36, see below.
5 For these Rabbah texts, Strack-Billerbeck, *Kommentar*, 2:615–16. English translation of the Rabbah texts from Numbers and Deuteronomy can be found in the collection *Midrash Rabbah* (Soncino edition), edited by H. Freedman and Maurice Simon. On this larger theme, Levinson, *The Holy Spirit*. 4Q161 and *T. Jud.* have the eschatological messiah possessing the Spirit, so the association of the Spirit with the end is widespread. *T. Jud.* 20:3–4 speak of any person's works written on the heart as part of an exposition of the two spirits (truth and error) doctrine. Nothing can be hidden because the works 'are written on the heart in the Lord's sight'.

course describes. It is not the law that goes inside the person but the presence of the one sent by God, actually the one sent by the Father. Second, is the theme that they do not need to come to know God because they do not need to teach one another because they all know God. In other words, they are all 'taught by God'. They are taught by God and him alone. It is only that teaching that counts, a point that might have a polemical dimension given the controversy Jesus' teaching here raises.

In Second Temple Judaism, the New Covenant fuelled this kind of future hope, though it was aimed in the direction of reestablishing Torah observance at Qumran (CD-B XX, 12).[6] The text was a part of national restoration hope coming out of a call for Israel to repent.

Ezekiel 36:22-31

This takes us to another text, Ezekiel 36:22-31. It describes the flock of God. In the midst of this text is the following in vv. 22-24:

> I will save my flock, and they shall no longer be ravaged; and I will judge between sheep and sheep. I will set up over them one shepherd, my servant David, and he shall feed them: he shall feed them and be their shepherd. And I, the LORD, will be their God, and my servant David shall be prince among them; I, the LORD, have spoken.

What follows is a description of the peace that will come to the people who make up the flock, those who benefit from the 'covenant of peace' (Ezek. 34:25). Notice the motif of feeding in the verse. Here it is the shepherd-servant David who feeds.

Beyond the later links noting Ezekiel 36 above in notes 4 and 5, this connection with Ezekiel and the link to a Davidic hope drops us into the host of passages that express the hope for a deliverer Messiah

---

6 Thompson, *Jeremiah*, 580. Ellingworth, *Hebrews*, 414; Beale and Carson, *Commentary*, 971.

in the eschaton.[7] Though this hope expressed itself with a great deal of variety, several of these images became central to the proclamation of realisation tied to the early church. Whether one thinks of the Davidic notes on fulfillment in the infancy materials, a text like John 10 about the great shepherd of the sheep, the centrality of texts like Psalm 2:7 or Psalm 110:1 in New Testament books ranging from the Gospels, Acts, and Hebrews, one can see this combination of deliverance, community, and peace became central to the early church's expression of the hope central to its kingdom theology and gospel.

Isaiah 8:14–16

Finally, there is Isaiah 8:14–16. This remark early in the book of Isaiah asks the question, who is being taught by what this prophetic book is teaching? The teaching is precious and should be bound up and sealed.[8] The command in Isaiah 8 is to seal up the teaching for the disciples. Isaiah 8:14–15 is also noting that this message will be controversial. They will stumble over the stone it represents. The idea of Isaiah 8:14–15 is alluded to in numerous NT texts, because the theme is associated with Psalm 118:22 and Isaiah 28:16. Matthew 21:42, Luke 2:34 and 20:18, Romans 9:32-33, and 1 Peter 2:8 connect to this idea.

What the prophet is announcing includes the deliverance tied to a rescuing figure of the Lord's disciples. Isaiah 8:15–16 is preparing to extol the arrival of a deliverer in Isaiah 9, who is a great light. He will sit on a throne where there is endless peace, a throne of David and a

---

7   Perhaps the best summary of the variety of themes tied to this idea within Jewish hope is found in Oegema, *The Anointed*. Note especially the charts found on pp. 33 and 300-02. He also helpfully notes 13 aspects that are tied to messianism that always come in various combinations with elements present and missing in any particular text (p. 31). They are (1) expectation; (2) Israel; (3) promise; (4) Davidic origin; (5) gift of the Spirit; (6) priesthood or kingdom; (7) end of days; (8) People of God; (9) liberation or salvation; (10) nations of the world; (11) justice; (12) peace; and (13) government. The chart on p. 33 noted Ezekiel 36 but curiously misses the Davidic link from this passage in Ezekiel. Ezekiel has five of these themes: gift of the Spirit, people of God, liberation, justice, and peace. We'd observe the Davidic link is also important to that text.
8   Oswalt, *Isaiah*, 235.

kingdom will be established with justice and righteousness (Isa. 9:7). It is followed by a call to wait on the Lord and to hope in him.

Conclusion

What we are seeing is very much a deeply embedded theme about being taught by God. This hope stands written 'in the prophets'. That teaching possesses many strands. The text declaring they are taught by God raises the question, what are they taught? What might Jesus be alluding to in John 6? They are taught about a covenant of peace that is fed to them by the Servant-King David. It is a covenant that works from the inside. It is a new covenant where God's presence is inside of them and sin is forgiven. It is a deep promise and truth that only some see. Those who see it are taught by God. Those who do not trip over it. Those who respond have no need of another teacher for they are drawn into and embrace the promise that teaching holds. John 6:45 may seem like a side remark but a tracing of the theme shows there is much there for those who will see it. Jesus is pointing the way to knowing God with him as the manna of life. What is taught goes far deeper than merely being taught by God because what is taught is food for the soul and the world.

Darrell L. Bock
Dallas Theological Seminary

Bibliography

Beale, G., and D. A. Carson — *Commentary on the New Testament Use of the Old Testament* (Grand Rapids, MI: Baker, 2007).

Bock, D. L. — *Acts* (Baker Exegetical Commentary on the New Testament; Grand Rapids, MI: Baker, 2007).

Braude, W. G. — *The Midrash on the Psalms* (2 vols.; New Haven, CT: Yale University Press, 1959).

Ellingworth, P. — *Commentary on Hebrews* (The New International Greek Testament Commentary; Grand Rapids, MI: Eerdmans, 1993).

Freedman, H., and M. Simon (eds.) — *Midrash Rabbah* (10 vols.; London: Soncino, 1983).

Keener, C. S. — *Acts: An Exegetical Commentary* (4 vols.; Grand Rapids, MI: Baker, 2012–15).

Levinson, J. — *The Holy Spirit in First Century Judaism* (Leiden: Brill, 2002).

Oegema, G. S. — *The Anointed and his People: Messianic Expectations from the Maccabees to Bar Kochba* (JSP Supplement Series, 27; London: Bloomsbury, T&T Clark, 1998).

Oswalt, J. — *The Book of Isaiah, Chapters 1—39* (New International Commentary on the Old Testament; Grand Rapids, MI: Eerdmans, 1986).

Plummer, A. — *The Gospel According to St. John* (Cambridge: Cambridge University Press, 1889).

Strack, H. L., and P. Billerbeck — *Kommentar zum Neuen Testament aus Talmud und Midrasch* (6 vols.; München: C. H. Beck, 1926).

Thompson, J. A. — *The Book of Jeremiah* (New International Commentary on the Old Testament; Grand Rapids, MI: Eerdmans, 1995).

Westcott, B. F. — *The Gospel According to John* (Cambridge: Cambridge University Press, 1881; repr. Grand Rapids, MI: Eerdmans, 1973).

GRACE THROUGH PAUL

Greek Shorthand in the Time of the New Testament

E. Randolph Richards

Abstract

The 1883 discovery of a fourth c. BC example of what appeared to be Greek 'shorthand' produced a flurry of scholarly discussion. Further discoveries and documentary arguments did not greatly impact the conclusions that shorthand began with Latin before Greek and a functional system was not available in New Testament times. More recent discoveries enable these conclusions to be questioned and the development to be reversed. In existence before Cicero and Tiro adapted it to Latin, a functional system of Greek shorthand was certainly available in the first century AD. We should not exclude the possible presence of shorthand writers in the New Testament world.

1. Introduction

Giving and taking dictation *at the speed of writing* was part of basic education even prior to New Testament times. Cicero notes dictating a letter syllable-by-syllable (*syllabatim*).[1] Seneca critiques a colleague who ridiculed the stammering Vinicius: 'he was pulling out individual words, as if he were dictating, not speaking'.[2] Rapid dictation, at the

---

1   Cic. *Att.* 13.25.3; Cicero was explaining (complaining) to Atticus over the care he had given a letter he composed to Varro. Pliny, *NH* 7.25.91, brags Julius Caesar could dictate seven letters at once.
2   Sen. *Ep.* 40.10.

speed of speech, however, requires a ταχυγράφος³ or σημειογράφος, or to use modern vernacular, a shorthand writer. The existence of a Greek system in New Testament times is disputed.⁴

2. Definition of Greek Shorthand

Perhaps the place to begin is to define what was meant here by 'tachygraphy' or shorthand, that is any system of continuous nonstandard writing employed in antiquity to increase the speed of writing, with the goal of attaining at least the speed of speech.⁵ For our purposes, we shall define shorthand as capable of reproducing a spoken text.

3. Early Scholarly Studies on Greek Shorthand

Perhaps due to the 1883 discovery of a fourth century B.C. marble gravestone on the Acropolis with what appears to be some early form of

---

3   LSJ, s.v. 'ταχυγράφος'. The earliest evidence they cite is Ioannis Lydi (6th Christian century).
4   Foat, 'Tachygraphy', 239. According to Gitlbauer, *Tachygraphie*, 25, the tenth Christian century had functioning Greek shorthand as seen in the appended scribal claim in MS Cod. Paris Graec. 1056: εγραψε γραμματα ες ταναγνωστου κονδυα ε θημισεα αυτα απιθανα ενακοσια ('that he wrote a passage 900 times by the water clock five times replenished'). This would be 27,290 words per hour, thrice the rate of normal speech. Even allowing for outrageous boasting, it would at least be shorthand. All subsequent scholarly references to MS 1056 merely cite Gitlbauer; no one else appears to have worked on this. It is not at all clear to me, however, where this 'appended scribal claim' is made, perhaps on the initial page: https://gallica.bnf.fr/ark:/12148/btv1b10722737x/f5.item. This and a few other marginal glosses were too faded for me to decipher, but I found nothing hinting at his text. Gitlbauer was responsible also for deciphering the tachygraphic text of Cod. Vat. Gr. 1809. His translation here was recently verified. Note the minuscule text on 255v ends midsentence with the tachygraphic text immediately following (255r); see https://digi.vatlib.it/view/MSS_Vat.gr.1809.
5   Joshua Parker, my former assistant and a bright young scholar, has done invaluable research on shorthand for this essay and has begun dabbling in deciphering Greek shorthand. I am indebted to him in this essay and he is rapidly outdistancing my inadequate tutelage. He was the one who succeeded in deciphering the tachygraphic text of Cod. Vat. Gr. 1809, confirming Gitlbauer's identification.

Greek tachygraphy,[6] a 20-year flurry of German scholarship on ancient Greek shorthand was led by the labours of Kopp, Blass, Gardthausen, Schmitz, Wattenbach, Lehmann, Ruess, Giry, Tardif, Chatelain, and especially Gomperz, Gitlbauer, and Wessely.[7] Hampered by very limited evidence, they nonetheless mounted considerable discussion. A few decades later, additional evidence was uncovered but no subsequent scholarly re-argumentation.

3.1 Archaeological Discoveries

By comparing the Acropolis-stone with shorthand texts of the tenth Christian century, some scholars argued the Acropolis-stone was some early form of Greek tachygraphy, perhaps syllabic.[8] A few papyrus fragments from the Fayum, dated to the fifth (sixth?) century B.C.,[9] provided additional examples of what might be a Greek syllabic system of shorthand, but not in any convincing manner. A gravestone inscription for Publius Aelius Actiacus uses the title σημειογράφος, which CIG translates as 'notary'.[10] It may be dated to the reign of either Hadrian (A.D. 117–138) or Aurelius (A.D. 180–192),[11] thus, post-New Testament. Although Egyptologists had recently uncovered better evidence, these new discoveries did not impact the early scholarly dis-

---

6   See Mentz, 'Grabschrift', 49. Foat, 'Tachygraphy', 246, later published a facsimile with an edited text. Although quite dated, the best summary of the developmental history of shorthand from ancient until modern times may still be Johnen, *Stenographie*, who concludes each period with a comprehensive bibliography, somewhat parallelled by Foat. Thompson, *Paleography*, 71ff. has a short discussion on tachygraphy and a good German bibliography, although pre-1906. See also Johnston, *Latin*, 27ff.
7   See Foat, 'Tachygraphy', 265–67, for complete bibliographic data. Just as Gitlbauer is the sole voice on the 10th century texts, Wessely is the basis for all subsequent discussion on the Ranier papyri (4th–6th century).
8   Mentz, *Kurzschrift*, 10–12, quickly disputed these claims, arguing it was an early attempt to reform the Greek language. Gardthausen, 'Akropolis-Steines', 81–84, summarises the debate.
9   P.Rain. 13.444; 3.9, 10.
10 CIG 3902d = Ramsay, *Phrygia* II 379, no. 208. Editors may be influenced by their opinion of the existence of shorthand and thus influenced in how they translate shorthand terminology, whether abbreviation instead of shorthand sign or notary instead of shorthand writer, as this text and translation illustrates.
11 Mentz, 'Grabschrift', 53.

cussions of a functional system of shorthand during New Testament times.[12]

3.2 Subsequent Documentary Arguments

Both the Septuagintal gloss ὀξυγράφος for סוֹפֵר מָהִיר in Ps. 45:1 [44:2] and Diogenes Laertius' [early 3rd Christian century] remark that Xenophon [426?–354 B.C.] was πρῶτος ὑποσημειωσάμενος τὰ λεγόμενα (*Vit. Xen.* 2.48) are too ambiguous to be evidence of Greek shorthand.[13] Xenophon's use of signs could refer to cryptic personal notes not recording dictation. Tarn, the noted scholar on Alexander the Great (356–323 B.C.) argues for an occasional 'genuine' speech, but '"Genuine", of course, does not imply a verbatim report; no such thing was known'.[14] Rather, Tarn argues a genuine speech might plausibly have come from ἀπομνημονεύματα.[15]

Nonetheless, three hundred years after Alexander, good notes seem insufficient to explain Arrian's (c. A.D. 96–180) *Discourses of Epictetus* (c. A.D. 50–120). Arrian specifically cites them as Epictetus's speeches. In fact, Arrian carefully delineates that it is not plagiarism (λογοκλοπία) of Epictetus but rather his notes of Epictetus's lectures: 'indeed, I acknowledge that I have not composed (οὐδὲ συγγράψαι) them at all. But whatever I heard him say I used to write down (γραψάμενος), word for word, as best I could....'[16] In a classic work on the nature of the Discourses, Hartmann argues forcibly, based upon an analysis of

---

12 This is not entirely correct. Although seemingly ignored, in 1905, Preisigke, 312, refers to P.Oxy. IV 724 and also comments, 310–311, that P.Oxy. II 293 (Nov. 15, A.D. 27) seems to distinguish between *gewöhnlicher* and *stenographischer Schrift*: οὐδεμίαν μοι φάσιν ἀπέστειλας περὶ τῶν ἱματίων οὔτε διὰ γραπτοῦ οὔτε διὰ σημέ[ι]ου...; see https://papyri.info/ddbdp/p.oxy;2;293. About forty years later, Mentz, *Kurzschrift*, 22, mentions 'der älteste bekannte stenographische Papyrus, der jetzt in Bremen ist, aus der Zeit zwischen 113 und 120 stammt'. He does not cite the bibliographic information, but we think he means P.Brem. 82.
13 So argues Milne, *Manuals*, 1; see also Kenyon, 'Tachygraphy', 1033.
14 Tarn, *Alexander*, 286.
15 Tarn, *Alexander*, 290–95.
16 According to Oldfather, the contrast here between γράφω and συγγράφω is quite intentional; Epictetus, *The Discourses as Reported by Arrian*, ed. W. A. Oldfather, LCL, 2 vols. (Cambridge, MA: Harvard University Press, 1925), 1: 5 n. 2.

Arrian's extant works, that Arrian was incapable of producing a work like the Discourses from mere recollection, adding Arrian's other works forbid an appeal to a great memory.[17] He argues Arrian must have been able to take rapid dictation, although he stops short of claiming Arrian knew shorthand.[18] Oldfather, twenty years later, is more bold: 'That Arrian's report is a stenographic record of the *ipsissima verba* of the master there can be no doubt',[19] adding (1) Arrian wrote in Attic, while the discourses are in the koine, (2) there was a marked difference in the style, especially in the use of several prepositions, and (3) the complete and utter difference in the spirit and tempo between the *Discourses* and the works of Arrian.

3.3 Early Conclusions against Greek Shorthand at the Time of the New Testament

Oldfather wrote after much of the discussion of Greek shorthand was over, and thus, Foat's and Mentz's assessment largely shaped the opinion of early scholarship. Foat had concluded early systems were not capable of writing Greek rapidly and would 'never have been of service for verbatim "reporting" of ordinary speech'.[20] Mentz places the synthesis of shorthand at the speed of speech with Seneca,[21] which would mean that Greek shorthand could not have gained meaningful traction in the first century since his changes would need to filter from Latin to Greek and then disseminate across the Empire. Mentz's conclusion continued to be cited as the authority in later discussions on

---

17   Hartmann, 'Arrian', 257.
18   Hartmann, 'Arrian', 275. Hartmann does not state it, but I would conclude that it was more likely the wealthy Arrian hired (or owned) a slave capable of taking Greek shorthand.
19   Oldfather, Epictetus (LCL), 1: XIII: 'the actual words'; Oates, *Philosophers*, XXII, expresses a similar sentiment: 'an apparently almost stenographic record of his lectures'. Oldfather wrote twenty years after Hartmann and after many papyri had been published.
20   Foat, 'Tachygraphy', 252.
21   Mentz, 'Entstehungsgeschichte', 386. Mentz, 369, uses the account in Isidore of Seville's Orig. 1.22 as a baseline, 'Romae primus Tullius Tiro Ciceronis libertus commentatus est notas, sed tantum praepositionum. Post eum Vipsanius Filagrius et Aquila libertus Maecenatis alius alias addiderunt'.

shorthand, especially regarding Tiro's connection to shorthand[22] and the alternate version of Cicero's speech *Pro Milone*.[23]

4. The Introduction of New Archaeological Evidence

The later works of Boge and Teitler (who examines notarii after A.D. 411) broached the topic again, noting some new archeological discoveries, but largely citing the older argumentation and reaching similar conclusions. A fresh but brief examination of new material appears in McNamee. Her focus is the marginalia in the only surviving papyrus with explanatory marginalia of Plato's Republic.[24] The marginalia is largely longhand with some literary abbreviation (where part of a word is written with only a few characters to represent the rest of the word). Although relying on Mentz primarily for interpretation, she cites several papyri that have come to light since he wrote (see below). Her discussion highlights that early conclusions about Greek shorthand were based upon some ambiguous archaeological data and some inconclusive documentary arguments. The few subsequent discoveries did not lead to altering the initial conclusion that there was no clear evidence of early functional Greek shorthand. It took rather decisive archaeological evidence to force a reconsideration of the topic.

4.1 The Oxyrhynchus Contract

A papyrus contract from Oxyrhynchus, dated A.D. 155, records a slave

---

22 See McDermott, 'M. Cicero and M. Tiro', 271-2 where McDermott dismisses Tiro having any involvement in shorthand on the basis of Isidore of Seville's account. McDermott points out several errors in Isidore's historiography, citing his unreliability as grounds for 'the great probability that shorthand does not precede an imperial date'. Isidore's unreliability, however, may only suggest that his evidence is inadmissible rather than that the opposite conclusion be the case.
23 See Settle, 'Milone', 276-7, who, using Mentz's article as proof, rules out shorthand as a possibility for explaining the alternative version's origin, opting instead to explain it as a forgery. See Marshall, 'Excepta Oratio', 735, who, also using Mentz's article, explains that the alternative version was a collection of notes that were compared and compiled since, per Mentz, shorthand was still being developed and was not 'capable of recording a delivered speech verbatim'.
24 P.Oxy. XV 1808 (dated A.D. 150-250); see McNamee, 'Plato', 97, but see the discussion below.

who was apprenticed to Apollonius, σημειογράφῳ. According to the editors, this very significant text reads:

> Panechotes also called Panares, ex-cosmetes of Oxyrhynchus, through his friend Gemellus, to Apollonius, writer of shorthand (σημ[ε]ιογράφῳ), greeting. I have placed with you my slave Chaerammon to be taught the signs which your son Dionysius knows, for a period of two years ... at the salary agreed upon between us ... you will receive at the end of the period when the boy writes fluently in every respect and reads faultlessly .... The 18th year of the Emperor Caesar Titus Aelius Iladrianus Antoninus Augustus Pius, Phamenoth 5.[25]

The contract meticulously noted the details: payment started when the slave started learning the signs (σημεῖων) and concluded when he writes fluently in every respect and reads faultlessly (ἐκ παντὸς λόγου πεζοῦ γράφοντος καὶ ἀναγεινώς[κον]τος ἀμέμπτως). The date of the papyrus is clear, mid-second century, but one must allow some time for an established apprenticeship system to reach a small town in provincial Egypt. Positing Greek shorthand in the first century in the leading cities of the Empire seems reasonable. We might further note this legal contract carefully explains benchmarks and payment details, but does not define σημειογράφος. The explanation of the speed and accuracy was not to explain what a σημειογράφος did but rather to establish the proficiency needed for final payment.

4.2 Other Shorthand Documents

Although this Oxyrhynchus papyrus was commonly cited as the oldest certain evidence of Greek shorthand,[26] McNamee cites an inscription

---

25 P.Oxy. IV 724; translation by Grenfell and Hunt.
26 So Bahr, 'Letter', 473; Haenchen, *Apostelgeschichte*, 39 n.3; Roller, *Formular*, 306–07; and Mentz, *Stenographie*, 19–20.

dated A.D. 103 and a few papyrus texts with shorthand.[27] We will also add a contemporary example from Judaea. At Wadi Murabbaʿāt, archaeologists uncovered documents dating to the second Jewish revolt. Benoit describes one parchment. In its present state, a piece of a parchment roll was apparently commandeered, perhaps as a scrap. It was folded along an original seam of the roll and then coarsely sewn along the two longer (opposite) sides to form a pouch, a common enough practice, probably to hold papyrus letters. The writing on the roll was tachygraphic.[28]

Without a translation, any conclusions about P.Mur. 164 remain tenuous. Nonetheless, two points may be made with reasonable certainty. One, while the content of P.Mur. 164 remains untranslated, it is clearly Greek shorthand.[29] A comparison of this text to those signs in Milne's *Manuals* reveals numerous signs in common as well as similarity in general appearance and the apparent use of the same shorthand rules.[30] Two, the parchment is most probably to be dated with the other

---

27 CIG 4763; see the text and untranslated drawing in A. Boeckhius, *Corpus inscriptionum graecarum* 3.1 (Berlin: ex officina academica, 1853), 3:384. McNamee, 'Plato', 104 n.26, lists Pack2 2771 = P.Har. 1 51 (first century), and several second century texts and commentaries, including P.Brem. 82 (102 n.17). To this we may add also P.Duk. inv. 311. She also cites PSI inv. 2013 = PSI Com 11 13 from the 3rd century, but it appears to be mainly a longhand text with several signs interspersed, per http://www.psi-online.it/documents/psi-com11-13.

28 P.Mur. 164; see Benoit, *Murabba'ât*, 275–79. Since this parchment was uncovered after Mentz wrote, it cannot be the same piece to which he referred.

29 So also the editors, *Murabba'ât*, 276–277.

30 Josh Parker has privately identified to me over 100 signs visually in common with Milne's list in the first 10 lines alone (out of the 48 lines in P.Mur. 164). Parker notes in a given line of about 23 characters on average, about a quarter match almost exactly to signs in Milne's manual, another half look similar but with some variation (longer/shorter tail, sharper/laxer curve, etc.), and the remaining quarter splits randomly per line between 1) signs not in the manual synthesised from simpler signs in the manual and 2) signs that seem foreign completely. Further, the system or grammar of shorthand described by Milne appears to be the same system in use in this document, as can be seen in the arrays of dots, small longhand letters, and small shorthand signs adorning the larger signs in many cases. Milne's lists come from 3rd–4th century and Milne's descriptions of the system come from 4th–5th century. These correlations betray a remarkable stability while still giving a nod to the century or more between them. We should also note the shorthand in P.Brem. 82 and P.Duk. inv. 311 both appear similar to P.Mur. 164.

papyrus letters found in the Wadi, that is, they probably date to the second Jewish revolt in the early second century.[31] Confidence in the date is possible because of the nature of the finds in Wadi Murabbaʿāt. It was a barren place of refuge, and thus the vast bulk of material dates around the revolt.[32] A text in this remote region from roughly the same time period as Egypt should be viewed as significant evidence for a more widespread use of Greek shorthand by the late first century.

To these early texts, we may add a later papyrus draft proclamation from the Fayum of a contest for youth (dated 18 January 323) where 'Some blank space is followed by the date in a different hand and tachygraphic characters'.[33] The editors note a date and three lines, but the digital image shows two additional lines of text by the same hand and then three lines of tachygraphy in a heavier hand, not translated.[34] There are a few other papyri and wax tablets from the second and third centuries, including what appear to be school exercises in tachygraphy.[35]

4.3 Conclusions

Regarding dating, McNamee identifies compelling evidence for Greek shorthand in the first century (P.Har. 1 51, *CIG* 4763), but she merely repeats Mentz's conclusion that Greek and Latin shorthand arose at about the same time without establishing priority. She then posits a theory of how shorthand developed. McNamee argued that Greek shorthand:

> originated in the creation of notes for common words from portions of capitals or cursively written letters. The creation of a systematic syllabary followed, about the

---

31 Benoit, *Murabbaʿāt*, 277.
32 The evidence is overwhelmingly from the early second century, although there were also a few Roman coins from the late second century, apparently lost by Roman soldiers garrisoned there. Since the parchments were recycled, to assume a date nearer the early end of the spectrum is very reasonable.
33 P.Oxy. I 42 = P.Lond. III 747 = Sel.Pap. II 238. The quotation and description is by the British Library editors, http://www.bl.uk/manuscripts/FullDisplay.aspx?ref=Papyrus_747, accessed May 28, 2021.
34 http://www.bl.uk/manuscripts/Viewer.aspx?ref=papyrus_747_f001r, accessed May 28, 2021.
35 BGU 5464 (https://berlpap.smb.museum/01610/); see Mentz, 'Tachygraphie', 37; Foat, 'Tachygraphy', 242–243; see also Kenyon, 'Tachygraphy', OCD, 1033–34.

beginning of the first Christian century, and then about A.D. 50, the creation of the Commentary. Certainly, it reached Egypt by the first century A.D. for we find it used already in an inscription of A.D. 103 (CIG 4763, Mentz[4], 39–40). It was then regularized in the course of the third century, when it assumed the form represented by Milne, although variant versions still circulated.[36]

5. Dating the Invention of Greek Shorthand

Clearly these later archaeological discoveries push Greek shorthand to the first Christian century, but arguments may be mustered to push the date back to the first century B.C. by addressing the question of priority between Greek and Latin shorthand.

5.1 The Case for Latin Shorthand

It is not disputed that the Romans had a working system of *Latin* shorthand by the first Christian century. Three examples from Seneca will suffice:

(1) When Suetonius was boasting the expertise of Titus, he adds: 'I have heard from many sources that he used also to write shorthand [*notis*] with great speed and would amuse himself by playful contests with his secretaries.'[37]

(2) We may push this back earlier from Seneca's comment that on the list of ingenuous inventions by slaves: 'What about signs for words, with which a speech is taken down, however rapid, and the hand follows the speed of the tongue?' To make sense of Seneca's point, the practice needed to be common enough that his hearers would not dispute it, and yet the practice still novel enough to engender marvel.[38]

---

36 McNamee, 'Plato', 102 n.17; also Mentz, *Stenographie*, 52–53.
37 Suet. *Tit.* 3.2.
38 Sen. *Ep.* 40.25 (c. A.D. 63/4).

(3) Seneca's remark about Janus implies the same skill: Janus was so eloquent that the 'secretary is not able to follow him'.[39] Seneca's purpose is to impress the reader with the oratorical skill of Janus, and thus we may assume a secretary could have followed a normal speech.

5.2 Dating Latin Shorthand

Seneca's comments allow us to date Latin shorthand unquestionably to at least the middle of the first Christian century, with a functional system so efficient that a secretary could even record a speech in the Roman Senate,[40] a considerably more difficult task than merely recording a dictated text or letter. The existence of Latin shorthand may perhaps be pushed back into the first century B.C. The earliest important text is found in Plutarch's discussion of the speech of Cato the Younger, which was delivered on December 5, 63 B.C.:

> This is the only speech of Cato which has been preserved, we are told, and its preservation was due to Cicero the consul, who had previously given to those clerks who excelled in rapid writing instruction in the use of signs [σημεῖα], which, in small and short figures, comprised the force of many letters; these clerks he had then distributed in various parts of the senate-house. For up to that time the Romans did not employ or even possess what are called shorthand writers [σημειογράφους], but then for the first time, we are told, the first steps toward the practice were taken.[41]

---

39 Sen. *Apocol.* 9.2, written shortly after the death of Claudius in A.D. 54. For the use of the term *notarius* for a shorthand writer, see also Sen. *Ep.* 90.25; Suet. *Tit.* 3; Paulus, *Digesta* 29.1.40 (c. A.D. 210); Ausonius, *Epigrammata* 146 (c. A.D. 395); and PW, s.v. 'Kurzschrift', by Weinberger, 11/2: 2217–31.

40 Both Mentz, *Noten*, 66, and Stein, 'Stenographie', 182, think Plutarch is referring to shorthand here. Other references, which alone are questionable, may be cited for additional support: Manilius, *Astronomicon* 4.197–99; Martial, *Epigrammata* 14.208 (c. A.D. 84/85); and Quint. *Inst.* 10.3.19.

41 Plut. *Cat. Min.* 23.3–5; see also Morgenstern, 'Cicero', 1–6. Plut. *Caes.* 17.4–5 may also imply shorthand, since it hardly seems noteworthy to say that Caesar was able to dictate slowly while in a carriage.

Plutarch's use of the term σημειογράφος may be an anachronism for the skill of writing shorthand,[42] but the historicity of Plutarch's account is not disputed[43] and 'the material in Plutarch rests ultimately on an eye-witness account'.[44] Bahr, however, argues that this particular text need not refer to true shorthand, arguing that Cicero used several secretaries to record the speech, because one secretary would not have been sufficient.[45] Cicero could then compared their texts and thereby, perhaps also with the aid of his own recollection, virtually recreate the original speech.

In response to Bahr's supposition, I would note the text isn't clear that Cicero was intending only to record Cato's speech. In fact, the context suggests that Cato's speech may have been unanticipated: 'Cato arose to give his opinion, and launched at once into a passionate and angry speech'.[46] We may assume taking dictation from Senate speakers required extra precision in exact vocabulary and grammar at an atypical speed. Employing multiple secretaries seems prudent. Expense was not a factor. A secretary could not interrupt a Senate orator to ask him to repeat what he said. Nevertheless, should one wish to dispute Cato's speech as an example of Latin shorthand, the recording of Cicero's speech in defense of Milo, eleven years later, is now widely accepted as an instance of functional shorthand.[47] Cicero apparently strongly propagated the use of Latin shorthand.[48] His connection to

---

42 So argues also Mentz, *Noten*, 83. Plutarch defines the term which may indicate that he doesn't expect all his readers to be familiar with the skill.
43 It was well established by Peter, *Quellen*, 65–68, and is also discussed in Mentz, *Noten*, 39.
44 Bahr, 'Letter', 471.
45 For further evidence of the use of several secretaries at once, see Cic. *Pro Sulla* 41–42 and Suet. *Caes.* 55.
46 Plut. *Cat. Min.* 23.1; Sen. *Apocol.* 9.2 (c. A.D. 54) also notes, a hundred years later, the challenge of taking dictation from an impassioned speaker.
47 Bahr, 'Letter', 472. He also cites Asconius Pedianus, *In Milonianum* 36.27–28 (c. A.D. 57/8), who in his discussion of this same speech adds 'Manet autem ilia quoque excepta eius oratio'. See Dyck, 'The Other *Pro Milone*', responding to Settle, 'Trial', and Marshall, '*Excepta Oratio*'; Dyck resolves the question of *excepta* meaning 'taken down in shorthand' versus 'interrupted' in favor of the former. After Dyck, the meaning of 'shorthand' is assumed in the writings of Gurd, 'Verres', and La Bua, 'Cicero's *Pro Milone*'.
48 See, e.g. Cic. *Att.* 10.8 and 2.2.1.

the rise of Latin shorthand is further strengthened by the strong tradition that his freedman and personal secretary, Tiro, was the inventor of the Latin system.[49] Tiro's name has since become synonymous with a system of Latin shorthand, Tironian Notes.[50]

5.3 The Case for Greek Shorthand Predating Latin Shorthand

Foat argues, through analogy from the Latin system, that a Greek system predates the Latin.[51] When Plutarch describes Cicero introducing (Latin) shorthand at Rome, he notes: 'For up to that time the Romans did not employ or even possess what are called shorthand writers [σημειογράφους], but then for the first time, we are told, the first steps toward the practice were taken.'[52] Naturally the Greek writer Plutarch refers to the practice with the Greek term—the earliest known occurrence of the word.[53] What is far more noteworthy is that Cicero in a *Latin* letter to Atticus inserts a Greek description (διὰ σημείων) when he refers to shorthand.[54] When would a Latin invention be described by a Greek name in a letter otherwise in Latin? Furthermore, Cicero uses the phrase without explanation.[55]

Rather, the argument is made that Cicero oversaw the borrowing and modifying of an existing Greek system. Cicero moved fluently

---

49 Eusebius, *Chronica* 156, and Isidor (c. 602–36) *Etymologiae* 1.22.1; Isidor notes that the system employed in his day had undergone revision since its invention by Tiro, although Isidor should be questioned (see n.22 above). See also Bahr, 'Letter', 472, n. 52. Dio Cassius, *Roman History* 55.7 credits Maecenas, the friend of Augustus, with the invention of a system of σημεῖα for speed writing. Dio is probably correct that Maecenas used such a system, but the texts dating the invention earlier to Tiro are to be preferred. Nonetheless, both texts place Latin shorthand prior to the New Testament.
50 Mentz, *Kurzschrift*, 18–19, in his discussion of the Tironian notes indicates that Jacques Gohory, a French scholar, first coined this term in 1550. The notes were first published in 1603 by Gruter, *Notae Romanorum Veterum quibus litera verbum Jacit, Tulii Tironis et Annaei Senecde erutasque nunc primum editaeque*. See also Mentz, *Noten*. Examples may be seen in Foat, 'Tachygraphy', 261 n.3.
51 'Tachygraphy', 242–61.
52 Plut. *Cat. Min.* 23.3–5.
53 According to Johnen, *Allgemeine*, 20; see also idem, *Stenographie*, 130.
54 Cic. *Att.* 13.32.
55 So also argue Bahr, 'Letter', 474; Milne, *Manuals*, 4–5; and Gardthausen, 'Griechen', 444–45.

between these languages.[56] His secretary was also fluent in both Greek and Latin.[57] Cicero's fluency in both languages, as well as that of his established secretary Tiro, facilitated this adaptation.[58] It seems most likely that Tiro adapted an existing Greek system to Latin rather than inventing a Latin system. So Milne concludes, 'And who more fit than he [Cicero], *utriusque linguae peritus,* to sponsor the transfer of a Greek invention to the Roman use?'[59]

6. Conclusions about Greek Shorthand at the Time of the New Testament

We may summarise a case for the existence of Greek shorthand during the time of the New Testament. First, it is undisputed that Latin shorthand was in use at that time in at least Rome. Second, the likeliest explanation is that the Latin system was modified from an existing Greek system. Third, there are literary comments about shorthand, both Greek and Latin, that predate the New Testament.[60] Most of these references are from the aristocratic elite in Rome, as are all other general comments about dictation, except for the legal illiteracy formulae. To these literary comments, we must add an inscription in A.D. 103 as well as several extant fragmentary texts of Greek shorthand that may be dated to the early second century and have a very wide geograph-

---

56 So Plut. *Cic.* 4.4–5, who indicated some of Cicero's Latin puns required knowledge of Greek (*Cic.* 25.4) and Cicero often assisted the transition of Greek philosophical ideas into Latin (*Cic.* 40.1–2).
57 Cic. *Att.* 12.4.
58 For a thorough discussion of Tiro and his relationship to Cicero, see McDermott, 'Cicero and Tiro', esp. 260–63.
59 Milne, *Manuals*, 1. He lists five points of similarity between Greek and Latin shorthand to buttress his point (p. 2). McDermott, 271–72, is quite emphatic that Tiro did *not* invent or even use shorthand, but he offers no real argument. He tends to be rather minimalist in all his conclusions.
60 Cicero notes *once* (*Att.* 13.25.3) that he chose specially to dictate *syllabatim*, indicating that usually he does not, preferring to dictate to Tiro who recorded 'whole sentences'. See also *Att.* 2.23.1; 4.16.1; 5.17.1; 7.13a.3; 8.12.1; 8.13.1; 10.3a.1; 13.25.3; 14.21.4; 16.15.1; *QFr.* 2.2.1; 3.1.19; 3.3.1. Some of these references are in or about letters *to* Cicero, not by him; e.g. *Att.* 6.6.4. Quintilian, *Inst.* 10.3.19 (35/40–95?), writes against the fashionable practice of dictation.

ical distribution: Rome, Greece, Asia Minor, the Judaean desert, and Provincial Egypt. Lastly we have the existence of a shorthand apprenticeship system in provincial Egypt (scarcely the aristocratic elite) by A.D. 155.

Thus, although originally lacking evidence, Foat's suggestion that Greek shorthand predated Latin shorthand appears justified:

> There did exist in post-classical, and accepting a reasonable hypothesis, also in classical times, a Greek tachygraphy. Its invention was thus, probably, anterior to that of the Roman system, which, with the accretions and corruptions of the Middle Ages, has descended to us as the '*notae Tironianae*'; and there are reasonable grounds for the belief that the original Roman system was directly derived from the hypothetical oldest Greek system.[61]

6.1. Prevalence of Greek Shorthand in New Testament Times

We may reasonably conclude Greek shorthand was fashionable among the wealthy elite in Rome by the middle of the first century B.C. In the following decades its use spread outward and downward economically until we find scattered texts in Egypt and the Judaean desert, as well as apprenticeships in the mid-second Christian century. We may assume in New Testament times the availability of shorthand in select major cities such as Corinth, Ephesus, Antioch, or Alexandria, perhaps Jerusalem. It might be unwise to assert that one could hire a σημειογράφος in Philippi or Iconium. Nonetheless, soon after the mid-first century, shorthand use had not only reached the more remote regions of the Empire but the practice was no longer rare but prevalent enough that an apprentice was able to convert his own text ἀμέμπτως,[62] at least if converted immediately.

While the services of a σημειογράφος were not common, it would be hasty to rule out their possible use in the New Testament. Since such

---

61 Foat, 'Tachygraphy', 264; see also 260, but Foat was skeptical of its speed, writing before the discovery of P.Oxy. IV 724.
62 P.Oxy. IV 724.

services were likely more expensive, we may conclude that most New Testament writers would not have seen the need for such an extravagance. Rather, most would value the editorial benefits of a secretary over their own *ipsissima verba*.[63] Unlike a Roman orator, New Testament writers were largely unskilled and composing in a second language. Thoughts return to Paul. He perhaps had the training (Phil. 3:4–6; Acts 22:3; contra 2 Cor. 10:10). He perhaps also had chutzpah to desire his exact words. If Paul had access to one, perhaps a fellow believer, then he may have availed himself. Was Tertius such a one (Rom. 16:22)? His Latin name and the likely conclusion he was known in Rome make this a possibility.[64] Nonetheless, with a possible exception for Romans, we may feel comfortable concluding the New Testament was composed from notes and went through a series of edits/revisions.[65]

6.2 Deciphering Greek Shorthand Texts

Milne produces essentially a critical edition of the shorthand manual as it was preserved in the third to sixth Christian centuries. The manual consists of the syllabary συλλαβαί, endings πτώσεις, monobola μονόβολα,[66] and the commentary κομεντάριον. The commentary has 810 shorthand signs. The relationship between these signs and the syllabary, endings, and monobola is not entirely clear (*pace* McNamee). For example, the sign ⟍ (Milne, sign 198) represents τὴν or the ending –ην. All extant signs of the commentary also have an accompanying list of four words (tetrads) also represented by the same sign. For example, our sign ⟍ has a tetrad of these four words: αλιευς, ενεδρευει, λοχα, κυνηγος.[67] If one of these alternative words is meant, a mark, often a

---

63 See the discussion in Richards, *Letter*, 74–77.
64 See the discussion in Richards, *Secretary*, 170–172.
65 For the practice of composing and editing, see Richards, *Letter*, 81–121.
66 Mentz and McNamee both call these μονοβολαί (from the noun μονοβολή), while Milne calls them, probably more correctly Parker argues, σημεῖα μονόβολα (from the adjective μονόβολος).
67 Milne, *Manuals*, 31. Some signs have five words such as sign 260 or 452, presumably with an additional position around the sign.

dot is placed in a quadrant around the sign.[68] Usually the first quadrant is at 9 o'clock and indicates the alpha-based word. The second quadrant is epsilon-based, the third is omicron-based (or omega or eta) and the fourth is upsilon-based (or iota).[69] According to Parker's analysis of P.Mur. 164, we find ·⌐ perhaps indicating it is the word αλιευς (fisherman).[70] Deciphering these texts is more complicated because shorthand writers also appear to have used abbreviations,[71] relying upon the associative faculties of the σημειογράφος. For example, the symbol ^ represents των. The σημειογράφος placed a δ underneath in the 6 o'clock position to indicate an iota-based word. The result was των δικων.[72]

McNamee speaks of additional signs for just declensional endings (πτώϲειϲ), but it is not clear whether the 'endings' represented a distinct set of signs or were the beginning signs for students learning shorthand, since we see the endings in Milne's section also appear in the commentary. If it was entry level shorthand, then it corresponds to McNamee's conclusion that the particular scribe of her Plato marginalia, who liberally used signs for endings of longhand words (but not much else), may have known some shorthand signs but was not a true

---

68 Milne's manual seems to indicate (at least) two starting places for the first quadrant, but seems to always follow the same sequence. Milne, *Manuals*, 18, shows the first position at 9 o'clock but the first plate in the commentary shows the first position at 2 o'clock.
69 According to Parker's analysis, the sequence of four words set by the vowels remain consistent, α, ε, o/ω/η, ι/υ, but the starting point may move from the 9 to the 2 o'clock position, perhaps based upon the shape of the sign. Diphthongs are covered by the initial vowel, except ει. There are other peculiarities, but such elaborations should await a publication from Parker.
70 Likewise, the sign / (Milne, sign 725) represents φημι μεν δη, with a tetrad of αποισει, εασας, οισει, συνοισει. Milne, *Manuals*, 62.
71 Abbreviations were commonly mixed in with shorthand and complicated translation. For example, a single letter can represent an entire word or the first and last letter can represent an entire phrase, as in εα is used for ἐν Σαλαμῖνι ναυμαχία. See Milne, *Manuals*, 5–6. See also Mentz, *Kurzschrift*, esp. the diagrams on pp. 15, 17, and 21, and Mentz, *Systeme*, 43, 54.
72 Due to the fragmentary nature of the manuals, where only the commentary has substantially survived, the exact function of the dots and other orbiting signs and how to determine the words behind the shorthand symbols must remain tentative. Explanations here are not definitive but rather to pique interest and to offer some hints at the system.

σημειογράφος.⁷³ For example, a scribe appended the sign ⸜ to the end of a stem for –ην.⁷⁴ We agree, since what McNamee identifies as shorthand is not true shorthand but rather a smattering of syllabary signs used for spelling shortcuts on the syllabic level. The manuscript contains no signs as μονοβολα nor as tetrads—none of the true grammar of shorthand. Either the scribe wasn't fully trained or he just used some signs as shortcuts for endings. Either way, her marginalia are not in true shorthand.⁷⁵

As the commentaries of Milne and Monserrat demonstrate, however, the system of shorthand with these various signs created a very efficient way of writing, certainly meeting the requirements of the σημειογράφος in the Oxyrhynchus papyrus. Yet, the conversion of a tachygraphic text into longhand required then, as it does now, some recall on the part of the tachygrapher.⁷⁶ It was expected the σημειογράφος converted his own notes soon after taking them. Thus, a shorthand text of one writer was not always convertible by another.⁷⁷ Foat's caution more than a hundred years ago is still justified: 'But such is the nature of tachygraphy that conjecture must be used with the utmost caution. Nothing is easier than to force a meaning, nothing more possible than for a plausible reading to be *toto caelo* wrong'.⁷⁸

7. Conclusion

What then shall we conclude about Greek shorthand? It appears to have been available during New Testament times, although it is unlikely

---

73 McNamee, 'Plato', 101–02.
74 So Mentz, *Systeme*, 26–7, 52–5. This practice may have survived as ligatures in minuscule manuscripts.
75 Based upon Parker's examination of the manuscript, there are 29 lines with a total of 99 'words', some of these are mixes of longhand and a syllabic shortcut. About 35% are longhand, 30% are abbreviated words, 17% are mathematical signs, leaving 17% (17 words) as these quasi-shorthand words.
76 So McNamee, 'Plato', 102–4. Her suspicions seem to correlate with the preliminary work by Josh Parker on the manuals of Milne and Montserrat.
77 As perhaps illustrated by Cicero: 'What I said about the ten legates, you did not fully understand. I suppose because I wrote it in shorthand [credo, quia διὰ σημείων scripserum]'; Cic. Att. 13.32.
78 Foat, 'Tachygraphy', 255.

it was used in the final composition of any actual New Testament document, with the *possible* exception of Romans. On the other hand, we would not wish to rule out some notes or ἀπομνημονεύματα or drafts may have been taken down by a σημειογράφος.

What should we do with the shorthand texts we have? For earlier scholars these were undecipherable (and currently remain so). Many scholars echo the pessimism of Foat:

> In the case of old Greek tachygraphy we are now in possession of the elements—the alphabet and a part of the syllabary; but we have no clue yet to the particular method in which abbreviation was developed. For that we must wait perhaps until there are more specimens of the full writing than have yet been recovered, or until tachygraphy shall find its own Rosetta stone![79]

Since more shorthand texts have been discovered, such as P.Mur. 164, P.Brem. 82 and P.Duk. inv. 311v,[80] we may wish to revisit Greek shorthand. Unlike most examples of shorthand, the Murabba'āt papyrus does not appear to be a syllabary, practice text, or a few lines of scribbled marginalia, but rather an actual shorthand text, perhaps a draft of a document. The parchment was part of a roll. Intriguingly, the editors do not describe it as a palimpsest, so was a roll used for a shorthand draft? According to Parker's preliminary analysis the same scribe wrote all the sections. Parker notes about twenty-three shorthand characters per line with about twenty-four lines in each of the three and a half columns that can still be discerned. At well over 1000 *shorthand* characters, the text is seemingly too long to be a typical letter or clerical document. Lastly, I repeat my observation from thirty years ago: there are a few intriguing signs within the text: what appears as a classic

---

79 Foat, 'Tachygraphy', 265.
80 P.Brem. 82, dates to 113–120, showing 1.5 columns of shorthand text (with the verso blank). It is unclear if it was part of a larger document. P.Duk. inv. 311v, the verso of a land measurement report in Egypt from the second century, contains running shorthand text. The original format of the shorthand text is unclear because the line ends are lost on both sides. All three texts appear to share similar shorthand.

Christian ChiRho in line 11 of P.Mur. 164a and what might be $\overline{\text{IC}}$ as a stylised nomen sacrum in line 11 of P.Mur. 164b. Such morsels will I hope tempt a scholar to take up this challenge.

E. Randolph Richards
Palm Beach Atlantic University

Bibliography

Arrian	ΑΡΡΙΑΝΟΥ ΑΛΕΞΑΝΔΡΟΥ ΑΝΑΒΑΣΕΩΣ, in P. A. Brunt (ed. and trans.), *Arrian, Anabasis of Alexander*, 2 vols., LCL (Cambridge, MA: Harvard University, 1976).
Bahr, G. J.	'Paul and Letter Writing in the First Century', *CBQ* 28 (1966), 465–477.
Benoit, P., J. T. Milik, and R. de Vaux.	*Les grottes de Murabba'ât*, DJD, no. 2 (Oxford: Oxford University, 1961).
Boge, H.	*Greichische Tachygraphie und tironische Noten,* Altertumswissenschaftliche Texte und Studien 2 (Hildesheim: George Olms, 1974).
Dyck, A. R.	'The Other *Pro Milone* Reconsidered', *Philologus* 146 (2002), 182–85.
Epictetus	Epicteti Dissertationes, in W.A. Oldfather (ed. and trans.), *The Discourses as Reported by Arrian, The Manual, and Fragments* (2 vols., LCL Cambridge: Harvard University, 1925–28).
Foat, F.W.G.	'On Old Greek Tachygraphy', *JHS* 21 (1901), 238–267.
Gardthausen, V.	'Tachygraphie oder Brachygraphie des Akropolis-Steines', *Archiv für Stenographie* 56 (1905), 81–84.
Gardthausen, V.	'Zur Tachygraphie der Griechen', *Hermes* 2 (1876), 444–445.
Gitlbauer, M.	*Die drei Systeme der griechische Tachygraphie,* Denkschriften der daiserliche Akademie der Wissenschaften, no. 44 (Vienna: C. Gerold's Son, 1896).
Grenfell, B. P., and A. S. Hunt (eds.)	*The Oxyrhynchus Papyri*. 51 vols. (London: Oxford University, 1898–1951).
Gurd, S.	'Verres and the Scene of Rewriting', *Phoenix* 64 (2010), 80–101.
Haenchen, E.	*Die Apostelgeschichte* (Göttingen: Vandenhoeck & Ruprecht, 1959).
Hartmann, K.	'Arrian und Epiktet', *Neue Jahrbücher für das klassische Altertum, Geschichte und deutsche Literatur und für Pädogogik* 8 (1905), 248–275.
Hitchcock, F. R. M.	'The Use of graphein', *JTS*, o.s., 31 (1930), 271–275.

Johnen, C.	*Allgemeine Geschichte der Kurzschrift* (4th ed. Berlin: F. Schrey, 1940).
Johnen, C.	*Geschichte der Stenographie: im Zusammenhang mit der allgemeinen Entwicklung der Schrift und der Schriftkürzung* (Berlin: F. Schrey, 1911).
Johnston, H. W.	*Latin Manuscripts: an Elementary Introduction to the Use of Critical Editions*, The Inter-Collegiate Latin Series (Chicago, IL: Scott, Foresman & Co., 1897).
Kenyon, F. G.	'Tachygraphy', 1033-34, in M. Cary, N. G. L. Hammond, and H. H. Scullard (eds.), *The Oxford Classical Dictionary* (2nd edn; Oxford: Clarendon, 1970).
La Bua, G.	'Cicero's *Pro Milone* and the "Demosthenic" Style', *Greece and Rome* 61 (2014), 29–37.
Lydi, I.	(Joannes Laurentius Lydus), in Ricardus Wuensch (ed.), *de Magistratibus populi Romani* (Leipzig: Teubner, 1903).
Malherbe, A.	'Introduction', in *The Cynic Epistles: a Study Edition*, SBLSBSS 12 (Missoula, MT: Scholars, 1977).
Marshall, B. A.	'*Excepta Oratio*, The Other *Pro Milone* and the Question of Shorthand', *Latomus* 46 (1987), 730–36.
McDermott, W. C.	'M. Cicero and M. Tiro', *Historia: Zeitschrift für Alte Geschichte* 21/2 (1972), 259–286.
McKenzie, J. L.	*Light on the Epistles: a Reader's Guide* (Chicago, IL: Thomas More, 1975).
McNamee, K.	'A Plato Papyrus with Shorthand Marginalia', *GRBS* 42 (2001), 97–116.
Mentz, A.	*Antike Stenographie* (AK 8. Munich: Ernst-Heimeran, 1927).
Mentz, A.	*Die Geschichte der Kurzschrift* (Wolfenbüttel: Heckners, 1949).
Mentz, A.	'Die Grabschrift eines griechischen Tachygraphen', *Archiv für Stenographie* 54 (1902), 49–53.
Mentz, A.	*Geschichte der Stenographie* (2nd edn. Berlin: Gerdes & Hödel, 1907).
Mentz, A.	*Geschichte und Systeme der griechischen Tachygraphie* (Berlin: Gerdes & Hödel, 1907).
Mentz, A.	*Die tironischen Noten: eine Geschichte der römischen Kurzschrift* (Berlin: de Gruyter, 1944).

Milne, H. J. M.	*Greek Shorthand Manuals: Syllabary and Commentary* (London: Oxford University Press, 1934).
Morgenstern, O.	'Cicero und die Stenographie', *Archiv für Stenographie* 56 (1905), 1–6.
Oates, W. J. (ed. and trans.)	*The Stoic and Epicurean Philosophers: the Complete Extant Writings of Epicurus, Epictetus, Lucretius, Marcus Aurelius* (New York, NY: Random House, 1940).
Peter, H. W. G.	*Die Quellen Plutarchs in die Biographien der Römer* (Halle: Waisenhaus, 1865).
Preisigke, F.	'Das σημεῖον', *Archiv für Stenographie* 56 (1905), 305–312.
Richards, E. R.	*Paul and First-Century Letter Writing* (Downers Grove, IL: IVP, 2004).
Richards, E. R.	*The Secretary in the Letters of Paul*, WUNT 2/42 (Tübingen: Mohr Siebeck, 1991).
Robinson, C. E.	*Everyday Life in Ancient Greece* (Oxford: Clarendon, 1933).
Roller, O.	*Das Formular der paulinischen Briefe* (Stuttgart: Kohlhammer, 1933).
Settle, J. N.	'The Trial of Milo and the other *Pro Milone*', *TAPhA* 94 (1963), 268–80.
Stein, A.	'Die Stenographie im römischen Senat', *Archiv für Stenographie* 56 (1905), 177–186.
Tarn, W. W.	*Alexander the Great. II: Sources and Studies* (Cambridge: Cambridge University, 1948).
Teitler, H. C.	*Notarii und Exceptores*, DMAHA 1 (Leiden: Brill, 1985).
Thompson, E. M.	*An Introduction to Greek and Latin Paleography* (Oxford: Oxford University Press, 1912; reprint, New York, NY: Burt Franklin, 1973).
Weinberger, W.	'Kurzschrift', in A. F. von Pauly and G. Wissowa (eds.), *Pauly's Real-Encyclopädie der classischen Altertumswissenschaft* (24 vols. Stuttgart: Druckenmuller, 1893–1963), 11/2, 2217–2231.

The Jews of Ancient Rome:
Their Burial Inscriptions and Implications for Paul's Letter to the Romans

Michael Trainor

Abstract

Professor Jim Harrison is the consummate scholar. His scholarly encouragement has been a true blessing to Australian researchers, like me, whom he has gently nudged to engage ancient inscriptions and uncover their importance for elucidating biblical texts. The results have been surprising, especially for their authors. It is with gratitude to Jim that I feel privileged to offer the following foray into the Jewish burial inscriptions of ancient Rome and suggest their contribution to Paul's *Letter to the Romans*.

1. The Jews of Rome

In the first century before the Common Era and in the centuries afterwards, Jews migrated to all parts of the Roman Empire, including Rome. We know about the presence of Rome's Jewish population around the turn of the first century C.E. In 38 C.E. the Alexandrian Jewish philosopher, Philo (c. 20 B.C.E. – c. 50 C.E.), came to Rome as part of a delegation to petition Gaius Caligula about the mistreatment of Alexandrian Jews by Aulus Avilius Flaccus (*Legatio ad Gaium*, 23, 155). Philo noted a significant Jewish population composed of enslaved prisoners of war, ransomed by co-religionists or manumitted by their owners. An earlier and more sanguine estimation of the Jewish population can be sifted from Cicero's speech in 59 B.C.E. defending Lucius Valerius Flaccus, accused of misappropriating gold collected by Rome's Jews intended for the maintenance of Jerusalem's Temple (*Pro Flacco*, 66–69).

The need for such a legal defence of Flaccus's alleged embezzlement, of which he was eventually acquitted, indicates the political influence of a reasonably sizeable Jewish population that necessitated such a public legal procedure (Josephus, *Antiquitates Judaicae*, 16.6.1–7). This coheres with the comment by Josephus of 8,000 Roman male Jews supporting a Jerusalem delegation to Augustus in 4 B.C.E. (*Antiquities*, 17.11.1. 300; *Bellum Judaicum*, 2.6.1.80). There is no definitive figure for Rome's Jewish population in the earliest centuries of the Common Era, though there are two proposals. If Josephus's number of presumably able-bodied mature Jewish males is accurate this would suggest a Jewish population of 40,000 to 50,000, about five percent of the total Roman population. Such a number would represent a significant though not large foreign group.[1] A second suggestion considers a much smaller Jewish population, less than two percent.[2] Whatever their population size, Rome's Jews were not without their influence, even though their average life expectancy was around twenty-two to twenty-five years, not unusual in comparison to Rome's other cultural groups.[3]

2. The 'Voice' of the Dead

Rome's inhabitants left their mark. Their voices echo in the remains of their monumental buildings, and in the inscriptions or epitaphs that have come to light in recent centuries and decades. These inscriptions, representing only one percent of Roman burials between 25 B.C.E. and 325 C.E., emerge from excavated sites and cemeteries and are supported, to a lesser extent, by literary works of commentators who lived in or visited Rome.[4] These writings, epitaphs, and inscriptions tell us about Rome's families, their desires for their deceased beloved, their socio-economic positions, and their relationship with others in a pop-

---

1 Leon, *Jews*, 135.
2 Rutgers, 'Reflections', 345–58.
3 Rutgers, 'Reflections'; Leon, *Jews*, 230.
4 Bodel, 'From Columbaria to Catacombs', 241–42.

ulation of approximately 1,000,000.[5] This material and literary evidence can offer something of a social, cultural, and historical snapshot of Rome's residents.

Most of Jewish burial inscriptions, over 500, come from six burial places, 'catacombs', that surround the city of Rome, close to the main thoroughfares that lead into the city. The oldest and largest of these is Monteverde, and inscriptions from other catacombs, dated between the third and fourth centuries C.E., fill out the picture.[6] Monteverde held a little under half of all identified Jewish inscriptions with burials from the first century B.C.E.[7]

These Jewish inscriptions and epitaphs, cautiously and judiciously analysed, are important for another reason. They help us conjecture about the social situation of those *members of the Jesus movement* who lived in Rome. The earliest generations of Jesus followers were Jewish.[8] They were first in Jerusalem in the 30s C.E. when the movement became established but, not many years later, if the Acts of the Apostles offers a level of historical plausibility, it expanded north, south, and west into Ethiopia, Syria, the Transjordan, Asia Minor, Macedonia, Greece, and finally Rome. It is here that Acts closes with Paul under house arrest (Acts 28:23–30) conceivably around the 60s, a generation or so before its author finalises the writing of Acts.[9]

Given limitations of space I summarise select inscriptional data from Monteverde and the other Jewish catacombs from Rome's Transtiberim region—a point to which I shall return shortly—that offer a snapshot of Jewish beliefs and their perception of the wider Roman world. Idiosyncratic anomalies in the inscriptions, the material on which they are written, and their location provide further suggestive evidence of Jewish economic and social status and congregational structure. In a concluding section, insights gleaned from the first pro-

---

5   Noy, *Foreigners*, 15–16.
6   From the six catacombs, 575 inscriptions have been identified. These include the 534 focused on by Leon who adds to and edits those initially catalogued by Frey, *Corpus*, hereafter *CII*.
7   Leon, *Jews*, 65–66, 74. Noy, *Foreigners*, 3–5; Frey, *CII*, 221–27.
8   Nanos, 'Jewish Context', 283–304.
9   For my conjectured dating and provenance of Acts, see Trainor, *Acts*, 3.

vide, with reservation, a way of intersecting with Paul's Letter to the Romans addressed to Roman Jesus followers, associates of their Jewish synagogal co-religionists.[10]

3. Transtiberim

Those who came to Rome gathered in the impoverished sections and poorer neighbourhoods of Rome, initially around Transtiberim ('Trastevere') between the Porta Capena and the Porta Esquilina. The area was defined by the Tiber and its demography.[11] It was where immigrants to Rome came. Slaves, the impoverished, citizens of low social status, artisans and the *peregrini* lived here.[12] Philo (*On the Embassy to Gaius*, 23.152–158.), and Martial (c. 38–c. 103 C.E.) corroborate the presence of Jews in this area. Martial described a Transtiberim populated by itinerants, the impoverished and cutthroats, if his commentary from the *Epigrams* can be believed.[13] His satiric remarks add to an already popular denigrating trope critical of the social standing of Transtiberim's Jews and their poverty (Juvenal, *Satire*, 3. 12–16, 296; 6. 159–160, 542–547, 588). If this was the domicile of Jews it was also the abode of Rome's Jewish Jesus followers.[14]

The fact that people bury their dead close to where they live and where they congregate for communal support and worship means that for the Jews and Jewish Jesus followers Transtiberim would also be where they buried their dead in the first century C.E., read the Torah, and sustained their faith life.[15] In this area, then, we find most of Rome's Jewish catacombs, located south-east and south-west of the city, and close to the arterial roads leading into the city.

---

10 Nanos, 'Jewish Context'.
11 Abrecht, 'Immigrant Neighbourhood, 2-22.
12 On the *peregrini*, see Noy, *Foreigners*, 24-5.
13 Roman, 'Martial', 88-117.
14 Lampe, *From Paul*, 19-65.
15 Nanos, 'Jewish Context', 285-86.

4. Inscription Summary

From the 500 inscriptions that have been identified most are written in Greek, the *lingua franca* of the ordinary Romans. A few are in Latin which reflects a more elite social context of the deceased. Many indicate that their commissioners were from a poor literacy background. Congregational leadership roles by the deceased on several indicate a level of organisational structure and status reflected by the offices and positions that they held and for which they were remembered.[16]

A complete study of the inscriptions is impossible. What emerges and is summarised in several studies is a recognition that the catacombs were close to where the Jews lived, in the more socio-economically deprived suburb of Rome's outskirts, Transtiberim. Inscriptional data further reveals that the Jews gathered in *proseuchai*, 'prayer halls', forming congregations called 'synagogues' which are given various names depending on location and other associations. The first and oldest synagogue was 'of the Hebrews'.[17] The mourners responsible for the inscriptions show a freedom to incorporate Jewish expressions of faith in symbols (menorah, shofar, ethrog, and lulab[18]) and wording ('sleep in peace',[19] 'house of eternity',[20] 'peace on Israel'[21]) even, though rarely, using Hebrew and Aramaic. Faith epithets ('righteous'—Gk. *dikaios*,[22] 'pious',[23] 'lover of child / sibling / synagogue'[24]) are also associated with those buried.[25] Their incorporation into these epitaphs of other non-Jewish Roman elements indicates a level of social integration and acculturation within their Roman urban world. Most revealing in the inscriptions are the various offices and honorific titles held by the deceased in their rela-

---

16 Noy, *Jewish Inscriptions*, 5.
17 Richardson, 'Augustan-Era Synagogues', 367–97; Leon, *Jews*, 139; *CII*, 1.291, 531; Noy, *Jewish Inscriptions*, 487.
18 Noy, *Jewish Inscriptions*, 97.
19 *CII*, 1.321, 433, 494.
20 *CII*, 1.337.
21 *CII*, 1.293, 397.
22 *CII*, 1.321, 363.
23 *CII*, 1.321, 363.
24 *CII*, 1.321, 363.
25 *CII*, 1.476, 36, 132, 380, 193, 111 and 509 offer examples of other virtuous epithets.

tionship to the synagogal gatherings. They were known with such titles as *archon*,[26] *exarchon*,[27] *archisynagogus*,[28] *phronistes*,[29] *grammateus*,[30] *prostates*,[31] and *gerusiarch*,[32] and honoured as 'mother'[33] or 'father' of a synagogue.[34] The titles reflect certain leadership, secretarial, organisational, and presidential functions within loosely confederated synagogues. There appears to be no overriding rabbinic authority or overseer over all Rome's synagogues. This would have allowed for a certain freedom, even difference in Torah teaching and halakic practice.

5. The Synagogue in Ostia

In the 1960s archaeological work in Ostia, Rome's ancient harbour port, under the directorship of Maria Floriana Squarciapino uncovered what was believed to be a synagogue.[35] Based on the masonry of the oldest section of the excavation, she proposed a date of the mid-first century C.E. A further study of other masonry types pushed the dating of the building to the late first century or early second century C.E. Second century C.E. additions reflected Jewish usage and activity.[36] Between the first and fifth centuries C.E., the building went through several phases of construction, initially as a two-storey domestic dwelling then later with subsequent renovations, remodelling, interior modifications, mosaic repair, additional rooms, a Torah shrine with enlargement of an *aedicula* platform, and repair of the floor.[37] The Ostia synagogue was the earliest outside of Rome, predating any *proseuchai* in Rome. Its renovations reflected Roman decorative appreciation.[38]

26 *CII*, 1.284, 337, 494, 503.
27 *CII*, 1.317.
28 Noy, '*Archisynagogoi*', 75-93; *CII*, 1.504.
29 *CII*, 1.337, 494.
30 *CII*, 1.284, 318, 351, 433, 456.
31 *CII*, I.365.
32 *CII*, 1.9, 119, 353, 504.
33 *CII*, 1.166, 496, 523.
34 *CII*, 1.494.
35 Floriani Squarciapino, 'La sinogaga di Ostia', 299-315.
36 White, 'Reading', 435-64.
37 White, 'Reading', 459.
38 White, 'Synagogue', 67.

Significant are two inscriptions. One in Latin dates from the early second century C.E. honours a synagogue member who donates a parcel of land for the construction of a 'monument' (synagogue?).[39] The epitaph celebrates three synagogue *gerusiarchs* who conceivably functioned at different times as head or president of the synagogue's *gerousia* ('assembly'). The role played by the *gerousia* in endorsing the donation and the officers to which this early inscription refers predates Jewish organisational structures that we note in Rome's later catacomb inscriptions.

A second inscription, with the opening line in Latin ('For the health of the Emperor') and its remainder in Greek, dates to the second or third centuries.[40] It was discovered in secondary use, originally from the vestibule of the synagogue, as part of a fourth century C.E. floor renovation. The original donator's name was scratched over, replaced by another who generously constructed the edifice or hall and set up the Torah ark. Both Ostia epitaphs mirror organisational features that we find later, almost a century later, in the catacomb inscriptions.

6. Implications for the Jesus Movement and the Letter to the Romans

The Roman Jewish burial inscriptions and the two from Ostia offer suggestive points of intersection with Paul's Letter to the Romans. The study of Ostia's synagogue and its inscriptions witness an organisational consistency across different time periods. This suggests that aspects of Judaism, evident in one era would have conceivably existed in an earlier period, and the earliest days of Jewish life in Rome. This has implications for Paul's Roman audience. The first Jesus followers who came to Rome were, like Paul, Jewish. There would have been several reasons for their presence: Jesus-members came as part of the general Jewish Mediterranean diaspora around the Roman Empire which, conjecturally, had a Jewish population of six to seven million.[41] Others, too, would have been slaves transported to Rome in the wake of the

---

39   *CII*, 1.533; Runesson, *Ancient Synagogue*, 224–25.
40   Runesson, *Ancient Synagogue*, 223; White, 'Synagogue', 53–5.
41   On the Jewish population in the Roman Empire see Leon, *Jews*, 135.

events that surrounded Israel in the first century C.E. and in the aftermath of the destruction of Jerusalem and its temple by Vespasian and Titus. Others, perhaps fewer, could have been Roman citizens, Gentiles initially attracted to Judaism as proselytes because of its high ethical standards later joined the Jesus movement.[42] It is possible, too, that a few would have been manumitted slaves who rose to the upper rung of Rome's social ladder. Whatever their economic status and social situation and their reasons for being in Rome, the inscriptional attestations from the Jewish catacombs offer us a tantalising view into how Jews and Jewish Jesus followers lived, their economic status and how they viewed death and their relationship to the non-Jewish Roman culture. It is even possible, if not probable, that Jewish Jesus followers were buried in the Jewish catacombs.

Paul writes his magisterial Letter to the Romans sometime in the late 50s C.E.[43] An overriding concern is the relationship between different groups of Rome's Jesus-members, Jews and non-Jews. These groups would initially identify with Rome's various synagogues.[44] Some non-Jewish Jesus followers would be linked to them with different levels of commitment (as 'proselytes' or 'God-fearers').[45] Other non-Jewish Jesus followers would have been independent of any synagogue affiliation. Paul's agenda is to address the differences of relationships to one another and the potential to dismiss each other's faith stance and heritage, especially if there has been a change of leadership within Rome's Jesus movement.[46] This might have been brought on as the power base moved from an original Jewish leadership to one that was non-Jewish after the purge of Jews from Rome that created a leadership vacuum filled later by Gentile Jesus-members.[47]

Inscriptional data from Rome's Jewish catacombs suggest a fluid

---

42   Brandle, 'Formation', 121–22.
43   On the dating of *Romans*, see Byrne, *Romans*, 9.
44   Fisk, 'Synagogue Influence', 175.
45   Brandle, 'Formation,' 121–22.
46   Such a change might have occurred with the expulsions of Jews in the time of Emperor Claudius c. 49 C.E. over 'Chrestus' as reported by Orosius (385–420 C.E.) in quoting Josephus (*Historiae adversum paganos* 7.6.15–16).
47   Rutgers, 'Roman Policy', 93–116.

and diverse situation amongst Rome's Jews and those recognised as their leaders and synagogue presidents. This context would have influenced those Jews attracted to the Jesus movement. The union 'in Christ' between Jews and non-Jews at Rome was central to Paul's letter. A key thematic in the letter concerns 'justification' (Gk. *dikaisune*) which, as we note on at least one inscription, was associated with Jewish faith expression. For Paul, communion with God, the fruit of religious practice, was God's gift and not dependent on fulfilling Torah observance (Rom. 1:16–17; 3:21–24). At the same time, Paul did not dismiss his Jewish heritage or the gifts which came from the Covenant or Torah practice, nor would he allow any room for non-Jews to act with a spirit of arrogance over Jewish members of Rome's Jesus gatherings. He clearly reminds the Gentiles about Israel's sacred history and their close relationship to their Jewish members. The Gentiles are like 'a wild olive shoot' grafted onto and supported by 'the rich root of the olive tree', that is, the Jewish people (Rom. 11:17). They are not to boast or act with arrogance (Rom. 11:18).

The background offered through the study of epitaphs in Rome and Ostia can fill out something of the picture and internal relationships that might have been operating amongst Rome's Christ followers. It alerts us to the delicacy of Paul's task in his writing to them. The letter is Paul's introduction to Rome's Jesus followers, whom he did not establish as in other parts of the Roman Empire. He entrusts his letter to Phoebe, a leader ('deacon') of a Jesus-gathering at Cenchreae, a harbour town south of Corinth from where Paul pens the letter (Rom. 16:1). Paul anticipates her meeting with the leaders of Rome's Jesus movement including those who held status in the synagogues in Transtiberim and who, years later, could be identified by Luke as those ('brothers') who meet Paul when he eventually arrives into Rome (Acts 28:14,17). Perhaps to some in Rome, Phoebe might be seen equivalently as an *archon, archisynagogus, gerusiarch,* or 'mother' of a Jesus synagogal gathering. In whatever way Phoebe's Roman audience would have perceived her, she would be received as one with authority and as Paul's legitimate representative.

In Paul's final chapter of the letter (Romans 16) it is obvious that he already knows several members of the Roman Jesus movement. He greets the whole group of Jesus believers, identifies twenty-four of them by name, two others through their relationship to others that Paul names, and their gatherings or 'households' (Rom. 16:5,10,11). This variety of households would echo a similar structure found amongst Rome's synagogue congregations. Of those whom Paul identifies, seven of them—the names, not the actual persons—will be found inscribed on epitaphs in the Roman catacombs. This similarity in names between those whom Paul mentions (Prisca, Maria, Herodion, Tryphaena, Rufus, Hermes, Julia) and what we find on inscriptions later testifies to Paul's strategy in Romans 16 that claims a close and beloved familiarity with the Roman situation and its members.[48]

7. Conclusion

Rome's catacomb inscriptions offer us insights into early Jewish life and religious organisational structures. Though not too many years removed from when Paul wrote to the Romans, the inscriptions from Rome and Ostia provide us with data for speculatively engaging Paul's letter, the relationship between his addressees and some of the theological issues with which they were grappling, especially their communion as households of Jesus followers and their association with various synagogal arrangements that could have exacerbated the divisions that Paul sought to address.

Michael Trainor
Australian Catholic University

---

48 The seven names appear in several inscriptions. The most frequent is 'Maria', nine times (in *CII*, 1.32, 169, 173, 203, 212, 289, 351, 375, 525).

Bibliography

Abrecht, R. — 'An Immigrant Neighbourhood in Ancient Rome', *Urban History* 47.1 (2020), 2–22.

Bodel, J. — 'From Columbaria to Catacombs: Collective Burial in Pagan and Christian Rome', in L. Brink and D. A. Green (eds.), *Commemorating the Dead Texts and Artifacts in Context: Studies of Roman, Jewish, and Christian Burials* (Berlin: Walter de Gruyter, 2008), 241–42.

Brandle, R. and E. W. Stegemann — 'The Formation of the First "Christian Congregations" in Rome in the Context of the Jewish Congregations', in K. P. Donfried and P. Richardson (eds.), *Judaism and Christianity* (Grand Rapids, MI: Eerdmans, 1998), 117–27.

Byrne, B. — *Romans* (Collegeville, PA: Liturgical Press, 1996).

Fisk, B. N. — 'Synagogue Influence and Spiritual Knowledge among the Christians of Rome', S. E. Porter (ed.), *As It Is Written: Studying Paul's Use of Scripture* (Atlanta, GA: SBL, 2008), 157–85.

Flexsenhar, M. — 'Jewish Synagogues and the Topography of Imperial Rome; The Case of the *Agrippesioi* and *Augustesioi*', *Journal for the Study of Judaism* 51 (2020), 367–97.

Floriani Squarciapino, M. — 'La sinogaga di Ostia: secondo campagna di scavo', in *Atti di VI Congresso internazionale di archeologial cristiana, 1962* (Rome: Pontifical Press, 1965).

Frey, J.-B. — *Corpus Inscriptionum Iudaicarum* (Vol. 1; Rome: Pontifical Institute of Christian Archaeology, 1936–1952).

Grayzel, S. — *History of the Jews: From the Babylonian Exile to the Present, 5728–1968* (New York, NY: Meridian, 1984).

Lampe, P. — *From Paul to Valentinus: Christians at Rome in the First Two Centuries* (New York, NY: Fortress, 2003).

Leon, H. — *The Jews of Ancient Rome* (Peabody, MA: Hendrickson, 1960).

Nanos, M. — 'The Jewish Context of the Gentile Audience in Paul's Letter to the Romans', *Catholic Biblical Quarterly* 61 (1999), 283–304.

Noy, D   'Archisynagogoi: Office, Title and Social Status in the Greco-Jewish Synagogue', *The Journal of Roman Studies*, 83 (1993), 75–93.

Noy, D.   *Foreigners at Rome: Citizens and Strangers* (London: Gerald Duckworth, 2000).

Noy, D.   *The City of Rome*. Vol. 2 of *Jewish Inscriptions of Western Europe* (Cambridge: Cambridge University Press, 2002).

Richardson, P.   'Augustan-Era Synagogues in Rome', in K. P. Donfried, and P. Richardson (eds.), *Judaism and Christianity* (Grand Rapids, MI: Eerdmans, 1998), 17–29.

Roman, L.   'Martial and the City of Rome', *The Journal of Roman Studies* 100 (2010), 88–117.

Runesson, A.   'The Synagogue at Ancient Ostia: The Building and Its History from the First to the Fifth Century', in B. Olsson, D. Mitternacht and O. Brandt (eds.), *The Synagogue of Ancient Ostia and the Jews of Rome: Interdisciplinary Studies* (Stockholm: Paul Astroms, 2001), 29–100.

Runesson, A., D. D. Binder, and B. Olsson *The Ancient Synagogue from Its Origins to 200 C.E.: A Source Book* (Leiden: Brill, 2008).

Rutgers, L.   'Reflections on the Demography of the Jewish Community of Ancient Rome', in M. Ghilardi, C. J. Goddard, and P. Porena (eds.), *Cités de l'Italie tardo-antique: IV- VI siècle: Institutions, économie, société, culture et religion* (Roma: École Française de Rome, 2006), 345–58.

Rutgers, L.   'Roman Policy toward the Jews: Expulsions from the City of Rome during the First Century C.E.', in K. P. Donfried and P. Richardson (eds.), *Judaism and Christianity* (Grand Rapids, MI: Eerdmans, 1998), 93–116.

Trainor, M.   *Acts: An Earth Bible Commentary* (London: T&T Clark, 2020).

White, M.   'Reading the Ostia Synagogue: A Reply to A. Runesson', *The Harvard Theological Review*, 92.4 (1999), 435–64.

White, M.   'Synagogue and Society in Imperial Ostia: Archaeological and Epigraphic Evidence', K. P. Donfried and P. Richardson (eds.), *Judaism and Christianity* (Grand Rapids, MI: Eerdmans, 1998), 30–68.

The Human Heart, the Centre of a Person, and The Holy Spirit
(Galatians 4:6; Romans 5:5; and 2 Corinthians 1:22)

Paul Trebilco

Abstract

Different languages associate parts of the body with different functions. In the New Testament, the heart is the centre of the inner life, including the understanding, emotions, will, and spiritual life. This is in contrast to contemporary English, where the heart is most strongly associated with the emotions alone. When Paul writes of the Spirit in connection with the human heart in Galatians 4:6, Romans 5:5, and 2 Corinthians 1:22, we can see in context that he is not simply thinking of the heart as the centre of emotions, but also as the centre of thinking, understanding, volition, and decision-making. Accordingly, contemporary readers risk misunderstanding the depths of what Paul is saying in these verses.

1. Introduction

I am delighted to have the opportunity to write this essay as a token of my appreciation to Jim for his friendship and his scholarship over many years.

In Biblical thought, different parts of the body are associated with different human characteristics. At times in the Hebrew Bible or the Greek New Testament, the parts of the body associated with a particular human characteristic are different from the association that that particular part of the body has in English. Perhaps the most obvious difference for us is that compassion is often associated with the bowels in the New Testament. In Philippians 1:8 the NRSV has: 'For God is my witness, how I long for all of you with the compassion of Christ Jesus', but the Greek word for 'compassion' here is σπλάγχνον, which literally means 'the viscera, *inwards parts, entrails*'[1] of one's being. However, the BDAG Lexicon tells us that σπλάγχνον is used 'of the seat of the emotions, in our usage a transference is made to the rendering *heart*', or it can be used 'of the feeling itself, pl. love, affection,'[2] which is the case in Philippians 1:8.[3] Hence the English translation of 'compassion' for σπλάγχνον is entirely appropriate, and a translation of 'entrails' would be unhelpful, to say the least.

When it comes to καρδία, literally 'heart', English readers need to be aware of a similar issue between Greek and English. Although the English dictionary meaning of 'heart' is very broad,[4] in my view, 'heart' in contemporary English usage is strongly associated with emotions. One example of this is the 'Head, Heart, Hands model', where the heart relates to the affective domain.[5] In contemporary usage, the 'heart' is most strongly associated with feelings and emotions, and so a phrase like 'my heart went out to them' refers to an emotional response to someone.

However, in the NT, as I hope to show, καρδία is used of a much wider range of facets of the human person than just the emotions. Here I will discuss three Pauline texts in which καρδία is mentioned in conjunction with the work of the Holy Spirit, since I think these passages are particularly open to misunderstanding today. It will be argued that the translation of καρδία as 'heart' risks seriously misleading contemporary readers. To argue this case, I need firstly to consider the use of καρδία in the Graeco-Roman world, the LXX, and the NT in general.

---

1 See BDAG, 938, italics original.
2 BDAG, 938, italics original.
3 See further Fee, *Philippians*, 94 n.104. A similar usage is found in Phlm. 12.
4 See, for example, *The Oxford English Dictionary Online*, accessed 22 March 2021.
5 See, for example, Jagannathan et al, 'The effectiveness', 53–62.

2. καρδία in the Graeco-Roman world and the LXX

In the Graeco-Roman world, καρδία was predominantly used for the heart in a physiological sense as the central organ of the human body. It was also used figuratively of the heart as the seat of emotions, such as anger, courage, or joy, as well as the seat of thought, or of the will.[6]

καρδία is predominantly used with a metaphorical sense in the LXX. Since this is the sense that it always has in the NT, it is generally agreed that the LXX is the key background when we discuss the use of καρδία in the NT,[7] and so we turn in more detail to the LXX.

καρδία is used over 900 times in the LXX. It is much more common in the LXX than it is in Greek literature in general, and this is because of the frequency in the Hebrew Bible of לב and לבב, both of which mean 'heart', and both of which are generally translated by καρδία. The range of nuances of these two Hebrew terms is found in the LXX usage of καρδία.[8]

καρδία can be used in the LXX of the physical heart (e.g. 2 Sam. 18:14; 2 Kgs 9:24). However, in the vast majority of occurrences, καρδία is used metaphorically.

It is used to refer to emotions and so the heart can be said to be glad (Judg. 16:25; 18:20), angry or 'hot' (Deut. 19:6), or weary (Ps. 60:2). But καρδία refers to much more than just emotions. It is often seen as the seat or home of mental abilities, understanding, and wisdom.[9] In Exodus 31:6 the heart is described as 'intelligent', in 1 Kings 3:12 it is 'prudent and wise', and in Ecclesiastes 1:17 it is connected to 'wisdom and knowledge'.[10] In Psalm 75:5 the heart is said to be 'stupid', and in Jeremiah 14:14 the heart is connected to lying. In Genesis 6:5 we read that in Noah's time people 'all think attentively in their hearts

---

6   See Baumgärtel and Behm, 'καρδία', 3: 608–9, with references; see also Silva, 'καρδία et al', 2:622–23.
7   See Sand, 'καρδία', 2:250; Silva, 'καρδία et al', 2:625; Baumgärtel and Behm, 'καρδία', 611; Jewett, *Paul's Anthropological Terms*, 312.
8   See Baumgärtel and Behm, 'καρδία', 609. English translations of the LXX are from NETS. Unless stated otherwise, translations of the NT are from the NRSV.
9   See Silva, 'καρδία', 624.
10 See also Prov. 10:8; Eccl. 8:5.

(διανοεῖται ἐν τῇ καρδίᾳ αὐτοῦ) on evil things all the days'.[11]

The heart is connected to matters of volition, will, and decision making. In 1 Kings 8:17 we read: 'And it was in the heart (ἐπὶ τῆς καρδίας) of my father David to build a house for the name of the Lord'.[12] But the heart can be 'hardened', as in the case of Pharaoh (Exod. 4:21; 7:3,22).[13]

The heart is also the place of awe and worship and of relationship with God. In Jeremiah 39:40 we read: 'And I will make an everlasting covenant with them, which I will not turn away from behind them, and I will assign my fear to their heart (εἰς τὴν καρδίαν αὐτῶν) so that they may not turn away from me'. People's hearts can be said to be far from God (Isa. 29:13), people turn or return to God 'with all your heart' (1 Sam. 7:3; 12:20; 1 Kgs 8:48; 2 Kgs 23:25; Joel 2:12), and 'a broken and humbled heart God will not despise' (Ps. 50:19). God's law is said to be in people's hearts (Isa. 51:7; Jer. 38:33), and 1 Chronicles 29:19 reads: 'And grant to Solomon my son a good heart (καρδίαν ἀγαθήν) to do your commandments'. In Jeremiah 24:7, God says: 'And I will give them a heart that they may know me'. Hence the heart is the place where humans meet God and encounter God's word and law.[14]

In addition, καρδία often 'means less an isolated function than the individual human life in its totality',[15] with the different functions of the heart being thought of together rather than treated in isolation.[16] Thus καρδία is used in a range of passages to refer to the inner and spiritual totality of a person's life. Psalm 22:26 reads: 'The needy shall eat and be satisfied, and those who seek him shall praise the LORD; their hearts (αἱ καρδίαι αὐτῶν) shall live forever and ever!' 1 Samuel 16:7 is similar: 'And the LORD said to Samuel, "Do not look on his appearance or on the posture of his size, because I have rejected him, for God will not look as a mortal will see, for a mortal will see into a

---

11 See also Deut. 29:4; Ps. 89:12.
12 Silva, 'καρδία', 624 comments: 'the will, and thus the carefully weighed intentions, originates in the heart'.
13 See also Exod. 14:5; Judg. 9:3; 1 Sam. 14:7; Prov. 6:18.
14 See also Ezek. 11:19; 2 Chr. 11:16; Prov. 23:26.
15 Silva, 'καρδία', 624.
16 See Lee, 'An exegetical-theological consideration', 605 n.11.

face, but God will see into a heart (ὁ δὲ θεὸς ὄψεται εἰς καρδίαν)'".[17]

Accordingly, we see that the heart is a term for the personality as a whole and for the inner person. It refers to the centre of a person's life, including life before God and the centre of the worship of God. It involves thinking and understanding, volition and decision making and emotion.[18]

3. Usage in the NT

Before discussing NT usage, we should note that there was debate in the first century C.E. about the location or seat of the intellect and of decision making in the human body. Followers of Plato and others located the seat of the intellect in the head or the brain, while Aristotelians and Stoics located it in the heart. Around the middle of the second century C.E. Galen undertook experiments which showed that the brain was the centre of will, cognition, and perception rather than the heart, and although this was a decisive contribution to the debate, he did not convince everyone and the issue remained contentious into the third century C.E.[19] When the New Testament was written, then, many people believed that what we would call the intellect and the will were located in the heart.

καρδία is used around 156 times in the NT,[20] and its meaning is strongly connected with the usage in the LXX. It is never used with a strictly literal meaning, although the physical sense is in the background in Luke 21:34; Acts 14:17, and James 5:5. It is used in the metaphorical sense to refer to the inner life, with BDAG giving the key meaning as the 'center and source of the whole inner life, w[ith] its

---

17 See also 1 Sam. 25:37; Ps. 72:26.
18 Baumgärtel and Behm, 'καρδία', 610 note καρδία 'relates to the unity and totality of the inner life represented and expressed in the variety of intellectual and spiritual functions'. See also Silva, 'καρδία', 624; Schroer and Staubli, *Body Symbolism*, 41–49.
19 See Tieleman, 'Head and Heart', 87–94. He notes of the first century (94): 'Those who assigned both cognition and emotion to the brain ... appear to have been a small minority'. See Martin, 'Performing', 75–78; Branson, 'Science', 231–232. For Galen's view see e.g. *Doctrines*, 7.3.2–10.
20 See Silva, 'καρδία', 625

thinking, feeling, and volition'.[21] This means that καρδία can be used to speak of a whole range of different 'activities' of the person.[22]

Firstly, καρδία is used of the emotions, desires and passions. Joy (John 16:22; Acts 2:26; 14:17), sorrow (John 16:6; 14:27; Rom. 9:2; 2 Cor. 2:4; Acts 21:13), anger (Acts 7:54), passion in a positive sense (Rom. 10:1; Luke 24:32), and lust (Rom. 1:24; Matt. 5:28) are all connected with καρδία.

Secondly, καρδία can refer to the centre of intellectual life, and so of understanding and thought. In Matthew 13:15b, quoting Isaiah 6:10, we read with regard to the people that: 'they might not look with their eyes, and listen with their ears, and understand with their heart (καὶ τῇ καρδίᾳ συνῶσιν) and turn—and I would heal them'. Luke 1:51 reads: 'he has scattered the proud in the thoughts of their hearts (διανοίᾳ καρδίας αὐτῶν)'.[23]

Thirdly, καρδία can refer to the will, the source of resolve, decision and intention. Note 2 Corinthians 9:7: 'Each of you must give as you have made up your heart[24] (τῇ καρδίᾳ), not reluctantly or under compulsion, for God loves a cheerful giver'. In 1 Corinthians 4:5 we read that the Lord: 'will bring to light the things now hidden in darkness and will disclose the purposes of the heart (τὰς βουλὰς τῶν καρδιῶν)'.[25] Evil intentions also come from the heart (Mark 7:21), and the intentions of the heart are judged by God's word (Heb. 4:12).

Fourthly, καρδία can refer to the centre of spiritual life, and so is spoken of as the part of a person where they encounter God or are encountered by God, in either a positive or a negative sense (Acts 8:21; Rom. 6:17; 1 Cor. 14:25; Heb. 3:12). Hearts can be hard and impenitent (Rom. 2:5) or senseless (Rom 1:21). It is in the heart that the deci-

---

21 See BDAG: 508.
22 The categories below are from Baumgärtel and Behm, 'καρδία', 611-13.
23 See also Matt. 9:4; 24:48; Mark 11:23; Luke 2:19, 35, 51; 24:38; John 12:40; Acts 7:23; 8:22; 28:27; Rom. 1:21; 10:6; 1 Cor. 2:9; Rev. 18:7. The strong relationship between καρδία and 'the mind' is shown in 2 Cor. 3:14-15, where νόημα ('mind') and καρδία are used with very similar meanings.
24 See further Jewett, *Paul's Anthropological Terms*, 331. The NRSV translates προῄρηται τῇ καρδίᾳ as 'made up your mind' here.
25 See also Luke 21:14; John 13:2; Acts 5:3-4; 11:23; 1 Cor. 7:37; 2 Cor. 8:16; Rev. 17:17.

sion for faith, or against it, occurs (Matt. 13:15; Mark 11:23; Luke 24:25; Acts 16:14; Rom. 10:8-10; Heb. 10:22), and one's heart can be hardened against God (Mark 3:5; 6:52; 8:17; 10:5; John 12:40).[26]

Finally, καρδία can also be used of the whole person in their totality,[27] to speak of a person as a thinking, feeling, willing whole. Jewett writes: 'Paul seems to use the word to depict the whole person in such a way that his Hebraic assumption of a psycho-somatic unity of man in thinking, willing, emoting, acting and responding to God and fellowman is clearly evident'.[28] Hence in 2 Corinthians 5:12 καρδία is used of the inner life as opposed to something outward or external: 'We are not commending ourselves to you again, but giving you an opportunity to boast about us, so that you may be able to answer those who boast in outward appearance and not in the heart'.[29] Note also 1 Peter 3:4: 'rather, let your adornment be the hidden heart of a person (ὁ κρυπτὸς τῆς καρδίας ἄνθρωπος)', with the last phrase being helpfully translated by the NRSV as 'the inner self', while the NIV gives 'your inner self'. Thus, a working gloss on καρδία in the NT is 'the centre of inner life, and so of understanding, emotions, will, and spiritual life'.

4. The Heart and the Spirit in Paul

I turn now to discuss three verses which refer to καρδία in relation to the Holy Spirit in which I think it is particularly important to understand that καρδία means much more than 'emotions'. These are passages which contemporary readers are particularly likely to mis-read and so miss a good deal of their theological importance.

For each of these passages, BDAG gives the meaning of καρδία as 'The human καρδία as the dwelling-place of heavenly powers and beings [...], of the Spirit'.[30] But why is the Spirit said to dwell in, or be poured into, the καρδία in particular in these passages? I will argue that

---

26   See also Matt. 13:19; Luke 8:12, 15; 16:15; 2 Cor. 5:6; Eph. 3:17; 1 Thess. 2:4; 3:11-13; 2 Thess. 2:16-17; 3:5.
27   See Jewett, *Paul's Anthropological Terms*, 305.
28   Jewett, *Paul's Anthropological Terms*, 313; see also Silva, 'καρδία', 625.
29   See also Mark 7:6; Rom. 2:29; 1 Thess. 2:17; Col. 2:2; 1 John 3:19-20.
30   BDAG, 509; this is meaning 1θ.

it is because the καρδία refers in these cases to the *whole* of the inner self of the person, and so the Spirit is said to come into the totality of the inner life. This can be seen to be the case because we can see that emotional, intellectual, volitional, and spiritual dimension of the inner life are all in play in the context of these verses. The Spirit is not being connected *only* to the emotions, but to the whole inner self, and the meaning of καρδία as 'the centre of inner life, and so of understanding, emotions, will, and spiritual life' is appropriate in these cases.

4.1 Galatians 4:6

In Galatians 4:6, Paul writes: 'And because you are children, God has sent the Spirit of his Son into our hearts (εἰς τὰς καρδίας ἡμῶν),[31] crying (κρᾶζον), "Abba! Father!"' I will argue that, in context, Paul is saying that the Spirit has been sent into 'the centre of inner life, and so of understanding, emotions, will, and spiritual life'.

In Galatians 4, Paul has said that while readers had previously been minors, and so enslaved to 'the elemental spirits of the world' (4:3), now, since God has sent his Son, readers have been adopted as children (4:5). But how do readers know this?[32] Galatians 4:6 gives the answer. Because readers are God's children, God 'has sent the Spirit of his Son εἰς τὰς καρδίας ἡμῶν, crying, "Abba! Father!"' This clearly shows knowledge of the Gospel tradition, evident in Mark 14:36, that Jesus called God 'Abba'. The Spirit of God's Son, Jesus Christ, now enables believers, as God's children, to also cry out to God as 'Abba, Father', just as Jesus did.

Paul says that the Spirit of the Son has been sent εἰς τὰς καρδίας ἡμῶν. My contention is that English readers see this as 'into the centre of our emotions'. The verb κρᾶζον might reinforce this reflex or 'default' view—that it is an emotional cry. Clearly, the believer's emotions are

---

31 There is a variant here, of ὑμῶν ('your') rather than ἡμῶν ('our'). ἡμῶν has the stronger external support and the change from 'you are children (ἐστε υἱοί)' at the beginning of Gal. 4:6 to 'our hearts', with ἡμῶν, towards the end of the verse is the more difficult reading and so is to be preferred; see Moo, *Galatians*, 271-272.
32 Dunn, *Galatians*, 219, notes 'the witness-bearing function of the Spirit' in the parallel in Rom 8:16 and suggests that here the Spirit is sent 'to act as witness in the formal act of *adoptio*'.

impacted here. As Moo writes of Paul's use of κρᾶζον here: 'Paul perhaps uses a word picture to convey the deep and emotional reaction within the believer's heart to the joyful conviction, brought by God's Spirit, that we are, indeed, God's sons'.[33] But the Spirit being sent εἰς τὰς καρδίας ἡμῶν involves much more than emotions. Given that καρδία also refers to understanding, will, and spiritual life, then the Spirit can be seen to impact each of these facets of the human personality. In this regard, Galatians 4:1–7 clearly involves the Spirit in bringing understanding of being an heir and so related to God, no longer as a minor or a slave, but now as a child of God.

The spiritual life is also hugely impacted, in that now the believer shares in Jesus' own filial relationship with Abba through the Spirit; this is a life of intimacy such that the believer can call God 'Abba' (4:6). Further, the believer's will or decision-making is impacted, because, while we were previously minors under guardians and trustees (4:1–2), as well as being enslaved to 'the elemental spirits of the world' (4:3), now believers have been adopted as children and redeemed (4:5) and so enter into the freedom of being children of God and heirs (4:7).[34] This freedom involves a whole new state, the transference from being under a guardian to being free, which Paul will elaborate on in Galatians 4:28—5:15. In the context of Galatians as a whole, this freedom brought by the Spirit being sent εἰς τὰς καρδίας ἡμῶν clearly has intellectual, volitional, emotional, and spiritual dimensions.

In context then, we can see that while the Spirit being sent 'into our hearts' does have an emotional dimension, it also clearly involves the intellect, the will and the spiritual life of the believer. Accordingly, Jewett notes that καρδία in Galatians 4:6 is:

> the center of man which stands open before God ... Since Christ is the son, he acts within the center of the human

---

33 Moo, *Galatians*, 270. Dunn, *Galatians*, 219, notes that the heart is 'the seat of the inner life, the inner experiencing "I", both as a rational, decision-making being, and as a being with emotions and desires', and adds (219–220), 'it is precisely Paul's point, that the reality of God's adoption/acceptance reaches to the motivating and emotive centre of the person'.
34 See Moo, *Galatians*, 270–71.

personality—the heart—to elicit an expression typical of a son, αββα ὁ πατήρ. The center of man is thus his heart; the heart's intentionality is determined by the power which rules it. In the case of Christian man, the direction of the heart's intentionality is determined by Christ's Spirit.[35]

Thus, a translation of Galatians 4:6 can be suggested: 'And because you are children, God has sent the Spirit of his Son into *the centre of our lives*, crying, "Abba! Father!"' A longer gloss would be 'God has sent the Spirit of his Son *into the centre of our inner lives, that is, our understanding, emotions, will, and spiritual life*, crying, "Abba! Father!"'[36]

4.2 Romans 5:5

In Romans 5:5 we read: 'hope does not disappoint us, because God's love has been poured into our hearts through the Holy Spirit (ἐν ταῖς καρδίαις ἡμῶν) that has been given to us'. Paul has been explaining the results of justification and that the believer exults, not only in the hope of sharing in God's glory, but also in sufferings because these sufferings produce hope. We can be certain that hope 'does not disappoint us' precisely because of the presence of the Holy Spirit ἐν ταῖς καρδίαις ἡμῶν.

Again, we can see an emotional dimension here, in that both hope and God's love clearly can and should impact our emotions, as experienced realities.[37] But we can see that the understanding, will and spiritual life are also involved or impacted. When Paul says 'but we also boast in our sufferings, knowing that suffering produces endurance, and endurance produces character, and character produces hope, and hope does not disappoint us' (5:3–5), he clearly draws on the understanding, since *in the midst of on-going suffering,* the believer is to *know* that suffering has a different outcome in hope.

Similarly, the will or volition is impacted. The believer knows that hope will not disappoint us because of the experience of God's love

---

35 Jewett, *Paul's Anthropological Terms*, 322-23.
36 Moo, *Galatians*, 263-64, notes that the closest parallel to Gal. 4:6 in the Pauline corpus is Rom. 8:15-16, where Paul locates the Spirit's activity in 'our spirit', which is clearly closely related to 'our inner life'.
37 See Fee, *God's Empowering Presence*, 496-97.

through the outpoured Spirit (5:5). This means that, in the midst of present suffering (5:3), the believer can stand fast and even exult or boast (5:3). This is clearly an act of the will, a decision to face suffering because of its outcome.

The spiritual life is similarly in view here, since the passage speaks of peace with God (5:1), access to God's grace (5:2), and the abundant out-pouring of God's love to the person (5:5).

Accordingly, in commenting on Romans 5:5, Jewett writes that the use of καρδία here shows that it is 'the center of the person where God chooses to reveal himself'.[38] In addition, that God's love flows into our hearts shows that love 'grasps humans at the innermost center of their selfhood'.[39] The breadth of the meaning of καρδία in Paul's usage needs to be kept in view here in order to understand what Paul means in this verse.

A suggested translation of Romans 5:5 is: 'hope does not disappoint us, because God's love has been poured into *the centre of our lives* through the Holy Spirit that has been given to us'. A longer gloss would be 'hope does not disappoint us, because God's love has been poured into *the centre of our inner lives, that is, our understanding, emotions, will, and spiritual life* through the Holy Spirit that has been given to us'.

4.3 2 Corinthians 1:22

In 2 Corinthians 1:21–22 we read: 'But it is God who establishes us with you in Christ and has anointed us, by putting his seal on us and giving us his Spirit in our hearts (ἐν ταῖς καρδίαις ἡμῶν) as a first instalment'.

The element of understanding is clear here. It is a mental attitude, an understanding of the work of God in establishing believers (1:21), that Paul is seeking to underline at this point. As Harris notes, in vv. 21–22: 'Paul points to the constant activity of God in producing stability in Paul *and* the Corinthians—those who have been brought into intimate and dynamic relation with Christ, who is God's secure and permanent "Yes"'.[40]

---

38 Jewett, *Paul's Anthropological Terms*, 310.
39 Jewett, *Romans*, 356, quoting Schlier.
40 Harris, *Second Epistle to the Corinthians*, 210, italics original.

Although the emotional dimension is not emphasised, Paul is seeking to counter the charge of inconsistency and lack of reliability created by his change of plans (1:15–18),[41] which was clearly (at the very least) unsettling for the Corinthians and seems to have led to them making some form of charge against him.[42] The presence of the Spirit ἐν ταῖς καρδίαις ἡμῶν is a key agent in overcoming this concern, and so has a role with regard to the Corinthians' emotions.

The will is also clearly impacted. As noted above, in 2 Corinthians 1:15-22 Paul is answering the charge that he has been vacillating in his plans to visit the Corinthians (1:17). They seem to think he says '"Yes, yes" and "No, no" at the same time' (1:17). Paul answers this by referring to God's promises being answered as 'Yes' in Christ. Paul shares in this certainty, of saying the 'Amen' (1:20) by being 'in Christ' (1:21), with the gift of the Holy Spirit ἐν ταῖς καρδίαις ἡμῶν as a 'first instalment' clearly playing a vital role here (1:22). In context, then, the given Spirit results in Paul having convictions of the will, such that his 'Yes' is dependable.

The spiritual dimension is also very clear. God has been active in establishing both Paul and the believers in Corinth in Christ (1:21), and in anointing them, sealing them and giving the Holy Spirit as an ἀρραβών (1:22). All these points relate to the believers' spiritual lives.

A suggested translation is thus: 'But it is God who establishes us with you in Christ and has anointed us, by putting his seal on us and giving us his Spirit in *the centre of our lives* as a first instalment'. A longer gloss would be 'by putting his seal on us and giving us his Spirit in *the centre of our inner lives, that is, our understanding, emotions, will, and spiritual life* as a first instalment.'[43]

---

41 See Thrall, *Second Epistle to the Corinthians*, 1:143.
42 Harris, *Second Epistle to the Corinthians*, 196 notes that ἐλαφρία in 1:17 is best translated as 'fickleness', and Paul 'is alluding to a charge that had been leveled against him by certain Corinthians'. He translates 1:17 (p.190) as 'Well, did I really show fickleness when I wanted to do this?'
43 Furnish, *II Corinthians*, 138, notes that 'in our hearts' is equivalent to ἡμῖν 'to us', the term Paul uses in 2 Cor. 5:5. This would suggest we could translate 2 Cor. 1:22 as 'by putting his seal on us and giving his Spirit *to us* as a first instalment'. But 'the centre of our lives' is to be preferred as giving more of a location for the presence of the Spirit.

5. Conclusions

In both the LXX and in the NT, καρδία refers to the centre of a person's being, involving the understanding, will, emotions, and the spiritual life. With this in view, I have considered three Pauline passages where the translations of καρδία as 'the heart' is, I think, misleading and unhelpful, since in English the connotations of 'the heart' focus on the emotions. In each case in context, we can see that the use of καρδία in relation to the Spirit impacts not just the believer's emotions, but also the understanding, will, and spiritual life. I believe a better translation in each case is to speak of the Spirit in 'the centre of our lives'. This translation also has the advantage of better representing the great significance of the work of the Spirit for Paul in these passages, for clearly Paul is underlining that the Spirit dwells in the centre of our being, at the centre of all we are as people, rather than just in one facet of our lives.

There is significant precedent for not always translating καρδία as 'heart', since in some NT passages καρδία is translated as 'mind'.[44] In these cases, translators have opted for an English word that better represents the actual connotations of καρδία in the passages concerned. This precedent suggests a translation such as 'the centre of our lives' should be used in these three passages.

There are a number of other Pauline passages which could be discussed, in which it is important to recognise the breadth of meaning of καρδία and to acknowledge that καρδία does not simply mean the centre of emotions.[45] But that is a topic for another day.

Paul Trebilco
University of Otago
Dunedin, New Zealand

---

44 See e.g. 1 Cor. 7:37, where καρδία is used of the centre from which decisions come, and so is appropriately translated as 'mind' in the NRSV. See also Luke 21:14; Rom. 1:21; 2 Cor. 3:15; 9:7.
45 See Rom. 2:29; 6:17; 10:8-10; 2 Cor. 3:2-3; 4:6; 1 Thess. 3:13.

Bibliography

Baumgärtel, F. and J. Behm   'καρδία, κτλ,' *TDNT* 3, 605–14.

Branson, R. D.   'Science, the Bible, and Human Anatomy', *Perspectives on Science and Christian Faith* 68 (2016), 229–36.

Dunn, J. D. G.   *The Epistle to the Galatians* (Black's NT Commentary; Peabody, MA: Hendrickson, 1993).

Fee, G. D.   *God's Empowering Presence: The Holy Spirit in the Letters of Paul* (Peabody, MA: Hendrickson, 1994).

Fee, G. D.   *Paul's Letter to the Philippians* (NICNT; Grand Rapids, MI: Eerdmans, 1995).

Furnish, V. P.   *II Corinthians: A New Translation with Introduction and Commentary* (AB; New York, NY: Doubleday, 1984).

Harris, M. J.   *The Second Epistle to the Corinthians: A Commentary on the Greek Text* (NIGTC; Grand Rapids, MI: Eerdmans, 2005).

Jagannathan, R. et al.   'The effectiveness of a head-heart-hands model for natural and environmental science learning in urban schools', *Evaluation and Program Planning* 66 (2018), 53–62.

Jewett, R.   *Paul's Anthropological Terms: A Study of Their Use in Conflict Settings* (AGJU 10; Leiden: Brill, 1971).

Jewett, R.   *Romans: A Commentary* (Hermeneia; Minneapolis, MN: Fortress Press, 2007).

Lee, S.-H.   'An exegetical-theological consideration of the hardening of the Jewish religious leaders' hearts in Mark 3:1–6', *Verbum et Ecclesia* 27 (2006), 596–613.

Martin, T. W.   'Performing the Head Role: Man is the Head of Woman (1 Cor 11:3 and Eph 5:23)', *Biblical Research* 57 (2012), 69–80.

Moo, D. J.   *Galatians* (BECNT; Grand Rapids, MI: Eerdmans, 2013).

Sand, A.   'καρδία', in H. Balz and G. Schneider (eds.), *Exegetical Dictionary of the New Testament* (Grand Rapids, MI: Eerdmans, 1991), 2:249–51.

Schroer, S. and T. Staubli *Body Symbolism in the Bible* (Collegeville, PA: Liturgical Press, 2001).

Silva, M. 'καρδία et al.', in M. Silva (ed.), *New International Dictionary of New Testament Theology and Exegesis* (Grand Rapids, MI: Zondervan, 2014), 2:622–27.

The Oxford English Dictionary Online https://www.oed.com/view/Entry/85068

Thrall, M. E. *A Critical and Exegetical Commentary on The Second Epistle to the Corinthians Volume 1* (ICC; Edinburgh: T & T Clark, 1994).

Tieleman, T. 'Head and Heart: The Pauline Corpus Considered against the Medical and Philosophical Backdrop', *Religion & Theology* 21 (2014), 86–106.

Reading Romans 9 on Election with the Rabbis and the Greek Fathers

Mark Reasoner

Abstract

Romans 9:1–23 is often read as a key locus for what Paul teaches about God's election of individuals by means of selected election texts from Genesis, Exodus, and Malachi. When rabbinic exegesis antecedent and contemporary to Paul of these Scriptures is considered, however, it is clear that these texts were interpreted as referring to the election of Israel vis-à-vis the nations. Since Paul is concerned with Israel throughout Romans, Tannaitic exegesis validates reading Romans 9 with this relationship of Israel and the nations in view, rather than metaphysical questions of how God's election relates to the human will more generally. Yet if we wish to extrapolate from the literal sense of Romans 9 to a spiritual sense regarding the election of individuals, the Tannaitic sages and Greek church fathers provide early and significant witness toward reading election in Romans 9 as intimately connected to human choices and behaviour.

Jim Harrison has completed the herculean labours of bringing the letter of Romans back to the house churches of Rome, helping us hear the letter as the first recipients of the letter heard it. Jim's research and publications have done much to prioritise what primary texts to use alongside our reading of Romans.[1] In honor of Jim's work and in appreciation for his friendship and inspiration to me, this essay extends Jim's project of prioritisation with a preliminary attempt to identify and illustrate from Romans 9:1–23 how the most relevant biblical commentators for reading Romans regarding election are the rabbis contemporary to Paul and the Greek fathers.

But Romans as a letter is not in the first place about election. Though Romans has been read by many as a letter for the reader as consumer, how the reader can get saved by faith, Romans is really about what God is doing in the cosmos. The obedience of faith that God brings through Jesus to all the nations (1:5), Paul's all-inclusive descriptions of his gospel's audience (1:14), his diachronic surveys of human history (5:12–15, 18–19; 7:9–11), and his grand vision of the material world (8:18–23) all prepare the reader for the cosmic focus even in chapters 9–11. In these chapters Paul extends the Old Testament prophets' reflection on how the God of Israel relates both to his own people and to the nations and develops within this reflection some guidelines on how the nations are to regard Israel. Specific points about God's election of individuals within Israel and the nations are secondary implications of Paul's discourse in chapters 9–11 about how God brings justice to the whole world through the faithfulness of Christ. So let it be known that this essay concerns a secondary matter in Paul's discourse, a matter that has weighed heavily on the minds of some exegetes, despite the utter lack of evidence in the letter that the questions of individuals' election concerned Paul.

Within these chapters, Romans 9:1–23 expresses Paul's grief over Israel's political and social displacement in the first century C.E. Mediterranean world (9:1–5), and offers two different interpretations of this displacement.[2] First, Paul uses his Scriptures to consider whether Israel should be defined by some other criterion than biological descent (9:6–13). This suggestion emerges at other points in the reflection

---

1   Among his many publications, see especially Harrison, *Paul's Language of Grace* and *Reading Romans with Roman Eyes*.
2   On the this-worldly dimensions of Paul's concern for Israel and its salvation he envisions, see Reasoner, 'The Salvation of Israel in Romans 9–11'.

through 11:6, but Paul drops it as he approaches his final conclusion.[3] Second, Paul engages in a diatribe to suggest that God elects individuals on earth only in regard to how God might display his glory, without consideration of the individuals' responsibility (9:14–23). This possibility also disappears from the discourse by 9:29, but it has held exegetes' attention for centuries, and thus will need consideration in this essay's look at 9:1–23.

The historical-critical method indicates that readers should read biblical texts in light of their literary genre and other contemporary writings in their milieu. For all Romans commentators' energies on the metaphysical implications of Paul's thoughts that seem to concern election in Romans 9, then, it makes sense to consider them in light of sources among the Zugot and the Tannaim, with special attention to the first half of the latter period, i.e. the first century C.E., in which Paul lived. And it also would be helpful to read Romans 9 not only in the light of Western commentators, but also in view of the Greek fathers, who read Romans 9 in their own language.

Tannaitic Readings of Paul's Election Texts

Paul's reference to God's regard only for Isaac, among Abraham's other sons, as the child of promise is the first scriptural argument Paul offers to show that God's word has not failed, even though most of Israel does not acknowledge Jesus as the promised Messiah. His next argument, from the oracle to expectant Rebekah that her older twin would serve the younger, concluding with Malachi's oracle about the nations of Judah and Edom, 'Jacob I have loved, Esau I have hated', seems at first reading, at least to those with any exposure to Reformed theology, to be evidence for a predestining God who has fixed people's destinies before they are born. Yet the rabbis and the Greek fathers have a different way of understanding these texts.

In *m. Avot* it is taught, 'A good eye and a humble spirit and a lowly

---

3   For a reading that sees Rom 9–11 as composed of disparate units of argument, not all of which function equally in Paul's final portrait of Israel, see Reasoner, 'Israel in the Outline of Romans 9–11'.

soul—[they in whom are these] are of the disciples of Abraham our father'.[4] This quotation, coming from a tractate with material that surely circulated in oral form in the first century C.E., illustrates that the rabbis around the time of Paul were considering who is a true follower or disciple of Abraham. This quest to define the disciples of Abraham is in the same general category as Paul's 'not all from Israel are Israel' in Romans 9:6b. Here in this context within *m. Avot*, a comparison is made between those Jews who are disciples of Abraham and those Jews who are disciples of the Gentile Balaam. The rabbis' answer, of course, is different from how Paul in Galatians 3 and Romans 4 describes the children of Abraham. But it shows that we could consider Paul's statement that the descendants of Abraham are not all his children (Rom. 9:7) not simply as Christian apologetics, but part of a quest among Jewish thinkers to understand in the conflicted circumstances of the first century what it meant to live as authentic children of Abraham.

When we consider how Paul presents God's choice of Jacob over Esau as a decision made before their birth, a relevant, albeit sectarian, text is *Jubilees*, written some time between 161 and 140 B.C.E.[5] This composition, highly focused on the Jewish calendar, spends considerable space portraying Jacob as righteous (29:14–16; 35:2–6,12) and Esau as wicked (29:18; 35:9–11,13–14). The divine election of Jacob over Esau seems to be narratively explained as arising from their behaviour, thus rendering the oracle to Rebekah an example of God's prescience.

This fits with how Jewish readers at the time of Paul read their Scriptures. For example, Pseudo-Philo's summary of barren Rebekah's conception of Esau and Jacob includes this interpreted quotation of Malachi: 'And God loved Jacob, but Esau he hated because of his deeds'.[6] That is, God must have known about Esau's deeds, and this resulted in God's rejection of him.

---

4   m.Avot 5.19, translation and bracketed phrase from Danby, *Mishnah*, 458.
5   Wintermute, '*Jubilees*', 44.
6   L.A.B. 32.5; trans. James, *Biblical Antiquities*, 175–76. This view of Esau's election continues into the Amoraic period; see, e.g., b.Yoma 38b.

The election of Isaac in first century C.E. Jewish sources as tied to a national consciousness is amply illustrated in Josephus's *Jewish Antiquities*. There we read that

> God appeared to [Abraham] and announced that he should have a son by Sarah, bidding him call him Isaac, and revealing how great nations and kings would spring from him, and how they would win possession, by war, of all Canaan from Sidon to Egypt. Furthermore, to the intent that his posterity should be kept from mixing with others, God charged him to have them circumcised and to perform the rite on the eighth day after birth.[7]

Josephus thus reflects the perspective shared by the rabbis and Paul: God's election of Isaac means God's election of the people of Israel. Paul believed in the merit of the fathers as did the rabbis of his day.[8] But since there is no evidence that the rabbis were concerned with the election of every individual, whether to a blissful afterlife or to eternal punishment in the afterlife, and since there is no evidence that Paul has the afterlife in view when he writes of Isaac, Jacob, Esau, and Pharaoh in Romans 9 or even of Israel's salvation in Romans 11:26–27, it is best not to import the concerns of Middle- and Neo-Platonism regarding the soul in an afterlife into any exegesis of the literal sense of Romans 9.

Paul's concluding quotation on Jacob and Esau's destinies, from Malachi 1:2, also points to the comparison that Paul is making between the nations that Jacob and Esau represent. We do not have evidence from the first century C.E. for the iconic valence of Esau/Edom for Rome. But the symbolic value of Esau/Edom for the nations surrounding Israel can be seen in the book of Obadiah, which also uses phrases like Mount Esau and the house of Esau for the nation of Edom. In Obadiah we read that the nations surrounding Judah will drink the same cup that Edom must drink (1:15–16). So though we cannot say

---

7   Josephus, *Ant.* 1.191–92.
8   Rom 9:5; 11:28, *Mek. Rab Ish.* Horovitz-Rabin, *Beshallach 2*, p.160.4 ('merit of Abraham, Isaac, and Jacob'; Lauterbach 2.102.7); Horovitz-Rabin, *Yitro 2*, p. 207.4 ('merit of Jacob ... merit of Israel'; Lauterbach 2.201.8–9).

that the Jacob and Esau comparison in Romans 9:10–13 is specifically a comparison between Judah and Rome, it is arguably the case that Paul has in mind Judaea and the nations when he invokes the Jacob and Esau texts. These help us see again that Paul is not primarily focused on the destiny of individuals. He is instead trying to understand the ebb and flow of Israel's place among the nations of the earth. Edom, the object of more opprobrium by Old Testament authors than the Babylonians who actually destroyed Jerusalem, functions by synecdoche to represent the nations in the Old Testament, and so Paul's use of a Jacob and Esau text that points to a difference between Israel and the nations is very appropriate here.

Another piece of the puzzle regarding Paul's selection of a text on Jacob and Esau, followed by a text on Pharaoh in the next paragraph, is illuminated by the Tannaitic text of the *Mekhilta de-Rabbi Ishmael*. In its exegesis of Exodus 15:6 'dashes in pieces the enemy', the enemy is identified as either Pharaoh or Esau.[9] So the others whom Paul names in his meditation on Israel vis-à-vis the nations fit with the ways the rabbis of his day identified Israel's archetypal enemy—a move we would expect given Paul's Israel-oriented descriptions of threats to God's people in Romans 8:35–36.

Paul also tracks with the rabbinic belief that God showed special mercy to the Pharaoh who ruled at the time of Israel's exodus, in order that God might be glorified among the nations. According to the rabbis in the *Mekhilta de-Rabbi Ishmael*, this Pharaoh was himself a firstborn son, but God spared him in the final plague.[10] And when Pharaoh and his army finally drowned, all the nations of the world heard, gave up their idols, and began worshipping God.[11]

---

9 *Mek. Rab Ish*. Horovitz and Rabin, *Beshallach 5*, p. 134.14 (Lauterbach 2.42.72). The rabbis understand Pharaoh or Esau to be 'the enemy' based on Exod. 15:9 and Ezek. 36:2. Cf. to Rom 9:13,17. The Mekhilta here calls attention to the future tense of the verb 'dashes'. Aaron Amit informed me that this is the rabbis' way of hinting that the enemy is an enemy in the Israelites' future, i.e. Rome (personal correspondence on December 27, 2021).

10 *Mek. Rab Ish*. Horovitz and Rabin, *Bo 13*, p. 43.6–11 (Lauterbach 1.97.18–98.25) in the exegesis of Exod. 12:29, with mention of Exod. 9:16. Cf. Rom. 9:22.

11 *Mek. Rab Ish*. Horovitz and Rabin, *Beshallach 8*, p. 142.2–7 (Lauterbach 2.59.6–60.15). Cf. Rom 9:23.

Results of Survey of Tannaitic Texts for Exegesis of Romans 9

The rabbis were concerned with Israel's relationship to the nations. When they refer to Isaac, Jacob, and Esau, and even Pharaoh, they consider them not as examples of how God elects individuals on earth. For the rabbis, these biblical characters are *dramatis personae* in the nation of Israel's story. Because the Christian doctrine of election is conceptually dependent on God's election of Israel, it is understandable how Christian exegetes can read Romans 9:6–29 as evidence for this doctrine. But based on Paul's recurrent references to Israel in Romans that lead up to chapters 9–11, it is clear that he is focused on how God relates to Israel and the Gentiles and not on the election of individuals.[12] The rabbis of the first century, including Paul of Tarsus, were not considering Jacob and Esau in order to make metaphysical claims on the continuum between divine determinism and human free will in the lives of individuals. They were simply trying to understand Israel's place in the world.

The rabbis were mostly concerned with the flourishing of the nation of Israel on earth, not with the eschatological status of Israelites in heaven, à la Revelation 7:1–8. Paul as well gives no evidence of being concerned with the status of souls in the afterlife. Based on the Scriptures Paul cites, his 'all Israel will be saved' in Romans 11:26 is a statement that the nation of Israel will experience renewed *shalom* on the earth. Tannaitic sages admittedly do speak of an individual's destiny after death. Thus the apostle Paul is arguably targeted as least in the kingdom of heaven.[13] And in another Tannaitic text, it is people like Paul who are possibly demoted further as having no share in the world to come, while the disciples of Abraham do enjoy life in the

---

12 Direct references to Israel include Rom. 1:16; 2:10–16; 3:1–4; 4:12; allusions include 7:9–13; 8:35–36.
13 Matt. 5:19. Paul admits to the criticism in 1 Cor. 15:9.

world to come.[14] So yes, some rabbis in the Tannaitic period could employ the category of life after death in their eschatology. But Paul does not signal that he is engaging in this category of discourse in Romans 9. The Old Testament texts he mentions all view Israel's salvation as its political and economic flourishing. In contrast, some Tannaitic sources make it explicit when they are concerned with a person's status after the resurrection. Still, the default setting among Tannaitic rabbis in discussions about 'salvation' is a consideration of life here on earth.

A third result of our look at the rabbis is that they do not display any proclivity toward reading Genesis as demonstrating that God chose Isaac and Jacob with no consideration of these patriarchs' lives. The dominant explanation of election of these individuals always connects their election to the righteous living these patriarchs exemplify, a connection not made in either the opening response to Israel's plight (9:6–13) or the following diatribe (9:14–23) in Paul's letter to the Romans.

Why Look Especially at the Greek Fathers?

Before we turn to the Greek fathers, it would be well to consider a question in some readers' minds:

Why consider the Jewish rabbis and Greek fathers on Romans 9 while mostly ignoring the later Latin fathers? The short answer to this question is that the Jewish rabbis and the Greek fathers help us avoid a more deterministic version of the individualised metaphysics that the Latin fathers, beginning with Augustine, have introduced into the exegesis of Romans 9. Augustine's paradigm was prompted by the questions Simplicianus asked.[15] Since Simplicianus was involved in the

---

14 The person who interprets Torah in ways that depart from *Halakhah* has no share in the world to come (*m.Avot* 3.12, in the name of Eliezer of Modiim who lived at the time of the Bar Kochba revolt, Danby 451). Disciples of Abraham will enjoy life in the world to come (*m.Avot* 5.19, Danby 458).
15 In 396, Augustine wrote his *Ad Simplicianum de diversis quaestionibus*, in response to Simplicianus's questions. Augustine deals with two questions in his response, the second of which is the interpretation of Rom. 9:10–29.

fusion of Platonism and Christianity in Milan, his questions were posed out of the ethereal worlds of Plato's forms and eternity as Christians conceived it. Origen had fallen out of favour in the Western Church, and it would be primarily Augustine and Pelagius who practically provided the foundations for the theology of the Latin Church.[16] This means that Origen's emphasis on the freedom of the will was not included in the Western church's first principles.

Augustine's frame and treatment of Simplicianus's request for an exegesis of Romans 9 revolve around the question of whether divine grace or the human will come first in the process of election. But a contextual reading of Romans, the rabbis' exegesis of the election texts in Genesis, and the Greek fathers' readings of Romans all indicate that Augustine's focus on the election of individuals is secondary to the literal sense of the text.

In the Donatist controversy, Augustine insisted against the Donatists' image of the Church as an ark that preserved the pure that the Church on earth was a reflection of the eternal reality of the Church, a neo-Platonic preparation for the predestination that would come to characterise the later Augustine's reading of Romans.[17] Augustine marshalled the Church's election and perseverance as weapons to fend off the spear thrust of Donatist skepticism about the Church's viability. In the Pelagian controversy, Augustine insisted on the election of individuals, in order to combat the optimistic anthropology of the Pelagians. Then with the inexorable advance of the northern tribes and with stories of people's apostasies in mind, Augustine more forcefully applied the allied doctrines of God's predestination and the perseverance of individual believers.[18] Almost in the very act of considering the Augustinian exegetical paradigm, an exegete can get pulled into the debate and spend one's energy arguing about questions that the

---

16   Brown, *Augustine*, 84, 147–48.
17   Brown, *Augustine*, 217–18. A similar argument to what I attempt in this paragraph—tracing how the pastoral and polemical concerns of Augustine pulled him away from the literal sense of election texts in Romans—is found in Bulgakov's eighth chapter, 'Augustinianism and Predestination', in his *Sophiology of Death*, 104–16.
18   Brown, *Augustine*, 408–10.

paradigm's categories have generated through the centuries: whether God elects only for salvation or also for damnation, whether election allows an individual to choose otherwise or whether one's choice is determined, and whether God willed the first sin and the Jews' later disinterest in Jesus. But these questions are not found in Romans. They reflect concerns in the early fifth century Western church.

A Survey of the Greek Fathers on Election in Romans 9

Now let us consider what the Greek fathers have to say about God's choice of Jacob over Esau, as found in Romans 9. As Augustine would do when writing against the Pelagians and Donatists, the Greek fathers had already assumed that the central issue of Romans 9 was election and the metaphysical questions associated with it. They viewed Israel as simply a test case or an example of Paul's real topic.[19] In this move they miss Paul's primary focus, but it is at least instructive for us to compare their exegesis of the election texts with Western fathers.

Unlike Augustine and those in the West who followed him, who see predestination in this chapter, Origen and the Greek fathers see Romans 9 as a meditation on God's prescience, rather than dealing with questions of predestination. Thus, Pharaoh's situation is simply that God foreknew that Pharaoh would harden his own heart.[20] Origen explains God's choice of Jacob over Esau before birth by hypothesising that in an earlier life, Jacob must have earned more merit than Esau.[21] Even if we cannot accept this, the principle is analogous to the foreknowledge that other Greek fathers see here. God knows something about the behaviour of Jacob and Esau, whether in a previous existence (Origen's position) or in their life after birth. Their natures are not irreversibly fixed. They are responsible to follow God, and can change from being a favoured vessel to being one that will receive judgement.[22]

Chrysostom asks how it could be, as the Old Testament texts

---

19 Parmentier, 'Greek Church Fathers', 11, citing Gorday, *Principles of Patristic Exegesis: Romans 9–11*.
20 Parmentier, 'Greek Church Fathers', 11.
21 Origen, *Princ.* 2.9.7.
22 Origen, *Princ.* 3.1.23.

quoted in Rom 9:12–13 indicate, that God would choose someone and reject another before they had performed any action. His answer is that God simply foreknew their actions.[23] As we have seen above, *Jubilees* addresses this difficulty by describing Jacob as righteous, the epitome of filial piety and opposite of evil Esau. Of course, there is some difficulty with this response, since Genesis does not portray Jacob as the paradigm of righteousness, particularly in how he plundered Esau's birthright.

Besides arguing for the human person's free will and the responsibility this implies, Chrysostom is also useful for his sense of the Greek text. In Romans 9:14–21, Chrysostom identifies some of the statements that others take as Pauline actually to be from a diatribe partner with whom Paul disagrees. Commentators since the sixteenth century have usually read Romans 9:16, in which a voice in the diatribe claims that only God's mercy matters in one's destiny, not one's will or behaviour, as though it represents Paul's position. Chrysostom correctly identifies this as an objection (ἀντίθεσις) that Paul voices, i.e., an objection that someone other than Paul might say to the line of argument Paul is pursuing.[24] More precisely, this objection is an incorrect inference that someone might draw from Paul's citations of the Isaac over Ishmael, Jacob over Esau examples, as well as God's self-proclaimed right to show mercy. How can we know that this is an incorrect inference at this point in the diatribe? We know this because the assertion that it does not depend on the one who wills or the one who runs does not cohere with Paul's insistence that God will judge people according to their works, which can actually influence one's destiny.[25] Romans 9:16 states that it does not depend on the one who runs, the same verb Paul employs in 1 Corinthians 9:26–27, in which he says that he runs, boxes, and disciplines his body lest he meet with disapproval at the judgement. Later Jewish thinkers would continue to wrestle with the question of how a merciful God still judges according to

---

23 *Hom.* 16 611B (Field, 279–80).
24 *Hom.* 16 613E (Field, 284).
25 Rom 2:5–11; Rom 14:10–12 and Byrne, *Paul and the Economy of Salvation*, 43–172.

works. But even the Talmud's 'and I will have mercy, even if they are not deserving,' does not go as far as Romans 9:16.[26] Paul is typically wary of those who will take one of his teachings to an extreme, and Romans 9:16 is an example of such an extreme, raised in the diatribe.[27] His emphasis on human responsibility in Romans 10:9–21 and 11:21–24 serves in the flow of his argument to correct the imagined conversation partner's false conclusion in Romans 9:16.

Again in the diatribe here, Romans 9:18—more extreme than the Scripture quotation in 9:15 in that it credits hardening to God—is spoken by someone who is taking Paul's insistence on God's right to show mercy to an extreme that Paul does not endorse at any point after this paragraph. This could be the same diatribe partner who speaks in Romans 9:16. Chrysostom labels this also an objection (ἀντίθεσις).[28] The net result of Chrysostom's identification of 9:16,18 as spoken by a dialogue opponent has the effect of softening any deterministic understanding of God's ways with the world. In Romans 2:17–29, the diatribe is not Paul's last word about Israel. Indeed, in the following context he says that Israel has great advantages over the nations (3:1–2). So here as well, whether one agrees with Chrysostom or not that the interlocutor rather than Paul is speaking in 9:16,18, it is clear that the diatribe in chapter 9 is not addressing the predestination of individuals and is not Paul's last word on the election of Israel.

Commentators today do not consistently interpret Romans 9:14–23 as a diatribe, though the paragraph does contain terms characteristic of the diatribe.[29] While Stowers does not go as far as Chrysostom in labelling sentences within 9:14–19 as objections, he does assert that this text does not teach that God arbitrarily elects some over others.

Paul does not raise the questions about God's justice in 9:14 and 19 in order to theoretically defend God or even less in order to say that God acts arbitrarily in his sovereignty. On the contrary, the whole

---

26 I am indebted to Aaron Amit for identifying this parallel in *b. Ber.* 7a.
27 Other examples of Paul's concern to head off extreme developments of his views are Rom 6:1–2,15–18; 14:14–15; 1 Cor 6:12; 8:4–13; 10:23; Gal 5:13.
28 *Hom.* 16 614B (Field, 284).
29 Bultmann, *Der Stil der paulinischen Predigt*, 90.

discussion in 9–11 supposes that God consistently acts for the greater good of those (Israel and the gentile peoples) to whom he has committed himself by promise.[30]

Of course, it would be a mistake to portray all of the Western commentators as opposed to the Eastern fathers' tendency to see prescience rather than predestination here. On Romans 9:12, where Paul suggests that God's choice of Jacob over Esau was simply due to God's call rather than human behavior, Pelagius cites Ezekiel 33:14–15, the text that describes how God will favourably respond to the condemned sinner who repents and lives virtuously, to support his point that God's foreknowledge is not predestination. Even near the end of his life, Jerome is as strong or stronger than Pelagius on the significance of the human's autonomous choice, writing in *Dialogue against the Pelagians* 3.6 that God can choose those whom he knows will turn out good and those who will make wrong choices. Thus the election of God is not determinative of how humans will respond to the invitation. It is possible that Jerome here is opposing Augustine's later teaching on predestination.[31]

Fifth century commentator Theodoret of Cyrrhus follows the approach of Chrysostom, declaring that God extends his promise toward those whom he foreknows will be righteous. He cites Isaac as an example of this, whom he says becomes a type for those who are righteous, since he was more righteous than Ishmael. Then he contends that the same principle explains why God can save some from among the Gentiles. It is because of the foreknowledge God has of the righteous judgement their lives will receive.[32] Even the early Augustine writes in his *Propositions on Romans*—one or two years before responding to Simplicanius's questions—that it is according to God's foreknowledge of someone's faith that election occurs. It is true that when responding to Simplicianus, he drops free will and simple foreknowledge as explanations by asserting that divine grace must precede any human response to God. Decades later, when writing his *Retractions*,

---

30 Stowers, *Rereading*, 300.
31 Scheck note 100 in his translation of Pelagius on Romans 9, citing Squires, 'Jerome on Sinlessness', 703.
32 Cramer, *Catena*, 321–22.

Augustine would mark his response to Simplicianus as the moment when he came to assert God's unilateral election, apart from a human's free will.[33] But still it is instructive for us that in his early reading of Romans, Augustine like the Greek fathers sees God's foreknowledge as the key to this text.

Diodore of Tarsus, who died ca. 390 C.E., explains that when Paul talks about how he chose Jacob over Esau, God foresaw the intentions of each of the brothers. So God's election is according to the human subject's intention; Paul is not talking about a disposition of God that is based on election.[34]

Regarding the 'Who are you to answer back to God?' question, Theodore of Mopsuestia (ca. 350–428 C.E.), interprets this not as a reprimand based on God's almighty power as creator. Rather, Theodore sees it as a rebuke of someone who is blaming God for determining one's life course, rather than taking responsibility to live in such a way that God will save that one. Parmentier regards this line of exegesis as 'an Antiochene invention', summarising what Theodore is saying as an appeal for a person to acknowledge that he or she as a human has great influence over one's life. Theodore goes on to say that the responsibility that a person has for his or her own destiny is seen in 2 Timothy 2:20–21 and 1 Corinthians 3:12.[35]

Conclusion

The rabbis help us see that the texts dealing with God's choice of Isaac over his half-siblings and Jacob over Esau always have Israel's place among the nations in view. This helps us affirm that Paul's foundational question in Romans 9 is how God works with the Jewish nation vis-à-vis the world. It also is strong evidence in support of the fact that Paul, their fellow rabbi, was really concerned about Israel and not about the metaphysics of Western thought, when writing Romans 9–11. The

---

33 *Exp. Quaest. Rom.* on Rom 9:15–21; *Div. Quaest. Simpl.* 1.2.21 (Ramsey, 204–5); *Retract.* 2.1.3 (Ramsey, 169).
34 Staab, *Pauluskommentare*, 98.7–12.
35 Parmentier, 'Greek Church Fathers', 13–14, summarizing from Staab, *Pauluskommentare*, 145.25–146.8.

Greek fathers' focus on the election of individuals in their exegesis of Romans 9 is something we must reject, along with the anti-Semitism that sometimes accompanies their reading of the literal sense of the text. But if we have to say what the spiritual sense of the text indicates about how God relates to humanity, the Greek fathers emphasise the free will of humans, and help us hear Paul's call to use that freedom wisely.

Mark Reasoner
Marian University, Indianapolis

Bibliography

Augustine — *Responses to Miscellaneous Questions* (trans. B. Ramsey; Works of St. Augustine 1.12 New York, NY: Augustine Heritage Institute, 2008).

Brown, P. — *Augustine of Hippo: A Biography* (new edn; Berkeley, CA: University of California Press, 2000).

Bulgakov, S. — *The Sophiology of Death: Essays on Eschatology: Personal, Political, Universal* (trans. R. J. De La Noval; Eugene, OR: Cascade, 2021).

Bultmann, R. — *Der Stil der paulinischen Predigt und die kynisch-stoische Diatribe* (FRLANT 13; Göttingen: Vandenhoeck & Ruprecht, 1910).

Byrne, B., S.J. — *Paul and the Economy of Salvation: Reading from the Perspective of the Last Judgment* (Grand Rapids: Baker Academic, 2021).

Field, F. — *Sancti Patris Nostri Joannis Chrysostomi Archiepiscopi Constantinopolitani in Divi Pauli Epistolam ad Romanos Homiliae XXXIII* (Oxford: J. H. Parker, 1849).

Gorday, P. — *Principles of Patristic Exegesis: Romans 9–11 in Origen, John Chrysostom, and Augustine* (New York, NY: E. Mellen, 1983).

Harrison, J. R. — *Paul's Language of Grace in Its Graeco-Roman Context* (WUNT 2.172; Tübingen: Mohr Siebeck, 2003).

Harrison, J. R. — *Reading Romans with Roman Eyes: Studies on the Social Perspective of Paul* (Lanham, MD: Lexington Books/Fortress Academic, 2020).

Josephus — *Jewish Antiquities Books I–IV* (trans. H. St. J. Thackeray; Loeb Classical Library; London: William Heinemann, 1930).

Mechilta d'Rabbi Ismael cum variis lectionibus et adnotationibus (eds. H. S. Horovitz and I. A. Rabin; 1931; reprint ed. Jerusalem: Shalem, 1997).

Mekhilta de-Rabbi Ishmael: A Critical Edition on the Basis of the Manuscripts and Early Editions with an English Translation, Introduction and Notes. (trans. J. Z. Lauterbach, 3 vols; Philadelphia, PA: Jewish Publication Society of America, 1933, 1935).

	The Mishnah: Translated from the Hebrew with Introduction and Brief Explanatory Notes (trans. H. Danby; Oxford: Oxford University Press, 1933).
Parmentier, M. F. G.	'Greek Church Fathers in Romans 9, pt. 2', *Bijdragen* 51 (1990), 2–20.
Pelagius	*Commentary on Romans* (trans. T. Scheck; 2021, unpublished).
Pseudo-Philo	*The Biblical Antiquities of Philo* (trans. M. R. James; London: SPCK, 1917).
Reasoner, M.	'Israel in the Outline of Romans 9–11', *Letter & Spirit* 10 (2015), 109–29.
Reasoner, M.	'The Salvation of Israel in Romans 9–11', in G. A. Anderson and J. S. Kaminsky (eds.), *The Call of Abraham: Essays on the Election of Israel in Honor of Jon D. Levenson* (Notre Dame: University of Notre Dame Press, 2013), 256–79.
Squires, S.	'Jerome on Sinlessness: A Via Media between Augustine and Pelagius', *HeyJ* 57 (2016), 697–709.
Staab, K.	*Pauluskommentare aus der griechischen Kirche: Aus Katenenhandschriften* (2nd edn; Münster: Aschendorff, 1984).
Stowers, S. K.	*A Rereading of Romans: Justice, Jews, and Gentiles* (New Haven, CT: Yale University Press, 1994).
Wintermute, O. S.	'Jubilees: A New Translation and Introduction', in J.H. Charlesworth (ed.), *Old Testament Pseudepigrapha* (Garden City, NY: Doubleday, 1985), 35–142.

Can Faith Be Measured?
Paul's Phrase 'The Measure of Faith' Reconsidered (Rom. 12:3)

Benjamin Schliesser

Abstract

Understanding what Paul means by 'the measure of faith' (Rom. 12:3) involves significant theological issues. This essay discusses four options, namely, the measure of charismatic faith; justifying faith; the norm to follow; or trusteeship, before proposing it to be a dynamic measure of a believer being in faith and contemplating some ecclesiological and theological consequences.

In the final section of his Letter to the Romans (Rom. 12:1—15:13), Paul talks about the consequences of his teaching for the Roman believers' way of life.[1] Before he takes a robust stance in the dispute between the 'strong' and the 'weak' (14:1—15:13),[2] he begins with a principal exhortation akin to a preamble that defines the fundamental relationship of believers to God and to the world. He then conveys a

---

1 An earlier version of this paper was presented at a conference at Oriel College (Oxford) under the auspices of the John Templeton Foundation project 'Trust in God', and I am grateful to the insightful discussion with the members of the research group. An important stimulus was Jim Harrison, who graciously invited me to contribute to the reference work *Ancient Literature for New Testament Study* (ALNTS) on '*Pistis* in Papyri and Inscriptions'. The present contribution, therefore, is a token of gratitude to Jim Harrison for his collegiality and friendship throughout the past years. His breadth of scholarship, which always keeps an eye on German- and French-speaking scholarship, and his concern to integrate historical, exegetical, and theological questions are inspiring. Thanks is owed to Dr. Travis Niles for improving the English style of this article.

2 On my interpretation of this section, see Schliesser, 'Konfliktmanagement'.

vigorous appeal 'spoken with prophetic authority or the authority of divine revelation' (cf. Gal. 1:9; 5:2)[3] and addressed to every single person among the Roman Christ-followers (Rom. 12:3, παντὶ τῷ ὄντι ἐν ὑμῖν). With rhetorical finesse, he plays with the word stem φρον-. This kind of paronomasia is frequently attested in Hellenistic prose.[4] The verbs σωφρονεῖν and ὑπερφρονεῖν form an antithesis: a 'wholesome' thinking and a 'self-overestimating' thinking are mutually exclusive. The cardinal virtue of 'prudence' (σωφροσύνη) shapes the thinking and striving of believers within the community.[5]

In the programmatic sentences in the beginning of his letter (Rom. 1:16–17), Paul had already made clear that πίστις is the linchpin and at the same time the point of contention of his deliberations. 'Faith'— even more so than the 'gospel' or 'righteousness' or 'salvation'—is the focal point of Paul's theological agenda: 'faith' binds together all the individual statements.[6] It is no surprise, therefore, that the readers of Paul's letter encounter πίστις in crucial statements and at all pivotal turns of thought. This is true also for our passage: Paul places his exhortations in the light of 'faith'. His wording, however, has puzzled interpreters throughout the centuries. He admonishes the Roman Christ-followers to 'think with sober judgement, each according to the μέτρον πίστεως that God has assigned' (Rom. 12:3, NRSV).

How should we understand the phrase 'measure of faith'? Is faith quantifiable? Do believers have different amounts of faith? What kind of 'faith' does Paul have in view here?

The most differentiated, albeit rather brief, treatment of the genitive compound μέτρον πίστεως was written by Charles Cranfield sixty years ago.[7] His list of interpretative options needs to be updated in

---

3 Dunn, *Romans 9–16*, 720.
4 See, e.g., Cranfield, *Romans*, 612.
5 Paul's disapproval of the ὑπερφρονεῖν echoes his warning to the Gentiles against falling into self-conceit in relation to the Jews: μὴ ὑψηλὰ φρόνει (Rom. 11:20).
6 Theobald, 'Der "strittige Punkt"', 283. I am well aware of the problems associated with the use of the term 'faith' as translation for πίστις, and I hope that my study of the phrase μέτρον πίστεως will also clarify its semantics.
7 Cranfield, 'ΜΕΤΡΟΝ ΠΙΣΤΕΩΣ'; Cranfield, *Romans*, 613-16.

view of the ongoing exegetical discussion and his conclusions need to be revised accordingly. Nevertheless, in his detailed analysis, he plays through each of the exegetical variables. I will draw here on Cranfield and add some nuances: What does Paul mean by the term μέτρον: 'quantifiable measure', 'standard' or 'norm', or 'limitation'? What is the sense of πίστις: 'charismatic faith', 'the faith by which one believes' (*fides qua*), 'the propositional content of faith' (*fides quae*), 'trust', 'trustworthiness', or 'trusteeship'? How is the genitive πίστεως to be determined? Addressing these questions is more than useless philological nitpicking; important theological issues are involved.

Possible and plausible combinations are manifold, but four serious options crystallise.[8] The expression μέτρον πίστεως could denote (1) the quantifiable measure of charismatic faith, which includes, for instance, the faith that moves mountains (partitive genitive); (2) the quantifiable measure of justifying faith or trust, which comes to each believer in a distinguishable form and quantity (partitive genitive); (3) the absolute measure, the norm which believers should follow, (genitive of apposition); and (4) the measure of trusteeship, according to which God confers on each one an individually measured portion (genitive of apposition). My own suggestion, (5) the dynamic measure with respect to a believer's being 'in faith', critically develops and reworks the mentioned options and (6) contemplates some noteworthy ecclesiological and theological consequences.

1. Charismatic Faith

Theophylact, archbishop of Ochrid and influential exegete of the 11th century, has interpreted πίστις against the backdrop of mountain-moving faith as the gift of a miracle-working faith. He expressly distinguishes between miraculous faith and justifying faith:

> [Paul] calls faith here a gift through which they worked miracles (ἐθαυματούργουν). Faith, in fact, is twofold ('Η γὰρ πίστις διττή): the one is ours, as in "Your faith has

---

8   Cranfield, 'ΜΕΤΡΟΝ ΠΙΣΤΕΩΣ', 347, lists a total of eight options.

healed you", the other is a gift of God through which there are also miracles, as in "If you have faith like a grain of mustard seed, say to this mountain, Transfer there, and it will be transferred."[9]

Accordingly, Paul is not talking (as usual) about justifying faith, but rather about a specific charismatic faith.

This view has been put forward very prominently by Theodor Zahn in his commentary on Romans. He argued that what is meant is 'not the faith which makes just and blessed, but the faith which Paul has placed under the χαρίσματα, the gifts wrought by the Spirit in the church in the field of natural life'. Saving faith

> may be called for as a trustful obedience to the gracious will of God, and has for its exclusionary antithesis sinful ἀπιστία and ἀπείθεια; however, faith as a charisma, like all other charismata, is merely a gift, which may well be asked for, cultivated, or neglected, but which cannot be enforced on oneself nor demanded from others, like the gift of prophecy or speaking in tongues or miraculous prayer. These two kinds of πίστις are related in that the charismatic faith, like the other charismatic gifts, is reserved for the community of believers and can be received only in connection with it.[10]

This type of interpretation, which has found quite a number of notable advocates,[11] must assume that some believers have received the miraculous 'special faith', whereas others have not. This contradicts the address of the appeal to all church members (παντὶ τῷ ὄντι ἐν ὑμῖν) and the statement that God has assigned the 'measure of faith' to everyone (ἑκάστῳ). It is not a special privilege, but a gift that belongs

---

9   Theophylact, *ad Romanos*, 501. Cf. already in this sense (Pseudo-)Oecumenius, *ad Romanos*, 565.
10 Zahn, *Römer*, 542 (with reference to 1Cor. 12:9 and 13:2).
11 See, e.g., Lagrange, *Romains*, 296: 'Il semble que Paul ... fasse ici allusion à une certaine plénitude de foi confiante capable d'opérer des actions surnaturelles; c'est la foi dont il est question I Cor. XII, 9; XIII, 2, où elle paraît nettement comme un don particulier'. Michel, *Römer*, 373, 375.

to all believers according to an individual measure. Furthermore, the interpretation presupposes that Rom. 12:3–8 is an 'admonition to the charismatics',[12] which is more than doubtful.

2. Justifying Faith or Trust

The interpretation (and at the same time limitation) of πίστις in the sense of an individually apportioned 'charismatic faith' has been criticised by Ernst Kühl and others as 'much too narrow for this comprehensive, general statement'.[13] A statement about the charisma 'faith' is ill-suited as a heading for a section on charismatic gifts as a whole. Rather, according to this criticism, the allotment of 'faith' parallels the gift of 'grace' (Rom. 12:6, κατὰ τὴν χάριν τὴν δοθεῖσαν). Thus, both πίστις and χάρις are superior categories compared to the individual charismatic gifts: 'all χαρίσματα have [...] in it [sc. faith] their source, their power, and their measure'.[14] Kühl concludes that Paul speaks of πίστις at this point in terms of saving faith. 'The stronger the saving faith, the greater the charismatic abilities: but all are given by God through grace'.[15]

Within the framework of her relational understanding of πίστις, which focuses on human trust and faithfulness, Teresa Morgan comes to a comparable conclusion:

> In an unusual phrase in chapter 12, Paul tells the Romans to 'think soberly, each according to μέτρον πίστεως apportioned by God' (12.3). [...] [T]his phrase, in context, surely refers to different quantities of *pistis* which God has apportioned [...] to different people as a gift or grace (12.6) and which allow them to exercise different ministries (12.6–8). *Pistis* here can be read straightforwardly as 'trust/faithfulness', the fundamental quality that allows one to become part of the body of Christ (12.5). Equally interesting for present purposes, and less discussed, is the

---

12 Michel, *Römer*, 373.
13 Kühl, *Römer*, 422.
14 Kühl, *Römer*, 422.
15 Kühl, *Römer*, 422.

next occurrence of *pistis* in this chapter, where Paul says that if our gift is for prophecy, κατὰ τὴν ἀναλογίαν τῆς πίστεως, 'in proportion to *pistis*', then we should practise it (12.6). This suggests that the stronger the trust of the faithful in God, the more strongly they may feel moved to communicate it to others, as a form of 'living (self) sacrifice' (12.1).[16]

Allowing for different grades of strength, Morgan explicitly sets herself apart from Cranfield's interpretation, which was dominating the discussion after he had published his aforementioned essay as well as his commentary and which gained ground even in the German-speaking world due to Ulrich Wilckens's commentary on Romans. Both object the view that πίστις refers to justifying faith or trust, and their objection should not be dismissed out of hand: Paul nowhere speaks of strong or weak faith and he does not define different quantities of faith or trust in terms of individual qualities. We will return to the question of how Paul differentiates modes of existence in πίστις. But first we give the floor to Cranfield and Wilckens.

3. Absolute Measure of Faith

Cranfield and Wilckens contend that the assumption of an individual intensity or quantifiable measure of faith is 'extremely unlikely'[17] and 'simply impossible'.[18] If this were Paul's intention, he would open the door to all sorts of (im)pious introspection and self-examination, which is poisonous for community life.[19] Both Cranfield and Wilckens therefore suggest that μέτρον should not be interpreted quantitatively but absolutely, as 'norm' or 'criterion'. The word 'πίστις either refers

---

16 Morgan, *Roman Faith*, 298–99. More recently, Morgan sympathises with the view presented as 'Measure of Trusteeship' (see below).
17 Cranfield, *Romans*, 614: 'It is surely extremely unlikely that Paul intended to imply this'.
18 Wilckens, *Römer*, 11.
19 Cf. Cranfield, *Shorter Commentary*, 300. 'A congregation, the members of which were carefully calculating their relative importance according to the amount of faith (of either sort) which they possessed, would have little chance of being a happy one'.

to the *fides quae creditur* or *fides qua creditur* in the sense that faith is given to every Christian as the standard for all conduct' (cf. Rom. 12:6).[20] The genitive is not to be understood as a partitive genitive, but as a genitive of apposition: Every Christian has received the same (saving) faith, and this faith is the standard which everyone needs to follow. The phrase 'ἑκάστῳ ὡς does not mean a measure of faith that is different in each individual case, but the one measure by which the charismata, each different from the other, are measured with a view as to how they are each brought to bear in Christian life'.[21]

In his *Shorter Commentary*, Cranfield summarises this view:

> [T]he sense of the verse is that every member of the church, instead of thinking of himself more highly than he ought, is so to think of himself as to think soberly, measuring himself by the standard which God has given him in his faith, that is, by a standard which forces him to concentrate his attention on those things in which he is on precisely the same level as his fellow Christians rather than on those things in which he may be either superior or inferior to them – for the standard Paul has in mind consists [...] not in the relative strength or otherwise of the particular Christian's faith but in the simple fact of its existence, that is, in the fact of his admission of his dependence on, and commitment to, Jesus Christ.[22]

In his earlier publication, Cranfield stated even more pointedly: 'The μέτρον πίστεως is really Jesus Christ himself as the Standard and Norm'.[23]

---

20 Wilckens, *Römer*, 11f. Cranfield, *Romans*, 615, suggests that *fides qua creditur* is meant.
21 Wilckens, *Römer*, 12.
22 Cranfield, *Shorter Commentary*, 300–301. Cf. Cranfield, *Romans*, 616: 'We conclude then that μέτρον πίστεως means "a standard (by which to measure, estimate, himself), namely, (his) faith"; but at the same time note that this does not mean that Paul is bidding the believer to estimate himself according to his fluctuating subjective feelings and personal opinions but that he is bidding him to estimate himself according to his God-given relation to Christ'.
23 Cranfield, 'ΜΕΤΡΩΝ ΠΙΣΤΕΩΣ', 351.

Cranfield's interpretation is a case in point that even a meticulous philological analysis is not immune to the influence of underlying theological presuppositions and preferences. What cannot be true according to certain dogmatic presuppositions—namely, that Paul has in mind individual portions of πίστις—is not true. As we will see below, the closest analogy to Paul's phrase in Romans 12:3 is 2 Corinthians 10:13, where Paul speaks of different spheres of missionary action, which God has apportioned. The verb μερίζειν clearly has distributive function. But before expanding on this parallel, we now turn to a view that was dominant for centuries: μέτρον πίστεως as measure of trusteeship.

4. Measure of Trusteeship

According to some of the earliest commentators, μέτρον πίστεως denotes the measure by which God has entrusted a believer with a gift. In the oldest extant commentary on Romans, written by Origen in the middle of the third century and translated by Rufinus in the beginning of the fifth, we already find this notion. After quoting the phrase, Origen explains: 'This means that each should know and understand what the measure of the grace of God is in himself, the measure that he has merited to attain through faith'. He lists specific gifts, such as being wise or showing mercy to the poor, and says: 'God has allotted each of these things to each one in accordance with their measure of faith'. Everyone should be aware of their respective gifts and not strive for those that God has not allocated to them.[24] We find a similar line of thought in Chrysostom's Homilies on Romans, probably preached in Antioch in the late fourth century. He records that Paul is speaking of πίστις as an entrusted good that God has apportioned, and he finds a pastoral point in this: as God is the agent, those who have received a lesser good are comforted and those who see themselves in possession

---

24 Origen, *ad Romanos* 9,2,12 (trans. Scheck).

of a greater good are repudiated.²⁵ God 'consoles the one who had the less, and humbles the one who had the greater share'.²⁶

This type of interpretation has been revived in current discussion. It is striking that these more recent new studies almost entirely ignore the comments of the church fathers, which had been authoritative well into the nineteenth century.²⁷ They argue that Paul means 'the entrusting of a gift or the entrusting of a task',²⁸ 'every man's measure of responsibility',²⁹ 'the measure of stewardship',³⁰ or 'the measure of a trusteeship'.³¹ John Goodrich, for instance, holds that 'that μέτρον πίστεως in Romans 12:3 refers to the believer's charism, addressed shortly and explicitly thereafter in 12:6'.³² According to Klaus Haacker, Romans 12:6 resumes the idea of being entrusted with regard to the gift of prophecy: those who received the gift of prophecy are urged to be prolific with their 'credit' and to use their gift for the benefit of the church, but at the same time they are warned against 'overdrawing their account', that is, against 'going beyond the messages entrusted to them by God and passing off their own desires and thoughts as proph-

---

25 Chrysostom, *ad Romanos* 21,3 (PG 60, 599): πίστιν ἐνταῦθα τὸ χάρισμα καλῶν. Cf. almost verbatim Theodoret of Cyrus, *Interpretatio* (PG 82, 188): Τὴν χάριν ἐνταῦθα πίστιν ἐκάλεσε. In the remainder of his remarks, Chrysostom does consider an alternative view, according to which πίστις denotes the faith through which miracles occur. This clue is taken up by Theophylact whose exegesis is oftentimes dependent on Chrysostom. Cf. Tholuck, *Römer*, 656, with further references to early church authors, e.g., Theodore of Mopsuestia and Photius.
26 Chrysostom, *ad Romanos* 21,3 (PG 60, 599).
27 Tholuck, *Römer*, 656, notes that this explanation, with some modifications, has remained the prevailing one until recent times. Cf., for instance, Baumgarten-Crusius, *Römer*, 345: 'Πίστις bezeichnet hier [...] ohne Zweifel die Geistesgabe (χάρισμα), nach der *objektiven* Bedeutung des Wortes *Anvertrautes* (πεπιστευμένον)'. Wolter, *Römer*, 265, who otherwise offers a fine interpretation of the phrase, writes that this interpretation has been added 'in recent years'.
28 Haacker, *Römer*, 303.
29 Black, *Romans*, 169.
30 Poirier, 'Measure of Stewardship'. Cf. Vanhoye, 'Problematic Reception'.
31 Goodrich, '"Standard of Faith"'. See the response Porter/Ong, '"Standard of Faith"' and the rejoinder Goodrich, 'Interpretation'.
32 Goodrich, '"Standard of Faith"', 753.

ecy.'[33] Teresa Morgan has revised her aforementioned interpretation and now holds that 'Paul could be referring here to the different degrees to which community members are entrusted: some with heavier responsibilities, such as apostolacy, and others with lighter'.[34]

No doubt there is plenty of literary and documentary evidence that πίστις and πιστεύειν can be used in the meaning of 'trusteeship' and 'to entrust', respectively. As Goodrich has shown in his analysis of Dio Chrysostom's discourse Περὶ Πίστεως, a trusteeship could consist 'of the formalization of a party's confidence in an individual by committing to him/her care of and responsibility for various persons, possessions, and/or tasks'.[35] The responsibilities associated with trusteeships came along with great cost for leaders and functionaries, and oftentimes 'the responsibility was irrevocable'.[36] Goodrich rightly refers to the expression ἐγχειρίζειν πίστιν, which appears in many inscriptions.[37] Notably, a comprehensive analysis of inscriptions containing πίστις and πιστεύειν is still lacking.[38]

The well-known honorific decree found on a stela from the city of Sestos in Thrace (c. 133–120 B.C.E.) (*OGIS* 339 = I. Sestos 1) honours the gymnasiarch Menas for his generosity to the gymnasium of Sestos, commending the remarkable civic loyalty of Menas, as he 'devoutly guarded the responsibilities (πίστεις) that were entrusted to him' (*OGIS* 339, ll. 11–12: τάς τ' ἐνχειρι[σ]- | θείσας ἑαυτῶι πίστεις).[39] Numerous inscriptions from Delphi document a so-called 'sacral manumission',[40]

---

33 Haacker, *Römer*, 305. Cf. ἐπιστεύθησαν in Rom. 3:2 (alongside 1 Cor. 9:17; 1 Thess. 2:4; Gal. 2:7).
34 Morgan, *Theology of Trust*, 298–99.
35 Goodrich, '"Standard of Faith"', 764.
36 Goodrich, '"Standard of Faith"', 767.
37 Goodrich, '"Standard of Faith"', 763–4 note 41.
38 See, for an overview, Schliesser, '*Pistis*', from which I adapt the following sections.
39 Danker, *Benefactor*, §17, provides a translation.
40 Traditionally, among private manumissions, scholars distinguish between 'secular manumissions', which remain in the civic sphere, and 'sacral manumissions', which involve the agency of the god.

using πιστεύειν in the sense of 'to entrust'.[41] The following is typical, as it contains the core formulaic elements (*SGDI* II 1685.1–5)[42]:

> Under the archonship of Thrasykleos, in the month of Herakleios, Athambos son of Athanion sold (ἀπέδοτο) to Pythian Apollo a female slave [lit. a female body] named Harmodika, from Elateia by origin, at the price of six silver minae, and he [sc. Athambos] received the whole price, since Harmodika entrusted (ἐπίστευσε) the purchase money to the god [sc. Apollo], under the condition that she is free and not to be claimed [as a slave] by anyone forever, and she can do whatever she wants and go wherever she wants. Guarantors according to the law of the city.

In these manumission records, the god acts as a broker for a slave, who cannot act as a party of a legal transaction. She has to entrust (πιστεύειν) her money to the god who in this legal play would hand it over to her master Athambos on her behalf. When the slave entrusts the money to the god, she trusts that he will fulfil his responsibility and transfer the money so that the manumission may be legally valid.

The reciprocal dynamics of entrusting someone with a gift and trusting in their responsible dealing with this gift also resonates in Paul's letters: he affirms that the Jews have been 'entrusted' with the oracles of God (Rom. 3:2: ἐπιστεύθησαν), and he describes himself as 'entrusted' with the gospel (1 Cor. 9:17; Gal. 2:7: πεπίστευμαι; 1 Thess. 2:4: πιστευθῆναι).[43] The linguistic problem remains, however, that Paul nowhere uses the noun πίστις in the sense of trusteeship or entrustedness in an unequivocal way.[44] Nevertheless, the idea of apos-

---

41 In Delphi, over 1200 manumissions are attested in around 1000 inscriptions, spanning from the beginning of the second century B.C.E. to the late first century C.E. Around 900 occurrences of the verb πιστεύειν have been verified. Cf. Mulliez, 'Les actes d'affranchissement delphiques'.
42 See, e.g., Lewis and Zanovello, 'Freedmen/Freedwomen'.
43 Morgan, *Theology of Trust*, 43: 'To be entrusted with something, in any sphere of life from politics to law, commerce, or cult, is an honourable and responsible position [...], but it is normally a means to an end, not an end in itself'.
44 Conceded also in Goodrich, '"Standard of Faith"', 754 note 4. See, however, Morgan, *Theology of Trust*, 283–91.

tolic entrustedness opens up a promising avenue for a further and final reflection on the phrase μέτρον πίστεως, starting from the parallel expression 2 Corinthians 10:13.

5. Individuality and Dynamics in Faith

In all of Paul's letters, there is only one parallel to the idea that God assigns a certain measure to a person: 2 Corinthians 10:13–16.[45] Here too, μέτρον is the direct object of μερίζειν. In his defensive speech against the attacks of his opponents, Paul mentions 'the measure of the sphere of action, which God has assigned to us as a measure' (τὸ μέτρον τοῦ κανόνος οὗ ἐμέρισεν ἡμῖν ὁ θεὸς μέτρου) (2 Cor. 10:13); by following this assignment, he had reached as far as Corinth, 'as far as you' (ἐφικέσθαι ἄχρι καὶ ὑμῶν). He stresses that his missionary activity is not based on his own commendation, but rather on the Lord's (2 Cor. 10:18). He is convinced that the fulfilment of the divine assignment, i.e., the missionary work in the geographical area that God has marked out for him, will bring him glory before God. However, he does not presume to take credit for areas in which he is not engaged in missionary work, for that would be going 'beyond proper limits' (2 Cor. 10:13,15, εἰς τὰ ἄμετρα). At the same time, he does not seem to assume that the boundaries of his field of activity are fixed unalterably. Rather, he seeks to evangelise beyond his previous territory, which for now extends to Corinth only (2 Cor. 10:16, εἰς τὰ ὑπερέκεινα ὑμῶν εὐαγγελίσασθαι).[46] The polyvalent noun κανών therefore carries both a spatial-geographical and an administrative connotation and should best be translated as 'assignment'.[47]

This corresponds to a noteworthy instance of κανών in a bilingual inscription from the region of Sagalassos in Pisidia from the beginning of the first century A.D. First published in 1976, it was Edwin Judge who five years later commented insightfully on its relevance for the

---

45 Noted also, for instance, in Jewett, *Romans*, 742; Goodrich, '"Standard of Faith"', 759–60.
46 If Paul already has certain regions in mind, he could be thinking of Spain (cf. Rom. 15:24, 28). Cf. Thrall, *II Corinthians VIII-XIII*, 651–52.
47 Cf. Kowalski, *Transforming Boasting*, 155.

'crux of Paul's *kanon*' in 2 Corinthians 10:13–16.[48] The edict of the provincial governor 'regulates travel in the area and seeks to protect locals against abuses by those using the imperial post'.[49] The governor defined responsibilities for transport services. The governor declares: 'I have promulgated in the individual cities and villages a schedule of what I judge desirable to be supplied' (SEG 26.1392 l. 29, κατὰ πόλιν καὶ κώμην ἔταξα κανόνα τῶν ὑπηρεσιῶν).[50] As Judge argued, κανών is 'the official schedule, in this case of the transport services to be supplied by the local community … The κανών in itself is not a geographical concept, but the services it formulates are in this case geographically partitioned'.[51] Paul and other protagonists in early Christian missions might well have been aware of such notices and applied it to the idea of their respective 'territorially-defined schedule of duties'.[52] In his quarrel with his opponents, Paul affirms that he acts on the basis of God's assignment and that he has no intention to go beyond his territorial commitment. As he serves within the limits of his responsibilities, he is convinced to receive due honour (2 Cor. 10:13,15–17), though he also makes clear that such limits are flexible and can be expanded (2 Cor. 10:16).

In my view, the linguistic parallel from 2 Corinthians 10:13, read against the backdrop of the Pisidian inscription, can help us to grasp the meaning of μέτρον πίστεως in Romans 12:3. To be sure, πίστις is not a geographical concept—κανών isn't either—but it is intriguing to play with the idea that Paul has in mind a sphere of πίστις in which believers act out their respective measure. God assigns to every believer a certain 'field of action', an 'area of responsibility' which they have to accept and to which they ought to adapt themselves. The spatial dimension that characterises Pauline missionary activity is also a char-

---

48 Cf. Judge, 'Regional κανών', 44.
49 Nasrallah, *Archaeology*, 94–5.
50 Note that the translation is based on the original Latin version, which has *formula* (l. 5) where the Greek reads κανών.
51 Judge, 'Regional κανών', 45. Judge's interpretation is accepted, e.g., by Thrall, *II Corinthians VIII-XIII*, 635, 647; Kowalski, *Transforming Boasting*, 202 note 58.
52 Thrall, *II Corinthians VIII-XIII*, 647.

acteristic of faith:⁵³ figuratively speaking, from the whole of faith, an individually measured section is assigned to the individual. It is crucial to go to the limits set by God, but not beyond these limits in unrestrained hubris (ὑπερφρονεῖν). Other believers also move in the space of faith, and there are overlapping 'territories'. Introspection at one's own 'measure of faith' (whether self-overestimating or self-shaming) is as detrimental as the evaluative sideways glances at other 'measures of faith'; it is more important to pay attention to the faith which a person has before God, as Paul would explain later on (cf. Rom. 14:22). But inasmuch as the boundaries of Paul's missionary territory are not fixed once and for all, believers should also strive beyond their area of faith as faith is able to 'grow' (2 Cor. 10:15).

The concrete realisation of the 'measure of faith' in individual life and in the community of believers, the way someone moves in the sphere of faith, is of a dynamic nature. Paul is aware of the existential and historical side of faith, and he reflects on the 'differences conditioned by individual gifts and situations'.⁵⁴ In the context of 2 Corinthians 10:13–16, Paul speaks of the Corinthians 'growing in faith' (αὐξανομένης τῆς πίστεως ὑμῶν, 2 Cor. 10:15). It is quite conceivable that the description of his missionary activity as one stretched to the limit is congruent with his thoughts of growing in faith. Earlier, Paul had attested to the Corinthians that they 'excel in everything', including their faith (2 Cor. 8:7, ἐν παντὶ περισσεύετε, πίστει ...). To the Thessalonians, he writes that he would finally pay them a visit to supplement the 'deficiencies of their faith' (1 Thess. 3:10, τὰ ὑστερήματα τῆς πίστεως ὑμῶν). He probably does not mean a defect that must disappear in order that perfection may be attained,⁵⁵ for 'perfection of faith' is not a category in Paul's thought and thus not the goal of his mission.⁵⁶ Rather, he seems to be concerned that through his apostolic presence, the Thessalonian believers be given the chance to

---

53 Referring to Rom. 12:3, Binder, *Glaube*, 58, programmatically speaks of faith as a 'topological' or 'oikological' entity: 'Sie [sc. πίστις] hat eine meßbare Ausdehnung (Röm. 12,3), sie nimmt einen Raum ein.'
54 Bultmann, 'πιστεύω κτλ.', 219, with reference to Rom. 12:3.
55 Cf. B-A, ὑστέρημα, 1692.
56 Quite differently, for instance, Hermas, mand., 5,2,3: τὴν πίστιν ἔχειν ὁλόκληρον.

fill out and expand their 'measure of faith'.

In two passages in Paul's letter to the Romans, we encounter the motif of 'becoming weak' or 'being weak in faith' (Rom. 4:19; 14:1). By stating that Abraham did not 'grow weak in faith' (μὴ ἀσθενήσας τῇ πίστει, Rom. 4:19), Paul indicates that the father of faith—though cognitively perceiving the biological toll of ageing (κατενόησεν)—remained steadfast in faith, and that his strength within the sphere of faith did not diminish even in the face of adverse circumstances. The case of the one who is weak in faith (Rom. 14:1, ὁ ἀσθενὴς τῇ πίστει) is somewhat different, for here Paul seems to assume that 'weakness' refers to a limited area of individual faith. To stay in the metaphor: For the 'weak' in faith, the phrase 'that nothing is unclean in itself' (Rom. 14:14) is beyond his currently allotted sphere. Paul does not refrain from saying that transcending this realm is possible and desirable. But he does not reproach the 'weak one' for not venturing to transcend this boundary at the moment. After all, according to Romans 12:3, it is up to God to set the limits for the individual.

6. Ecclesiological and Theological Afterthoughts

According to Paul, God is the origin and giver of the power experienced in πίστις not only in a believer's conversion, but also remains the subject of growing (2 Cor. 10:15), of flourishing (1 Thess. 3:13), of becoming strong (Rom. 4:20), and of the individual measure (Rom. 12.3).[57] The 'measure of faith' received by each believer is embraced by divine activity, related to the contingencies of life, and operative in the manifold areas of Christian existence: knowledge and ethical judgment (Rom. 14:1—15:13), trust (Rom. 4:19), the acceptance of certain propositions of faith (*fides quae*; cf. 1 Thess. 3:10; 2 Cor. 10:15), confession (Rom. 10:9–10; 1 Thess. 3:13), miraculous activity (1 Cor. 13:2), and spiritual gifts (Rom. 12:6) are differentiated according to the specific measure of faith.

In his almost forgotten commentary, August Meyer insightfully

---

57 Cf. von Dobbeler, *Glaube als Teilhabe*, 237.

reflected on the practicalities of variegated 'faith':

> This is the subjective condition [...] of that which everyone can and ought to do in the Christian life of the church. According, namely, as faith in the case of individual Christians is more or less living, practical, energetic, efficacious in this or that direction, – whether contemplative, or manifesting itself in the outer life, in eloquence and action, etc., – they have withal to measure their appointed position and task in the church. He, therefore, who covets a higher or another standpoint and sphere of activity in the community, and is not contented with that which corresponds to the measure of faith bestowed on him, evinces a wilful self-exaltation, which is without measure and not of God [...]. The πίστις is therefore to be taken throughout in no other sense than the ordinary one: *faith in Christ*, of which the essence indeed is alike in all, but the individually different *degrees of strength* (comp. 1 Cor. xiii.2), and *peculiarities of character* in other respects (vv. 4 ff.), constitute for individuals the μέτρον πίστεως in quantitative and qualitative relation.[58]

Paul does not differentiate between different kinds of faith or separate areas of faith, such as 'charismatic faith' or 'saving faith', but takes for granted that the *one* faith, πίστις Χριστοῦ, encompasses and takes shape in all areas of life. Those who are 'in Christ' and have their identity defined by the Christ-event actively participate in the space of faith in the way intended for them individually. Paul does not shy away from quantifying a person's individual 'extension' in the realm of faith. However, he warns against two intertwined misconceptions: the first is to overestimate oneself and one's own possibilities at the expense of the community. According to Paul, such behaviour falls under the rubric of 'sin'.

---

58 Meyer, *Romans*, 470–71.

> Sin arises [...] when one goes beyond the gift of God, instead of attending to one's own μέτρον πίστεως, and thus falls into ὑπερφρονεῖν. Faith is a concrete orientation to the lordship of Christ which grasps it, which in its breadth leaves room for the particularities of the members, which does not impose uniformity.[59]

The second misconception is to declare one's own measure of faith to be the 'measure of all things' and to impose it on the other believers, putting at risk the unity of the community.[60] Whoever acts in this way thwarts the other's relationship to God and risks divisions in the community. The fact that individual members of the Roman church fell victim to both dangers and got into disputes over differently formatted measures of faith is shown in Romans 14:1—15:13.

For Paul, being a believer means being 'in Christ' (ἐν Χριστῷ) and being 'in faith' (ἐν πίστει). There are two ways, and only two ways, to relate to Christ-faith (πίστις Χριστοῦ): one either participates in it or one does not; one is either inside or outside. In Paul's world of thought, there is no being in between, no being torn back and forth, no wavering between 'yes' and 'no'. And yet Paul does not lump believers together. There is an individuality in faith, insofar as God apportions to all believers their respective 'measure of faith'. Experience confirms—in Paul's time as well as ours[61]—that not everyone believes and trusts in the same measure, and that not everyone is entrusted with gifts and responsibilities in the same measure. The personal history of individual believers affects the actual intensity of their πίστις. Paul does not disregard the existentiality of faith, and he frequently has in mind 'the living and dynamic aspect of faith rather than the mere fact'.[62] The dynamism and differentiation of faith affects, in fact, all areas of life. In various places in Paul's letters, dimensions shine forth

---

59 Käsemann, *Romans*, 379.
60 Cf. Jewett, *Romans*, 742.
61 Cf. Dunn, *Theology*, 557 note 137: 'By "the measure of faith" Paul probably refers to different apportionments of faith; it is the same faith/trust, but experience then (as now) no doubt confirmed that not all trusted to the same extent'.
62 Bultmann, 'πιστεύω κτλ.', 212.

that have an ethical or epistemological (Rom. 14:1), fiducial (Rom. 4:19), doxastic (1 Thess. 3:10; 2 Cor. 10:15), confessional (Rom. 10:9–10; 1 Thess. 3:13), thaumaturgical (1 Cor. 13:2), charismatic (Rom. 12:6), and possibly even physical (Rom. 4:20) emphasis.[63]

Only a dogmatically biased view of faith will consider the idea of an individually assigned measure of faith 'simply impossible'.[64] Believers differ in the way in which they participate in faith and how they move in the space of faith; they have received an individual quantum of faith, linked to specific purposes and responsibilities. There is a negative determination of πίστις insofar as no one has full or perfect faith, and there is a positive determination of πίστις insofar as everyone is entrusted with a particular share.[65] Paul does not praise the 'strong in faith' for their strength and neither rebukes the 'weak in faith' for their weakness. Rather, he calls the (supposedly) strong to self-examination: 'So if you think you are standing, watch out that you do not fall' (1 Cor. 10:12), because strength in faith never becomes a possession of the believer. It remains dependent on God, who gives the 'measure of faith'. The (supposedly) weak should remember: 'And they will be upheld, for the Lord is able to make them stand' (Rom. 14:4).

Let me conclude with a significant insight of the jubilarian, which he expressed in his introduction to the 2017 reprint edition of his seminal study *Paul's Language of Grace in its Graeco-Roman Context*:

> [T]he study of grace in systematic and biblical theologies had remained for a very long while caught in a "time warp"

---

63 Jewett's comments are even more far-reaching, *Romans*, 742: 'There are political, ideological, racial, and temperamental components that are legitimately connected with faith, comprising the peculiar "measuring rod" that each person in the church been given. By making these unique faith relationships the "measure of all things", so to speak, Paul defines "sober-mindedness" as the refusal to impose the standard of one's own relationship with God onto others. The same thought is reiterated in 14:4, 22–23 in the admonition not to interfere with the faith relationships that other believers have with the Lord. This verse therefore stands as a bulwark against elitist conceptions of "divine-men", superleaders and geniuses who claim precedence over others because of their gifts and benefactions'.
64 Wilckens, *Römer*, 11.
65 Cf. Tholuck, *Römer*, 658.

of Reformation dogmatics and has only recently been substantially challenged by the 'New Perspective' [...] For too long there has been a disinclination on the part of theological exegetes to enter sympathetically and imaginatively into the struggles of mid-first-century Roman believers when they heard Paul's papyrus letter being read out aloud for the first time in their house churches.[66]

What is true for our reflection on 'grace'[67] is also true for 'faith'.[68]

Benjamin Schliesser
University of Bern

---

[66] Harrison, *Grace*, xx.
[67] Cf. Rom. 12:6: κατὰ τὴν χάριν τὴν δοθεῖσαν ἡμῖν.
[68] Cf. Rom. 12:3: ὁ θεὸς ἐμέρισεν μέτρον πίστεως.

Bibliography

Baumgarten-Crusius, L. F. O. *Kommentar über den Brief Pauli an die Römer* (ed. E. J. Kimmel; Jena: Mauke, 1844).

Binder, H. *Der Glaube bei Paulus* (Berlin: Evangelische Verlagsanstalt, 1968).

Black, M. *Romans* (NCB; Grand Rapids, MI: Eerdmans, 1973).

Bultmann, R. 'πιστεύω κτλ.' *TDNT* 6:174–82, 197–28.

Chrysostom *In epistulam ad Romanos* (PG 60, 391–682).

Cranfield, C. E. B. *A Critical and Exegetical Commentary on the Epistle to the Romans, vol. 2: Commentary on Romans IX-XVI and Essays* (ICC; Edinburgh: T&T Clark, 1975).

Cranfield, C. E. B. 'ΜΕΤΡΟΝ ΠΙΣΤΕΩΣ in Romans XII. 3', *NTS* 8 (1961/1962), 345–51.

Cranfield, C. E. B. *Romans: A Shorter Commentary* (Grand Rapids, MI: Eerdmans, 1985).

Danker, F. W. *Benefactor: Epigraphic Study of a Graeco-Roman and New Testament Semantic Field* (St. Louis, MO: Clayton, 1982).

Dobbeler, A. von *Glaube als Teilhabe. Historische und semantische Grundlagen der paulinischen Theologie und Ekklesiologie des Glaubens* (WUNT 2, 22; Tübingen: Mohr Siebeck, 1987).

Dunn, J. D. G. *Romans 9—16* (WBC 38B; Waco, TX: Word, 1988).

Dunn, J. D. G. *The Theology of Paul the Apostle* (Grand Rapids, MI: Eerdmans, 1998).

Goodrich, J. K. '"Standard of Faith" or "Measure of a Trusteeship"? A Study in Romans 12:3', *CBQ* 74 (2012), 753–72.

Goodrich, J. K. 'The Interpretation of μέτρον πίστεως in Romans 12.3— A Rejoinder to Porter and Ong', *JGRCJ* 9 (2013), 213–20.

Haacker, K. *Der Brief des Paulus an die Römer* (THKNT 6; 4th edn, Leipzig: Evangelische Verlagsanstalt, 2012).

Harrison, J. R. *Paul's Language of Grace in Its Graeco-Roman Context* (2nd edn; Eugene, OR: Wipf and Stock, 2017).

Jewett, R. *Romans. A Commentary* (Hermeneia; Minneapolis, MN: Fortress, 2007).

Judge, E. A.	'The Regional κανών for Requisitioned Transport', in G. H. R. Horsley (ed.), *New Documents Illustrating Early Christianity*, vol. 1: *A Review of the Greek Inscriptions and Papyri Published in 1976* (North Ryde,NSW: Macquarie University, 1981), 36–45.
Käsemann, E.	*Commentary on Romans* (London: SCM, 1980).
Kowalski, M.	*Transforming Boasting of Self into Boasting in the Lord: The Development of the Pauline Periautologia in 2 Cor 10—13* (Studies in Judaism; Lanham, MD: University Press of America, 2013).
Kühl, E.	*Der Brief des Paulus an die Römer* (Leipzig: Quelle & Meyer, 1913).
Lagrange, M. J.	*Saint Paul. Epître aux Romains* (Études Bibliques; 6th edn; Paris: Gabalda, 1950).
Lewis, D. M., and S. Zanovello	'Freedmen/Freedwomen: Greek', in *The Oxford Classical Dictionary* (online edition, 2017). <https://doi.org/10.1093/acrefore/9780199381135.013.8019>
McLean, B. H.	*An Introduction to Greek Epigraphy of the Hellenistic and Roman Periods: From Alexander the Great to the Reign of Constantine* (323 BC–AD 337) (Ann Arbor, MI: University of Michigan Press, 2002).
Meyer, H. A. W.	*Critical and Exegetical Handbook to the Epistle to the Romans* (trans. J. C. Moore and E. Johnson; New York, NY: Funk & Wagnalls, 1884).
Michel, O.	*Der Brief an die Römer* (KEK 4; 5th edn; Göttingen: Vandenhoeck & Ruprecht, 1978).
Morgan, T.	*Roman Faith and Christian Faith. Pistis and Fides in the Early Roman Empire and Early Churches* (Oxford: Oxford University Press, 2015).
Morgan, T.	*The New Testament and the Theology of Trust* (Oxford: Oxford University Press, 2022).
Mulliez, D.	'Les actes d'affranchissement delphiques', *Cahiers du Centre Gustave Glotz* 3 (1992), 31–44.
Nasrallah, L. S.	*Archaeology and the Letters of Paul* (Oxford: Oxford University Press, 2019).
(Pseudo-)Oecumenius	*Pauli Epistola ad Romanos* (PG 118, 323–636).

Origen	*Commentary on the Epistle to the Romans*, Books 6—10 (trans. T. P. Scheck; The Fathers of the Church 104; Washington, DC: The Catholic University of America Press), 2002.
Poirier, J. C.	'The Measure of Stewardship: Πίστις in Romans 12:3', *TynB* 59 (2008), 145-52.
Porter, S. E. and H. T. Ong	'"Standard of Faith" or "Measure of a Trusteeship"? A Study in Romans 12:3—A Response, *JGRChJ* 9 (2013), 97-103.
Schliesser, B.	'Konfliktmanagement in der stadtrömischen Christenheit. Eine neue Sicht auf die "Starken" und "Schwachen" in Rom', in U. E. Eisen and H. Mader (eds.), *Talking God in Society: Multidisciplinary (Re)constructions of Ancient (Con)texts* (Festschrift Peter Lampe; Göttingen: Vandenhoeck & Ruprecht, 2021), 83-104.
Schliesser, B.	'*Pistis* in Papyri and Inscriptions', in *Inscriptions and Papyri* (ALNTS 10; Grand Rapids, MI: Zondervan, forthcoming).
Theobald, M.	'Der "strittige Punkt" (Rhet. a. Her. I,26) im Diskurs des Römerbriefs. Die propositio 1,16f und das Mysterium der Errettung ganz Israels', in *Studien zum Römerbrief* (WUNT 136; Tübingen: Mohr Siebeck, 2001), 278-323.
Theodoret of Cyrus	*Interpretatio in xiv epistulas sancti Pauli* (PG 82, 36-877).
Theophylact	*Epistolae Divi Pauli ad Romanos Expositio* (PG 124, 335-560).
Tholuck, A.	*Commentar zum Brief an die Römer* (5th edn; Halle: Anton, 1856).
Thrall, M. E.	*A Critical and Exegetical Commentary on the Second Epistle to the Corinthians, vol. 2: Commentary on II Corinthians VIII-XIII* (ICC; Edinburgh: T&T Clark, 2000).
Vanhoye, A.	'The Problematic Reception of πίστις in Romans 12.3, 6', in P. McCosker (ed.), *What Is It That the Scripture Says? Essays in Biblical Interpretation, Translation and Reception* (FS H. Wansbrough; LNTS 316; London: T&T Clark, 2006), 102-10.
Wilckens, U.	*Der Brief an die Römer, vol. 3: Röm 12-16* (EKK 6, 3; 3rd edn; Neukirchen-Vluyn: Neukirchener Verlag, 2005).
Wolter, M.	*Der Brief an die Römer, vol. 2: Röm 9—16* (EKK.NF 6, 2; Göttingen: Vandenhoeck & Ruprecht, 2018).
Zahn, T.	*Der Brief des Paulus an die Römer* (Kommentar zum Neuen Testament 6; 2nd edn; Leipzig: Deichert, 1910).

Paul in Illyricum

Richard S. Ascough

Abstract

Although there is no way to know with any certainty whether Paul spent time in Illyricum, his claim to have proclaimed the gospel "as far around as" that province (Rom 15.19) invites some speculation as to what such efforts might have looked like had he gone there. Drawing on data from occupational associations in the area as well as the trends among mobile traders using networks to facilitate travel and work, this paper imagines what someone like Paul might have done in order to establish Christ groups in Illyricum.

In his book on *Paul's Language of Grace in its Graeco-Roman Context*, Jim Harrison convincingly demonstrates, among many other things, how Paul's use of *charis* both reflected and contrasted with practices of benefaction in the voluntary associations of that time.[1] This builds upon an earlier article Jim wrote on 'Paul's House Churches and the Cultic Associations,'[2] that was both affirming of my own work on associations at the time while pushing me to think more broadly. Although I did not know Jim personally then, later meetings confirmed for me his commitment to experimentation and pushing boundaries in New Testament interpretation by drawing on the rich repository of epigraphic and papyrological work that too often is ignored in more classical exegesis. In that spirit, and in recognition of both his acumen

---

1 Harrison, *Paul's Language of Grace*, esp. 29-33 and 280-83.
2 Harrison, 'Paul's House Churches'.

and his willingness to take risks, I offer up an admittedly speculative suggestion of the nature of Paul's work in the Roman province of Illyricum, about which very little information is provided by Paul or other New Testament writers, and on which very few commentators elaborate beyond debating whether Paul went there.[3]

1. On The Road To Illyricum

There are two mentions of Illyricum in the New Testament. In the first, Paul boasts that 'from Jerusalem and as far around as Illyricum I have fully proclaimed the good news of Christ' (Rom. 15:19), suggesting that he personally had been involved in establishing Christ groups in this area. In the second reference, written pseudepigraphically at least a generation or two after Paul, the writer imagines that there is a Christ group in 'Dalmatia', the southern part of Illyricum, to which Titus can travel: 'Demas, in love with this present world, has deserted me and gone to Thessalonica; Crescens has gone to Galatia, Titus to Dalmatia' (2 Tim. 4:10). While it might be that the writer is imagining that Titus is making the first missionising foray into this area, this seems unlikely since the author is complaining of his abandonment and the other two places named—Thessalonike and Galatia—already have Christ groups in place.

The first reference to Paul's having preached 'as far around as' (μέχρι) Illyricum has led to a lot of interpretive debate. Most commentators read μέχρι to indicate that Paul preached up to the borders of Illyricum rather than entering the province,[4] but they do not often say when or how this took place.[5] Meeks is representative of this position:

---

3 Murphy-O'Connor does suggest that Paul spent at least a year there following a failed visit to Spain (*Paul*, 363), but this was not his initial trip to the area, which had happened much earlier.
4 Jewett, for example, sees it as a reflection of the types of maps used in antiquity (*Romans*, 912-13).
5 E.g. Dunn, *Romans*, 864; Schreiner, *Romans*, 769; Longenecker, *Romans*, 1041; see further the discussion in Chapple, 'Paul and Illyricum', 23-25, incl. nn. 15 and 21; Chapple thinks Paul did work in Illyricum (p.25).

Paul's mention of Illyricum has perplexed commentators since antiquity. Quite enough ink has already been wasted in speculation whether Paul really set foot within the boundaries of this Roman province, and if so, when. It is sufficient to note that here the naming of Illyricum is, as Fitzmyer says, 'a rhetorical flourish'.[6] Illyricum functions as a terminus, hyperbolically marking the bounds of Paul's eastward mission, as now he announces a new terminus, to the West. That terminus is Spain, which appears suddenly, without preparation, in Paul's description of his forthcoming travel to Rome.[7]

Meeks, or for that matter Fitzmyer, does not explain why Illyricum is 'hyperbole' but Spain is a very real plan. Clearly Paul intended to go to Spain, since he expressed his hope that the Romans would help fund that trip (Rom. 15:23–24). But why discount so quickly that he went to Illyricum, particularly since he had demonstrated an aptitude for travel and the funding thereof?

That Paul would travel to Illyricum is certainly possible, particularly following his time in Thessalonike. In 1 Thessalonians 3:1–3, Paul mentions that Timothy was dispatched to Thessalonike from Athens and has now returned with news that the Thessalonian Christ adherents are doing okay. This aligns with the account in Acts 17 that, following their time in Thessalonike, Paul and his companions headed south to Athens. Most interpreters have accepted this timeline as it seems on the surface to align with the letter. Yet, if Paul were to have traveled to Illyricum, one obvious time to do so would be shortly after

---

6 Fitzmyer, *Romans*, 714.
7 Meeks, 'Jerusalem to Illyricum', 174.

visiting Thessalonike.⁸ The Via Egnatia ran from the Hellespont on the east, through Philippi, Thessalonike, Beroea, and across to Dyrrachium on the Adriatic Sea coast. Paul could have followed this route and spent some time in Illyricum before heading south to Athens using the Via Flavia. This would extend the gap between his time in Thessalonike and the writing of 1 Thessalonians. Doing so would then give more time for the dissemination of news about 'the reception' that Paul and his companions had among the Thessalonians through Macedonia and Achaia (1 Thess. 1:7). These were not, as I have argued elsewhere, missionising activities by the Thessalonians but rather the spreading of news about their honouring of a new god and benefactor via networks of traders, artisans, and other travellers.⁹ The solidifying of adherence to a new god by an association in Thessalonike, followed by the news of such flowing through networks to the south takes time, and a detour by Paul to Illyricum would expand the time available.

In arguing that Paul spent time in Illyricum, Chapple points to the importance of key cities as nodal for trade by sea and/or by land, including Epidaurum, Narona, and especially Salona, whose 'prosperity was based on import and export traffic between the hinterland, the interior, and the Adriatic', so much so that 'it was a "flourishing centre

---

8   In traditional dating this would put it around 49–50 C.E. Schnabel thinks Paul was in Illyricum in summer 56, after visiting Corinth and travelling in Macedonia. From Illyricum Paul returned to Corinth via ship from Illyrian Apollonia to Corinth, from where he wrote Romans (Schnabel, *Early Christian Mission*, 47, 52, 1250, 1254; Murphy-O'Connor, *Paul*, 316–17). Jewett (*Romans*, 913–14) argues that Paul visited Illyricum in the summer and fall of 56 C.E., 'after meeting Titus in Macedonia (2 Cor. 7:5–16)', which he also links to the connection of Titus with Dalmatia in the Pastoral epistles. Like Jewett, Moo places Paul's visit into Illyricum during his 'third' missionary journey, thus using Acts as normative for a Pauline chronology (*Romans*, 894–95 n. 64). Towner (*Timothy and Titus*, 624) dates Paul's work in the area 'prior to his arrest' but also suggests that Titus was to meet Paul in Nicopolis, either 200 miles south of Dalmatia or in the area itself (citing Titus 3:12). Chapple sees this later dating as unlikely, pointing out that this does not align with the sequence of visits referred to in 1 and 2 Corinthians. A more likely dating, he suggests, is after Paul's Macedonia visit and before wintering in Corinth, although here Chapple draws upon the reliability of Acts, especially 20:1–3 ('Paul and Illyricum', 27–28). I am suggesting the earlier date since Paul was already travelling on the main artery into the region.
9   Ascough, 'Redescribing'.

of commerce" in Caesar's time'.[10] Although it would be simplistic to make a straight correlation between the trade routes and the spread of the Christ cult, it most likely is a major contributing factor insofar as these well-worn trade routes 'would have created circumstances conducive to the spread of private cults'.[11] Humphries points to one particular location as key for the growth of foreign cults: the city of Aquileia in northern Italy, which bordered the northern edge of the province of Illyricum.[12] It was an important trade hub, given its access to the sea and to the roads and as such, according to Herodian in the early third century C.E., 'has acted as a trading post (emporion) for [northern] Italy by providing sea traders with a market for goods from inland by land or river' (8.2.3), confirming the description of Strabo some three centuries earlier (5.1.8; 4.6.10). Populated by migrants from across the Empire, the epigraphic record shows that 'private soteriological cults are unusually well represented, with dedications to deities such as Magna Mater, Mithras and Isis' along with 'a thriving Jewish community'.[13]

There is no evidence for a Christian community in Aquileia before the Council of Arles in 314 C.E., but at that time there existed a massive complex of well-decorated buildings that enlarged an earlier structure, indicating that the community there 'was already extremely wealthy in the opening decades of the fourth century'.[14] Humphries goes so far as to suggest, 'in a city which had made its fortune on trade, such an ostentatious display by the Christians of Aquileia arouses suspicions that some of them were associated with the commercial life in the city in some way, perhaps as traders themselves'.[15] Although not

---

10   Chapple, 'Paul and Illyricum', 26, citing Wilkes, *Illyrians*, 209. Schnabel suggests Paul established a Christ group in Dyrrachium, or at least one was there in the first century (*Early Christian Mission*, 1531).
11   Humphries, 'Trading Gods', 203-14.
12   For the Romans Illyricum was viewed as a border area between Italy and the East (Valeva and Vinos, 'Balkan Peninsula', 325).
13   Humphries, 'Trading Gods', 215, citing Calderini, *Aquileia romana*, 123-37, and Ruggini, 'Ebrei e orientali', 192-213.
14   Humphries, 'Trading Gods', 216; cf. Valeva and Vionis, 'Balkan Peninsula', 329, who point to the ecclesiastical architecture in Eastern Illyricum in the early third century.
15   Humphries, 'Trading Gods', 216.

directly in Illyricum, the presence of Christ groups in this northern border city circumstantially can align with the possibility of a (relatively) robust presence of Christianity in the preceding centuries. More importantly, the evidence

> points to a strong connection between its Christian and trading communities [...]. Extending out of the city, there were Christian networks of influence which followed precisely the trade routes used most frequently by merchants operating out of the city [...]. If these connections stretch back to the very beginnings of Christianity in the city [...] then it seems that at Aquileia Christian origins were profoundly influenced by the city's importance in ancient trade networks.[16]

Humphries seems to have an unstated assumption that the Christ groups along the trade routes emanated from Aquileia, but I want to suggest that at least some of the flow might have been into the city from the south, from Illyricum proper. To appreciate the development of the robust communities, we must step back in time to their point(s) of origin.

2. Making Contact

Here, I want to use Paul's claim as a speculative jumping off point.[17] As we noted, we cannot know with any amount of certainty whether Paul entered the region of Illyricum at all, and if so what he did there. Yet the later presence of Christ groups in the area means that *someone*

---

16   Humphries, 'Trading Gods', 218-19.
17   One of the benefits *and* drawbacks of choosing Illyricum as the focus is the lack of data for Christ groups in the earliest period. Outside of Paul's oblique reference to proclamation in or near the province, we have no other data from the first century. The downside is obvious, but on the upside, neither do we have over two thousand years of theological dogma ingrained into set interpretations of New Testament datapoints, as so often is the case with Christ groups in other cities or areas. This allows us the freedom to imagine one (and only one of many) possible scenarios based on the developing scholarly understanding and trends about how people used networks to facilitate travel and work.

did, and as far as we know Paul was the only one making the claim. But of more interest to me is the social dynamic of the founding of one or more Christ groups in this province. In fact, it is the very lack of evidence from actual letters of Paul or from the Book of Acts that gives us the freedom to imagine at least one possible scenario as a way of testing the waters for (non-theological) readings of the establishing of Christ groups in major urban areas. By focusing on Illyricum, I am in part attempting a 'thought experiment' in filling gaps in Paul's biography and in part examining 'micro-realties' or at least province-wide realties to test some of the recent conclusions on the intersection of economic life and associative social structures in antiquity, as Liu rightly calls for.[18]

Based on work done on Paul's activities in Thessalonike and Corinth, it is clear that the artisan's workshop was a key location for recruitment. Chapple notes this in passing but leaves it unexplored:

> there is evidence for the existence of a number of trade guilds in Salona. In many ways this thriving city is likely to have reminded Paul of Corinth. If so, this would only reinforce the perception that this would be a strategic centre for reaching Ilyricum with the gospel.[19]

Narona and especially Salona provide the evidence for occupational associations in Illyricum, with the bulk of the inscriptions coming from the latter city. From Narona there are three attestations for one or more guilds of craftsmen (*collegium fabrum*), with the earliest dating in the mid-first century C.E., although more securely perhaps in

---

18 Liu, 'Professional Collegia', 204.
19 Chapple, 'Paul and Illyricum', 27. Chapple goes further to speculate why Paul would venture into this province as a precursor for his trip to Rome and preparation for going to Spain, something there is no room to explore more in this essay. On Paul's use of the workshop in his recruitment strategy see further Hock, 'Workshop'; Ascough, 'Thessalonian Christian Community'.

the second century which is the dating of the other two.[20] The longest inscription is a funerary stele set up by the spouse of a man who served as scribe of his guild:

> D(is) M(anibus) | Pactumeio Euty|chiano srib(a)e col(legii) | fab(rum) iu(dici?) beni(gno) infelici | qui vixit annos p(lus) m(inus) | LXIII mes(es) XI dies VI | [Pu]blicia Marcella | marito
>
> To the God-Spirits of the dead. For Pactumeius Eutychianus, scribe of the guild of craftsmen, benign iudex(?), the unfortunate who has lived more or less 63 years, 11 months, 6 days. Publicia Marcella (has set up this monument) to her husband. (*CIN* II 110, II C.E.).[21]

It is unclear what the designation 'iudex' points to here, although it seems to be a position within the guild that Pactumeio held as well as serving as scribe. The guild itself is designated as *fabrum*, most likely comprised of workers in the building and construction trades.

From Salona there are at least fifteen association texts that date to the first through third centuries C.E., with the bulk lying in the second century, and six having a terminus of the mid-second century C.E. They are either honorifics for patrons or funerary texts recognising a member, often a well-to-do member, of the association. Those dated earliest are rather fragmentary yet attest to *fabri* ('builders'; *CIL* III 884 and *CIL* III 8819, both I–III C.E.), *dendrophoroi* ('tree-carriers'; *CIL* III 8823, II–III C.E.), and *centonarii* ('clothmen'; *CIL* III 8829, II C.E.). From the second century there is an interesting honorific set up by two occupational associations:

---

20 Although most of the inscriptions discussed here post-date Paul's lifetime, the presence of evidence of occupational guilds in the second century is a good indication that they were forming in the first century or earlier, as was the case in other places throughout the Roman empire. My argument is not that Paul was connected to any one or more of the attested associations, but that the phenomenon of associations facilitated his recruitment activities.
21 All texts and translations are from the Ghent Database of Roman Guilds (https://gdrg.ugent.be). The other two inscriptions from Narona are *ILJug* III 1889 (51–150 C.E.) and *CIL* III 1829 (101–250 C.E.).

> M(arco) Ulpio M(arci) f(ilio) | Sabino eq(uo) p(ublico) | dec(urioni) col(oniae) Sal(onitanorum) | IIviro iure | dicundo praef(ecto) bis | coll(egii) fabr(um) et cen|tonariorum | patrono col(legii) | s(upra) s(cripti) ob industriam | adque(!) sing(ula)rem | eius innocent|am et integritatem | defensionem|que ex aere col|lato coll(egium or -egia) s(upra) s(criptum).
>
> To Marcus Ulpius Sabinus, son of Marcus, (endowed) with the public horse, decurion of the colony of Salona, twice prefect of the guild(s) of the craftsmen and of the clothmen, patron of the guilds. The above-mentioned guilds (have set up this monument) for his dedication and singular uprightness and integrity, and protection with collected money. (ILJug III 2109, 126–75 c.e.)

From the same period, we have evidence for each of these guilds named independently,[22] including the craftsmen association's honorifics for men who served as both prefect and patron.[23] The text quoted above, however, is the only attestation in which two associations are joined in honouring a man who seemingly served or perhaps even united both groups. Much depends on whether one reconstructs *coll* as singular or plural. If these two guilds were separate, as is the case with individualised attestations, it is not clear whether Marcus Ulpinus Sabinus served them simultaneously or sequentially, although the fact that they could work together to collect money in his honour does suggest that there was a symbiosis between them that might well have been brokered by Marcus himself given his position of prestige and power in the city.

We see this again in a later inscription where the same two guilds honour another equestrian decurion of Salona for his prefecture of the 'guild(s) of craftsmen and clothmen' (*ILJug* II 678, 201–326 c.e.).[24]

---

22 Craftsmen: *CIL* III 8824, 150–300 c.e.; *CIL* III 8837, 176–225 c.e. Clothmen: *ILJug* III 2115, 151–300 c.e.
23 *CIL* III 2026 and on the reverse of the same stone *CIL* III 2087, both dating to 101–50 c.e. In this case, it seems that two men merited honour for their service, likely sequentially.
24 On the links between elite magistrates and associations see Verboven, 'Guilds', 201.

From this later period we have yet another example:

> [Au]r(elius) Quintianus dec(urio) coll(egii) fab(rum) et | [ce]nt(onariorum) qui vixit ann(os) p(lus) m(inus) LI men(ses) V d(ies) X | [viv]us sibi posuit et Aur(eliae) Ianuari(a)e | [co]niugi suae cot(!) si quis aeam(!) arcam | [po]st mortem eorum aperire vo|[lu]eri[t inferet] decuriae meae | (denarios) XXV
>
> Aurelius Quintianus, decurio of the guild of craftsmen and clothmen who has lived more or less fifty-one years, five months, ten days has set up (this monument) to himself during his lifetime and to Aurelia Ianuaria his wife. If anyone should want to open this coffin after their death, let him pay twenty-five denarii to my *decuria*. (*CIL* III 2107)

In this case, however, it is a funerary stele rather than an honorific, and it was erected by the deceased on his own behalf, and with his own funds, rather than by the guild(s).

Unfortunately, to date there is no evidence for associations of leatherworkers—the profession with which Paul can most likely be affiliated (see Acts 18:3)—although such guilds are attested elsewhere in the Roman empire.[25] It is clear, however, that Paul used his skills as an artisan in his recruitment efforts.[26] In order to ply his trade as an independent, itinerant contractor, Paul would have relied on the trade networks along the Roman road and sea system, which was extensive and filled with travellers, including migrant workers.[27]

---

25 See, for example, *AGRW* 131 (Thyatira, late I c.e.); *IEph* 596 (Ephesos, II c.e.); *TAM* V 79 (Saittai, Lydia, 152/153 c.e.); *IGR* IV 790 (Apameia Kelainai, Phrygia, ca. 160 c.e.); *IEph* 2080 (Ephesos 200-10 c.e.); *AGRW* 259 and *IG* XII, 2 109 (both Mytilene, Lesbos, undated); *CIL* VI 9053 (Rome, 70-200 c.e.). On the east side of the forum of corporations in Ostia (regio II,VII,4) the guild of leather merchants identified itself as *corpus pillion[um] Ost[iensium] et Port[ensium]* (*CIL* XIV 4549, 2). On Paul as a leatherworker, the material out of which tents and awnings (σκηνοποιός) were made, see Still, 'Paul', 781. Paul makes a similar connection not based on shared ethnicity but perhaps on status as working professionals in meeting with Lydia the purple-dealer at Philippi (Acts 16:12-15).
26 1 Thess. 2:9; 1 Cor. 4:9, 9:6; 2 Cor. 11:27; cf. Acts 18:3.
27 Casson, *Travel*, 127; de Ligt and Tacoma, 'Approaching Migration', 9-10.

In order for mobile artisans such as Paul and his companions to navigate the process of finding paid work when arriving at a new city, network connections provided by common ethnicity and common trade were critical.[28] As Holleran notes, 'comparative material demonstrates the importance of [...] networks not only in stimulating movement, but also in assisting migrants with finding housing and work upon arrival in a particular location.'[29] Occupational associations such as those described above would be particularly important for making connections. Not only did they provide an income, but affiliation with a guild would ensure that the migrant worker was treated as someone who was trustworthy and dependable.[30] This, in turn, would open doors for Paul and his companions to speak with others, both in the workshop and beyond as they entered the broader social and occupational networks afforded by their connections in the guild. Such informal networking was probably a primary concern of associations, where members aided one another socially and financially as they navigated life in the city.[31] For Paul and his companions, these sorts of connections would be critical in establishing a 'matrix of social interactions' that would result in drawing people, or even groups of people, into the cult of Christ.[32]

3. Conclusion

I have used 'Paul' as an example of a person who might have been instrumental in the diffusion of Christ groups in Illyricum, in part because we know he did such work elsewhere and in part because he claimed to have done so in this province. Certainly, there were Christ groups there by the second century, so clearly somebody took part in the diffusion. But the 'who' is much less important to the growth than

---

28 Further on mobile traders and the role of associations in facilitating trade networks, see Ascough, 'Working with the Gods'.
29 Holleran, 'Getting a Job', 117.
30 Verboven and Laes, 'Work, Labour, Professions', 16.
31 Bollmann, *Römische Vereinshäuser*, 38; Broekaert, 'Joining Forces', 222.
32 Cf. White, 'Expansion', 115–18; Kloppenborg, *Christ's Associations*, 337.

the circumstances that allowed for and encouraged the growth.[33] It is the circumstances of mobile traders and trade networks that I am primarily interested in exploiting in this regard. That Paul was directly involved is only circumstantial, at best, and is more a fabrication to make concrete the process. But that should not take away from the primary argument that trade networks and those who travelled along trade routes played an important part in the expansion and growth of early Christ groups, even into Illyricum.

Richard S. Ascough
Queen's University
Kingston, Canada

---

33 Humphries, 'Trading Gods', 206. As Humphries points out, according to Acts 28:13, when Paul arrived at Puteoli he found there an already established Christ group, which is not a surprise when one recognises that it was the key port and market on the Bay of Naples and the major port of Rome ('Trading Gods', 207). Whoever helped establish the groups to which Paul wrote the letter to the Romans most likely entered the area through this port city, much as did Paul, on a ship that followed the trade routes of the day (Humphries, 'Trading Gods', 207). Moving forward in time, Humphries shows that by the Council of Ariminum in 359 c.e. the cities represented by the bishops were for the most part also important commercial centres and hubs on major road or shipping networks.

Bibliography

Ascough, R. S. — 'Re-describing the Thessalonians' "Mission" in Light of Graeco-Roman Associations', *New Testament Studies* 60 (2014), 61–82.

——— 'The Thessalonian Christian Community as a Professional Voluntary Association', *Journal of Biblical Literature* 119 (2000), 311–28.

——— 'Working with the Gods: Occupational Associations and Early Christ Groups', in B. Longenecker (ed.), *Associations, Deities, and Early Christianity* (Waco, TX: Baylor University Press, 2022), 49–64.

Bollmann, B. — *Römische Vereinshäuser: Untersuchungen zu den Scholae der römischen Berufs-, Kult- und Augustalen-Kollegien in Italien* (Mainz: Philipp von Zabern, 1998).

Broekaert, W. — 'Joining Forces: Commercial Partnerships or Societates in the Early Roman Empire', *Historia* 61 (2012), 221–53.

Calderini, A. — *Aquileia romana: Ricerche di storia e di epigrafia* (Milan: Societa Editrice Vita e Pensiero, 1930).

Casson, L. — *Travel in the Ancient World* (Baltimore, MD: The Johns Hopkins University Press, 1994).

Chapple, A. — 'Paul and Illyricum', *Reformed Theological Review* 72/1 (2013), 20–35.

de Ligt, L., and L. E. Tacoma. — 'Approaching Migration in the Early Roman Empire', in L. de Ligt and L. E. Tacoma (eds.), *Migration and Mobility in the Early Roman Empire* (Studies in Global Social History 23/7; Leiden: Brill, 2016), 1–22.

Dunn, J. D. G. — *Romans* (WBC 38; Dallas, TX: Word, 1988).

Fitzmyer, J. A. — *Romans: A New Translation with Introduction and Commentary* (AB 33; New York, NY: Doubleday, 1993).

Harrison, J. R. — 'Paul's House Churches and the Cultic Associations', *Reformed Theological Review* 58 (1999), 31–47.

——— *Paul's Language of Grace in its Graeco-Roman Context* (WUNT II/172; Tübingen: Mohr Siebeck, 2003).

Hock, R. F. — 'The Workshop as a Social Setting for Paul's Missionary Preaching', *Catholic Biblical Quarterly* 41 (1979), 438–50.

Holleran, C. — 'Getting a Job: Finding Work in the City of Rome', in K. Verboven and C. Laes (eds.), *Work, Labour, and Professions in the Roman World* (Impact of Empire 23; Leiden: Brill, 2017), 87–103.

Humphries, M. — 'Trading Gods in Northern Italy', in H. Parkins and C. Smith (eds.), *Trade, Traders and the Ancient City* (Oxford: Routledge, 1998), 203–24.

Jewett, R. — *Romans: A Commentary* (Hermeneia; Minneapolis, MN: Fortress, 2007).

Kloppenborg, J. S. — *Christ's Associations: Connecting and Belonging in the Ancient City* (New Haven, CT: Yale University Press, 2019).

Liu, J. — 'Professional Collegia', in P. Erdkamp (ed.), *Cambridge Companion to the City of Rome* (Cambridge: Cambridge University Press, 2013), 352–68.

Longenecker, R. N. — *The Epistle to the Romans* (NIGTC; Grand Rapids, MI: Eerdmans, 2016).

Meeks, W. A. — 'From Jerusalem to Illyricum, Rome to Spain: The World of Paul's Missionary Imagination', in C. K. Rothschild and J. Schröter (eds.), *The Rise and Expansion of Christianity in the First Three Centuries of the Common Era* (Tübingen: Mohr Siebeck, 2013), 167–81.

Moo, D. J. — *The Epistle to the Romans* (NICNT; Grand Rapids, MI: Eerdmans, 1996).

Murphy-O'Connor, J. — *Paul: A Critical Life* (Oxford: Clarendon, 1996).

Ruggini, L. — 'Ebrei e orientali nell'Italia settentrionale tra il IV e il VI secolo d. C', *Studia et Documenta Historiae et Iuris* 25 (1959), 186–308.

Schnabel, E. J. — *Early Christian Mission* (2 vols.; Downers Grove, IL: InterVarsity Press, 2004).

Schreiner, T. R. — *Romans* (BECNT; Grand Rapids, MI: Eerdmans, 1998).

Still, T. D. — 'Did Paul Loathe Manual Labor? Revisiting the Work of Ronald F. Hock on the Apostle's Tentmaking and Social Class', *Journal of Biblical Literature* 125 (2006), 781–95.

Towner, P. H.   *The Letters to Timothy and Titus* (NICNT; Grand Rapids, MI: Eerdmans, 2006).

Valeva, J., and A. K. Vionis.   'The Balkan Peninsula', in W. Tabbernee (ed.), *Early Christianity in Contexts: An Exploration across cultures and Continents* (Grand Rapids, MI: Baker, 2014), 321–78.

Verboven, K.   'Guilds and the Organisation of Urban Populations During the Principate', in K. Verboven and C. Laes (eds.), *Work, Labour, and Professions in the Roman World* (Impact of Empire 23; Leiden: Brill, 2016), 173–202.

Verboven, K., and C. Laes.   'Work, Labour, Professions. What's in a Name?', in K. Verboven and C. Laes (eds.), *Work, Labour, and Professions in the Roman World* (Impact of Empire 23; Leiden: Brill, 2016), 1–19.

White, L. M.   'Adolf von Harnack and the "Expansion" of Early Christianity', *Second Century* 5 (1985), 97–127.

Wilkes, J.   *The Illyrians* (The Peoples of Europe; Oxford: Blackwell, 1992).

Abbreviations

AGRW   *Associations in the Greco-Roman World: A Sourcebook*, R. S. Ascough, P. A. Harland, and J. S. Kloppenborg (Waco: Baylor University, 2012).

CIL   *Corpus Inscriptionum Latinarum*, Theodor Mommsen et al. (eds.) (Berlin: Reimerum, 1863–).

CIN   *Corpus Inscriptionum Naronitanarum*, Emilio Marin et al. (eds.) (2 vols. Tivoli: Tipigraf, 2000–20).

IEph   *Die Inschriften von Ephesos*, H. Wankel and H. Engelmann (eds.) (8 vols., IGSK 11–17 Bonn: Rudolf Habelt, 1979–84).

IG XII   *Inscriptiones insularum maris Aegaei praeter Delum*, R. Hiller von Gaertringen, W. R. Paton, J. Delamarre, and E. Ziebarth (eds.) (9 parts; Berlin: Georg Reimer, 1895–1915).

IGR   *Inscriptiones graecae ad res romanas pertinentes*, R. L. Cagnat, J. F. Toutain, V. Henry, and G. L. Lafaye (eds.) (4 vols. Paris: E. Leroux, 1911–1927).

ILJug   *Inscriptones Latinae quae in Iugoslavia inter annos MCMXL et MCMLX repertae et editae sunt*, A. and J. Šašel (3 vols. Ljublijana: Narodni muzej, 1963–86).

TAM   *Tituli Asiae Minoris*, Osterreichische Akademie der Wissenschaften (Vienna: Hoelder-Pichler-Tempsky, 1901–).

Intimations of Democracy in early Christ groups

John S. Kloppenborg

Abstract

Private associations in the Hellenistic and early Roman periods tended to imitate both civic structures and practices, and also the civic value of democratic autonomy. These practices and values persisted even with the decline of civic autonomy in the imperial period. Many of the practices of Christ groups can be regarded as emulations of these democratic values such that Christ groups might be treated as 'mini-democracies'.

For much of his career, James R. Harrison has devoted himself to understanding the ethos of early Christ groups, in particular as they are found in the cities of the Empire. From his first monograph on *Paul's Language of Grace in its Graeco-Roman Context*, Harrison has been at pains to show on the one hand the indebtedness of Paul's language to the cultural *lingua franca* of the Empire, but on the other, the variety of ways in which Paul's language also struck out in new and rather unprecedented directions. In addition, assuming the editorship of *New Documents Illustrating the History of Early Christianity* in 2012, Harrison has been instrumental, along with Larry Welborn, in bringing the six-volume *The First urban Churches* (2015–2021) to publication,[1] with its detailed essays on the many urban sites in which Christ groups were found. More is undoubtedly to come.

In this age of shrinking democracies and their displacement by corporatism and autocracies, I wish to turn to another aspect of the ethos of early Christ groups, their 'democratic' practices. Christ assemblies, almost from the beginning, acted as though they had autonomous political agency over their own affairs and it is in this limited sense that they might be thought of as 'playing at democracy'.

The invention of democracy in late sixth century B.C.E. Athens was a virtually unprecedented development. In most of ancient world, monarchies, aristocracies, oligarchies, and theocracies were the orders of the day. Nevertheless, the virtues that emerged in the reforms of Cleisthenes proved to be not only durable but contagious: *isonomia*—all being subject to the same laws—and *isēgoria*—the right of all citizens (Herodotus means of course free males)—to voice their opinion on matters of political significance, and *parrhēsia*, the right of free speech.[1] In spite of various threats to democracy, citizen assemblies in the East lasted well into the third century C.E.

It is commonly observed that the many private associations that began to appear at least by the late fifth century B.C.E. in Achaia tended to imitate the structures and practices of the *polis*. In Athens, but elsewhere too, this imitation included mimicry of the democratic practices of the Athenian *ekklēsia*. The honorific decrees of Athenian private associations had the same morphology as decrees of the Athenian assembly and were presented as the consensus decision of members. The leadership of private Athenian associations mimicked that of the *polis*, with supervisors elected yearly. The regular meeting of the assembly was called ἀγορὰ κυρία or ἐκκλησία κυρία; and the vocabulary and formulae of democratic practices abound. The decisions of these associations were treated as sovereign, and steps were taken to prevent those decrees from being overturned or vacated by subsequent motions.

Recognising the imitation of civic structures by associations, Foucart suggested these mini-democracies might be limited to cities that had a democratic tradition.[2] One might also surmise that as Athens progressively came under the control the Macedonians and then Rome, the democratic constitutions of its private associations might also wane.

---

1 See Herodotus 3.80.6 and 5.78 and Ober, *The Athenian Revolution*, chap. 4.
2 Foucart, *Des associations religieuses*,51.

Yet this does not seem to have been the case. As Nicholas Jones argued, the rise of private associations in the fourth and third centuries B.C.E. was as much a response to the flaws and limitations of Athenian democracy as it was an imitation of it.³ Jones pointed out that the ideology of egalitarianism was countered by the continued existence of elite clubs, that the council of 500 was in no way representative of political opinion, even though each of the demes sent members, that minority citizen participation was impossible given the geography of Attica and the physical constraints on the seating capacity of the *ekklēsia*, and that non-citizens, women, and slaves were excluded from participation.⁴ In this context, the development of private associations that were inclusive of those persons and groups that Athenian democracy had excluded can be viewed as a response to the limitations of democracy and perhaps a realisation of equality and participation that Athens, as a large *polis*, could not in fact implement.⁵

One might suppose that with the arrival of Rome, all traces of democratic practices would have disappeared. But as Steven Payne has shown, there is robust evidence of the continued existence of citizen assemblies that continued to pass decrees until well into the third century C.E., not merely in the hellenistic period, during which it is possible to identify democratic assemblies in parts of the eastern Mediterranean.⁶ The nature of the data—all epigraphical—does not allow us to peer very far into the practices of these polities to determine whether *eisonomia*, *parrhēsia*, and *isēgoria* were fully practised. Almost two-thirds (81) of the inscriptions are honorific decrees approved by the *boulē* and *dēmos*, and another twelve percent are decisions on cultic and financial matters. These data indicate, however, that in spite of the fact that *poleis* were under the direct control of Roman governors, citi-

---

3   On the limitations of Athenian democracy, see Ober, *Mass and Elite*, 293–403.
4   Jones, *Associations of Classical Athens*, 47–50, (SEG 49:14, 100, 159, 162).
5   Contrast Connor, 'Civil Society', who argues that associations mediated the formation of Athenian democracy. This view—hardly to be disregarded—is similar to recent political sociologist such as Putnam, *Bowling Alone*, who has argued for a strong relationship between small local associations and the ability to sustain democracies.
6   Payne, 'Spiritual Bodies', 586–98.

zen assemblies continued to exercise a degree of autonomy in voting honours and regulating certain aspects of their political life.[7]

One might suppose that the practice of voting of honours to a benefactor was hardly an index of democracy, since such honours were virtually automatic and hence in no way qualify as an exercise of autonomy on the part of the *polis*. As Onno van Nijf has pointed out, however, the exchange between benefactors and the cities that honoured them was a symbolic exchange and rested on the fiction that the benefactor was disinterested and that the client freely honoured the benefactor; otherwise, it would seem a commercial transaction of the benefactor simply buying recognition.[8] The notable instances of cities refusing to honour a benefactor indicate that the process of honouring benefactors was both imagined to be an autonomous act and in some instances was in fact an autonomous act of the *polis*.[9] That is, even though cities no longer enjoyed full political rights, *ekklēsiai* continued to act as though they were autonomous and could choose to honour benefactors or not.

If *poleis* continued to act as though they had political rights, so too did private associations, including many associations outside of Athens. Four examples from the imperial period exemplify the mimicry of democratic practices. In 142 C.E. the Artists associated with Dionysos of Nysa (Roman Asia) inscribed a decree honouring a benefactor, using common democratic formulae. Like civic decrees, their decree distin-

---

7 See now Thomsen, *Politics of Associations*, chap. 4, who has shown that Rhodian private associations exemplified democratic practices: 'there can be little doubt that all were committed to a democratic form of internal government. The one activity attested for practically all private associations in Rhodes ... was the passing of honorific decrees awarding crowns of gold or foliage to a benefactor and recorded by the benefactor himself in a monument to his own social importance. Each ... gives evidence of a procedure intimately connected to democratic institutions: a decision in the form of a formal motion proposed by a member of an association and subsequently debated in an assembly, before it was eventually passed by a majority and effectuated by magistrates charged with procuring the crown and proclaiming it to the members of the association and perhaps beyond' (pp. 98–99).
8 Van Nijf, *Civic World*, 119. See also the critical review of Paul Veyne's view of disinterested benefaction by Andreau, Schmitt, and Schnapp, 'Review'.
9 See the case of Vedius Antoninus and the council of Ephesus, discussed by Zuiderhoek, *Politics of Munificence*, 108–9.

guished between the one who introduced the motion ([ε]ἰσηγησαμένου) and the member who actually moved it (ἐπιψηφισαμένου) in the assembly; the motion was introduced by ἐπειδή with typical descriptions of the honoree's achievements; and it was then approved by the membership (ἐψηφίσαντο) who ordered that the decree be inscribed.[10]

In the early first century C.E., an association (*synodos*) of priests of Asklepius from Matinea in Arcadia (Peloponnese) voted honours to Iulia Eudia, who had benefitted the group variously. The morphology of the inscription leaves little doubt that the priests were mimicking democratic practices: the decree begins with ἐπειδή; the formula δεδόχθαι τοῖ[ς] ἱερεῦσι implies collective approval of the decree; there is a warning against future failures to follow the decree; and a the magistrate was deputed to oversee the enacting of the decree, which is called a ψήφισμα.[11]

In the Latin West, one does not find decrees that take the form of Athenian decrees, but it is common to encounter decisions of a collegium to 'elect' or 'coopt' a patron or patroness as a matter of unanimous consent of the membership. Thus, a collegium of builders (*fabri*) in Pisaurum in 256 C.E., having already 'elected' Petronius Victorinus as a patron, decided with the 'agreement of all [members' (*universoru(m) consensu*, l. 5) and with 'easy unanimity' (*prono consensu*, l. 13) to coopt his wife as a patroness.[12] This formulation of course disguises the fact that the patrons involved had to agree to this relationship and may even have initiated the offer of patronage. Yet from the point of view of the private association, they were 'electing' a patron by assertion of their autonomous rights to act.

A final example is offered by a mid-second century C.E. Roman association devoted to the cult of Aesculapius and Hygia. Their by-laws, recorded on a large plaque, are framed as a matter of consent of all the members (*ex decreto universorum*, l. 8). A provision on the distribution

---

10 I.Eph. 22 (Nysa, 142 CE) = GRA II 144.
11 IG V,2 269 (Matinea [Arcadia]) [CAPInv 432].
12 CIL 11.6335 (Pisaurum [Umbria: Regio VI] 256 C.E.). Similarly, CIL 11.5750 (Sentium 260 C.E.): the election of a patron by the 'unanimous vote' (*communis voti*, l. 9) of the collegium of cloth dealers (*centonarii*).

of sportulae was approved 'on the condition that the full assembly agrees' (*ea condicione, qua in conventu placuit universis*, l. 16), and the by-laws reiterated that they were approved by 'a roster of our members' (*ordini n(ostro) placuit*) in a full meeting (*in conventu pleno*, l. 23).[13] Although not all associations left decrees that mimicked the morphology of the democratic enactments of the Athenian *ekklēsia*, there are many other indications of democratic practices among private associations. Of course, it is impossible to claim that all associations engaged in democratic practices. There are sufficient indications, however, that many did and some reason to believe that one of the appeals of membership was the sense of autonomy in decision-making that membership afforded.

An association of coppersmiths from Lycia (150-100 B.C.E.) issued its by-laws, which ends with the statement (face C):

ἐπὶ δὲ τοῖς προγεγραμ-
μένοις πᾶσιν εὐδόκησεν τὸ κοινὸν
25 τῶν χαλκέων· ἀναδοθείσης ψήφου, ἐ-
κρίθη πάσαις·

The *koinon* of coppersmiths agreed to everything written above. When a vote was taken, it was unanimously approved. (SEG 58:1640 = GRA II 149).

In Ptolemaic and Roman Egypt the decisions of private associations required the formal assent of members in order to come into effect, either unanimous consent or a majority of those voting.[14] Association by-laws from the Ptolemaic period appear to have required unanimous approval.[15] The original impulse for this practice is probably not imitation of democratic practices, but rather legal considerations. Since many of these by-laws empowered the president to impose fines or to seize sureties from membership who defaulted on their obligations, and since the by-laws imposed upon the association duties toward the

---

13 CIL 6.10234 (Rome, 153 C.E.).
14 Paganini, 'Decisional Practices', 1889–1901.
15 De Cenival, *Les associations religieuses*, 147–48.

membership, signed copies of the by-laws could be used to guarantee the legal undertakings listed in the by-laws. Associations routinely collected a funeral fee (ταφικόν) from members and in turn the association agreed to participate in and contribute to funeral costs. Two late-third century B.C.E. papyri register official complaints by relatives of the members of associations that the association question had failed in this obligation. Hence, the *stratēgos* could examine an archival copy of the association's by-laws to determine whether there was in fact a funeral provision and whether the member in question belonged to the association.[16] Closer to the imperial period, an association of grave-diggers complained that contrary to the agreement that 'all the grave-diggers of the association (ἔθνος)' had made, some members had acted in contravention of that agreement.[17] In such a case, the prefect could examine the contract and confirm that the culprits were in fact signatories to the agreement, and take the appropriate action.

Egyptian associations not only approved their own by-laws by unanimous consent, but also honorific decrees where there was no likelihood of a legal challenge and hence no need to stipulate those who approved the motion. Yet an honorific decree in the Delta does precisely this: it notes the decree was enacted at the meeting of the group and that it received unanimous approval.[18] Another decree honouring the president of an association notes that a 'majority of members were present' and insists that each of the members undersign the decree: 'This decree in duplicate is undersigned in order to be valid and enforceable' (τό τε δόγμα τοῦτο δισσὸν ὑπογραφὲν ἔστω κύριον καὶ βέβαιον).[19]

---

16 See, e.g., P. Enteux. 20, 20 (= GRA III 189, 190).
17 P.Ryl. II 65 (Oxyrhynchus, 67 B.C.E.?).
18 I.Prose I 40.2, 47-49 = GRA III 160 (Psenamosis, 67–63 B.C.E.). The end of the inscription reads ὑφ' ὃ καὶ ὑπέγραψαν πάντες εὐδοκοῦντες, 'at the bottom are written (the names) of everyone who approved'. There is no list of names at the bottom of the inscription nor space for names. Paganini, 'Decisional Practices', 1899, suggests that 'their names obviously appeared in the original copy of the decree, presumably written on papyrus, but they were eventually not carved on stone, either for economy or other reasons'.
19 I.Prose I 49.6, 46-47, 52-53 = GRA III 170 (Psenamosis, 5 B.C.E.). Paganini, 'Decisional Practices', 1893 n.12, is probably right that τοῦ Ἀπολλωνίου τὰ δόγματα means the decisions pertaining to the president, Apollonios, rather than all the future decisions of the president.

The practice of including an 'approval list' at the end of by-laws continued into the Imperial period. In the by-laws of a guild of sheep and donkey herders the text ends with the statement κύριος ‹ἔ›στω{ι} ὁ νόμος ὑπογραφεὶς ὑπὸ τῶν πλείστων, 'the law will be valid when signed by the majority (of members)'. The document ends with the names of sixteen members, each using the formula, 'I Sōtērichos son of Sōtērichos approve' (P.Mich. V 243 = GRA III 206, Tebtynis, time of Tiberius). Several other by-laws from the same period show the same approval practice.[20]

As I have suggested, the impulse for unanimous consent to the enactments of Egyptian associations was not originally a matter of the imitation of democratic practices. Yet, by the early imperial period this practice was attested in honorific decrees in which the point of the approval lists did not serve a legal end, but was rather a part of honorific exchange in which it was important for the association to represents its honorific acts as a matter of the free consensus of members. And whether or not the unanimous approval of association by-laws originated out of a democratic urge, by the imperial period it had the *effect* of implying that all members were governed by common rules that each member had approved.[21]

In the Latin West there is no evidence of by-laws that were renewed yearly with lists of names attached. Yet the idea that each member had to agree to the by-laws was nonetheless critical. A Roman association

---

20 P.Mich. V 244 (= GRA III 212; Tebtynis, 43 c.e.]; P.Mich. V 246 (= GRA III 211; Tebtynis, 43–49 c.e.]. P.Mich. V 247 (=GRA III 209; Tebtynis, early I c.e.) and P.Mich. V 248 (=GRA III 213, Tebtynis 45–47 c.e.) lack the texts of the by-laws, but include a list of names which ends with the first part of approval lists in the form ‹hand 2› Ἡρακλῆς νεώτερο(ς) Ἡρώδου ἐψήφισμαι. ‹hand 3› Ἁρμιῦσις Ὀννώφρι‹ο›ς ἐψήφισμαι), 'I, Heraklēs the younger, son of Herōdes, have voted; Harmiysis son of Onnophris have voted....' etc.
21 Paganini, 'Decisional Practices', 1901, also rejects the notion that this practice originated under democratic impulse, but nevertheless argues the 'the adoption of (pseudo-)democratic or egalitarian procedures was probably a typical feature that was more or less naturally adopted by groups of people who gathered together in association and had to take some decision: every single member felt their duty to be responsible for what was carried out in the association and to contribute individually to the good of the group, because of their sense of belonging to the club'.

devoted to the cult of Diana and Antinoüs, insisted:

> You who want to enter this *collegium* as a new member, first read the by-laws (*lex*) in their entirety and enter in such a manner that later you may not make a complaint or leave a dispute to your heir.[22]

The result of these various approval practices was *isonomia*, the old Athenian virtue of all being governed by the same laws.

Another aspect of associations' assertion of autonomy was their insistence that matters of dispute among members must be adjudicated in-house. From the late third century B.C.E. the by-laws of Demotic associations included provisions to fine any member who took a legal dispute to a civil authority that could be settled by the association itself.[23] As Monson has argued, the immediate reason for these and other provisions was to foster a sense of mutual trust within the association and to discourage free-riding.[24] A very fragmentary set of Greek by-laws from the first century appears to have a similar provision: 'it is no lawful for anyone to ... a private debt ... not to prosecute him (μηδ' ἐνκαλεῖν αὐτῶι)... against him ... he might meet just terms'.[25] About the same time the guild of sheep and donkey herders in Tebtynis imposed fines on any member who prosecuted or calumniated another member (P.Mich. V 243.12 = GRA III 206). A century later the by-laws of the Athenian Iobakchoi imposed a twenty-five denarii fine on anyone who appealed to the public courts instead of going to the association's priest or *archibakchos* (IG II² 1368.90–94 = GRA I 51).

The provisions, although they may have arisen for diverse reasons as strategies for reducing internal conflict and enhancing group solidarity, had the effect of asserting the autonomy of the group in respect

---

22 CIL 14.2112.19-20 (Lanuvium [Latium et Campania: Regio I],136 C.E.).
23 P.Lille.dem. I 29 = GRA III 188 (Pisais, 223 B.C.E.); P.Cair. 30606 = GRA III 191 (Tebtynis, 158/157 B.C.E.); P.Cair. 31179 (Tebtynis, 147 B.C.E.); P.Cair. 30605 (Tebtynis, 145 B.C.E.); P.Prague.dem (Tebtynis, 137 B.C.E.). On these, see de Cenival, *Les associations religieuses*.
24 Monson, 'Ethics and Economics', 234, citing Tilly, *Trust and Rule*.
25 BGU XIV 2371 = GRA III 253 (Herakleopolis, I B.C.E.). There are striking similarities of these by-laws to P.Lond. VII 2193 = GRA III 199 (Philadelphia, 69–58? B.C.E.).

to legal matters. They constituted the association as a mini-*polis*, able to formulate and approve its own bylaws and able to administer and police those bylaws.

Christ Assemblies playing at democracy

Christ groups quickly adopted the term *ekklēsia*, first as a term for a local assembly of Christ devotees (e.g. 1 Thess. 1:1; 1 Cor. 1:2; Phil. 4:15; Phlm. 2), but later as a term embracing all Christ devotees as constituting a 'spiritual' assembly (2 Clem. 14:2).

Whether Christ groups appropriated the term *ekklēsia* from the LXX (where it translates *qahal*) or from the language of the civic assembly is rather beside the point.[26] At least in the case of 1 Thessalonians and 1 Corinthians, addressed as they are to non-Jews, it seems rather unlikely that Paul expected his addressees to see *ekklēsia* as a Septuagintalism. Given the widespread use of the term in Greek cities, *ekklēsia* was entirely legible to Macedonians and Corinthians as a term belonging to civic vocabulary. It is also unsurprising that Christ groups adopted other vocabulary that was perfectly legible within a civic context: *episkopos* (Phil. 1:1), *politeuma* (Phil. 3:20), and *presbyteros* (Acts; 1 Tim.; James; 1 Peter; Rev.), irrespective of their putative sources.

When the practices of Christ groups are read in the context of the democratic practices of a variety of ancient private associations, one can see various gestures towards democratic practices. Most obvious as the several references to the election (χειροτενέω) of officers and ambassadors (Did. 15.1; Ignatius, Phil. 10.1; Smyrn. 11.2; Pol. 7.2) and the Didache's reference to the vetting (δοκιμάζω) of candidates for office (15.1), a standard practice in the democratic Greek cities. Less obvious, but no less significant, are the references in Paul's letters to disciplinary practices that are enacted by the entire group. Thus, he acknowledges than an offender was punished 'by the majority' (2 Cor. 2:6), which recalls association bylaws that prescribe that punishments for infractions of the bylaws should be in accord with 'whatever the association

---

26 See Trebilco, 'Why Did the Early Christians?'; van Kooten, ''Εκκλησία τοῦ θεοῦ', 522–48.

decides' (P.Mich. V 243.3; IG XII,3 330.254–255). When considers the matter of Corinthian members taking each other to the civic courts, he insists, like some private associations, that such matters should be settled in house (1 Cor. 6:1–7). This is not only a strategy to control the fractiousness what was endemic in associations of all kinds, but an assertion of quasi-civic autonomy over judicial and disciplinary matters.

Finally, as Harrison has noted, Paul's insistence on ἰσότης as the rationale for contributing to the collection for the poor of Jerusalem was a fundamental element of δημοκρατία.[27] A very similar rational appears in an epidosis for the poor of Iasos in a time of famine. Contributions to the common good reinforced democracy.[28]

While the tendencies toward democratic practices in early Christ groups were not the only tendencies at work—the eventual cultivation of patronage by elite members resulted had an opposite effect—early Christ groups, like many private associations, carried the fruits of the political experiment born in Athens six centuries earlier.

John S. Kloppenborg
University of Toronto

---

27 Harrison, 'Review: Ralph Korner'. See also Welborn, '"That There May Be Equality"'; Welborn, 'Paul's Place'; Welborn, 'How "Democratic" Was the Pauline Ekklēsia?'; and Miller, *Corinthian Democracy*.
28 I.Iasos 244 (Iasos, II b.c.e.): 'These, wishing from their own free will to reinforce democracy from their own resources, have contributed funds for the purchase of grain so that the *dēmos* will always live happily, having an abundance of grain, with all the citizens having a supply of grain from the common fund, in accordance with decree'. (A list of names follows).

Bibliography

Ammitzbøll Thomsen, Christian   *The Politics of Associations in Hellenistic Rhodes* (New Approaches to Ancient Greek Institutional History; Edinburgh: Edinburgh University Press, 2020).

Andreau, Jean, Pauline Schmitt, and Alain Schnapp   'Review: Paul Veyne et l'évergétisme', *Annales. Histoire, Sciences Sociales* 33.2 (1978), 307–25.

Connor, W. Robert   'Civil Society, Dionysiac Festival, and the Athenian Democracy', in Josiah Ober and Charles W. Hedrick (eds.), *Demokratia: A Conversation on Democracies, Ancient and Modern* (Princeton, NJ: Princeton University Press, 1989), 217–26.

De Cenival, Françoise   *Les associations religieuses en Égypte d'après les documents démotiques* (Publications de l'Institut français d'archéologie orientale du Caire. Bibliothèque d'étude 46; Cairo: Institut français d'archéologie orientale, 1972).

Foucart, Paul   *Des associations religieuses chez les Grecs—Thiases, éranes, orgéons, avec le texte des inscriptions rélatives à ces associations* (Paris: Klincksieck, 1873).

Harrison, James R.   'Review: Ralph Korner, *The Origin and Meaning of Ekklēsia in the Early Jesus Movement* (Leiden: Brill, 2017)', *RBL* 7 (2020), https://www.sblcentral.org/home/bookDetails/12808?search=korner&type=0.

Jones, Nicholas F.   *The Associations of Classical Athens: The Response to Democracy* (London and New York: Oxford University Press, 1999).

Miller, Anna C.   *Corinthian Democracy: Democratic Discourse in 1 Corinthians* (Princeton Theological Monograph Series 220; Eugene, OR: Pickwick Publications, 2015).

Monson, Andrew   'The Ethics and Economics of Ptolemaic Religious Associations', *Ancient Society* 36 (2006), 221–238.

Ober, Josiah   *Mass and Elite in Democratic Athens: Rhetoric, Ideology, and the Power of the People* (Princeton, NJ: Princeton University Press, 1989).

Ober, Josiah   *The Athenian Revolution* (Princeton, NJ: Princeton University Press, 1996).

Paganini, Mario C. D. 'Decisional Practices of Private Associations in Ptolemaic and Early Roman Egypt', in T. Derda, A. Łajtar, and J. Urbanik (eds.), *Proceedings of the 27th International Congress of Papyrology* (JJP Supp 28; Warsaw: Taubenschlag Foundation, 2016), 1889–1901.

Payne, Steven T. 'Spiritual Bodies and the Afterlives of Ancient Democracy in Early Paulinism' (PhD Thesis; New York, NY: Fordham University, 2019).

Putnam, Robert D. *Bowling Alone: The Collapse and Revival of American Community* (New York, NY: Simon & Schuster, 2000).

Tilly, Charles *Trust and Rule* (Cambridge Studies in Comparative Politics; Cambridge and New York: Cambridge University Press, 2005).

Trebilco, Paul R. 'Why Did the Early Christians Call Themselves ἡ ἐκκλησία?' NTS 57.3 (2011), 440–60.

van Kooten, 'George H. Ἐκκλησία τοῦ θεοῦ: The "Church of God" and the Civic Assemblies (ἐκκλησίαι) of the Greek Cities in the Roman Empire: A Response to Paul Trebilco and Richard A. Horsley', *NTS* 58.4 (2012), 522–48.

Van Nijf, Onno *The Civic World of Professional Associations in the Roman East* (Dutch Monographs on Ancient History and Archaeology 17; Amsterdam: J. C. Gieben, 1997).

Welborn, L.L. 'How "Democratic" Was the Pauline Ekklēsia? An Assessment with Special Reference to the Christ Groups of Roman Corinth', *NTS* 65.3 (2019), 289–309.

Welborn, L.L. '"That There May Be Equality": The Contexts and Consequences of a Pauline Ideal', *NTS* 59.1 (2012), 73–90

Welborn, L.L. 'Paul's Place in a First-Century Revival of the Discourse of "Equality"', *HTR* 110.4 (2017), 541–62.

Zuiderhoek, Arjan J. *The Politics of Munificence in the Roman Empire: Citizens, Elites, and Benefactors in Asia Minor*, Greek Culture in the Roman World (Cambridge and New York: Cambridge University Press, 2009).

The Materiality of Grace:
Paul's Collection for the Poor

L. L. Welborn

'Without bread, you can't appreciate roses.'
Lynn Steger Strong, *Want*.

Abstract

The essay focuses upon relatively neglected 'material' aspects of Paul's grace-filled project: the collection for the poor in Jerusalem. First, the language which Paul employs in speaking of the collection in 1 Corinthians, 2 Corinthians, Galatians, and Romans is scrutinized, leading to recognition that the eagerness of interpreters to discover Paul's theological motivations has largely silenced economic resonances of Paul's vocabulary. Second, recent studies of the financial practices of individuals and groups in Greco-Roman society are examined, in order to assess whether donative inscriptions and records of private associations cast light upon the collection, administration, and distribution of funds in Pauline communities.

I

The last two decades have witnessed a dramatic increase in studies devoted to Paul's collection for the poor among the saints in Jerusalem.[1]

---

1 Among numerous studies: Joubert, *Paul as Benefactor*; Wan, 'Collection for the Saints'; Lindemann, 'Hilfe für die Armen, 199-216; Kim, *Die paulinische*; Schmithals, 'Die Kollekten', 78-106; Downs, *The Offering of the Gentiles*; Heil, '"Die Armen nicht vergessen"', 86-103; Friesen, 'Paul and Economics', 24-54; Longenecker, *Remember the Poor*; Klein, 'Die Begründung, 104-30; Sänger, '"Jetzt aber führt auch das Tun zu Ende"', 257-82; Ogereau, 'The Jerusalem Collection', 360-78; Tucker, 'The Jerusalem Collection', 52-70; Kloppenborg, 'Fiscal Aspects of Paul's Collection', 153-98; Kloppenborg, 'The Collection', 245-64.

The motivation for these studies is doubtless complex and difficult to disentangle—whether, that is, Pauline scholars are concerned about the impoverishment of the masses in an era of globalised capital,[2] or whether scholars are finally determined to do justice to the project that summed up Paul's theology, apostleship, and ministry as a whole.[3] In any case, the recent studies share a tendency with the older works by Dieter Georgi, Keith Nickle, and Klaus Berger: namely a concentration upon the theological significance of the collection for the poor.[4] According to Bruce Longenecker, Paul sought to promote spirited generosity to the poor as a key component of righteousness toward Israel's deity, making the collection the most important application of Paul's general caritative principle.[5] David Downs seeks to demonstrate that Paul presents the collection for Jerusalem as a religious offering, an act of corporate worship that will result in thanksgiving and praise to God.[6] To be sure, none of the recent interpreters of the collection entirely ignore Paul's intention to provide material relief for impoverished believers at Jerusalem, although Longenecker judges that it is unproductive to consider whether Paul hoped that his collection would bring about improvements in the economic circumstances of the Jerusalem Jesus-followers, insisting that, for Paul, the collection was symbolic;[7] and Downs concludes that Paul's metaphorical presentation of the collection as an act of cultic worship functioned rhetorically to obscure and downplay the role of the collection as a mundane benefaction.[8]

Without diminishing the theological significance (caritative, ecumenical, eschatological) that the collection acquired in the course of

---

2   Vassiliadis, 'Equality and Justice', 51-59; Horrell, 'Paul's Collection', 74-83; Welborn, '"That There May Be Equality"', 73-90.
3   Cullmann, *Message to Catholics*; Munck, *Paul and the Salvation*; Beckheuer, *Paulus und Jerusalem*.
4   Georgi, *Geschichte der Kollekte*; Nickle, *The Collection*; Berger, 'Almosen für Israel', 180-204. To be sure, these studies contained many important sociological insights, alongside the concern for Paul's theological motivation.
5   Longenecker, *Remember the Poor*, 187.
6   Downs, *Offering of the Gentiles*, 28-29, 120-21.
7   Longenecker, *Remember the Poor*, 315 n.38.
8   Downs, *Offering of the Gentiles*, 158.

its administration, the present essay will focus upon relatively neglected material aspects of Paul's grace-filled project. We shall begin with the language Paul employs in speaking of the collection in 1 Corinthians, 2 Corinthians, Galatians, and Romans. We shall see that the eagerness of interpreters to discover Paul's theological motivations has largely silenced economic resonances of Paul's vocabulary. Second, we shall examine recent studies of the financial practices of individuals and groups in Graeco-Roman society, to assess whether donative inscriptions and records of private associations cast light upon the collection, administration, and distribution of funds in the Pauline communities.

II

In what is probably the earliest reference to the collection in the Pauline corpus, in 1 Corinthians 16:1–4, Paul gives instructions for the implementation of the project, in response to the Corinthians' inquiry.[9] The term λογεία, by which the collection is designated here, has been taken by Keith Nickle, among others, as a kind of 'tax' imposed by the Jerusalem church, on the analogy of the didrachma tax collected for the maintenance of the sacrifices offered in the temple at Jerusalem.[10] While it is undeniable that λογεία is used of the collection of taxes,[11] the meaning 'contribution' seems most apposite in the context of 1 Corinthians 16:1-4, where it is clear that the offering is in response to a solicitation. It is this sense of a solicited contribution that is found in a first-century C.E. papyrus from Oxyrhynchus: a certain Epimachus swears by Nero Caesar that he has not asked for contributions (λογεῖαι) of any kind toward becoming the headman of his village.[12] As Grenfell and Hunt observe, 'the word λογεία [in this instance] refers to irregular

---

9 On περὶ δὲ τῆς λογείας τῆς εἰς τοὺς ἁγίους as a letter response formula, see Hurd, *The Origin of 1 Corinthians*, 200–206. For the chronological priority of 1 Corinthians over Galatians, see Lüdemann, *Paul*, 47.
10 Nickle, *The Collection*, 74–93.
11 Frequently in tax receipts on ostraca, so Moulton and Milligan, *The Vocabulary of the Greek Testament*, 377 s.v. λογεία; Arzt-Grabner, Kritzer, Papathomas, and Winter, *1. Korinther*, 506.
12 P.Oxy II.239 (66 C.E.; Moulton and Milligan, *Vocabulary of the Greek Testament*, 377 s.v. λογεία.

local contributions, as opposed to regular taxes'.[13]

Recently, Downs has argued that, in applying the term λογεία to the collection, Paul drew upon language associated with monies donated to temples and deities, thus framing the collection metaphorically as a religious offering.[14] To be sure, a number of instances are attested in which λογεία is used of a collection for sacred purposes, as in a first-century ostracon in which a certain Psenamounis, a προστάτης of god, acknowledges receipt of four drachmae and one obol as a 'contribution' (λογεία τοῦ θεοῦ) from a worshipper.[15] Yet, Paul advises the Corinthians that the contributions set aside by each person out of his or her earnings on the first day of the week are to be kept 'individually' (παρ' ἑαυτῷ).[16] There is no indication that these small weekly sums are to be deposited in the common fund of the *ekklēsia* during Sunday worship, as Downs urges us to believe.[17] That individual accounts are envisioned by Paul, rather than contributions to a central ecclesiastical chest, is indicated by the use of the plural λογεῖαι in 1 Corinhians 16:2. In sum, the verdict of Georgi on the meaning of λογεία in 1 Corinthians 16:1–2 still seems justified: 'λογεία in this context means a collection

---

13 Grenfell and Hunt, *The Oxyrhynchus Papyri 2*.
14 Downs, *Offering of the Gentiles*, 129–31.
15 PSI 3.262 (58 c.e.); Arzt-Grabner, *1. Korinther*, 507, with additional examples.
16 Kloppenborg, 'Fiscal Aspects of Paul's Collection', 170: 'That these presumably smaller weekly sums should not immediately be given to the ekklēsia but be kept individually (παρ' ἑαυτῷ) meant only that the bookkeeping connected to the collection could be kept separate from whatever other funds the ekklēsia administered'.
17 Downs, *Offering of the Gentiles*, 128–29, argues that the prepositional phrase παρ' ἑαυτῷ qualifies the preceding subject ἕκαστος ὑμῶν, rather than the following verbal clause τιθέτω θησαυρίζων, so that 'Paul instructs each member of the church in Corinth individually to donate to the common fund on the first day of the week', appealing to Llewelyn, 'The Use of Sunday, 205–223. But see the counter to Llewelyn's interpretation by Young, '"The Use of Sunday": A Response', 111–22. Cf. Conzelmann, *Der erste Brief an die Korinther*, 365: 'Auch eine Kollekte beim Gottesdienst ist nicht vorgesehen, wenn jeder das Seine bei sich selbst "deponieren" soll'.

of funds, nothing else'.[18]

The second term by which Paul designates the collection in 1 Corinthians 16 is χάρις. Given the complex and subtle ways in which Paul employs this term in subsequent appeals to the Corinthians for partnership in the collection, it is understandable that interpreters should take the meaning to be fundamentally theological. In 2 Corinthians 8 and 9, Paul uses χάρις of the manifestation of divine favour (8:9), the effects of God's grace in the lives of believers (8:1; 9:8,14), and human gratitude and thanksgiving to God (8:16; 9:15), building upon the extraordinary semantic versatility of the word.[19] Nevertheless, in 1 Corinthians 16:3, χάρις refers unambiguously to the collection for the Jerusalem saints, in the sense of a 'gift', a 'benefaction'—the meaning which the word also has in 2 Corinthians 8:6,7 and 19.[20] James Harrison has elucidated this sense of the term in his thorough examination of honorific inscriptions registering the disposal and return of χάριτες by benefactors and beneficiaries,[21] such as the first-century stele erected by the people of Cardamylae recompensing Poseidippos for the benefits he had bestowed upon the citizens with their never-ending gratitude (ἀτελῆ χάρις).[22] In a discourse delivered in his native Prusa, Dio Chrysostom laments that his promise of a gift (χάρις) to embellish the city had soured into an obligation because of his tardiness in making the payment.[23] Moreover, the verb which Paul uses in speaking of the conveyance of the Corinthians' gift to Jerusalem in 1 Corinthians 16:3 adds a nuance of reciprocity that has gone unnoticed by the commentators: ἀποφέρω in an economic context has the sense of

---

18 Georgi, *Remembering the Poor*, 53, referencing Kittel, 'λογεία', 282–83. Cf. Arzt-Grabner, *2. Korinther*, 392 n.704: 'Was die paulinische Kollekte betrifft, fällt zwar auf, dass Paulus nie explizit von "Geld" (ἀργύριον, χρύσιον) spricht, der Terminus λογεία in 1 Kor 16:1 ist aber durchaus als monetärer Begriff aufzufassen'.
19 Moulton and Milligan, *Vocabulary of the Greek Testament*, 684 s.v. χάρις; Schulz, *The Meaning of Charis*, 63; Harrison, *Paul's Language of Grace*, 294.
20 Conzelmann, *Der erste Brief an die Korinther*, 366; Georgi, *Remembering the Poor*, 53–54; Betz, *2 Corinthians 8 and 9*, 42, 54 n.119, 58, 76; Harrison, *Paul's Language of Grace*, 294, 300–301, 313.
21 Harrison, *Paul's Language of Grace*, 314–22.
22 SEG XI.948; Harrison, *Paul's Language of Grace*, 51–52, 316.
23 Dio Chrysostom Or. 40.3-4; Harrison, *Paul's Language of Grace*, 312.

'pay back', 'return', and hence 'pay what is due'.[24] That is, the obligation of the Corinthian believers to recompense the Jerusalem saints for the spiritual benefits they had received, an obligation finally made explicit in Romans 15:26–27, is already implicit in 1 Corinthians 16:3.

The final sentence of the paragraph on the implementation of the collection at Corinth discloses another material aspect that is overlooked by recent commentators. To his instructions for accumulating monies, Paul adds a promissory incentive: 'if [the collection] is sufficiently large', he himself will convey it to Jerusalem, and the delegates of the Corinthian *ekklēsia* will accompany him (16:4). The conditional clause, ἐὰν δὲ ἄξιον ᾖ, is taken by most recent interpreters to lodge the decision about the conveyance of the collection with the Corinthians, and so translated 'if it seems advisable', that is, 'to you'.[25] But Johannes Weiss argued for an interpretation that refers the conditional clause to the amount of the collection, reflecting the sense of ἄξιος as 'worth' or 'value', a meaning that is well attested by the papyri.[26] Thus, Weiss translates, 'Wenn es der Mühe wert ist', and comments, 'nur wenn eine glänzende Sammlung zusammen- gekommen ist, will er es tun'.[27] We have, then, in 1 Corinthians 16:4 the first indication of the large role which Paul anticipates the Corinthians will play in the success of the collection for the

---

24 Liddell-Scott-Jones, *Greek-English Lexicon*, 226 s.v. ἀποφέρω II.2, Herodotus 1.196; 4.35; 5.84; Thucydides 5.31, etc. The sense of 'return' or 'give back' is also present in the papyri, e.g., P.Cair.Zen. I.59120, 4-5 (256 B.C.E.); P.Fuad. I Univ. App. I.3-4 (229 B.C.E.?); Arzt-Grabner, *1. Korinther*, 509.
25 So, for example, Barrett, *The First Epistle to the Corinthians*, 251; Conzelmann, *1 Corinthians*, 294; Fee, *The First Epistle to the Corinthians*, 816; Collins, *First Corinthians*, 589. But as recently as 1966, Nickle (*The Collection*, 16) could observe: 'It is usual to refer ἄξιον to the amount of the collection, translate it "worthwhile", or some similar term, and make Paul's decision to travel to Jerusalem dependent upon the generosity of the collection'. Nickle rejects this interpretation on moralistic, rather than linguistic, grounds: 'it unjustifiably imputes to Paul a pettiness and a shallow appreciation of the significance of the collection, a profound lack of confidence in the Corinthians, and a willingness to manipulate his churches in a rather crude fashion'.
26 Weiss, *Der erste Korintherbrief*, 382. For the sense of ἄξιος as 'worth' or 'value' in the papyri, see Moulton and Milligan, *Vocabulary of the Greek Testament*, 50–51 s.v. ἄξιος. Cf. Arzt-Grabner, *1. Korinther*, 510 n.27: 'Generell wird ἄξιος in den Papyri meist attributive in Verbindung mit Menschen oder Gegenständen ("würdig, wert") gebraucht'.
27 Weiss, *Der erste Korintherbrief*, 382.

poor, on account of their greater prosperity—an expectation that is expressed more clearly in 2 Corinthians 8:14 and 9:8.

Paul's deployment of the word-field describing 'abundance'— περισσεία, περισσεύω, περίσσευμα—in 2 Corinthians 8 and 9 is, if anything, more rich and subtle than his use of χάρις in these chapters.[28] Recently, Ryan Schellenberg has asserted that the rhetoric of 2 Corinthians 8 complicates the assumption that Paul is speaking of economic plenty in his use of περίσσευμα and its cognates.[29] Rhetoric to be sure (!), conspicuously displayed in the striking oxymoron with which Paul motivates his appeal to the Corinthians in 2 Corinthians 8:2: 'because the poverty (πτωχεία) [of the Macedonians] has overflowed (ἐπερίσσευσεν) into the wealth of their generosity'.[30] But it is, or should be, incontestable that in 2 Corinthians 8:14, where the Corinthians' περίσσευμα is set opposite the ὑστέρημα of the Jerusalem saints, Paul is speaking of material abundance and material lack. Paul's usage is well illustrated by a second-century inscription from Sparta in which the president of the Caesarean and Eurykleian games is described as 'having handed over to the city the whole surplus (περισσεία) of the monies (χρήματα) for the direction of the games'.[31] Thus, Hans Dieter Betz comments on 2 Corinthians 8:14: 'At the literal level, Paul certainly intended the material abundance of the Corinthians and the material poverty of the Jerusalem church'.[32] Indeed, the inference that seems warranted with respect to Paul's manipulation of the word-group denoting 'abundance' is the exact opposite of that drawn by Schellenberg: namely, the economic surplus enjoyed by the Corinthians is the assumptive basis upon which Paul skilfully erects an emotional, ethical, and ideological superstructure that proleptically justifies his appeal for the redistribution of resources.

---

28 Windisch, *Der zweite Korintherbrief*, 244; Theobald, *Die überströmende Gnade*, 301–34; Betz, *2 Corinthians 8 and 9*, 43.
29 Schellenberg, 'Subsistence, Swapping, and Paul's Rhetoric of Generosity', 215–34, here 228 n.59.
30 Bauer, *Greek-English Lexicon*, 805 s.v. περισσεύω 1.γ; Betz, *2 Corinthians 8 and 9*, 44.
31 *CIG* 1.1378; Deissmann, *Light from the Ancient East*, 80.
32 Betz, *2 Corinthians 8 and 9*, 68.

This conclusion regarding the meaning of περίσσευμα and its cognates is reinforced by Paul's use of the term ἁδρότης in 8:20 to describe the 'abundant' or 'lavish' gift the Corinthians are being asked to entrust to his administration.[33] Diodorus Siculus employs the cognate term in describing the 'abundant gifts and honors' that Ptolemy promised to give to the commander of the garrison at Tyre.[34]

The term ἁπλότης by which Paul describes the quality of the Macedonians' unexpected gift in 2 Corinthians 8:2 ingeniously evokes both moral and material aspects of the Macedonians' response to divine grace, exploiting the range of meanings embraced in the word.[35] To be sure, a number of interpreters insist that only the moral sense of the term as 'sincerity' is lexically warranted. Thus, Joseph Amstutz argues for the translation 'spontane Einfalt',[36] while Stephan Münch refers the term exclusively to the inner, spiritual attitude of the giver, not to the generosity of the gift.[37] But the cognate ἁπλοῦς is well attested in the documentary papyri in an economic sense, in reference to the repayment of a marriage dowry and the payment of loan interest.[38] In the *Testament of Issachar*, entitled Περὶ ἁπλότητος, the patriarch observes: 'the ἁπλοῦς does not crave gold, he does not defraud his neighbor' (4:2), making clear that ἁπλότης is not only an inner disposition, but a concrete action.[39] A Greek epitaph found at Rome praises a young man, affectionately nicknamed 'Raven of the Rocks' by his friends, because 'he practiced generosity' (ἤσκι τὴν ἁπλότητα).[40] Thus, commentators from Hans Windisch to Thomas Schmeller are justified

---

33   Bauer, *Greek-English Lexicon*, 21 s.v. ἁδρότης; Windisch, *Der zweite Korintherbrief*, 265; Furnish, *II Corinthians*, 424.
34   Diodorus Siculus 19.86; Liddell-Scott-Jones, *Greek-English Lexicon*, 25 s.v. ἁδρός I.
35   Bauer, *Greek-English Lexicon*, 104 s.v. ἁπλότης, where 2 Cor. 8:2 is placed under two meanings: 'ingenuousness' and 'generosity.' See further the insightful comments of Windisch, *Der zweite Korintherbrief*, 245; Betz, *2 Corinthians 8 and 9*, 44.
36   Amstutz, ἉΠΛΟΤΗΣ, 103-11.
37   Münch, *Das Geschenk der Einfachheit*, 93-94.
38   E.g. P.Gen. I.21; Moulton and Milligan, *Vocabulary of the Greek Testament*, 58 s.v. ἁπλοῦς.
39   *T. Issachar* 4:2; cited by Betz, *2 Corinthians 8 and 9*, 44 n.35.
40   Kaibel, *Epigrammata Graeca ex lapidibus conlecta*, no. 716.

in concluding that ἁπλότης in 2 Corinthians 8:2 has the meaning 'generosity'—open-hearted liberality.[41] The economic sense of ἁπλότης is even clearer in 2 Corinthians 9:11 where Paul explains that the Achaians' wealth is intended for 'the greatest generosity', and in 9:13 where Paul anticipates that the Jerusalem saints will praise God for 'the generosity of the partnership benefiting them and all'.[42]

The expressions by which Paul further characterises the gift of the Macedonians in 2 Corinthians 8:3 have unmistakable economic resonances. The phrase κατὰ δύναμιν appears frequently in the documentary papyri with the sense 'according to one's financial capability'—as in a marriage contract from the time of Augustus in which a certain Dionysius pledges 'to feed and clothe Isidora as wedded wife κατὰ δύναμιν'.[43] The financial meaning of Paul's contrasting phrase, παρὰ δύναμιν, is well illustrated by an Oxyrhynchus papyrus of the first century C.E. in which a certain Tryphon complains against the wife who abandoned him, employing the semantic equivalent ὑπὲρ δύναμιν: 'I for my part provided for her what was suitable and even beyond my resources'.[44] Indeed, the term δύναμις in an economic context simply means the 'value' or 'worth' of money, as illustrated by several passages in Plutarch's *Lives*.[45] Paul emphasises the eagerness of the Macedonians' contribution by means of the adjective αὐθαίρετος, 'voluntary', 'of one's own accord'.[46] The same usage appears on a first-century inscription from Cyprus praising the gymnasiarch Adrastus who provided oil at his own expense and exercised his office αὐθαίρετος.[47]

---

41 Windisch, *Der zweite Korintherbrief*, 244–45; Furnish, *II Corinhians*, 400; Betz, *2 Corinthians 8 and 9*, 44–45; Martin, *2 Corinthians*, 253; Thrall, *The Second Epistle to the Corinthians*, 523–24; Harris, *The Second Epistle to the Corinthians*, 563; Schmeller, *Der zweite Brief an die Korinther*, 46.
42 Betz, *2 Corinthians 8 and 9*, 87, 116, 124–25.
43 BGU IV.1050; Moulton and Milligan, *Vocabulary of the Greek Testament*, 171 s.v. δύναμις.
44 P.Oxy II.252 (30–35 C.E.); Moulton and Milligan, *Vocabulary of the Greek Testament*, 171 s.v. δύναμις.
45 Plutarch *Lyc*. 9; *Sol*. 15; Liddell-Scott-Jones, *Greek-English Lexicon*, 452 s.v. δύναμις III.2.
46 Windisch, *Der zweite Korintherbrief*, 245.
47 OGIS 583 (29 C.E.); Moulton and Milligan, *Vocabulary of the Greek Testament*, 91.

The undertaking in which the Macedonians sought to participate is described by Paul in 2 Corinthians 8:4 as ἡ διακονία τῆς εἰς τοὺς ἁγίους, 'the relief work for the saints'. As Windisch observed, the repetition of this formula in 2 Corinthians 9:1,12–13 indicates that this was the official name by which the collection was known in the Pauline *ekklēsiai*, an abbreviation of the fuller description of the project given to the Roman believers in Romans 15:25–26: ἡ διακονία εἰς τοὺς πτωχοὺς τῶν ἁγίων τῶν ἐν Ἰερουσαλήμ.[48] Victor Furnish adduced a striking parallel to the language of 2 Corinthians 8:4 in the *Testament of Job* 11:1–3, where the patriarch tells his children:

> And there were also certain strangers who saw my zeal [to help the poor] and they also desired to assist in this service (διακονία). And there were some others at that time without resources and unable to spend a thing. And they came urging me (παρακαλοῦντες) and saying:
>
> 'We beg you (δεόμεθά σου), since we could also engage in this service (διακονία), but own nothing, show mercy on us and furnish us money so we may depart for distant cities and, by engaging in trade, we may be able to do the poor a service (τοῖς πένησιν δυνηθῶμεν ποιήσασθαι διακοίαν)'.[49]

From this text and others, such as Acts 6:1, Furnish concluded that Greek-speaking Judaism had come to use the term διακονία in a technical sense for supplying the needs of the poor.[50]

The relationship between the Macedonians and the Jerusalem saints is described in 2 Corinthians 8:4 as a κοινωνία. The same word is used in 2 Corinthians 9:13 to designate the agreement with the Jerusalem saints which Paul urges upon the Achaians, and retrospectively in Romans 15:26 in reporting to the Romans the decision of the Macedonians and Achaians to take part in the collection. In his meticulous examination of hundreds of inscriptions and papyri, Julien

---

48 Windisch, *Der zweite Korintherbrief*, 246.
49 Furnish, *II Corinthians*, 401. Text and translation of T. Job 11:1-3 in Kraft, *The Testament of Job*.
50 Furnish, *II Corinthians*, 401.

Ogereau has demonstrated that the term κοινωνία and its cognates κοινωνέω and κοινωνός often denote an economic partnership of some kind.[51] The nature of the partnership that Paul sought to establish between the Achaians and the Jerusalem saints is disclosed by the formulaic language of 2 Corinthians 9:13. As Betz observed, the vocabulary of this verse is legal.[52] The term ὁμολογία is very common in the papyri in the sense of 'contract' or 'agreement': a first-century papyrus from the Fayum acknowledges the sale of a priest's chamber within a temple κατὰ τήνδε τὴν ὁμολογίαν, 'in accordance with this agreement';[53] another first-century contract from the Fayum records a ὁμολογία between a labourer and the owner of an oil-press to provide services for the harvest season.[54] Thus, ὁμολογία in 2 Corinthians 9:13 does not mean 'confession', as elsewhere in the New Testament, but 'contractual agreement'.[55] The phrase ἐπὶ τῇ ὑποταγῇ τῆς ὁμολογίας ὑμῶν indicates that the Achaians have entered into a contractual agreement with the Jerusalem saints by means of their contribution. Whether such a contract existed, and whether Paul's language reflects the wording of a document, as Betz suggested,[56] must remain an open question. But that Paul chose to represent the relationship as economic and juridical, by means of the technical vocabulary he employs, seems undeniable.

In 2 Corinthians 9:12 Paul characterises the relief work for the saints in Jerusalem as a λειτουργία. The verb form of the same word is used in Romans 15:27, where Paul explains why the Gentiles are reciprocally obligated to the Jerusalem saints. Recently, Downs has argued that λειτουργία and λειτουργέω refer to religious or cultic activities: thus, the phrase ἡ διακονία τῆς λειτουργίας in 2 Corinthians 9:12 urges

---

51 Ogereau, *Paul's Koinonia with the Philippians*.
52 Betz, *2 Corinthians 8 and 9*, 122.
53 *P. Ryl.* 2.161 (81 C.E.).
54 *P. Fay.* 91 (99 C.E.)
55 Contra Bauer, *Greek-English Lexicon*, 709 s.v. ὁμολογία 1: 'professing', 'confessing'. For ὁμολογία as 'contractual agreement' in the papyri, see Arzt-Grabner, *2. Korinther*, 441.
56 Betz, *2 Corinthians 8 and 9*, 123–25, with the assessment by Arzt-Grabner, *2. Korinther*, 441–42.

the Achaians to view their participation in the collection as an act of priestly service offered to God.⁵⁷ In support of this interpretation, Downs adduces inscriptions from the Hellenistic and Roman periods in which λειτουργία appears in cultic contexts, and claims that most commentators understand λειτουργία in 2 Corinthians 9:12 in a cultic sense.⁵⁸ But these assertions misrepresent both the breadth of lexical evidence and the diversity of scholarly opinion. In literary sources from Athens and elsewhere (Lysias, Demosthenes, Polybius, et al.), λειτουργία designates a 'public service performed by private citizens at their own expense'.⁵⁹ In the documentary papyri, as well, λειτουργία refers to a voluntary service rendered in the interest of the state or the common good, according to Ruth Kritzer and Peter Arzt-Grabner in their papyrological commentary on 2 Corinthians.⁶⁰ Moreover, commentators—from Georg Heinrici to Betz, including Windisch and Celas Spicq—recognise the political and economic usage of λειτουργία in 2 Corinthians 9:12 as the performance of a public service.⁶¹ Alfred Plummer may speak for the group: 'Λειτουργία is used here in a sense closely akin to the meaning of the "aids" which wealthy citizens rendered to the public in financing various projects'.⁶² This is not to deny

---

57 Downs, *Offering of the Gentiles*, 144–45.
58 Downs, *Offering of the Gentiles*, 144 n.81, referencing *IG* V/1.1390; *IMagnMai* 98; *IG* II².1028, 1039, and adducing in support the commentaries of Meyer, *Der zweite Brief an die Korinther*, 245–46; Bachmann, *Der zweite Brief des Paulus an die Korinther*, 330; Furnish, *II Corinthians*, 451; Harris, *Second Epistle*, 648–49; Furnish, *II Corinthians*, 443, although Furnish asserts: 'A *leitourgia* was any act of public service, whether of wealthy citizens who supported civil events and institutions, of civil magistrates, or of priestly officials who conducted the ceremonies of religious cults'.
59 Andocides 4.42; Lysias 21.19; Demosthenes 20.2; Polybius 6.33.6; Liddell-Scott-Jones, *Greek-English Lexicon*, 1036 s.v. λειτουργία.
60 Arzt-Grabner, *2. Korinther*, 439: 'Unter einer Liturgie ist in den dokumentarischen Papyri Ägyptens in erster Linie—wie in griechischen 'Mutterland'—ein ehrenamtlich, im Interesse des Staates oder Gemeinwohls zu leistender Dienst zu verstehen'.
61 Heinrici, *Der zweite Brief an die Korinther*, 307: 'eine gemeinsame öffentliche Angelegenheit füf die Gläubigen'; Windisch, *Der zweite Korintherbrief*, 281–82; Strathmann, 'λειτουγέω, κτλ.', 227; Betz, *2 Corinthians 8 and 9*, 117. See also Spicq, *Notes de lexicographie néotestamentaire* 1, 479; Danker, *Benefactor*, 330–31.
62 Plummer, *A Critical and Exegetical Commentary*, 265.

that Paul skilfully invokes the cultic connotations of λειτουργία in 2 Corinthians 9:12 through repeated reference to the thanksgiving which is the return of grace received from God. But the economic aspect of λειτουργία is fundamental, and is highlighted in Romans 15:27, where Paul makes clear that the respect in which the Gentiles are obligated to render service (λειτουργῆσαι) to the Jerusalem saints is in 'material things' (τὰ σαρκικά).[63]

Finally, Paul's characterisation of the Jerusalem saints as 'the poor', οἱ πτωχοί, in Romans 15:26 (cf. Gal. 2:10). As is well known, Karl Holl argued that the Jerusalem believers referred to themselves as οἱ πτωχοί, a title which gave expression to the group's sense of utter dependence upon divine resources, rather than a description of their destitute condition.[64] Holl's suggestion was taken up by Rudolf Bultmann and Karl Ludwig Schmidt, among others, and was tentatively endorsed by Keith Nickle.[65] But in two articles published in the 1960s, Leander Keck decisively refuted Holl's claim that οἱ πτωχοί was a self-designation of the earliest Jerusalem Christians, serving as a synonym for 'the righteous'.[66] That the term denotes material poverty is indicated by Paul's repeated reference to the 'want' (ὑστέρημα) of the Jerusalem saints in 2 Corinthians 8:14 and 9:12. Nor should it go unnoticed that Paul uses πτωχός rather than πένης to describe the poor among the saints in Jerusalem: the πτωχός is a destitute beggar, not merely a poor person who lives at the level of subsistence.[67] As Aristophanes observes in the *Plutus*, 'the πτωχός possesses nothing at all; the πένης lives thriftily and is attentive to his work'.[68]

Who were 'the poor among the saints in Jerusalem' (Rom. 15:26)? The sources of our knowledge about the poor of Jerusalem are entirely

---

63 Peterman, 'Romans 15:26', 457–63, here 463; Blanton IV, 'The Economic Functions of Gift Exchange', 279–306.
64 Holl, 'Der Kirchenbegriff des Paulus', 920–47.
65 Nickle, *The Collection*, 138.
66 Keck, 'The Poor among the Saints in the New Testament', 100–29; Keck, 'The Poor among the Saints in Jewish Christianity and Qumran', 54–78.
67 Liddell-Scott-Jones, *Greek-English Lexicon*, 1550 s.v. πτωχός.
68 Aristophanes *Pl.* 552.

literary.[69] Mark's Gospel portrays a 'poor widow' (χήρα πτωχή) who put two small coins, amounting to the quarter-piece of a Roman *as*, into the treasury of the temple (Mark 12:42). Mark's Jesus explains to the disciples that this miniscule offering was 'everything she had, her whole livelihood' (Mark 12:44).[70] The author of Acts describes a 'lame man' (ἀνὴρ χωλός) who lay daily beside the Beautiful Gate of the temple asking for alms (Acts 3:2, 3, 10).[71] Should one assume that the historicity of these accounts, with their fleeting glimpses of the impoverished of Jerusalem, is enhanced by the fact that they derive from sources which were produced by the non-elite?[72] The underlying cause of poverty in Jerusalem was generally the same as in the other cities of the early Empire: the concentration of resources in the hands of the land-owning elite led to deprivation of the general population.[73] Locally, the economic situation of Galilee and Judaea deteriorated after the death of Herod in 4 B.C.E., as major building projects began to wind down and jobs disappeared.[74] The plight of the poor in Jerusalem was exacerbated by the famine of 46 or 47 C.E., which occasioned the distribution of grain and money 'to the needy' (τοῖς ἐνδεέσι) by Helena, queen of Adiabene, and her son Izates.[75] The social anomie of Judaea in the early years of Nero is proxy evidence of impoverishment: a widespread dislocation of persons whom Josephus labels 'bandits' (λῃσταί) and 'imposters' (γόητες).[76]

A thorough treatment of the material aspects of Paul's language in speaking about the collection would take account of the changes in vocabulary—from the bald, denotative term λογεία employed in the

69   Jeremias, *Jerusalem in the Time of Jesus*, 109-19.
70   Collins, *Mark*, 586-90.
71   Barrett, *A Critical and Exegetical Commentary on the Acts of the Apostles* 1, 174-85.
72   Welborn, 'The Polis and the Poor', 189-244, esp. 192-93, 223-31.
73   Scheidel, 'Stratification, Deprivation and Quality of Life', 40-59; Harris, 'Poverty and Destitution in the Roman Empire', 27-56; Bang, 'Predation', 197-217.
74   Jeremias, *Jerusalem in the Time of Jesus*, 120-44; Theissen, *Sociology of Early Palestinian Christianity*, 33-46; Stegemann and Stegemann, *The Jesus Movement*, 104-25; Syon, *Small Change in Hellenistic-Roman Galilee*, 171-99.
75   Josephus A.J. 20.51-53; cf. Winter, 'Acts and Food Shortages', 59-78.
76   Josephus A.J. 20.98, 167-68; cf. Theissen, *Sociology of Early Palestinian Christianity*, 42-45, 49-50, 60-61.

first mention of the project in 1 Corinthians 16, through the richly evocative word χάρις used in the rhetorical appeals of 2 Corinthians 8 and 9, to the forthrightly political term λειτουργία deployed in 2 Corinthians 9 and Romans 15, reflecting the dynamics of Paul's turbulent relationship with the Corinthians. Such an undertaking lies beyond the scope of the present essay. But a promising effort in this direction has already been made by Stephan Joubert who pays attention to the complex and shifting ways in which Paul represents his relationship with the Jerusalem church in his appeals to Gentile groups for partnership in the collection.[77] Our purposes will have been served if we have given audibility to some of the economic resonances in Paul's language about the collection—resonances muted by interpreters eager to emphasise moral, spiritual, and cultic connotations.

III

Recent studies of the financial practices of individuals and groups in Greek cities provide instructive analogies to the Pauline collection in several respects. John Kloppenborg has focused attention upon the *epidoseis*, or public subscriptions, which called upon all residents—not only citizens, but *metics*, and even foreigners—to contribute to a variety of projects: the construction or repair of public buildings and sanctuaries, the support of games and festivals, the purchase of grain in times of shortage, etc.[78] *Epidoseis* are attested throughout Greece and Asia Minor, in Cyrenaica, Sicily, and Egypt, dating from the fourth century B.C.E. to well into the imperial period.[79] Ordinarily, these organised contributions were not ongoing payments for routine civic expenses, but collections raised to meet special needs.[80] The amounts solicited

---

77 Joubert, *Paul as Benefactor*, 114–15, 132, 139, 217 and *passim*.
78 Kloppenborg, 'Fiscal Aspects of Paul's Collection', 164–73; Kloppenborg, *Christ's Associations*, 248–52.
79 Kuenzi, ΕΠΙΔΟΣΙΣ; Migeotte, *Les souscriptions publiques* and Chaniotis, 'Public Subscriptions' for public subscriptions, and upon Migeotte, 'Les souscriptions dans les associations privées', 113–27 for *epidoseis* in private associations.
80 Chaniotis, 'Public Subscriptions', 91; Kloppenborg, 'Fiscal Aspects of Paul's Collection', 169; Kloppenborg, *Christ's Associations*, 248.

varied considerably: some subscriptions set no maximum donation, while others set both a maximum and a minimum; in a few cases, all subscribers contributed the same (usually quite small) amount.[81] The mechanism by which the funds were collected is made clear by several inscriptions: first, a subscriber would 'promise' or 'announce' the amount of his or her contribution, denoted by the verb ἐπαγγέλεσθαι; then, at some point in the future, the subscriber was expected to 'fulfil or 'complete' his pledge, indicated by the verb συντελεῖν; in some cases, the subscriptions were paid in instalments.[82] When all monies had been collected, an inscription was cut listing the names of the contributors, often in descending order, according to the amounts contributed.[83]

Kloppenborg perceptively notes several similarities between the public subscriptions of Greek cities and the Pauline collection. First, Paul's expectation that all, or most, of the Corinthians would contribute to the collection for the saints, indicated by the phrase ἕκαστος ὑμῶν παρ' ἑαυτῷ in 1 Corinthians 16:2, resembles the aim of the *epidoseis* that all residents, and not only the wealthy ones, should have the opportunity to participate in a common project for the benefit of the *polis*.[84] Second, the gap between promise and fulfilment in the *epidoseis*, allowing for payment of the promised amount in regular instalments, bears comparison with Paul's instructions to the Corinthians that each should lay aside something from whatever he had managed to earn on the first day of every week, so that collections need not be taken when he arrived (1 Cor. 16:2).[85] Finally, Paul's insistence that the Corinthians bring to completion the collection they had willingly begun, signalled by repetition of the verb ἐπιτελεῖν in 2 Corinthians 8, finds a counter-

---

81 E.g. *IG* II².791, 2332, 2334; VII 3191–3192; *SEG* 48.1103; *I.CosPH* 387, 404; Kloppenborg, *Christ's Associations*, 249–50.
82 E.g. *SEG* 50.1050; *ILindos* 2, no. 252.3, 6; Kloppenborg, *Christ's Associations*, 250.
83 *IEph.* 20; Harland, *Greco-Roman Associations*, 127; cf. *IG* II².2332; Migeotte, *Les souscriptions publiques*, no. 19; Kloppenborg, 'Fiscal Aspects of Paul's Collection', 169.
84 Kloppenborg, 'Fiscal Aspects of Paul's Collection', 170; Kloppenborg, *Christ's Associations*, 252.
85 Kloppenborg, 'Fiscal Aspects of Paul's Collection', 170; Kloppenborg, *Christ's Associations*, 252.

part in the emphasis upon the fulfilment of the promised contributions—marked by συντελεῖν—in the *epidosis* inscriptions, where those who reneged on their promises might be publicly shamed.[86]

Perhaps the *epidosis* inscriptions permit a further inference about the amounts of money contributed to the Pauline collection by various members of the Christ groups at Corinth. Paul's advice regarding the accumulation of funds in 1 Corinthians 16 directs that money be set aside each week from whatever extra each person has earned. But in 2 Corinthians 8, Paul speaks of the 'abundance' (περίσσευμα) of the Corinthians and of the 'lavish sum' (ἁδρότης) being entrusted to his administration. If the latter terms are not rhetorical exaggerations, Paul must have expected that some at Corinth with larger surplus resources—the patrons of the house churches—would supplement the small weekly sums saved by ordinary believers, so that the collection might be deemed 'sufficient' (ἄξιος).[87] An *epidosis* from Tanagra in Boeotia solicits contributions from women, in order to relocate the temple of Demeter and Kore to a better part of the city. The decree sets the maximum donation at a very low amount—five drachmae—and stipulates that if sufficient money is not produced from the promises of the women, the treasurer for sacred funds shall provide whatever additional money is needed.[88] A fragmentary *epidosis* from Iasos records the names of citizens who contributed voluntarily to the creation of a fund for the purchase of grain in times of shortage. One large contribution of 600 drachmae by a certain Menesthenes is afforded first place on the donor list, followed by a series of smaller contributions of declining size.[89] Evidently, Paul set neither a minimum nor a maximum contribution to the collection. Nor does Paul mention the

---

86 *ILindos* 2, no. 252.3, 6; Isaeus 5.37-38 on the shaming of those who reneged on their promises; Kloppenborg, 'Fiscal Aspects of Paul's Collection', 185-86; Kloppenborg, *Christ's Associations*, 252.
87 On the social status of Chloe, Crispus, Gaius, and Stephanas, the putative patrons of the house churches, see Theissen, *The Social Setting of Pauline Christianity*, 57, 73-75, 83-89, 92-93; Meeks, *The First Urban Christians*, 57-59; Chow, *Patronage and Power*, 88-90, 94-95.
88 *SEG* 43.212A = Sokolowski, *Lois sacrées des cites grecques*, no. 72.
89 *I.Iasos* 244; Hicks, 'Iasos', 83-118, here 100-101.

names of wealthier donors. But their existence seems to be presupposed, and the Corinthians would have known who they were.

A second area in which Kloppenborg has adduced analogies to the Pauline collection is the security and audit of monies raised by private associations.[90] Kloppenborg cites an inscription of an association of Herakleiastai in Attica pertaining to the management of funds for sacrifices and banquets.[91] Of special relevance to Paul's instructions in 1 Corinthians 16 is the requirement that the treasurer of the association provide a detailed account of income and expenses, along with a provision for the appointment of auditors:

> Likewise, when the treasurer renders an account, after a meeting has been called, they shall appoint three auditors (ἐγλογισταί) and the auditors shall swear by Herakles and Demeter and Kore [....] And let the account be closed when the auditors, having taken an oath, return the account to the president of the association, and indicate whether the treasurer owes anything.[92]

As Kloppenborg correctly observes, there are two salient parallels between the provisions of this association inscription and Paul's instructions in 1 Corinthians 16:3: first, Paul's assurance that the collection will be conveyed to Jerusalem by 'those whom you approve' (οὓς ἐὰν δοκιμάσητε); and second, Paul's promise that the Corinthian envoys will travel with letters from him.[93] That the representatives of the Corinthian *ekklēsia* have an official role to play related to their trustworthiness in delivering the collection is indicated by Paul's use of the verb δοκιμάζειν, which is a technical term for the testing and approval of candidates for civic office and for membership in private

---

90 Kloppenborg, 'Fiscal Aspects of Paul's Collection for Jerusalem', 164–73; Kloppenborg, *Christ's Associations*, 252–59.
91 *SEG* 31.122; Kloppenborg, *Christ's Associations*, 252–53.
92 *SEG* 31.122, lines 29–30, 40; translation in Ascough, Harland, and Kloppenborg, *Associations in the Greco-Roman World*, 9.
93 Kloppenborg, 'Fiscal Aspects of Paul's Collection for Jerusalem', 171; Kloppenborg, *Christ's Associations*, 254–55.

associations.⁹⁴ And that the letters which Paul promises to send with the envoys are financial accounts like those rendered by the treasurer of the *Herakleiastai* is suggested by the language of Romans 15:28, where Paul outlines the proper steps to be taken in the completion of the collection: specifically, the verb σφραγίζειν, by which Paul describes the 'sealing' or certification of the gift for Jerusalem, is often found in the papyri in connection with the authentication of letters and documents for security against fraud.⁹⁵

Again, we may build upon Kloppenborg's research by examining Paul's commendation of an unnamed brother as an agent in the completion of the collection at Corinth in 2 Corinthians 8:18–21. To be sure, Paul does not use the technical term λογιστής, 'auditor', to describe the brother whom he is sending along with Titus, but the language by which Paul affirms and justifies the inclusion of this brother in the delegation to Corinth makes clear that he is intended to conduct an audit and to allay any suspicion of misappropriation of funds. First, Paul acknowledges that the brother enjoys the 'approval' (ἔπαινος) of all the churches and has, in fact, been 'elected' (χειροτονηθείς) by the Christ assemblies (2 Cor. 8:18–19). The verb χειροτονεῖν is a technical term, attested in numerous inscriptions, describing the process of electing officials by a show of hands in the assembly.⁹⁶ Paul further characterises the brother as his συνέκδημος (2 Cor. 8:19), another term used in a technical sense to denote a person accompanying a public mission, as in a first-century B.C.E. inscription from Samothrace.⁹⁷ Indeed, Paul

---

94 Moulton and Milligan, *Vocabulary of the Greek Testament*, 167 s.v. δοκιμάζω: 'In the inscriptions indeed the verb is almost a term. tech. for passing as fit for a public office'. Further, Kloppenborg, 'The Moralizing of Discourse in Greco-Roman Associations', 215–28, here 216–19; Kloppenborg, 'Fiscal Aspects of Paul's Collection for Jerusalem', 171.
95 Deissmann, *Bible Studies*, 238–39; Moulton and Milligan, *Vocabulary of the Greek Testament*, 617–18 s.v. σφαγίζω; Kloppenborg, 'Fiscal Aspects of Paul's Collection for Jerusalem', 172.
96 Moulton and Milligan, *Vocabulary of the Greek Testament*, 687 s.v. χειροτονέω; Betz, *2 Corinthians 8 and 9*, 74–75 n.287; Arzt-Grabner, *2. Korinther*, 408–409; Kloppenborg, *Christ's Associations*, 294.
97 IG XII/8. 186; Moulton and Milligan, *Vocabulary of the Greek Testament*, 605 s.v. συνέκδημος; Betz, *2 Corinthians 8 and 9*, 75; Kloppenborg, *Christ's Associations*, 294.

acknowledges that the brother has a certain amount of control over the collection, 'in association with this charitable work being administered by us' (σὺν τῇ χάριτι ταύτῃ τῇ διακονουμένῃ ὑφ' ἡμῶν).[98] Especially revealing is Paul's explanation that the appointment of the brother is a precautionary measure, guarding against a potential accusation of embezzlement: 'acting in this way, we avoid the possibility that someone should complain against us in view of the large sum of money being administered by us' (2 Cor. 8:20).[99] Thus, a close reading of the paragraph authorising the activity of the brother appointed by the churches confirms and reinforces Kloppenborg's suggestion that the provisions made for the security and audit of the Pauline collection find instructive analogies in inscriptions documenting the proper management of funds by private associations.

Perhaps we may also build upon Harrison's insightful comparison of inscriptions honouring civic benefactors with Paul's appeal for partnership in the collection. Harrison has called attention to the purpose clauses in honorific inscriptions, marked by the particles ἵνα and ὅπως, for the light that these clauses cast upon the ideology of civic munificence.[100] In Hellenistic decrees, the ἵνα and ὅπως clauses in the resolution proper give expression to the ethical aims of the exchange of gifts and honours between benefactors and the *polis*;[101] these clauses also articulate the greater good accruing to the community as a result of the participation of citizens and residents in a reciprocal relationship.[102] Harrison details several respects in which the purpose clauses of honorific decrees reinforced civic virtues and motivated generous behaviour: first, in maintaining the reputation of the city for repaying honours to those who conferred benefits upon the people;[103] second, in stimulating healthy competition between those who sought to serve the

---

98 Betz, *2 Corinthians 8 and 9*, 75–76.
99 For this construction of στελλόμενοι τοῦτο, μή τις ἡμᾶς μωμήσηται κτλ. in 2 Cor. 8:20, see Rengstorf, 'στέλλω κτλ.', 588–90; s, *Der zweite Korintherbrief*, 265; Furnish, *II Corinthians*, 423; Betz, *2 Corinthians 8 and 9*, 76–77.
100 Harrison, *Paul's Language of Grace*, 315–18.
101 Harrison, *Paul's Language of Grace*, 315–16.
102 Harrison, *Paul's Language of Grace*, 316–17.
103 E.g. *SIG* 613A.

common good;[104] third, in inspiring zealous imitation of benefactors by persons who have not yet been involved in public munificence.[105]

In 2 Corinthians 8:13–15, Paul explains the rationale for the collection by appealing to the principle of 'equality' (ἰσότης) which, Paul stipulates, is both the ground and goal of relations between Christ believers—between those who enjoy abundance and those who suffer lack. Paul's argument is formulated in ἵνα and ὅπως clauses: first, with respect to the assumptive basis of the collection; then, with respect to the desired result.

> For the purpose [of the collection] is not (οὐ γὰρ ἵνα) that there [should be] relief for others and affliction for you, but rather [it should be] on the basis of equality (ἐξ ἰσότητος). At the present time, your abundance should supply their lack, in order that (ἵνα) their abundance may supply your lack, so that there may be equality (ὅπως γένηται ἰσότης).

One wonders how readers in Roman Corinth, accustomed to seeing ἵνα and ὅπως clauses in honorific inscriptions, would have understood Paul's appeal to 'equality', employing precisely these formulae. It seems likely that the effect of Paul's argument would have been startling, given the extraordinary rarity of the term ἰσότης in the entire corpus of Greek inscriptions.[106] In contrast to the egalitarian assumptions and objectives of Paul's argument, the donative inscriptions promulgate an ideology in which wealthy benefactors are honoured by the bouleutic elite. Thus, in the inscription from Cardamylae mentioned above, a stele was set up in the gymnasium for Poseidippos, 'in order that (ἵνα) those who confer benefits may receive favor in return for love of honor'.[107] Similarly, an inscription from Attica decrees a crown for a benefactor 'in order that (ὅπως) there may be competition among those who strive eagerly to offer themselves in the common interest, when they see that they receive favors worthy of whatever kindnesses

---

104 E.g. *SEG* XXI.419.
105 E.g. *IG* VI/2.2712 (37 C.E.).
106 Only a handful of instances are found in the *Searchable Greek Inscriptions* of The Packard Humanities Institute: e.g. *IG* XII.4; XII.6; *Halikarnassos* 95.
107 *SEG* XI.948.

they have performed'.[108] The honorific decrees structure an exchange of honours for benefits, symbolic capital for material capital, which ultimately serves to re-inscribe social hierarchy. By contrast, Paul argues for a redistribution of goods between rich and poor on the basis of the democratic principle of equality.

IV

As Paul wrote his letter to the Romans, he was planning to travel to Jerusalem to deliver the collection (Rom. 15:25, 28). Paul was evidently anxious about the reception of his gift and asked the Romans to join him in prayer that his gift might be 'acceptable to the saints' (Rom. 15:30–31).[109] The fate of the collection is unknown. Some scholars interpret the silence of the author of Acts as an indication that the collection was refused.[110] However that may be, our exposition of Paul's concern for material aspects of the ministry to the saints makes it likely that, whatever the reception, Paul would have found a way to distribute the funds that he collected for the poor among the saints in Jerusalem.[111]

L. L. Welborn
Fordham University

---

108 *SEG* XXI.419.
109 Joubert, *Paul as Benefactor*, 208, 213–15; Jewett, *Romans*, 936–37.
110 Lüdemann, *Opposition to Paul in Jewish Christianity*, 61; Légasse, *Paul Apôtre*, 203; Jewett, *Romans*, 937.
111 Georgi, *Remembering the Poor*, 120, 125–26.

Bibliography

Amstutz, J.	ΑΠΛΟΤΗΣ. *Eine begriffsgeschichtliche Studie zum jüdisch-christlichen Griechisch* (Bonn: Hanstein, 1968).
Arzt-Grabner, P.	*2. Korinther. Papyrologische Kommentare zum Neuen Testament, Band 4* (Göttingen: Vandenhoeck & Ruprecht, 2014).
Arzt-Grabner, P., R. E. Kritzer, A. Papathomas, and F. Winter	*1. Korinther. Papyrologische Kommentare zum Neuen Testament, Band 2* (Göttingen: Vandenhoeck & Ruprecht, 2006).
Ascough, R. S., P. A. Harland, and J. S. Kloppenborg	*Associations in the Greco-Roman World: A Sourcebook* (Waco: Baylor University Press, 2012).
Bachmann, P.	*Der zweite Brief des Paulus andie Korinther* (Leipzig: Deichert, 1909).
Bang, P.	'Predation' in W. Scheidel (ed.), *The Cambridge Companion to the Roman Economy* (Cambridge: Cambridge University Press, 2012), 197–217.
Barrett, C. K.	*A Critical and Exegetical Commentary on the Acts of the Apostles, Volume 1: Acts 1–14* (London: T & T Clark, 2004).
_____.	*The First Epistle to the Corinthians* (New York: Harper, 1968).
Beckheuer, B.	*Paulus und Jerusalem: Kollekte und Mission im theologischen Denken des Heidenapostels* (Frankfurt am Main: Peter Lang, 1997).
Berger, K.	'Almosen für Israel', *New Testament Studies* 23 (1977), 180–204.
Betz, H. D.	*2 Corinthians 8 and 9: A Commentary on Two Administrative Letters of the Apostle Paul* (Philadelphia: Fortress Press, 1985).
Blanton, T. R., IV	'The Economic Functions of Gift Exchange', in T. Blanton and R. Pickett (eds.), *Paul and Economics* (Minneapolis: Fortress Press, 2017), 279–306.
Chaniotis, A.	'Public Subscriptions and Loans as Social Capital in the Hellenistic City: Reciprocity, Performance, Commemoration', in P. Martzavou (ed.), *Epigraphical Approaches to the Postclassical Polis: Fourth Century BC to Second Century AD* (Oxford: Oxford University Press, 2013), 89–106.

Chow, J. K.	*Patronage and Power: A Study of Social Networks in Corinth* (Sheffield: Sheffield Academic Press, 1992).
Collins, R.	*First Corinthians* (Collegeville: Michael Glazier, 1999).
Collins, A. Y.	*Mark: A Commentary* (Minneapolis: Fortress Press, 2007).
Conzelmann, H.	*Der erste Brief an die Korinther* (Göttingen: Vandenhoeck & Ruprecht, 1981).
_____.	*1 Corinthians: A Commentary on the first Epistle to the Corinthians* (Philadelphia: Fortress Press, 1975).
Cullmann, O.	*Message to Catholics and Protestants* (Grand Rapids: Eerdmans, 1959).
Danker, F. W.	*Benefactor: Epigraphic Study of a Graeco-Roman and New Testament Semantic Field* (St. Louis: Clayton, 1982).
Deissmann, A.	*Bible Studies* (Edinburgh: T & T Clark, 1923).
_____.	*Light from the Ancient East: The New Testament Illustrated by Recently Discovered Texts of the Graeco-Roman World* (New York: Hodder and Stoughton, 1910).
Downs, D. J.	*The Offering of the Gentiles: Paul's Collection for Jerusalem in Its Chronological, Cultural, and Cultic Contexts* (Tübingen: Mohr Siebeck, 2008).
Fee, G. D.	*The First Epistle to the Corinthians* (Grand Rapids: Eerdmans, 1987).
Friesen, S. J.	'Paul and Economics: The Jerusalem Collection as an Alternative to Patronage' in Mark D. Given (ed.), *Paul Unbound: Other Perspectives on the Apostle Paul* (Peabody: Hendrickson, 2010), 24–54.
Furnish, V. P.	*II Corinthians* (Garden City: Doubleday, 1984).
Georgi, D.	*Remembering the Poor: The History of Paul's Collection for Jerusalem* (rev. and exp. edn; Nashville: Abingdon, 1992 [German, 1965]).
Grenfell, B. P., and A. S. Hunt	*The Oxyrhynchus Papyri, Vol. 2* (London: Egypt Exploration Society, 1899).
Harland, P. A.	*Greco-Roman Associations: Texts, Translations, and Commentary, II: North Coast of the Black Sea, Asia Minor* (Berlin: Walter de Gruyter, 2014).
Harris, M. J.	*The Second Epistle to the Corinthians* (Grand Rapids: Eerdmans, 2005).

Harris, W. V.	'Poverty and Destitution in the Roman Empire', in W. V. Harris (ed.), *Rome's Imperial Economy* (Oxford: Oxford University Press, 2011), 27–56.
Harrison, J. R.	*Paul's Language of Grace in its Graeco-Roman Context* (Tübingen: Mohr Siebeck, 2003).
Heil, C.	'"Die Armen nicht vergessen": Die Kollekte des Apostels Paulus für die Armen in Jerusalem', in Leopold Neuhold (ed.), *Muss arm sein? Armut als Ärgernis und Herausforderung* (Innsbruck: Tyrolia, 2008), 86–103.
Heinrici, C. F. G.	*Der zweite Brief an die Korinther* (Göttingen: Vandenhoeck & Ruprecht, 1900).
Hicks, E. L.	'Iasos', *Journal of Hellenic Studies* 8 (1887), 83–118.
Holl, K.	'Der Kirchenbegriff des Paulus in seinem Verhältnis zu dem der Urgemeinde', *Sitzungsberichte der preussischen Akademie der Wissenschaften* (Berlin: Verlag der Akademie der Wissenschaften, 1921), 920–47.
Horrell, D.	'Paul's Collection: Resources for a Materialist Theology,' *Epworth Review* 22 (1995), 74–83.
Hurd, J.	*The Origin of 1 Corinthians* (London: SPCK, 1965).
Jeremias, J.	*Jerusalem in the Time of Jesus: An Investigation into Economic and Social Conditions during the New Testament Period* (Philadelphia: Fortress Press, 1969).
Jewett, R.	*Romans: A Commentary* (Minneapolis: Fortress Press, 2007).
Joubert, S.	*Paul as Benefactor: Reciprocity, Strategy and Theological Reflection in Paul's Collection* (Tübingen: Mohr Siebeck, 2000).
Kaibel, G.	*Epigrammata Graeca ex lapidibus conlecta* (Berlin: Reimer, 1878).
Keck, L. E.	'The Poor among the Saints in Jewish Christianity and Qumran', *Zeitschrift für die neutestamentliche Wissenschaft* 57 (1966), 54–78.
———.	'The Poor among the Saints in the New Testament', *Zeitschrift für die neutestamentliche Wissenschaft* 56 (1965), 100–29.
Kim, B.	*Die paulinische Kollekte* (Tübingen: Franke, 2002).
Kittel, Gerhard	'λογεία', *Theological Dictionary of the New Testament* IV (Grand Rapids: Eerdmans, 1967), 282–83.

Klein, H.   'Die Begründung für den Spendenaufruf für die Heiligen Jerusalems in 2Kor 8 und 9', in Dieter Sänger (ed.), *Der zweite Korintherbrief: Literarische Gestalt—historische Situation—theologische Argumantation* (Göttingen: Vandenhoeck & Ruprecht, 2012), 104–30.

Kloppenborg, S. J.   *Christ's Associations: Connecting and Belonging in the Ancient City* (New Haven: Yale University Press, 2019).

———.   'Fiscal Aspects of Paul's Collection for Jerusalem', *Early Christianity* 8 (2017), 153–98.

———.   'The Moralizing of Discourse in Greco-Roman Associations, in C. J. Hodge (ed.), *'The One Who Sows Bountifully',* (Providence: Brown Judaic Studies, 2013), 215–28.

Kraft, R. A.   *The Testament of Job* (Missoula: Scholars Press, 1974).

Kuenzi, A.   ΕΠΙΔΟΣΙΣ: *Sammlung Freiwilliger Beiträge* (Bern: Haupt, 1922).

Légasse, S.   *Paul Apôtre: Essai de biographie critique* (Paris: Cerf, 2000).

Lindemann, A.   'Hilfe für die Armen: Zur ethischen Argumentation des Paulus in den Kollektenbriefen II Kor 8 und II Kor 9', in Christl Maier (ed.), *Exegese vor Ort* (Leipzig: Evangelische Verlagsanstalt, 2001), 199–216.

Llewelyn, S. R.   'The Use of Sunday for Meetings of Believers in the New Testament', *Novum Testamentum* 43 (2001), 205–223.

Longenecker, B. W.   *Remember the Poor: Paul, Poverty, and the Greco-Roman World* (Grand Rapids: Eerdmans, 2011).

Lüdemann, G.   *Paul: The Founder of Christianity* (Amherst: Prometheus Books, 2002).

———.   *Opposition to Paul in Jewish Christianity* (Minneapolis: Fortress Press, 1989).

Martin, R. P.   *2 Corinthians* (Waco: Word Books, 1986).

Meeks, W. A.   *The First Urban Christians: The Social World of the Apostle Paul* (New Haven: Yale University Press, 1983).

Meyer, H. A. W.   *Der zweite Brief an die Korinther* (Göttingen: Vandenhoeck & Ruprecht, 1870).

Migeotte, L.   'Les souscriptions dans les associations privées', in P. Fröhlich (ed.), *Groupes et associations dans les cites grecques (IIIe siècle av. J.-C. – IIe siècle ap. J.-C.)* (Geneva: Librairie Droz, 2013), 113–27.

———. *Les souscriptions publiques dans les cites grecques* (Quebec: Éditions du Sphinx, 1992).

Moulton, J. H., G. Milligan *The Vocabulary of the Greek Testament, Illustrated from the Papyri and Other Non-Literary Sources* (Grand Rapids: Eerdmans, 1957).

Munck, J. *Paul and the Salvation of Mankind* (Atlanta: John Knox, 1977).

Münch, S. *Das Geschenk der Einfachheit: 2 Korinther 8,1-15 und 9,6-15 als Hinführung zu dieser Gabe* (Würzburg: Echter, 2012).

Nickle, K. F. *The Collection: A Study in Paul's Strategy* (Naperville: Allenson, 1966).

Ogereau, J. M. *Paul's Koinonia with the Philippians: A Socio-Historical Investigation of a Pauline Economic Partnership* (Tübingen: Mohr Siebeck, 2014).

———. 'The Jerusalem Collection as Κοινωνία: Paul's Global Politics of Socio-Economic Equality and Solidarity', *New Testament Studies* 58 (2012), 360–78.

Peterman, G. W. 'Romans 15:26: Make a Contribution or Establish Fellowship?', *New Testament Studies* 40 (1994), 457–63.

Plummer, A. *A Critical and Exegetical Commentary on the Second Epistle of St. Paul to the Corinthians* (Edinburgh: T & T Clark, 1915).

Rengstorf, Karl Heinrich 'στέλλω', *TDNT* 7 (1971), 588–90.

Sänger, D. '"Jetzt aber führt auch das Tun zu Ende": Die korinthische Gemeinde und die Kollekte für Jerusalem', in Dieter Sänger (ed.), *Der zweite Korintherbrief: Literarische Gestalt—historische Situation—theologische Argumantation* (Göttingen: Vandenhoeck & Ruprecht, 2012), 257–82.

Scheidel, W. 'Stratification, Deprivation and Quality of Life' in M. Atkins (ed.), *Poverty in the Roman World* (Cambridge: Cambridge University Press, 2006), 40–59.

Schellenberg, R. S. 'Subsistence, Swapping, and Paul's Rhetoric of Generosity', *Journal of Biblical Literature* 137 (2018), 215–34.

Schmeller, T. *Der zweite Brief an die Korinther. Teilband 2, 2 Kor 7,5-13,13* (Neukirchen-Vluyn, 2015).

Schmithals, W. 'Die Kollekten des Paulus für Jerusalem', in Cilliers Breytenbach (ed.), *Paulus, die Evangelien und das Urchristentum* (Leiden: Brill, 2004).

Schulz, T. N.　　　*The Meaning of Charis in the New Testament* (Genova: Laterna, 1971).

Sokolowski, F.　　*Lois sacrées des cites grecques* (Paris: E. de Boccard, 1969).

Spicq, C.　　*Notes de lexicographie néotestamentaire*, Vol. 1 (Fribourg: Editions universitaires, 1978).

Stegemann E. W., and W. Stegemann　　*The Jesus Movement: A Social History of Its First Century* (Minneapolis: Fortress Press, 1999).

Strathmann, Hermann　　'λειτουγέω, λειτουργία, λειτουργός, λειτουργικός', *TDNT* IV (Grand Rapids: Eerdmans, 1967), 215–222, 226–232.

Syon, D.　　*Small Change in Hellenistic-Roman Galilee: The Evidence from Numismatic Site Finds as a Tool for Historical Reconstruction* (Jerusalem: Israel Numismatic Society, 2015).

Theissen, G.　　*The Social Setting of Pauline Christianity. Essays on Corinth* (Philadelphia: Fortress Press, 1982).

_____.　　*Sociology of Early Palestinian Christianity* (Philadelphia: Fortress Press, 1978).

Theobald, M.　　*Die überströmende Gnade: Studien zu einem paulinischen Motivfeld* (Würzburg: Echter, 1982).

Thrall, M.　　*The Second Epistle to the Corinthians, Volume II: 2 Corinthians 8-13* (Edinburgh: T & T Clark, 2000).

Tucker, J. B.　　'The Jerusalem Collection, Economic Inequality, and Human Flourishing: Is Paul's Concern the Redistribution of Wealth, or a Relationship of Mutuality (or Both)?', *Canadian Theological Review* 3 (2014), 52–70.

Vassiliadis, P.　　'Equality and Justice in Classical Antiquity and in Paul: The Social Implications of the Pauline Collection', *St. Vladimir's Theological Quarterly* 36 (1992), 51–59.

Wan, S.　　'Collection for the Saints as Anticolonial Act: Implications of Paul's Ethnic Reconstruction', in Richard H. Horsley (ed.), *Paul and Politics: Ekklesia, Israel, Imperium, Interpretation* (Harrisburg: Trinity, 2000), 191–215.

Weiss, J.　　*Der erste Korintherbrief* (Göttingen: Vandenhoeck & Ruprecht, 1910).

Welborn, L. L.	'The Polis and the Poor: Reconstructing Social Relations from Diverse Genres of Evidence', in J. R. Harrison and L. L. Welborn (ed.), *The First Urban Churches 1: Methodological Foundations* (Atlanta: SBL Press, 2015), 189–244.
_____.	'"That There May Be Equality": The Contexts and Consequences of a Pauline Ideal', *New Testament Studies* 59 (2013), 73–90.
Windisch, H.	*Der zweite Korintherbrief* (Göttingen: Vandenhoeck & Ruprecht, 1970).
Winter, B. W.	'Acts and Food Shortages', in D. W. J. Gill (ed.), *The Book of Acts in Its Graeco-Roman Setting* (Grand Rapids: Eerdmans, 1994), 59–78.
Young, N. H.	'"The Use of Sunday for Meetings of Believers in the New Testament": A Response', *Novum Testamentum* 45 (2003), 111–22.

Charis, Charisms and the 'Greater Gifts' in 1 Corinthians 12

Louise A. Gosbell

Abstract

This chapter addresses the relationship between Paul's use of the language of grace (*charis*) and the grace-gifts (*charisma*) in the letters of Paul. In his work on *charis*, James R. Harrison asserts the significance of this theme in the letters of Paul and the way in which Paul depicts *charis* as overturning the obligations of the Graeco-Roman reciprocity system. *Charis* is demonstrated most clearly in the Christ-event but is now also displayed in the relationships between the members of the Body of Christ. Building upon James R. Harrison's assessment of *charis* in the Pauline literature, this chapter explores the impact of his interpretation of *charis* on an understanding of Paul's references to the *charisma*, the grace-gifts. Although not semantically equivalent terms, the relationship between *charis* and *charisma* is significant. The *charisma* are God's grace-gifts given to believers through the Spirit so that believers are equipped to be benefactors to one another: interdependent and living in mutuality and service to one another and to God. This chapter will explore the bearing of Harrison's research of *charis* on the concept of the *charisma* in Paul's letters, especially Paul's language of the Body of Christ in 1 Corinthians 12 where the language of the *charisma* is most heavily concentrated. In light of this, the chapter will also explore the implications of these conclusions on Paul's alleged imperative in 1 Corinthians 12:31 to 'zealously seek the greater gifts'.

1. Introduction

In his now seminal work *Paul's Language of Grace in its Graeco-Roman Context*, James R. Harrison assesses Paul's use of the language of grace (*charis*) against the backdrop of the Graeco-Roman reciprocity system for which the language of *charis* had become the 'central leitmotif'.[1] Harrison's thesis is that, although Paul's use of *charis* in his letters invokes the language and ideals of this reciprocity system, Paul's language indicates an 'implicit critique' of this system.[2] Where the Graeco-Roman reciprocity system burdened people with the obligations of benefaction, Paul beckons believers to be shaped by God's great act of benefaction in the Christ-event which 'operates on the basis of His overflowing grace over against the obligation of reciprocity'.[3] Harrison asserts that while Paul certainly 'expects believers to live worthily of God'[4] in light of this overflowing grace, God's beneficence is 'unilateral', unburdening believers of any need for reciprocity.[5] Instead, Harrison argues, '(f)or Paul, it is love that subverts the dynamics of the Graeco-Roman reciprocity system',[6] creating 'an alternative vision of social relations by the means of his theology of grace'.[7] It is here in the *ekklesia*, the Body of Christ, where we see this 'alternative vision of social relations' enacted. In the Body of Christ, we see that patronage is not limited to the wealthy and elite, but now '(a)ll believers are equipped by divine grace to be benefactors and are called to abandon the dependency fostered on the benefaction system'.[8] Now believers are indebted to one another, equipped through the Spirit with grace-gifts (*charisma*) to be benefactors to one another: interdependent, both using and receiving the grace-gifts for the mutual benefit and functioning of the whole Body of Christ.

While Harrison does address briefly the implications of his study

---

1 Harrison, *Paul's Language*, 2.
2 Harrison, *Paul's Language*, 311.
3 Harrison, *Paul's Language*, 348.
4 Harrison, *Paul's Language*, 348.
5 Harrison, *Paul's Language*, 348.
6 Harrison, *Paul's Language*, 349.
7 Harrison, *Paul's Language*, 311.
8 Harrison, *Paul's Language*, 349.

of the language of *charis* on that of the *charisma*,[9] the 'grace-gifts' mentioned in the Pauline letters, this discussion was tangential to the main aims of his investigation. In this essay, I would like to explore further Harrison's findings on *charis* and its bearing on the language of *charisma* employed in Paul's letters, especially in 1 Corinthians 12 and Paul's depiction of the *ekklesia* as the Body of Christ. In light of this investigation, I would then like to assess potential implications for this study of Paul's alleged imperative in 1 Corinthians 12:31 to 'zealously seek the greater gifts'.

2. The Relationship between *Charis* and *Charisma*

As has been recorded by Harrison among other scholars,[10] there is little evidence of the word *charisma* prior to Paul. The earliest extant usage of *charisma* from Greek literary sources is from the second century A.D. in Alciphron's *Epistles* 3.17.4. In terms of Jewish literature, *charisma* does not appear in the LXX, although it does appear twice in the Jewish apocrypha with no reference to God[11] and once in the pseudepigraphic work the *Sibylline Oracles* which Harrison, among others, argues post-dates the Pauline literature.[12] *Charisma* does appear twice in Philo referring to the 'free grace of God'.[13] However, Harrison contends that this 'probably represents the first time in antiquity that the word was used with theological reference'.[14] Robert J. Banks also asserts that occurrences of *charisma* in the papyri are limited with all extant examples post-dating the New Testament literature.[15] In this respect, Enrique Nardoni proposes that Paul borrowed the language of *charisma* from colloquial language, where the term must have been used with the meaning of 'gift' or 'present'[16] and he imbued it with new

---

9 Harrison, *Paul's Language*, 279–83.
10 Harrison, *Paul's Language*, 279.
11 Sir. 7:33 [cod.B] and 38:30 [cod.S]).
12 Harrison, *Paul's Language*, 279, argues that the text is clearly a 'Christian interpolation'.
13 Philo, *Alleg. Interp.* 3.78.
14 Harrison, *Paul's Language*, 279.
15 Banks, *Paul's Idea*, 79.
16 Nardoni, 'Charism', 69.

theological import shaped by the Christ-event. For this reason, Paul is often credited with being the inventor of this usage of *charisma*.[17]

It is evident from his use of this terminology that Paul did not consider *charis* and *charisma* to be semantically equivalent words.[18] However, as Nardoni suggests, *charisma* are a direct result of God's *charis* and a 'concrete materialization of God's grace'.[19] For this reason, Dunn contends that the word *charisma* in Paul 'denotes the result of gracious giving (*charizesthai*, "give graciously")'.[20] Dunn says that '(f)or Paul the archetypal *charisma* was the gracious act of Christ on the cross',[21] however, God's *charis* is now demonstrated in word and deed through the expressions of the various *charisma* gifted to believers by God.

This link between *charis* and *charisma* is made explicit in the opening chapter of 1 Corinthians where Paul offers thanks to God for the Corinthians because of God's 'grace (χάρις) given you in Christ' (1 Cor. 1:4) which has meant they 'have been enriched in every way' not lacking 'any grace-gift (χάρισμα) as (they) eagerly wait for our Lord Jesus Christ to be revealed (1 Cor. 1:5,7). Likewise, in Paul's use of the Body of Christ imagery in Romans 12, he states: 'We have different grace-gifts (χάρισμα), according to the grace (χάρις) given to each of us' (Rom. 12:6). The relationship between *charis* and *charisma* is also evident in the only usage of *charisma* in the New Testament outside of the Pauline corpus whereby 1 Peter 4:10 asserts that, 'Each of you should use whatever grace-gift (χάρισμα) you have received to serve others, as faithful stewards of God's grace (χάρις) in its various forms'.

---

17 E.g. Dunn, *Jesus and the Spirit*, 206, states that '"charisma" is a concept which we owe almost entirely to Paul'.
18 Harrison, *Paul's Language*, 280, says the terms are not simply 'interchangeable'. Contra Fitzmyer, *First Corinthians*, 464, who states that *charis* and *charisma* 'are etymologically only remotely related'.
19 Nardoni, 'Charism', 74; cf. Carson, *Showing the Spirit*, 19, states that *charisms* are 'concretizations of grace'.
20 Dunn, *Theology of Paul*, 553.
21 Dunn, *Theology of Paul*, 559.

3. *Charisma* and the Body of Christ in 1 Corinthians 12

3.1 Paul's Presentation of the Body of Christ in 1 Corinthians 12

It is apparent that one of Paul's motivations in writing 1 Corinthians is to address the dissension that had arisen in the Corinthian church.[22] Throughout the letter, Paul appeals to the Corinthians to bring an end to the church's factionalism for the sake of ecclesial unity. He urges them to have 'no divisions (σχίσμα)' among them but that they would instead 'be perfectly united (καταρτίζω) in mind and thought' (1 Cor. 1:10) by putting aside their 'jealousy and quarrelling (ζῆλος καὶ ἔρις; 1 Cor. 3:3)'. While it is likely these schisms were the result of numerous theological as well as social factors, it is well established in scholarship on 1 Corinthians that social stratification of the members of the church was a contributing factor to these schisms.[23] Paul cites a number of interactions which reveal this social dissension, including the disputes amongst the 'have' and 'have nots' in the church in respect to the participation in the Lord's Supper (1 Cor. 11),[24] litigation amongst the rich and the poor (1 Cor. 6), as well as the disagreements between the 'weak' and the 'strong' concerning food offered to idols (1 Cor. 8–10). Close examination of 1 Corinthians thus reveals the church as a heterogenous community composed of people from a range of social strata, importing into the church the values of the Graeco-Roman world on matters of social status, honour, and power.[25]

Throughout his letter, Paul attempts to remind the Corinthian church that the *ekklesia* does not function as the world does. It has its own set of behaviours and values modelled on the 'honoured and glorified Christ' who 'suffered total dishonour in his crucifixion [...] leaving aside the glory of his heavenly riches and assuming the impoverishment of broken humanity'.[26] Rather than seeking power and honour for

---

22 Although I am familiar with the debates about the integrity of 1 Corinthians (e.g. Welborn, *Paul*, 13) for the purposes of this chapter, I have assumed compositional unity of 1 Corinthians.
23 E.g. Theissen, 'Social Stratification', 69–119; Meeks, *First Urban Christians*, *passim*.
24 Theissen, 'Social Conflicts', 377–81.
25 E.g. Judge, *Social Pattern*; Meeks, *First Urban Christians*, 51–73.
26 Harrison, 'Erasure of Distinction', 85.

himself, Christ became like a dishonoured slave, put to death in the way of a shameful criminal (Phil. 2:6–8). Likewise in 1 Corinthians, Paul describes himself in vocabulary usually reserved for those of low social status (e.g. 1 Cor. 4:10). It is from his position as one of low honour that he charges the Corinthians to imitate him as he imitates Christ (1 Cor. 11:1). Paul reminds the Corinthians that in the gospel, 'God chose the foolish (μωρός) things of the world to shame (καταισχύνω) the wise ... the weak (ἀσθενής) things of the world to shame (καταισχύνω) the strong ... so that no one may boast before him' (1 Cor. 1:27–29).

One method Paul employs to address the dissension and reframe the way in which the church distributed honour is through an adaptation of the well-known body metaphor employed in Graeco-Roman *homonoia* ('concord') speeches. These speeches employed the image of the human body as a metaphor for a corporate body such as a particular city-state, or political or civic group.[27] The body politic metaphor was used to encourage unity among the members but it did so by promoting adherence to the existing hierarchy with a reminder that all members of the body were positioned by Nature to fulfil their particular role for the benefit of the whole body.[28] While some members were naturally stronger and more valuable than others, this was as Nature designed it. Despite the inequity, all members must fulfil their particular role within the body to maintain order and unity. Any attempt to 'deviate from the prescribed duties' meant a disturbance to 'the natural order.'[29]

In 1 Corinthians 12,[30] Paul likewise employs the image of a physical body to represent a corporate body—in this case, the body represents the *ekklesia*, the church. The parallels between Paul's usage of the metaphor with other extant examples from Graeco-Roman antiquity are immediately apparent. Like the numerous examples from Graeco-Roman *homonoia* speeches, Paul's usage of the body metaphor also

---

27 The most well-known example of the body politic metaphor comes from the Greek fabulist Aesop entitled *The Belly and the Members* (Zipes, *Aesop's Fables*, 58).
28 Martin, *Corinthian Body*, 92.
29 Peterlin, 'Stomach', 67.
30 See also Rom. 12:3–8; Eph. 4:1–16; Col. 1:15–20.

seeks to promote concord and unity amongst the disparate members of a body where members all have their own unique skills and roles. Paul's depiction echoes many of the features commonly seen in body politic imagery including conversations among body parts (1 Cor. 12:15–16), mention of the strategic placement of members (1 Cor. 12:14), and in particular, the threat of schisms in the body if all the members do not fulfil their designated roles (1 Cor. 12:25).

For this reason, some scholars see in Paul's metaphor a similar appeal for adherence to authority and the maintenance of the status quo as seen in other examples of the *topos* from Graeco-Roman antiquity. Jerome Neyrey, for example, sees in Paul's Body of Christ metaphor a clear call to the maintenance of hierarchy within the body. Like Aesop's fable of *The Belly and the Members*, Neyrey argues Paul depicts the members of the Body of Christ as clearly ranked with some parts of the body 'greater' than others with the 'ranking of differentiated parts [...] related to the roles ascribed to the members of the church'.[31] Others, however, see in Paul's body *topos* an adoption of similar language and themes but with the intention of inverting the order of priority. Dale Martin, for example, states that Paul's rhetoric in 1 Corinthians 12 'pushes for an actual reversal of the normal, "this-worldly" attribution of honor and status'.[32] Given Paul's critique of the Corinthian elites and the way they prized the gifts of 'exultation and visible demonstrative "success"',[33] Paul attempts to outline a new method of distributing honour in the *ekklesia* that was not built on status, power, or wealth. Paul uses the image of the body, as Ben Witherington argues, to

> relativise the sense of self-importance of those of higher status, making them see the importance and necessity of the weaker, lower-status, Corinthians Christians. Paul questions the usual linking of high social status and honor by saying that God gives more honor to the 'less presentable' members.[34]

---

31 Neyrey, *Paul*, 139.
32 Martin, *Corinthian Body*, 96.
33 Thiselton, *First Corinthians*, 1023.
34 Witherington, *Conflict and Community*, 258.

These divergent interpretations will be explored further as we examine Paul's use of *charisma* in 1 Corinthians 12.

3.2 *Charisma* and Body of Christ in 1 Corinthians 12

It is within the context of Paul's Body of Christ imagery in 1 Corinthians 12 that the language of *charisma* is most heavily concentrated. Paul begins this section with referring to the Corinthians' use of *pneumatika* (1 Cor. 1:1). It appears that Paul locates in his discussion first in *pneumatika* as a means of adopting the language that the Corinthians themselves used to desribe spiritual gifts.[35] Paul then shifts vocabulary from *pneumatika* to *charisma* in order to offer a 'theological corrective',[36] repositioning the focus from individual abilities to God's abundant grace in his distribution of gifts. The language of *charisma* emphasises that these are 'grace-gifts'[37] and not connected to human ability, wealth, or status. The distribution of the gifts to all believers at God's bidding means there is no scope for individuals to boast in their spiritual gifts because each gift has been given by God to be used in service to him and to the whole body. It is the Spirit of God that helps believers to understand the gifts that have been given (1 Cor. 2:12) and it is God who animates those gifts (1 Cor 12:7). The *charisma* for Paul thus 'display the operative presence of grace in the Spirit'.[38]

The model of reciprocity demonstrated in Graeco-Roman antiquity favoured wealthy benefactors who utilised their positions of power and wealth to keep weaker and more vulnerable people beholden to them. However, God's demonstration of *charis* in the Christ-event unburdened believers of the kind of reciprocity that existed between a powerful benefactor and an indentured beneficiary. Instead, as recipients of God's grace, Christians have entered into 'a reciprocal exchange that mutually strengthens and encourages' all members of the Body of Christ.[39] Through God's great act of benefaction in the Christ-event

---

35 Collins, *First Corinthians*, 452.
36 Collins, *First Corinthians*, 452.
37 Garland, *1 Corinthians*, 575; Carson, *Showing the Spirit*, 19.
38 Barclay, *Paul*, 126.
39 Harrison, *Paul's Language*, 281.

and the gracious distribution of gifts, all believers are now benefactors and beneficiaries of grace through the use of the grace-gifts in the *ekklesia*.[40] In this respect, Edwin Judge observes that '(t)he body of Christ remains a figure of the intimate web of obligations that binds believers to him and to each other through the gifts of the Spirit'.[41]

God's grace is demonstrated not only in the generous pouring out of gifts upon believers irrespective of social standing or human ability, God's grace is also visible in the Body of Christ by the broad variety of gifts God makes available to believers. Paul critiques the Corinthians' fixation on *glossolalia* above other gifts not simply because *glossolalia* only edifies the speaker while prophesy 'edifies the church' (1 Cor. 14:4) but also because this narrow valuation of gifts fails to recognise the diversity of gifts God has provided to believers.[42] While there are four lists of spiritual gifts in the Pauline literature (1 Cor. 12:7–11; 28; Rom. 12:6–8; Eph. 4:11),[43] no two lists are identical indicating that no list is meant to be exhaustive.[44] Paul wishes to expand the Corinthians' understanding of the wide variety of gifts God has made available to believers. Thus Banks' assertion that the lists are shaped by Paul to respond to the particular *Sitz im Leben* of the individual church community to whom he is writing is likely correct.[45]

Paul's first list of *charisma* in the 1 Corinthians 12:7–11 includes those gifts for which the accompaniment of visible manifestations was possible and might even have been expected by the Corinthians. These gifts, which include 'messages of wisdom (λόγος σοφίας)', 'miraculous powers (ἐνεργήματα δυνάμεων)', and 'gifts of healing (χαρίσματα ἰαμάτων)', could all have been used in a performative way when believers met together in the *ekklesia*. As such, these appear to be the kinds

---

40 Harrison, *Paul's Language*, 349.
41 Judge, 'Demythologising the Church', 585.
42 Garland, *1 Corinthians*, 577, says that Paul 'is intent on broadening the Corinthians' understanding of spiritual gifts to include humbler forms of expression such as everyday acts of service'.
43 Although Ephesians 4 refers to the gifts as *domata* rather than *charisma*.
44 Banks, *Paul's Idea*, 82; cf. Barclay, *Paul*, 126; Carson, *Showing the Spirit*, 35; Collins, *First Corinthians*, 451; Dunn, *Theology of Paul*, 557; Fee, *First Epistle to the Corinthians*, 585.
45 Banks, *Paul's Idea*, 82.

of gifts which would have had an appeal to the Corinthians. It is notable that this list omits some of the less visibly impressive gifts Paul lists elsewhere, such as gifts of mercy or financial aid even though such *charisma* appear on his list in Romans 12 where Paul also employs the Body of Christ metaphor.

Following his extended illustration of the Body of Christ, Paul offers a second list of grace-gifts which has some overlap with the first but which also appears to develop the initial list (1 Cor. 12:28). It is also the only enumerated list of gifts in the Pauline corpus. The list begins however, not with gifts but with roles: 'God has placed in the church first of all apostles, second prophets, third teachers' (12:28a). These roles are then followed by a return to listing particular *charisma* with Paul then adding 'miracles, then gifts of healing, of helping, of guidance, and of different kinds of tongues' (12:28b). While this list does include gifts such as 'miracles (δυνάμεις)' and 'gifts of healing (χαρίσματα ἰαμάτων)', Paul appears to supplement this list with some gifts which the Corinthians may have believed less valuable due to their lack of observable spectacle such as 'helping (ἀντίλημψις)' and 'guidance (κυβέρνησις)'. It is certainly possible the Corinthians viewed the roles of apostles and teachers as likewise lacking in demonstrable power which is part of Paul's motivation for placing them first on the list while the Corinthians' preoccupation with *glossolalia* leads Paul to placing them at the end.

In reflecting on Paul's enumerated list in 1 Corinthians 12:28, many scholars assert that the numbering of the *charisma* is representative of a hierarchy of gifts.[46] While some scholars are at pains to argue that a member's gifts do not impact their value or worth in the body,[47] it is clear that many scholars read the enumeration of gifts in 12:28 in conjunction with Paul's imperative for believers to 'ζηλοῦτε the greater gifts' in 1 Corinthians 12:31 thus establishing that the 'greater' gifts

---

46 Banks, *Paul's Idea*, 83; Brock and Wannenwetsch, *Therapy*, 122; Collins, *First Corinthians*, 451; Fitzmyer, *First Corinthians*, 483.
47 E.g. Hiramatsu says that while the gifts 'do not convey status', he states that '(s)ome gifts are greater than others, and (Paul) encourages the Corinthians to seek them (12:31)', 'Paul's Theology', 82.

are those ranked higher on Paul's hierarchy in 12:28: apostles, prophets, and teachers. Dunn, for example, states that prophecy is 'the most valuable of all the charisms for Paul'.[48] Blanton likewise suggests that the role of apostles has been 'assigned preeminent position'.[49] Ciampa and Rosner assert that Paul's enumeration of apostles, prophets, and teachers clearly indicates that these are the 'three most valuable gifts'.[50] While they suggest that these gifts do not represent a 'hierarchy of authority' they do reflect a 'hierarchy of value or profitability, with value or profitability measured in terms of the ability to edify a church'.[51] By interpreting Paul's reference to 'greater gifts' as a descriptor for the enumerated gifts listed in 12:28, these verses are determined by many scholars to mean that there is a hierarchy of *charisma* and that believers are called to 'eagerly desire (ζηλοῦτε)' (12:31, NIV) these more valuable gifts over others.

It is the view of many scholars that Paul is promoting an alternative hierarchy of grace-gifts, a hierarchy that offers primacy of gifts based on the potential impact a gift has to edify the members of the *ekklesia*. This view is promoted by Banks, for example, who argues that the ranking of gifts is measured 'on the basis of their effect'.[52] Those gifts which have the potential to build up greater numbers of people in the church are the greater gifts. Similarly for Martin, Paul's list is 'explicitly hierarchical',[53] however, it is a hierarchy which inverts the valuation of gifts demonstrated by the Corinthians. This inversion means that '(g)reater honor [...] should be given to those normally considered to be of low status'.[54] According to Martin, Paul places apostles in the preeminent position in the list only after dedicating much space in his epistle to what Paul's view is of being an apostle. Martin argues that Paul's description of apostles is such that is shows them 'as of low status—when judged, that is, by the standards of normal society [...] The

---

48 Dunn, *Theology of Paul*, 556.
49 Blanton, *A Spiritual Economy*, 109.
50 Ciampa and Rosner, *First Letter to the Corinthians*, 609.
51 Ciampa and Rosner, *First Letter to the Corinthians*, 610.
52 Banks, *Paul's Idea*, 83.
53 Martin, *Corinthian Body*, 102.
54 Martin, *Corinthian Body*, 96.

apostles are last, in the position of criminals, a spectacle before angels and human beings, foolish, weak, dishonored. They are the hungry, thirsty, naked, reviled, manual laborers of the world, society's "scum" (4:9–12)'.[55] Paul's call to 'eagerly desire' the greater gift of apostleship then is a call to the kind of 'self-abasement (4:16–21)'[56] which Paul has voluntarily taken upon himself for the sake of the gospel.

While it is certainly true that Paul is exhorting the Corinthians to defy the world's methods of attributing honour and value, there is still a danger in interpreting 1 Corinthians 12:28 as promoting a hierarchy of *charisma* even if that hierarchy is an inverted version of the one promoted by the Corinthians. It is evident from 1 Corinthians 12—14 that Paul certainly does consider some gifts to have greater potential to edify the church, however, this is quite different to creating an immutable, fixed heirarchy of gifts. The very existence of a hierarchy would naturally lead members of the *ekklesia* to value some gifts over others which is precisely what Paul is attempting to redress in 1 Corinthians. Members who were in possession of the higher ranked gifts of apostleship, prophecy, and teaching would thus be considered as contributing more to the Body than those in possession of gifts of 'helping' or 'guidance'. However, the fact that the list in 12:28 is not exhaustive and does not include many *charisma* Paul refers to elsewhere in his letters—including the gift of interpretation of tongues which Paul mentions in 12:10 and again in 14:5—must indicate that this cannot be deemed an alternative hierarchy of gifts.

In recognising the apparent incongruity of interpreting the gifts hierarchically, some scholars have offered alternative means of understanding Paul's enumeration of gifts in 12:28. Richard B. Hays suggests that the numbering of gifts is a reference to 'the temporal order in which these gifts come into play in the construction of the Christian community'.[57] Thomas R. Schreiner concurs, adding that the enumerated roles are those which are 'necessary for the establishment and

---

55 Martin, *Corinthian Body*, 102-103.
56 Martin, *Corinthian Body*, 103.
57 Hays, *First Corinthians*, 217.

maintenance of the church.'[58] Blomberg also promotes an interpretation of 'chronological priority' asserting that

> (t)o establish a local congregation requires a church planter. Then the regular proclamation of God's word must ensue. Next teachers must supplement evangelism with discipleship [...] Only at this point does a viable Christian fellowship exist to enable the other gifts to come into play.[59]

This interpretation of a 'chronological priority' appears much more tenable in light of Paul's presentation of the Body of Christ thoughout 1 Corinthians 12.

It is also possible that what Paul is attempting to do with the list in 12:28 is to counter the Corinthians' hierarchy of gifts, not by offering an alternative hierarchy, but simply by challenging the existence of theirs as a means of bringing equilibrium. As I have argued elsewhere,[60] it is well known from medical writings of Graeco-Roman antiquity that imbalances in the body were corrected through the application of the opposite element. For example, the Hippocratic author of *Aphorisms* states that 'diseases caused by repletion are cured by depletion; those caused by depletion are cured by repletion.'[61] In a continuation of his body metaphor, I suggest Paul is promoting this same technique of 'curing' imbalance within the Body. Paul is wishing to 'treat' the imbalance of power and honour in the Corinthian church by the complete reversal of the methods used to attribute honour. It is in the process of offering honour to the most unlikely of recipients, to the 'unpresentable parts' and to those who possess gifts unvalued by the Corinthian church, that balance would be restored to the stratified Corinthian church. Paul is not advocating for an alternative hierarchy but a means of redressing imbalance and ensuring redistribution of honour among all the members of the Body. This interpretation aligns far better with

---

58 Schreiner, *1 Corinthians*, 269.
59 Blomberg, *1 Corinthians*, 247; cf. Talbert, *Reading Corinthians*, 85, says that Paul here 'enumerates sequence' and there is no ranking. This is likewise the view of Gardner, *1 Corinthians*, 548.
60 Gosbell, 'Disability', 299–300.
61 Hippoc. *Aph.* 2.22 (LCL: Jones).

Paul's depiction of Jesus as the antithesis of Graeco-Roman ideals and his own self-portrait as an apostle who is considered foolish by the world (1 Cor. 3:18; 4:10), the 'scum of the earth' (1 Cor. 4:13), and garbage (1 Cor. 4:13). Any depiction of himself as one who was then in possession of the 'greater gifts' would then have been completely at odds with Paul's depiction of himself throughout the letter. In this way, 1 Corinthians 12:28 is Paul's attempt to recalibrate the Corinthians' valuation of the gifts by placing those gifts at the top which the Corinthians deemed of little value and placing tongues, which the Corinthians considered the most impressive of the *charisma*, at the bottom.

As already noted, the traditional body politic *topos* was employed in *homonoia* speeches as a means of maintaining hierarchy and status quo. In extant examples from Graeco-Roman antiquity, the hierarchicalisation of members of a body politic was assumed with some members of the body clearly ranked above others. Paul, in contrast, appears to eschew such a hierarchical view of the members in the Body of Christ. Paul's depiction of the *ekklesia* as a body is one where all the members serve one another in mutuality and interdependence. Unlike other representations of the body politic where members are clearly ranked in terms of those who are the weaker and stronger parts, Paul here speaks only of those parts which '*seem* to be weaker' (v. 22) and 'the parts that *we think* are less honourable' (v. 23). Paul speaks about the relative weakness and honourability of members only in terms of human perception of value, not in actuality. By measuring one another by worldly standards, some members of the Corinthian church were perceiving others to be weak and without honour. Paul then exhorts the Corinthians not to allocate value or honour by human standards but by recognising that God has poured out his grace in equal measure on all members. Any attempt to then hierarchicalise the gifts listed by Paul in 1 Corinthians 12 is incompatible with the rest of Paul's argument about the nature of God's *charis* and the grace-gifts.

If 1 Corinthians 12:28 is not offering an alternative hierarchy of grace-gifts, what does Paul mean by the 'greater gifts' and how are we to interpret Paul's exhortation ζηλοῦτε? The challenges with the interpretation of 12:31 are two-fold. Firstly, there are a range of suggestions from scholars on the way in which the word ζηλοῦτε should be interpreted in 12:31. Secondly, if, as I suggest, the 'greater gifts' is not a reference to a hierarchy of gifts in 12:28, what is Paul referring to when speaking of these 'greater gifts' in 12:31?

While it is possible that ζηλοῦτε could be read as either an indicative or an imperative, the vast majority of scholars and translators opt for reading it as the latter. This is particularly the case for those who read 12:28 as a hierarchy of the 'greater' or more valuable *charisma*. For those who suggest Paul is promoting a hierarchy of gifts, it is a logical next step that Paul would then exhort the Corinthians to 'eagerly desire' those more valulable gifts. And yet, in 12:29–30, Paul asks a series of rhetorical questions: 'Are all apostles? Are all prophets? Are all teachers? Do all work miracles? Do all have gifts of healing? Do all speak in tongues? Do all interpret?' It is evident from the way the questions are framed in Greek that 'the only appropriate response would be "no".'[62] If this is the case and the gifts are distributed by God as he pleases, we must ask the question with Garland: 'But how does one strive for or eagerly desire something that can only be given' by God?[63]

In attempting to address this tension, some scholars thus consider ζηλοῦτε to be an imperative but one that is ironic. J. F. M. Smit, for example, argues for this position thus rendering the phrase something akin to 'continue to strive for the greater gifts! It will be to your ruin!'[64] However, other scholars are sceptical of this reading, questioning whether Paul would introduce a chapter on love with a statement of irony.[65] Alternatively, others prefer an indicative reading of ζηλοῦτε. Gardner, for example, proposes that reading ζηλοῦτε as an indicative would result in interpreting 12:31 as 'now you are earnestly desiring the greater grace-gifts and I will show you an even greater way.'[66] In this way, it is a critique of the Corinthians' attitude towards *charisma* pointing them to love as the priority over and above the existence and

---

62 Ciampa and Rosner, *First Letter to the Corinthians*, 614.
63 Garland, *1 Corinthians*, 602.
64 Smit, 'Two Puzzles', 247–55.
65 Garland, *1 Corinthians*, 601.
66 Gardner, *1 Corinthians*, 552; Other proponents of an indicative reading include Bittlinger, *Gifts*, 73–75; Iber, 'Zum Verständnis,' 43–52; Louw, 'Function of Discourse,' 331; Talbert, *Reading Corinthians*, 85.

use of *charisma*. Such an interpretation appears to lead well into Paul's discussion of love in 1 Corinthians 13. However, the concern of some scholars with an indicative reading is that when ζηλοῦτε is used again by Paul in 1 Corinthians 14:1 and 14:39, in both cases, it is clearly used as an imperative.[67]

Alternatively, Willem C. Van Unnik argues that it is best to render ζηλοῦτε as an imperative, but rather than translating this as 'eagerly desire', that it is more appropriate to translate it as something like 'put zealously into practice'.[68] Van Unnik argues convincingly for this translation based on the use of ζηλόω in a range of ancient sources where it is translated as 'devoting oneself to something', of ' zealously doing something', or 'zealously practicing something'.[69] Van Unnik thus concludes that what Paul is saying is that those who have received 'the various gifts of the Spirit should be zealous in them, that is to say: zealously practice them, and that not in an ordinary way, but as much as they can, even to the highest degree'.[70] In a similar vein, Thiselton proposes that the verse should be considered to mean 'Do not stop being zealously concerned about the "greatest" gifts, provided that you follow me in transposing and subverting your understanding of what counts as "the greatest"'.[71]

Translating ζηλοῦτε in 12:31 to mean 'be zealous in using the grace-gifts' aligns much better with Paul's rhetorical questions in 12:29–30 where Paul again reminds the Corinthians—as he has done on four previous occasions in the chapter (12:11; 12:18; 12:24; 12:28)—that the grace-gifts are allocated by God at his discretion for the edification of the church. In this respect, Paul is charging the

---

67 Lappenga, *Paul's Language of* Ζῆλος, 153.
68 Van Unnik, 'The Meaning of 1 Corinthians', 151.
69 Van Unnik, 'The Meaning of 1 Corinthians', 152. Diodorus Siculus refers to Asclepius who 'devoted himself to the science of healing (ζηλῶσαι τὴν ἰατρικὴν ἐπιστήμην)' (*Hist.* IV 71; LCL: Oldfather). Likewise Josephus recalls Ananias speaking to King Izates who had become a convert to Judaism saying that he need not have to be circumcised in order to show himself 'a devoted adherent of Judaism (εἴγε πάντως κέκρικε ζηλοῦν τὰ πάτρια τῶν Ἰουδαίων)' (*Ant.* 20.4; LCL: Thackeray).
70 Van Unnik, 'The Meaning of 1 Corinthians', 154.
71 Thiselton, *First Epistle*, 1024.

Corinthians to be devoted to using or putting into practice the grace-gifts that have been allocated to them. There is no need for the members of the body to 'strive' after the greater gifts as such striving is unneccesary and at odds with God's placement of members 'just as he wanted them to be' (12:18). There is no need for any sense of competition where some believers have gifts higher on a hierarchy than others, but each member should be satisfied with the grace-gifts that have been allocated to them by God and be diligent in using them in service to the Body of Christ.

That said, Paul does refer to 'greater gifts' both in 12:31 and again in 14:6. It is clear then that Paul does consider some gifts to have a further reach in terms of the edification of the Body of Christ. Part of Paul's concern with the overuse of *glossolalia* in the Corinthian church rests on the fact that *glossolalia* is limited in its ability to edify the whole Body of Christ. However, even though Paul says in 1 Corinthians 14:5 that he would 'rather have (the Corinthians) prophesy' than use *glossolalia* because of the wider benefit of prophesy for the people of God, he qualifies this by saying that 'the one who prophesies is greater than the one who speaks in tongues, *unless someone interprets*, so that the church may be edified' (1 Cor. 14:5).[72] Paul does not universally see prophecy as the most superior gift and tongues the least valuable as is suggested by those scholars who read 12:28 as a heirarchy of gifts. Instead, at times when the interpretation is available, *glossolalia* may prove to have greater potential for the edification of believers. In this respect, Paul does not see the *charisma* as having fixed values in a set heirarchy of gifts, but he acknowledges that in different circumstances, different gifts are going to be of greater value for the edification for the whole church. Such a view reduces any temptation for members to fix the valuation of some gifts over others, thus continuing to replicate the issue which had arisen in the Corinthian church of offering greater honour to those deemed to be in possession of more valuable gifts.

---

72 Emphasis is mine.

4. Conclusion

As Harrison's work has demonstrated, Paul's depiction of God's *charis* reframes the conventions of beneficence known and practised througout Graeco-Roman anitquity. While the Graeco-Roman reciprocity system required commensurate return for acts of *charis*, Paul instead stresses that God's *charis* is 'unilateral', unburdening believers of any need for reciprocity.[73] Although Paul continues to 'affirm the obligation of believers to each other and to their Graeco-Roman neighbours', he does so by 'transform(ing) the dynamic of reciprocity by means of the debt of love'.[74]

In addition to the Christ-event, God's *charis* continues to be demonstrated in his generous outpouring of *charisma*, grace-gifts, distributed amongst believers at God's discretion, for the edification of the Body of Christ. This *charis* is demonstrated not only in the abundant variety of grace-gifts he makes available to believers, but also in the distribution of these gifts in a way that defies the Graeco-Roman benefaction system. Gifts are not distributed in greater measure to those of higher status or wealth, but rather all believers are endowed with *charisma* which are to be used in service to God and the community of believers. In the Body of Christ, all believers undertake the simultaneous roles of both benefactor and beneficiary, being obligated to one another and mutually participating in the use of their grace-gifts for the edification of the whole body.

In contrast to the Graeco-Roman depictions of the body *topos*, the Body of Christ is not a hierarchical body with some members possessing higher ranked gifts than others. In relaying his vision of the Body of Christ in 1 Corinthians 12, Paul does not depict this Body as a rigid hierarchy with some members being in possession of more valuable gifts than others. Instead, Paul emphasises the mutuality and interdependence of all the members. In this way, the 'hierarchical structure of the (Graeco-Roman) honour system is radically overturned: all believers are endowed with χαρίσματα; the weak, not the strong, are to be

---

73 Harrison, *Paul's Language*, 348.
74 Harrison, *Paul's Language*, 343.

given the first place of honour; all believers are slaves of Christ who must serve each other'.[75] In critiquing the Corinthians' prioritisation of some gifts over others, Paul does not simply offer an alternative hierarchy that he wishes the Corinthians to adhere to as such a response would be counter-productive. A new hierarchy of gifts would simply result in the Corinthians continuing along the same trajectory: valuing and honouring some gifts over others. Instead, the list of grace-gifts in 1 Corinthians 12:28 is offered by Paul as a corrective to the Corinthians' valuation of the more visibly impressive gifts. His intention was not to provide a fixed, immutable list of valuable gifts as an alternative to their present hierarchy, but it was to help expand the Corinthians' understanding of the variety of gifts God makes available while also challenging the Corinthians to rethink their valuation of some gifts over others. The 'greater gifts' are not those which are demonstrable or impressive in their usage, but those which afford greater edifcation for the community of believers.

Paul writes not to encourage the Corinthians to strive after those gifts which appear at the top of a hierarchy of valuable gifts, but instead he exhorts them to zealously practise those gifts which have been allocated to them by God. The Corinthians are to eschew the world's priorities of visibly impressive gifts and instead to give priority to those gifts which have the greatest capacity for building up others in the Body of Christ. There is no scope for envying others' gifts or striving to possess gifts others have because the gifts have been allocated by God to fulfil his purposes. Paul seeks to remind the Corinthians that God's *charis* means they are indebted to one other, equipped through the Spirit with grace-gifts for the mutual benefit and functioning of the whole body.

Louise A. Gosbell
Mary Andrews College, Sydney

---

75   Harrison, *Paul's Language*, 349.

Bibliography

Ancient Sources:

Aesop *Aesop's Fables* (Jack Zipes, trans.; London and New York: Penguin, 1996).

Josephus *Jewish Antiquities, Volume I: Books 1—3* (LCL 242; H. St. J. Thackeray, trans.; Cambridge: Harvard University Press, 1930).

Diodorus Siculus *Library of History, Volume I: Books 1—2.34* (LCL 279; C.H. Oldfather, trans.; Cambridge: Harvard University Press, 1933).

Hippocrates *Nature of Man. Regimen in Health. Humours. Aphorisms. Regimen 1-3. Dreams. Heracleitus: On the Universe. Volume 4.* (LCL 150; W. H. S. Jones, trans.; Cambridge: Harvard University Press, 1931).

Modern Sources:

Banks, R. J. *Paul's Idea of Community: Spirit and Culture in Early House Churches* (3rd edn.; Grand Rapids, MI: Baker Academic, 2020).

Barclay, J. M. G. *Paul and the Power of Grace* (Grand Rapids, MI: Eerdmans, 2020).

Bittlinger, A. *Gifts and Graces: A Commentary on 1 Cor 12—14* (H. Klassen, trans.; Grand Rapids, MI: Eerdmans, 1968).

Blanton, T. R. *A Spiritual Economy: Gift Exchange in the Letters of Paul of Tarsus* (New Haven, CT: Yale University Press, 2017).

Blomberg, C. L. *1 Corinthians* (NIVAC; Grand Rapids, MI: Zondervan, 1994).

Brock, B., and B. Wannenwetsch *The Therapy of the Christian Body: A Theological Exposition of Paul's First Letter to the Corinthians* (Vol. 2; Eugene, OR: Cascade, 2018).

Carson, D. A. *Showing the Spirit: A Theological Exposition of 1 Corinthians 12—14* (Moore Theological College Lecture Series; Homebush West: Lancer, 1988).

Ciampa, R. E., and B. S. Rosner *The First Letter to the Corinthians* (PNTC; Grand Rapids, MI: Eerdmans, 2010).

Collins, R. F.	*First Corinthians* (SP 7; Collegeville, PA: Liturgical Press, 1999).
Dunn, J. D. G.	*Jesus and the Spirit: A Study of the Religious and Charismatic Experience of Jesus and the First Christians as Reflected in the New Testament* (Grand Rapids, MI: Eerdmans, 1975).
Dunn, J. D. G.	*The Theology of Paul the Apostle* (Grand Rapids, MI: Eerdmans, 1998).
Fee, G. D.	*The First Epistle to the Corinthians* (NICNT; Grand Rapids, MI: Eerdmans, 1987).
Fitzmyer, J. A.	*First Corinthians: A New Translation with Introduction and Commentary* (New Haven, CT: Yale University Press, 2008).
Gardner, P.	*1 Corinthians* (ZECNT; Grand Rapids, MI: Zondervan, 2018).
Garland, D. E.	*1 Corinthians* (BECNT; Grand Rapids, MI: Baker Academic, 2003).
Gosbell, L. A.	'A Disability Reading of Paul's Use of the "Body of Christ" Metaphor in Romans 12:3–8 and 1 Corinthians 12:12–31', in P. G. Bolt and J. R. Harrison (eds.), *Romans and the Legacy of St Paul: Historical Theological and Social Perspectives* (Macquarie Park: SCD Press, 2019), 281–335.
Harrison, J. R.	*Paul's Language of Grace in its Graeco-Roman Context* (WUNT II 172; Tübingen: Mohr Siebeck, 2003).
Harrison, J. R.	'The Erasure of Distinction: Paul and the Politics of Dishonour', *TynB* 67.1 (2016), 63-86.
Hays, R. B.	*First Corinthians* (Interpretation; Louisville, KY: Westminster/John Knox, 2011).
Hiramatsu, K.	'Paul's Theology of Weakness in 1 Cor 8:1—14:40', *HBT* 41.1 (2019), 71-91.
Iber, G.	'Zum Verständnis von 1 Cor 12:31', *ZNW* 54 (1963), 42-52.
Judge, E. A.	*The Social Pattern of Christian Groups in the First Century* (London: Tyndale, 1960).
Judge, E. A.	'Demythologising the Church: What is the Meaning of "the Body of Christ"?', in E. A. Judge, *The First Christians in the Roman World* (J. R. Harrison, ed.; WUNT 229; Tübingen: Mohr Siebeck, 2008), 568-85.
Lappenga, B. J.	*Paul's Language of Ζῆλος: Monosemy and the Rhetoric of Identity and Practice* (Leiden: Brill, 2016).

Louw, J. P.   'The Function of Discourse in a Sociosemiotic Theory of Translation Illustrated by the Translation of *zēloute* in 1 Corinthians 12.31', *BT* 39 (1988), 329-35.

Martin, D.   *The Corinthian Body* (New Haven, CT: Yale University Press, 1995).

Meeks, W. A.   *The First Urban Christians: The Social World of the Apostle Paul* (New Haven, CT: Yale University Press, 1983).

Nardoni, E.   'The Concept of Charism in Paul', *CBQ* 55.1 (1993), 68-80.

Neyrey, J. H.   *Paul in Other Words: A Cultural Reading of his Letters* (Louisville, KY: Westminster, 1990).

Peterlin, D.   'Stomach, Hands, Legs, Feet, Eyes, Ears, Mouth, Upper and Lower Teeth, Molars, Eyebrows and Head: The Unity of Christians and the Ancient *Topos* of Body and Members', *Evangelical Journal of Theology* 4.1 (2010), 63-83.

Schreiner, T. R.   *1 Corinthians* (TNTC; Downers Grove, IL: IVP, 2018).

Smit, J. F. M.   'Two Puzzles: 1 Corinthians 12:31 and 13:3: A Rhetorical Solution', *NTS* 39 (1993), 246-64.

Talbert, C. H.   *Reading Corinthians: A Literary and Theological Commentary on 1 and 2 Corinthians* (New York, NY: Crossroad, 1987).

Theissen, G.   'Social Conflicts in the Corinthians Community: Further Remarks on J. J. Meggitt, Paul, Poverty, and Survival', *JSNT* 25 (2003), 371-91.

Theissen, G.   'Social Stratification in the Corinthian Community: A Contribution to the Sociology of Early Hellenistic Christianity', in G. Theissen (ed.), *The Social Setting of Pauline Christianity: Essays on Corinth* (Philadelphia, PA: Fortress, 1982), 69–119.

Thiselton, A. C.   *The First Letter to the Corinthians* (NIGTC; Grands Rapids, MI: Eerdmans, 2000).

Van Unnik, W. C.   'The Meaning of 1 Corinthians 12:31', *NovT* 35.2 (1993), 142-59.

Welborn, L. L.   *Paul, the Fool of Christ: A Study of 1 Corinthians 1-4 in the Comic-Philosophic Tradition* (London: T&T Clark, 2005).

Witherington, B., III,   *Conflict and the Community in Corinth: A Socio-Rhetorical Commentary on 1 and 2 Corinthians* (Grand Rapids, MI: Eerdmans, 1995).

'But by the Grace of God I Am What I Am' (1 Corinthians 15:10a): Pauline Identity in Theological Perspective

Stephen C. Barton

Abstract

Taking its cue from Paul's testimony in 1 Corinthians 15 that he is who he is 'by the grace of God', this essay is an exploration of Paul's sense of self. The essay is in three parts. The first part offers an exegesis of 1 Corinthians 15:10a as a key to Paul's sense of self as the unworthy beneficiary of divine grace. The second asks what it is about grace, understood as gift, that is so determinative of Paul's sense of self. The third discusses Paul's practice and pedagogy of prayer—especially prayers of thanksgiving—as one of the ways grace is formative of his language and life.

Introduction

In a letter written to counter party-spirit among the Christ-followers in Corinth and to consolidate them as 'one' in God, Christ and the Spirit (cf. 1 Cor. 12:4–6,12–13,27),[1] Paul's autobiographical statements in 1 Corinthians play a significant part. Time and again, Paul offers his personal narrative as a significant point of reference for the ongoing conversion of life of the believing community. Critical to the persuasive intent of this narrative is the way in which Paul represents his experience as an embodiment of the primordial divine reality of gift and call—of divine beneficence with its attendant reciprocal obligations—into which both he and the Corinthians have been drawn.

---

1   For a magisterial treatment see Mitchell, *Paul*.

The word he uses for that reality is *charis* (χάρις), normally translated, 'grace'.

In this essay, written in honour of my lifelong friend Jim Harrison, a scholar who has devoted his life to the study of the semantics and historical-contextual explication of grace (and much else!) in the world of the apostle Paul,[2] what I seek to explore is the meaning of grace for *Paul's sense of self*, his sense of who he is. In relation to Paul's 'I' in his autobiographical statements, this may be expressed as a decentring and recentring, effected by and commensurate with the gift. And insofar as Paul's 'I' is offered for imitation by the 'you' of the association of Christ-followers, what Paul says about the gift-relation constitutes a judgement on self-seeking and party-spirit and a call to a life of other-regard and mutual recognition in/as the body of Christ.

'But by the grace of God I am what I am' (1 Cor. 15:10a)

A brilliant example of the appeal to divine grace and gift as constitutive of Paul's sense of self along with its wider implications occurs in 1 Corinthians 15:1–11. In the preceding section of the letter (11:2—14:40), Paul offers instruction aimed at countering disorder and strengthening the unity of the fellowship when the Christ-followers 'come together' to celebrate their eschatological existence by the exercise of various kinds of Spirit-inspired 'gifts' (χαρίσματα). He then proceeds to another controverted and divisive matter also related to eschatological existence—namely belief about death, resurrection, and the afterlife, with its implications for how to live now (15:32b–34,58; cf. 6:14). Here, in order to bolster their common faith in the gospel of Christ crucified *and risen*—and simultaneously to remind them of his (i.e. Paul's) agency for their benefit as the gospeller of the gospel (15:1–2)—Paul adduces authority-bearing testimony: first, that of the scriptures (15:3–4), and then that of eyewitnesses, including his own (15:5–11).

The list of eyewitnesses follows a temporal order (characterised by the repetition of ἔπειτα) which also has about it something of a peck-

---

2   See, *inter alia*, Harrison, *Paul's Language*; and, more recently, Harrison, *Paul*.

ing order marked, not only by the sequencing, but also by the adducing of personal names and status-sensitive technical terms: Cephas, the Twelve ... James (presumably, the Lord's brother), and 'all the apostles'. This builds to an ironic climax (in 15:8–11), where what comes at the tail-end—Paul's self-confessedly ambiguous testimony—receives the most extensive, and most theologically developed, attention:

> Last of all, as to one untimely born, he [i.e. Christ] appeared also to me. For I am the least of the apostles, unfit to be called an apostle, because I persecuted the church of God. But by the grace of God I am what I am, and his grace toward me has not been in vain. On the contrary, I worked harder than any of them—though it was not I, but the grace of God that is with me. Whether then it was I or they, so we proclaim and so you have come to believe.[3]

To grasp something of the significance of this testimony in its paraenetic context, I offer the following observations.

First, this is one of a number of autobiographical testimonies in 1 Corinthians, each of which plays a vital role in Paul's pedagogy, reflecting as they do the importance of leading by personal example, not least when the lesson Paul seeks to impart is controversial or likely to meet resistance. Thus, in 1 Corinthians 9, in an autobiographical 'digression' in the context of sensitive matters to do with the exercise of Christian freedom (in respect of 'food sacrificed to idols') in a culturally plural environment (cf. 1 Cor. 8—10), Paul appeals to his apostolic status and rights only to show that his status and rights are *relative* to a higher consideration (and to what defines his apostleship in the first place), namely, his obligation to 'endure anything rather than put an obstacle in the way of the gospel of Christ' (9:12b). Likewise, in another autobiographical interlude (in chapter 13), Paul names exceptional Spirit-inspired gifts and virtues familiar to him, only to argue that, practised without the other-regard of love (ἀγάπη), they are an expression, not of personal worth and spiritual maturity, but of a kind of self-negation conveyed in the twofold verdict, 'I am nothing ... I gain nothing' (13:2,3). Signifi-

---

3 Unless indicated otherwise, all biblical quotations are from the NRSV.

cantly, a common thread running through each of these testimonies is a decentring of the Pauline 'I' and a threefold recentring: on God (or Christ or the Spirit), on the gospel, and on the people of God.

Second, in 15:8–9, the language Paul uses of himself is the language of deliberate—even shocking—self-abasement.[4] i. He is 'last of all' to be the recipient of a revelation of the risen Christ. ii. In relation to Christ's vivifying resurrection appearance to him, he is like 'a miscarried, aborted foetus' (ὡσπερεὶ τῷ ἐκτρώματι)[5]—even though, as he says elsewhere, he was set apart by God while in his mother's womb (Gal. 1:15; cf. Isa. 49:1). iii. He is 'the least [ἐλάχιστος] of the apostles', a ranking which, in everyday terms, puts him at a severe social disadvantage. iv. He is 'unfit' [οὐκ ... ἱκανός; literally, 'not sufficient'] to have apostolic title, status and credentials—another damning admission. v. And, as the climax of this catalogue of self-abasements, the reason why he is 'unfit'—as everyone will have known—is because he committed the heinous sin of *opposing God* as a persecutor of the *ekklēsia tou theou*.

Third, in relation to the immediately preceding, v.10 represents a radical reversal which gives Paul's testimony a clear rhetorical structure. The move is from what disqualifies him to what (or better, who) now qualifies him. The reversal is marked grammatically by the adversative particle δέ ('But'). More importantly, it is marked with massive intensity by the threefold repetition of the terminology of divine *charis* (χάρις). i. Although he persecuted the church *of God* (τοῦ θεοῦ) it is by the grace or beneficence of the same God (χάριτι δὲ θεοῦ) that Paul has been re-made. ii. The divine grace shown to Paul was not given 'in vain' (οὐ κενή), a truth evidenced in gospel labours exceeding those of the apostles he has listed previously. iii. But (and in a further testimony to decentring) even these labours were performed, not by his agency alone, but by the enabling 'grace of God' (ἡ χάρις τοῦ θεοῦ) present with him. In sum, it is *a story of personal revivification* by God and, as

---

4 What Paul says of himself here is comparable to the kind of language he uses of himself (and Apollos) in 4:9–13. As Mitchell puts it (in *Paul*, 285 n.556): 'In both places ghastly pictorial images describe the lowest depths of humility.'
5 I follow here the formulation of Thiselton, *Corinthians*, 1208–10, himself drawing *inter alios* on Nickelsburg, 'An *ektrōma*'.

such, totally appropriate to a paraenetic context in which what is at issue is unity grounded in a shared belief in the sovereign power of God to give life to the dead.

Fourth, Paul's claim that God's grace towards him was not 'in vain' (οὐ κενή; 15:10a) is important. It resonates with several other occurrences of the expression in close proximity: 'if Christ has not been raised then our proclamation has been in vain [κενόν], and your faith has been in vain [κενή]' (15:14); and, at the conclusion of the entire argument for unity in resurrection faith, 'Therefore, my beloved, be steadfast, immovable, always excelling in the work of the Lord, because you know that in the Lord your labor is not in vain [οὐκ ἔστιν κενός]' (15:58).[6] The language is that of purpose, result, or benefit. The implied sense is that the grace of God and connection with the risen Lord is *efficacious*—and can be seen to be so.

Finally, by way of drawing this foundational statement (in vv. 1–11) to a conclusion, and in a further expression of personal decentring, Paul brings the argument full circle (cf. 11:1-2). Reminding the Corinthians of the resurrection faith they had embraced and which they held in common, Paul says, '*Whether then it was I or they* [εἴτε ... εἴτε], so we proclaim and so you have come to believe' (v.11). It is as if Paul's identity (along with that of God's other apostolic messengers) is of relative importance only. What is most important is not the preacher—and therefore not factional allegiance to one apostle in preference to another—but the gospel preaching and the unity in faith, hope, and love it enables.

Overall, what is striking is the way in which Paul's rhetoric of personal decentring in the direction of self-abasement does two things. First, and most importantly, it creates space, as it were, for making God and the vivifying, eschatological grace of God the centre of attention, a recentring entirely consistent with the theocentric thrust of the letter as a whole.[7] Second, insofar as Paul is a model for imitation in the life of the community (cf. 11:1; also, 4:16),[8] what he says by way of per-

---

6 Similarly, in 2 Cor. 6:1: 'As we work together with him, we urge you also not to accept the grace of God in vain'.
7 On Paul's theocentrism, see Ciampa and Rosner, 'The Structure and Argument'.
8 On the *imitatio Pauli*, see Fiore, 'Paul'.

sonal apostolic testimony offers the basis for a group ethos characterised by a kind of critical self-awareness—a subjectivity tutored in humility and other-regard, and therefore beneficial for enhancing communal harmony.

Who is Paul now?

In the light of Paul's testimony that, 'by the grace of God I am what I am' (15:10a), it seems reasonable to pursue further the question of Paul's identity.[9] Given the decentring impact on Paul of God's disruptive grace, *who is Paul now?* Certainly, in the immediate context, Paul's 'I am' is an assertion of his identity and status *as an apostle*, the last in the line of apostolic recipients of a resurrection appearance (1 Cor. 15:8,10b–11). Paul is an apostle because God in God's sovereign freedom has called him from being a persecutor of God's *ekklēsia* to being one of God's agents for the proclamation of the liberating gospel of the crucified and risen Christ; and the persuasive weight of his resurrection testimony is a function of that apostleship.[10]

But may we press the identity question beyond its relevance to Paul's status and calling as an apostle? When Paul says, 'by the grace of God I am what I am', is he giving expression to a self-understanding open to exploration and articulation on a wider front and a deeper level?[11] Certainly, the assertive and highly personal quality of the double εἰμι (in εἰμι ὅ εἰμι)—unique in the Pauline corpus—hints in that direction.

The beginnings of an answer must lie in the legitimating phrase χάριτι δὲ θεοῦ ('by the grace of God'). At this point, of course, we are on the brink of a discussion of *the* most important and dynamic aspect of Paul's experience, thought, and practice. Suffice it to say, especially on the

---

9   For current scholarly interest in identity definition and formation in antiquity generally, see Niehoff and Levinson, (eds.) *Self*. For early Judaism, see Putthoff, *Ontological Aspects*. For Paul, see Eastman, *Paul*.
10 For further expressions of Paul's self-understanding as an apostle, see, among multiple examples, 1 Cor. 1:1; 4:9; 9:1–2; 2 Cor. 1:1; 12:12; Gal. 1:1; Rom. 1:1; 11:13. For a succinct account, see Dunn, *The Theology of Paul*, 571–80.
11 Indeed, may not Paul's statement of his own identity in terms of grace express a truth fundamental to the identity of his fellow-believers also? For affirmation, see Thiselton, *Corinthians*, 1211.

basis of what Paul says about χάρις in Galatians and Romans (cf. Gal. 1:15–16; Rom. 3:21–26; 5:15–16), that Paul is who he is by virtue of a *gift relationship*, where the gift is Christ, union with whom in his death and resurrection radically reconstitutes Paul's sense of self in eschatological terms. As he says in Galatians, 'I have been crucified with Christ; and it is no longer I who live, but it is Christ who lives in me' (Gal. 2:19–20); and, in relation to highly significant symbols of cultural and religious distinction, 'For neither circumcision nor uncircumcision is anything; but a new creation [καινὴ κτίσις] is everything!' (Gal. 6:15).[12]

That the gift of the Christ-relation is reconstitutive of Paul's sense of self arises above all from his recognition of the *incongruity* of the gift, as John Barclay has shown.[13] Given that 'incongruity' in the context of gift-relations and gift-exchange denotes a gift 'given without condition, that is, *without regard to the worth of the recipient*',[14] God's gift of God's Son imparted by revelation to Paul, even though he 'was violently persecuting the church of God ... trying to destroy it' (Gal. 1:13b; cf. 1 Cor. 15:9b), becomes for Paul a point of radical dislocation in his personal narrative. What has given him his sense of worth up to now is *recalibrated*. Indeed, in writing to the believers in Philippi, Paul makes explicit use of the language of accounting to express the transformation in his symbolic world, system of values and sense of self which the gift of the Christ-relation has brought about. Having listed his seven(!) claims to self-worth, social honour, and divine blessing—claims which he could enter previously in the credit column—he proceeds to transfer them to the debit column:

> Yet whatever gains [κέρδη] I had, these I have come to regard as loss [ζημίαν] because of Christ. More than that, I regard everything as loss [ζημίαν] because of the surpassing value [ὑπερέχον] of knowing Christ Jesus my Lord. For his sake I have suffered the loss of all things [πάντα ἐζημιώθην], and I

---

12 Cf. 2 Cor. 5:17, 'So if anyone is in Christ, there is a new creation [καινὴ κτίσις], everything old has passed away; see, everything has become new [καινά]!'
13 Barclay, *Paul and the Gift*, 331–561; and, for a popular summary, Barclay, *Paul and the Subversive Power of Grace*.
14 Barclay, *Paul and the Gift*, 72–73. Italics in the original.

regard them as rubbish [σκύβαλα], in order that I may gain Christ [Χριστὸν κερδήσω] and be found in him, not having a righteousness of my own that comes from the law, but one that comes through faith in Christ. (Phil. 3:7–9)

If we ask *how* the Christ-relation, the being 'found in him', could effect a change of such a catastrophic kind (in terms of Paul's inherited social norms and cultural values), what Paul says points not only to the incongruity of the gift, but also to the identity of the giver and the substance of the gift.

That the gift is given without regard to the worth of the recipient—whether worth is calibrated in terms of ethnicity, social status, or gender—has the effect of *destabilizing* the time-honoured norms, values, and identity-markers of the society of Paul's day, creating space for *creativity and innovation*, for seeing, doing, and feeling differently. Here, Paul himself—whom F. F. Bruce memorably called, 'apostle of the heart set free'[15]—is exemplary.

But it is important to emphasize first, that the degree of incongruity is grounded in and magnified by the fact that the One who gives without regard to human ascriptions of worth is *God* who gives in love primordially and superabundantly; and second, that the gift given is *Christ crucified*, a 'gospel' (εὐαγγέλιον) elaborated in paradoxical and world-changing terms as 'the power of God and the wisdom of God' (1 Cor. 1:24) and, as such, constitutive of an apocalyptic epistemology which offers, as a corollary, a distinctive hermeneutic of personhood, both individual and communal.

A praying self

Given that, fundamental to Paul's sense of self is his recognition that he is the (unworthy) recipient of divine benefaction, an important manifestation of that selfhood—and one that may not have received the attention it merits—is what Paul expresses both in the prayers he

---

15   The phrase is the title of Bruce's theology of Paul: *Paul: Apostle of the Heart Set Free*.

reports and in his prayer pedagogy.[16] Krister Stendahl's comment on the prayer-full character of Paul's discourse is pertinent:

> What we have in Paul is ... a style of writing that is saturated by prayerful language. His gratitude, his greetings, his farewells, his hopes, his admonitions, his worries, his travel plans are all often cast in a language that borders on prayer, a language shaped and informed by his awareness of divine presence, divine activity.[17]

For present purposes, what Paul's prayer discourse displays is that his sense of self, as the recipient of the heavenly gift, is oriented towards God and Christ *in thanksgiving*,[18] the felt form of which is *joy*—with attendant implications for the communal subjectivity and ethos of Paul's hearers and readers.

Suggestive here, by way of analogy, is Carol A. Newsom's substantial essay on the ways in which the language and structure of the Thanksgiving Hymns (or Hodayot) from Qumran, with introductory formulae taking the form, 'I thank you, O Lord, that ...', constitute a rhetoric for the formation of a sense of self among members of the sect.[19] The following points are especially relevant: i. On the concept of 'selfhood' itself (at least as understood within cultural anthropology): a person's sense of self 'is constructed through the symbolic practices of a person's culture'.[20] Such practices are both linguistic and non-linguistic. ii. In a sectarian context such as the Qumran community, language practices, including the 're-accentuation' of traditional idioms (such as those found in the biblical psalms), play a critical rhetorical role in the formation of a distinctive and alternative subjectivity. iii. 'The language of prayer with its address to an absolute "you" is a very powerful instrument for the formation of subjectivity' among sect members.[21] iv. The prayers of the Hodayot cast the relationship between God and the

---

16 For a valuable survey, see Hunter, 'Prayer'.
17 Stendahl, 'Paul at Prayer', 151.
18 O'Brien, 'Thanksgiving', is pertinent.
19 Newsom, 'Apocalyptic Subjects'.
20 Newsom, 'Apocalyptic Subjects', 4.
21 Newsom, 'Apocalyptic Subjects', 14.

sect member as, above all, one of benefaction, with the pray-er as the recipient of a gift, such as deliverance, pardon, election, and so on. v. In consequence, the reader of these texts is oriented to thanksgiving 'as the paradigmatic mode of experience'.[22] vi. In offering thanksgiving, the pray-er is a witness, such that 'an important part of the speaker's subjectivity [is] in this very act of declaring. The speaker encounters himself, comes to experience himself, as one who praises God'.[23]

Like the author(s) of the Hodayot, Paul's prayer reports along with his prayer pedagogy testify to his sense of self as a beneficiary of divine grace, and therefore as one *given over* to thanksgiving and doxology.[24] The following texts, the first two of which are taken from the letter introductions, are exemplary.

1. The opening of 1 Thessalonians, Paul's earliest extant letter, is a case in point. On the basis of the Thessalonians' new, existential location 'in God the Father and the Lord Jesus Christ', Paul begins, not with the conventional opening of a letter of friendship—χαῖρε/χαίρετε ('Greetings!')—but with a prayer of benediction: χάρις ὑμῖν καὶ εἰρήνη ('Grace to you and peace'). Then, having located his addressees in the sphere of divine benefaction, he offers an extended, first-person prayer report in the form of a thanksgiving:

> We always give thanks to God [Εὐχαριστοῦμεν τῷ θεῷ πάντοτε] for all of you and mention you in our prayers, constantly remembering before our God and Father your work of faith and labor of love and steadfastness of hope in our Lord Jesus Christ. For we know, brothers and sisters, beloved by God, that he has chosen you ... (1:2-4).

The evident hyperbole ('always', 'all of you', 'constantly') need not distract us from acknowledging that Paul's sense of self, shaped by the

---

22 Newsom, 'Apocalyptic Subjects', 15.
23 Newsom, 'Apocalyptic Subjects', 16.
24 Of course, that prayers of thanksgiving and praise are not the only forms of prayer practised and taught by Paul is suggested by 1 Tim. 2:1, where the writer urges that 'supplications, prayers, intercessions, and thanksgivings be made for everyone'. For the evidence of Acts regarding Paul's practice of prayer, see Acts 9:11; 14:23; 16:13,25; 20:36; 21:5; 22:17; 28:8, cited in Hunter, 'Prayer', 725-726.

obligations arising from his relationships both heavenly and earthly, finds categorical expression in the language of a prayer of thanksgiving. Furthermore, insofar as the prayer is 'overheard' by his addressees when the letter is read in the assembly, it orients them also towards thanksgiving as (what Newsom calls) 'the paradigmatic mode of experience'. This sense is reinforced towards the letter's end. Here, on the basis of Paul's assurance (in language of apocalyptic dualism particularly relevant in a context of persecution) that he together with his addresses are 'children of the light and children of the day ... not of the night or of the darkness' (5:5), he commands: 'Rejoice always [Πάντοτε χαίρετε], pray without ceasing [ἀδιαλείπτως προσεύχεσθε], give thanks in all circumstances [ἐν παντὶ εὐχαριστεῖτε]; for this is the will of God in Christ Jesus for you' (5:16–18).[25]

2. Paul's prayer of benediction and first-person report of thanksgiving at the beginning of 1 Corinthians follow a similar pattern (cf. also Phil. 1:3–5; Col. 1:2b–3; 2 Thess. 1:2–3; Phlm. 3–5; Rom. 1:7b–10). Once again, grace/gift language is intense and pervasive:

> Grace to you [χάρις ὑμῖν] and peace from God our Father and the Lord Jesus Christ.
> I give thanks to my God [Εὐχαριστῶ τῷ θεῷ μου] always because of the grace of God that has been given you [ἐπὶ τῇ χάριτι τοῦ θεοῦ τῇ δοθείσῃ ὑμῖν] in Christ Jesus, for in every way you have been enriched [ἐπλουτίσθητε] in him ... so that you are not lacking in any spiritual gift [χαρίσματι] (1 Cor. 1:4,7a).

Evoking the three-way relation of 'I', 'you' (plural), and God/Christ Jesus, Paul's prayer expresses a privileged participation in the *circle and circulation of grace*, a participation into which he seeks to enclose his addressees by witnessing to his thanksgiving to God for what God, in Christ Jesus, has given them. Noteworthy, in respect of what ensues in the letter, is that Paul's orientation of himself and his addressees

---

25 Cf. Gaventa, *Thessalonians*, 8, who points out that, remarkably, each of the three main letter sections ends with a prayer (1:2–10; 3:11–13; 5:23–24); and comments: 'prayerful thanksgiving dominates 1 Thessalonians'.

towards God and Christ in thanksgiving is a rhetorical nudge *away from* perverse, narcissistic preoccupation with the self.

3. This God-ward orientation in prayerful thanksgiving recurs at the rhetorical climax of Paul's argument concerning resurrection in 1 Corinthians 15, discussed earlier. Building upon apocalyptic imagery of Endtime cosmic battle with Death, Paul exclaims, 'But thanks be to God [τῷ δὲ θεῷ χάρις], who gives us the victory [τῷ διδόντι ἡμῖν τὸ νῖκος] through our Lord Jesus Christ' (1 Cor. 15:57). The gift (noting the use of δίδωμι) is victory effected by Christ in his death and resurrection; and this calls forth a reciprocal gift (noting χάρις) in the rhetorical form of thanksgiving. Significantly, χάρις as gift evokes χάρις in return. There is a circularity of χάρις which binds benefactor and beneficiary together. Indeed, in this eschatological scenario, the beneficiary is an 'us', Paul and the community of Christ-followers. They are, by grace, a community of resurrection hope made articulate in the prayer of thanksgiving.

4. Still within the ambit of Paul's relations with the Corinthian Christ-followers is his testimony to his practice of prayer in response to a gift of a very different kind. Having 'boasted'—under duress and with considerable circumspection—of being the beneficiary of 'visions and revelations of the Lord' (2 Cor. 12:1), including an experience of religious ecstasy in the form of a rapture to Paradise (12:3–4), Paul says: 'a thorn was given me [ἐδόθη μοι] in the flesh, a messenger of Satan to torment me, to keep me from being too elated' (12:7). Whatever the 'thorn' refers to, what is significant is that Paul places it, remarkably, in the context of the relationship of divine benefaction, epitomised by χάρις: 'Three times I appealed to the Lord [τὸν κύριον παρεκάλεσα] about this, that it would leave me, but he said to me, "My grace is sufficient for you [ἀρκεῖ σοι ἡ χάρις μου], for power is made perfect in weakness."' (12:8–9). Here, no doubt in part with an eye towards confusing and confounding the honour system of his cultured despisers in the assembly, Paul acknowledges openly that three times he besought the risen Christ in prayer for deliverance and in response receives, not deliverance, but the gift of a revelatory word which takes his experience of adversity to a deeper level, allowing him to *re-interpret* his adversity christologically and eschatologically, such that he can boast 'most gladly' (noting the superlative, ἥδιστα, in vv. 9b and 15) of

weaknesses which make Christ's power present.[26]

Examination of Paul's prayer reports and prayer pedagogy could be taken further,[27] but enough has been said to make in regard to Paul's sense of self what Newsom says of the selfhood of the author of the Hodayot, that, arising out of a profound sense of being the beneficiary of divine grace, '[t]he speaker encounters himself, comes to experience himself, as one who praises God'.[28]

Conclusion

According to Edwin Judge, '[t]he trouble with Paul has always been to put him in his place'.[29] Few have done more than Jim Harrison to respond to his respected mentor's challenge by seeking to locate Paul more firmly, not least through attention to the evidence about the urban world of Paul revealed in the non-literary, as well as the literary, sources.[30] In terms of Paul's subjectivity, his sense of self, my suggestion here is that Paul is to be 'found'—and 'finds' himself—above all in persons and relationships heavenly and earthly. That would seem to be a fair inference from Paul's prayers. It would seem a fair inference also from his testimony, 'by the grace of God, I am what I am'.

Stephen C. Barton
University of Manchester

---

26 Nor is this the only occasion where Paul invokes prayer, including thanksgiving, in situations of adversity. See, for example, 1 Thess. 3:7–10; 2 Cor. 1:3–4; Phil. 1:3,18–19; Rom. 8:14–17.
27 Illuminating, especially for its comparison of Pauline thanksgiving with Graeco-Roman thanksgiving conventions displayed in the honorific inscriptions, is Harrison, *Paul's Language*, 269–272.
28 Newsom, 'Apocalyptic Subjects', 16.
29 Judge, 'St Paul', 73.
30 Exemplary in this respect are the multiple volumes in the series on urban Christianity, co-edited by Harrison and Welborn, beginning with *The First Urban Churches 1*, and currently ongoing.

Bibliography

Barclay, J. M. G. — *Paul and the Gift* (Grand Rapids, MI: Eerdmans, 2015).

Barclay, J. M. G. — *Paul and the Subversive Power of Grace* (Cambridge: Grove Books, 2016).

Bruce. F. F. — *Paul: Apostle of the Heart Set Free* (Grand Rapids, MI: Eerdmans, 1977).

Ciampa, R. E., and B. S. Rosner — 'The Structure and Argument of 1 Corinthians: A Biblical/Jewish Approach', *NTS* 52 (2006), 205–218.

Dunn, J. D. G. — *The Theology of Paul the Apostle* (Grand Rapids, MI: Eerdmans, 1998).

Eastman, S. G. — *Paul and the Person. Reframing Paul's Anthropology* (Grand Rapids, MI: Eerdmans, 2014).

Fiore, B., S. J. — 'Paul, Exemplification, and Imitation', in J. P. Sampley (ed.), *Paul in the Greco-Roman World* (Harrisburg, PA: Trinity Press International, 2003), 228–257.

Gaventa, B. R. — *First and Second Thessalonians* (Louisville, KY: Westminster John Knox Press, 1998).

Harrison, J. R. — *Paul's Language of Grace in Its Graeco-Roman Context* (Tübingen: Mohr Siebeck, 2003).

Harrison, J. R. — *Paul and the Ancient Celebrity Circuit. The Cross and Moral Transformation* (Tübingen: Mohr Siebeck, 2019).

Harrison, J. R., and L. L. Welborn (eds.) — *The First Urban Churches 1. Methodological Foundations* (Atlanta, GA: SBL Press, 2015).

Hunter, W. B. — 'Prayer', in G. F. Hawthorne, et al. (eds.), *Dictionary of Paul and his Letters* (Downers Grove, IL: InterVarsity Press, 1993), 725–734.

Judge, E. A. — 'St Paul and Classical Society', in D. M. Scholer, (ed.), *Social Distinctives of the Christians in the First Century. Pivotal Essays by E. A. Judge* (Peabody, MA: Hendrickson, 2008), 73–97.

Mitchell, M. M. — *Paul and the Rhetoric of Reconciliation* (Louisville, KY: Westminster John Knox, 1992).

Newsom, C. A. 'Apocalyptic Subjects: Social Construction of the Self in the Qumran Hodayot', *JSP* 12.1 (2001), 3–35.

Nickelsburg, G. W. E. 'An *ektrōma*, Though Appointed from the Womb: Paul's Apostolic Self-Description in 1 Cor 15 and Gal 1', *HTR* 79 (1986), 198–205.

Niehoff, M. R., and J. Levinson, (eds.) *Self, Self-Fashioning and Individuality in Late Antiquity* (Tübingen: Mohr Siebeck, 2019).

O'Brien, P. T. 'Thanksgiving and the Gospel in Paul', *NTS* 21 (1974–75), 144–155.

Putthoff, T. L. *Ontological Aspects of Early Jewish Anthropology: The Malleable Self and the Presence of God* (Leiden: Brill, 2017).

Stendahl, K. 'Paul at Prayer', in K. Stendahl, *Meanings* (Philadelphia, PA: Fortress, 1984), 151–161.

Thiselton, A. *The First Epistle to the Corinthians* (Grand Rapids, MI: Eerdmans, 2000).

Grace, Gratitude, and Glory in 2 Corinthians 4:15

Bradley J. Bitner

Abstract

Paul is an apostle of grace and of glory. Yet his ministry was marked by opposition, suffering, and fragility. In 2 Corinthians 4:15–16 Paul takes courage because he perceives the tangible effects of his Christ-gospel among the Corinthians. Gratitude in the growing community is the nexus binding gift and glory. Graeco-Roman and Jewish forms of gratitude, and especially the text of 1 and 2 Corinthians, show that these acts of gratitude consisted in sung hymns, prayers, and monetary gifts. Such forms of gratitude were themselves glorifying to God. And they were, for Paul, manifestations of the new creational transformation wrought in and among the Corinthian believers.

1. Grace, Gratitude, and Glory in the work of J. R. Harrison

Grace was the focus of James R. Harrison's important first monograph.[1] Jim saw that the overflow of grace in Paul is interrelated with the concepts of gratitude and glory:

> Paul consistently associates the return of gratitude with the motif of abundance: τὴν εὐχαριστίαν περισσεύσῃ (2 Cor. 4:15b); περισσεύουσα διὰ πολλῶν εὐχαριστιῶν τῷ θεῷ (9:12b); περισσεύοντες ἐν εὐχαριστίᾳ (Col. 2:7b). The return of thanks, however, cannot be measured against the

---

1 Harrison, *Paul's Language of Grace*.

infinite generosity of the divine Benefactor: 'For what thanksgiving can we return to God ...?' (1 Thess. 3:9: τίνα γὰρ εὐχαριστίαν δυνάμεθα τῷ θεῷ ἀνταποδοῦναι). Instead, for Paul, εὐχαριστία simply abounds! Christian gratitude spontaneously responds to the divine blessing (τὸ χάρισμα) that comes from the answered prayers of fellow Christians (2 Cor. 1:11); it rejoices in the extension of divine grace (ἡ χάρις πλεονάσασα) through the suffering apostles to others (4:15 [cf. vv. 7-11]); it celebrates the spiritual maturity and generosity of the Gentile Christians as they meet the needs of their impoverished Jewish brethren (9:11b-12).[2]

2 Corinthians 4:15[3] is a text that underlines divine grace as the ground of Christian gratitude.[4] And Paul interweaves a third strand: glory.[5] Grace, gratitude, and glory, especially in Graeco-Roman epigraphical perspective, are recurrent themes in Harrison's scholarship. So, it seems fitting in this expression of εὐχαριστία καὶ τιμή to probe the relations among these three concepts as they are correlated in 2 Corinthians 4:15 and its context. I offer this exegetical reflection as a token of gratitude for Jim's abiding generosity as a scholar, mentor, and friend who models in his own life an unabashed return of gratitude and glory to his gracious God and Saviour.

---

2   Harrison, *Paul's Language of Grace*, 271.
3   Note how 2 Cor. 4:15 and other texts from 2 Corinthians dominate the paragraph just cited.
4   Harrison, *Paul's Language of Grace*, 271, affirms as 'inescapable' the judgement of Zeller: 'Gnade ist der Grunde der εὐχαριστία'. See Zeller, *Charis bei Philon und Paulus*, 196.
5   Glory in Paul also features prominently in several of Harrison's studies, e.g., Harrison, 'Paul and the Roman Ideal of Glory'; Harrison, 'The Brothers as the "Glory of Christ"'.

2. The Puzzle of 2 Corinthians 4:15

Paul often interrelates grace, gratitude, and glory with the language of abundance and overflow[6] and in relation to suffering.[7] This coalesces strikingly in 2 Corinthians 4:15. But this verse presents a syntactical puzzle to the interpreter.[8] 2 Corinthians 4:15 consists of a short independent clause followed by a long dependent clause beginning with ἵνα. It is the relations of syntax within the ἵνα clause that are challenging. The text reads

τὰ γὰρ πάντα δι' ὑμᾶς, ἵνα ἡ χάρις πλεονάσασα διὰ τῶν
πλειόνων τὴν εὐχαριστίαν περισσεύσῃ εἰς τὴν δόξαν τοῦ θεοῦ.

The general sense is clear. According to Chrysostom, 'For the entirety (τὸ πᾶν) is from God, who desires to give graciously to many (πολλοῖς χαρίσασθαι), with the result *that grace might appear the greater* (ὥστε μείζονα ὀφθῆναι τὴν χάριν)'.[9] But what is 'the entirety' in view? And how, precisely, is grace amplified to 'appear the greater'? Any answer must begin by understanding the overflowing syntax with which Paul praises God's abounding grace and its effects.

Among the many proposals for interpreting the syntax of the ἵνα clause in 4:15, I find most persuasive the line taken by Thomas Schmeller (following, *inter alia*, Margaret Thrall, and Hans Windisch).[10] Visually, this interpretation might be represented as follows:

---

6 Grace (χάρις) and glory (δόξα): Rom. 5:2; 2 Cor. 8:19; Eph. 1:6; grace (χάρις) and gratitude (εὐχαριστία; εὐχαριστέω): 1 Cor. 1:4; 10:30; gratitude (εὐχαριστία) and glory (δοξάζω.): Rom. 1:21; grace, gratitude, and/or glory with abound (πλεονάζω), surpass (ὑπερβάλλω), and/or overflow (περισσεύω; περισσεία): Rom. 3:7, 6:1; 5:15, 17; 2 Cor. 3:9-10; 8:7-15; 9:8-15; Eph. 1:7-8; 2:7; Phil. 4:17-20; Col. 2:7; 2 Thess. 1:3.
7 Suffering (πάθημα) and/or tribulation (θλίψις) with abundance (πλεονάζω) and overflow (περισσεύω): 2 Cor. 1:4-5; 8:1-2.
8 Collange, *Énigmes*,167: 'Cette proposition est un vrai casse-tête'.
9 Chrysostom, *Hom. 2 Cor.* (PG 61.461); italics mine.
10 Schmeller, *Der zweite Brief*, 268-69. Cf. Windisch, *Der zweite Korintherbriefe*, 150-51; Thrall, *2 Corinthians*, 344-47.

A ἵνα ἡ χάρις
B πλεονάσασα διὰ τῶν πλειόνων
C τὴν εὐχαριστίαν περισσεύσῃ εἰς τὴν δόξαν τοῦ θεοῦ.

A in order that grace—
B having increased by the agency of the many—
C might cause thanksgiving to abound unto the glory of God.

The syntactical and exegetical decisions behind this rendering are as follows.[11] Πλεονάσασα (line B) is adjectival and intransitive. As a nominative participle in agreement with χάρις, it describes the prior and (ongoing) general character of grace in Paul's ministry. In context, this divine grace is a new-creational (4:4–6; cf. 5:17), life-giving (4:11–14), and renewing power (4:16). Its operation of increase is expressed intransitively by the participle. The modifying prepositional phrase (διὰ τῶν πλειόνων) specifies an intermediary agency that amplifies the increase. Through and *by means of* 'the many' (and not merely *among* the many), the subject χάρις finds its verbal expression in the aorist subjunctive περισσεύσῃ. That is, grace *causes thanksgiving to abound*. Εὐχαριστία is most naturally connected to the closest verb (περισσεύσῃ; which follows in this case; cf. περισσεύουσα in 2 Cor. 9:12). The final prepositional phrase (εἰς τὴν δόξαν τοῦ θεοῦ) is telic (or resultative), expressing divine glory as the purpose or end of the combined operations of grace and gratitude.[12] Thrall offers this translation of v. 15: 'For everything is for your sake, so that grace, having enlarged its scope through the growing numbers, may cause the thanksgiving to increase to the glory of God'.[13] In other words, according to Schmeller, the Corinthian community, created by divine grace and by its growing numbers amplifying gratitude, 'is part of this ever growing movement of grace'.[14] The question I want to raise in this

---

11 Options and discussion, see Thrall, *2 Corinthians*, 345–47; Schmeller, *Der zweite Brief*, 268.
12 Windisch, *Der zweite Korintherbriefe*, 151: 'der letzte Zweck dieser Tatigkeit, die Verherrlichung Gottes'.
13 Thrall, *2 Corinthians*, 321; cf. the paraphrase in Schmeller, *Der zweite Brief*, 269: 'Die Gnade, die im Dienst des Paulus und seiner Evangeliumsverkündigung wirksam ist, soll grosser warden, indem immer mehr Menschen bekehrt warden; dadurch nimmt der Dank an Gott zu, der zu seiner Verherrlichung führt'.
14 Schmeller, *Der zweite Brief*, 269.

essay is 'how so'? With these syntactical pieces of the puzzle in place, what form(s) of gratitude did Paul envision?

3. Gratitude, Tending to Glory

Commenting on 2 Corinthians 4:15, Calvin noted that, 'When [Paul] makes the overflowing of God's gift consist in gratitude, tending to the glory of its Author, he admonishes us, that every blessing that God confers upon us perishes through our carelessness, if we are not prompt and active in rendering thanks'.[15] Calvin does not here specify the form(s) which rendering thanks might have taken in the Corinthian assembly. But he rightly says that *gratitude, tending to glory* lies at the heart of Paul's statement. Just how might Paul and the Corinthians have understood this gratitude? Several inscriptions, and some texts from Philo, may offer some help.

3.1 ISestos 1—Gratitude for the Grace and Glory of Menas

The first inscription is one which Harrison has drawn on repeatedly. ISestos 1 (c.133-120 B.C.) comprises 106 lines of text preserved on a *stele* from the city of Sestos in Thracian Cheronese on the Dardanelles.[16] It belongs to the period of turbulence after the death of the Seleucid ruler Attalos III. In the midst of turmoil and danger, a leading citizen and ambassador named Menas is honoured and thanked by the city for his generosity, embassies, and example. Menas is praised thus:

> Menas, in word and deed continued to discharge his responsibilities in superb fashion by dedicating himself unstintingly to everything that would be advantageous to the city, and

---

15 Calvin, *Commentary*, 210.
16 IK 19 Sestos 1 (= OGIS 339); now in the British Museum collection (no. 1877,0815.1); broken at the top; dimensions: 1.6m (h) x 60cm (w). *Ed. pr.* Curtius, 'Inschrift aus Sestos'; Krauss, *Die Inschriften von Sestos*, 14-63 (no. 1). English translations in Austin, *The Hellenistic World*, 435-38 (no. 252) and Danker, *Benefactor*, 92-97 (no. 17). Harrison draws on this text, though not in direct connection with 2 Cor. 4:15: 'Paul and the Gymnasiarchs'; 'The Brothers as the "Glory of Christ"', 166-67; *Paul and the Imperial Authorities*, 208; *Paul and the Ancient Celebrity Circuit*, 153-55.

undertook wholeheartedly his embassies ... (*ll*. 18–21).¹⁷

On the whole, the inscription is a striking instance of what one scholar has recently labelled the 'theatre of public generosity' in which we see a clear pattern of grace, gratitude, and glory.¹⁸ Most relevant for our purposes are the three moments in the decree where the language and forms of gratitude figure prominently. First, we learn that Menas

> constantly wishes through his own zeal to supply something useful to the people and thereby through the thanksgiving that constantly redounds to him from the multitude (διὰ τῆς ἀπαντωμένης ἐκ τοῦ πλήθους εὐχαριστίας), aims to acquire for himself and his family imperishable glory (δόξαν ἀίμνηστον περιποεῖν, *ll*. 8–10).¹⁹

The gratitude (εὐχαριστία, *l*. 9) of the city is noteworthy. This gratitude comes repeatedly 'from the multitude' (ἐκ τοῦ πλήθους, *l*. 9).²⁰ Thanksgiving arises not only from the *boulē* and the *demos*; it is amplified through many people in the city and—in what follows—is expressed in a variety of forms. In addition, gratitude and glory are strikingly juxtaposed in *l*. 9 (... εὐχαριστία δόξαν ...). Rhetorically and discursively, the decree highlights the fact that Menas aims for civic gratitude *and* personal glory. In fact, the former is the means by which he intends to achieve the latter.

Later in the decree we glimpse another moment of gratitude:

> [Because of Thracian assaults ...] the resulting unremitting dearth of grain inflicted distress on the public as a whole and on the citizens individually, among whom also Menas

---

17 Μηνᾶ[ς] καὶ λέγων καὶ πράσσων διετέλει τὰ ἄριστα καὶ κάλλιστα, διδοὺς ἀπροφασίστως ἑαυτὸν εἰς πάντα τὰ συνφέροντα τῆι πόλει, τάς τε πρεσβείας ἀνεδέχετο προθύμως. Cf. 2 Cor. 5:20. Translations slightly modified from Danker, *Benefactor*.
18 von Reden, 'The Politics of Endowment', 115: The [Menas] 'text is replete with verbs of seeing and beholding, pointing to the visibility of civic virtue ... and the reciprocal processes of which the decree was a part'.
19 βουλόμενός τε τῶι μὲν δήμωι διὰ τῆς ἰδίας σπουδῆς ἀεί τι τῶν χρησίμων κατασκευάζειν, ἑαυτῶι δὲ καὶ τοῖς ἐξ ἑαυτοῦ διὰ τῆς ἀπαντωμένης ἐκ τοῦ πλήθους εὐχαριστίας δόξαν ἀίμνηστον περιποεῖν.
20 Danker, *Benefactor*, 96, comments on these lines: 'Compare 2 Corinthians 4:15, but note the variation in motivation'.

found himself hard pressed in many ways, but ignoring his own situation and secure in his awareness that the people were appreciative (... θεωρεῖν τὸν δῆμον εὐχάριστον ὄντα) and knew how to honor good men, he surpassed himself in his contributions ... (*ll.* 55-61).[21]

The backdrop is again Menas's generosity. As before, he is described as heedless of his own affliction and driven by concern for the city. Love of glory and anticipation of civic gratitude drive him on to further benefactions.

A summary moment in the decree is telling:

> Therefore, in order that all might know that Sestos is hospitable to men of exceptional character and ability, especially those who from their earliest youth have shown themselves devoted to the common good and have given priority to the winning of a glorious reputation (φιλοδοξεῖν), and [in order] that the people might not appear remiss in their gratitude (καὶ ἐν χάριτος ἀποδόσει μὴ λείπηται) ... be it resolved ... (ll. 86-92).[22]

Yet again the city presents its resolution as a public offering of gratitude commensurate with the benefactions of Menas. In fact, in this section especially, Sestos's gratitude is held up as a model to be emulated. Conversely, a lack of gratitude would lessen Menas's glory and bring shame on the city.

Altogether, what forms of gratitude do we witness? From *l.* 94 onward they are multiple: shields dedicated in his honour (*l.* 94), a crown bestowed (*l.* 95), a proclamation heralded (*ll.* 96–97), a statue

---

21 αἴ τ' ἐπιγενόμεναι κατὰ τὸ συνεχὲς ἀφορίαι τοῦ σίτου εἰς ἀπορίαν κατὰ κοινόν τε τὸν δῆμον ἤγαγον, καθ' ἰδίαν τε ἕκαστον τῶν πολιτῶν· ἔνθα καὶ Μηνᾶς ἐν πολλοῖς τεθλειμμένος, πάντα δὲ ταῦτα παραιτησάμενος τῶι θεωρεῖν τὸν δῆμον εὐχάριστον ὄντα καὶ τιμᾶν τοὺς ἀγαθοὺς ἄνδρας ἐπιστάμενον [ὑ]περέθετο ἑαυτὸν ταῖς τε δαπάναις καὶ τῆι λοιπῆι φιλοδοξίαι·

22 ἵνα οὖν καὶ ὁ δῆμος φαίνηται τοὺς καλοὺς καὶ ἀγαθοὺς τῶν ἀνδρῶν τιμῶν καὶ τοὺς ἀπὸ τῆς πρώτης ἡλικίας φιλοτίμους γινομένους περὶ τὰ κοινὰ καὶ φιλοδοξεῖν προαιρουμένους ἀποδεχόμενος καὶ ἐν χάριτος [ἀ]ποδόσει μὴ λείπηται ... δεδόχθαι ...

erected and its base inscribed (*ll.* 98–99),[23] and the entire decree inscribed on a *stele* and set up in the gymnasium (*ll.* 105–106). These acts of gratitude are tightly connected to glory in the case of Menas. Indeed, gratitude *was* glorifying. Gratitude arose *from the multitude* in Sestos in forms both aural and visual.

3.2 An Inscribed Thanksgiving Stele or (εὐ)χαριστήριον

A second example of gratitude in action comes in the form of a pair of inscriptions. Both are representative of a much larger set of short epigraphical dedications. Typically, this kind of dedication designates itself as a (εὐ)χαριστήριον, or thanksgiving-*stele*.[24] These are widespread, found from the Hellenistic through the Roman and early Christian periods and in every region of the Mediterranean world.[25] Several examples are gathered in a recent collection of inscriptions from Lydia in Asia Minor.[26]

Malay and Petzl, no. 6 – Thank-offering to a deity or deities
Date: 1st or 2nd century A.D.

[*ca.* 4 -]ιστις Μενεκρά-	... -*istis, daughter [? wife ?] of Menekrates,*
[του] ὑπὲρ αὐτῆς καὶ	*on behalf of herself and*
[ἀν]δρὸς αὐτῆς καὶ τέ-	*her husband and (her) children*
4 κνων καὶ βίου εὐχαρισ-	4 *and (her) property*
τήριον ἀνέθηκεν.	*set up (this) thanksgiving.*

---

23 At Menas's own expense!
24 Such dedications are often seen as a subset of dedicatory or *ex-voto* (i.e. emerging from a vow) offerings. See McLean, *An Introduction to Greek Epigraphy*, 246–59. I have in mind here the numerous inscriptions, frequently small pillars or columns, that explicitly identify themselves with the term (εὐ)χαριστήριον.
25 Although there are many scattered throughout epigraphical publications, I have been unable to find a definitive collection or treatment of such inscriptions. Marijana Ricl informs me, *per litteras*, that neither she nor Gil Renberg is aware of such a study.
26 Malay and Petzl, *New Religious Texts from Lydia*, nos. 6, 19, 38, 39.

The inscription calls itself a thanksgiving (εὐχαριστήριον) in *ll.* 4-5. Together with the verb of dedication (ἀνέθηκεν), this is formulaic.[27] The stone was inscribed and set up as an act of piety by (possibly) the daughter of Menekrates. She meant it to be a focused act of gratitude for herself and on behalf of her family (and even because of her possessions[28]). And although her thanks to the god or goddess may have been uttered in a sanctuary or other public setting, it is the tangible nature of text on stone that rendered this a monument of gratitude in perpetuity.

Malay and Petzl, no. 39 – Dedication to Meter Aneitis and Meis Tiamou

Date: 3–2 B.C.

Ἔτους β' καὶ π', μηνὸς Ὑπερβερεταί-	*Year 82, month of Hyperberetaios*
ου ις'· Ἑρμογένης Ἀττάλου ΜΕ	*16; Hermogenes son of Attalos ME*
ΓΑΛΥΝΙΝC Μητρὶ Ἀν{είτ}ιδι καὶ Μην{ὶ}	*GALUNINS to Meter Aneitis and Men*
4 {Τι}αμου χαριστήριον,	4 *Tiamou (dedicated this) thanksgiving,*
ὅτι με ἐξ ἀνελπίστων ἤγαγον	*because they led me out of hopelessness*
εἰς ἐλπίδας καὶ ἐπόησάν μ{ε μετὰ}	*to hope and did (this with respect to) me with*
γυναικὸς οὕτως κα{ὶ τ}έκνων.	*(my) wife so also (with my) children.*

This *stele* also designates itself as a thanksgiving (χαριστήριον, *l.* 4). Hermogenes dedicated it to the goddess (Meter Aneitis) and god (Meis Tiamou). Part of the visually preserved gratitude in this case was three reliefs above (wreath) and in the middle (female bust, moon crescent, between *ll.* 4 and 5) of the inscribed text. From *l.* 5 we hear the reason or basis (ὅτι) of the act of gratitude. Hermogenes and his family were 'led ... out of hopelessness to hope' (ἐξ ἀνελπίστων ἤγαγον εἰς ἐλπίδας, *ll.* 5-6) by divine action of some kind. As above, Hermogenes's experience led him to inscribe and erect this *stele* as an act of personal piety. He modelled his gratitude in a palpable form for his community.

---

27 Sometimes the verb is ἀπέδωκα.
28 The editors rightly interpret βίος in *l.* 4 as 'private property' (cf. 1 John 2:16) and not as a proper name.

3.3 Junia Theodora—Testimonials of Gratitude

A third example of gratitude, consists of a dossier of five inscriptions from first-century Corinth itself.[29] The dynamics of thanksgiving in the well-known Iunia Theodora inscription are similar to those seen in the Menas decree. The key difference is that Theodora is being honoured and thanked *in* Corinth and *by* Corinth *at the behest of* members of the Lycian federation and cities who have benefited from her hospitality and support.[30] Probably she was originally from Lycia herself but had Roman and (likely) Corinthian citizenship. As a result, the gratitude stimulated by her Lycian compatriots amplified her status in Roman Corinth. This gratitude took a variety of forms. Two brief samples will suffice:

In the second letter of the dossier, we hear that a delegation from the Lycian city of Myra went to Corinth and testified (ἐμαρτύρουν, *l*. 16) concerning Theodora. This letter concludes by specifying the desired result (*ll*. 20–21): 'And we have decided also to write to you (Corinth), *so that you may know the gratitude* (εὐχαριστίαν) *of the city (Myra)*'.[31] Then, in the third letter of the dossier, the Lycian city of Patara sends the text of a decree. Its stated purpose was to make Theodora and the Corinthians aware of their loyalty and thereby to exalt her in Corinth (*ll*. 36–40). They are quite explicit (*ll*. 31–36):

> Therefore our people in gratitude (εὐχάριστον ὄντα) agreed to vote to commend (ἐπαινέσαι) Iunia and acknowledge her generosity (διαμαρτυρῆσαι αὐτῇ) to our native city and her goodwill, and to invite her to extend her loyalty in the certainty that in its turn our people will not show any negligence in its devotion and gratitude to her (οὐθὲν ἐνλείψει

---

29 Kearsley, 'Women in Public Life'. She dates Theodora to the mid-50s A.D.
30 Kearsley, 'Women in Public Life', 194: 'The reasons for the gratitude of the Lycians to Theodora are, in brief, her concern for, and care of, all Lycians coming to Corinth whether on private or official business. She extended to them hospitality in her own home, especially on their arrival in the city, and she actively assisted them in their various needs (*ll*. 18–19, 28–29, 50, 75–76) ... she sheltered and cared for certain exiles from Lycia (*l*. 58) ... [and used her] influence in official circles on behalf of the Lycians (*ll*. 5, 52)'.
31 ἐχρείναμεν δὲ καὶ ὑμεῖν γράψαι, ὅπως εἴδετε τὴν τῆς πόλεως εὐχαριστίαν.

τῆς εἰς αὐτὴν εὐνοίας καὶ χάριτος), and will do everything for the excellence and glory (πρὸς ἀρετὴν αὐτῇ καὶ δόξαν) she deserves.

Altogether, Iunia Theodora is shown wave upon wave of gratitude[32] by means of letters and testimonials delivered before the Corinthian people, magistrates, and council. She is thanked, too, with a gold crown, saffron, a gilded portrait.[33] And, as in the case of Menas, it is a gratitude that is explicitly designed to redound to Theodora's glory.[34]

3.4 Gratitude in Philo—Prayers and Hymns of Praise

A final example comes not from an inscription, but from Philo (who may, however, suggest practices of inscribing *stelai* in the contexts of Jewish synagogues or προσευχαί, see *Legat.* 133). In *Plant* 126, in the context of discussing the proper response to Mosaic instruction, Philo speaks of praise. For Philo, the pre-eminent virtue involved in returning such praise is thanksgiving (εὐχαριστία δὲ ὑπερβαλλόντως).[35] But how is this gratitude to be expressed? God is not genuinely shown gratitude (γνησίως εὐχαριστῆσαι) through buildings or dedications and sacrifices. Instead, Philo declares that thanksgiving 'must be expressed by means of hymns of praise (δι' ἐπαίνων καὶ ὕμνων), and these not such as the audible voice shall sing, but strains raised and re-echoed by the mind too pure for the eye to discern'. Prayers of praise, then, are the purest expression of gratitude for Philo.[36] Leonhardt-Balzer, in her detailed treatment of prayer and praise in Philo, notes that overall, 'Philo describes the singing of hymns as an especially appropriate way to express one's gratitude, of equal importance [for Jews] to prayers and sacrifices.'[37]

---

32 εὐχαριστῶ-language: *ll.* 21, 25, 3132, 61, 84; πᾶς-language: *ll.* 3, 18, 29, 35, 48, 53, 69; χάρις-language: *ll.* 29–30, 35, 61.
33 For these latter, tangible gifts see *ll.* 63–68.
34 For the politics of thanksgiving in Roman Corinth, see Bitner, *Paul's Political*, 137-96.
35 Philo, *Plant* 126.
36 For a more extensive treatment of grace and gratitude in Philo (and Paul), see McFarland, *God and Grace*. He briefly treats 2 Cor. 4:15 at 212, 220.
37 Leonhardt-Balzer, *Jewish Worship*, 168.

3.5 Summary and Implications

As these brief examples demonstrate, gratitude could take a diversity of forms in the Graeco-Roman world. In many ways, we see here three distinct yet overlapping paradigms of gratitude in relation to gift and glory.

3.5.1 The Civic Reciprocity Paradigm

What we might call the *civic reciprocity paradigm* of gratitude is evident in the inscriptions honouring Menas and Iunia Theodora. In both, we see a fitting return of thanksgiving in a civic context, a return that comes because of the generous gift(s) of a benefactor.[38] Although this is a well-known paradigm, there are some pertinent observations with regard to 2 Corinthians 4:15. First, there is a strikingly mimetic function aimed at stimulating ongoing civic participation. Menas and Theodora were held out as exemplars of generosity and virtue to be imitated. But even more, the reciprocal cycle encouraged civic involvement and encouragement on the part of others.[39] The gift and its result(s) were amplified through 'the many'. Second, and especially visible in the Menas inscription, gratitude—in whatever aural or tangible shape it took—was itself the modality of glory. Gratitude in all its apposite forms glorifies the giver. Overall, then, Menas and Theodora help us to grasp what is often overlooked in NT appeals to the dynamics of civic reciprocity. That is, a focus on the reciprocal relation between gift and obligatory return risks missing the diverse particularities and forms the return might take. It may also obscure the encouragement the gift is intended to stimulate towards an increased civic participation by 'the many'. And it sometimes overlooks the tight connection between gratitude and glory.

3.5.2 The Personal Piety Paradigm

A second pattern, which might be labelled the *personal piety paradigm*, is reflected especially in the thanksgiving *stelai*. As we glimpsed in two brief examples, these expressions of gratitude are often familial. They

---

38 See Barclay, *Paul and the Gift*.
39 In this instance, the *neoi*; see Wallace, 'The Evolution of the Hellenistic Polis', 57.

are deeply personal, offering thanks in relation to spouses, children, and even property. A χαριστήριον was personal but not private. These thank offerings, once inscribed and erected, were visible, tangible, and strategically located. They therefore served a catechetical purpose in respect of the larger village or community who worshiped the same god/dess.[40] And finally, the emphasis in these short texts is on a highly affective return (*you brought me from hopelessness to hope*). Offering a script for others, these small but powerful testimonials of gratitude resulted in glory for the deity.[41]

3.5.3 The Communal Prayer and Praise Paradigm

A third pattern of gratitude, visible particularly in Philo, is the *communal prayer and praise paradigm*. This overlaps somewhat with the personal piety paradigm above. But gratitude in Philo is largely in response to the Mosaic *Torah*, God's revealed instruction and wisdom. And this gratitude, although perhaps sometimes inscribed, was expressed chiefly in hymns and prayers of praise. Given Philo's philosophical bent, he preferred silent, mental praise. Nevertheless, we glimpse in Philo and other early Jewish sources the communal *locus* (synagogue or prayer house) of these prayers and sung offerings of praise which suggests they were shared and offered audibly.

4. Εὐχαριστία Simply Abounds

We saw initially that Harrison, in reflecting on 2 Corinthians 4:15, noted the impossibility in Paul of matching 'the return of thanks' to 'the infinite generosity of the divine Benefactor'. Thus, Harrison noted, 'for Paul, εὐχαριστία simply abounds!'[42] But if we expand our focus from the asymmetrical relationship of gift and return to the forms and functions of gratitude available to Paul and the Corinthians, we are perhaps able to say slightly more about how thanksgiving abounds in 2 Corinthians 4:15.

---

40 Belayche, 'Fonctions', 268.
41 Chaniotis, 'Ritual performances', 131–38.
42 Harrison, *Paul's Language of Grace*, 271.

4.1 Gratitude Comprehends the Gift

What precisely is the 'gift' in 2 Corinthians 4:15? For Calvin the χάρις of 4:15 was the 'deliverance' described in 4:8–9. It was daily, sustaining, preserving grace that allowed Paul, even in suffering, to minister the gospel of grace to the Corinthians, to their great benefit.[43] Barnett glosses χάρις as 'Paul's speaking and suffering'.[44] That is, Paul's gospel message of new creation glory in Christ (4:1–6), ministered through his own fragile body so closely identified with Jesus' death (4:7–14), is the gift that overflows among the Corinthians. In his 'Lexicon of Gift', John Barclay defines the χάρις of 4:15 as 'the gift itself', namely, the overlap between 'God's *act* of beneficence towards the world in Christ ... [and] Christ himself'.[45] This is not semantic overload. Rather, it is the interpretation of 'grace' required by the near context of 2 Corinthians 4:1–15 and the larger context of the epistle. Such a conclusion is bolstered by Paul's opening τὰ γὰρ πάντα δι' ὑμᾶς in 4:15.

It is this Christ-gift—effecting new creation, preserving Paul in his ministry, salvific and sustaining and overflowing among the Corinthians—that calls forth the gratitude of which Paul speaks. He is confident that Corinthian gratitude will comprehend the greatness of the gift. Within Barclay's matrix of perfections, this gift in 2 Corinthians 4:15 runs along the lines of perfections one (superabundance: 'the overflowing nature of the gift') and five (efficacy: the gift 'fully achieves what it was designed to do').[46] And the comprehension of that overflow together with the on-going, on-giving power of the gift, continually achieves its goal by means of gratitude.

4.2 A Tremendous Symphony of Thanksgiving

We have seen variable forms gratitude might have taken in response to χάρις in Paul's world. But what form(s) did he envision it taking among

---

43 Calvin, 210.
44 Barnett, *The Second Epistle*, 244.
45 Barclay, *Paul and the Gift*, 577.
46 Barclay, *Paul and the Gift*, 70–75. Χάρις in 2 Cor. 4:15 does *not* align with Barclay's perfection six (non-circularity); gratitude is clearly the obligatory return in response to the gift.

the Corinthians? Hans Windisch suggested that:

> Paul has in mind a twofold work of grace ... one the one hand, the constant expansion of its sphere of activity among men, then, the ultimate purpose of this activity, the glorification of God. The mediation between the two works and the means of the latter is the fulfillment of the converts with a sense of gratitude, which is discharged in constant prayers of thanks or in a tremendous symphony of thanksgiving.[47]

Truly, the return of gratitude was amplified by 'the many'. And its amplification was along the lines of what we have already glimpsed in Philo: prayers and hymns of praise. For Ambrosiaster, 4:15 signified that 'Paul was to preach to all so that more could believe, with the result that the overflowing gift of God would not, because of so few thanks, be diminished'.[48] It was God's glory at stake in the apposite gratitude of the Corinthians. Theodoret interpreted the gratitude as a fitting response of sung praise: 'it is fitting for us without ceasing to render in return hymns (ὕμνοις ἀμείβεσθαι)'.[49]

Other interpreters agree. And they note confirming evidence in 2 Corinthians. Most recently, Deibert has pointed to the correspondences in vocabulary and even syntax among 2 Corinthians 4:15, 1:8–11, and 9:11–14.[50] On the basis of 2 Cor. 1:11, we see that prayers comprise part of the gratitude of 4:15. And in light of 9:11–14, it is likely that the tangible material support of generous contributions to Paul's ministry and collection was also part of the εὐχαριστία of 4:15. There is a rumble of amplified material generosity and consequent thanksgivings (*plural*; 9:14 ... ἀλλὰ καὶ περισσεύουσα διὰ πολλῶν εὐχαριστιῶν τῷ θεῷ).

---

47 Windisch, *Der zweite Korintherbrief*, 151.
48 Ambrosiaster, *Commentary*, 222.
49 Theodoret, *Interp. Ep. 2 ad Cor* [PG 82.404].
50 Deibert, *Second Corinthians*, 187-88. Note, in comparison to 4:15, the ἵνα clause and similar prepositional phrases (ἵνα ἐκ πολλῶν προσώπων, διὰ πολλῶν) in 1:11, ἵνα ἐκ πολλῶν προσώπων τὸ εἰς ἡμᾶς χάρισμα διὰ πολλῶν εὐχαριστηθῇ ὑπὲρ ἡμῶν. See also Windisch, *Der zweite Korintherbrief*, 150-51.

In addition to the forms of gratitude suggested by these other passages in 2 Corinthians, we should also recall 1 Corinthians 14:13–18. There, too, Paul speaks of thanksgiving. In 14:15–16, both praying (προσεύχομαι) and singing (ψάλλω) intelligibly in the assembly are referred to as acts of praise (εὐλογέω) and thanksgiving (εὐχαριστία). In fact, the idea of intelligible spoken and sung gratitude punctuates the passage and is expected to result in a verbal 'Amen!' from the outsider and in the edification of all those in assembly (14:16–17).[51] In short, Calvin did not quite grasp the entirety of the gratitude Paul envisioned in 4:15 when he commented, 'They were also admonished, that, since they could not aid Paul otherwise, they should, at least, help him by their prayers and sympathy'. There was indeed aid in addition to prayers and sympathy. The εὐχαριστία 'through the many' that Paul had in mind consisted in sung praises, verbal utterances, and monetary gifts. These were the specific forms of gratitude that responded appropriately to God's grace in Christ. And these responses were precisely the modes in which glory redounded to the Giver.

4.3 Gratitude Amplifies the Gift and the Glory

In the Graeco-Roman and Jewish examples above, we saw that forms of gratitude were themselves modalities of glory. Paul communicates this clearly in 2 Corinthians 4:15—grace overflows and the thanksgiving of the many redounds unto divine glory. But how does gratitude amplify both the gift and the glory?

Erasmus, in his paraphrase of the verse, points to the spread of Paul's gospel as that which is most amplified:

> [A]ll things are done for your sake in order that the truth of the gospel may be disseminated more widely among you and that the more there are who come to their sense and repent, the more there may be to give thanks, not to us, but to God, for it pertains to his glory that the faith, which he wished all to share, be propagated as widely as possible.[52]

---

51 Boobyer, 'Thanksgiving', 78–81.
52 Erasmus, *Paraphrases*, 225.

This captures Paul's meaning in part. But the context suggests further, specific connections tying gratitude both to χάρις and δόξα. Firstly, glory is explicitly tied to Paul's gospel of Christ in 4:4,6. The gospel gift in Christ has a glory, one that effects a glorious result in the Corinthians.[53] And as that new creational power spreads among more Corinthians, the glory of God in the face of Christ elicits multiple and multiplying thanksgivings. Glory in the gospel amplifies itself through them.

Furthermore, as Paul continues, despite suffering, to maintain his confidence to speak in 4:7–15, he highlights a key facet of the glory of God in Christ: resurrection from the dead. Paul's cry of faith with the Psalmist in 4:13 (Ps. 115:1 LXX) is on the basis of God's resurrection power in Christ (4:14, causal participle εἰδότες). Indeed, Beale argues that '[t]he reason why Paul wants to affirm this resurrection faith is that the spreading of this message about resurrection and its reality will lead to "the giving of thanks ... to the glory of God" (4:15)'.[54] The power of resurrection, at work in and through Paul (despite all appearances) is central to the gift. Resurrection empowers and amplifies the gratitude, and results in glory to the Giver. In this manner, as Windisch argues (appealing also to 2 Cor. 9:12): 'God establishes and preserves the whole work of salvation in order to create and increase his honor: the glorification of God as the beginning and end of the whole history of salvation'.[55] We might say, therefore, that gratitude in 4:15 is the fulcrum in the community. By it, Paul hopes they will by moved continually from grace to glory. Glorifying gratitude is for Paul the chief manifestation of the new creational transformation wrought in and among the Corinthians.

53 4:4 τὸν φωτισμὸν τοῦ εὐαγγελίου τῆς δόξης τοῦ Χριστοῦ; 4:6 πρὸς φωτισμὸν τῆς γνώσεως τῆς δόξης τοῦ θεοῦ ἐν προσώπῳ Ἰησοῦ Χριστοῦ.
54 Beale, *A New Testament Biblical Theology*, 269.
55 Windisch, *Der zweite Korintherbrief*, 151: '... dass Gott das ganze heilswerk einrichtet und im Gang erhalt, um seine Ehre zu schaffen und zu mehren: die Verherrlichung Gottes Anfang und Ende der ganzen Heilsgeschichte'. Collange, *Énigmes*, 168, plausibly detects a polemical edge to the final phrase 'the glory of God' (i.e., *not* the glory of others).

4.4 Therefore, We Do Not Lose Heart

Grace, gratitude, and glory—all expressed so powerfully and compactly in 2 Corinthians 4:15—actually serve a larger purpose in Paul's discourse. If gratitude offered to the glory of Menas aimed to encourage an ongoing civic culture of generous benefaction, gratitude in Corinth also served to bolster encouragement. But it is an encouragement of a different quality. Twice in 2 Corinthians 4 Paul asserts, 'Therefore, we do not lose heart' (4:1,16). His second disavowal of discouragement is a direct result (Διὸ οὐκ ἐγκακοῦμεν ..., 4:16) of the potent nexus of grace, gratitude, and glory in 4:15. How is this inference possible?

We may perceive the logic of Paul's thought by noting the connections of his discourse. Within the section 4:7–15 the most prominent element comes in 4:13 (the Ἔχοντες δὲ carries the discourse forward from vv. 7–12). Despite suffering and opposition, despite the weakness of his own dying body, Paul sees his ministry as effecting life in the Corinthians. He then cries out with a spirit of faith, taking the words of the Psalmist on his own lips. He says, in effect: despite appearances, I believe in the resurrection power of Christ at work through my ministry and therefore I will carry on speaking of him. We saw above that the immediate grounds in 4:14 for this cry of faith comes from the knowledge of resurrection power and glory in Christ ('because we know ...'). But the ultimate grounds for Paul's confident cry of faith and continued ministry of gospel proclamation in this passage is signalled by the γάρ of 4:15 ('For all things are on your account ...'). Paul's vision of glorious, new creational grace swelling the numbers of grateful Corinthians who then engage in various acts of thanksgiving unto the glory of God is what provides explanatory support for his unlikely outburst of faith in 4:13. And on that basis, clear-eyed about his own weakness and fragility as an ambassador for Christ, Paul can keep going and assert, 'Therefore we do not lose heart'.

5. The Glory of Thy Gratitude

In his poem 'A Song to David', the eighteenth century English poet Christopher Smart wrote, 'Sweeter with every grace endu'd / The glory of thy gratitude, / Respir'd unto the Lord'.[56] Smart's insight into the glory of a gratitude that comes in response to grace and is itself enabled by grace resonates with what we see in 2 Corinthians 4:15. In response to divine grace, Paul envisions thanksgiving being amplified among the Corinthian believers and redounding to divine glory. In this light, I conclude by tying the results of this exegesis to the stated theme of this volume honouring Jim Harrison: grace inscribed on the human heart. It is evident in 2 Corinthians 4 that grace is inscribed indelibly on Paul's heart. Grace is written all over his paradoxically glorious and grueling ministry. Strikingly, it is evidenced in the cry of faith issuing from his dying body and in the proclamation of Christ in his fragile ministry. The very personal knowledge Paul has of the Giver and his new creational, resurrection gift grants him a spirit of faith that sustains him (4:13–14). Clearly, the grace revealed in the glorious, life-giving gospel of the resurrected Lord Jesus is one of the primary reasons why Paul does not lose heart (4:1–6; 16–18).

But Paul is not an apostle of grace only but of glory also. He is zealous for the glory of the Lord who grants such a glorious gift (3:18; 4:4–6). And he perceives that *acts of gratitude in the transformed and growing community* are the nexus binding gift and glory. Thus, according to 4:15, of paramount encouragement to Paul (4:16) is the manner in which this same saving and sustaining grace of the Lord Jesus has abounded in his ministry *for the Corinthians*. He has seen its message and its power inscribed on more and more hearts. He has seen its resurrection, new-creational reality give life to increasing numbers. And now Paul takes courage to see that grace and its effects rise and swell in the multiplying, grateful hymns, prayers, and gifts of the Corinthian believers, for the advance of his gospel ministry, yes, but most of all to the great glory of the Giver.

Bradley J. Bitner
Westminster Seminary California

---

56 For the theme of gratitude in the poetry of Christopher Smart, see Guest, *A Form of Sound Words*.

Bibliography

Ambrosiaster	*Commentary on Romans and 1–2 Corinthians* (Ancient Christian Texts; Translated and edited by G. L. Bray; Downers Grove, IL: IVP Academic, 2009).
Austin, M. M.	*The Hellenistic World from Alexander to the Roman Conquest: A selection of ancient sources in translation* (2nd edition; Cambridge: Cambridge University Press, 2006).
Barclay, J. M. G.	*Paul and the Gift* (Grand Rapids, MI: Eerdmans, 2017).
Barnett, P.	*The Second Epistle to the Corinthians* (Grand Rapids, MI: Eerdmans, 1997).
Beale, G. K.	*A New Testament Biblical Theology* (Grand Rapids, MI: Baker, 2011).
Belayche, N.	'Fonction de l'écriture dans les inscriptions religieuses de l'Anatolie romaine: du *monumentum* a l'écriture efficace', *Revue de l'histoire des religions* 2 (2013), 253–72.
Bitner, B. J.	*Paul's Political Strategy in 1 Corinthians 1–4: Constitution and Covenant* (SNTSMS 163; Cambridge: Cambridge University Press, 2015).
Boobyer, G. H.	*"Thanksgiving" and the "Glory of God" in Paul* (Borna-Leipzig: R. Noske, 1929).
Calvin, J.	*Commentary on the Epistles of Paul to the Corinthians, Vol. 2.* (Edited and translated by J. Pringle. Grand Rapids, MI: Eerdmans, 1948).
Chaniotis, A.	'Rituals performances of divine justice: the epigraphy of confession, atonement and exaltation in Roman Asia Minor', in H. M. Cotton, et al. (eds.), *From Hellenism to Islam: Cultural and Linguistic Change in the Roman Near East* (Cambridge: Cambridge University Press, 2009), 115–53.
Collange, J.-F.	*Énigmes de la deuxième épître de Paul aux Corinthiens: étude éxégetique de 2 Cor. 2:14–7:4* (SNTSMS 18; Cambridge: Cambridge University Press, 1972).
Curtius, C.	'Inschrift aus Sestos', *Hermes* 7 (1873), 113–39.
Danker, F. W.	*Benefactor: Epigraphic Study of a Graeco-Roman and New Testament Semantic Field* (St. Louis, MO: Clayton, 1982).

Deibert, R. I. — *Second Corinthians and Paul's Gospel of Human Mortality* (WUNT 2.430; Tübingen: Mohr Siebeck, 2017).

Erasmus — *Collected Works of Erasmus. Paraphrases on the Epistles to the Corinthians, Ephesians, Philippians, Colossians, Thessalonians* (Edited by R. D. Sider; Translated and annotated by M. O'Mara and E. A. Phillips, Jr.; Toronto: University of Toronto, 2009).

Guest, H. — *A Form of Sound Words: The Religious Poetry of Christopher Smart* (Oxford: Clarendon, 1989).

Harrison, J. R. — 'Paul and the Gymnasiarchs: Two approaches to pastoral formation in antiquity', in S. E. Porter (ed.), *Paul: Jew, Greek, and Roman* (Pauline Studies, Vol. 5; Leiden: Brill, 2009), 141–78.

Harrison, J. R. — 'Paul and the Roman Ideal of Glory in the Epistle to the Romans', in U. Schnelle (ed.), *The Letter to the Romans* (BETL 226; Leuven: Peeters, 2009), 329–69.

Harrison, J. R. — 'The Brothers as the "Glory of Christ" (2 Cor. 8:23)', *NovT* 52 (2010), 156–88.

Harrison, J. R. — *Paul and the Ancient Celebrity Circuit: The Cross and Moral Transformation* (WUNT 1.430; Tübingen: Mohr Siebeck, 2019).

Harrison, J. R. — *Paul and the Imperial Authorities at Thessalonica: A Study in the Conflict of Ideology* (WUNT 1.273; Tübingen: Mohr Siebeck, 2011).

Harrison, J. R. — *Paul's Language of Grace in Its Graeco-Roman Context* (WUNT 2.172; Tübingen: Mohr Siebeck, 2003).

Kearsley, R. A. — 'Women in Public Life in the Roman East: Iunia Theodora, Claudia Metrodora and Phoebe, Benefactress of Paul', *Tyndale Bulletin* 50 (1999), 189–211.

Krauss, J. — *Die Inschriften von Sestos und der thrakischen Chersones* (Inschriften griechischer Städte aus Kleinasien, 19; Bonn: Habelt, 1980).

Malay, H. and G. Petzl. — *New Religious Texts from Lydia* (Ergänzungsbände Tituli Asiae Minoris 28. Wien: Österreichischen Akademie der Wissenschaften, 2017).

McFarland, O. — *God and Grace in Philo and Paul* (NovTSupp 164; Leiden: Brill, 2015).

McLean, B. H.	*An Introduction to Greek Epigraphy of the Hellenistic and Roman Periods from Alexander the Great down to the Reign of Constantine (323 B.C.–A.D. 337)* (Ann Arbor: University of Michigan, 2002).
Schmeller, T.	*Der zweite Brief an die Korinther (2Kor 1,1–7,4)* (EKKNT Bd. 8/1; Neukirchen-Vluyn: Patmos, 2010).
Thrall, M. E.	*2 Corinthians 1–7: A Critical and Exegetical Commentary, Volume 1* (Reprint; London: T&T Clark, 2005).
von Reden, S.	'The Politics of Endowment', in M. D. Gygax and A. Zuiderhoek (eds.), *Benefaction and the Polis: The Public Gift in the Greek Cities from the Homeric World to Late Antiquity* (Cambridge: Cambridge University Press, 2021), 115–36.
Wallace, C. R.	'The Evolution of the Hellenistic Polis: Case Studies in Politics and Political Culture' (Unpublished PhD thesis, University of Toronto, 2012).
Windisch, H.	*Der zweite Korintherbriefe* (KEK; Göttingen:Vandenhoeck & Ruprecht, 1924).
Zeller, D.	*Charis bei Philon und Paulus* (Stuttgarter Bibelstudien 142; Stuttgart: Katholisches Bibelwerk, 1990).

Ephesian Mysteries

Paul W. Barnett

Abstract

After discussing the authorship, place of origin, and manner of delivery, this essay notes that Ephesians is a circular letter to the Asian churches, but written with with a clear focus to reassure Gentiles of their place in the people of God alongside Jewish believers.[1]

The Letter to the Ephesians is an impressive text. It is closely argued and falls into separate equal halves, the one addressing theological matters, the other consequential ethical directions, including a comprehensive 'house table'.

Yet, for all its admirable qualities, there are significant issues to be addressed. There is the question of its authorship. While it is attributed to Paul most authorities claim that it is non-Pauline. Then there is the matter of its provenance. The letter is written from prison, but from which city? What prompted the author to write this letter?

Three Letters written from Prison

It is generally agreed that there is a relationship between these letters written from prison—Philemon, Colossians and Ephesians.

These are the opinions of scholars in summary regarding authorship:

    Philemon: Pauline authorship not generally doubted.

---

[1] This short paper is written in deep appreciation for the unique scholarship of Professor James Harrison. His interest in Ephesus seeks to connect with his profound understanding of that city on the basis of its inscriptions.

Colossians:	Pauline authorship doubted by a majority of scholars.
Ephesians:	Pauline authorship is overwhelmingly doubted:[2]

Analysis of the three letters yields the following results:

1. *Each is written from prison*
Philemon	9,10,13
Colossians	4:3,18
Ephesians	3:1; 4:1; 6:20

2. *In prison with Paul*
Epaphras	Philemon 23

3. *Co-sender of the letters*
Philemon	Timothy	Philemon 1
Colossians	Timothy	Colossians 1:1
Ephesians	—	

4. *Senders of greetings*
Epaphras, Mark, Aristarchus, Demas, Luke	Philemon 22–23
Aristarchus, Mark, Epaphras, Luke, Demas, Jesus Justus	Colossians 4:10,14

5. *Specifically greeted*
Archippus	Philemon 2; Colossians 4:17

6. *Envoy for the three letters*
Philemon	Tychicus	Colossians 4:7; Philemon 12
Colossians	Tychicus	Colossians 4:7
Ephesians	Tychicus	Ephesians 6:21

---

2 For discussion of Pauline authorship of the prison epistles (Colossians, Philemon and Ephesians) see McDonald and Porter, *Early Christianity*, 471–488.

References to Tychicus in Colossians and Ephesians are almost identical:

Ephesians 6:21-22

So that you also may know how I am and what I am doing, *Tychicus* the *beloved brother and faithful minister* in the Lord will tell you everything. ²² *I have sent him to you for this very purpose, that you may know how we are, and that he may encourage your hearts.*

Colossians 4:7-8

Tychicus will tell you all about my activities. He is *a beloved brother and faithful minister* and fellow servant in the Lord. ⁸ *I have sent him to you for this very purpose, that you may know how we are and that he may encourage your hearts...*

Based on the above the following can be concluded:

1. The Letter to Philemon and the Letter to the Colossians were written at the same time and from the same place with greetings from and to the same people.[3] Since it is generally agreed that Paul wrote the Letter to Philemon it follows that he also wrote Colossians.
2. Since Tychicus was the envoy for the three prison letters it is reasonable to assume that Ephesians was written at the same time and place as the other two.
3. So, with respect to the authorship question, my argument is (a) because Paul's authorship of the Letter to Philemon is almost universally accepted, it follows (b) that because of their commonalities Paul was also author of the Letter to the Colossians, so that (c) because Tychicus was bearer of all three letters, it follows that Paul was author and sender of all three letters.

---

3 See Wright, *Paul and the Faithfulness of God*, 7-8, for argument that Philemon was written from Ephesus and for relationship between Ephesians and Colossians. Cf. *Paul: A Biography*, 239-40, 264-66.

There is also significant commonality of interest in Colossians and Ephesians:

	Colossians	Ephesians
Christology	1:15–20; 2:9–10	1:3–4,21–22
Ecclesiology	1:18, 24	1:22–23; 3:8–10; 5:22–23
Moral Theology	1:14; 2:13; 3:13	1:7; 2:1–3
Eschatology	1:11–14; 2:12–13; 3:1–3	1:20; 2:4–6

Nevertheless, although the two letters have much in common, they have fundamentally different 'tones'. Paul wrote Colossians to address a heretical teaching that was capturing the church. As I will suggest shortly, while Ephesians is more serene and placid, it too addresses an issue in the churches in Paul's Asian mission. Nevertheless, scholars have rightly proposed that Ephesians is a circular letter.[4]

Provenance: Ephesus

Let me reflect now on the letters' place of origin. From the Acts of the Apostles we know of Paul's imprisonments in Philippi (c. A.D. 50; overnight), Caesarea (c. A.D. 57–60) and Rome (c. A.D. 60–62; 63–65). Second Corinthians which was written c. A.D. 57 refers to 'imprisonments',[5] some of which may have been for short periods, as at Philippi. On the other hand, however, if the whole of Ephesians and its associated texts Colossians and Philemon were written at the same time it would mean that Paul, with his associate Epaphras, would have been incarcerated for many weeks.

It is widely held and assumed that Paul wrote these three letters from a prison in Rome, in c. A.D. 62–65. However, there are substantial difficulties with the 'prison in Rome' theory.

---

4   The letter itself implies that Paul did not know all his readers (1:15; 3:2-3). There is also an absence of personal references, apart from Tychicus (6:21-22).
5   2 Corinthians 11:23.

Is it reasonable to imagine that Timothy, Epaphras, Mark, Aristarchus, Jesus called Justus, Luke, and Demas were each in Rome at that time, able to have Paul send their greetings to the Colossians congregation and to Philemon's house church?

Is it feasible to think that the slave Onesimus walked from Colossae to Ephesus (130 miles), travelled by ship to Corinth, then caught another ship to Brundisium, then walked (400 miles) to Rome via the Appian Way? This would be a precarious venture for a runaway slave. Having arrived in a strange city how likely would it be for that slave accidentally to find Paul in prison[6] and through him become a convert? Paul writes somewhat airily about visiting Philemon and staying in his guest room.[7] That is conceivable if Paul was writing from (say) Ephesus which is a four day journey to Colossae, but not from Rome.

Few subscribe to the view that Paul wrote the Asian letters from Ephesus for the very simple reason that there is no record of Paul having been in prison in Ephesus. An imprisonment in Ephesus, however, is consistent with the many problems Paul faced in that city. He writes, 'I am in danger every hour' and have 'fought with beasts' (we assume metaphorically) and 'there are many adversaries'.[8] His forthright preaching that 'gods made with hands are no gods' was taken to be as his attack on Artemis, Ephesus's much loved and revered patron deity.[9] So effective was Paul's preaching that the income of artisans who manufactured silver shrines for the goddess was affected.[10] This issued in a city-wide riot from which Paul narrowly escaped and which Paul called 'a sentence of death'.[11]

Given the many problems Paul suffered in Ephesus it is reasonable to believe that he was subjected to an imprisonment in that city, even

---

6 Philemon 10.
7 Philemon 22.
8 1 Corinthians 15:30,32; 16:9.
9 Acts 19:23-27.
10 Acts 19:21-27.
11 2 Corinthians 1:8-9; Acts 19:30.

for a brief period. There are the remains of a prison on Mt Pion which some local tour guides believe was the location of Paul's imprisonment.

Epaphras and the Province of Asia

According to the book of Acts Paul remained in Ephesus where he engaged in debate daily in the 'hall of Tyrannus'. These meetings were well attended, so that 'all the residents of Asia heard the word of the Lord, both Jews and Greeks'.[12]

Paul had not personally visited the city of Colossae.[13] The believers there owed their conversions to Epaphras who was a native of that region:

> ... the gospel which has come to you ... just as you learned it from Epaphras our beloved fellow servant. He is a faithful minister of Christ on your behalf and has made known to us your love in the Spirit.[14]
>
> Epaphras, who is one of you, a servant of Christ Jesus, greets you, always struggling on your behalf in his prayers, that you may stand mature and fully assured in all the will of God. For I bear him witness that he has worked hard for you and for those in Laodicea and in Hierapolis.[15]
>
> Epaphras, my fellow prisoner in Christ Jesus, sends greetings to you ...[16]

From these few references we infer that Epaphras established churches in the major cities in the Lycus Valley (Colossae, Laodicea, and Hierapolis). When joining Paul in prison (in Ephesus) he would have brought greetings from the Christians in Colossae, Laodicea, Hierapolis and from Philemon.

---

12 Acts 19:10; cf. 19:20 ('the word of the Lord continued to increase and prevail mightily'.)
13 Colossians 2:1.
14 Colossians 1:7.
15 Colossians 4:12.
16 Cf. Philemon 19.

Epaphras and Tychicus

Epaphras would have been the source of information to Paul regarding problems in Colossae and in the other Asian churches. Paul with Timothy and perhaps also Epaphras and Tychicus wrote the three letters in prison in Ephesus. Because of Epaphras's imprisonment with Paul he was unable to deliver the letters. That responsibility was entrusted to the ever-reliable Tychicus, an Asian leader.[17]

A Circular Letter to the Asian Churches

In addition to the Asian churches known from the Letter to Philemon and to the Colossians (Laodicea, Hierapolis, Colossae, Philemon's church) there may have been others like Troas and those addressed in Revelation—Smyrna, Pergamum, Thyatira, Sardis, Philadelphia. Ignatius sent letters to Magnesia and Tralles a few decades later. These may have been part of the network of churches in Paul's day. Asia was a large, wealthy and heavily populated province.

There is little doubt that the letter we call 'Ephesians' was a circular letter to the churches of the province of Roman Asia. Its title 'Ephesians' is possibly explained by its provenance, Ephesus, and by the fact that there were house churches in that city.[18]

Whilst recognising the letter as an encyclical a particular issue needs to be noticed. It appears that gentile believers experienced some difficulty recognising that they were truly part of God's people, a privilege they seem to have thought was reserved to the Jewish believers.[19]

The pronouns are important. Paul uses 'me', 'we', and 'us' for Jewish believers like him and 'you' and for gentile believers.

---

17 Acts 20:4; Ephesians 6:21–22; Colossians 4:7; Titus 3:12; 2 Timothy 4:12.
18 Acts 20:20.
19 Jewish exclusivity was criticised, for example by Tacitus: But the rest of the world they confront with the hatred reserved for enemies. They will not feed or intermarry with gentiles. Though a most lascivious people, the Jews avoid sexual intercourse with women of alien race. Among themselves nothing is barred. They have introduced the practice of circumcision to show that they are different from others. Proselytes to Jewry adopt the same practices, and the very first lesson they learn is to despise the gods, shed all feelings of patriotism, and consider parents, children and brothers as readily expendable (*Histories* 5.3).

Ephesians 1:11

In him *we* have obtained an inheritance, having been predestined according to the purpose of him who works all things according to the counsel of his will, [12] so that *we* who were the first to hope in Christ might be to the praise of his glory. [13] In him *you* also, when you heard he word of truth, the gospel of your salvation, and believed in him, were sealed with the promised Holy Spirit...

Ephesians 2:11

Therefore remember that at one time *you* Gentiles in the flesh, called 'the uncircumcision' by what is called the circumcision, which is made in the flesh by hands— [12] remember that *you* were at that time separated from Christ, alienated from the commonwealth of Israel and strangers to the covenants of promise, having no hope and without God in the world. [13] But now in Christ Jesus *you* who once were far off have been brought near by the blood of Christ.

Ephesians 3:1

For this reason I, Paul, a prisoner for Christ Jesus on behalf of you Gentiles—[2] assuming that *you* have heard of the stewardship of God's grace that was given *me* for *you*, [3] how the mystery was made known to me by revelation, as I have written briefly.

Ephesians 3:7

Of this gospel I was made a minister according to the gift of God's grace, which was given *me* by the working of his power. [8] To *me*, though I am the very least of all the saints, this grace was given, to preach to the Gentiles the unsearchable riches of Christ, [9] and to bring to light for everyone what is the plan of the mystery hidden for ages in God who created all things, [10] so that through the church the manifold wisdom of God might now be made known to the rulers and authorities in the heavenly places.

These passages, which are very important in the first half of the letter, invite an interpretation along ethnic-religious lines. It seems that many of the Asian churches had mixed ethnic membership, but that gentile believers felt that they were inferior to their Jewish brethren and thus not full members of the churches which they attended.

This may have been such an issue in the Asian churches that Epaphras brought it to Paul's attention during their time of common imprisonment in Ephesus.

In prison in Ephesus Paul, and his three colleagues Timothy, Epaphras, and Tychicus set about writing the three letters—to Philemon, to the Colossians, and the circular (the so-called 'Ephesians'). Perhaps, too, friends like Mark and Luke had access to the prisoners and may have contributed to the writing of 'Ephesians'.

The task completed Tychicus set out for Colossae, accompanied by Onesimus.

Then Tychicus would have travelled to nearby churches in the Lycus valley, Laodicea and Hierapolis. Tychicus would have read and explained the letter in each church and then arranged for a copy to be made for the ongoing use by each church. Because copying was a laborious and time-consuming task Tychicus would have stayed for several weeks in each place. He would then move on to other churches in that large and populous province. Tychicus's pastoral journey may have taken many months.

Paul's Letter to the Ephesians is a circular, but it was a circular that addressed a specific pastoral issue for gentile believers in the churches of Asia, and for the equality of membership of the churches.

Conclusion

Common details in the three prison letters—to Philemon, to the Colossians, and the circular 'Ephesians'—establish that they were written in the same place and at the same time. Despite a lack of reference to an imprisonment in Ephesus there is, nevertheless, good reason to recognise that city as the provenance for those letters. The widespread reference to Rome as the origin of these letters is problematic. Although 'Ephesians' is clearly a circular, it is a focused circular. The first half of the letter implies gentile angst about belonging to God's people as equals with the Jewish believers. Paul's loving words were written to allay such anxiety and encourage their sense of full membership of the churches.

Paul W. Barnett
Moore College (Emeritus)

Bibliography

McDonald, L. M. and S. Porter   *Early Christianity and its Sacred Literature* (Peabody, MA: Hendrickson, 2000).

Wright, N. T.   *Paul and the Faithfulness of God* (London: SPCK, 2013).

Wright, N. T.   *Paul: A Biography* (London: SPCK, 2018).

Adoption into the Family of God:
Ephesians 1:5 in light of Roman Adoption

Joseph D. Fantin

Abstract

Ephesians 1:3–14 is not a theological treatise. I suggest that a much more common conceptual framework undergirds this passage, namely the family. This focus is made clear in Ephesians 1:5 when the author introduces the concept of adoption. However, simply imposing our modern view of adoption upon this passage will lead to misunderstanding. Here I will briefly explore ancient Roman adoption and the implications that this institution would have had on this passage. I will focus on aspects important to the ancient concept such as inheritance and the personal nature of adoption. In addition, I will explore the impact of well-known adoptions upon the text. These insights will result in a better understanding of Ephesians 1:5 and contribute towards the larger suggestion that Ephesians 1:3–14 is best understood with a family concept as its background (context).

0. Introductory Remarks on the Occasion of this Article

It is a privilege to write an article in honour of the academic life and ministry of J. R. Harrison.[1] His bibliography speaks for itself. Jim's scholarly contributions are significant. However, scholarship is not the only area in which he has left a legacy. Jim has also left and continues

---

1   An early version of this article was presented at the 2018 Evangelical Theological Society's annual meeting in Denver at the Greco-Roman Backgrounds session of which J.R. Harrison is a coordinator. I wish to thank participants of that session for their feedback. Finally, I wish to thank Carrie Cooper, Jillian Fantin, and Ricardo Uriegas for reading this article and providing helpful feedback.

to leave an impact on many who have had the privilege to know him over the years. I am one such individual. My friendship with Jim goes back to my PhD student days where, with no prior introduction, he was so generous as to find time to help guide my research. Our friendship has grown from there. I thank Jim for being a constant example of a godly scholar. He truly is committed to the field of New Testament studies, excellence, and his Lord. Having read many of Jim's works, I find his mastery of both primary sources and secondary literature a standard to which to strive. I am thankful that his example will always be there as encouragement and a challenge. I could go on. However, given Jim's and my mutual interest in imperial cults, I will be in danger of crossing a line with my tribute. I know this is something that Jim would not want me to do.

1. Introduction

We are reading Ephesians 1:3–14 incorrectly!

Actually, this statement is too strong but it grabs one's attention more than: 'I am going to discuss an aspect of the context of Ephesians 1:3–14 that will provide clarification and insight into the passage'. Packed with terms like 'election', 'predestination', 'redemption', etc., we often assume that Ephesians 1:3–14 is some type of theological treatise. However, to assume that systematic theology is the key to understanding this passage is misleading. I suggest that a much more common conceptual framework undergirds this passage, namely the household or family.

A number of words in this passage draw one's attention to family. These include but are not limited to: 'father', 'adoption', 'inheritance', even 'redemption' which has a connection to slavery (also a household concept). Full development of this thesis would demand extensive discussion of these and other terms as well as relevant contextual information. I will focus here on only one such concept, namely, the ancient Roman family practice of adoption. This is only one step in demonstrating the larger family background of this passage. Nevertheless, it is a central concept on which this broader reading is dependent.

Further, I will focus on adoption for a number of other reasons. First, the topic of adoption in Ephesians 1:3–14 is important enough to warrant significant discussion. Second, there is a substantial difference between ancient adoption in the first-century Roman empire and modern forms. This disconnect can result in unwittingly importing foreign, modern notions into the passage. Third, understanding Ephesians 1:5 from the perspective of the ancient practice will result in significant application that is often missed due to modern assumptions of adoption.

In this study I will first reconstruct relevant aspects of the cognitive environment shared by the author and his readers that have a bearing on interpretation. This includes ancient adoption as understood by first-century Romans. I will highlight areas of differences between the ancient forms of adoption and their modern counterparts. I will then consider Ephesians 1:5 in light of these factors.

1.1 Preliminary matters

First, it is well known that the authorship of Ephesians is disputed. Because this study focuses primarily on a cultural practice, its conclusions are not dependent upon a particular author. Nevertheless, dating is affected. Adoption will generally be understood in the same way during the entire potential dating range. However, different noteworthy adoptions will have occurred at various times. Such adoptions may forefront the practice in their context. In this study I will prioritise Pauline authorship and a date in the early 60s. This is not an unreasonable conclusion.[2] Nevertheless, although a later date will weaken one point of my argument, the overall strength of the conclusion will be only minimally affected and accommodation will be noted for a later-date position.[3]

---

2   This is the conclusion of Arnold, *Ephesians*, 50, 52; Barth, *Ephesians 1–3*, 41, 51; Baugh, *Ephesians*, 1–8, 30–31; Cohick, *The Letter*, 25, 47; Hoehner, *Ephesians*, 60–61, 96; Thielman, *Ephesians*, 19. Hoehner includes a thorough discussion of the topic including a helpful table identifying positions of important figures in the debate from Erasmus to 2001 (*Ephesians*, 2–61). Finally, for further defence of this date and authorship, see Fantin, *The Lord*, 275–85.
3   Important voices for pseudonymity and a later date include Best, *Ephesians*, 45 (A.D. 80–90) and Lincoln, *Ephesians*, lx, ('post-apostolic period', 'For second-generation Pauline Christians', p.lxxxv). However, Best suggests that if authentic, it would have been written in the 'early sixties' (*Ephesians*, 46).

A second well-known introductory dispute involves the identification of the book's original addressees. Most significant is whether or not the phrase ἐν Ἐφέσῳ is original in verse 1. Despite less manuscript evidence, our earliest and best manuscripts including P[46] (A.D. 200), ℵ (iv century), and B (iv) omit this phrase. The earliest examples of its inclusion are A (v) and D (v). These are both inferior witnesses and D has a tendency to expand. Stylistically, it is somewhat awkward without an explicit destination or something else in its place. However, this is not an insurmountable problem. Thus, it seems reasonable to consider this a circular letter likely intended for various churches in Asia Minor. The association with Ephesus likely occurred because it was the most important church among the recipient assemblies.[4]

Third, from a methodological perspective, I acknowledge that we cannot enter the mind of the author. However, I maintain that a careful study of the historical and social context of the letter can provide insight into the audience. Assuming Paul knew his audience, some access to Paul's intention can be gleaned from these observations. My approach is based on an application of relevance theory, a communication theory which emphasises inference and intention in communication.[5] Thus, I am attempting to critically use information about the first-century context to reconstruct a shared 'cognitive environment' (knowledge about the world shared and often assumed among a group of people at a specific time and in a specific place) among those involved in the original communicative event. I acknowledge that this can never be complete. One must always be open to revision based on new information and new methodology(s). Thus, caution is demanded. Caution is a superior approach to simply rejecting this information due to uncertainty.

---

4 Paul spent more than two years in Ephesus (see Acts 19:8–11). The circular nature of this letter may help explain why Paul did not include his usual personal greetings.

5 The foundational work is Sperber and Wilson, *Relevance*. See also the more recent, Wilson and Sperber, *Meaning*. Helpful introductory works include Wilson and Sperber, 'Relevance Theory'; Gutt, *Relevance Theory* (dated, but still helpful as an introduction). For a basic introduction to communication and relevance theory aimed at biblical scholars and students, see Fantin, *Greek Imperative Mood*, 43–60. For an example of relevance theory used in a major New Testament study, see Pattemore, *People of God*.

Fourth, my conclusion is not exclusive. Communication and language are multi-layered. I am adding a specific layer to our understanding. In other words my conclusion makes no comment on whether more traditional understandings of Ephesian 1:5 are also valid.

Fifth, in addition to the acknowledgement of the multi-layered nature of communication and language, my approach to communication results in the need to make another presupposition explicit. When describing an ancient concept or practice, it is almost always possible to find exceptions to the more common understanding of the practice. This does not make the 'stereotypical' understanding of the practice invalid. It does however demand caution and acknowledgment of potential exceptions. In fact, I would argue that society generally thinks in the realm of 'stereotypical' even when exceptions are understood. For example, many Americans, when asked about their view of Congress reply, 'Congress is corrupt', but when asked about their own congressperson, they often answer positively, 'they are a good public servant'.

Sixth, generally our sources come from the elite. Thus, getting into the experience of the more representative population including the poor, voiceless, marginalised, and so on is not always straightforward. This reality does not mean that our sources are irrelevant. Often the elite set the tone for the culture.[6] In the case of adoption, it is difficult to know how common this practice was among people with little means.[7] However, even if not common, it is likely that the population was aware of the practice among the elite. As we will see, it was rather 'high profile' at the time of our date of Ephesians.

2. Adoption

Before discussing ancient examples and Ephesians 1:5, a brief understanding of Roman adoption is necessary.

Although there were three potential backgrounds for Paul's use of

---

6   Downing, 'A bas les aristos', 212–30.
7   Dixon suggests that 'it did not seem to have extended often beyond the ruling class' (*The Roman Family*, 113). Gardner states, 'Outside the imperial house, very few adoptions are directly attested in the sources for the imperial period' (*Familia*, 143).

adoption, I am assuming a 'flexible' Roman adoption. I acknowledge that there is debate here. Greek adoption predates Roman in Asia Minor, the area to which Ephesians was written. However, the area was strongly Romanised by the first century. Nevertheless, I do not rule out influence from the Greek practice making its way into the first century, especially in a historically Greek area such as Asia Minor. In many ways, Greek adoption was similar to Roman.[8] It was certainly influential.[9] Concerning a Jewish background, although υἱοθεσία does not occur in the LXX, it cannot simply be dismissed.[10] Conceptual parallels (e.g. Moses becoming Pharaoh's daughter's son [Exod 2:10]) may exist without lexical parallels and the author of Ephesians was Jewish.[11] This would also fit well with a more communal interpretation of adoption (adoption of a group such as Israel or the church). However, given the readership of Ephesians, Roman adoption is more probable.[12] One needs to reflect on what context is most likely understood by the intended audience. Without specific textual evidence otherwise, addressees of a circular letter within a Romanised Greek area would likely be most familiar with the most common practice of the day. Of course, particular modification needs to occur as necessary. This is the 'flexibility' in my identification.

Before proceeding, it is worth mentioning a fourth option, one adopted by many modern students of the Bible today, namely a modern Western notion of adoption. This is not an option here. It did not exist 2000 years ago. Specific differences between ancient Roman and modern Western adoption will be made clear below. However, it is worth noting that the basic motivation of adoption was generally different. Modern adoption is usually adoptee-focused, as parents desire

---

8 Lindsay, *Adoption*, 35-61.
9 Lindsay, *Adoption*, 35-61.
10 See Scott, *Adoption*.
11 Scott, *Adoption*, 75-117.
12 However, see Heim, *Adoption*, 115.

to adopt in order to nurture a child.[13] In the first-century Roman world, the major purpose of children generally, and thus adopted individuals, focused on the parents or household.[14] Childless parents needed someone to take care of them and provide for their burial.[15] Further, they needed someone to continue the household, that is, someone to continue the family sacred rites and to inherit their estate.[16]

2.1 Types of Roman Adoption

There were different types of adoption in the Roman world. Most relevant for us are *adoptio* and *adrogatio*, but it is also worth noting *testamentary*.[17] The difference between the main two forms, *adoptio* and *adrogatio*, was that the former involved adopting someone still under the authority (*patria potestas*) of another and the latter was the adoption of an independent individual.[18] *Testamentary* adoption should likely be seen as a form of *adoptio* and *adrogatio*.[19] It occurs through

---

13 The Australian Institute of Health and Welfare is representative. Their website states, 'Adoption in Australia aims to provide a nurturing, safe, and permanent family for children and young people. Adoption is seen as a service for the child or young person, and decisions about an adoption are to be made with their best interests—both in childhood and later life—as the primary consideration' ('Adoptions, About').
14 Dixon, *The Roman Family*, 108-9.
15 Dixon, *The Roman Family*, 108-9.
16 Lindsay, *Adoption*, xi-xii, 4, 21.
17 Lindsay, *Adoption*, 48. I am unaware of Greek parallels to these technical Latin terms for types of adoption. Lindsay organizes these differently: 1. *inter vivos* (includes *adoptio* and *adrogatio*), 2. adoption by will (*testamentary*), and 3. posthumous (pp. 43-54). The latter is not included here since the notion of God, the adoptive parent in Ephesians, cannot die and thus would not be considered in the context. The same may be said about *testamentary* adoptions but because of Octavian's *testamentary* adoption, it would have been widely known and relevant to many.
18 Lindsay, *Adoption*, 48.
19 Lindsay sees this as a 'development' of the other two forms of adoption (*Adoption*, 48) and Gardner suggests scholars use this label for 'a form of posthumous *adrogatio*' (*Familia*, 128).

a will and is executed after the death of the adopting individual.[20] However, in all cases, one aspect remains constant: a person is legally moved from the pre-adoption position or state into a new family unit.[21] I suspect that not all people in the Roman empire fully grasped the legal complexities of adoption but most would have understood the notion that adoption involved the transference of an individual into a new family unit as well as the privileges and responsibilities connected with this new status. Thus, we can assume that Paul and our original readers of Ephesians shared at least this 'imprecise' view of the practice. This is not unlike modern adoption. Few know all the legal intricacies involved but everyone has a basic understanding of the practice. Essentially, an adoptee is legally separated from his or her pre-adopted family relationships and is now in a new legal familial relationship.

2.2 Relevant Aspects of Roman Adoption for our Study

I have briefly described Roman adoption with its parent or household focus. A full description of Roman adoption, legal and practical, is beyond the scope of this essay.[22] Also, one must consider potential irretrievable local emphases and individual experiences. With the general foundation laid, I will focus on aspects of the practice most relevant for this study.

First, adoption was an important strategy for securing heirs.[23] Lindsay notes, 'In Greece and Rome the head of the family had a special responsibility for ensuring continuity'.[24] If a natural heir was

---

20 Gardner rejects this as a valid form of adoption. Among other reasons, she notes a lack of legal evidence for this practice (*Familia*, 128-30). Further, when discussing a *testamentary* adoption, she describes it as 'not a legal "adoption" at all' (p.144). Given the example of Octavian discussed below, whether or not there is legal precedent, I will consider this a valid practice. It may be best to see it simply as a posthumous form of adoption more generally. Lindsay acknowledges that any posthumous adoption is 'vulnerable' and thus is weak (*Adoption*, 46-49).
21 Gardner, *Familia*, 117.
22 For detailed discussions of Roman adoption see, Lindsay, *Roman Adoption* and Knust, *Römische Adoption*. For a discussion of adoption procedures, see, Gardner, *Familia*, 126-32.
23 Lindsay, 'Adoption and Heirship', 346-48; 354-55.
24 Lindsay, 'Adoption and Heirship', 346.

unavailable, he could look elsewhere (adoption) to fulfil this need.

The second major reason for adoption in ancient Rome was the present and after-death care of ageing parents. An important responsibility of a child was to assure one's parents' care, fulfil after-death responsibilities, and continue the family cults.[25] For parents with no surviving heirs, adoption was a means of assuring the fulfilment of these important social functions.

Third, in contrast to many modern adoptions that focus on the present care and nurture of the child, ancient Roman adoption was future-focused.[26] However, similar to modern adoption, inheritance was an important aspect of adoption. The adopted individual would inherit the parent's estate and carry on the family line.

Fourth, as a result of the future and parental focus of the practice, adult males were usually the objects of adoption.[27] Although not unheard of, girls and infants were not normally adopted.[28] Males had the power in the Roman culture to fulfil the necessary responsibilities and infants were much more susceptible to perish before reaching an age where they could be useful to the adoptive parents. Lindsay states, 'The bias in the Roman situation must have favoured the adoption of adults, since it was only through survival to adulthood that maintenance of the *sacra* could be assured'.[29] Further, given the purpose for adoption, parents would not want to leave a gap in time in which they could die before the child reaches the appropriate age.[30]

Although males were the common recipients of adoption, we should not make too much of any postulated etymology of the word 'adoption' (υἱοθεσία) in Ephesians 1:5 which includes υἱός ('son'). The practice of adopting adult males was pragmatic. There were other

---

25 Lindsay, *Adoption*, 41; Lindsay, 'Adoption and Heirship', 355–56, 359.
26 Lindsay, *Adoption*, 41.
27 Gardner, *Family*, 115; Lindsay, *Adoption*, 48.
28 For a discussion of women as adoptees, see Gardner, *Familia*, 130, 159–65. Because stability of the ruling family was important, imperial adoptions may involve infants (Lindsay, *Adoption*, 69). Gardner discusses some non-imperial infant adoptions but these are primarily family strategies and not out of concern for the infants' well-being (*Familia*, 195).
29 Lindsay, *Adoption*, 25; 21–22.
30 Lindsay, *Adoption*, 25.

terms in which women could be so referred (for example, θυγατροποία, τενοθεσία). However, such terms appear to be rare and likely referred to exclusively female adoptions. The masculine, υἱοθεσία, was likely used because it was both common and could refer to all.[31]

Fifth, ideally, adoptees were somehow related to the adoptive parents' kinship unit or (less popularly I assume) from their friendship group.[32] Generally, those in need of the services of an adopted child looked first to their relatives.[33] Although not unheard of, it was rare to adopt freedpeople or other non-relatives.[34]

Sixth, adoptees were not chosen at random but often the potential adoptee had proven himself in some manner that would make them attractive additions to a family. Lindsay notes that adult adoptions provide the opportunity for the adoptive father 'to become thoroughly acquainted with the character and capacities of his chosen adoptee'.[35] Also, this aspect is related to the previous point in which family standing contributed to the choice of an individual.

These points are all related. Thus, the legal and practical procedures of adoption were developed in order to maintain family stability which had ramifications on society more generally. Stable societies depend on a clear and worry-free transfer of power from generation to generation. Concerns over care, burial, the survival of the family cults, and the continuation of the family line were significant and adoption provided a means for assuring these basic needs when a natural heir was not available.

2.3 An Imperial Aspect

Unrelated to the imperial adoptions that will be noted below, in Paul's letters, adoption had an important anti-imperial nuance. Space does

---

31 See the discussion in *New Documents* 3, 16–17 (entry 3). For further discussion on words for adoption, see, Baugh, *Ephesians*, 85, n.58.
32 Gardner, *Familia*, 115. Lindsay, 'Adoption and Heirship', 358–59; Corbier, 'Divorce and Adoption', 67–68.
33 Gardner, *Familia*, 190–99.
34 See Lindsay, *Adoption*, 134–37. For an extensive discussion of adoption and freedmen, see Gardner, 'Adoption of Roman Freedmen', 236–57.
35 Lindsay, *Adoption*, 48.

not provide full development of this polemical use in Paul.³⁶ However, given Jim Harrison's scholarly output on this subject, at least some discussion has to be included here. In 2 B.C., Augustus received the title *Pater Patriae* ('Father of his country') (Suetonius, *Augustus* 58.1), a title accepted by most other emperors.³⁷ Interestingly, many initially rejected this title,³⁸ including Nero (Suetonius, *Nero* 8). A polemic is evident in that Caesar was the ultimate or superlative 'father'. For Paul to claim this role for God, a rival to the Roman pantheon and to the Caesars themselves who were considered gods, a challenge on some level is likely intended.³⁹

2.4 Summary

Adoption at the time of Paul shared many features with the adoption practices that most of us are familiar with today. This includes the fundamental aspect of membership in a new family. However, important differences were present. Without an understanding of these differences, the modern interpreter is in danger of misunderstanding certain aspects of Paul's message to Ephesians.

Differences that are important for our purposes include the almost exclusive future-focused purpose, the general practice of adopting adult males, the preferred adoption of extended family, the choice of a known individual, and the choice of a proven individual (or from a proven family). Also, given the wider sociological context and the role of the emperor as 'Father' of his country, a further imperial nuance may come into play if adoption terminology was in any way perceived

---

36   For an illuminating discussion of Roman 8:15 in its Roman imperial context, see Lewis, *Paul's 'Spirit of Adoption'*.
37   Purcell, 'Pater Patriae', 1089.
38   Purcell, 'Pater Patriae', 1089. See for example Tiberius (who never accepted it) (Suetonius, *Tiberius* 26.2; 67.2) and Vespasian (Suetonius, *Vespasian* 12).
39   See also Lewis, *Paul's 'Spirit of Adoption'*, where he discusses the importance of religious experience, 'spirit', and other terminology to argue for an anti-imperial polemical interpretation of Romans 8:12–17. For a discussion of a similar type of polemic in Paul to what is described here, see Fantin, *The Lord*. I argue that in some contexts, where Jesus is being claimed as a superlative Lord (κύριος), Paul intends a polemic against the living Caesar. As Caesar was the assumed superlative Lord in the culture, he was also the superlative Father.

as suggesting that another was usurping the emperor's role as *Pater Patriae*.

3. Examples

Roman adoption appears to have been common.[40] O. Salomies was able to devote an entire monograph to the nomenclature of the practice in the republic and early empire.[41] Various sources, both literary and epigraphical, reveal numerous examples of adoption in the Roman world.[42] Gardner has suggested that adoption was rare outside of the imperial family during the imperial period.[43] Gardner is focusing on the legal adoptions with explicit evidence. It seems helpful for my purposes to grant more informal examples as well. Before considering Ephesians, it is worthwhile to briefly discuss a few examples of ancient Roman adoption in order to gain an appreciation of how this practice was understood in the empire. Adoption, like so many cultural practices, had many nuances and each example in some ways is unique. No attempt here is made to comprehensively account for uniquenesses. In some ways our goal is to allow the modern reader to get a basic understanding of what the ancient reader would have understood by this practice.

If we can grant that adoptions among the non-elite were rather rare,[44] it is worth noting that our evidence that emphasises imperial adoptions is convenient. These would be the most well known. Also, few would ever dream of adoption into the most prestigious family in the empire. This context will illuminate our Ephesians text.

3.1 General Adoptions in Rome

Our sources are primarily from the elite. However, in this case, this may prove helpful. It is unknown how common the practice was

---

40   Lindsay, *Adoption*, 2-3.
41   Solomies, *Adoptive and Polyonymous Nomenclature*.
42   Solomies, *Adoptive and Polyonymous Nomenclature*, 15-19.
43   Gardner, *Familia*, 143.
44   We must remain open to more informal practices among the populace and a lack of surviving evidence to account for this. However, with the present evidence, we cannot assume such practices.

among the non-elite. It seems reasonable that many in the Roman world would not have had the means, possessions, and so on to warrant a formal adoption. However, this assumption can be taken too far. The elite often provided the standards for society. Thus, with caution we can consider examples of elite adoption that could be relevant for the common people. Even if adoption was not common, knowledge of the practice was likely prevalent. And who knows, like modern fairy tales, it is possible some dreamed of adoption into a noble family.

First, the great Roman Aemilius Paullus (approximately 230–160 B.C.) had four sons. He gave up for adoption his first two sons with whom he shared with his first wife Papiria. Unfortunately, after he remarried, his two other sons died (Plutarch, *Aemilius Paullus* 35; Livy, *History* 44.35.14; 45.40.7–8 [*adoptionem*]).

Second, it appears that Pliny the Younger (approximately A.D. 61–113) was adopted by his uncle, Pliny the Elder (*Epistle* 5.8.5). Gardner suggests that this is *testamentary* and thus not a legal adoption.[45] However, Pliny himself calls this *adoptionem*. Thus, this provides evidence for the popular understanding of the practice which for our purposes is not dependent upon legality.

There are not many details about these adoptions in our sources. Thus, a discussion of purposes and results is not forthcoming here.[46] The imperial adoptions provide more details. This is helpful because imperial adoptions occurred during the time period suggested for the composition of Ephesians and we can be confident that such high-profile adoptions were well known.

3.2 Adoptions in the Imperial Family

Although we know little of the practice among the common people, we are confident that they would be aware of the practice most dramatically in the examples of the high-profile adoptions among the imperial family. Here we will discuss two extremely important imperial adoptions that were likely to have been well known and evoked various opinions.

---

45 Gardner, *Familia*, 143–44.
46 For a general discussion of adoptions in Roman history, see Gardner, *Familia*, 133–45. For a more examples, see Lindsay, *Adoption*, 138–68.

Imperial adoptions are very important for understanding the New Testament. Various reasons for this exist. The most important reason may simply be their prominence in the first century. Imperial adoptions were attested to on coins, inscriptions, and other means of propagating imperial ideology.[47] It was in the emperor's best interest to make his adoption known, especially if he was the adoptee of a divine emperor. He was the 'son of (a) god'.

3.2.1 Overview

For the Julio-Claudian dynasty which ruled from Augustus (31/27 B.C.) through Nero (A.D. 68), adoption was the primary means of succession (described below). This strategy has advantages. Cassius Dio's epitome (tenth or eleventh century summary of the third century work [could include actual excerpts]) has the emperor Hadrian explaining this advantage:

> Now there is this difference between the two methods—that a begotten son turns out to be whatever sort of person Heaven pleases, whereas one that [has] adopted a man takes to himself as the result of a deliberate selection. Thus by the process of nature a maimed and witless child is often given to a parent, but by process of selection one of sound body and sound mind is certain to be chosen ... (69.20.1–3; tr. Cary).

An overview of the Julio-Claudian dynasty with reference to adoption is as follows: prior to becoming the first Roman emperor, Octavian, later Augustus, learned that he was adopted by his great-uncle, Julius Caesar, after the dictator's death (44 B.C.). Octavian capitalised on this association in many ways including the use of the title 'son of god'. This was possible because Julius had been declared a god by the

---

47 For helpful and foundational discussions of imperial cults and the divinity of the Roman emperor, see Price, *Ritual and Power*, Gradel, *Emperor Worship*, Friesen, *Twice Neokoros*. Friesen also has a helpful introduction to imperial cults in *Imperial Cults*, 23–121.

Roman state.[48] After establishing the empire, Augustus (ruled 31 B.C. – A.D. 14), without a direct male heir of his own, adopted Tiberius (A.D. 14–37). Tiberius adopted Caligula (A.D. 37–41). Caligula was assassinated young and thus made no provision for succession. His uncle Claudius was chosen to succeed him (A.D. 41–54). Here is where it becomes interesting. Claudius had a natural heir (Britannicus) but adopted Nero, the son of his present wife. Nero ultimately succeeded Claudius (A.D. 54–68). Although this history points to the strategy, I will focus on the two most relevant examples for the author and readers of Ephesians in the early 60s. It is worth noting that the main reason for adoption as a strategy for succession was because that, in most cases, there was no other option. No natural heir was available. Although it clearly was an effective strategy, it remained a secondary option. Augustus attempted to provide a natural heir through grandchildren. Tiberius had a grandson who was too young to rule. The Flavian dynasty (A.D. 69–96) had natural heirs and succession took place in the traditional manner. Finally, Hadrian's high praise for the practice of adoption noted above in the quotation from Cassius Dio could be a rationalisation. Hadrian had no natural heir. I suspect that if a natural son existed, that son would have succeeded Hadrian.

3.2.2 Augustus

Augustus is the paradigmatic example of a succession adoption. His rule overshadows much of what was to come. The advisor of Herod the Great, Nicolaus of Damascus (born approximately 64 B.C.), wrote

---

48 For the deification of Julius Caesar, see Cicero, *Philippics* 2.110; Appian, *Civil Wars* 2.106; Cassius Dio 44.4-6; Suetonius, *Caesar* 76.1; 84.2. The nature and timing of Caesar's deification are disputed. Weinstock seems to maintain deification began during Caesar's lifetime (*Divus Julius*, 401); Price seems to disagree (*Rituals*, 54 n.3). Gesche takes a mediating position suggesting that agreement to deification was made while Caesar was alive and was to be implemented after his death (*Die Vergottung Caesars*, 48–53). It seems best to conclude some sort of deification was already functioning at Caesar's death but not fully formalized until after. See Gradel, *Emperor Worship*, 56–61; Fantin, *Lord*, 108. However, the issue and interpretation of the primary sources are disputed. See discussions in the above mentioned sources and Fishwick, *The Imperial Cult* 1.1, 56–67.

a biography of Augustus while the emperor was still alive. His *Bios Kaisaros or Life of Augustus* can be dated after A.D. 4 and may have used Augustus' own (non-extant) autobiography (Suet. *Aug* 85.1) and his personal contact with the emperor.[49]

Nicolaus tells us that Julius Caesar was impressed by his great-nephew Octavian (*Life of Augustus* 23–25) and 'greeted him with an embrace, as if he were his son' (24; tr. Toher). After Caesar's assassination, Octavian learned that he had been adopted and made heir in his great-uncle's will and was encouraged by his mother and others for his own safety not to accept the inheritance (*Life of Augustus* 52–53). Nevertheless, undeterred and backed by the enthusiasm of the people, Octavian went on to claim his inheritance. Nicolaus continues:

> the whole land shared his enthusiasm and was summoning him to his paternal rights on the clearest basis of justice. For by nature and by law these powers belonged to him as Caesar's nearest relation by blood and as his adopted son (παιδὶ τεθειμένῳ) and above all it was most in accord with justice that he avenge and extract punishment for what Caesar had suffered [...] After learning from all his friends about the matter, without hesitating Caesar accepted the name and his adoption (υἱοθσίαν) with good fortune and under a favorable omen (*Life of Augustus* 53–55; tr. Toher).

This most famous of adoptions has many of the aspects of adoption mentioned above. Octavian was an adult male relative, chosen for his abilities to carry on Caesar's line (he even received Caesar's name) and inherit much of Caesar's estate. At first glance, it seems like this lacks the important responsibility for end-of-life and after-life care. However, as Nicolaus makes clear above, 'and above all it was most in accord with justice that [Octavian] avenge and exact punishment for what Caesar has suffered' (53; tr. Tohen). For a man in Julius Caesar's position, traditional end-of-life care and burial were not really necessi-

---

49 Toher, *Nicolaus of Damascus*, 27. Toher persuasively argues against an earlier date (pp.22–28).

ties. He died while still somewhat in his prime and his supporters and/or the state would likely be responsible for and assure his burial. What he did need was someone to avenge his death and continue his programs for (rule over) Rome. Octavian was aware of his responsibilities and fulfilled them.

3.2.3 Nero

Nero's path to the royal family was not smooth. His mother, Agrippina, was banished (Suet. *Nero* 6.3) and he was brought up by his aunt in a measure of poverty (Suet. *Nero* 6.3). When Claudius became emperor, he restored Nero's mother to favour and Nero himself began to prosper (Suet. *Nero* 6.3–4). Claudius married Agrippina (A.D. 49) and later adopted her son Nero in A.D. 50. Tacitus (early second century A.D.) states:

> the adoption of Domitius [Nero] was swiftly pushed ahead through Pallas' influence. Pallas felt bound to Agrippina as the arranger of her marriage, and later because of a sexual relationship, and he now kept urging Claudius to take thought for the good of the state and provide protection for Britannicus in his early years.

Convinced by this, Claudius set Domitius [Nero], who was three years older, ahead of his own son (Tacitus, *Annals* 12.25; tr. Yardley).

Tacitus's record reveals that Nero's adoption is peculiar. Nevertheless, a number of characteristics are present, such as adoption of an adult male relative, and succession. Interestingly, Pallas argues for Nero's adoption on the basis of merit, and protection for Claudius' own son.

Unlike Octavian's adoption, this seems unnecessary and the result of manipulation. There are three reasons to consider Nero's adoption here. First, it is likely that this adoption caused a measure of scandal in the empire. Tacitus goes on to say, 'When this was done, there was nobody so heartless as not to be touched by sadness for Britannicus' lot' (*Annals*, 12.26; tr. Yardley). Even granting Tacitus's likely anti-Nero bias, such a response seems natural for a son who seems to have been rejected. Second, this high-profile adoption and the scandal that would have ensued likely resulted in highlighting the practice of adoption in the cognitive environment. Third, assuming Pauline authorship, Nero would have been the emperor at the time the letter to Ephesians was written.

3.2.4 Summary

The adoptions of Augustus and Nero were well known throughout the empire and certainly familiar to the readers of Ephesians. Augustus's adoption may have been seen with reverence and awe. This also may have been true of Nero's. After all, they we both 'sons of god' (Claudius was deified). However, it is also possible that given the peculiar nature of Nero's adoption, it would have been viewed in a tabloid-type manner as well. Further, given the date of Ephesians, this would have been relevant. Even though Nero may have gotten 'lucky', no reader would have ever hoped for or dreamed of an adoption into such a noble family.

3. Ephesians 1:5 in Light of Roman Adoption

Our overview of Roman adoption has provided a number of observations that when applied to our understanding of Ephesians 1:5 specifically, and Ephesians 1:3–14 more generally,[50] suggests insights unavailable from a twenty-first-century perspective.[51] A number of

---

50   For discussions of the adoption metaphor in Romans 8:15, 23; 9:4, and Galatians 4:5, see Burke, *Adopted* (to some extent also deals with Eph 1:5); Byrne, *'Sons of God'* (broad but still deals with adoption); Heim, *Adoption*; Lewis, *Paul's 'Spirit of Adoption'*; Scott, *Adoption*; Trick, *Abrahamic Descent* (focuses on testamentary adoption and Galatians); Watson, *Paul*. For a theological approach to the doctrine of adoption, see Garner, *Sons*.
51   Some modern commentators acknowledge that understanding the Roman family and adoption contribute to understanding this passage. See Hoehner, *Ephesians*, 196, and especially (by implication given the space devoted to the topic) Baugh, *Ephesians*, 84–88. However, no one of whom I am aware goes so far as to suggest that these practices are the main background of the entire passage, Eph 1:3–14. Cohick's discussion is also more involved than most (*The Letter*, 97–98).

these will be noted as we work through the passage.[52]

Ephesians 1:3 introduces this long sentence (1:3–14). God is blessed and identified as 'the Father'. Although such titles can be used in various contexts, here it opens up the possibility of a familial context. Ephesians 1:4 continues, 'just has he chose (ἐξελέξατο) us in him before the foundation of the world'.[53] Although the verb ἐκλέγομαι[54] is used here and elsewhere of God choosing people for something,[55] it simply means 'choose'. For example, Mary 'chose' (ἐξελέξατο) to listen to Jesus (Luke 10:42) and guests 'chose' (ἐξελέγοντο) places of honour (Luke 14:7).[56] The term can but does not necessarily demand a 'special choice' meaning. Such an interpretation is gleaned from context, not the lexical form itself. Although the verb is not found in the active voice in the New Testament, it has an active form elsewhere and thus

---

52   No attempt is made here to provide a comprehensive exegesis of this passage. The aim here is to highlight contributions that a knowledge of Roman adoptions makes to the exegesis of this passage. Also, in light of concepts like the sonship of Israel (Deut. 14:1; Ps. 82:6; Jer. 3:19) and the church as the people of God (Rom. 9:26; Heb. 4:9; 11:25; 1Pet. 2:10; Rev. 21:3), the suggestion that this passage refers to the adoption of the community as a whole is possible. However, communities are made up of individuals and it seems like such a communal association would also have individual implications. Even in these communal interpretations, I do not think the individual can be removed entirely from this passage. Nevertheless, given the personal nature of Roman adoption, the individual interpretation seems most probable.
53   Unless otherwise noted, all scripture translations are my own.
54   The verb is used twenty-two times in the New Testament. Apart from Eph. 1:4, it only occurs two other times in Paul (1Cor. 1:27–28). With the exception of Jas 2:5, all other occurrences appear in the Gospels and Acts. All Bible statistics are from Logos Bible Software 9.
55   See for example, Mark 13:20; John 13:18; 15:16; Acts 15:7; 1Cor. 1:27–28; Jas 2:5; LXX Num. 16:5; LXX Deut. 14:2; 18:5; LXX 1Kgdms 2:28; LXX 1Chron. 15:2; LXX Ps. 104:26; LXX Isa. 41:8. Ephesians 1:4 also is an example of God choosing people.
56   See also LXX Gen. 13:11 2 (Lot 'chose' [ἐξελέξατο] the area around the Jordan), LXX 3Kgdms 17:40 (David 'chose' [ἐξελέξατο] five stones), LXX 3Kgdms 18:25 (Elijah tells the prophets of shame [Baal] to 'chose' [Εκλέξασθε] one young bull for sacrifice), and the Epistle to Barnabas 3.1, 3 (God is mentioned as having 'chosen' [ἐξελεξάμην] approved fasts).

should not be so considered with the traditional label 'deponent'.⁵⁷ The middle voice often has a nuance of self-interest.⁵⁸ This fits both the meaning of ἐκλέγομαι and its use in this context.⁵⁹

Finally, to continue the quotation of the Epitome of Cassius Dio quoted above, Cassius Dio has or records Hadrian using the same term regarding his initial selection of Lucius as his adopted son, 'For this reason I selected (ἐξελέξαμην) Lucius before all others—a person such

---

57 Recently the entire notion of deponency has been challenged (for a brief history, see Campbell, *Advances*, 91–104; for a helpful discussion of why deponency is likely now an obsolete category, see Mathewson, *Voice*, 70–71). Since I do not think that this is a middle-only form, this debate is irrelevant here.
58 See Louw-Nida, *Greek-English Lexicon*, 30.86 (general meaning) and 30.92 (usage with contextual 'special' nuance). Other words can be used in 'special' selection contexts as well. For example, Louw-Nida 30.91 mentions αἱρέομαι (2 Thess 2:13) and the related term αἱρετίζω (Matt 12:18). BDAG may go too far listing Eph. 1:4 under a category describes as 'to make a choice in accordance with significant preference'. Louw-Nida does not list Eph. 1:4 in their 'special' choice entry for ἐκλέγομαι (30.92; the reference for ἐκλέγομαι in Eph. 1:4 is not listed in their lexicon). Rather, the middle voice reflects some measure of 'self-interest'. Wallace states, 'in general, in the middle voice the subject *performs* or *experiences the action* expressed by the verb in such a way that *emphasizes the subject's participation*. It may be said that the subject acts "with a vested interest"' (*Greek Grammar*, 414–15; emphasis original; for a recent more detailed discussion of the middle voice, see Mathewson, *Voice*, 63–73). Moulton and Milligan's *Vocabulary* list the word under its active form and has no hint of any 'special' nuance. Like Moulton and Milligan, classical lexicons consulted list the word in its active form (ἐκλέγω). LSJ makes no attempt to specify any 'special' nuance in its general gloss but uses the theological 'elect' with 'choose' when listing Eph. 1:4. *The Brill Dictionary of Ancient Greek* includes Eph. 1:4 and mentions the word in its middle form and labels the category 'to select *(for oneself)*' (italics original). This lexicon also adds the more theological term 'elect'. Neither lexicon gives any justification for the special use under the more general category and thus likely reflects translation and theological history rather than any intended 'special' meaning. *The Cambridge Greek Lexicon* also suggests the middle means 'pick out for oneself' and gives no indication of any 'special' nuance. For other unjustified suggestions of the theological meaning, see Eckert, 'ἐκλέγομαι', *EDNT*, 1.416–17. Although still too theological, Silva discusses the more theological usages in a section called 'theological reflection' ('ἐκλέγομαι', *NIDNTTE*, 2.149–52). This is somewhat in line with the purpose of the work that considers word groupings and focuses on concepts. The discussion of the verb alone is more descriptive (p.2.149). After a brief and descriptive section on the verb ('ἐλέγομαι', *TDNT*, 4.144), Schrenk describes the theological concept generally focusing on the noun (pp. 4.145-92).
59 Schrenk 'ἐλέγομαι', *TDNT*, 4.144.

as I could never have expected a child of my own to become' (69.20.3; tr. Cary).

The author of Ephesians continues, 'he predestined us to adoption'. Again, like 'choose', the participle προορίσας ('predestined'; here translated as a finite verb) should not distract us. The word προορίζω means 'decide upon beforehand, *predetermined*' (BDAG; italics original). These words, ἐκλέγομαι and προορίζω, have come to represent theological concepts beyond their use in this text. The words themselves are not special, it is the one who does the choosing and predestining that does remarkable things. Do not misunderstand me, I am not saying that election and predestination are not valid Christian doctrines. However, these doctrines should not be read back into the text here. Rather, Ephesians 1:4–5 contributes to these doctrines. In fact, in reading the theological concepts into the text, we risk missing Paul's teaching here.

As noted, I do not believe that the original readers would have considered these terms in a systematic theological framework. Rather, readers would be awaiting some type of anchor to make sense of them. Once the term 'adoption' (υἱοθεσία) is read,[60] things become clear.[61] The concepts represented by 'choose' and 'predestine' would now have

---

60 In all biblical Greek literature, the word υἱοθεσία is only used by Paul (Rom. 8:15, 23; 9:4; Gal. 4:5). Our general meaning of adoption is acceptable (see BDAG; Louw-Nida, *Greek-English Lexicon*, 35.53; Moulton and Milligan, *Vocabulary*; LSJ; and the *Brill Dictionary of Ancient Greek*) and the discussion of Roman adoption above is relevant here. The word is omitted in a handful of manuscripts from Romans 8:23: the western D (vi century), F,(ix) G (ix) majuscules. It is also lacking in the late minuscule, 614 (xiii) and the Old Latin manuscript t (vii-xi). At least one copy of Ambrosiaster (wrote late iv) also seems to lack it. Most importantly, although damaged, it seem clear that our oldest manuscript, P[46] does not have the word (see the image on the website of *The Center for the Study of New Testament Manuscripts*, 'P[46]' and the older transcription in Kenyon, *The Chester Beatty Biblical Papyri*, 3. Although P[46] is strong evidence and the omission is the shorter reading, the inclusion of the term in the important fourth-century majuscules ℵ and B seems to slightly favor the inclusion. It may have been omitted to avoid confusion since this passage is forward looking. Romans 8:15 suggests adoption has already occurred. Likely it reflects Paul's already/not yet approach to salvation.

61 Arnold acknowledges that the readers would have this legal practice in mind when this term is read (*Ephesians*, 82).

a familiar and understandable context. A familiar framework would be evoked. I have explored the nature of Roman adoption. Adoption is a father's choice of bringing another into his family. As I discussed above, Roman adopters generally targeted adult, kinship-related, proven, male individuals. Also, given a date of A.D. 60–62, I have suggested that the peculiar, but not entirely impossible, example of the ruling emperor Nero's adoption would have placed Roman adoption generally, and Nero's unlikely adoption specifically, into the current cognitive environment in the form of news and/or gossip.

Essentially, Nero's adoption into Claudius's royal family was unlikely but not impossible. He was part of Claudius's kinship unit. In contrast, the readers, who had no connection to God, are now told that they are adopted children in the family of God. This family is far superior to anything on earth, including the Julio-Claudian family. I do not think we can overestimate the impact of this powerful statement. Believers have a 'privileged new relationship [...] with God'.[62] The readers of Ephesians are told that they are legitimate heirs that can expect the protection of their father, the creator of the universe, and can expect an inheritance much greater than that of adoption into the Roman royal family.

In addition to implications that we as modern readers can appreciate (e.g. inheritance), there are a number of features with implications that may escape immediate notice. Three are worth noting.

First, as suggested above, the primacy of kinship adoption would suggest that the readers' adoptions are the result of a special act on God's part. He is incorporating strangers into his family. This would not be expected by the original readers. More dramatic would be the reception of this message by slaves and women members of groups from which adopted individuals rarely came.

Second, God is not randomly choosing people. Although not always the case, those involved in modern adoptions are simply looking for a child to adopt. They are not looking for a specific pre-known individual. Roman adoption is personal. God does not just want any-

---

62 Lincoln, *Ephesians*, 25.

one. He knows and wants the Ephesian readers specifically. Or, more pointedly for readers today, he wanted and chose you and me.

Third, and problematically, the choice of an adoptee is often based on some type of proven worth. Hadrian's quote about the superiority of adoption above and Caesar's positive impression of his great-nephew demonstrate this. This aspect of adoption causes pause. Is Paul introducing merit into the selection (salvation) process? This seems to contradict the general theme of salvation by grace through faith in Ephesians (most pointedly stated in Ephesians 2:5b,8–9). Should this implication simply be ignored since we know it does not fit the remainder of the teaching of the book? Can I be taking this metaphor too far? Although metaphors can be overextended, I do not think so. This is made clear as the author continues. The next statement removes any notion of merit (or familial connection) on the part of the adoptees, the readers are adopted 'through Jesus Christ to him [God]'[63]. Thus, if the readers mistakenly believe that there is anything that they have done to attract God's notice, Paul makes it clear that we were adopted through the agency of Jesus Christ.[64] It is the result of Christ's work that makes our new position possible. Just like our kinship did not make us good candidates for adoption (who we are), our acceptability for adoption is not based on what we have done. It is based in Christ himself. Thus, this contrast between the culture's criteria of one's worthiness for selection for adoption and our deficiency fits the book's context well. It highlights the role of Christ. All of this is pleasing to God, or, 'according to the pleasure of his will' (Eph. 1:5).[65]

I acknowledge that many date Ephesians later than A.D. 60–62. This affects my conclusion but only minimally. The background of Roman adoption and all its implications apply equally to later-proposed dates. This background is most relevant for my argument. What does impact my argument is that the example of Nero is not relevant

---

63   The phrase εἰς αὐτόν refers to God (Arnold, *Ephesians*, 82-83; Best, *Ephesians*, 126; Hoehner, *Ephesians*, 197-98). Thielman states 'the goal of the adopted sonship of believers is a relationship with God similar to that of Jesus's own filial relationship with God' (*Ephesians*, 52).
64   Hoehner, *Ephesians*, 197; Lincoln, *Ephesians*, 25.
65   Fowl, *Ephesians*, 42.

for later dates. This weakens one supporting argument. Assuming a later first-century date,[66] a contemporary royal adoption would not be in the cognitive environment for these later readers. In response, I suggest that since the Flavian dynasty (A.D. 69–96) did not lack potential heirs, adoption would stand in contrast to the present royal method of succession and thus highlight the practice in a different manner. Nevertheless, I acknowledge that confidence in my position is weakened.

4. Conclusion

Considering Roman adoption, the understanding of Ephesians 1:5 is enhanced. The readers of Ephesians were not being told that they were objects of an impersonal adoption process. Rather, despite nothing to warrant membership into God's family, Paul tells his readers that they specifically have been adopted into God's family through Christ (with superior wealth, prestige, and security) and enjoy all the responsibilities and benefits associated with that new family.

Joseph D. Fantin
Dallas Theological Seminary

---

66 Royal adoptions would be relevant for early to mid-second century dates since they would again become common. The dramatic example of Nero would not be as readily available but the notion of royal adoption would again be current.

Bibliography

Arnold, C. E. — *Ephesians* (ZECNT; Grand Rapids: Zondervan, 2010).

Australian Institute of Health and Welfare — 'Adoptions, About' (2021) <https://www.aihw.gov.au/reports-data/health-welfare-services/adoptions/about> [accessed 23 October 2021].

Barth, M. — *Ephesians: Introduction, Translation, and Commentary on Chapters 1—3* (AB 34; New York, NY: Doubleday, 1974).

Bauer, W. — *A Greek-English Lexicon of the New Testament and Other Early Christian Literature* (BDAG), revised and edited by Frederick Danker (3rd ed.; Chicago, IL: University of Chicago, 2000).

Baugh, S. M. — *Ephesians* (Evangelical Exegetical Commentary; Bellingham, WA: Lexham, 2016).

Best, E. — *Ephesians* (ICC; London: T & T Clark, 1998).

Burke, T. J. — *Adopted into God's Family: Exploring a Pauline Metaphor* (New Studies in Biblical Theology 22; Downers Grove, Il.: InterVarsity, 2006).

Byrne, B. — *'Sons of God'—Seed of Abraham: A Study of the Idea of Sonship of God of All Christians against the Jewish Background* (Analecta Biblica 83; Rome: Biblical Institute, 1979).

Campbell, C. R. — *Advances in the Study of Greek: New Insights for Reading the New Testament* (Grand Rapids, MI: Zondervan, 2015).

Cassius Dio. — *Dio's Roman History, vol. 8: Books LXI-LXX* (translated by E. Cary; LCL 179; London: Heinemann, 1925).

Center for the Study of New Testament Manuscripts. — 'P46' (n.d.) <https://manuscripts.csntm.org/Manuscript/Group/GA_P46> [accessed 23 October 2021].

Cohick, L. H. — *The Letter to the Ephesians* (NICNT; Grand Rapids, MI: Eerdmans, 2020).

Corbier, M. — 'Divorce and Adoption as Roman Familial Strategies (Le Divorce et l'adoption "en plus")', in B. Rawson (ed.), *Marriage, Divorce, and Children in Ancient Rome* (Oxford: Oxford University Press, 1991), 47–78.

Diggle, J., et al., (eds.) — *The Cambridge Greek Lexicon* (2 vols.; Cambridge: Cambridge University Press, 2021).

Dixon, S.	*The Roman Family* (Baltimore, MD: Johns Hopkins University Press, 1992).
Downing, F. G.	'A bas les aristos: The Relevance of Higher Literature for the Understanding of the Earliest Christian Writing', *NovT* 30 (1988), 212–30.
Eckert, J.	'ἐκλέγομαι', in H. Balz and G. Schneider (eds.), *Exegetical Dictionary of the New Testament* (EDNT) (vol. 1; Grand Rapids, MI: Eerdmans, 1990; tr. from German, 1978–80), 416–17.
Faithlife	*Logos Bible Software* (version 9.8.0.0008; Faithlife: Bellingham, Washington, 2021) [faithlife.com].
Fantin, J. D.	*The Greek Imperative Mood in the New Testament: A Cognitive and Communicative Approach* (Studies in Biblical Greek 12; New York, NY: Peter Lang, 2010).
Fantin, J. D.	*The Lord of the Entire World: Lord Jesus, a Challenge to Lord Caesar?* (New Testament Monographs 31; Sheffield: Sheffield Phoenix, 2011).
Fishwick, D.	*The Imperial Cult in the Latin West: Studies in the Ruler Cult of the Western Provinces of the Roman Empire* (vol. 1.1; 2nd edn.; Études préliminaires aux religions orientales dans l'Empire Romain; Leiden: Brill, 1993).
Fowl, S. E.	*Ephesians* (NTL; Louisville, KY: Westminster John Knox, 2012).
Friesen, S. J.	*Imperial Cults and the Apocalypse of John: Reading Revelation in the Ruins* (Oxford: Oxford University Press, 2001).
Friesen, S. J.	*Twice Neokoros Ephesus, Asia, and the Cult of the Flavian Imperial Family* (Religions in the Graeco-Roman World 116; Leiden: Brill, 1993).
Gardner, J. F.	'The Adoption of Roman Freedmen', *Phoenix* 43 (1989), 236–57.
Gardner, J. F.	*Family and Familia in Roman Law and Life* (Oxford: Clarendon, 1998).
Garner, D. B.	*Sons in the Son: The Riches and Reach of Adoption in Christ* (Phillipsburg, NJ: P&R, 2016).
Gesche, H.	*Die Vergottung Caesars* (Frankfurter Althistorische Studien 1; Kallmünz/Opf.: Michael Lassleben, 1968).

Gradel, I.   *Emperor Worship and Roman Religion* (Oxford Classical Monographs; Oxford: Oxford University Press, 2002).

Gutt, E.-A.   *Relevance Theory: A Guide to Successful Communication in Translation* (Dallas, TX and New York, NY: Summer Institute of Linguistics and United Bible Societies, 1992).

Heim, E. M.   *Adoption in Galatians and Romans: Contemporary Metaphor Theories and the Pauline Huiothesia Metaphors* (Biblical Interpretation 153; Leiden: Brill, 2017).

Hoehner, H. W.   *Ephesians: An Exegetical Commentary* (Grand Rapids, MI: Baker, 2002).

Hornblower, S., A. Spawforth, and E. Eidinow (eds.)   *The Oxford Classical Dictionary* (4th ed.; Oxford: Oxford University Press, 2012).

Horsley, G. H. R. (ed.)   *New Documents Illustrating Early Christianity: A Review of the Greek Inscriptions published in 1978* (*New Documents*, vol. 3) (North Ryde, NSW: Macquarie University, 1983).

Kenyon, F. G.   *The Chester Beatty Biblical Papyri* (Descriptions and Texts of Twelve Manuscripts on Papyrus of the Greek Bible; fasc 3, supp. Pauline Epistles; London: Emery Walker, 1936).

Kunst, C.   *Römische Adoption: Zur Strategie einer Familienorganisation* (Frankfurter althistorische Beiträge 10; Hennef, Germany: Marthe Clauss, 2005).

Lewis, R. B.   *Paul's 'Spirit of Adoption' in Its Roman Imperial Context* (LNTS 545; London: T. & T. Clark, 2016).

Liddell, H. G., and R. Scott (comps.)   *A Greek-English Lexicon* (LSJ), revised and augmented by Henry Stuart Jones and Roderick McKenzie (9th ed. with a revised supplement, 1996, ed. R. G. W. Glare and A. A. Thompson. Oxford: Clarendon, 1940).

Lincoln, A. T.   *Ephesians* (WBC 42; Dallas, TX: Word, 1990).

Lindsay, H.   *Adoption in the Roman World* (Cambridge: Cambridge University Press, 2009).

Lindsay, H.   'Adoption and Heirship in Greece and Rome', in Beryl Rawson (ed.), *A Companion to Families in the Greek and Roman Worlds* (Blackwell Companions to the Ancient World; Malden, MA: Wiley-Blackwell, 2011), 346–60.

Louw, Johannes P., and E. A. Nida (eds.)   *Greek-English Lexicon of the New Testament Based on Semantic Domains* (2 vols.; New York, NY: United Bible Societies, 1988).

Mathewson, D. L.   *Voice and Mood: A Linguistic Approach* (Grand Rapids, MI: Baker, 2021).

Montanari, F., I. Garofalo, and D. Manetti   *The Brill Dictionary of Ancient Greek,* revised and edited by M. Goh and C. Schroeder (Leiden: Brill, 2015 [Italian: 2013]).

Moulton, J. H., and G. Milligan   *The Vocabulary of the Greek Testament: Illustrated From the Papyri and Other Non-Literary Sources* (London: Hodder and Stoughton, 1930. Reprint, Grand Rapids, MI: Eerdmans, 1985).

Nicolaus of Damascus   *The Life of Augustus* and *the Autobiography*, edited with introduction, translations and historical commentary by M. Toher (Cambridge: Cambridge University Press, 2017).

Page, T. E., W. H. D. Rouse, E. Capps, et al.   The Loeb Classical Library (London and New York, NY: Heinemann and Macmillan, 1912—). [unless otherwise noted, used for classical sources]

Pattemore, S.   *The People of God in the Apocalypse: Discourse, Structure, and Exegesis* (SNTSMS 128; Cambridge: Cambridge University Press, 2004).

Price, S. R. F.   *Rituals and Power: The Roman Imperial Cult in Asia Minor* (Cambridge: Cambridge University Press, 1984).

Purcell, N.   'Pater Patriae', in S. Hornblower, A. Spawforth, and E. Eidinow (eds.), *The Oxford Classical Dictionary* (4th ed.; Oxford: Oxford University Press, 2012).

Salomies, O.   *Adoptive and Polyonymous Nomenclature in the Roman Empire* (Commentationes Humanarum Litterarum 97; Helsinki: Societas Scientiarum Fennica, 1992).

Schrenk, G.   'ἐκλέγομαι', in Kittel (ed.), *Theological Dictionary of the New Testament* (TDNT) (vol. 4; Grand Rapids, MI: Eerdmans, 1964 [German, n.d.]), 144–92.

Scott, J. M.   *Adoption as Sons of God: An Exegetical Investigation Into the Background of ΥΙΟΘΕΣΙΑ in the Pauline Corpus* (WUNT 2.48; Tübingen: Mohr Siebeck, 1992).

Silva M. (ed.)	'ἐκλέγομαι', in *New International Dictionary of New Testament Theology and Exegesis* (NIDNTTE) (vol 2; Grand Rapids, MI: Zondervan, 2014), 145–52.
Sperber, D., and D. Wilson	*Relevance: Communication and Cognition* (2nd edn; Oxford: Blackwell, 1995).
Tacitus	*The Annals: The Reigns of Tiberius, Claudius, and Nero* (translated by J. C. Yardley with Introduction and Notes by A. A. Barrett; Oxford World's Classics; Oxford: Oxford University Press, 2008).
Thielman, F.	*Ephesians* (BECNT; Grand Rapids, MI: Baker, 2010).
Toher, M.	See Nicolaus of Damascus above.
Trick, B. R.	*Abrahamic Descent, Testamentary Adoption, and the Law in Galatians: Differentiating Abraham's Sons, Seed, and Children of Promise* (Supplements to Novum Testamentum 169; Leiden: Brill, 2016).
Wallace, D. B.	*Greek Grammar beyond the Basics: An Exegetical Syntax of the New Testament* (Grand Rapids, MI: Zondervan, 1996).
Watson, E. W.	*Paul, His Roman Audience, and the Adopted People of God: Understanding the Pauline Metaphor of Adoption in Romans as Authorial Audience* (Lewiston, NY: Mellen, 2008).
Weinstock, S.	*Divus Julius* (Oxford: Clarendon, 1971).
Wilson, D. and D. Sperber	'Relevance Theory', in L. R. Horn, and G. Ward (eds.), *The Handbook of Pragmatics* (Malden, MA: Blackwell, 2004), 607–632.
Wilson, D. and D. Sperber	*Meaning and Relevance* (Cambridge: Cambridge University Press, 2012).

Grace and Faith in Ephesians 2:8–10:
Engaging Barclay and Bates

Constantine R. Campbell

Abstract

Paul's language of grace and faith have received focused attention in recent scholarship. This essay explores two of the major contributors on these themes, namely Barclay and Bates, and reads their contributions in conversation with the text of Ephesians 2:8–10, in which both themes are prominent and intertwined.

Introduction

The subject of grace has been of explosive importance in Pauline and Judaism studies in recent decades, culminating in the magisterial work of John Barclay, *Paul and the Gift*, published in 2015.[1] James Harrison sketches the resurgence of scholarship on the role of grace in Paul's thought in the introduction to the 2017 reprint edition of his book, *Paul's Language of Grace in Its Graeco-Roman Context*.[2] Harrison has provided the most extensive discussion of grace against the Graeco-Roman backdrop, while Barclay's study is grounded in Second Temple Judaism, which is the primary interest in this essay because of its direct interaction with the New Perspective on Paul. As Barclay summarises, in Christian tradition,

---

1 Barclay, *Paul and the Gift*.
2 Harrison, *Paul's Language of Grace in Its Graeco-Roman Context*.

Paul's theology of grace has often been interpreted as the antithesis of Judaism, as if by Paul's day Judaism had corrupted its biblical theology of grace with a soteriology of 'works-righteousness' and reward. Paul's language [...] has been conscripted to differentiate Christianity from Judaism on these terms, and to diminish the latter. On this reading, Paul was the premier theologian of grace who resisted the 'legalism' of 'late' Judaism, a works-based religion that amounted to auto-salvation.[3]

Scholars associated with the so-called New Perspective on Paul have challenged this negative image of Judaism, presenting it as a religion of grace, demonstrating how grace is widely prevalent within Second Temple literature, making Paul's contribution unremarkable.[4] But, as Barclay asks, if 'grace' is everywhere in Second Temple Judaism, is it everywhere the same? 'Is there evidence for diversity, even debate, regarding the generosity of God [...]? If so, where should Paul be placed within this Jewish diversity?'[5]

Barclay situates grace in its sociological, theological, and Second Temple Judaism context, attempting to move the discussion beyond the impasse of traditional Reformed theology and the New Perspective on Paul. The results of Barclay's magnum opus have been summarised for wider access in his 2020 publication, *Paul and the Power of Grace*, which adds discussion of Ephesians—while the former work focused primarily on Galatians and Romans.[6] Barclay defines 'gift' as 'the sphere of voluntary, personal relations characterized by goodwill in the giving of a benefit or favor, which generally elicits some form of reciprocal return that is necessary for the continuation of the relationship'.[7] In most cultures, 'gifts are part of a circular exchange, an ongoing cycle where the gift is intended to create or maintain a social relationship'.[8]

---

3   Barclay, *Paul and the Gift*, 2.
4   The most prominent figures are E. P. Sanders, J. D. G. Dunn, and N. T. Wright. Barclay, *Paul and the Gift*, 2.
5   Barclay, *Paul and the Gift*, 2.
6   Barclay, *Paul and the Power of Grace*.
7   Barclay, *Paul and the Power of Grace*, 2.
8   Barclay, *Paul and the Power of Grace*, 3.

Barclay demonstrates that God's grace tends to be analysed in terms of six concepts, with different interpreters emphasising some over others: (1) *superabundance*—the size of the gift; (2) *singularity*—the pure benevolence of the gift; (3) *priority*—giving at the ideal time; (4) *incongruity*—lack of merit in the recipient; (5) *efficacy*—the ability of the gift to achieve its intended purposes; (6) *noncircularity*—the absence of obligation to reciprocate by giving a gift in return.[9] The only one of these that Paul does not endorse is (6) *noncircularity*, since it is argued that he expects the recipients of God's grace to respond with devotion and obedience. For Paul, Christ is 'the ultimate gift of God to the world, to be given without regard to the worth, and in the absence of the worth—an unconditioned or incongruous gift that did not match the worth of its recipients but created it'.[10]

If correct, Barclay's understanding calls into question the rhetoric that sometimes characterises discussion about God's grace as a 'free gift' without any obligation or expectation.[11] Rather, God's grace does indeed warrant a reciprocal response from its recipients. Such a claim might elicit the charge of semi-Pelagianism, in which believers are saved by God's grace in combination with their own works.[12] However, this would be a mistaken interpretation of Barclay's claims. The important points are that God's grace *is* a gift, but that this gift opens a relationship with its recipients, who in turn maintain their new relationship with God through various forms of reciprocation. Reciprocation does not diminish the gift, but coheres with its relational intent.

---

9   Barclay, *Paul and the Power of Grace*, 13–16; Barclay, *Paul and the Gift*, 70–75. This summary of Barclay's 'six perfections of grace' comes from Bates, *Salvation by Allegiance Alone: Rethinking Faith, Works, and the Gospel of Jesus the King*, 104.
10 Barclay, *Paul and the Power of Grace*, xviii.
11 Barclay contends that the notion of a 'pure gift' without any expectation of reciprocity is a relatively modern Western notion that anthropologists and most cultures would not recognise as a gift at all; Barclay, *Paul and the Power of Grace*, 9–11.
12 Incidentally, Barclay claims that 'Pelagius did not believe in grace *less than* Augustine; he simply believed in it *differently*'. Barclay, *Paul and the Power of Grace*, 18.

For Paul, such reciprocity comes through transformation: the Christ-gift 'remolds the self and recreates the community of believers. The social effects of this divine gift in human gift-practices are, therefore, a *necessary* component of grace'.[13] In Ephesians 2:8–10 this is abundantly clear, since salvation is by God's grace, not by human works, and yet once saved, believers are to walk in the good works that God has prepared for them. Salvation does not come through any human contribution; it is the incongruous gift of God. But that gift *transforms* its recipients, bringing them from spiritual death to life, and from divine alienation to new creations in Christ. Good works are expected as an expression of this new creation—not as a contributing factor to God's gift but as an expression of the new relationship that has been forged between God and those in Christ.

Alongside a renewed understanding of grace stands a renewed appreciation of faith. In his book, *Salvation by Allegiance Alone*, Matthew Bates argues that the Greek word normally translated 'faith' or 'trust'—*pistis*—'included ideas that aren't usually associated in our contemporary culture with belief or faith, such as reliability, confidence, assurance, fidelity, faithfulness, commitment, and pledged loyalty'.[14] He contends that the translations 'faith' and 'trust' mislead believers into a truncated sense of how we are saved and how we ought to respond to God's gift of salvation.

Key to Bates's argument is how the gospel is understood. Rather than reducing the gospel to statements about how we are saved through Jesus's death for our sins—as it typically is reduced in contemporary discourse—the gospel properly understood refers to Jesus' reign as king. And this in turn affects how we should understand faith: 'The gospel reaches its zenith with Jesus' installation and sovereign rule as the Christ, the king. As such, *faith* in Jesus is best described as *allegiance* to him as king'.[15]

Bates supports this claim with the following four points:

---

13 Barclay, *Paul and the Power of Grace*, 125 (emphasis original).
14 Bates, *Salvation by Allegiance Alone*, 3.
15 Bates, *Salvation by Allegiance Alone*, 77 (emphasis original).

First, although *pistis* does not always mean allegiance, it certainly does carry this exact meaning sometimes in literature relevant to Paul's Letters and the rest of the New Testament. Second, since Paul regards Jesus above all else as the king (the Christ) or the Lord, this is the most natural way to speak of how the people of God should relate to Jesus. Third, allegiance makes better sense of several otherwise puzzling matters in Paul's Letters. Fourth, the proclamation 'Jesus is Lord' resonated with Graeco-Roman imperial propaganda, so that *pistis* as allegiance fits into the broader cultural milieu of the New Testament world.[16]

Bates accepts Barclay's observations about God's grace (above) and argues that popular contemporary notions of grace fail to account for the *effective* nature of grace, which sets believers free from slavery to sin and the evil powers, and transforms them into new creations in Christ.[17] Receiving God's gift by 'faith' therefore entails a new allegiance, loyalty, and devotion to God's gift—Christ.

Exploring Ephesians 2:8–10

We turn now to explore the preeminent passage for the interrelationship of grace and faith in the Pauline canon—Ephesians 2:8–10.[18] As anticipated in Ephesians 2:5b, in 2:8 Paul draws the inevitable conclusion of the argument that has been developed from 2:1-7. Since believers were once spiritually dead—cut off from God and following the ways of the world, the devil, and their desires (2:1-3)—and God took initiative to raise them with Christ from spiritual death because of his mercy and love (2:4-6), granting them a position in the heavens with Christ (2:7), there can be no other conclusion: salvation is entirely by the grace and gift of God.

The meaning of grace in Paul's world has been the subject of exten-

---

16 Bates, *Salvation by Allegiance Alone*, 78.
17 Bates, *Salvation by Allegiance Alone*, 104.
18 While I accept Pauline authorship of the letter to the Ephesians, this position is not essential to the discussion that follows.

sive recent discussion, as addressed in the introduction above. Whatever else may be said about the meaning of grace, it is clear from the context of this passage that it describes the unmerited, unprompted, and God-initiated action to save the spiritually dead from the wrath that was their fate until his intervention. It is the movement of 2:1–7 that most clearly shapes our understanding of grace in 2:8.

Salvation by grace is mediated 'through faith'.[19] Paul does not define what is meant by faith in this context, but it has also been the topic of recent scholarly discussion (see the introduction of this essay). Faith has a wide range of possible meanings, including faithfulness and reliability, trust and confidence, allegiance, and the contents of belief (i.e., doctrine).[20] The most likely sense of faith here is within the 'allegiance' field of meaning. This means that faith is much more than mere mental assent, as though a believer is simply someone who agrees with the notion that God exists—even the demons believe this, and they shudder (Jas. 2:19). Allegiance differs from mere mental assent in that it conveys a level of commitment—a person with allegiance to Christ offers his or her devotion and obedience, while also trusting him. In this sense, faith in the Lord Jesus (cf. Eph. 1:15) is not genuine faith if the 'believer' has not switched allegiances from self and the forces of evil (2:2–3) to Christ. Since Jesus is presented as the 'Lord', genuine faith in him can involve nothing less than genuine devotion and allegiance.

However, it will be noted that in Ephesians 2:8, faith has no object. Paul does not say, 'For you are saved by grace through faith *in Christ Jesus*'. Believers are saved by grace *through faith*. But we are on safe ground to assume that Christ is the object of faith here. In 1:15, Paul refers to his readers' 'faith in the Lord Jesus',[21] which is an unambiguous instance of Jesus as the object of faith. Chapter 1 contains two other references to believing (1:13,19),[22] but these do not specify objects, like 2:8. However, given their close proximity to 1:15, it would be quite natural for readers to assume that Jesus is the object of believing in

---

19 διὰ πίστεως.
20 BDAG, s.v. 'πίστις', 818–20.
21 ὑμᾶς πίστιν ἐν τῷ κυρίῳ Ἰησοῦ.
22 In Greek, 'believing' and 'faith' share the same lexical root: πιστεύω, πίστις.

those instances too (cf. 3:12,17; 4:5,13; 6:16). As such, given that Jesus is explicitly named the object of believers' faith in 1:15, and no other object of faith is named anywhere else in the letter, it is reasonable to conclude that faith *in Christ Jesus* is meant in Ephesians 2:8.

Quite a different reading is possible, as Cohick explores, regarding the so-called subjective genitive debate, in which 'faith' is the main noun, qualified by 'Christ' in the Greek genitive case.[23] Interpreters have long wrestled over phrases that can be translated 'through/from *faith in (Jesus) Christ*' or 'through/from *the faithfulness of (Jesus) Christ*'.[24] Though Ephesians 2:8 is not technically an example of this, since 'faith' has no genitive qualifier, the debate has some bearing here. In short, the 'subjective genitive' reading (admittedly in the absence of any genitive) would render 'faith' as the *faithfulness of Jesus*, rather than believers' *faith in (allegiance to) Jesus*. That would mean that Ephesians 2:8 teaches that Christians are saved by grace through the faithfulness of Jesus, which is not from themselves, but is the gift of God. As Cohick notes, the subjective genitive reading suggests that Paul 'wants to create a picture in his listeners' minds that puts Christ in the forefront, and not themselves.'[25] While this reading would no doubt unsettle some of the inheritors of the Protestant Reformation, for whom 'salvation by grace through (our) faith' is a bedrock, if anything the subjective genitive reading only further underscores the work of Christ in our salvation—even our faith is not depicted as part of the equation (though it is elsewhere, of course; cf. 1:15). Without going further into the details of the debate, the objective genitive reading seems more likely here, with Christ understood as the object of believers' 'faith' (as traditionally understood). This is simply due to the fact that Christ is *not* mentioned as a qualifier of 'faith' and must therefore be supplied.[26] And since he *is* mentioned elsewhere in the letter as the object of faith

---

23 See Bird and Sprinkle, *The Faith of Jesus Christ: Exegetical, Biblical, and Theological Studies*.
24 διὰ/ἐκ πίστεως ('Ιησοῦ) Χριστοῦ (Rom. 3:22,26; Gal. 2:16; 3:22; Phil. 3:9).
25 Cohick, *The Letter to the Ephesians*, 162.
26 Best, *A Critical and Exegetical Commentary on Ephesians*, 226.

(and never its subject), this seems most plausible overall.[27]

The following phrase 'and this is not from yourselves; it is God's gift' is sometimes understood to qualify faith, so that even faith cannot be regarded as a kind of 'work' that may contribute to salvation (cf. 2:9).[28] But such an understanding does not account for the details of the Greek text. The pronoun translated 'this' (from '*this* is not from yourselves') is grammatically neuter,[29] and therefore does not match the grammatically feminine 'faith'.[30] Thus, when Paul says, 'you are saved by grace through *faith*, and *this* is not from yourselves', *this* does not refer to *faith*. Regardless of whether or not human faith is a gift of God from a theological perspective, that is not the point in this verse. So, then, what does *this* refer to, if not faith? Being grammatically neuter, it most likely refers to the entirety of the statement, 'for you are saved by grace through faith'. The whole idea that you are saved by grace through faith is God's gift.[31] This means that salvation by grace through faith 'is not from yourselves'—Paul's point is that the entire concept is from God, rather than believers' faith specifically.

Ephesians 2:9 adds further specification to the phrase 'this is not from yourselves; it is God's gift' in 2:8. Being the gift of God, salvation is not derived 'from yourselves', and this includes your 'works'. Rather than understanding 'not from works'[32] as another way to say 'not from yourselves', it is more likely a subset of it. Of all that a person might have hypothetically contributed to their salvation, their works are singled out. Indeed, a person's works or deeds are not the only elements

---

27 Though Foster tentatively argues that 3:12 contains a subjective genitive, which then influences his reading of 2:8 in that direction also. Foster, 'Πίστις Χριστοῦ Terminology in Philippians and Ephesians', in Bird and Sprinkle, *Faith of Jesus Christ*, 91–109. In contrast, and in the same volume, Bell argues that 3:12 contains an objective, rather than subjective, genitive. Bell, 'Faith in Christ: Some Exegetical and Theological Reflections on Philippians 3:9 and Ephesians 3:12', in Bird and Sprinkle, *Faith of Jesus Christ*, 111–25.
28 E.g. Hodge, *A Commentary on the Epistle to the Ephesians*, 18–19, as well as some ancient interpreters such as Chrysostom, Theodoret, and Jerome. Arnold, *Ephesians*, 139.
29 τοῦτο.
30 πίστις.
31 Arnold, *Ephesians*, 139.
32 οὐκ ἐξ ἔργων.

that someone might boast about. Ethnicity, heritage, pedigree, wealth, and elect status are all elements about which someone might boast, alongside works.

In Romans and Galatians, 'works' (often found in the phrase, 'works of the law')[33] refers to specifically Jewish elements that give expression to that privileged ethnic and religious status—circumcision being a prominent example—along with obedience to the law of Moses (e.g., Rom. 3:20; Gal. 2:16). In those contexts, Paul counters the Jewish view that God's final judgement will be based on Israel's election and obedience.[34] If such an understanding of 'works' applies here, then it might be argued that salvation is not grounded on any of the markers of Jewish identity and elect status, rather than on general good deeds. But that is why it is important to see the phrase 'not from works' as a subset of 'not from yourselves' in 2:8—markers of Jewish identity (if that is how 'works' are to be understood) are but a subset of all that is 'from yourselves'. Jews might claim such identity-markers, but gentiles might claim other boast-worthy elements. Regardless of what might be boasted, 2:8 disqualifies anything 'from yourselves' as a factor of salvation, and 2:9 specifically rules out 'works'.[35]

Having said that, however, it is unlikely that 'works' refers to Jewish identity-markers in this context. First, there is no contextual reason to read specifically Jewish overtones into this term. The passage does not engage the Jew–gentile polemic seen in Romans and Galatians.[36] Second, the passage begins with gentiles in view (Eph. 2:1–2) with Jews then added into view (2:3). With both people-groups now in view Paul states that their salvation is not dependent on their works, so it makes little sense to narrow the focus to Jews only—unless it is to let gentiles know that they suffer no disadvantage in comparison to believing Jews. Third, there is a deliberate wordplay at work with 2:10 in

---

33 ἔργων νόμου.
34 Arnold, *Ephesians*, 139–40; see also Gathercole, *Where Is Boasting? Early Jewish Soteriology and Paul's Response in Romans 1–5*, 248–51.
35 Arnold, *Ephesians*, 140.
36 The absence of justification language, which normally occurs in such polemic contexts, underscores the nonpolemic tone of Eph. 2:1–10. Arnold, *Ephesians*, 140.

which saved humanity is regarded as God's 'workmanship',[37] thus indicating that salvation of humanity in Christ is God's 'work' not ours. These factors demonstrate that 'works' in 2:9 refer generally to human deeds, power, and resources, rather than to specific markers of Jewish identity and obedience.[38]

The language of boasting also may be understood generally.[39] First it should be noted that boasting is not necessarily wrong; it involved ascribing value to something, recognising its worth, and treating it as superior 'symbolic capital'.[40] Paul speaks positively of boasting when it is boasting in God, in the Lord, and in the cross of Christ (Rom. 5:2,11; 1 Cor. 1:31; Gal. 6:14). Rather than ruling out all boasting, Paul's concern in 2:9 is that believers might boast in themselves, and so dishonour God, to whom belong all praise and glory.[41] While it is known that some Jews of Paul's day boasted in their ethnic and religious credentials, this fact does not mean that Paul addressed such boasting alone. It is conceivable that gentiles also might have indulged their own boasting for reasons that made sense to them. Indeed, in Graeco-Roman Ephesus, 'buildings were replete with notices (i.e., "boasts" to Paul) of the lavish deeds of various benefactors'.[42] Instead of choosing those with worldly boasts, God has called and chosen the 'foolish', the 'weak', the 'low', and the 'nothings' of the world to exclude human boasting (1 Cor. 1:26–30; cf. 4:7b).[43] Paul's wording here leaves the matter open since 'no one' can boast—neither Jew nor gentile.

The conclusion of this section of Ephesians, found at 2:10, focuses again on the theocentric and christocentric nature of salvation. The anthropocentric side is downplayed as God's workmanship is contrasted to the inefficacy of human works (cf. 2:9). Instead of producing

---

37 ποίημα. While different words are used for believers 'works' (ἔργων) and God's 'workmanship' (ποίημα), there is an obvious synonymity between them. See BDAG, s.v. 'ἔργον', 390-91 (esp. §3); BDAG, s.v. 'ποίημα', 842.
38 Baugh, *Ephesians*, 162.
39 BDAG, s.v. 'καυχάομαι', 536.
40 Barclay, *Paul and the Gift*, 469.
41 Cohick, *Ephesians*, 164–65.
42 Baugh, *Ephesians*, 162.
43 Thielman, *Ephesians*, 144.

their own salvation, saved people are the product that God produces.[44] We are *his* workmanship, created in Christ Jesus.[45] Saved people are created by God in Christ Jesus (cf. 2 Cor. 5:17) because it is through participation with Christ that believers have been made alive, raised, and seated in the heavens (2:5–6). This participation with Christ is central to the saving work of God. Without it, believers would remain spiritually dead, severed from relationship with God.

Strikingly, believers are created in Christ Jesus 'for good works'.[46] Having just stressed the inefficacy of works in 2:9, it may seem somewhat jarring that believers have been created for them.[47] But three things must be acknowledged here. First, it is only after stressing the inefficacy of works for salvation that Paul will acknowledge a positive role for them. Once it is clear that people are not saved by their works, it is possible to understand their proper place, which is for those who have already been saved by the grace of God. Second, despite the negative references to works in 2:9 it is clear that human works *are* important to God. They do not contribute to salvation, but it is nevertheless God's intention that humans will do works that are pleasing to him once they have been saved. Third, it is only after establishing salvation by grace, apart from works, that human works are called 'good'. Prior to their salvation, human works cannot be regarded as good, since their subjects remain dead to God. No matter what the spiritually dead may do, they are unable to please God because they are still cut off from him. Their works are therefore incapable of being received as good by God.

Lest believers yet slip into boasting about their good works, we see

---

44   Schnackenburg, *Ephesians: A Commentary*, 98.
45   The placement of αὐτοῦ at the beginning of the clause (αὐτοῦ γάρ ἐσμεν ποίημα) is an example of 'main clause emphasis', in which the most important element(s) of the main clause are put in a position of prominence in order to attract attention to it using a change in word order. Runge, *Lexham Discourse Greek New Testament*. The effect of the placement of αὐτοῦ is to emphasize the fact we are *his* workmanship, rather than the product of our own works (cf. 2:9).
46   Allen points out the relative rarity of the term 'good works' in Paul's writings, appearing elsewhere only in his letters to Timothy and Titus (1 Tim. 2:10; 5:10,25; 6:18; Titus 2:7,14; 3:8,14). Allen, *Ephesians*, 45.
47   Roberts, *Ephesians*, 68.

that these have been prepared by God ahead of time (cf. 1:4).[48] It is not clear when these works were prepared ahead of time—at the foundation of the world or at the point of conversion.[49] But, with Best, the Greek prefix 'pro' ('pre-' or 'before')[50] in the word translated 'he prepared'[51] is seen in 1:4,5,9,11, pointing to a precreation timeframe in the wider context.[52] This suggests the likelihood that good works were prepared by God even before the creation of the world.[53] Thus, there is a double God-dependence for good works.[54] First, believers are only capable of doing 'good' works because God has mercifully saved them. Second, the good works themselves have been prepared by God for believers to execute. Thus, even our good works are a product of God's grace. As Barclay comments, 'obedience is not instrumental (it does not acquire the gift of Christ, nor any additional gift from God), but is integral to the gift itself'.[55]

Finally, believers will execute these God-ordained good works by *walking* in them. Though often hidden in translation, 2:10 uses the language of walking rather than doing.[56] This then creates an *inclusio* with 2:1–2, where we saw that the spiritually dead walked according to the ways of the world and the devil.[57] Now walking appears again, but this time believers are able to walk according to God's ways, according to the deeds he has preordained for them to walk in. Thus, God's salvation not only produces new creations in Christ, but completely reorients believers' activity. They are no longer subjected to life under the authority of sin, death, and the devil; they are now free to please God in their actions as they conduct themselves in line with his intentions for them.

48 BDAG, s.v. 'προετοιμάζω', 869.
49 Cohick, *Ephesians*, 167.
50 προ-.
51 προητοίμασεν.
52 πρὸ καταβολῆς κόσμου ('before the foundation of the world'; 1:4); προορίσας ἡμᾶς ('predestining us'; 1:5); προέθετο ἐν αὐτῷ ('he purposed in him'; 1:9); προορισθέντες ('having been predestined'; 1:11); κατὰ πρόθεσιν ('according to the plan'; 1:11).
53 Best, *Ephesians*, 232.
54 Hoehner, *Ephesians: An Exegetical Commentary*, 349.
55 Barclay, *Paul and the Gift*, 518.
56 περιπατήσωμεν.
57 Heil, *Ephesians: Empowerment to Walk in Love for the Unity of All in Christ*, 107.

Conclusion

The conclusions of Barclay on grace and Bates on faith fit together like hand in glove, and they offer a compelling reading of Ephesians 2:8–10. Of Barclay's six concepts to describe God's grace, the first five are clearly in view in the wider passage of 2:1–10. Superabundance is seen in the dramatic resurrection and ascension of the spiritually dead with Christ (2:4–6). Singularity is seen in the sheer benevolence of God's action, prompted only by his mercy and love (2:4). Priority is seen in the rescuing of the spiritually dead before they befall the wrath of judgement (2:5b,8). Incongruity is seen in the gift of heavenly ascension for those who had utterly rejected God through their trespasses and sins (2:6–7). Efficacy is seen in the total transformation of the spiritually dead to new creations in Christ (2:10). Noncircularity, however, is arguably not present, since believers have been created in Christ Jesus for good works. Their new identity comes with good works wrapped in.

As for Bates's faith as allegiance, this also makes good sense in 2:8–10. Believers are saved by God's grace through their allegiance to Christ. Clearly such allegiance is not regarded as human works so that no one can boast (2:9). But it is regarded as one side of being 'with' Christ. God has raised believers with Christ, and their participation with him is of central significance in the passage (2:5–6). Allegiance to Christ is simply the ongoing reality of remaining with him in loyal dependence on the one who keeps them with him in the heavens (2:6–7). This allegiance expresses itself as those created anew in Christ Jesus perform the good works that God has prepared in advance for them to walk in (2:10). Their conduct has been reoriented, along with their direction and destination. They have been transformed by the grace of God in Christ.

Constantine R. Campbell
Sydney College of Divinity

Bibliography

Allen, M.	*Ephesians* (Brazos Theological Commentary on the Bible; Grand Rapids, MI: Brazos Press, 2020).
Arnold, C. E.	*Ephesians* (Zondervan Exegetical Commentary on the New Testament 10; Grand Rapids, MI: Zondervan, 2010).
Barclay, J. M. G.	*Paul and the Gift* (Grand Rapids, MI: Eerdmans, 2015).
Barclay, J. M. G.	*Paul and the Power of Grace* (Grand Rapids, MI: Eerdmans, 2020).
Bates, M. W.	*Salvation by Allegiance Alone: Rethinking Faith, Works, and the Gospel of Jesus the King* (Grand Rapids, MI: Baker Academic, 2017).
Baugh, S. M.	*Ephesians* (Evangelical Exegetical Commentary; Bellingham, WA: Lexham Press, 2016).
Bell, R. H.	'Faith in Christ: Some Exegetical and Theological Reflections on Philippians 3:9 and Ephesians 3:12', in M. F. Bird and P. M. Sprinkle (eds.), *The Faith of Jesus Christ: Exegetical, Biblical, and Theological Studies* (Peabody, MA: Hendrickson, 2009), 111–125.
Best, E.	*A Critical and Exegetical Commentary on Ephesians* (ICC; London: T&T Clark, 1998).
Bird, M. F., and P. M. Sprinkle, eds.	*The Faith of Jesus Christ: Exegetical, Biblical, and Theological Studies* (Peabody, MA: Hendrickson, 2009).
Cohick, L. H.	*The Letter to the Ephesians* (NICNT; Grand Rapids, MI: Eerdmans, 2020).
Foster, P.	'Πίστις Χριστοῦ Terminology in Philippians and Ephesians', in M. F. Bird and P. M. Sprinkle (eds.), *The Faith of Jesus Christ: Exegetical, Biblical, and Theological Studies* (Peabody, MA: Hendrickson, 2009), 91–109.
Gathercole, S. J.	*Where Is Boasting? Early Jewish Soteriology and Paul's Response in Romans 1–5* (Grand Rapids, MI: Eerdmans, 2002).
Harrison, J. R.	*Paul's Language of Grace in Its Graeco-Roman Context* (Repr., Eugene, OR: Wipf & Stock, 2017).
Heil, J. P.	*Ephesians: Empowerment to Walk in Love for the Unity of All in Christ* (SBLStBL; Atlanta, GA: Society of Biblical Literature, 2007).

Hodge, C.	*A Commentary on the Epistle to the Ephesians* (New York, NY: Carter, 1856. Repr., London: Banner of Truth, 1964).
Hoehner, H. W.	*Ephesians: An Exegetical Commentary* (Grand Rapids, MI: Baker Academic, 2002).
Roberts, M. D.	*Ephesians* (Story of God Bible Commentary; Grand Rapids, MI: Zondervan, 2016).
Runge, S. E.	*The Lexham Discourse Greek New Testament* (Bellingham, WA: Lexham Press, 2008–2014).
Schnackenburg, R.	*Ephesians: A Commentary* (Translated by H. Heron. Edinburgh: T&T Clark, 1991).
Thielman, F.	*Ephesians* (BECNT; Grand Rapids, MI: Baker Academic, 2010).

The Value of the Local

Peter Oakes

Abstract

This article discusses ways in which studies that are 'local', in various senses, can contribute fruitfully to understanding the early Christian movement and its texts. This approach, of which Harrison is a leading exponent, is illustrated using work on Philippi and, as a contrasting type of case, Pompeii. The article suggests three situations in which local studies can be particular useful: when a place has a historical connection to an early Christian text or event; when a place offers extensive evidence that is culturally local to early Christian settings; when a place offers controlled sets of data for analysis of topics in early Christian studies.

Among the key contributions that Jim Harrison's work has made to study of the New Testament and the early Christian movement has been a strengthening of the understanding and significance of factors local to places associated in some way with early Christian texts. This can be seen in his studies ranging from 'Paul and the Imperial Gospel at Thessaloniki' to *Reading Romans with Roman Eyes*. It is also seen particularly in the edited series, *The First Urban Churches*, working with Larry Welborn. This series has had, and undoubtedly will continue to have, a major long-term influence on understanding sites associated with early Christian texts, especially in comprehension of how those locations can help in thinking about those texts.

I was delighted to be invited to participate in two of the volumes of the series, on Philippi and Galatia, and particularly appreciated the

SBL seminars at which many contributors' papers were discussed. One feature that became evident in each discussion was the wide variety of ways in which local factors could be significant for historical and textual understanding. There was also discussion at various points, both about the extent to which local factors could, or could not, be learned, and about the extent to which they were, or were not, relevant for understanding an associated early Christian text. For my research, answers to these questions looked different for Philippi and for Galatia. Reflecting on that also made me think of the different type of location that I focused on between Philippi and Galatia, namely, Pompeii. To what extent can local evidence be relevant if it is from a place not associated with an early Christian text? I and others such as David Balch and Carolyn Osiek[1] have spent a great deal of time on understanding detail local to Pompeii and Herculaneum. Editors of works such as the *Dictionary of the Bible and Ancient Media*, that seek to contextualise biblical texts, commission articles on topics such as the Villa of the Papyri at Herculaneum.[2] To what extent does this kind of local evidence have value for understanding the early Christian movement and its texts? What should we make of the differences in relation between place and text involved in locations such as, on the one hand, Philippi, a place directly associated with NT missions and NT text, and, on the other hand, Pompeii, a place yielding dense first-century cultural evidence but lacking direct connection with NT events or texts? For each of these locations, what is the value of the local for those wishing to understand early Christianity and its texts?

1. Philippi: Historically Local, Culturally Local, and a Controlled Data Set

Local factors at Philippi have been brought into NT study for a long time. The main reason has to do with it being a Roman colony. However, it was not the historical fact of being a Roman colony that initially triggered NT scholars' interest, but the fact of the city being

---

1 E.g. Osiek and Balch, *Families*.
2 Oakes, 'Villa', 439–41.

specified as a colony in Acts (16:12). Paul's mission in Acts had actually already taken him to several Roman colonies, such as Pisidian Antioch, and was about to reach a particularly famous colony, Corinth, to which he also sent letters, but it was the colony specified in Acts that was interpreted as such. Appian's *Civil Wars* IV—and probably Shakespeare's *Julius Caesar*—then led scholars to think about Philippi as the site of the decisive battle of 42 B.C.E. and as the type of colony founded by settlement of veteran Roman soldiers.

On this Classical basis, a scholar such as D. Karl Bornhäuser could frame Philippians as a letter specifically designed to appeal to veteran soldiers.[3] Bornhäuser's book is an extreme example of a pattern still common among popular commentators and preachers: archaeological discoveries at Philippi are not a significant factor, instead, Acts 16:12 is combined with knowledge, ultimately from Classical literature, of Philippi as a Roman veteran colony, to yield a view of Philippians as a letter written for retired Roman soldiers.[4]

In this way, a certain amount of local knowledge has led many interpreters smartly up the garden path. An aim of my monograph on Philippians was to debunk this type of reading, which generally forgets the passage of a century between the colonisation and Paul's letter, casually assumes a male audience for the letter, and effectively buys into various elements of imperial ideology such as 'myth of the empty land' ideas, implicit in comments such as Gordon Fee's that 'Octavian honored Philippi by "refounding" it as a Roman military colony'.[5] There was such a thing as honorific designation as a colony but that was not what happened at Philippi, where there will have been mass expropriation and redistribution of prime agricultural land.[6]

Scholars do often handle the idea of Philippi as a Roman colony effectively. Lukas Bormann, for instance, rightly argues that political control at Philippi was firmly Roman and that ongoing involvement of

---

3   Bornhäuser, *Jesus*.
4   E.g. *The NIV Study Bible*, 1767.
5   Fee, *Philippians*, 25.
6   Oakes, *Philippians*, 24–29, citing the well-documented parallel cases of expropriation (and associated protests) in Italy as part of the same 42 B.C.E. programme of colonisation (Appian, *B.Civ.* V.12).

veteran soldiers in governance would have been a substantial factor right up to Paul's time.[7] Even though, as Peter Pilhofer argues, Romans would probably have been in a minority in the Philippi of Paul's day[8] and, as I argue, the proportion of the mid-first-century C.E. Romans who were freshly settling veteran soldiers is bound to have been very small, veterans who did do so were likely to have been influential in colonial governance and, more broadly, the city would still have had a colonial ethos. This point is strongly reinforced by the archaeology. Finds in the central area of the town, and civic finds generally, remain markedly Roman until well after the first century C.E.. They also include evidence of strong civic support of Roman institutions such as a Latin library and a publicly funded troop of Latin mime actors.[9]

Two substantial collections of essays have recently been published on Philippi, with many of the contributors seeking to relate local evidence to early Christian texts, especially Acts and Philippians. In the Harrison and Welborn edited *First Urban Churches* volume on Philippi,[10] Harrison's own two pieces in the volume are both contributions drawing substantively on local evidence. In his first essay, he particularly presents epigraphic evidence of religious life in villages around Philippi, then considers ways in which that might shed light on aspects of Philippians.[11] In the essay that closes the volume, Harrison uses honorific inscriptions from Philippi to illustrate a discussion on the Roman *cursus honorum*, which in turn sheds light on Paul's boasting in Philippians 3:4–6.[12] Another essay using Philippian epigraphy is that by Julien Ogereau. He studies Philippian Christian inscriptions of the fourth to sixth centuries that carry some socio-economic evidence. This enables him to discuss very directly the situation of the Christians who provide evidence of that kind, albeit the number is limited.[13] Paul Holloway's contribution to the volume combines evidence local to

---

7   Bormann, *Philippi*, 28.
8   Pilhofer, *Philippi* I, 90.
9   Oakes, *Philippians*, 35–40; Pilhofer, *Philippi* II, nrs 233, 476.
10 Harrison and Welborn, eds., *The First Urban Churches. 4. Roman Philippi*.
11 Harrison, 'Excavating', 15–30.
12 Harrison, 'From Rome', 334–62.
13 Ogereau, 'The Social Constituency', 87–110.

Philippi with evidence from Vindolanda, in northern Britain, to argue about the significance of the term 'Praetorium' in Philippians 1:13.[14] Should the documents known as the Vindolanda Tablets be seen in any sense as 'local evidence' for study of Philippians? This counter-intuitive question raises issues that will be discussed below in relation to Pompeii. Local study has clearly taken place at Vindolanda. We understand the material from there so well because the quantity and quality of co-located preserved evidence is so great that we can build up a very 'thick', socially and culturally specified picture.[15] A similarly rich (but in different ways) collection at the other end of the empire is that from Mons Claudianus, with its mass of ostraca offering evidence of daily life.[16] In both cases, the depth of the local study paradoxically enables broad conclusions to be drawn about life at various levels in the Roman empire. These local studies are relevant to understanding the culture in which Paul writes, even though they are not local to Paul himself.

The second substantial recent collection of work on Philippi is the volume resulting from a major gathering held at Philippi in 2015. Scholars met from a range of disciplines involved in archaeological, historical or textual study of the city and texts connected to it.[17] Among the papers, a number work at drawing local evidence into conversation with early Christian texts. Jennifer Quigley and Laura Nasrallah use evidence of donation amounts in the inscriptions at the sanctuary of the god Silvanus to reflect on the entwining of religious devotion and economics in Philippians.[18] Looking at the idea of 'local' through the other end of the telescope, Cavan Concannon specifies the location of Philippi by mapping the city's connections to other places, in trade and other forms of contact, as indicated by several types of evidence: Philippian inscriptions and inscriptions elsewhere that mention Philippi; inscriptions relating to traders; and imported ceramics. He then uses that to discuss the patterns of contact between Ignatius,

---

14   Holloway, 'Vindolanda Tablet'.
15   Bowman, *Life*; Geertz, 'Thick Description'.
16   Bingen, *Mons Claudianus*.
17   Friesen *et al.* (eds.), *Philippi from Colonia Augusta to Communitas Christiana*.
18   Quigley and Nasrallah, 'Cost', 221–28.

Polycarp, and Philippi.[19] Angela Standhartinger brings the early Christian remains in Philippi into conversation with the set of early Christian texts connected to the city.[20]

My own contribution to the volume draws on the local in two ways. The article is a study of funerary epigraphy from the vicinity of Philippi in the Roman period.[21] It gathers the available textual and iconographic evidence (as collected in Pilhofer's catalogue of Philippian inscriptions),[22] of all types, on monuments in and immediately around the town. It then adds the countryside around the town, this time specifically analysing text and imagery that may relate to afterlife or its absence. The results of this local analysis, especially its indication of a reasonably widespread practice of representing the dead in 'heroic' terms, are put to work in two ways. First, the local evidence is compared with the 'local' text. Afterlife language in Paul's letter to the Philippians is compared with the extent and nature of afterlife evidence in the local funerary epigraphy. The conclusion is that the most distinctive afterlife expressions in Philippians would fit with elements familiar to inhabitants of Philippi, although few of them would have been from social locations where they would have been likely to have put such representations on their own, or their family's funerary monuments. Second, the local evidence acts as a controlled gathering of data to contribute to broader questions about ancient beliefs regarding afterlife. By analysing all of the extensive data we gain some analytical control in what has been a rather chaotic debate, commonly involving uncontextualised quoting of instances that support a particular conclusion about Greek or Roman views on afterlife, without any sense of what proportion of funerary monuments (or other forms of representation) fitted with one view or another.

All in all, consideration of Philippi suggests three ways in which local study of a place associated with a NT text or event may be useful for understanding of NT texts and early Christianity. First, there may

---

19   Concannon, '"Let us Know"'.
20   Standhartinger, '"The Beloved Community"'.
21   Oakes, 'Popular Heroization'.
22   Pilhofer, *Philippi* II.

be something specific to that text or event which relates to the location. Occasionally, historical or archaeological evidence about the place relates directly to a NT text. The identification of Philippi as a colony in Acts 16:12 is directly supported by literary and archaeological evidence; that evidence then expands on the nature of the colony. Less directly, the epigraphic study above concludes that an expression such as in Philippians 3:21, 'who will transform our lowly bodies into the likeness of his glorious body', can be understood in relation to depiction on Philippian gravestones of the deceased transformed into the likeness of a hero or deity.[23] Whether or not the same was true in other places, there is exegetical interest in seeing whether aspects of a NT text are comparable to evidence local to the place of composition or intended destination of the text.

Second, local study of Philippi may be useful because the place is in the same cultural sphere as various NT texts and early Christian groups. Study of Philippian funerary epigraphy is valuable for consideration of first-century views on afterlife. This makes it useful for discussion of early Christian views on the subject. The local study is valuable beyond the immediate location. Because the study is local, it is not the only relevant contribution on a broad first-century topic. However, it is of value.

Third, the study of Philippian funerary epigraphy shows how a local study can provide a controlled set of data on a topic. It would be extremely hard to gauge what percentage of all first-century gravestones expressed views suggestive of afterlife, but we can do so for Philippi. Again, being local means that this is far from being the only relevant contribution on the topic. However, local studies are usually the main practical route to providing a reasonably controlled set of data to contribute to a debate.

---

23 Oakes, 'Popular Heroization', 273-75.

2. Pompeii: Culturally Local and a Controlled Data Set (with Rich Data)

Pompeii was not associated with any NT texts or events. There may have been Christians there prior to the eruption in 79 C.E. but evidence that might demonstrate that looks to me to be very thin.[24] However, the date of the sudden destruction of Pompeii, Herculaneum and other nearby locations puts evidence from there right in the heart of the period of production of NT texts. Given the degree of commonality between archaeological evidence from the Vesuvian towns and that from Roman-influenced towns around the empire, it looks safe to describe Pompeii as being, to a significant degree, culturally local to many NT texts and events.[25]

Local study of Pompeii, like local study of Philippi, also provides some very reasonably controlled data sets for study of topics relevant to study of NT texts and early Christian groups. One of my favourites is Henrik Mouritsen's study of locations of election *programmata*: political slogans painted on Pompeian street walls. These can be analysed as a full set (within the areas so far dug). We can see how many supported (or attacked) each candidate. We can map their location. We can analyse how the locations related both to main circulation routes and, in some cases, even to the location of the candidate's residence, identifiable through named belongings found there.[26] I have argued elsewhere that this offers evidence for mapping of patronage networks in Pompeii. This in turn offers input to a range of recent and current debates about NT texts and patronage.[27]

This example also shows why local studies of the Vesuvian towns are particularly important for understanding first-century life: the density of data available there is at least an order of magnitude higher than at almost any other sites. Even though there is always a certain level of distinction to be made between Pompeii and any site directly linked to

---

24 For a contrasting argument that the evidence for there being Christians there is compelling, see Longenecker, *The Crosses*.
25 Oakes, *Reading Romans*, 89–97.
26 Mouritsen, *Elections* 50–56, 69.
27 Oakes, 'Urban Structure', 182–83.

the NT, the detail of the Pompeian evidence makes local study of Pompeii a vital tool for research into NT and early Christian groups. Indeed, it already lies behind much NT research that is meant to be specific to sites directly associated with NT texts. In my own research on Philippi, I repeatedly discovered that a method that the archaeologists were using to interpret structures (and similarly other finds) was to decide which Pompeian structure the Philippian example most closely resembled, then interpret the Philippian instance from the Pompeian evidence.

3. Conclusion

Generalised study of a phenomenon across a wide geographic range is often ideal in principle, but very problematic in practice. To make effective progress, local study is usually needed. In fact, we can go further than this. Local study is always needed, even in principle: an empire-wide study of a phenomenon is only the aggregation of studies of local phenomena, which need to be interpreted as such. Local studies can also provide the added value of reasonably controlled data sets and, in some cases, arguable direct connection to an element of a NT text. All this means that the type of locally focused work that Jim Harrison has exemplified, commissioned, and tirelessly promoted will always remain a crucial element of study of our discipline.

Peter Oakes
University of Manchester

Bibliography

Bingen, J. — *Mons Claudianus: ostraca graeca et latina* (Le Caire: Institut Français d'Archéologie Orientale, 1997).

Bormann, L. — *Philippi: Stadt und Christengemeinde zur Zeit des Paulus* (Supplements to Novum Testamentum 78; Leiden: Brill, 1995).

Bornhäuser, D. K. — *Jesus imperator mundi (Phil 3, 17–21 u. 2,5–12)* (Gütersloh: Bertelsmann, 1938).

Bowman, A. K. — *Life and Letters on the Roman Frontier: Vindolanda and Its People* (London: British Museum Press, 1994).

Concannon, C. — '"Let us Know Anything Further which you have Heard", Mapping Philippian Connectivity', in S. J. Friesen, M. Lychounas, and D. N. Schowalter (eds.), *Philippi from Colonia Augusta to Communitas Christiana: Religion and Society in Transition* (Novum Testamentum Supliments 186; Leiden, E. J. Brill: 2021), 185–207.

Fee, G. D. — *Paul's Letter to the Philippians* (New International Commentary on the New Testament; Grand Rapids, MI: Eerdmans, 1995).

Friesen, S. J., M. Lychounas, and D. N. Schowalter (eds.) *Philippi from Colonia Augusta to Communitas Christiana: Religion and Society in Transition* (Supplements to Novum Testamentum 186; Leiden: E. J. Brill, 2021).

Geertz, C. — 'Thick Description: Toward an Interpretive Theory of Culture', *The Interpretation of Cultures: Selected Essays* (New York, NY: Basic Books, 1973), 3–30.

Harrison, J. R. — 'Excavating the Urban and Country Life of Philippi and Its Territory', in J. R. Harrison and L. L. Welborn (eds.), *The First Urban Churches 4: Roman Philippi* (Atlanta: SBL Press, 2018), 1–61.

Harrison, J. R. — 'From Rome to the Colony of Philippi: Roman Boasting in Philippians 3:4–6 in Its Latin West and Philippian Epigraphic Context', in J. R. Harrison and L. L. Welborn (eds.), *The First Urban Churches 4: Roman Philippi* (Atlanta: SBL Press, 2018), 307–70.

Harrison, James R., and L. L. Welborn (eds.) *The First Urban Churches. 4. Roman Philippi* (Atlanta: SBL Press, 2018).

Holloway, P. A.   'Vindolanda Tablet 2.154, *RPC* 1651, and the Provenance of Philippians', in J. R. Harrison and L. L. Welborn (eds.), *The First Urban Churches 4: Roman Philippi* (Atlanta: SBL Press, 2018), 123–37.

Longenecker, B. L.   *The Crosses of Pompeii: Jesus-Devotion in a Vesuvian Town* (Minneapolis, MN: Fortress, 2016).

Mouritsen, H.   *Elections, Magistrates and Municipal Élite: Studies in Pompeian Epigraphy* (Analecta Romana Instituti Danici— Supp XV; Rome: 'L'Erma' di Bretschneider, 1988).

Oakes, P.   *Philippians: From People to Letter* (Society for New Testament Studies Monograph Series 110; Cambridge: Cambridge University Press, 2001).

Oakes, P.   'Popular Heroization in Philippian Funerary Epigraphy and Paul's Letter to the Philippians', in S. J. Friesen, M. Lychounas, and D. N. Schowalter (eds.), *Philippi from Colonia Augusta to Communitas Christiana: Religion and Society in Transition* (Supplements to Novum Testamentum 186; Leiden: E. J. Brill, 2022), 252–77.

Oakes, P.   *Reading Romans in Pompeii: Paul's Letter at Ground Level* (Minneapolis, MN: Fortress/ London: SPCK, 2009).

Oakes, P.   'Urban Structure and Patronage: Christ Followers in Corinth', in D. Neufeld and R. E. DeMaris (eds.), *Understanding the Social World of the New Testament* (London: Routledge, 2010), 178–93 (= Oakes, *Empire, Economics, and the New Testament* [Grand Rapids, MI: Eerdmans, 2020], 109–22).

Oakes, P.   'Villa of the Papyri, Herculaneum', in T. Thatcher, C. Keith, R. F. Person Jr., E. R. Stern (eds.), *Dictionary of the Bible and Ancient Media* (London: Bloomsbury, 2017), 439–41.

Ogereau, J. M.   'The Social Constituency and Membership of the First Christian Groups at Philippi: A Literary and Epigraphic Survey', in J. R. Harrison and L. L. Welborn (eds.), *The First Urban Churches 4: Roman Philippi* (Atlanta: SBL Press, 2018), 79–122.

Osiek, C. and D. L. Balch   *Families in the New Testament World: Households and House Churches* (Louisville, KY: Westminster John Knox, 1997).

Pilhofer, P.   *Philippi* I: *Die erste christliche Gemeinde Europas* (Wissenschaftliche Untersuchungen zum Neuen Testament 87; Tübingen: Mohr Siebeck, 1995).

Pilhofer, P.   *Philippi* II: *Katalog der Inschriften von Philippi. 2. überarbeitete und ergänzte Auflage* (2nd edn; Wissenschaftliche Untersuchungen zum Neuen Testament 119; Tübingen: Mohr Siebeck, 2009).

Quigley, J. and L. Nasrallah   'Cost and Abundance in Roman Philippi', in S. J. Friesen, M. Lychounas, and D. N. Schowalter (eds.), *Philippi from Colonia Augusta to Communitas Christiana: Religion and Society in Transition* (Supplements to Novum Testamentum 186; Leiden: E. J. Brill, 2022), 208–32.

Standhartinger, A.   '"The Beloved Community" after Paul: Early Christianity in Philippi from the Second to the Fourth Century', in S. J. Friesen, M. Lychounas, and D. N. Schowalter (eds.), *Philippi from Colonia Augusta to Communitas Christiana: Religion and Society in Transition* (Supplements to Novum Testamentum 186; Leiden: E. J. Brill, 2022), 316–35.

The NIV Study Bible (UK edn; London: Hodder and Stoughton, 1987).

Christ and Alexander the Great
Philippians 2 compared with Plutarch's Tractate *De Alexandri Magni fortuna aut virtute*

Samuel Vollenweider

Abstract

The essay draws some parallels between two Early Imperial portraits of the universal king (*kosmokrator*), namely Christ in Paul's letter to the Philippians 2:6–11 and Alexander in Plutarch's *De Alexandri Magni fortuna aut virtute,* both written in epideictic style. Both rulers are contrasted with a negative figure (usurper or selfish tyrant). Both have a mission for universal unification. A remarkable difference between the two portraits consists in the assessment of the relationship between human and divine agency: Plutarch represents a synergistic model whereas Paul offers a monergistic model of God's efficacy in saving believers through Christ.

In 1752 Johann Jakob Wettstein drew the attention of biblical scholars to a remarkable parallel between the portrait of Jesus Christ in Philippians 2 and a description of Alexander in Plutarch's *De Alexandri Magni fortuna aut virtute* (1:8. 330c/d).[1] Some two hundred years later, Arnold Ehrhardt tried to outline some striking analogies between early Christology and some conventional features of the

---

1   Wettstein, *Novum Testamentum,* vol. 2, 269b. Another one who connects the passage in Plutarch and Phil. 2 is Wyttenbach in his Plutarchean Index, vol. 8.1, 252.

Hellenistic traditions about Alexander.[2] Finally, thirty years ago, Dieter Georgi dealt with the comparison between Plutarch's treatise and the New Testament.[3]

The main purpose of my paper in honour of James R. Harrison is to put these somewhat accidental parallels into a wider framework, thus taking into consideration the complexity of how Alexander was portrayed both in Hellenistic and Roman historiography or biography and in popular imagination.[4] The material is so rich that we must content ourselves only with a fresh look at Plutarch's declamations on Alexander with respect to their rhetorical character and use of older traditions about the Macedonian king. At several points, we will discuss associations with the portrait of Christ in Philippians 2. We have here the rare opportunity to compare two early imperial portraits of an ideal ruler in encomiastic rhetoric.

Plutarch's two treatises about Alexander's fortune (περὶ τῆς Ἀλεξάνδρου τύχης) confront the reader with numerous difficulties—complicated challenges which are not easier to overcome than the well-known exegetical problems within Philippians 2. First of all, we know nearly nothing about the circumstances under which the treatises have been written.[5] Secondly both treatises may be incomplete.[6] Thirdly there is no clearly identifiable relation between the two declamations. Probably both treatises are to be regarded as exercises performed by the young Plutarch which have never been definitely developed and completed.[7] At least the genre can be clearly defined: The two treatises belong to the epideictic genos and may be classified as declamations, as enkomia of

---

2   Ehrhardt, 'Jesus Christ'. The author had a clear awareness of the significant political dimensions of Phil. 2:5-11, unlike most of his contemporaneous exegetical scholars. See his monumental magnum opus: *Politische Metaphysik* (esp. vol. 2: 8, 26).
3   Georgi, 'Reflections'.
4   I intend to present much more detail in a separate study.
5   The latest state of the art is offered by Italian scholarship, esp. two excellent editions: D'Angelo, *Plutarco. La fortuna*; Cammarota, *Plutarco. La fortuna*. See also Cecchet, *La fortuna*.
6   See Schröder, *Alexanderreden*.
7   Both treatises together with similar ones (esp. *De Fortuna Romanorum, De gloria Atheniensium*) are most often regarded as Plutarch's 'Schriften der rhetorischen Jugendperiode' (so Ziegler, *Plutarchos*, 716-17).

Alexander. Like the related tractate *De Romanorum fortuna* they mainly work with elements of the 'competition of speeches' (ἀγὼν λόγων), namely the contest between fortune and virtue.[8] It is interesting that later on in the series of his famous biographies, Plutarch also wrote a Life of Alexander comparing the great Macedonian king with the Roman Julius Caesar. The variations caused by the different types of literature are remarkable: Whereas the declamations praise Alexander as an outstanding paradigm of virtue, the biography offers a more 'realistic' bios including some negative, unpleasant aspects of Alexander the Great.[9]

In addition, we shall also focus on the portrait of Christ in Philippians 2:6–11. The question whether Paul is the author of this praise of Jesus Christ or simply its transmitter will not be discussed in this essay. Nevertheless, an attentive reader will notice a certain kind of 'surplus' of this text in relation to its context. Especially the second part of the praise of Christ (vv. 9–11) is not explicitly put to good advantage in the argumentation Paul develops later in his letter. Thus, 2:9–11 is about exaltation, but the partially related passage 3:10–21 is about resurrection. Paul seems to be working with a carefully crafted text—either drafted by himself or derived from older tradition—characterised by an outstanding elevated, sublime prose and composed independently from the specific situation in which he addresses the Philippians as a prisoner. Whether it is a hymn depends on how one defines this genre.[10] In what follows, I am content to speak simply of 'praise'.

At the least, the epideictic character of both Philippians 2 and Plutarch's declamations already form a narrow bridge between Paul, the apostle, and Plutarch, the Delphic philosopher and priest.

1. Fortune or Virtue

There are two basic conceptions underlying both of Plutarch's treatises. One of them is the traditional Hellenistic antithesis between fortune

---

8   See Cammarota, *Tradizione*.
9   See Cammarota, 'Espressione retorica'. In the whole *Corpus Plutarcheum*, Alexander 'is a controversial figure, with positive and negative sides' (Muccioli, 'Search', 129).
10 See Vollenweider, 'Hymnus'.

and virtue (τύχη vs. ἀρετή). The primary intention of Plutarch is to depict Alexander as a perfect example of virtue in contrast to being a product of mere fortune.[11] It is very interesting to notice what Plutarch associates with Tyche: It offers supremacy as 'as a pure gift' (προῖκα) and is not 'won by the price' of suffering and effort.[12] Products of Tyche are kings like Darius, Xerxes, Hannibal and others; 'the royal diadem came to their doors (ἐπὶ θύρας)',[13] whereas Alexander had to strive for it. Even more intriguing and thought-provoking: It was Tyche who elevated Darius from his position of a servant to the position of the lord:[14]

> Darius was your handiwork: he who was a slave and courier of the king, him did you make the mighty lord of Persia (ὃν ἐκ δούλου καὶ ἀστάνδου βασιλέως κύριον Περσῶν ἐποίησας).

Plutarch denies that Alexander received his dominion as an unexpected luck. Yet such was a widespread interpretation of Alexander's numerous victories: According to a proverb, retained in comedic literature, an Ἀλεξανδρῶδες meant an unexpected occurrence, as if an event or a person, desperately longed for, suddenly happens or appears.[15]

Whereas the first discourse is exclusively based on the antagonism between Tyche and virtue, the second works with a more 'synergistic' conception of their relation:[16] The way Tyche manifests itself depends on the actor's behaviour; it offers possibilities which may be accepted

---

11 Alexander has often been portrayed against the background of the polarity between virtue and fortune: 'Das in den beiden Vorträgen behandelte Thema von Alexanders Glück oder Tugend ist in der antiken Literatur seit den Lebzeiten des Königs und besonders in den Rhetorenschulen unablässig traktiert worden', Ziegler, 'Plutarchos', 723.
12 Plut., fort. Alex. 1:1. 326d. Cf. 2:9. 340e. – The translations are from: Babbitt, LCL, unless otherwise noted.
13 Plut., fort. Alex. 2:8. 340b.
14 Plut., fort. Alex. 1:2. 326e
15 Menand., frg. 751, quoted by Plut., Alex. 17:4: "How Alexander-like, indeed, this is; and if I seek someone,/ spontaneous he'll present himself (ὡς Ἀλεξανδρῶδες ἤδη τοῦτο· κἂν ζητῶ τινα, αὐτόματος οὗτος παρέσται)."
16 Plut., fort. Alex. 2:4. 336e/f, 2:7–8: 339a–340a (τῇ Τύχῃ καλῶς κέχρηται). Cf. the conception of Tyche as a supporting force in Plut., Alex. 20:7, 26:14, 58:2. Cf. Eckholdt, Vorsehung, esp. 330–31; 442.

or rejected. Nevertheless, the second discourse is marked by the mentioned antagonistic relationship as well; Tyche even seems to become the opposing evil power Alexander has to face.[17] The king therefore displays his wounds caused by his battle with fortune, his στίγματα so to speak, thus boasting with his bravery in front of the whole world.[18]

If we now turn to Philippians 2 we are faced with a very different configuration: *Prima vista* the main opposition is not the one between an ambivalent external power (as Tyche) and one's own virtue, but rather between an attitude of self-centredness versus an attitude of obedience and dedication to God's will (cf. 2:1–5). To put it concisely: Reliance on an external instance is judged negatively by Plutarch, but highly valued in the Pauline text. Such is the case in vv. 6–8 and in vv. 9–11 as well. The striking parallel to Philippians 2:9–11 (God raises Jesus from servant to Lord) in the already quoted passage about Darius (326e) unmistakably illustrates this fact.

At first glance there seems to be a harsh disagreement between Plutarch and Paul, between the Greek call for autonomy and the Jewish-Christian adherence to heteronomy. However, the appeal to look to one's own strengths and efforts is not Plutarch's last word. Piety is one of the distinctive features of an active philosopher like Alexander. In contrast to the God-attacking Homeric hero Diomedes, Alexander believed the gods to be the ultimate authors of all success, particularly of all his victories:[19]

> He was more reverent than Diomedes; for Diomedes was ready to fight with gods, but Alexander believed the gods to be the authors of all success (ὁ δὲ πάντα τοὺς θεοὺς ἐνόμιζε κατορθοῦν).

This not only coincides with the second part of our praise of Christ (vv. 9–11), where the power over the whole world is the distinct gift

---

17 See esp. the speech of *parrhesia* against Tyche in 2:9. 340e, which runs until 2:10. 340d, if not until the end of the discourse.
18 Plut., fort. Alex. 1:9. 331c (he 'bore them with him openly as symbolic representations, graven on his body, of virtue and manly courage'). Those 'signs' are also mentioned in 1:2. 327a, 2:9. 341a/b.
19 Plut., fort. Alex. 2:12. 343b.

of God, but also with the conclusion Paul wants to draw from these verses, namely in verse 13.

Admittedly such statements are quite rare here in Plutarch's declamations on virtue, whereas concerning the author of Philippians, they have to be considered as one of his basic apostolic convictions. But if we take the whole oeuvre of the Delphic priest into consideration, the picture becomes considerably more multifaceted.[20] Plutarch is convinced that the gods are 'dispensers of good' (ἀγαθῶν δοτῆρες)[21] above all else:

> (God) is our guide to all blessings, the father of everything honourable (ὡς πάντων μὲν ἡγεμὼν ἀγαθῶν πάντων δὲ πατὴρ καλῶν).[22]

In other words, for the philosopher, unlike for the apostle, there is no fundamental alternative between human self-activity and divine agency. In terms of theology, Plutarch may be considered to represent a basic synergistic position: Good comes about when the benevolent God and virtuous man cooperate. This position certainly allows the emphasis to be placed on God's activity. The fact that the primary role and honour are due to the gods corresponds precisely to Plutarch's personal religion, his piety.

In Philippians 2 we are faced with the much-disputed question of whether Christ receives his position of sovereignty in vv. 9–11 as a reward for his humility (formally comparable to Alexander's virtue) or as a mere gift (formally comparable to a gift from Tyche). I will come back to this point at the end of the essay.

---

20 See e.g. Valgiglio, *Divinità*, 26–30; Frazier, 'Göttlichkeit'; Roig Lanzillotta, 'Idea', 138–44; Hirsch-Luipold, 'Plutarch', 27–34 ('a theology of Plutarch'); Brenk, 'Plutarch's Monotheism'.
21 See esp. Plut., adv. Stoic. 14. 1065e, 32. 1075e.
22 Plut., non poss. 22. 1102d. Cf. 23. 1103c ('what comes from the gods is excellent as well; but its coming as a divine gift is itself a great source of pleasure and unbounded confidence and of a pride and joy that are like a gentle radiance illuminating the good').

2. Universal power

Let us now look at the second main feature concerning the figure of Alexander in Plutarch's declamations, i.e. the figure of the cosmocrator, the ruler of the world. Here we are confronted with some remarkable encomiastic statements belonging to a wider range of ancient traditions regarding Alexander, the outstanding paradigm of a ruler, especially in the Roman imperial age. In the following we shall focus on four points.

1. The portrait of the king as the unifier of the East and the West, of Greeks and barbarians, is a traditional one. In his discourses Plutarch oscillates between a more Hellenocentric view—with the barbarians reduced to objects in need of cultural refinement—and a view pointing to an integration and reconciliation of both cultures into a single universal society; here the Greek Plutarch possibly adopts a Roman element of political propaganda.[23] Alexander appears as a mediator:[24]

> But, as he believed that he came as a heaven-sent governor to all, and as a mediator for the whole world (ἀλλὰ κοινὸς ἥκειν θεόθεν ἁρμοστὴς καὶ διαλλακτὴς τῶν ὅλων νομίζων), those whom he could not persuade to unite with him, he conquered by force of arms, and he brought together into one body all men everywhere (εἰς ταὐτὸ συνενεγκὼν τὰ πανταχόθεν), uniting and mixing in one great loving-cup, as it were [...]. He bade them all consider as their fatherland the whole inhabited earth (πατρίδα μὲν τὴν οἰκουμένην προσέταξεν ἡγεῖσθαι πάντας), as their stronghold and protection his camp, as akin to them all good men, and as foreigners only the wicked (συγγενεῖς δὲ τοὺς ἀγαθούς, ἀλλοφύλους δὲ τοὺς πονηρούς).

The garments Alexander used to wear on certain occasions, a mixture of Macedonian and Persian style, especially illustrate this universal programme. We shall come back to this point later on. By the way, we can notice an amazing analogy with the deutero-Pauline conception of

---

23 See Asirvatham, 'Classicism'; Asirvatham, 'Alexander', 368–370; cf. also Balch, 'Origin', 498.
24 Plut., fort. Alex. 1:6. 329b/c. Cf. Badian, 'Alexander'.

the church as a universal synthesis of both Jews and Greeks mediated by Christ (Eph. 2:14–18; cf. Col. 1:20).

2. The characterisation of the Alexander Empire as the 'incarnation' of both the Stoic cosmopolis and the Platonic ideal state is also traditional.[25] This universal reign is governed by one logos and one common law.[26]

3. Alexander is portrayed as a delegate sent by the heavenly gods; he appears as a 'heaven-sent governor' and is called back by the gods somewhat too early.[27] Alexander is also depicted as a figure resembling Hercules and Bacchus:[28] 'I imitate Heracles, and emulate Perseus, and follow in the footsteps of Dionysus, the divine author and progenitor of my family.'

4. The virtues of Alexander as an ideal king are praised, in particular his magnanimity and his philanthropy (μεγαλοψυχία, φιλανθρωπία). We are here in full accordance with both the epideictic traditions and the prince's mirror-admonitions.[29] Alexander therefore even excels the Homeric heroes. As a ruler he rejects luxury and indulgence in favour of harmony, peace, and community.[30] Was he not charged with the duties of a king, he would fight for the simplicity and frugality personified by Diogenes.[31]

In one way or another we come across all these features in Philippians 2 as well. This is not by accident since Philippians 2 can be charac-

---

25 Plut., fort. Alex. 1:6. 329a/b (Zeno), 1:5. 328e (Plato). Plutarch's reference to the Stoic cosmopolis is not merely a rhetorical ornament (so Babut, *Plutarque*, 84–85; D'Angelo, *Plutarco. La Fortuna*, 26), since the reason-guided ideal city is a widely shared (utopian) conception in later Hellenism.
26 Plut., fort. Alex. 1:8. 330d (see below) and, just quoted, 2:5. 329c.
27 Again, Plut., fort. Alex. 1:8. 330d and 2:5. 329c. It seems that Plutarch does not owe this conception to his sources dealing with Alexander: See D'Angelo, *Plutarco. La Fortuna*, 206 ('Plut. è il solo a parlare della"missione divina" di cui Alex. si riteneva investito'). Georgi, 'Reflections', 30, overstates the case when he interprets Alexander's role in a decidedly soteriological way.
28 Plut., fort. Alex. 1:10. 332a.
29 See esp. Hadot, 'Fürstenspiegel'.
30 Plut., fort. Alex. 2:9. 330e.
31 Plut., fort. Alex. 1:10. 332a.

terised as a text revealing the 'archetype' of the one and only just and divine ruler that is Christ as the cosmocrator.

The first two points may be dealt with as one. In short, Philippians 2 can be interpreted as a text struggling primarily with the oneness of God and therefore displaying a kind of 'Christological monotheism' as indicated by the intentional use of Isaiah 45:23.[32] But at the same time all beings in heaven, earth, and the world of the dead are for their part united in their confession of Jesus Christ as the Lord. In the immediately preceding context Paul appeals to the Philippians for unity and solidarity (2:1–5), referring to the wide-spread rhetoric of homonoia (concordia).[33] Hellenistic Jews like Philo and Josephus emphasise the essential relation between the belief in One God and the unity of his believers. So at least the background of the praise of Christ in Philippians 2 allows us to make out a remarkable analogy to Plutarch's Alexander: Both 'heroes' are represented as unifiers of the whole world.

In the third point, Plutarch's Alexander and the pre-existent and incarnated Christ are so obviously linked with each other by the notion of the god-sent king so that we do not have to mention it in particular. And yet we have to admit that this conception is not a basic one for Plutarch, whereas among early Christians the belief in the divine origin of Jesus is definitely a fundamental conviction.

Finally and fourth, the attitude of the pre-existent Christ can be interpreted as a radical transformation of the 'prince's mirror' traditions. Obviously renouncing the pleasures of a high status, such as Christ in heaven did, comes close to what was expected from a good ruler and king.[34] Nevertheless the radical depiction of Christ's kenosis turns the whole ancient cultural system of values upside down, as

---

32 See my article: 'Monotheismus', 28–29.
33 See my article: 'Theologie'; furthermore Thraede, 'Homonoia'; Thériault, *Culte*.
34 Harrison, *Celebrity Circuit*, 243, has drawn particular attention to 'Plutarch's discussion of the acceptance or rejection of absolute power by rulers and the quality of rule that emerged from their decision', both as an analogy and as a contrast to Phil. 2:5–11.

shown by Christ's humiliation, self-enslavement and crucifixion.[35]

3. 'Not like a robber'

We are now well prepared to integrate all the mentioned aspects regarding power over the whole world as we now proceed to a comparison of Philippians 2 with its most famous counterpart in Plutarch's treatise:[36]

> For he (i.e. Alexander) did not overrun Asia like a robber nor was he minded to tear and rend it, as if it were booty and plunder bestowed by unexpected good fortune (οὐ γὰρ ληστρικῶς τὴν Ἀσίαν καταδραμὼν οὐδ' ὥσπερ ἅρπαγμα καὶ λάφυρον εὐτυχίας ἀνελπίστου σπαράξαι καὶ ἀνασύρασθαι διανοηθείς), after the manner in which Hannibal later descended upon Italy, or as earlier the Treres descended upon Ionia and the Scythians upon Media. But Alexander desired to render all upon earth subject to one law of reason and one form of government and to reveal all men as one people, and to this purpose he clothed himself (ἀλλ' ἑνὸς ὑπήκοα λόγου τὰ ἐπὶ γῆς καὶ μιᾶς πολιτείας, ἕνα δῆμον ἀνθρώπους ἅπαντας ἀποφῆναι βουλόμενος, οὕτως ἑαυτὸν ἐσχημάτιζεν). But if the deity that sent down Alexander's soul into this world of ours had not recalled him quickly, one law would govern all mankind and direct them to one rule of justice, as if it were the universal light (εἰ δὲ μὴ ταχέως

---

35 Cf. Harrison, *Celebrity Circuit*, 258-59; comparable with Paul's inversion of 'contemporary models of exemplary virtue' (p.343). Nevertheless, there are interfaces to ancient and especially Roman political models, which Harrison, *Imperial Authorities*, 176, has pointed out: On the one hand, a voluntary renunciation of power (as with Augustus), on the other hand, a public dishonour (as with Q. Fabius Maximus). Both models, however, do not play a role in any Alexander tradition, to my knowledge.
36 Plut., fort. Alex. 1:8. 330c/d. Babbitt's translation has been slightly modified. Especially at the end of the passage, it is advisable to follow—against the leading BSGRT-edition—the manuscript tradition (ἐπέβλεπε ... διωκεῖτο) and refrain from shifting the verbs along with a conjecture (ἐπέβλεπον); see Giangrande, 'Testo', 52-53; D'Angelo, *Plutarco. La Fortuna*, 217-18. The edition of Frazier/Froidefond, *Plutarque*, 123, does not even indicate the use of replacements respecting conjectures.

ὁ δεῦρο καταπέμψας τὴν Ἀλεξάνδρου ψυχὴν ἀνεκαλέσατο δαίμων, εἷς ἂν νόμος ἅπαντας ἀνθρώπους ἐπέβλεπε καὶ πρὸς ἓν δίκαιον ὡς πρὸς κοινὸν διῳκεῖτο φῶς). But as it is, that part of the world which has not looked upon Alexander has remained without sunlight.

The following points must be emphasised:

1. We encounter again the unification topic. Alexander unifies the world into a whole, ruled by a common nomos and logos.[37] This is an embodiment of the stoic cosmopolis. There is even a kind of an eschatological perspective in Plutarch's text: Due to the fact that Alexander was called back so early, several parts of the earth still wait for the benefits of his conquest.[38] Likewise, Philippians 2:10–11 can easily be interpreted in terms of eschatology: The Kyrios-confession of every creature of heaven, earth and underworld is not realised in the present age yet, but refers to the world to come.[39]

2. In Plutarch as well as in Paul we are faced with the conception of a being sent from above and returning there. While De Fortuna remains almost entirely silent in this regard, the Vita Alexandri offers the popular traditions of Alexander's sonship of God (Zeus; Ammon). However, Plutarch is conspicuously reticent here as well.[40] Furthermore our Greek intellectual has a remarkably critical attitude towards self-deification and the ruler-cult in general, not only in these early declamations, but also in other writings.[41]

3. The micro contexts are instructive. Plutarch gives an explanation why Alexander wears his Macedonian-Persian garments (as explic-

---

37 About Alexander as Lawgiver see Koulakiotis, 'Lawgivers', 411–12.
38 On the projection of Alexander's power to the west compare Gilley, *Damn*, 278-79.
39 See e.g. Bockmuehl, *Philippians*, 146 ('One day [...] that acknowledgement of Christ's lordship will be offered by all creatures everywhere. It is in keeping with the eschatology both of Deutero-Isaiah and of the NT').
40 See esp. Plut., Alex. 28:6; cf. Hamilton, *Plutarch*, lxii, 69–70, 73–75.
41 Plut., fort. Alex. 2:5. 338a; cf. Scott, 'Plutarch'.

itly mentioned in the beginning of the section, 329f):[42] Alexander's Graeco-oriental dress is judged very differently in the ancient sources; here in our declamation it symbolises the ecumenical character of his reign. The change of clothes (μετασχηματισμός) can be called a political-symbolic accommodation of the world ruler to the ruled peoples.[43]

The theme of clothing provides an inviting bridge to Philippians 2.[44] Paul's narrative works with elements of the metamorphosis genre[45]—especially the depiction of a transfiguration from a godlike being into a human being with an extremely low status (and, implicitly, vice versa: again to an exalted being, even with a superior position of dominion). The topic of metamorphosis embraces the metaphoric of garments and their change, thus impressively demonstrating the change of status. Jesus changes his μορφαί like clothes—one feels reminded of the Gnostic Hymn of the Pearl referring to the garments of light.[46]

It is noticeable that there is another small story in our declamation that is specifically close to Christ's exaltation in Philippians 2:9: A simple gardener is made king by Alexander. The change of status is symbolised by a change of clothes: Abdalonymus exchanges his simple dress for the royal robe.[47] Here, however, we are faced with the type of status given by Tyche, which is just different from that which Alexander laboriously acquires.

4. We have to focus on 'robbery'. Since the days of Wettstein this appeared to be one of the most striking parallels between the texts of Plutarch and Paul. Obviously Plutarch defends his philosophical

---

42   The translations are sometimes too vague at this point: ἑαυτὸν ἐσχημάτιζεν is to be referred specifically to Alexander's clothing and not (only) to a general attitude or conduct. So in my view the translation of D'Angelo is appropriate, 117 ('abbigliò in questo modo'); less precise are Babbitt, 405 ('he made himself conform'); Frazier/Froidefond, 123 ('il conformait son personnage'; cf. 221 n.5: 'les calculs qui auraient motivé tous les actes d' Alexandre'); Cecchet, 617 ('conformò le proprie scelte').
43   The version in the biography (45:1–4) is much more complex and deliberately ambivalent, see Whitmarsh, 'Hellenism', 191.
44   Cf. Wojtkowiak, *Christologie*, 88–89.
45   See Holloway, *Philippians*, 48–52, 115–16, and Vollenweider, 'Metamorphose'.
46   Acts Thom. 109–13 (Elliott, *Apocryphal NT*, 488–91).
47   Plut., fort. Alex. 2:8. 340c–e. Cf. Diod. Sic., hist. 17:47:3–6; Curt., Alex. 4:1:22.

king against heavy attacks originating in a strongly negative trajectory within the ancient traditions about Alexander. The Macedonian king was depicted as a tyrant both brutal with his subordinates and lacking in self-control. His main vices were supposed to be alcoholism, wrath, pride, thirst for glory, susceptibility to flattery, etc. The effusive praise of Alexander, which is entirely in keeping with panegyric rhetoric, forms an antithesis to the negative Alexander topic, as it were to the Alexander rebuke. One of the important negative topoi is that of the robber.[48] This is best illustrated by an apophthegm transmitted by Augustine:[49]

> It was a pertinent and true answer which was made to Alexander the Great by a pirate whom he had seized. When the king asked him what he meant by infesting the sea, the pirate defiantly replied: 'The same as you do when you infest the whole world; but because I do it with a little ship I am called a robber, and because you do it with a great fleet, you are an emperor.

The story gains profile against a broad background of political theory: empires and their rulers are disqualified as predators.[50] With such an apophthegm Augustine illustrates his thesis: 'Justice removed, then, what are kingdoms but great bands of robbers (magna latrocinia)?'

Plutarch's Alexander offers a counter-image to the type of despot as a political brigand.

Turning now to Philippians 2, we are confronted with the enigmatic phrase οὐχ ἁρπαγμὸν ἡγήσατο. An overwhelming majority

---

48 See e.g. Curt., Alex. 7:8:19; Seneca, ben. 1:13:3 (*latro gentiumque vastator*); Lucan, bell. 10:21 (*felix praedo*); cf. Hoffmann, *Porträt*, 18, 54–55, 74–75, 110; Koulakiotis, *Genese*, 33, 113; Moore, *Companion*, 45, 75, 307, 488. Negative judgements are found especially in the Romans Seneca and Lucan; see Fears, 'View'; Lassandro, 'Figura'.

49 Augustine, civ. 4:4 (transl. R.W. Dyson). Augustine probably refers to Cicero, who in turn echoes the philosopher Carneades, see Cic., rep. 3:24 ('for when he was asked what wickedness drove him to harass the sea with his one pirate galley, he replied: "The same wickedness that drives you to harass the whole world."'); cf. La Penna, 'Bandito'.

50 For more material see Vollenweider, 'Raub', 277–78.

of modern exegetes take it as an idiom with the meaning 'something to seize upon' (ἁρπαγμός being a synonym of ἅρπαγμα).⁵¹ This distinctive resolution of a notorious crux interpretum, however, faces four serious problems: 1. The idiom, if it exists at all, is attested only from the fourth century AD onwards—the main witness, Heliodorus of Emesa, most probably belongs to this period.⁵² 2. As a master of elaborate narrative technique and sophisticated style, the latter uses the idiom specifically where sex and crime are staged.⁵³ 3.This particular denotation, conversely, suggests that Paul, himself an idiosyncratic but talented stylist, would not use it for his description of the divine, delivered in solemn epideictic rhetoric. 4. In early Jewish as well as early Christian literature (to use Walter Bauer's term: in 'our literature'),⁵⁴ the word family ἁρπαγ- is almost entirely determined by negative semantics.

Therefore, Plutarch's declamation, working with the common political semantics of robbery, offers a much better exegetical alternative to the interpretation of Philippians 2:6a as an idiom. This is not without irony: Early in the twentieth century, our Plutarchean text, of all things, was the main driver for the hypothesis of an idiom and served as its crown witness.⁵⁵ In the meantime, this hypothesis has completely detached itself from the Plutarchean passage (that does not contain the double accusative construction, constitutive of the postulated idiom).⁵⁶ In turn, Plutarch offers us today a valid exegetical and religious-historical alternative to the claimed idiom.

Now, neither Plutarch's Alexander nor Paul's Christ intended to act as robbers. However, the object of the robbery is different. Alexander refused to rob other peoples' and nations' property, whereas the case of Christ is notoriously more intricate. According to an old exegetical hypothesis the pre-existent Christ refused to 'rob' a godlike

---

51 See the cloud of witnesses in: Martin, 'ἁρπαγμός', 176 n.3.
52 See the hints in: Morgan, 'Heliodoros', 417–21; Whitmarsh, 'Hellenism at the Edge', 111.
53 Heliodorus, Aeth. 7:11:7, 7:20:2; cf. 8:7:1.
54 Bauer, 'Introduction', xiv.
55 Jaeger, 'Studie', 550–51.
56 Hoover, 'Harpagmos'; Martin, 'ἁρπαγμός'.

position. If such is the reference of 'robbing' the parallel between Plutarch's Alexander and Paul's Christ seems relatively superficial. However, we have again to consider the whole range of ancient traditions about Alexander, in particular the description of him as a man transgressing all human limitations and boundaries. Admittedly the declamations of Plutarch do not explicitly mention this feature. But many other traditions deal with this subject. In Alexander's career one of the most disputed points is his attitude towards self-deification.[57] Both his expedition to the oracle of Ammon in the Egyptian desert and the troubles related to his call for proskynesis in Bactria were interpreted negatively, i.e. as an expression of hubris and arrogance. So there are at least some signs for portraying Alexander as usurper of divine honours. This is explicitly the case in a record of Curtius Rufus.[58] Plutarch himself does not mention the subject of self-deification in his declamations. However, in the biography of Alexander, he can no longer avoid this matter, but tries to play it down.[59]

5. In short: Both Paul and Plutarch take a stand against a type of ruler who aspires only to the exploitation of high status (existing or aspired to). Both argue in each case for the abandonment of, or at least a cautious handling of, such a position. Plutarch's Alexander is caught up in a harsh fight against the attacks and temptations of Tyche and suffers heavy and almost deadly hardships. Paul's Christ follows the path of humility and even suffers crucifixion and death.

4. Conclusion

We have tried to draw some parallels between two early imperial portraits of an excellent ruler, painted by Plutarch and Paul. Of course, these portraits are embedded in very different literary, social, cultural, and religious constellations. Nevertheless, both have a common back-

---

57 See esp. Badian, 'Deification'.
58 Curt., Alex. 8:5:5: 'He began to consider how he might usurp divine honours (*quonam modo caelestes honores usurparet coepit agitare*). He wished, not only to be called, but to be believed to be the son of Jupiter.'
59 See above nn.40 and 41.

ground, namely the experience of the Roman Empire as a global realisation of universal power.[60]

1. In both Plutarch and Paul, the theme of universal kingship predominates, and the epideictic form fits this theme exactly.

2. Both Alexander and Christ are portrayed as paradigms of royal virtues. Both are contrasted with the negative figure of the usurper. In Plutarch's case, the antagonist seems to be a selfish tyrant; in the case of Philippians, a king full of hubris (cf. Isa. 14; Ezek. 28).

3. Several connotations are linked with the royal figure, namely universal unification and a mission carried out from above. Whereas the latter point seems to be marginal in Plutarch, it is outlined as a paradoxical and disturbing change of status in Philippians 2.

4. The difference in the assessment of the relationship between human and divine agency is remarkable. Plutarch puts all the emphasis on the king's own activity; Alexander owes his status not to Tyche but to his virtuous performance. But if one takes into account the comprehensive literary context, the entire oeuvre of Plutarch, a synergistic model suggests itself: a virtuous and pious life owes itself to the cooperation of God and man.

In Philippians 2:5–11 we have left open the question of whether Jesus' exaltation is to be understood as a reward for his obedience or as a mere gift. The former is suggested by the inferential conjunction διό and the sapiential sayings-tradition (Matt. 23:12/Luke 14:11, 18:14), the latter by the emphasised verb ἐχαρίσατο and by the subsequent application (Phil. 2:13). Again, the broad literary context, the Pauline collection of letters, indicates a distinctive direction: In contrast to Plutarch's pious synergism, Paul develops a monergistic theory of God's efficacy in saving believers through Christ's cross and resurrection (Rom. 1:16–17; 1 Cor. 1:18).[61] As a phenomenon of resonance, all the

---

60 See esp. Spencer, *Alexander*, about 'Alexander as an archetype for power and imperialism in the Roman world' (xv; cf. 165–203).
61 In Josephus' *interpretatio graeca* of the Jewish religious groups, Paul comes close to the Essene doctrine (Ant. 13:171, 18:18).

believers' conduct is a gift from God (cf. 1 Cor. 4:7; Rom. 9:16). Christology is also placed under a theocentric premise; Paul's praise of Christ ends, therefore, with the praise of God (Phil. 2:11d).

Samuel Vollenweider
University of Zurich (Emeritus)

Bibliography

Asirvatham, S. R.   'Classicism and Romanitas in Plutarch's *De Alexandri fortuna aut virtute*', *AJP* 126 (2005), 107–125.

Asirvatham, S. R.   'Plutarch's Alexander', in K. R. Moore (ed.), *Brill's Companion to the Reception of Alexander the Great* (Leiden: Brill, 2018), 355–376.

Babbitt, F. C. (ed.)   Plutarch. *Moralia* (LCL, vol. 4; Cambridge, MA: Harvard University Press / London: Heinemann, 1936; repr. 1962).

Babut, D.   *Plutarque et le stoicisme* (Paris: Presses Univ. de France, 1969).

Badian, E.   'Alexander the Great and the Unity of Mankind', in: *Collected Papers on Alexander the Great* (London: Routledge, 2012), 1–19.

Badian, E.   'The Deification of Alexander the Great', in *Collected Papers on Alexander the Great* (London: Routledge, 2012), 244–81.

Balch, D. L.   'The Cultural Origin of "Receiving All Nations" in Luke-Acts: Alexander the Great or Roman Social Policy?', in J. T. Fitzgerald, et al. (eds.), *Early Christianity and Classical Culture: Comparative Studies in Honor of Abraham J. Malherbe* (NovTSupp 90; Leiden: Brill, 2003), 483–500.

Bauer, W.   'An Introduction to the Lexicon of the Greek New Testament', in BDAG, xiii–xxix.

Bockmuehl, M.   *The Epistle to the Philippians* (BNTC; London: A & C Black, 1997).

Brenk, F.E.   'Plutarch's Monotheism and the New Testament', in: R. Hirsch-Luipold (ed.), *Plutarch and the New Testament in Their Religio-Philosophical Contexts. Bridging Discourses in the World of the Early Roman Empire* (Brill's Plutarch Studies 9; Leiden: Brill, 2022), 66–83.

Cammarota M. R.   'Il De Alexandri Magni fortuna aut virtute come espressione retorica: il panegirico', in I. Gallo (ed.), *Ricerche plutarchee* (Napoli: Università degli Studi di Salerno, 1992), 105–124.

Cammarota M. R.   'La tradizione retorica in tre declamazioni di Plutarco: De Alexandri Magni fortuna aut virtute, De fortuna Romanorum, De Gloria Atheniensium', in L. van der Stockt

	(ed.), *Rhetorical Theory and Praxis in Plutarch* (Louvain-Namur: Peeters, 2000), 69–86.
Cammarota, M. R. (ed.)	*Plutarco. La fortuna o la virtú di Alessandro Magno. Orazione 2* (Corpus Plutarchi moralium 30; Napoli: M. D'Auria, 1998).
Cecchet, L.	'La fortuna o la virtù di Alessandro', in E. Lelli and G. Pisani (eds.), *Plutarco. Tutti i Moralia* (Firenze: Giunti, 2017), 610–643, 2622–26.
D'Angelo, A. (ed.)	*Plutarco. La fortuna o la virtú di Alessandro Magno. Orazione 1* (Corpus Plutarchi moralium 29; Napoli: M. D'Auria, 1998).
Eckholdt, J.-F.	*Von göttlicher Vorsehung bis Zufall: "Tyche" im Werk des Plutarch von Chaironeia* (Prismata 22; Berlin: Lang, 2019).
Ehrhardt, A. A. T.	'Jesus Christ and Alexander the Great', *JThS* 46 (1945), 45–51; reprint in: A. A. T. Ehrhardt, *The Framework of the New Testament Stories* (Manchester: Manchester University Press, 1964), 37–43. German version: 'Ein antikes Herrscherideal. Phil. 2,5–11', *EvTh* 8 (1948), 101–10; 'Nochmals: Ein antikes Herrscherideal', *EvTh* 8 (1948) 569–72.
Ehrhardt, A. A. T.	*Politische Metaphysik von Solon bis Augustin* (3 vols. Tübingen: Mohr Siebeck, 1959–1969).
Elliott, J. K. (ed.)	*The Apocryphal New Testament. A Collection of Apocryphal Christian Literature in an English Translation* (Oxford: Oxford University Press, 1993, 2005).
Fears, J. R.	'The Stoic View of the Career and Character of Alexander the Great', *Philologus* 118 (1974), 113–130.
Frazier, F. and C. Froidefond (eds.)	*Plutarque. Oeuvres morales* (vol. 5.1; Budé ; Paris: Belles Lettres, 1990).
Frazier, F.	'Göttlichkeit und Glaube. Persönliche Gottesbeziehung im Spätwerk Plutarchs', in R. Hirsch-Luipold (ed.), *Gott und die Götter bei Plutarch* (RVV 54; Berlin: de Gruyter, 2011), 112–137.
Georgi, D.	'Reflections of a New Testament Scholar on Plutarch's Tractates *De Alexandri Magni fortuna aut virtute*', in B. A. Pearson et al. (eds.), *The Future of Early Christianity: Essays in Honor of Helmut Koester* (Minneapolis, MN: Fortress, 1991), 20–34.

Giangrade, G.	'Testo e lingua nel De Alexandri Fortuna auf Virtute plutarcheo', in I. Gallo (ed.), *Ricerche plutarchee* (Napoli: : Università degli Studi di Salerno, 1992), 39–84.
Gilley, D. L.	'Damn with Faint Praise. A Historical Commentary on Plutarch's On The Fortune or Virtue of Alexander The Great' (Ph.D. Diss. University of Missouri, 2009).
Hadot, P.	'Fürstenspiegel', *RAC* 8 (1972), 555–632.
Hamilton, J. R.	*Plutarch. Alexander. A Commentary* (Oxford: Oxford University Press, 1969).
Harrison, J. R.	*Paul and the Ancient Celebrity Circuit: The Cross and Moral Transformation* (WUNT 430; Tübingen: Mohr Siebeck, 2019).
Harrison, J. R.	*Paul and the Imperial Authorities at Thessalonica and Rome: A Study in the Conflict of Ideology* (WUNT 273; Tübingen: Mohr Siebeck, 2011).
Hirsch-Luipold, R.	'Plutarch and the New Testament. History, Challenges and Perspectives', in: R. Hirsch-Luipold (ed.), *Plutarch and the New Testament in Their Religio-Philosophical Contexts. Bridging Discourses in the World of the Early Roman Empire* (Brill's Plutarch Studies 9; Leiden: Brill, 2022), 11–48.
Hoffmann, W.	*Das literarische Porträt Alexanders des Grossen im griechischen und römischen Altertum* (Leipzig: Quelle & Meyer, 1907).
Holloway, P.	*Philippians* (Hermeneia; Minneapolis: Fortress, 2017).
Hoover, R. W.	'The Harpagmos Enigma: A Philological Solution', *HTR* 64 (1971), 95–119.
Jaeger, W. W.	'Eine stilgeschichtliche Studie zum Philipperbrief', *Hermes* 50 (1915), 537–53.
Koulakiotis, E.	*Genese und Metamorphosen des Alexandermythos im Spiegel der griechischen nichthistoriographischen Überlieferung bis zum 3. Jh. n. Chr.* (Xenia 47; Konstanz: Universitätsverlag, 2006).
Koulakiotis, E.	'Greek Lawgivers in Plutarch: A comparison Between the Biographical Lycurgus and the Rhetorical Alexander', in A. G. Nikolaidis (ed.), *The Unity of Plutarch's Work: Moralia Themes in the Lives, Features of the Lives in the Moralia* (Millennium Studies 19; Berlin: de Gruyter, 2008), 403–422.

La Penna, A.	'Il bandito e il re', *Maia* 31 (1979), 29–31.
Lassandro, D.	'La figura di Alessandro Magno nell'opera di Seneca', in M. Sordi, (ed.), *Alessandro Magno tra storia e mito* (Milano: Jaca Book), 155–168.
Martin, M. W.	'ἁρπαγμός Revisited: A Philological Reexamination of the New Testament's "Most Difficult Word"', *JBL* 135 (2016), 175–194.
Moore, K. R. (ed.)	*Brill's Companion to the Reception of Alexander the Great* (Leiden: Brill, 2018).
Morgan, J. R.	'Heliodoros', in G. Schmeling (ed.), *The Novel in the Ancient World* (Mnemosyne Supp 159; Leiden: Brill, 1996), 417–56.
Muccioli, F.	'In Search of the Many Images of Alexander at Chaeronea. Historical and Literary Traditions in Plutarch's Corpus', in K. Nawotka et al. (eds.), *The Historiography of Alexander the Great* (Classica et Orientalia 20; Wiesbaden: Harrassowitz, 2018), 119–129.
Roig Lanzillotta, L.	'Plutarch's Idea of God in the Religious and Philosophical Context of Late Antiquity', in L. Roig Lanzillotta and I. Muñoz Gallarte (eds.), *Plutarch in the Religious and Philosophical Discourse of Late Antiquity* (AMMTC 14; Leiden: Brill, 2012), 137–150.
Schröder, S.	'Zu Plutarchs Alexanderreden', *MH* 48 (1991), 151–57.
Scott, K.	'Plutarch and the Ruler Cult', *TAPA* 60 (1929), 117–135.
Spencer, D.	*The Roman Alexander: Reading a Cultural Myth* (Exeter: Exeter University Press, 2003).
Thériault, G. (ed.)	*Le Culte d'Homonoia dans les cités grecques* (Série Épigraphique et Historique 3; Lyon: Maison de l'Orient Méditerranéen and Quebec: Éditions du Sphinx, 1996).
Thraede, K.	'Homonoia (Eintracht)', *RAC* 16 (1994), 176–289.
Valgiglio, E.	*Divinità e religione in Plutarco* (Genova: Compagnia dei Librai, 1988).
Vollenweider, S.	'Der "Raub" der Gottgleichheit. Ein religionsgeschichtlicher Vorschlag zu Phil 2,6–11)', in S. Vollenweider, *Horizonte neutestamentlicher Christologie* (WUNT 144; Tübingen: Mohr Siebeck, 2002), 263–284.

Vollenweider, S.	'Die Metamorphose des Gottessohns. Zum epiphanialen Motivfeld in Phil 2,6–8', in S. Vollenweider, *Horizonte neutestamentlicher Christologie* (WUNT 144; Tübingen: Mohr Siebeck, 2002), 285–306.
Vollenweider, S.	'Hymnus, Enkomion oder Psalm? Schattengefechte in der neutestamentlichen Wissenschaft', in S. Vollenweider, *Antike und Urchristentum. Studien zur neutestamentlichen Theologie in ihren Kontexten und Rezeptionen* (WUNT 436; Tübingen: Mohr Siebeck, 2020), 275–297.
Vollenweider, S.	'Politische Theologie im Philipperbrief?', in S. Vollenweider, *Antike und Urchristentum. Studien zur neutestamentlichen Theologie in ihren Kontexten und Rezeptionen* (WUNT 436; Tübingen: Mohr Siebeck, 2020), 227–238.
Vollenweider, S.	'Vom israelitischen zum christologischen Monotheismus. Überlegungen zum Verhältnis zwischen dem Glauben an den einen Gott und dem Glauben an Jesus Christus', in S. Vollenweider, *Antike und Urchristentum. Studien zur neutestamentlichen Theologie in ihren Kontexten und Rezeptionen* (WUNT 436; Tübingen: Mohr Siebeck, 2020), 21–31.
Wettstein, J. J. (ed.)	*Novum Testamentum Graecum* (2 vols. Amsterdam 1751/52; repr. Graz: Akademische Druck- u. Verlagsanstalt, 1962).
Whitmarsh, T.	'Alexander's Hellenism and Plutarch's Textualism', *ClQ* 52 (2002), 174–192.
Whitmarsh, T.	'Hellenism at the Edge: Heliodorus', in T. Whitmarsh (ed.), *Narrative and Identity in the Ancient Greek Novel: Returning Romance* (Greek Culture in the Roman World; Cambridge: CUP, 2011), 108–35.
Wojtkowiak, H.	*Christologie und Ethik im Philipperbrief* (FRLANT 243; Göttingen: Vandenhoeck & Ruprecht, 2012).
Wyttenbach, D. (Hg.)	Index graecitatis, in *Plutarchi Chaeronensis Moralia, id est opera, exceptis vitis, reliqua*. 8 vols. (Oxford: Typogr. acad., vol. 8: 1795–1830).
Ziegler, K.	'Plutarchos 2', *PW* 21.1 (1951), 636–962.

Become Fellow-Imitators Together with Me (Phil 3:17)
Embodying Christ in the Face of Enemies of the Cross

Kathy Ehrensperger

Abstract

With relevance to whether Paul faced a Jewish problem at Philippi, this essay re-examines Paul's vocabulary of 'dogs' and 'evil workers', as well as the word κατατομή (3:2), often taken as a sharp contrast to περιτομή (3:3). The derogatory term 'dogs' could refer to idolators, perhaps associated with Diana. 'Evil workers' could refer to those involved in local cults, perhaps supportive of Roman power. The word κατατομή can refer to an inscription, perhaps the local carvings associated with Diana? In contrast to local idolators, the Christ-followers now join the περιτομή, alongside the Jews, as worshippers of the one true God. Rather than being oriented to the values of those around them, they are oriented by the values of the cross.

Paul's appeal to the Philippians to imitate him and others (3:17) functions to counter-balance people he labels as 'enemies of the cross' (3:18). In recent interpretations the Roman-dominated[1] and in

---

1 James R. Harrison emphasised in an exemplary way the importance of in depth understanding not only of Roman elite culture but especially of Roman everyday life as is evident particularly in material culture for understanding Paul. I am grateful to contribute this piece in honour of a great colleague and fellow traveller! As far as Philippi was concerned, he noted that the Roman dominance was prevalent mainly at the public level of the colony and does certainly not mean to ignore the presence of the Greek and Thracian population in the colony and surrounding rural areas. For details see his excellent chapter 'Excavating the Urban', 1–62. Also Wojtkowiak, *Christologie*, 51–63.

terms of cult, the pagan context of the Philippian Christ-following group has been highlighted, thus acknowledging that little literary or archaeological evidence of a Jewish presence in Philippi in the first century has been found.[2] Nevertheless, Philippians 3:2–11 seems to indicate that there was a Jewish problem in Philippi or at least a problem with the perception of the value of Jewish credentials, including a potential risk of Judaising influences.[3] Combined with Paul's self-references pertaining to the law, the occurrence of the term κατατομή (3:2) is taken as a clear indication that Paul sets up a dichotomy to περιτομή (3:3).[4] This identification of a Jewish problem, or Judaising opponents, despite the predominantly non-Jewish context of Philippians is puzzling. In this paper I will explore the function of Philippians 3:2–11 as part of chapter 3, in particular in relation to vv. 17–18 in the wider context of the letter and propose an alternative to a Jewish or potentially Jewish related problem in Philippi.

Aspects of the Reception History

The emphasis in interpretations since 1945 has been on identifying the opponents behind the conflict which is addressed in Philippians 3. Thus, it is taken for granted that in this chapter there is evidence of a conflict or of a potential conflict in the Christ-following group in Philippi. Since this appears to be out of tune with other parts of the canonical letter, partition theories have been proposed with chapter 3 in particular being assigned to a different letter.[5] Irrespective of partition theories, different proposals for identifying opposition have been made. In some approaches three different opposition positions are identified, in others there are two, and an increasing number of interpreters identify one oppositional position only. Thus, Lohmeyer

---

2   Pilhofer, *Philippi I*, 232–34. Only an inscription dating from the 3rd to 4th century mentions a synagogue.
3   See discussion in Woytkowiak, *Christologie*, 35–38.
4   E.g. John Reuman who states that 'The key term for understanding the nature of the enemies in Phil 3 is "circumcision" (v.3) and its parody term in v 2 "*the incision*"...' (*Philippians*, 472). Also Betz, *Studies*, 52.
5   Cf. Standhartinger, *Der Philipperbrief*, 14–23.

considers vv. 2–11 as formulated against Jewish agitators who are the initiators of persecutions in Philippi, with vv. 12–16 addressing internal risks of overstating the value of martyrdom. The 'enemies of the cross' (v. 18) are identified as former members of the Christ-movement who had left the group due to experiences of persecution.[6] Betz presents a variation to this theory, identifying the 'enemies of the cross' as other Christian communities which had developed a different lifestyle. In Betz's view, earlier differences had turned to bitter enmity towards the cross of Christ.[7]

Even where it is noted that there is actually little internal or external evidence for a Jewish presence in Philippi, or in the group of Christ-followers, it is taken for granted that Paul argues against opponents who promote Jewish practices.[8] Mikael Tellbe, for instance, argued that despite the fact that Paul does not 'explicitly reveal the identity of the agitators, it is most likely that they were travelling Jewish missionaries, that is, Judaizers'.[9] The reasons provided for this identification are based on the assumption that the labels in 3:2 (τοὺς κύνας (dogs), τοὺς κακοὺς ἐργάτας (evil workers), and τὴν κατατομήν (incision), are all 'inversions of Jewish boasts',[10] and the reference to κατατομή in particular is seen as 'a blatantly sarcastic wordplay on the Jewish practice of circumcision'.[11] The following positive affirmation of περιτομή now with reference to Christ-followers is seen as confirmation that κατατομή is Paul's perception of circumcision, thereby asserting that they 'do not need this Jewish form of circumcision that amounts to mutilation'.[12]

Despite more careful formulations that 'the references to κατατομή in 3:2 refer to no one in particular'[13] and that they are merely meant to caution the Philippians of a potential rather than an actual danger, this

---

6   Lohmeyer, *Der Brief an die Philipper*, 122–54.
7   Betz, *Studies*, 63.
8   Cf. e.g. Ascough, *Paul's Macedonian Associations*, 201–04.
9   Tellbe, 'Sociological Factors', 100.
10 Telbe, 'Sociological Factors', 98.
11 Heil, *Let Us Rejoice*, 118.
12 Heil, *Let Us Rejoice*, 119.
13 Lamoureaux, *Ritual*, 121.

vague reference to a potential risk is restricted to the actual situation in Philippi. Despite this being considered a general warning, these potential (rather than actual) opponents are identified as Judaisers, in some cases based on supposed past experience of Paul particularly in Galatia.[14] Thus, although it is being acknowledged (by scholars like Osiek, Lamoureaux, and others), that actual opponents cannot be identified in Philippi, those who potentially might cause problems in the future are clearly considered to be Jews or Christ-followers with a Judaising agenda.[15] Those so clearly identified in v. 2 are seen as the same people later labelled as 'enemies of the cross', rendering Jewish identity diametrically opposed to an important emphasis in Paul's understanding of the Christ-event.[16] If those labelled in v. 2 are not seen as identical with 'the enemies of the cross' the problem of more than one opposing group emerges, which leads to the question of how such a multitude of opposition could occur within such a short time and limited space. These attempts at identifying the problem or the opponents in Chapter 3 remain unsatisfactory, irrespective of partition theories.

In my view it is hardly credible to think of two or more problematic groups in Philippi. Those labelled dogs, evil workers, and mutilation/incision in v. 2, and those labelled enemies of the cross, most likely are not different people but different labels for the same group of people.

Based on this presupposition it is necessary to consider the first three labels before proceeding to the last. Interpretations which see Jewish opponents or agitators as the target of vv. 2–3 see 'dogs' and 'mutilation/incision' in particular as mutually explanatory, with 'dogs' being an inversion of a derogatory term used by Jews at the time for non-Jews/pagans, and 'mutilation/incision' as providing not only a *paranomasia*, but also carrying Paul's negative valuation of circumcision. Hence the two interpretations are seen as mutually supporting the proposed perception of Jewish opponents or agitators.

Mark Nanos has proposed a reading, taking the pagan context of

---

14 Cf. e.g. Vollenweider, 'Politische Theologie', 460.
15 Thus, e.g Hooker, 'Philippians', 377–95; Bockmuehl, *Philippians*, 232.
16 Vollenweider argues for a double-reference here, with Paul possibly having in view both, Jewish as well as Roman aspects, 'Politische Theologie', 466.

Philippians generally acknowledged for the letter as the basic presupposition also for Chapter 3.[17] Changing the perspective and hermeneutical presuppositions in tune with what is presupposed with other parts of the letter is a convincing step. Why should different hermeneutical parameters guide the reading of this chapter compared with others? If it is recognised that the polytheistic/pagan context is decisive in Philippians, it seems rather arbitrary to postulate a different scenario just for Chapter 3. The mere presence of the terms κατατομή and περιτομή, rather than leading to envisaging a Judaising scenario, should be read guided by the same hermeneutical presuppositions as the other parts of the letter. Even if this is a composite letter, the context of these letters most likely would not be different, which means that the pagan environment would still be decisive for interpretation. Having already argued for one target group in this chapter rather than two or more, it is necessary to interpret v. 17 (the enemies of the cross) in light of the labels used in v. 2.

The Dogs

That 'dogs' is not a reversal of a Jewish derogatory term for non-Jews now applied to Jewish opponents has convincingly been demonstrated by Mark Nanos.[18] He has provided extended evidence that 'dogs' is not a specific term used by Jews but a general derogatory term used by Romans, Greeks, and Jews alike. Nevertheless, specific connotations may resonate with each particular use of the term. The cultural codes the term carries may vary according to the respective cultural context in which it is used.[19] Thus it is at times used by Jews for non-Jews, but it is far from being the standard Jewish way of labelling these. If it is presupposed that Paul argues from within a Jewish perception of the world, then the question concerning the range of meaning of 'dogs' in this perspective arises afresh. If this is not a reversal of a meaning (for which there is no evidence in the first place) but a rather general

---

17 Nanos, 'Paul's Polemic ', 142-91.
18 Nanos, 'Paul's Reversal', 448-82.
19 See Ehrensperger, *Paul*, esp. 59-62.

straightforward negative label, some more specific aspects come into view: there are some rabbinical traditions which indicate that idolatry is referred to by the name of a dog.[20] Dogs appear metaphorically as enemies and oppressors in the Psalms (22:17; 22:21; 59:15; cf. also Jer. 15:3), a use also found in 1 Enoch where dogs are mentioned among those wild animals that threaten and oppress the sheep, that is, Israel (1 Enoch 89:42–49; 90:4).[21] Philo uses dogs with reference to detestable behavior (*Contempl.* 40), with reference to oppressors (*Spec.* 89–91), and in relation to idolatry (*Leg.* 139). These few examples indicate that an argument for a Jewish use of the term as to some extent distinct from a non-Jewish use can be made. 'Dogs' can indicate oppression or idolatry (or a combination of both), but there is no evidence that 'dogs' was a general derogatory label for non-Jews as the neutral uses of the term prevail.

However, Paul certainly does not exchange pleasantries in 3:2, and the Philippians are cautioned to watch out for those labelled 'dogs' here. There is no reason or indication in the text not to consider these to be locals in Philippi, people the addressees know, rather than any group from outside which may constitute a threat now or in the future. In accordance with Jewish uses of this label, and taking the local context into account, 'dogs' could refer to those who dominate the colony at the time, that is, the Roman elite which had taken over control over the public sphere and land since the establishing of the *Colonia Victrix Philippensium* by Antonius in 42 B.C.E. and after the latter's defeat by Octavian of its refoundation as *Colonia Iulia Augusta Philippensis* in 31 B.C.E.[22] More specifically, it cannot be ruled out that the cult of Diana might be in view, who as a hunter was accompanied by dogs, or the cult of Hekate, to whom dogs were offered. The rock carvings which have been found in the hills right behind Philippi which depict Diana/Artemis/Bendis with dogs supports such a trajectory of interpretation.[23]

---

20 Schwartz, 'Dogs', 273.
21 On the symbolism of the Animal Apocalypse, see my 'The Pauline Ἐκκλησίαι', 183–216.
22 On the Roman dominance see Oakes, 'The Economic Situation', 65–71.
23 For details see Nanos, 'Paul's Polemic', 160–65.

As noted, the label 'dog' in Jewish references can imply either oppression or idolatry or possibly both combined, since those under whose rule the Jewish people lived over the centuries worshipped numerous deities, and thus in Jewish eyes were idolators, or as Paul might label them elsewhere ἐξ ἐθνῶν ἁμαρτωλοί. This perception might indicate in what direction the subsequent labels could be understood.

Evil Workers

This is the label which has left interpreters puzzled the most.[24] The term seems to generally indicate some negatively depicted activities on the parts of those so labelled, and evidently the addressees should avoid such. If the hermeneutical presuppositions direct the interpreter to presumed Judaisers, solutions like 'wandering missionaries' who are or might in the future try to influence the Philippians are being suggested. If they are to be found in Philippi, their identity is mostly derived from the identity of the 'dogs' and the 'mutilation' combined, hence the label 'evil' is seen as confirming that Paul considers Jewish practice as 'evil work' in opposition to being in Christ.[25] However, if the non-Jewish cultural and socio-political context is the guiding parameter this might well refer to actual pagan practices the addressees were most familiar with from their lives before they joined the Christ-movement. The dominating Roman influence on the official everyday life of the colony at the time has been noticed and although this influence certainly did not render Greek and Thracian culture and language irrelevant,[26] at the official public and also at the economic level Roman dominance cannot be denied for the period in question.[27] Thus it is noteworthy that a key emphasis in Roman cult practice was the 'right' performance of the rite (νόμος), that is, the correct 'doing' of all aspects of ritual performance. Respect for the gods was expressed foremost in orthopraxy, that is in the correct performance of a rite. One was con-

---

24　Cf. discussion of the terms by Standhartinger, *Der Philipperbrief*, 216-20, 255-58.
25　See, e.g. Holloway, *Philippians*, 149-53.
26　See Oakes, *Philippians*, 32.
27　Brawley, 'Alternative Community', 225-29.

cerned with 'savoir-faire' rather than 'savoir-penser'.[28] With this emphasis on 'doing' or 'performing' the terminology of ἔργον may well point to the performance of rituals in relation to beings the Christ-followers from the nations should no longer respect as deities.

It is indeed plausible that those who 'do' or perform these rites as a means to establish and maintain the 'peace with the gods' are meant here. Most important, these were the practices of everyday life, performed at home or at the street corners and in neighbourhood shrines.[29] At the public level, in the major temples, such Roman cult performance aimed at legitimising and stabilising Roman imperial domination which in Roman perspective was god-given. From the perspective of Jews and now also those non-Jews who worshipped the one God of Israel through Christ, such cult performance was, in Paul's terminology, based on confusion at best ('No, I imply that what pagans sacrifice, they sacrifice to demons and not to God', 1 Cor 10:20). In any case it was foolish and the result of darkened minds who had 'exchanged the glory of the immortal God for images resembling a mortal human being or birds or four-footed animals or reptiles' (Rom 1:23). Performing rites honouring deities other than the one God could well be described as performing evil works or of being an evil worker. If the label 'dogs' does imply a reference to worshippers of Artemis/Diana, Hekate or possibly Dionysios,[30] the labels cohere well and actually point in the same direction, namely to practices the addressees should have left behind. It combines aspects of oppression and idolatry found in some Jewish uses of the label 'dogs' as noted above. With the addressees most likely not being part of the dominating Roman elite but rather from among those who had been affected by Roman colonising appropriation of their land, some of them at least were most likely alienated from this dominating power before joining the Christ-movement. They had little option to envisage or live alternatives in their lives between accommodation and resistance. Brawley makes a convincing case that although 'primary Roman coloni-

---

28 Scheid, *Quand Faire C'est Croire*, 15–57.
29 For more details see Ehrensperger, 'Between Polis, Oikos, and Ekklesia', 105–32, now also in my *Searching Paul*, 159–80.
30 Iconography of Dionysios also involves dogs as part of frugal scenes.

zation occurred three generations before Paul's epistle, the colonized certainly carried the loss of land in their cultural memory'.[31] 'Evil workers' thus can be seen also as referring to practitioners of cults in relation to, and in support of the dominating Roman power.

Mutilation/ κατατομή

This is the one term which has led most clearly to the identification of opponents as Jews or Judaisers with the supposed sound analogy to περιτομή thus sarcastically ridiculing Jewish identity. If this were Paul's view of circumcision this passage would certainly strongly support the view that Paul had rejected Jewish tradition and opposed all aspects of Jewish identity when he joined the Christ-movement.[32] This strand of interpretation then leads almost inevitably to an understanding of περιτομή in v. 3 as the 'true' circumcision, that is, those in Christ. A dichotomy between a 'true' περιτομή over against 'wrong' circumcision or rather κατατομή is set up, the κατατομή thus being identified as those Jews who do not consider Jesus to be the messiah. The question that needs to be raised is whether κατατομή actually constitutes this sarcastic refutation of the Jewish marker of identity, that is of their trust and loyalty in God. Nothing in the letter or even in Chapter 3 gives any indication that Paul would have referred to περιτομή in such a derogatory way. Even in Galatians where he is using decisively firm and emotionally charged language in order to prevent the assemblies of ἔθνη in Christ from getting circumcised, he never uses such language in relation to περιτομή.[33] In Philippians circumcision is not an issue at all, and it would be utterly strange to find such a strong negative expression out of nowhere for what Paul in v. 5 embraces as part of his credentials, which are far from abrogated in Christ. It is difficult to envisage that he could consider his own περιτομή to be actually κατατομή. Although he considers his own credentials to be recalibrated as all of life is reca-

---

31 Brawley, 'Alternative Community', 226.
32 Cf. e.g. Vollenweider, 'Rivals, 298–300, similarly also Nikki, *Opponents*, 159–79.
33 Brawley, similarly notes, 'The warning to look out for the mutilation … can hardly be a vicious parody of Israelite circumcision', 'From Reflex', 144.

librated in light of the dawning of the age to come, this is something entirely different from abrogated.[34] It is thus necessary to consider other options for κατατομή—and there are a number of possibilities here.

There are indications in the LXX which tune in with what I have already argued concerning the labels 'dogs' and 'evil workers' as referring to other cult practices rather than having any relation to Jewish life and practice. It has been noticed that the lexeme κατατέμνω is used in LXX Lev 21:5 and 1 Kgs 18:28 with reference to cult practices in relation to other deities (Baal in the second case in particular). Although these passages have been refuted as irrelevant and foreign for interpreting Phil 3:2,[35] a reference to idolatry and oppression is not foreign at all in this context. It is more obvious to look for something associated with it in the pagan context of Philippi rather than with reference to Jewish practice.[36]

As mentioned above, Nanos has drawn attention to rock carvings in a quarry in close proximity to Philippi which depict Diana, including her dogs. He notes that 'the word we translate 'mutilation' (κατατομή) is lexically most commonly used not for 'mutilation' at all but to denote an 'inscription', 'carving', 'incision', 'notch', or 'groove', including specifically the cutting of a rock face or quarry—which is precisely where the reliefs are found!'[37] There are thus a number of options to which κατατομή could refer right in the local context of the addressees. There is no need to introduce outside invaders to produce a problem Paul addresses in Philippi! It seems rather obvious that the three labels are being used consistently within the passage, and in the wider context of the letter. Paul addresses an issue the addressees are familiar with, something that possibly is a temptation. The people thus labelled are most likely known to the Philippians, they are located in

---

34 On this see Campbell, 'I Rate All Things', 39–61; now also in Campbell, *Unity*, 203–23.
35 Cf. Nanos, 'Paul's Polemic', 155.
36 I am not convinced that it refers directly to devotees of Cybele who castrated themselves as has been proposed by Nanos, 'Paul's Reversal', 475–81, and Brawley, 'From Reflex', 144.
37 Nanos, 'Paul's Polemic', 160.

the civic and social space which they share, and in which to some extent they still are embedded. It would possibly not have been easy to give up all the familiar practices and sever all the ties with people they had associated with. A scenario which envisages pagan referents for the three terms of v. 2 fits the widely shared consensus that the Christ-following group predominantly encompassed people from the ἔθνη, that is, people who had formerly been loyal to other deities, or as god-fearers were at least not exclusively loyal to the one God.

Περιτομή

The phrase 'we are the circumcision' in v. 3 is traditionally interpreted as referring to the Christ-followers. It is evident that the Christ-followers are in view here but the emphasis certainly does not allow for the insertion found in many translations of the word 'true' or the likes. In light of the arguments presented above, the juxtaposition is rather between those identified as worshippers of other deities, and those who worship the one God alongside and linked with the people of Israel. In that sense the Christ-followers are qualified as those who worship God through the spirit—ἡμεῖς γάρ ἐσμεν ἡ περιτομή, οἱ πνεύματι θεοῦ λατρεύοντες καὶ καυχώμενοι ἐν Χριστῷ Ἰησοῦ καὶ οὐκ ἐν σαρκὶ πεποιθότες,— which I would translate as follows: *For we are that circumcision, that worship God through the spirit and boast in Christ Jesus rather than trusting in flesh.* The emphasis is on who they are—positively in relation to God, but in distinction from loyalties to other gods rather than in opposition to any Jewish way of expressing such loyalty and trust.[38] William S. Campbell has presented thorough arguments that Paul's reference to his own credentials in vv.5-6 should not be read as rejecting his Jewish identity, but rather, when it comes to referring to these he actually has much to offer. But in relation and comparison with Christ, all of life is recalibrated.[39] He could not give any other example than himself to support the Philippians' understanding of what the implications of being in Christ mean in relation to status and honour in the civic order of Roman

---

38 Thus also Brawley, 'Alternative Communities', 239.
39 Campbell, 'I Rate All Things'.

society. The analogy for the addressees would be respective Roman credentials which certainly were propagated at the time, as inscriptional evidence from Philippi demonstrates. Significantly most inscriptions of the first century C.E. were in Latin, a fact which changes after this century with Greek becoming the dominating inscription language again.[40] It has been noted that the reference to ἐκ γένους Ἰσραήλ resonates with the designation of a *civis Romanus* as Roman citizen, the reference to φυλῆς Βενιαμίν resonates with the accompanying necessary belonging to a Roman neighborhood, that is, a tribal designation (*Tribus Voltinia*). The reference to "Ἑβραῖος ἐξ Ἑβραίων could equal the reference to the father in Latin inscriptions whereas the reference to circumcision on the eighth day may be seen in analogy to the *toga virilis*, the official gown of a free adult male Roman citizen. The additional acquired credentials mentioned by Paul resonate with what a free Roman citizen would need to add to his birth nobility by acquired achievements.[41] By analogy the Philippians are led to understand that such honour and status related positions or perceptions are not what life in Christ actually ought to be, that such aspirations for status and honour are not the guiding parameters. It is not decisive that the addressees would be in positions that would enable them to actually climb the ladder of the *cursus honorum*, this ideal that is prevalent in the Roman-dominated public sphere. The presence of a rather small Roman and possibly a cooperating Greek elite in Philippi, with significant numbers of Greek and Thracian inhabitants of lower status actually constituting the majority of the colony and its surroundings, would render this interpretation of Paul's arguments rather credible. Precisely these non-elite groups are encouraged not to orient themselves on a Roman-driven perception of honour and status, but to orient themselves on Paul's embodiment of life in Christ which is characterised in the Christ-hymn of Chapter 2. The decisive aspect is that these non-Jewish addressees now are loyal to the one God of Israel. In that sense they are περιτομή—not in opposition to the Jewish people, but rather in association with them.

---

40   Brélaz, *Philippes*, 73–77.
41   Pilhofer, *Philippi I*, 124–27, also Harrison, 'From Rome', 334–43.

The Enemies of the Cross

To refer to those called enemies of the cross in v. 17 fits the scenario depicted above on a number of levels.

On the one hand, the status and honour credentials identified are those of Roman citizenship. Roman rule introduced with establishing the Roman colony of Philippi after the turmoil of the civil war was hardly on sympathetic terms with a group which affirms its loyalty to someone who was executed on a Roman cross. Roman military domination can easily be referred to as being hostile to the cross of Christ.

That the term enemies here should indicate any former closeness of those so labelled with the Christ-followers seems a strange way of trying to either identify them as a group of opponents different from those in v. 2, some kind of former insiders who have turned away or adhere to a different form of being in Christ, or to align them as Judaising insiders. Since, as noted, there are no Judaisers in sight at the beginning of the chapter it would be rather strange to find them now suddenly here.[42] That it is former insiders who might be more generally in view is deduced from the mentioning of tears in v. 18 which is taken as indicating some emotional attachment or involvement on Paul's part.

What is clear is that the enemies are qualified as enemies of the cross, and this should be taken specifically into account when trying to identify those so labelled. They are not enemies of Paul: he is not arguing in the mode of personal defence as in 2 Corinthians. They are enemies of the cross. The cross is certainly a means to exercise terror over conquered provinces, which is precisely what the purpose of the crucifixion of Jesus was in Roman perspective. It is the perspective which Cicero summarised in Pro Rabirio 5.16 as follows:

> The mere word 'cross' should be removed not only from the person of a Roman citizen, but from his thoughts, his eyes and his ears. For it is not only the actual occurrence of these things or the endurance of them, but liability to them, the expectation, indeed the mere mention of them, that is unworthy of a Roman citizen and a free man.

---

42 Cf. also Bockmuehl, *Philippians*, 231.

In light of the Christ hymn of Philippians 2 the reference to enemies of the cross can also be a qualification of those people who draw their status and honour precisely from the dominating values of elite Roman society, in promoting domination and superiority over others. It is not that these enemies of the cross necessarily inflicted suffering on others but they avoided the implications that are inherent to a movement that aligns itself with someone who stood by the ethos of his people to the point of death imposed by imperial violence, and was vindicated by God. They walk in the way of life prevalent in the Roman context of the movement, and by embodying those ideals and values they are actually enemies of the cross. According to Paul their fate is destruction (τὸ τέλος ἀπώλεια, 3:19). This is a term he never uses for his fellow Jews but only for non-Jews outside of the Christ-movement. 'All who have sinned apart from the law will also **perish** apart from the law, and all who have sinned under the law will be judged by the law' (Rom. 2:12).[43] Jews who do not share in Paul's perception of the Christ-event are being judged but they are not being destroyed. Together with the label 'enemies of the cross' this in my view clearly indicates that Paul has non-Jews in view here, as in the opening of this chapter as well as in 1:28.[44]

The addressees are admonished not to orient themselves and their way of life on these people but rather as in the hymn of Chapter 2 on Christ, and as they can also see it embodied by Paul and his colleagues (possibly referring to Timothy and Epaphroditus). The negative reference to honour and shame is seen as an indication that these enemies of the cross orient themselves on the high esteem of status and honour in the Roman dominated colony, that is, earthly, belly-filling aspects of life.[45] The emphasis in 1:27—2:18 on ταπεινοφροσύνη (2:3) is diamet-

---

43 Cf. also 1 Cor. 5:5 and 1 Thess. 5:3.
44 Wojtkowiak also sees this as a decisive indicator for identifying who Paul has in view, and is of the view that they cannot be part of the community as this would contradict Paul's perception of *ekklesia* space as sin-free space. Members of the community would not be referred to in the terminology of destruction, hence they must be outsiders, in Wojtkowiak's view former Christ-followers, which would explain the emotional aspect here in the language of weeping. *Christologie*, 196.
45 Wojtkowiak, *Christologie*, 195.

rically in opposition to those status credentials held in such high esteem in the public discourse of the colony.

It has been proposed that these enemies could have been insiders or former insiders, even when it is acknowledged that they are not Jewish. If they were former Christ-followers they might have left the movement because they could not cope with the struggles that it implied in their context, and so they went back to their former pagan ways of life. A variation to that theme could be a scenario where these former pagans who might have been God-fearers before they had joined the Christ-movement either reverted or never entirely gave up their loyalty to other deities. Continuing to participate in worshipping local or Roman deities would certainly avoid the problem inherent in giving up all such loyalty expressions for non-Jews.[46] It is possible that such former non-Jewish Christ-followers are in view here, although this would mean that those targeted in vv. 1–2 would be a different group, a scenario which I consider unlikely.

But it is highly likely that those the addressees should keep in view are people in their immediate context, neighbours, possibly even family members who continued to live their lives loyal to their deities. As mentioned, that Paul uses his own Jewish credentials in an exemplary way in his attempt to show the addressees how all of life is recalibrated in light of the Christ-event does not indicate any Jewish opponents nor some theological juxtaposition of Jewish practice and tradition to being in Christ. For former pagans the recalibrating of life means different things than for a Jew like Paul. But it does not mean that all of a sudden there is a *tabula rasa* or as some formulate, an obliteration of all and everything. As Phil. 4:8 demonstrates, there are aspects of the life of ἔθνη which are compatible with life in Christ: 'Finally, beloved, whatever is true, whatever is honorable, whatever is just, whatever is pure, whatever is pleasing, whatever is commendable, if there is any excellence and if there is anything worthy of praise, think about these things'. Paul trusts the addressees that they are able to discern what this implies. Their own wisdom is required to work this out, but it clearly

---

46 Wojtkowiak, *Christologie*, 200.

means that in that sense Paul does not set up a counter-cultural dichotomy between being in Christ and the Greek, Roman, Thracian, or other cultures, inasmuch as he does not set up a dichotomy to Jewish tradition and practice. There must be significant aspects of the life of ἔθνη that are seen as compatible with life in Christ, if Paul's insistence that they should not become Jews is in any way sensible. Of course, in order to learn how to relate to the one God of Israel, their main point of orientation is Jewish tradition, but not in opposition to what is compatible with their new loyalty and trust.

In my perspective there is no indication in Philippians, including Chapter 3, that Paul addresses issues concerning so-called Jewish opponents or the like. A scenario entirely consistent with the noted emphasis and context of the letter as dealing with civic and political (Roman and pagan) issues of the colony can be envisaged also for Chapter 3. In my view this is a far more likely scenario than any introduction of potential or anticipated Judaising opponents who might possibly eventually arrive by means of the Via Egnatia from Galatia, or who were on the way back from Corinth. Such scenarios seem anachronistic as they have to argue for highly hypothetical options, which have no hint of an indication in the text of the letter, or the context reconstructed by most contemporary interpretations. There is no need and there is no convincing argument for Judaising or Jewish opponents. There are significant arguments for problems at the very doorsteps of the addressees, issues that arise from their everyday life with and among pagan, Greek, Thracian, and Roman neighbours in the colony. These Paul sees as causing the community to lose sight of the alternative values they are called to embody, hence his urge that they become co-imitators with him and those whom they have seen embracing the values of the movement.

Kathy Ehrensperger
Abraham Geiger Kolleg,
University of Potsdam

Bibliography

Ascough, R. — *Paul's Macedonian Associations* (Tübingen: Mohr Siebeck, 2003).

Betz, H. D. — *Studies in Paul's Letter to the Philippians* (Tübingen: Mohr Siebeck, 2015).

Bockmuehl. M. — *The Epistle to the Philippians* (Black's New Testament Commentary; London: A&C Black, 1997).

Brawley, R. — 'An Alternative Community and an Oral Encomium: Traces of the People in Philippi', in Joseph A. Marshal (ed.), *The People Beside Paul. The Philippian Assembly and History from Below* (Atlanta, GA: SBL Press, 2015), 223–46.

Brawley, R. — 'From Reflex to Reflection: Identity in Philippians 2.6–11 and its Context', in Kathy Ehrensperger and J. Brian Tucker (eds.), *Reading Paul in Context. Explorations in Identity Formation. FS for William S. Campbell* (London, New York, NY: T&T Clark, 2010), 128–46.

Brélaz, C. — *Philippes, colonie romaine d'Orient: Recherches d'histoire institutionelle et sociale* (Athens: École fraînçaise d'Athènes, 2018).

Campbell, W. S. — '"I Rate All Things as Loss". Paul's Puzzling Accounting System: Judaism as Loss, or the Re-evaluation of All Things in Christ', in Peter Spitaler (ed.), *Celebrating Paul: Festschrift in Honor of Jerome Murphy-O'Connor and Joseph A Fitzmyer* (Washington, DC: Catholic Biblical Association, 2012), 39–61.

Campbell, W. S. — *Unity and Diversity in Christ: Interpreting Paul in Context* (Eugene, OR: Cascade, 2013).

Ehrensperger, K. — 'Between Polis, Oikos, and Ekklesia: The Challenge of Negotiating the Spirit World (1 Cor 12.1–11)', in J. R. Harrison and L. L. Welborn (eds.), *The First Urban Churches. Vol 2: Roman Corinth* (Atlanta, GA: SBL Press, 2016), 105–32.

Ehrensperger, K. — *Paul at the Crossroads of Cultures: Theologizing in the Space-Between* (London, New York, NY: T&T Clark, 2013).

Ehrensperger, K. — *Searching Paul: Conversations with the Jewish Apostle to the Nations* (Tübingen: Mohr Siebeck, 2019).

Ehrensperger, K.	'The Pauline 'Εκκλησίαι and Images of Community in Enoch Traditions', in G. Boccacini and C. Segovia (eds.), *Paul the Jew: Rereading the Apostle as a Figure of Second Temple Judaism* (Minneapolis, MN: Fortress, 2016), 183–216.
Harrison, J. R.	'Excavating the Urban and Country Life of Roman Philippi and Its Territory', in J. R. Harrison and L. L. Welborn (eds.), *The First Urban Churches 4. Roman Philippi* (Atlanta, GA: SBL Press, 2018), 1–62.
Harrison, J. R.	'From Rome to the Colony of Philippi: Roman Boasting in Philippians 3.4–6 in Its Latin West and Philippian Epigraphic Context', in J. R. Harrison and L. L. Welborn (eds.), *The First Urban Churches 4. Roman Philippi* (Atlanta, GA: SBL Press, 2018), 307–62.
Heil, J. P.	*Let Us Rejoice in Being Conformed to Christ* (Atlanta, GA: SBL Press, 2010).
Holloway, P. A.	*Philippians* (Minneapolis, MN: Fortress 2017).
Hooker, M.	'Philippians: Phantom Opponents and the Real Source of Conflict', in I. Dunderberg, et.al. (eds.), *Fair Play: Diversity and Conflicts in Early Christianity. FS for Heikki Räisannen* (Leiden: Brill, 2002), pp..
Lamoureaux, J. T.	*Ritual, Women, and Philippi: Reimagining the Early Christian Community* (Eugene, OR: Cascade 2013).
Lohmeyer, E.	*Der Brief an die Philipper* (4th edn; Göttingen: Vandenhoeck & Ruprecht, 1974).
Nanos, M. D.	'Paul's Reversal of Jews Calling Gentiles, Dogs (Philippians 3:2): 1600 Years of an Ideological Tail Wagging an Exegetical Dog?', *BibInt* 17 (2009), 448–82.
Nanos, M. D.	'Paul's Polemic in Philippians 3 as Jewish Sub-Group Vilification of Local Non-Jewish Cultic and Philosophical Alternatives', in Mark D. Nanos (ed.), *Reading Corinthians and Philippians within Judaism. Collected Essays Vol 4* (Eugene, OR: Cascade, 2017), 142–91.
Nikki, N.	*Opponents and Identity in Philippians* (Leiden: Brill, 2019).
Oakes, P.	'The Economic Situation of the Philippian Christians', in Joseph A. Marshal (ed.), *The People Beside Paul. The Philippian Assembly and History from Below* (Atlanta, GA: SBL Press, 2015), 63–82.

Oakes, P.	*Philippians: From People to Letter* (Cambridge: Cambridge University Press, 2001).
Pilhofer, P.	*Philippi I, Die erste christliche Gemeinde Europas* (Tübingen: Mohr Siebeck, 1995).
Reuman, J.	*Philippians: A New Translation with Introduction and Commentary* (The Anchor Yale Bible; New Haven, CT: Yale University Press, 2008).
Scheid, J.	*Quand Faire C'est Croire. Les rites sacrificiels des Romains* (Paris: Flammarion, 2011).
Schwartz, J.	'Dogs in Jewish Society in the Second Temple Period and in the Time of the Mishna and the Talmud', *JJS* 55.2 (2004), 246–77.
Standhartinger, A.	*Der Philipperbrief* (Handbuch zum Neuen Testament 11/I; Tübingen: Mohr Siebeck, 2021).
Tellbe, M.	'The Sociological Factors behind Philippians 3.1–11 and the Conflict at Philippi', *JSNT* 55 (1994), 97–121.
Vollenweider. S.	'Politische Theologie im Philipperbrief?', in D. Sänger and U. Mell (eds.), *Paulus und Johannes* (Tübingen: Mohr Siebeck 2006), 457–69.
Vollenweider, S.	'Rivals, Opponents, and Enemies: Three Kinds of Theological Arguments in Philippians', in J. R. Harrison and L. L. Welborn (eds.), *The First Urban Churches 4. Roman Philippi* (Atlanta, GA: SBL Press, 2018), 291–306.
Wojtkowiak, H.	*Christologie und Ethik im Philipperbrief: Studien zur Handlungsorientierung einer Frühchristlichen Gemeinde in Paganer Umwelt* (Göttingen: Vandenhoeck & Rurprecht, 2012).

Greetings In Stone:
Shifting the Accent from Papyri to Epigraphy in Colossians 4:15–17

Alan H. Cadwallader

The greetings sections of the Pauline corpus have become increasingly surveyed since Jeff Weima's ground-breaking monograph published in 1994.[1] The study of the salutations has relied on two main points of intersection—an intra-comparative analysis based on the canonical Pauline corpus,[2] and an inter-comparative investigation based on the thousands of letters surviving on papyri and ostraka, mainly from Egypt, with some Judean additions and a minuscule number fortuitously preserved on lead or wood from various locations.[3] The first approach is problematic because of a tendency to homogenise the greetings sections of letters, even though Weima had noted that for all of the structural similarity, 'the apostle regularly shapes and adapts his letter closings'.[4] The letter to the Colossians stands out as an example of distinctive emphasis. Questions of pseudepigraphy aside, the instructions for the synoiketic reading of two letters plus an enigmatic instruction to Archippos are unique in the Pauline corpus. Here I want to hone in on the valuable assistance that epigraphy can deliver. It is, I hope, a fitting tribute to Jim Harrison whose gentle yet assiduous scholarship has for decades sought to gain bread from stones.

---

1 Weima, *Neglected Endings*; see also his 'Sincerely Paul', 307–45.
2 This approach is distilled in Francis and Sampley, *Pauline Parallels*.
3 There has been an industry of delving into the papyri for insights into the Pauline letters. For two recent examples focused on narrow issues of letter carriage and secretarial insertions, see, respectively, Head, 'Onesimus', 628–56, and Cadwallader, 'Tertius', 378–96.
4 Weima, 'Sincerely, Paul', 345.

I lay a foundation in the particularity of Colossians 4:15–17, move to the wider context of the inter-polis tensions that operated in the Lycus Valley once Colossae lost its hegemony over the entire area in the Hellenistic to early Roman period, and then examine how some inscriptions that record greetings and their delivery might contribute to an understanding of this small sub-section of the letter to the Colossians.

A turn in the greetings

When commentators address the greetings section in the letter (Col. 4:10–18), the overarching assumption is that it reflects congenial relationships and operates to cement them. The particular personnel are of course different, say as between Romans 16 and Colossians 4:10–17.[5] And even by comparison with Philemon where the same names are found with the addition of Apphia and Philemon,[6] the notable difference is that the names in Colossians are given expanded descriptive predicates. Aristarchus is now ὁ συναιχμάλωτός μου, 'my fellow prisoner' (Col. 4:10, cf. Phlm. 24), Mark is specified as ὁ ἀνεψιὸς Βαρναβα ..., 'the cousin/nephew of Barnabas concerning whom you have received instructions: if he comes to you, welcome him' (Col. 4:10, cf. Phlm. 24), Epaphras is now ὁ ἐξ ὑμῶν ... 'one of yourselves ...' with multiple additional credentials (Col. 4:12–13, cf. Phlm. 23) and Luke now has an occupation: ὁ ἰατρὸς ὁ ἀγαπητός 'the beloved doctor' (Col. 4:14, cf. Phlm. 24). Only Demas is left unadorned

---

5 The absence of any of the names in the greetings section of Colossians and Philemon from those in Romans 16 (taken as an integral part of the letter) precludes any notion that Philemon (and certainly Colossians) were written with a Roman or Italian destination in mind, or, probably, from a Roman provenance. Pace, Balabanski, 'Where is Philemon?, 131–50.

6 Huttner has raised the possibility that Apphia and Philemon were unimpressed by Paul's letter and left: 'The Development of Christianity'; Arzt-Grabner however considers that they had died (an alternative admitted by Huttner): Arzt-Grabner, 'Everyday Life', 214–16.

(Col. 4:14 cf. Phlm. 24).[7] This marks a shift from the relatively personal letter to Philemon, where greetings are to him (σε, Phlm. 23) notwithstanding the inclusion of an address to 'the church in your [s.] house' (Phlm. 2) and the plural recipients of the final benediction (Phlm. 24).

The more formal letter to the Christ-followers at Colossae clearly has a plural address throughout, including the greetings.[8] This is not a personal letter. Indeed, the plurality of address is compounded once the secondary readership at Laodikeia is included (Col. 4:16). This becomes a critical consideration when considering Col. 4:15, which is almost universally taken as the epistolary Paul relying on the Colossian Christ-followers to pass on his greetings to those at Laodikeia. As Paul Foster has written, reaffirming the assumption of collegiality, 'Presumably, these [greetings] are on Paul's behalf and are not because they have been negligent in relations with the Laodikeian community'.[9]

It will be helpful now to give the text of Col 4:15–17, before proceeding further.

15 Ἀσπάσασθε τοὺς ἐν Λαοδικείᾳ ἀδελφοὺς καὶ Νύμφαν καὶ τὴν κατ' οἶκον αὐτῆς ἐκκλησίαν

16 καὶ ὅταν ἀναγνωσθῇ παρ' ὑμῖν ἡ ἐπιστολή, ποιήσατε ἵνα καὶ ἐν τῇ Λαοδικέων ἐκκλησίᾳ ἀναγνωσθῇ, καὶ τὴν ἐκ Λαοδικείας ἵνα καὶ ὑμεῖς ἀναγνῶτε

17 καὶ εἴπατε Ἀρχίππῳ Βλέπε τὴν διακονίαν ἣν παρέλαβες ἐν κυρίῳ, ἵνα αὐτὴν πληροῖς.

---

7 Strictly Demas has been denuded in Colossians; in Phlm., he is included in the designation οἱ συνεργοί μου. See Lightfoot, *Colossians, Philemon*, 38. The intrigue about the defection of a Demas in 2 Tim. 4:9–10 and the outright deception and hostility of Demas in A.Thecla 1,4,12,14,16 cannot be resolved. The name is relatively rare and thereby intensifies the possibility that the same person is meant, certainly above any equation of the Onesimos, a ubiquitous name, of Phlm. 10 with the same name in Col. 4:9. LGPN for Asia shows 42 instances for Demas and 378 for Onesimos. Both names are attested in the Colossian district in the first to second century: Audollent, *Defixiones*, 14A (Onesimos); SEG 61.1160 (Demas).

8 As a sample of the second person plural pronoun only, see Col. 1:2,3,4,5,6,7,8.

9 Foster, *Colossians*, 435.

The greetings of verse 15 confirm the plurality of address. 'The comrades / friends / fellows' (the likely meaning of οἱ ἀδελφοί here: cf. Col. 1:2) and the narrowed focus on one named Christ-follower along with the church in her house points to an expansive range of people, not to be folded into one group. But why Nympha is named and no others generates a puzzle, even though, in formal stylistics, it matches the house-church of Philemon (καὶ τῇ κατ᾽ οἶκόν σου ἐκκλησίᾳ, Phlm. 2, cf. Rom. 16:5). After all, Paul's lengthy acknowledgement of membership of the Roman churches in Romans 16 is part of his rhetorical demonstration of some familiarity with a church he has never visited.[10] A similar situation confronts the epistolary Paul with the Laodikeians whom he also has not seen (so Col. 2:1, cf. 4:7). That the house-owner, Nympha, is singled out must therefore carry some particular significance.[11] It hints at the possibility of a distinction between Nympha and her house-church and the ethnically-defined brothers (that is, those generally in Laodikeia). This distinction is not necessarily adversarial or tensile. It may be that the author is simply recognising Nympha's capacity as a benefactor. As Steven Friesen has shown, women benefactors were frequently sought out by male petitioners concerned to advance their own interests.[12] That Nympha owned her own house in Laodikeia, supported a gathering of Christ-followers, and was greeted by name strongly signals her authority at Laodikeia.

The writer does not name her and her credentials without reason or without interest. Indeed, as Margaret MacDonald has observed, Nympha appears to operate at some distance from the authority struc-

---

10 See Fitzmyer, *Romans*, 55–65; Byrne, *Romans*, 29.
11 The debate over whether Nympha or Nymphas is the householder need not detain us here—the integrity of αὐτῆς is in my view decisive. Corsten recently argued for the masculine name: Νυμφᾶς: 'Mann oder Frau', 215–19. No attestation of male or female name is found at Laodikeia; however a Νυμφώ daughter of Ξενόστρατος (not mentioned by Corsten) is found in a recently-discovered inscription containing a list of women's names (association/cult membership or census roll?); see Aytaçlar and Akıncı, 'A List of Females', 113.
12 Friesen, 'Junia', 203–26.

tures contained in the household code.¹³ She may have been a widow. She may have been granted autonomous operations as the mother of three children (if she was, in local transactions, subject to Roman law).¹⁴ She may, like some Phrygian women, have been able to exercise greater agency than other women in the Empire.¹⁵

These possibilities are background contextual informants that gain no trace in the text. But the text moves on, compelling us to avoid quarantining one verse. Nympha and the church in her house as well as the Laodikeian Christ-followers generally are tied by the καί that opens verse 16 to a specific expectation, namely that the letter to the Colossians, after it has been read in the Christ-followers' gathering(s) in Colossae, be read at Laodikeia. Significantly, the ἐκκλησία defining the Laodikeians has no parallel at Colossae. There is, unusually, no ἐκκλησία mentioned in the epistolary address (unlike Gal. 1:2, 1 Thess. 1:1, 2 Thess. 1:1 but cf. Rom. 1:7, Phil. 1:1); rather the ἅγιοι καὶ πιστοί ἀδελφοί are syntactically set off from the city, as if the locality is not to define the Christ-followers at Colossae. Rather their anchorage is ἐν Χριστῷ (Col. 1:2, cf. 3:1,3). ἐκκλησία only enters the body of the letter as a universal category (Col. 1:18, 24).

There is an emphasis on reading—ἀναγνωσθῇ ... ἀναγνωσθῇ ... ἀναγνῶτε. It suggests that whatever the relationship between the Christ-followers of Colossae and those of Laodikeia, reading has a key role to play. Indeed, there is an imperative that it occur—ποιήσατε.

---

13   MacDonald, 'Can Nympha Rule This House?', 99–120. This raises the difficult question of the purpose of the household code, especially in an Asian context where family structures bear little relationship to the paterfamilial nuclear family portrayed. See, Standhartinger, 'The Origin', 117–30; Cadwallader, 'Family Life'.

14   The assertion of autonomy (αὐτεξουσία) by reason of child-bearing (ius (trium) liberorum) meant that a woman could act without a κύριος, a guardian, (the Lex Iulia and Lex Papia Poppaea). It is known to have been accessed across the empire, and even awarded to those who may not have been able to display the children that had grounded the privilege: I.Aphrodisias 2007 11.413 (3rd century CE), SB 18.13305 (Karanis, 271 CE). Pliny, at the turn of the second century, suggests it had already become honorific (quaere in the first century) rather than necessarily factual Ep. 2.13.

15   Of c.32 known women sponsors of civic bronze coinage in Roman imperial times, 9 are from Phrygia.

The Colossians are to ensure that it be read among the Laodikeians and they are to read the letter that comes from Laodikeia. Whether that letter is a letter from epistolary Paul to the Laodikeians or one which emanates from the Christ-followers at Laodikeia, the Colossians have the agency of reading imposed on them. But the double passive leaves the lector seemingly unnamed.

This is where the second imperative εἴπατε with the connective καί amplifies the importance of the final verse of this section of the text. Foster correctly underscores the connective here but thinks that there is a sudden shift of focus from Laodikeia to some local difficulty at Colossae.[16] He considers the instruction has a 'rebarbative' tone, suggesting that Archippos has somehow slackened in his duties.

This is where some attention on the name and the epithet is helpful. Archippos is not a name familiar in Phrygia, nor in the west of the empire. Its 234 instances in the LGPN reveal a concentration in Greece, the Aegean islands, and Magna Graeca. The single instance outside of Christian literature (Col. 4:17, Phlm. 2 and the derivative reiteration in the story of St Michael of Chonai) occurs as the name of a Laodikeian recorded as having visited the sanctuary of Apollo at Claros.[17] The name reflects an aristocratic background or elitist aspiration.[18] This suggests that Archippos is not from a Phrygian (or specifically Colossian) origin. Vicki Balabanski affirms that the description of Archippos as 'our fellow soldier' (ὁ στρατιώτης ἡμῶν, Phlm. 2) aligns Archippos with Paul not Philemon and Apphia, even though he is, for some period, located at Colossae. Rather, on the basis of Phil. 2:25, where the epithet is applied to Epaphroditos, the term indicates someone who is delegated to specific assignments. He is mobile.[19] This suggests that εἴπατε is better understood in the sense of commission or instruction and βλέπε, in the opening of the commission, operating to foreground the commission by the verbal aspect of the present tense.[20]

---

16 Foster, *Colossians*, 442–5.
17 I.Claros mémoriaux 17.
18 Dubois, 'Hippolytos and Lysippos', 42.
19 Balabanski, 'Where is Philemon?' 138.
20 Contrà Foster (*Colossians*, 444) who highlights the older understanding of the present as continuous arguing that it suggests no one-off action was meant.

Indeed, the importance of what is given to him is further emphasised by ἵνα αὐτὴν πληροῖς, a doubling of the personal address to Archippos from the Christ-followers at Colossae. On this understanding, the mention of Archippos comes as the culmination of the section (Colossians 4:15–17) where greetings to the Laodikeian Christ-followers including Nympha and her house-church and the reading of epistles is to occur. Archippos is tied to the previous two verses. This has the potential to provide a specific content to the διακονία that has been assigned to him ἐν κυρίῳ. But this assignment comes as an address from the Christ-followers at Colossae (albeit themselves operating under the instruction of epistolary Paul). It has all the hallmarks of a communal commissioning of a delegate.

These three verses of a discrete section of the greetings conclusion of the letter have raised some significant issues—the importance of Nympha, the emphasis on greetings and letter-reading, and the role of Archippos. These three issues beg the question of the fundamental problem—what is prompting such concerns? Here a review of the relationships between the cities of the Lycus Valley is important, including what hints we can gather about the nature and quality of inter-Christian connections.

Inter-city rivalry in the Lycus Valley

There was a time when the territory of Colossae stretched from the eastern entrance of the Lycus Valley to the confluence of the Lycus with the Maeander River in the West.[21] The earliest inscription (267 BCE) from the Lycus has been traditionally credited to Laodikeia even though it predates the foundation of Laodikeia (256/255 BCE) by a decade.[22] Part of the reason for the assignment has been the naming of the gods Zeus and Apollo, even though these are gods associated with villages (Kiddioukome and Babakome). Laodikeia in the late Roman Republic and early imperial period claimed Zeus as its foundational

---

21 Herodotos 7.30; Michael Choniates Or. 2.39.
22 I.Laodikeia 1.

god,[23] and so a retrospective trajectory is traced.[24] These villages were probably part of an estate owned by Achaios (also mentioned in the inscription), a leader with close familial ties with the Seleucids. At the time, however, the only controlling city for the territory (inherited from a Persian satrapy) was Colossae, whose Seleucid commander, Helenos, is mentioned in the inscription. Colossae's bronze coins of the third and second centuries BCE feature Zeus, Apollo, and Artemis-with-Herakles, in diminishing weights, thereby signaling Zeus as the primary god of the city, with Apollo next in line.[25] Here a closer temporal influence can be traced for this early inscription. Moreover, frequently overlooked is that an earlier foundation story for Laodikeia told of Antiochos II being instructed by Zeus that he had delegated authority to Hermes to guide the location and construction of the new city,[26] named in honour of Antiochos's estranged wife, Laodike. Certainly the firing up of a Laodike cult by Antiochus III (193 BCE) was reflected in the dominant bronze coins of Laodikeia's Seleucid-Attalid period with Laodike portrayed as Aphrodite and Hermes's caduceus accompanying a cornucopia. This suggests that Laodikeia later changed its foundation story to accommodate the new Roman realities, upgrading the prominence of the eagle-standard borne by Jupiter (Zeus).

The consequence of the foundation of Laodikeia was, firstly, that settlements within close proximity to the new city were separated from the supply and control of Colossae; secondly, that the conceptual cartography was re-focused from the east to the west, with Laodikeia in

---

23 See Huttner, 'Wolf und Eber', 93–109. The god is sometimes, wrongly, described as Zeus Laodicensus, a misnomer for Zeus Aetophoros; see Metcalfe, *The Cistophori of Hadrian*, 70.
24 Corsten, 'The Foundation of Laodikeia', 131–36.
25 See Cadwallader, *Fragments*, 52, 65–8.
26 Stephanus Byz. *Ethnika* 11.37, sometimes sourced to the second century Phlegon of Tralles.

206 BCE being located within Caria not Phrygia;[27] and, thirdly, that Colossae's religious identity was also abrogated by Laodikeia as it increasingly tied its fortunes to the Roman juggernaut.[28] Laodikeia was rewarded with the assize centre of the Kibyran conventus, at least by the time of Cicero.[29] Laodikeia became, as Pliny compiled its epithets (rather than giving names for its earlier settlements), Diospolis.[30] Commentators have been content to assert that the establishment of Laodikeia was the beginning of Colossae shuffling off the Lycus stage. However, given the evidence we have of other neighbouring Hellenistic cities,[31] it is far more likely that the dominant response was one of rivalry and tension rather than sniveling retirement.

Laodikeia made extensive use of its prestige with Rome to garner imperial support over against its neighbours. In 114 CE, an edict of the governor of Asia was delivered to Laodikeia designed to protect the city's water supply. Significantly, water security was extended beyond the city to the countryside (l.24),[32] that is into the upper hinterland on the lower reaches of the Taurus range. If, as seems likely, this was the feeder area for the Kapros and Asopos Rivers that run on the eastern

27 I.Magnesia 59 = Rigsby nr 109 = I.Laodikeia 4. A list of five cities of Caria is appended to the long inscription in the dossier of inscriptions adorning walls of the agora at Magnesia-on-Maeander, probably indicating that these cities cohered with Laodikeia's support for Magnesia's aspirations for asylia status. It points to Laodikeia's recognised royal pre-eminence. It was a status in regard to Caria that Laodikeia never forgot, claiming in one coin in the mid-third century to metropolitical leadership over both Caria and Phrygia (RPC online 8.ID 58864 temp.), significantly, in the legend, described as ἀνανέωσις, 'renewal'.
28 Note the statue and bilingual inscription placed on the Capitoline Hill in Rome that Laodikeia renewed at least once: CIL 1² 728. See also, for coins, Theophilos, 'Employing Numismatic Evidence', 270–77.
29 Cicero ad Fam. 3.7, 15.4; ad Att. 5.15, 21. The delegate of the Cibyran conventus joining a dedication to Caligula in connection with a new temple in Miletus was Glykon son of Euarches, a Laodikeian (I.Didyma 148, l.16; 37 or 41 CE).
30 So, Ramsay, *The Cities and Bishoprics of Phrygia* (vol 1), 35. A second epithet, Rhoas, probably reflects the ubiquity of poppies in the Laodikeian environment. Poppies are also found on Laodikeia's coins and in architectural reliefs: RPC 3.2337, 4.2.2088 temp, 4.2.2138 temp.; Düşen, et al., 'Laodikeia', 370, 383.
31 See Heller, 'Les bêtises des Grecs'.
32 Guizzi, 'Edict on the Aqueduct', 149.

and western borders of the city proper, then this broaches Colossae's territory. The editor of the inscription, Francesco Guizzi, considers it likely that Laodikeia, under the armory of a proconsular edict, expropriated the water resources of other cities[33]—most probably Colossae and possibly Trapezopolis. If so, neighbourliness is unlikely to be the defining characteristic of the relations between proximate cities.

Any reservations over specific inter-city conflict disappeared in 130–31 CE, when Lycus Valley tensions bubbled over. Hierapolis, Tripolis (strictly on the Lydian side of the Maeander River but connected by a main road to Hierapolis) and Laodikeia were embroiled in a dispute over fishing rights on a lake that lay between Laodikeia and Hierapolis. So intense was the feeling that a decision was referred to the emperor Hadrian. Laodikeia won the rights to fish but Hadrian ensured some marketing rights to the other two cities.[34] Two significant elements stand out. Firstly, the relaying of Hadrian's decision comes from non-identical letters sent to each of the feuding cities. The extant letter, to Hierapolis, makes reference to 'the matters I have written to the Laodikeians' which Hadrian assumes the Hierapolitans will know (ll.6–7). Secondly, there is reference to the intensity of feelings, not only the agôn between the cities, but the quarrels, disputes, and disruptive words that have characterised their dealings (ll.14–15, 22). Concord between the cities was required to be demonstrated (l.19). Significantly this is the only time Hierapolis and Laodikeia expressed a homonoia relationship in their coinage.[35] Both Hierapolis and Laodikeia expressed concord with other cities many times afterwards, but never again with one another. We need to be cautious in assuming that simply because Laodikeia and Hierapolis might be named together (Col 4:13),[36] the connection was cordial.

---

33   Guizzi, 'Edict on the Aqueduct', 154.
34   Ritti, *Hierapolis*, 388–95.
35   Franke and Nollé, *Die Homonoia-Münzen Kleinasiens*, nrs 799–801, 1148–1151; BMC Phryg, 256 nr 162 = 325 nr 270; see also RPC 3.2356, 2357, 2358.
36   Laodikeia and Hierapolis were sometimes conjoined in the Roman imperial view: see Christol and Drew-Bear, 'Un senateur de Xanthos', 213; cf TAM II 194.

Ironically, the avowal of homonoia relationships appears frequently to have had a competitive edge, especially when some high honour was bestowed on a nearby city. Thus, when Laodikeia received its first senatorial award of neokorate status in 180 CE, Aphrodisias and Colossae immediately proclaimed their own cultural standing, as well as affirming their own loyalty to the valorised Roman virtue of concordia by entering a sister-city agreement with one another, expressed, as often, in a homonoia coin.[37] Colossae minted a series of bronze coins at that time that stand out for their artistic excellence. It was as if the ruling elite of Colossae felt the need to reassure the populace that, even though Laodikeia had achieved high honours, Colossae's historic eminence was undiminished.

Again, when Laodikeia's neokorate status was reaffirmed by Caracalla and promulgated by Elagabalus early in the third century, Colossae produced a flurry of coins all visually espousing homonoia, even if formal alliance relationships with the cities evoked by the symbolism on the coins (Ephesos, Smyrna) were not in fact negotiated. One of the coins in particular squared off against Laodikeia in the affirmation of territorial boundaries. Ulrich Huttner's study of Laodikeia's wolf and wild-boar coins had seen these as visual personifications of the Lycus (wolf) and Kapros (wild-boar) rivers, topographical features marking out polis-state possessions if not boundaries.[38] One Laodikeian bronze, with the head of the emperor Antoninus Pius on the obverse, removed any doubt. Two river gods were featured on the reverse supporting a seated Tyche holding a statue of Zeus Aetophoros in her right hand and a staff in her left. This time the rivers were named by legends in the field of the coin: ΛΥΚΟC and ΚΑΠΡΟC.[39] The coin was repeated with Commodus's image on the obverse a decade or so later.[40] But when Colossae struck a bronze coin with almost identical features during the reign of Elagabalus, it was clear that disputes over territorial boundaries, and, especially, access to water supplies were

---

37 RPC online 4.2.2446 temp.
38 Huttner, 'Wolf und Eber', 100.
39 RPC online 4.2.2086 temp.
40 RPC online 4.2.2065 temp.

lying in the background.⁴¹ Significantly, Colossae's seated Tyche held a statue of Artemis Ephesiaca in her right hand—evoking a strong tie with the province's metropolis—and a cornucopia in her left. Colossae's famous fecundity was dependent not only on the river Lycus but on the Kapros. And she was not sympathetic to any ambit Laodikeian claim.

Once we narrow our attention from civic disputation to intra-Christian tensions, conflict is clearest in the popular story of St Michael of Chonai. This was probably written down in the aftermath of the c. 365 CE Synod of Laodikeia's anathematisation of the worship of angels (Canon 35), which appears to have targeted the healing shrine about three kilometres to the south of the city of Colossae.⁴² In return, the story distorted the etymology of the ethnic Laodikeians into 'people of unrighteousness', the 'lawless mob', accusing them of idolatry—the very charge leveled in the synodical canon.⁴³ Ulrich Huttner sees in such inter-Christian rivalry the Christian version of the agonistic competition for prestige and preference that characterised relationships between Greek poleis.⁴⁴

The question is whether such inter-Christian tensions are visible in the letter to the Colossians. Theodoret of Cyrrhus certainly thought so. He surmised that the two letters—one to the Colossians and one from the Laodikeians to Paul (his interpretation of τὴν ἐκ Λαοδικείας in 4:16)—indicated that Paul wrote in response to a letter of accusation from the Laodikeians. Theodoret was certainly influenced by the Synod of Laodikeia's indictment of what he saw as continuing Colossian failures (Col. 2:18).⁴⁵

However, the tensions may lie closer to the first century in the difference in the demography of Laodikeia and Colossae. Older scholarship had seen references to festival, new moon, and Sabbath in Colossians 2:16 as a warrant to build an entire heterodox philosophy that combined Jewish ideas with other influences as a threat to the

---

41 RPC online 6.10900 temp.
42 So Theodoret of Cyrrhus, Comm. Col. 2:18 (PG 82.613, also 620).
43 Michael of Chonai 3.15, 9.9-10, 11.10 (ed. Bonnet). See Cadwallader, 'Intercity', 109-28.
44 Huttner, *Lycus Valley*, 190-95.
45 Theodoret Comm. Col. 4:16 (PG 82.625D).

Christ-followers at Colossae. More recently, two perspectives have gained traction. The first is that the inability of scholars to reach any consensus about the nature and accents of this supposed oppositional group to Pauline teaching and communities may point to the absence of any such group at all. Rather the epistolary Paul is seeking to situate the Christ-followers in a competitive environment that offered multiple, unintegrated alternatives to various aspects of his teaching.[46]

Secondly, it has been recognised that there is no evidence of a Jewish presence in Colossae until the twelfth century.[47] In fact, in the polemical narrative already mentioned, the Story of St Michael of Chonai, Jews might readily have been drawn into use as despised protagonists just as they are in a number of canons of the Synod of Laodikeia (Canons 29, 37, 38, perhaps also 16); but they are completely absent. I have dealt with the question of Jews at Colossae at length elsewhere.[48] Here I underscore that Laodikeia and Hierapolis both have considerable evidence for a long-standing Jewish presence.[49] If the use of κατοικίᾳ ... κατοικούντων in one Jewish epitaph at Hierapolis has its usual polis meaning, then it points to a past settlement that secured a recognised political presence for Jews in that city.[50] The expatriation of Jews by Antiochus III is likely to have been directed towards establishing supporters in Seleucid cities such as Hierapolis and Laodikeia,[51] rather than in those holding a memory of Achaemenid hegemony, such as Colossae.

When the letter to the Colossians was read in / to the ἐκκλησία in Laodikeia (including but not confined to Nympha's house gathering), any Jewish references and allusions in the Colossians letter would have been more likely to excite an intra-community recognition and reaction than at Colossae. Colossae would by contrast have recognised the

---

46 So Balabanski, *Colossians*, 111–12; Foster, *Colossians*, 280–82.
47 Michael Choniates Or. 2.88.
48 Cadwallader, 'Greeks in Colossae', 224–41; 'On the Question', 105–51. See also Foster, *Colossians*, 10–16.
49 See the epigraphical evidence assembled by W. Ameling: IJO 2.187–209 (Hierapolis); 2.212–3 (Laodikeia). See also Fine, 'The Menorah', 31–50.
50 IJO 2.205, l.4. See Williams, 'Semitic Name-Use', 177–78.
51 See, in general terms, Josephus Ant. 12.148–153.

synagogue and its disseminated practices as characterising Laodikeia and Hierapolis 'over there' rather than 'here'. The inclusion of such references and allusions in the letter to the Colossians may well have had the secondary readership (at Laodikeia) in mind from the beginning.[52] It may also provide the reason for carefully seeking the support of a woman with a decidedly Greek name, namely Nympha. We certainly know that there were fierce debates about the legacy of Jewish beliefs and practices in early Christianity in this region. The letters to the seven churches in Revelation (Rev. 2:1–3:22), one of which names Laodikeia though all are to be read together (Rev. 1:11), prescribe an expression of belief and practice with closer ties to Judaism than Pauline Christianity (note especially Rev. 2:14–15, 20–1). Colossians, by contrast, places Greek *before* Jew (Col. 3:11), uniquely in the New Testament.[53]

There is some speculation here, but it seeks to make sense of the letter in its variegated and contesting Lycus context. The long-standing inter-city rivalry between Laodikeia and its neighbours, notably Colossae, is unlikely to have left the population unaffected, even if many in the lower level of society were simply observers at best, collateral damage at worst, of the wrangles of elite power-brokers and mercantile proprietors (cf. Rev. 3:17a). While reliance on or fear of Rome acted to keep the most blatant conflicts in check,[54] this was hardly a resource that the early Christ-followers could mine for the resolution of their own conflicts, except perhaps in imitation.

But there was already a long-standing cultural and political Hellenistic heritage that shaped dealings between contesting poleis upon which they could draw to assist their efforts at reconciliation.

---

52 Compare the bipartite readership of Colossians proposed by Severian of Gabala in the late fourth century. He too saw different takes on the letter depending on whether the reader was Greek or Jew, even though considering both to have been in the Colossian demographic. His comment is only known in catenae; see Cramer, *Catenae Graecorum Patrum* (vol. 6), 292; Staab, *Die Pauluskommentare*, 315.
53 Cadwallader, 'Greeks in Colossae', 227–29.
54 See Ager, 'Roman Perspectives', 15–43.

Archippos and instruments of Hellenistic diplomacy

Three decades ago, Margaret Mitchell introduced Hellenistic typologies of diplomacy into the way in which Christian envoys might be understood. Mitchell's concentration was on the identity of the present envoy with the absent sender and the authority of the envoy to speak as the commissioning subject.[55] However, the conventions and practices governing diplomacy between Hellenistic cities and even in Roman utilisation of those conventions were far more widespread. In a context where poleis and their territories adopted a stance of autonomy (even when part of a kingdom), diplomacy was crucial to negotiate disputes, arrange for a negotiated peace, resolve high-level legal cases, develop, maintain or extend alliances, or seek to advance recognition and status. The primary point of scholarly access to this crucial method of cultivating and repairing inter-city relations comes from inscriptions. In Asia Minor and the Aegean there are a number of caches of materials that have proved invaluable.

The largest comes from Magnesia-on-Maeander dated to the turn of the third to the second century BCE. The city authorities were intent on gaining recognition from kings, city-states, and associations ostensibly for the festival of Artemis Leukophryne, their city goddess, and her promotion of the city's desire for the status of asylia—that is, to be an inviolable city. Such status of course meant multiple alliances that avowed support through times of war and peace, of need and plenty. Multiple ambassadors were dispatched armed with letters and instructions. Multiple decrees and letters, themselves borne by the envoys of answering cities, were received.[56]

This might appear temporally distant from our needs. However, the practices continued into the early Roman imperial period. As Werner Eck notes, 'In all probability, ... such embassies were routine, but necessary, if one wanted to get what was needed for a community'.[57] More significantly, these letters were etched in stone to adorn the

---

55 Mitchell, 'New Testament Envoys', 641–62 (644–51).
56 See Rigsby, *Asylia*, nrs 66–131.
57 Eck, 'Diplomacy', 206.

agora of the city of Magnesia, and remained there. Not only was this memorialising effort turned into an on-going function of identity-formation/reinforcement for the Magnesians. But cities whose letters and resolutions of support for the Magnesians' ambitions were also clearly named, a constant reminder of their support and a reciprocal building of their own importance in relation to Magnesia, a 'means of self-assertion through multi-faceted processes of memory making'.[58]

Laodikeia—then distinguished as Laodikeia in Caria, but understood as Laodikeia on the Lycus—was one of more than 160 cities involved. While the inscription detailing the exchange between Magnesia and Laodikeia is fragmentary, it tells of Laodikeia's own participation in the public memorialisation of the diplomatic exchange. Laodikeia committed to the erection of a white stele 'in the most conspicuous place in the agora' (ἐν τῆι ἀγοραῖ ἐν τῶι ἐπιφανεστάτωι τόπωι b ll.12–13, as reconstructed) that contained its own self-aggrandising record including, probably, notice of other related expenditures as well.[59] These lasting public displays reinforced the practice and the elements of the pageantry and performance of the actual diplomatic engagements long since consigned to memory.[60] Although we have nothing resembling the detail of the Magnesian efforts to secure asylia status, a recent inscription reveals the previously unknown award of that status to Hierapolis.[61] Similar diplomatic efforts would have accompanied the preliminary positioning required to secure it. All this confirms that diplomacy and its code of key elements would have been familiar to the inhabitants of the Lycus Valley. And these two cities with a known heritage in diplomacy, Laodikeia and Hierapolis, are those named in the letter to the Colossians (Col. 4:13).

Envoys (theoroi / presbeutai) were crucial to the diplomatic enterprise. They were almost always named (often becoming the focus of honorific inscriptions after the fulfilment of their charge). Also named

58 Amendola, 'Presbeutikoi and Enteuktikoi Logoi', 98.
59 I.Magnesia 59 = I.Laodikeia 4.
60 Ceccarelli, 'Letters and Decrees', 149.
61 Ritti, *Hierapolis*, 294–98. The award of ἀσυλία seems to have been a late Hellenistic achievement since it is confirmed by Hadrian (SEG 55.1415, l.12, 117 CE).

were those individuals or occasionally cities who were (sometimes) needed to act as proxenoi, sympathetic delegates, when certain procedures (such as preparatory sacrifices) were required to be observed. These envoys, once permission had been granted, presented their commissioned task before the key city institutions, the boulê and the demos, but most significantly, in the assembly (the ekklêsia).[62] The commissioned task most frequently entailed the reading out of a city's resolution or letter and delivering an address based on that document. Frequently, the inscriptions are careful to note that the envoys' oral delivery 'followed closely' the matters given in the letter or decree of the sending community: καὶ αὐτοὶ διελέχθησ[αν] ἀκολούθως τοῖς γεγραμμένο[ις].[63]

What has gained increasing attention in recent scholarship is the rhetoric of diplomacy, especially the elements that make up the proper pursuit of the diplomatic task. These elements can only be outlined briefly here. Crucial to the establishment of the mutuality was the delivery of greetings. Of course, when a letter was read out, the ubiquitous χαιρεῖν concluded the formal opening address. However, when an oral presentation was given greetings from the authorising body were a crucial opening—here the language is ἀσπάζεσθαι usually with a plural agency, παρ' ὑμῶν / αὐτῶν.[64] The island of Kos received a diplomatic mission from an unknown city that formally communicated its gratitude for the adjudication delivered in its city by a Koan judge:

> In order that the Koans too shall know the respect (προαίρεσις) our Demos has determined to show, it was decided to appoint two representatives (πρεσβευτές) who, upon their arrival in Kos, shall deliver the resolution (ψήφισμα) and, having come before the council (βουλή) and assembly (ἐκκλησία) and passed on the greetings (ἀσπασάμενοι) of our people (πλῆθος), shall thank the Koans for their sending (ἀποστολή) of the judge and beseech (παρακαλέσουσιν) them, who are our friends

---

62 I.Magnesia 73b, I.4 (as one example among many).
63 I.Magnesia 23, II.10-11.
64 For example, I.Magnesia 19, II.3-4.

(φίλοι), to preserve their goodwill (εὔνοια) towards our polis ....[65]

The formalities also included some reprise of historical proofs of the connection and of benefactions that had tied the cities and groups together.[66] These are almost always based on assertions of familiarity and kinship ties. Different language is used—οἰκειώτης, συγγενεία, φιλία, ἀδελφία[67]—but the purpose was to intimate that the two groups share common interests and that these should be strengthened.

When we apply these elements to Colossians 4:15-27 the resonances are clear, including the purpose behind the extended reference to Epaphras in 4:12-13. There is a named envoy (Archippos 4:16) who is given an official commission by a community (4:16 ποιήσατε ἵνα ...; v. 17 εἴπατε, both plural imperatives). That community is the sending and greeting community (ἀσπάσασθε, 4:15), the plural imperative (like the succeeding two) suggesting that the Colossians themselves are to give greetings not act as conduits for those of the epistolary Paul (which would make superfluous the greeting of 4:18).[68] There is also a named member of the addressed community (Nympha, 4:15) who in a diplomatic perspective, would be relied upon to enable a positive reception for, and due observance of local requirements by, the envoy. The two communities are reminded of their kinship ties (ἀδελφοί v.15),[69] and the past efforts (πολὺν πόλλον v. 13) that have been made in three cities—Colossae, Laodikeia, Hierapolis. This

---

65 IG XII, 4, 1.177 = SEG 49.1119, II. 9-19; translation adapted from Rubinstein, 'Spoken Words', 168.
66 Note especially I.Magnesia 53, II.47-66.
67 IG XII, 9.1186; I.Magnesia 61; SEG 38.1476. This last example even speaks of 'divinely instituted kinship' (συγγενεία ... ἀπὸ τῶν θεῶν II.20-1). See Jones, Kinship.
68 Hence, contra McKnight, Colossians, 394, who ties v. 15 to the previous greetings, adds an implied ἐμοῦ or ὑπὲρ ἐμοῦ (or ἡμῶν if Timothy is included) and does not see that v. 18 equally applies to the secondary audition at Laodikeia (v. 16). He is far from alone. Foster's alternative reading interpreting the greetings as fostering 'a close relationship with another Pauline community' is closer to the meaning and syntax of the text (Colossians, 435).
69 McKnight is correct in seeing 'fictive family language' here, Colossians, 394, but this also properly belongs in diplomatic efforts to foster relationships between cities and groups (Ceccarelli, 'Letters and Decrees', 149).

strong affirmation (μαρτυρῶ ... αὐτῷ) generates the sense that the contemporary engagement by Archippos, acting as envoy of Colossae, is an expansion of previous labour for the Christ-followers in these cities by Epaphras.[70] In the tight sequence of Colossians 4:15–17, Archippos's substantial responsibility was, as of all envoys, the reading of the letter sent with him, that is, the letter to the Colossians. He is the authorised agent implied by the passive ἀναγνωσθῇ, at least in the second instance in verse 16. It is likely that his oral performance of the letter as lector was accompanied by additional oral explanations, not least as the one who delivered the greetings of verse 15. Given that diplomacy requires the exchange of letters and deliveries if there is to be any expectation of success,[71] this raises the real possibility that the letter of Laodikeia that the Colossians are to read (τὴν ἐκ Λαοδικείας ἵνα καὶ ὑμεῖς ἀναγνῶτε) is not a letter of Paul sent to Laodikeia but rather the expected response to the Colossian 'initiative'.

This raises two critical issues. It is clear that the epistolary Paul is setting up the diplomatic exchange, for all that substantial parallels with Hellenistic practice can be demonstrated. This shifts the entire enterprise closer to the letter of Hadrian to Hierapolis previously noted where Hadrian requires all parties in the dispute over fishing rights to (re-)establish concordant relations. The ending of the letter to the Colossians places the epistolary Paul into a similar authoritative position, requiring contending communities in two cities to restore (perhaps meaning establish) harmonious relations. Here we are returned to one of Jim Harrison's favourite pursuits, that of discerning the 'collisions and convergences' in Pauline Christianity.[72]

And so we are left to ponder a second issue, namely the question of the success of the diplomatic mission. Here there is a decided ambiguity. On the one hand, there is no extant letter of the Laodikeians from the first century.[73] However, responses to the key instruments of a dip-

---

70 Compare Amendola, 'Presbeutikoi and Enteuktikoi Logoi', 91.
71 This is very apparent in I.Magnesia 53, ll. 47–66.
72 Harrison, *Paul*, 146.
73 The pseudpigraphal 'Letter to the Laodikeians' was composed as a letter of Paul, not one from the Laodikeians. See Lightfoot, *Colossians, Philemon*, 272–98. It is dated to the fourth century.

lomatic mission, namely the letter and/or decree (and perhaps parts of the oral delivery), frequently made use of the very language of those instruments; this would have been an expectation given the diplomatic code. So, there may need to be an investigation that the letter to the Ephesians is in fact the letter *of* (not *to*) the Laodikeians in response to the Colossian mission, a response that made such critical use of the Colossian letter. This would confirm that the mission was a success. After all, the accredited first bishop of the Church of Laodikeia was none other than ... Archippos![74]

Alan H. Cadwallader
Australian Centre for Christianity and Culture,
Charles Sturt University, Canberra

---

74 *Apostolic Constitutions* 7.46. This is not the only claim on Archippos: see Huttner, *Lycus Valley*, 273.

Bibliography

Ager, S. L. — 'Roman Perspectives on Greek Diplomacy', in C. Eilers (ed.), *Diplomats and Diplomacy in the Roman World* (Leiden: Brill, 2009), 15–43.

Amendola, D. — 'Presbeutikoi and Enteuktikoi Logoi in Hellenistic Interstate Relations. Some Further Thoughts from an Epigraphical Perspective (c. 306–205 B.C.)', *Ktèma* 44 (2019), 87–103.

Arzt-Grabner, P. — 'Everyday Life in a Roman Town Like Colossae: The Papyrological Evidence', in J. R. Harrison and L. L. Welborn (eds.), *The First Urban Churches 5: Colossae, Hierapolis, and Laodicea* (Atlanta, GA: SBL, 2019), 187–238.

Audollent, A. — *Defixionum Tabellae* (Paris: Fontemoing, 1904).

Aytaçlar, P. Ö. and E. Akıncı — 'A List of Female Names from Laodicea on the Lycos', *EA* 39 (2006), 113–16.

Balabanski, V. — *Colossians: An Eco-Stoic Reading* (London: T & T Clark, 2020).

Balabanski, V. — 'Where is Philemon? The Case for a Logical Fallacy in the Correlation of the Data in Philemon and Colossians 1.1–2; 4.7–18', *JSNT* 38 (2015), 131–50.

Byrne, B. — *Romans* (Sacra Pagina 29; Collegeville, MN: Liturgical, 1996).

Cadwallader, A. H. — 'Family Life in Asia Minor', in R. Richards, and J. R. Harrison (eds.), *Ancient Literature for New Testament Study: Inscriptions, Graffiti, Documentary Papyri, Ostraca, Coin Legends* (Grand Rapids, MN: Zondervan, 2022 [forthcoming]).

Cadwallader, A. H. — *Fragments of Colossae: Sifting through the Traces* (Adelaide: ATF, 2015).

Cadwallader, A. H. — 'Greeks in Colossae: shifting allegiances in the Letter to the Colossians and its context', in D. C. Sim, and J. S. McLaren (eds.), *Attitudes to Gentiles in Ancient Judaism and Early Christianity* (London / NY: Bloomsbury, 2013), 224–41.

Cadwallader, A. H.   'Inter-city Conflict in the Story of St Michael of Chonai', in W. Mayer, and B. Neil (eds.), *Religious Conflict from Early Christianity to the Rise of Islam* (Arbeiten zur Kirchengeschichte 121; Tübingen: de Gruyter, 2013), 109–28.

Cadwallader, A. H.   'On the Question of Comparative Method in Historical Research: Colossae and Chonai in Larger Frame', in J. R. Harrison, and L. L. Welborn (eds.), *The First Urban Churches 5: Colossae, Hierapolis, and Laodicea* (Atlanta, GA: SBL, 2019), 105–51.

Cadwallader, A. H.   'Tertius in the Margins: A Critical Appraisal of the Secretary Hypothesis', *NTS* 64.3 (2018), 378–96.

Ceccarelli, P.   'Letters and Decrees, or Idioms of Power in the Hellenistic Period', in P. Ceccarelli et al (eds.), *Letters and Communities: Studies in the Socio-Political Dimensions of Ancient Epistolography* (Oxford: Oxford University Press, 2018), 148–83.

Christol, M. and T. Drew-Bear   'Un senateur de Xanthos', *Journal des Savants* 3 (1991), 195–226.

Corsten, T.   'The Foundation of Laodikeia on the Lykos: An Example of Hellenistic City Foundations in Asia Minor', in H. Elton and G. Reger (eds.), *Regionalism in Hellenistic and Roman Asia Minor* (Bordeaux: Ausonius, 2007), 131–6.

Corsten, T.   'Mann oder Frau: Nympha oder Nymphas in Laodikeia?' in J. Verheyden, M. Öhler and T. Corsten (eds.), *Epigraphical Evidence Illustrating Paul's Letter to the Colossians* (WUNT 411; Tübingen: Mohr Siebeck, 2018), 214–19.

Cramer, J. A.   *Catenae Graecorum Patrum in Novum Testamentum* (vol. 6; Oxford: Academic Typographer, 1844).

Dubois, L.   'Hippolytos and Lysippos: Remarks on some Compounds in Ἱππο-, -ιππος', in R. W. V. Catling, and F. Marchand (eds.), *Onomatologos: Studies in Greek Personal Names, Presented to Elaine Matthews* (Oxford: Oxbow, 2010), 41–52.

Düşen, O, U. Sarpkaya, B. Gürcan, and Ö. Gül   'Laodikeia Antik Kenti'nin Floristik Yapısı', in C. Şimşek (ed), *10. Yalındı Laodikeia (2003–2013 Yılları)* (Istanbul: Ege, 2014), 369–86.

Eck, W.   'Diplomacy as Part of the Administrative Process in the Roman Empire', in C. Eilers (ed.), *Diplomats and Diplomacy in the Roman World* (Leiden: Brill, 2009), 193–207.

Fine, S.   'The Menorah and the Cross: Historiographical Reflections on a Recent Discovery from Laodicea on the Lycus', in E. Carlebach and J. J. Schacter (eds.), *New Perspectives on Jewish-Christian Relations: In Honor of David Berger* (Leiden, Boston: Brill, 2012), 31–50.

Fitzmyer, J. A.   *Romans* (AB 33; New York, NY: Doubleday, 1993).

Foster, P.   *Colossians* (London: Bloomsbury, 2016).

Francis F. O and J. P. Sampley   *Pauline Parallels* (2nd edn; Minneapolis: Fortress, 1984).

Franke, P. R. and M. K. Nollé   *Die Homonoia-Münzen Kleinasiens unter der thraksichen Randgebeite: I Katalog* (Saarbrücken: Saarbrücker Verlag, 1997).

Friesen, S.   'Junia Theodora of Corinth: Gendered Inequalities in the Early Empire', in S. J. Friesen, S. A. James, and D. N. Schowalter (eds.), *Corinth in Contrast: Studies in Inequality* (Leiden: Brill, 2014), 203–26.

Guizzi, F.   'An Edict of a Proconsul of Asia on the Aqueduct of Laodikeia (114/115 CE?)', in C. Şimşek (ed.), *15. Yalındı Laodikeia (2003–2018)* (Istanbul: Ege, 2019), 143–64.

Harrison, J. R.   *Paul and the Ancient Celebrity Circuit: The Cross and Moral Transformation* (Tübingen: Mohr Siebeck, 2019).

Head, P. M.   'Onesimus the Letter-Carrier and the Initial Reception of Paul's Letter to Philemon', *JTS* 71 (2020), 628–56.

Heller, A.   *'Les bêtises des Grecs': Conflits et rivalités entre cités d'Asie et de Bithynie à l'époque romaine (129 s.C –234 p.C)* (Bordeaux: de Boccard, 2007).

Huttner, U.   *Early Christianity in the Lycus Valley* (Leiden: Brill, 2013).

Huttner, U.   'The Development of Christianity in the Lycus Valley: socialization and violence', in J. R. Harrison et al. (eds.), *New Documents Illustrating the History of Early Christianity vol 12: The Lycus Valley* (Grand Rapids, MN: Eerdmans, 2023 [forthcoming]).

Huttner, U.   'Wolf und Eber: die Flüsse von Laodikeia in Phrygien', in J. Nollé, B. Overbeck, and P. Weiss (eds.), *Internationales Kolloquium zur kaiserseitlichen Münzprägung Kleinasiens* (Nomismata 1; Milan: Ennerre, 1997), 93–109.

Jones, C. P.   *Kinship Diplomacy in the Ancient World* (Cambridge, MA: Harvard University Press, 1999).

Lightfoot, J. B.   *Colossians and Philemon* (9th ed.; London: Macmillan, 1890).

MacDonald, M. Y.   'Can Nympha Rule This House? The Role of Domesticity in Colossians', in W. Braun (ed.), *Rhetoric and Reality in Early Christianities* (Waterloo, ON: Wilfred Laurier University Press, 2005), 99–120.

McKnight, S.   *The Letter to the Colossians* (Grand Rapids, MI: Eerdmans, 2018).

Metcalfe, W. E.   *The Cistophori of Hadrian* (New York, NY: American Numismatic Society, 1980).

Mitchell, M.   'New Testament Envoys in the Context of Greco-Roman Diplomatic and Epistolary Conventions: The Example of Timothy and Titus', *JBL* 111 (1992), 641–62.

Ramsay, W. M.   *The Cities and Bishoprics of Phrygia* (2 vols; Oxford: Clarendon, 1895, 1897).

Rigsby, K. J.   *Asylia: Territorial Inviolability in the Hellenistic World* (Berkeley: University of California Press, 1996).

Ritti, T.   *Hierapolis di Frigia IX: Storia e istituzioni di Hierapolis* (Istanbul: Ege, 2017).

Rubinstein, L.   'Spoken Words, Written Submissions and Diplomatic Conventions: The Importance and Impact of Oral Performance in Hellenistic Inter-polis Relations', in C. Kremmydas, and K. Tempest (eds.), *Hellenistic Oratory, Continuity and Change* (Oxford: Oxford University Press, 2013), 165–99.

Staab, K.   *Die Pauluskommentare aus der griechischen Kirche* (Münster: Aschendorff, 1933).

Standhartinger, A.   'The Origin and Intention of the Household Code in the Letter to the Colossians', *JSNT* 79 (2000), 117–30.

Theophilos, M. P.   'Employing Numismatic Evidence in Discussions of Early Christianity: A Case Study from Laodicea', in J. R. Harrison, and L. L. Welborn (eds.), *The First Urban Churches 5: Colossae, Hierapolis, and Laodicea* (Atlanta, GA: SBL, 2019), 257–92.

Weima, J. A. D.   *Neglected Endings: The Significance of the Pauline Letter Closings* (Sheffield: JSOT Press, 1994).

Weima, J. A. D.   'Sincerely, Paul: The Significance of the Pauline Letter Closings', in S. E. Porter and S. A. Adams (eds.), *Paul and the Ancient Letter Form* (Leiden: Brill, 2010), 307–45.

Williams, M. H.   'Semitic Name-Use by Jews in Roman Asia Minor and the Dating of the Aphrodisias Stele Inscriptions', in E. Matthews (ed.), *Old and New Worlds in Greek Onomastics* (Oxford: Oxford University Press, 2007), 173–98.

Πίστις, Ἀγάπη, and Ἐλπίς in 1 Thessalonians: New Insights from Old Stones

Julien M. Ogereau

Abstract

This paper explores the significance of the triad πίστις, ἀγάπη, and ἐλπίς, found in 1 Thessalonians 1:3 in light of epigraphic documents. It adduces a number of inscriptions which illustrate the different semantic nuances the terms could acquire in civic, domestic, and cultic contexts. It suggests new ways to interpret how the verse might have been initially intended by the author and understood by a first-century audience. Thereby it aims to demonstrate the enduring relevance of epigraphic material for the study of the New Testament.[1]

Besides offering the earliest attestation to the *parousia* of Christ and to the resurrection of the dead (5:15–16), Paul's first letter to the Thessalonians also introduces for the very first time the triad πίστις, ἀγάπη, and ἐλπίς, a trio of virtues which he will later enshrine as quintessentially Christian in 1 Corinthians 13:13. In 1 Thessalonians 1:3, Paul indeed begins his epistle with a heartfelt thanksgiving as he remembers the Thessalonians' active loyalty (ἔργον τῆς πίστεως), labour of love (κόπος τῆς ἀγάπης), and enduring hope (ὑπομονὴ τῆς ἐλπίδος) in Christ, before concluding in 5:8 with an exhortation to

---

1 Earlier versions of this paper were presented at the 'Papyrology, Epigraphy, and the New Testament' seminar of the 75th general meeting of the *Studiorum Novi Testamenti Societas* (Leuven, 2021), and at the 'Documentary Texts and Literary Interpretation (DTLI)' seminar of the annual meeting of the Society of Biblical Literature (San Antonio, 2021). Thanks are due to the respondents for their careful review and critical observations.

put on the breastplate of faithfulness and love (θώραξ πίστεως καὶ ἀγάπης), and saving hope as a helmet (περικεφαλαία ἐλπίδα σωτηρίας). Traditionally, commentators have been keen to explore the possible pre-Pauline origins and theological significance of this unusual cluster of terms, which is otherwise unattested in biblical or Greek literature.[2] While trying to determine its possible origin remains an elusive, and indeed speculative, enterprise,[3] S. Légasse has nonetheless observed that similar series of virtues (or vices), in which either πίστις, ἀγάπη, and/or ἐλπίς at times feature, do occur in moral discourses in earlier or contemporary literature, including in Jewish sources.[4]

This suggests that the three terms (which are in no way specific to the Septuagint) might not necessarily have had the theological connotations—i.e. faith (in God), (divine/self-sacrificial) love, (eschatological) hope—that they subsequently acquired in Christian literature and that modern interpreters generally assume.[5] In fact, it is almost certain that the terms did not bear the theological import they now possess and that commentators might be tempted to impose upon them in their exegetical analyses. This in turn raises the questions as to how the terms might have been (variously) meant and used in the first-century C.E., and how a Graeco-Roman audience such as the Thessalonians might have understood them. What concepts—theological, moral, or otherwise—might it have evoked in Gentile hearers who were likely not familiar with Jewish thought, literature, and traditions? Drawing from the research conducted in preparation for an epigraphic commentary on *1 Thessalonians*, this paper proposes to shed new light on these questions by paying greater attention to the social-cultural background of Paul's audience as illustrated by epigraphic documents.

---

2 See esp. Söding, *Die Trias*, 31–103; Weiß, 'Glaube–Liebe–Hoffnung'. Cf. Dibelius, *Thessalonicher I*, 3–4; Best, *Thessalonians*, 67; Bruce, *Thessalonians*, 12; Légasse, *Thessaloniciens*, 75–77; Holtz, *Thessalonicher*, 44; Malherbe, *Thessalonians*, 109.
3 Cf. Malherbe, *Thessalonians*, 109; Légasse, *Thessaloniciens*, 76.
4 See Légasse, *Thessaloniciens*, 76 (with nn. 4–5).
5 Cf. s.v. in *PGL*.

1. Τὸ ἔργον τῆς πίστεως

The expression τὸ ἔργον τῆς πίστεως is, as far as one can tell, not encountered in inscriptions, although the two lexemes are widespread in epigraphic sources. The same can be said of the phrases κόπος τῆς ἀγάπης and ὑπομονὴ τῆς ἐλπίδος, and of the Pauline triad πίστις, ἀγάπη, and ἐλπίς (outside of Christian inscriptions), on which the genitive τοῦ κυρίου ἡμῶν Ἰησοῦ Χριστοῦ hangs.[6]

While the term ἔργον designates any type of work, deed, activity, or occupation in general,[7] in inscriptions it mainly refers to architectural constructions (or the building work itself) such as temples,[8] funerary monuments,[9] road works,[10] public infrastructures,[11] or Jewish and Christian buildings.[12] Understandably, it can sometimes be used in a more general sense as well.[13] Ἔργον, however, rarely refers to one's athletic, artistic, and/or moral achievements,[14] let alone one's 'pious works' (εὐσεβέων ἔργων),[15] or one's 'works of discretion' (ἔργα σαοφροσύνης).[16]

The substantive πίστις is not as common as ἔργον and, in Roman

---

6   The relation of the genitive to the triad remains debated. See Von Dobschütz, *Thessalonicher-Briefe*, 65; Rigaux, *Thessaloniciens*, 369; Richard, *Thessalonians*, 46; Holtz, *Thessalonicher*, 43.
7   Cf. s.v. LSJ and BDAG.
8   E.g. *IG* X 2,1.31 (Thessalonica, 27 B.C.E.–14 C.E.); *I.Ephesos* 18B (II C.E.); *I.North Galatia* 209B (Kalecik, III C.E.?).
9   E.g. *IGBulg* IV 2254 and 2268 (Neine/Parthicopolis, undated); *SEG* 15.796 (Phrygia, IV C.E.).
10 E.g. *I.Ephesos* 3157 (II C.E.).
11 E.g. *I.Ephesos* 20 (I C.E.) and 633 (II C.E.); *I.Aphrodisias* 2007 nos. 11.508 (II C.E.), 12.909 (II–III C.E.), 12.1111 (II C.E.).
12 E.g. *I.Smyrna* 844 (IV–V C.E.); *I.Mylasa* 621 (VI C.E.); *SEG* 37.1275 (Anemurium, VI C.E.).
13 E.g. *TAM* V,2.945 and *TAM* V,2.991 (Thyatira, III–IV C.E.): τὸ ἔργον τῶν βαφέων; *REG* 112 (1999): 2–17, ll. 49–50 (Claros, III B.C.E.): τὸ δὲ ἔργον τῆς κατασκευῆς τῆς στήλης καὶ τῆς ἀναγρα||[50]φῆς τῶμ ψηφισμάτων; *I.Ephesos* 2101 (undated): ῥητορικῆς ἔργα.
14 See, e.g. *SEG* 41.1407 B (Seleukeia on the Kalykadnos, II C.E.), which celebrates a wrestler for his many victories and 'deeds of great wrestling' (μεγάλης ἔργα παλαισμοσύνης), or *I.Tralleis* 110 (I–III C.E.), which praises a winner of Asian contests for the 'superiority of his accomplishment' and the 'orderliness of his character' (διά τε τὴν | τοῦ ἔργου ὑπεροχὴν καὶ τὸ κόσμιον τοῦ ἤθους).
15 *I.Aphrodisias* 2007 no. 15.347 (IV–VI C.E.). The expression is not reserved to Christian inscriptions. See *I.Tomis* II 380 (III–IV C.E.): εὐσεβὲς ἔργον | ἔδρασε.
16 *I.Ancyra* II 367 (V–VI C.E.).

times, is most frequently employed in honorary, civic, and diplomatic contexts to express faithfulness or loyalty to one's spouse, ancestors, city, state, or political allies.[17] For example, a decree from Maroneia concerning an embassy sent to Claudius evokes the 'good will and loyalty' the Maroneians kept towards the Romans continually and incessantly (ἵν' οἱ πάντοτε καὶ ἀδιαλείπτως τὴν πρὸς Ῥωμαίους εὔ|νοιαν καὶ πίστιν φυλάξαντες; B, ll. 17–19).[18] A dedication to the god M(e)is Tiamou Artemidorou, on the other hand, exposes a spouse who 'was not faithful' to her husband but committed a fault against him (οὐκ ἐτήρησε τὴν πίστιν τ|ῷ Γαείῳ ἀλλ' ἐξήμαρτεν; ll. 5–6).[19] In particular, it can refer to the trust or confidence a magistrate, a civic benefactor, or a priest, might have been entrusted with by the council and/or the people in the conduct of civic affairs, or by a divinity in the conduct of cultic activities. An honorary decree from Eretria, for instance, congratulates a gymnasiarch for conducting himself in a manner worthy of his ancestors and of the confidence entrusted to him by the people (ἐνδόξως ἀνεστράφη καὶ ἀξίως ἑαυτοῦ τε καὶ τῶν προγό|νων καὶ τῆς ἐγχειρισθείσης αὐτῶι ὑπὸ τοῦ δήμου πίστεως; ll. 3–4).[20] Another decree from Smyrna honours a *chresmologos* for being worthy both of the trust of the god and of the ambition of the people (ἄ[ξιον αὐτὸν παρέχε]|ται

---

17 Also encountered are more commercial or legal senses of the term such as 'pledge of good faith' or 'security' (e.g. IG XII 7.62; I.Cret. IV 285), or 'good faith/*bona fide*' (καλῇ πίστει; I.Ano Maked. 186, Orestis, II c.e.). Cf. Morgan's exhaustive survey of fides/πίστις in the Principate (*Roman Faith*, 36–122). Names formed on the Πιστ- stem are plenty as well. See s.v. in Fraser and Matthews, Lexicon.
18 I.Thrake Aeg. E180 (SEG 53.659; Samothrace, 41–54 c.e.). Cf. the decree in honour of Hermagoras Klasios from Rhodos, who demonstrated 'good will and loyalty' (εὔνοιαν καὶ πίστιν) towards the emperor Titus, the Senate, and the people of Rome (IG XII 1.58; I c.e.), or the Aphrodisian decree concerning the election of ambassadors 'who were loyal and well-disposed towards the Romans' (πρεσβευτὰς ἄνδρας ... πίστιν ἐχόντων καὶ εὐνοϊκῶς πρὸς Ῥωμαίους διαχειμένων; I.Aphrodisias 2007 no. 8.3; 88 b.c.e.).
19 SEG 57.1159 (Dima/Kerbia, Lydia; late imperial period). See also the honorary decree for a prominent woman from Sardis who was praised for her nobility (ἀξία τοῦ γένους), moral quality (ἦθος), and loyalty to her ancestors (πίστιν δὲ προγόνων; I.Sardis I 44; 26–130 c.e.).
20 IG XII 9.235 (Eretria, I b.c.e.).

καὶ τῆς τοῦ θεοῦ πίστεως καὶ τῆ[ς τοῦ δήμου]|| φιλοτιμίας; *ll*. 13–15).[21] In epitaphs and honorific inscriptions, πίστις can often stand for a moral or philosophical virtue. At Patras, a certain Phaedrus was celebrated for his 'goodwill and faithfulness' (τὴν σὴν εὔνοιαν καὶ | πίστιν) as to the 'rules of life' (ἐν βιοτῆς μέτ||ροις),[22] while at Corinth a client put up a marble base in honour of his friend and patron on account of his 'virtue and trustworthiness' (ἀ[ρετ]ῆς ἕνεχ[α]|| κ[αὶ] πίστεως).[23] Similarly, at Sparta a gymnasium trainer (ἀλείπτης) was commended for his 'trustworthiness' towards the athletes under his care (ἀλείπτην,| πίστεως τῆς περὶ || τοὺς ὑπ' αὐτῷ γεγε{ι}ν<η>|μένους ἀθλητὰς | ἕνεκα),[24] while a teacher (διδάσκαλος) from Rhodos was remembered on his epitaph as having been appointed as 'a steward of mysteries' (ἐπιστάτης μυστικῶν) by Hermes and Hekate on account of his 'complete trustworthiness' (πίστεως πά[σ]ης χ[άριν]).[25] Similar inscriptions praising prominent citizens for their 'virtue and trustworthiness' have been found at Tralleis,[26] Aphrodisias,[27] and Maionia.[28]

As far as the extant evidence goes, πίστις never seems to be used in the sense of 'trust' or 'faith' in a divinity outside of Christian inscriptions.[29]

---

21 SEG 42.1065 (Claros; II B.C.E.). The confidence of Apollo towards Menophilos is, in context, made evident by the god's call to the presidency of the *manteion* by virtue of his piety (cf. *ll*. 6–8). Cf. Robert and Robert, 'Décret de Colophon', 280, 290–91.
22 *CIG* 1553 (Patras, I–II C.E.).
23 *Corinth* VIII 3.265 (II C.E.).
24 *IG* V 1.491 (Sparta, Roman period).
25 *IG* XII 1.141 (Rhodos, I B.C.E.).
26 *I.Tralleis* 80 (post 127 C.E.).
27 *I.Aphrodisias 2007* nos. 11.212 (I C.E.) and 5.204 (II–III C.E.).
28 *TAM* V,1.514 (I B.C.E.).
29 See, e.g. the famous third-century epitaph of the bishop of Hierapolis in which he affirms that πίστις led and sustained him throughout his life (Πίστις π[άντη δὲ προῆγε]|| καὶ παρέθηκε [τροφὴν]|| πάντη; SEG 30.1479, Hierapolis, ante 216 C.E.), or that a fourth-century soldier from Lycaonia who confessed holding fast unto 'the faith of Christians' (τὴν τῶν Χρειστιανῶν πίστιν φυλάσσων) despite his many tortures (MAMA I 170; Laodikeia Katakekaumene, IV C.E.). For additional examples, see *I.Chr. Macédoine* 234 (ἐν τῇ ὀρθῇ [πί]στι; Philippi, IV CE); *IG* IX 1², 4.1191 (πίστιν βασίλιαν; Kerkyra, V C.E.); *I.Ephesos* 1353 ([πάσαις ταῖς ἐκκλη]σίαις τῆς ὀρθοδόξου πίστεως; VI C.E.); and the many late antique epitaphs from Zoora put up for Christians of 'good name and good faith' (μετὰ καλοῦ ὀνόματος καὶ καλῆς πίστεως; e.g. *I.Zoora* Ia 95, etc.).

This might be because polytheists never felt the need to articulate their πίστις/*fides* in cultic activities or to advertise it on monumental structures, and/or because the personification of confidence and good faith (Πίστις/*Fides*) was herself worshipped as a goddess (often in association with Zeus/Jupiter).[30]

In the light of the predominant use of πίστις in inscriptions, it is therefore questionable whether the sense of 'faith' or even 'belief' (in God) is what would have immediately jumped to the audience's mind. Indeed, given the occurrence of both terms in honorific inscriptions, the phrase ἔργον τῆς πίστεως might have been more readily understood as referring to the exercise of a virtue 'before God' (ἔμπροσθεν τοῦ θεοῦ, 1:3),[31] rather than to some 'work of faith (in God)' as is commonly translated.[32] That is, the Thessalonians might have taken it as a commendation for their faithful attitude towards Christ (thus taking the distant genitive τοῦ κυρίου ἡμῶν Ἰησοῦ Χριστοῦ in 1:3b as objective), which they practically demonstrated by holding fast unto Paul's teaching and by living a life worthy of the gospel (cf. 4:1–2).[33]

2. Ὁ κόπος τῆς ἀγάπης

Contrary to the lexeme ἔργον, the term κόπος, which emphasises the trouble and weariness involved in work,[34] is much rarer and, as noted above, is never encountered with ἀγάπη. In most cases, it is used to express one's 'own (or joint) efforts' (ἐκ τῶν ἰδίων/κοινῶν κόπων)

---

30 See, e.g. a marble stele recording the appointment of Straton as priest of Roma and Pistis (Ἱερεὺς ἀπε|δείχθη Ῥώμη|ς καὶ Πίστεως | Στράτων Ἐσ||τιαίου; *ll.* 1–5; *BCH* 19 [1895]: 554; Teos, imperial era), a dedication to Πίστις and Ὁμόνοια from Pergamon (*MDAI[A]* 35 [1910]: 460 no. 42; II c.e.), or the statue of Πίστις dedicated by the Kompetaliastai to the gods at Delos (Κομπεταλιασταὶ γενόμενοι | τὴν Πίστιν vac θεοῖς vac ἀνέθηκαν; *I.Délos* 1761, *ll.* 18–19; 98/7 b.c.e.). Cf. Otto, 'Fides', *PW* 6 (1909): 2281–86; Bernert, 'Pistis', *PW* 6 (1950): 1812; Freyburger, *Fides*, 229–317; Morgan, *Roman Faith*, 123, 128–37. According to Morgan, 132, the cult of Πίστις reached the Greek East in II c.e..
31 Cf. Légasse, *Thessaloniciens*, 76.
32 See, e.g. NIV, NAS, ESV.
33 Cf. Frame, *Thessalonians*, 76; Schreiber, *Thessalonicher*, 95–96.
34 See s.v. in LSJ and BDAG.

in preparing a funerary monument for a loved one or for oneself.³⁵ Well-attested in Macedonia in the Roman era, the expression likely implied that one acted independently of testamentary obligations, that is, at one's own expense (ἐξ ἰδίων δαπανῶν),³⁶ and thus out of a sense of responsibility and affection for the deceased. On rare occasions, the phrase can also be used to indicate one's efforts in setting up a votive for a deity.³⁷ Similarly, benefactors can sometimes be congratulated for their munificence towards the city. An honorary decree from Apollonia Pontica, for instance, praises a benefactor for sparing neither efforts nor expenses in his service to the city (μήτε κόπου φεισάμε|νος μήτε δαπάνης; *ll.* 10–11).³⁸ Ordinary persons could also be rewarded. A freedwoman received her sepulture as an 'eternal gift' (δῶρον ἀθάνατον) in recognition of her 'toils and goodwill' towards her former master (ἀντὶ τῶν κόπων σου καὶ τῆς ἰς ἐμὲ εὐνοί||ας; *ll.* 4–5).³⁹

Compared to the lexemes φιλία and φιλανθρωπία which occur hundreds of times, the noun ἀγάπη (as well as the adjective ἀγαπητός) is seldom attested in inscriptions (or even in papyri),⁴⁰ even though personal names formed on the Ἀγάπ- stem are not uncommon in the late Roman period (especially among Christians).⁴¹ This is not entirely surprising given that the term became familiar only progressively

---

35 See, e.g. a sarcophagus from Thessalonica paid out of the deceased's 'common efforts': Αἰλεία Θεοφίλα Αὐρηλείῳ Σαβίνῳ τῷ γλυκυτάτῳ συνβείῳ ἐκ τῶν | κοινῶν κόπων μνείας χάρειν καὶ ἑαυτῇ ζῶσα (*ll.* 6–7; *IG* X 2,1.531; III c.e.). Cf. *IG* X 2,1.443, 445, 478, 495, 546, etc. (Thessalonica, I–III c.e.); *I.Kato Maked.* 262 (Edessa, II–III c.e.), 539 (Pella, II–III c.e.); *SEG* 45.774 (Cassandreia, II–III c.e.).
36 E.g. *IG* XIV 1882 (Rome, undated); *IG* XII 2.443 (Mytilene, undated).
37 See, e.g. a votive for Zeus Ombrios put up 'out of the joint efforts of the first cohors': Διε<ὶ> τῷ ὁμ|βραρῷ λε|γεῶνος | τρίτης Γα||λλικῆς | Οὐαλέριος | Κάσσιος (ἑκατόνταρχος) ... ἐκ | κοιν(ῶν) κό(πων) χ|ώρτης πρώ|της ἀνέθη||καν (*ll.* 1–15; *IGLS* 3,1.741; Gunduzli, III c.e.).
38 *IGBulg* I² 390 (Apollonia Pontica, II–I b.c.e.). See also a monument from Aphrodisias honouring the president of an athletic association (ξυστάρχης) for his financial support (δα|[π]ανήμασιν ἱκανοῖς) and his 'many efforts' (κόπῳ πολλῷ) in organising an athletic contest in Pisidian Antioch (*I.Aphrodisias* 2007 no. 12.920 i.a.32; 138–169 c.e.).
39 *IG* X 2,1.691 (Thessalonica, 147 c.e.).
40 Arzt-Grabner, *Philemon*, 177; Kreinecker, *2. Thessaloniker*, 115. Cf. Wischmeyer, 'Agape', 218–24.
41 See s.v. in Fraser and Matthews, *Lexicon*. Cf. Wischmeyer, 'Agape', 224–27; Bons, *Lexicon of the Septuagint*, 43, s.v. ἀγάπη.

(whereas the verb ἀγαπάω was already well established in common parlance by III B.C.E. and the translation of the LXX).[42] The noun is mostly employed in epitaphs to refer to the affectionate character of the deceased who can, for example, be remembered as a wife 'full of affection and love for her husband' (πολλῆς στοργῆς καὶ ἀγά|πης ἀνδρί; *ll.* 1–2),[43] or who is sometimes said to be of 'beloved memory' (χάριν μνείας ἀγαπητῆς).[44] Nevertheless, as a virtue, love is primarily encountered in Christian inscriptions (often alongside πίστις and ἐλπίς).[45] Allusions to the ἀγάπη of a deity, let alone to one's love *for* a deity, are unattested and exceptional even in Christian inscriptions.[46] And so are mentions of the love of a native land for its inhabitants, as can be read on the epitaph of a decurion from Tiberias (ἢ τίς ὑπὸ πάτρης τόσσην ἔσχ᾽ ἀγάπην; *l.* 6).[47]

Although the origin and significance of ἀγάπη have often been debated, there is little linguistic evidence to suggest that the term ever had a specific theological connotation (e.g. 'self-sacrificing' or 'self-giving love'), so that its broad semantic range is now generally accepted.[48] The little extant epigraphic evidence confirms this conclusion and highlights the importance ἀγάπη gained in Christian thought in late antiquity. No familiarity with the LXX would have therefore been required to make sense of the expression κόπος τῆς ἀγάπης, which the audience might not necessarily have understood vis-à-vis Christ. This is all the more so since ἀγάπη is seldom used in inscriptions to characterise one's relationship with a deity, and since the position of the geni-

---

42 See Joly, *Le vocabulaire chrétien de l'amour* (on ἀγάπη specifically, see 35, 48); Barr, 'Love', 7–8, 14; Swinn, 'Ἀγαπᾶν'; Lee, 'Septuagint', 107. Literary attestations of ἀγάπη prior to the LXX are rare. A quick search of the *TLG* returns only eight occurrences. This is not the case with the verb ἀγαπάω which was already in use in Homeric and Classical Greek. Cf. Barr, 'Love', 8; Bons, *Lexicon of the Septuagint*, 41–42, s.v. ἀγάπη.
43 *IG* XII 9.856 (Eretria, Roman period).
44 *TAM* V,2.1289 (Hierocaesarea, undated).
45 E.g. *I.Perinthos* 285 (IV–V C.E.); *TAM* V,2.1406 (Lydia, 358–378 C.E.); *I.Mus. Iznik* 550 (IV–VI C.E.); *IGLS* 3,1.727 (Rhosos, undated); *IGLS* 4.1460–1461 (El-Bâra, undated) and 1732 (Šeyh Barak, undated).
46 E.g. *I.Chr. Bulgarien* 207 (Philippopolis, IV C.E.): ἀγάπην ἔχων παρὰ θ(εο)ῦ (*l.* 4).
47 *SEG* 8.11 (Peek, *GVI* 730; Tiberias, III C.E.).
48 See Barr, 'Love'; *DGE* s.v. Cf. Lee, 'Septuagint', 107–108; Aitken, *No Stone*, 68–69.

tive τοῦ κυρίου ἡμῶν Ἰησοῦ Χριστοῦ leaves a margin of ambiguity. Here as well, the praiseful allusion to the Thessalonians' 'labour of love' may thus have been primarily intended, and understood, in reference to their virtuous efforts at loving one another (and their contemporaries), even though the distant genitive τοῦ Χριστοῦ leaves the alternative reading a possibility.

3. Ἡ ὑπομονὴ τῆς ἐλπίδος

As far as our evidence goes, the noun ὑπομονή is principally observed in (a handful of) Christian inscriptions from late antiquity either as a (rare) personal name or in the general sense of 'endurance'.[49] The only non-Christian attestation comes from the decree by Octavian granting Roman citizenship and exemption from taxes to a fleet commander for his military assistance in war and his endurance in dangers (οὐδενὸς φεισάμενος τῶν πρὸς ὑπομονὴν δεινῶν; *l.* 14).[50]

Predominantly encountered in civic and funerary contexts, the substantive ἐλπίς offered a large range of possibilities to express one's hope(s) in general, or to refer more specifically to the object(s) of one's hope (which, of course, could vary depending on circumstances).[51] In civic or honorific decrees, it often evokes the 'greater hopes' (μεγίστων ἐλπίδων, πλήονας ἐλπίδας),[52] the 'better hopes' (εἰς βελτείονας ἐλπίδας),[53] the 'many good hopes' (πολλῶν ἐλπίδων ἀγαθῶν),[54] or even 'the most beautiful hopes' (τὰς ἀρίστας ἐλπίδας),[55] that citizens could have for their city, native land, or personal life, and which benefactors could fulfil through their good deeds.[56] A classic example is an honorary inscrip-

---

49 E.g. *I.Chr. Egypte* 467 (Hermonthis, undated); *IG* XIV 531 (*CIG* 9474; Catania, IV–V c.e.); *SEG* 39.1023 (Syracuse, IV–VI c.e.); *ICUR* IV 9911 (undated).
50 *IGLS* 3,1.718 (Sherk, *RDGE* 58; Rhosos, 42–30 b.c.e.).
51 Cf. s.v. in LSJ, BDAG, DGE, TLNT 1:482–90 (the distinction between 'secular' and 'religious' objects of hope in the latter is unnecessary). For papyrological material, see Kreinecker, *2. Thessaloniker*, 186–88.
52 *IG* IV² 1.83 (Epidauros, ca. 40–42 CE); *I.Byzantion* 3 (I c.e.).
53 *I.Tomis* 2 (II–I c.e.).
54 *IG* XII 7.239 (Amorgos, undated). Cf. *I.Kibyra* 56 (I b.c.e.–I c.e.); *SEG* 2.713 (Pednelissos, II–III c.e.).
55 Robert, *Claros*, 11–17 (V, 22).
56 Cf. Robert, *BE* 1960.93.

tion from Iasos in which the *boule*, the *demos*, and the local Roman *negotiatores* praise the priest of Agrippa Postumus and Hermes for fulfilling the 'great hopes' of the *demos* (τὰς μεγίστας παρεχόμενον | ἐλπίδας τῶι δήμωι; *ll*. 5–6).[57]

What the *demos*' expectations consisted of is generally not specified, but it must have related to the welfare of the city. In the so-called calendar inscription of Priene, for example, the 'hopes' (τὰς ἐλπίδας, *l*. 37) which Augustus is said to have exceeded ([ὑπερ]|έθηκεν) through his benefactions were most certainly aspirations for peace, prosperity, and good fortune, as is made clear by the decree itself (*ll*. 30–77) and by the proconsular letter prefacing it (*ll*. 1–30).[58] Alternatively, a benefactor himself might come to embody the aspirations of the people, as in the honorary inscription for the Galatarch T. Claudius Procillianus who was acclaimed as the 'new hope of (his) native city' (νέαν ἐλπίδα τῆς πατρίδος).[59] Occasionally, ἐλπίς could also indicate a more mundane object of hope. A decree from Elis, for instance, simply alludes to a wrestler's hope of winning a sacred crown in athletic contests at Olympia (ὡς πρόδηλον | εἶναι τὴν ἐλπίδα τῆς ἐπὶ τὸν ἱερώτατον στέφανον | αὐτῶι).[60]

More frequently, ἐλπίς is employed in funerary contexts to express parents' crushed hopes in the loss of a child.[61] In an epitaph from Beroia, for example, the parents of a young daughter deplore that Envy and Pluto have snatched their 'golden flower' (χρύ|σεον ἄνθος) and

---

57 *I.Iasos* 90 (cf. *BE* 1973.427; 4/7 C.E.).
58 *I.Priene* B-M 14 (9 B.C.E.).
59 *I.Ancyra* 83 (ca. 150 C.E.). As Mitchell notes, this may have been a way of 'expressing a wish both that he should pursue a career in his native city, and that he was prepared to take up his father's mantle as a civic benefactor' (246). Cf. decree X in *I.Sardis* I 8 (2 B.C.E.) in which the son of a benefactor is said to have been born 'with the fairest hopes' (ταῖς καλλίσταις ἐλπίσιν) of becoming an illustrious citizen as well.
60 *I.Olympia* 54 (*Syll.*³ 1073; II C.E.). See also an honorary decree for a student of rhetoric whose hopes to gain an education were crushed as he died prematurely (δείλαιος οὐδὲ τῆς ἐλπί|ίδος ἀπολαύσας ἐπὶ | πλέον ἔφθη; *I.Klaudiupolis* 70, Roman period).
61 Cf. Strubbe, 'Epigrams', 47–48.

dashed their 'good hopes' (χείρας γονέων | ἐλπίδας ἐσθλοτάτας).[62] In another from upper Macedonia, Hades is blamed for his lack of mercy and for cutting down the hopes of a twelve-year-old's parents (ἐλπίδας ἐκκόψας ἡμετέρων τοκέω[ν]).[63] What hopes the child was supposed to carry is generally not told, but a funerary epigram from Chios makes it explicit: parents expected to be nurtured in old age (τὰς γὰρ ἀφ' ὑμῶν || Ἅιδης γηροτρόφους ἐλπίδας ὠρφάνισεν; *ll.* 9–10).[64] Similarly, two epitaphs from Phrygia and Syria respectively describe a daughter and a lost son as being their father's cherished 'hope in old age' (ἐλπίδα εἰς γῆρας/γήρους).[65]

Tombstones could also be occasions for more existential reflections about the fragility and futility of human life, or to voice one's 'endless hopes' (ἀτέλεστοι | ἐλπίδες) in, presumably, a blessed afterlife.[66] Others, however, are more cynical in their outlook and bemoan the absurdity of human hopes,[67] or deride the aspirations of mortal men as being 'uncertain' and as 'staring into the unknown' (ἄστατοι ἐλπίδες εἰσὶ βροτῶν ἰς ἄ|δηλα βλέπουσαι), leaving those who die 'cheated of all hopes' (πάσαις ἐλπίσι | ψευσαμέναις).[68] Curses to avert tomb desecration were likewise common and could be called to frustrate one's 'hopes of (bearing) children' (τέκνων ἐλ|πίδας μὴ σχοῖ).[69]

Significantly, expressing one's hope in a deity (by means of an objective genitive, i.e. ἐ. τοῦ θεοῦ) does not seem to have been a common practice in inscriptions, possibly because the personification of

---

62 *I.Beroia* 404 (II c.e.). Cf. a similar expression (ἐλπίδας ἀθλοτάτας) in the funerary epigram *SEG* 35.630 (Larissa, II c.e.).
63 *I.Ano Maked.* 193 (Orestis, I–II c.e.).
64 *CIG* 2240 (Chios, I c.e.).
65 *Steinepigramme* III 16/31/17 (Appia, III–V c.e.) and *SEG* 26.1622 (Seleukeia, undated).
66 *IG* XII 8.38 (Lemnos, II c.e.).
67 See, e.g. a gnomic funerary inscription found in a hypogeum at Kos: ἄστοχον ἐλπίδε[ς]| εἰσὶν ἐν ἀνθρώποις | ἰδίου ἅμα καὶ βίου (*ll.* 1–3; *IG* XII 4,4.3408; *I.Cos Segre* EF 346; *SEG* 57.794; II–III c.e.).
68 *SEG* 40.1090 (Lydia/Phrygia, 154/5 c.e.).
69 *I.Hierapolis Judeich* 155 (undated). Cf. *I.Hierapolis Judeich* 339 (*ll.* 10–13) for a similar curse.

'good hope' herself could be worshipped as Ἐλπίς Ἀγαθή,[70] or simply because it was itself implied in the act of offering a votive. Still, the term is occasionally found in cultic contexts. In a rare votive from Thracia, for example, two stablemen in charge of (imperial?) draft animals dedicated a plate to the (otherwise unattested) god Kellon 'for their hope' (ὑπὲρ | τῆς ἐνθήκ[ης] καὶ αὐτῶν ἐλπίδος; *ll*. 3–4).[71] A curse tablet from Athens 'restrains'—'binds' (literally)—the hopes of the cursed victims and the help they could gain from gods and heroes: καταδήω (names of twelve persons), τούτων τῶν ἀνδρῶν καὶ | γυναικ[ῶ] ν καὶ ἐλπίδας | καὶ παρὰ θεῶν καὶ πα<ρ>' ἡρώ|ων καὶ ἐργασίας [ἁ] πάσας; *ll*. 1–11).[72] More explicit still is a so-called confession inscription from Lydia in which the dedicant acknowledges his own fortune as a source of hope in the face of Zeus Oreites's punishment (ἡ δὲ ἐμὴ Τύχη ἐλπίδαν | ἔδωκε).[73] In a similar vein, the sacred law of Antiochos I instituted several religious regulations to be observed in honour of the king himself and for the 'blessed personal hopes of [the people's] fortune' (οὐ μόνον εἰς τιμὴν ἡμετέραν | ἀλλὰ καὶ μακαριστὰς ἐλπίδας ἰδίας ἑ|κάστου τύχης, *ll*. 107–109).[74]

While the idea of placing one's hope in a particular deity (for whatever benefit) is rarely articulated in inscriptions, it is unlikely that the Thessalonians would have been unfamiliar with the general concept (especially given the numerous votive offerings discovered in the tem-

---

70 See, e.g. the dice oracle *I.Pisidia Central* 5 §33 (Nollé, *Losorakel*, Kr, pp. 68–77; Kremna, 117–138 C.E.), of which at least eight other copies are known (cf. *SEG* 31.1285; *TAM* III,1.34). Ἐλπίς was the only one not to escape the *pithos* opened by Pandora according to Hesiod (*Op*. 90–105), and the last benevolent god to remain on earth according to the poet Theognis of Megara (1135–1146 E).
71 *IGBulg* III 1519 (Cillis, Roman era). See also a votive altar found near Aizanoi offered to Hosios as a votive 'for the hopes' of the dedicant (['O]σίῳ εὐχὴν ὑπὲρ τῶν ἐλπίδων; *EA* 18 [1991]: 38 no. 83; II C.E.).
72 'I bind (so and so), and the hopes of these men and women, and all the deeds from gods and heroes'. Audollent, *Defixiones*, no. 72 (III–II B.C.E.). See also Audollent, *Defixiones*, no. 73: καταδήω Πάνφιλον καὶ | ἐλπίδας τὰς Πανφίλου ἁ|πάσας καὶ ἐργασίας πάσας (*ll*. 1–3).
73 *SEG* 38.1236 (ca. 200 C.E.).
74 *IGLS* 1 (Nemroud Dagh; ca. 31 B.C.E.).

ple of the Egyptian gods, for instance).[75] What inscriptions highlight nonetheless is the tendency of citizens to put their hope in the hands of civic and royal or imperial benefactors for the welfare of their city and nation, and to reward these with monumental honours when they proved worthy of their expectations.[76] What they also poignantly illustrate are the existential aspirations of the ordinary people in the face of death, and how children carried the hopes of their parents for their posterity and care in old age. Against this background, Paul's allusion to the Lord Christ as the object and source of the Thessalonians' hope would have undoubtedly struck a chord with his audience. On the one hand, they might have taken it as an encouragement to continue to view him as their principal (κύριος) benefactor to whom, by implication, they should turn for all their earthly aspirations. On the other hand, it would have reminded them that only Christ could address their existential aspirations and give them hope in their current eschatological distress.

4. Conclusion

By way of conclusion, let me reiterate that 1 Thessalonians 1:3 presents us with the earliest Pauline attestation of the triad of virtues πίστις, ἀγάπη, ἐλπίς, which are combined here in a unique fashion with the substantives ἔργον, κόπος, and ὑπομονή (and with θώραξ and περικεφαλαία in 5:8). As inscriptions have illustrated, none of these virtues is uniquely Pauline and each would have strongly resonated with a first-century Graeco-Roman audience. In this respect, the epigraphic context of Greek cities provides us with a rich background against which Paul's thanksgiving might be heard afresh. It also helps us better appreciate how Paul appropriates moral and philosophical concepts that were popular and occasionally promoted on public monuments, redefines them teleogically with Christ as a reference point, and

---

75 E.g. *IG* X 2,1.75-123. Cf. Steimle, *Religion*, 79-132; Falezza, *I santuari della Macedonia*, 266-80. For papyrological examples, see Kreinecker, *2. Thessaloniker*, 188.

76 On the social dynamics of civic euergetism (or patronage), see the classics by Veyne, *Le pain et le cirque*; and Gauthier, *Les cités grecques*.

applies them to the communal and spiritual life of the Thessalonian *ekklesia*. In effect, Paul's thanksgiving can therefore be read as a commendation for maintaining their loyalty to Christ, for striving to support one another in love, and for persevering in the hope that Christ will sustain them in the midst of adversity (cf. 1:6, 2:14, 3:3).

Julien M. Ogereau
Universität Wien

Bibliography

For all epigraphic sources, see the AIEGL's *List of Abbreviations of Editions and Works of Reference for Alphabetic Greek Epigraphy* at https://www.aiegl.org/newsreader/grepiabbr.html.

Adrados, F. R. et al. (eds.) — *Diccionario griego-español* (7 vols.; Madrid: Consejo Superior de Investigaciones Cientificas, 1980–).

Aitken, J. K. — *No Stone Unturned: Greek Inscriptions and Septuagint Vocabulary* (Critical Studies in the Hebrew Bible, 5; Winona Lake, IN: Eisenbrauns, 2014).

Arzt-Grabner, P. — *Philemon* (Papyrologische Kommentare zum Neuen Testament, 1; Göttingen: Vandenhoeck & Ruprecht, 2003).

Barr, J. — 'Words for Love in Biblical Greek', in L. D. Hurst and N. T. Wright (eds.), *The Glory of Christ in the New Testament: Studies in Christology in Memory of George Bradford Caird* (Oxford: Clarendon, 1987), 3–18.

Bauer, W. — *A Greek-English Lexicon of the New Testament and Other Early Christian Literature* (3rd edn; Chicago, IL: University of Chicago Press, 2000).

Best, E. — *A Commentary on the First and Second Epistles to the Thessalonians* (Black's New Testament Commentaries; London: Black, 1972).

Bons, E. (ed.) — *Historical and Theological Lexicon of the Septuagint*, vol. 1: *Alpha–Gamma* (Tübingen: Mohr Siebeck, 2020).

Bruce, F. F. — *1 and 2 Thessalonians* (Word Biblical Commentary, 45; Waco, TX: Word Books, 1982).

Dibelius, M. — *An die Thessalonicher I, II; An die Philipper* (3rd rev. edn; Handbuch zum Neuen Testament, 11; Tübingen: J. C. B. Mohr [Paul Siebeck], 1937).

Dobschütz, E. von. — *Die Thessalonicher-Briefe* (Kritisch-exegetischer Kommentar über das Neue Testament, 10; Göttingen: Vandenhoeck & Ruprecht, 1909).

Falezza, G. — *I santuari della Macedonia in età romana: Persistenze e cambiamenti del paesaggio sacro tra II secolo a.C. e IV secolo d.C.* (Rome: Quasar, 2012).

Frame, J. E. *The Epistles of St. Paul to the Thessalonians* (The International Critical Commentary; Edinburgh: T. & T. Clark, 1912).

Fraser, P. M., and E. Matthews (eds.) *A Lexicon of Greek Personal Names* (5 vols.; Oxford: Clarendon, 1987–2010).

Freyburger, G. *Fides: Étude sémantique et religieuse depuis les origines jusqu'à l'époque augustéenne* (Paris: Les Belles Lettres, 1986).

Gauthier, P. *Les cités grecques et leurs bienfaiteurs* (Bulletin de correspondance héllénique Supplément, 12; Paris: de Boccard, 1985).

Holtz, T. *Der erste Brief an die Thessalonicher* (3rd edn; Evangelisch-Katholischer Kommentar zum Neuen Testament, 13; Zürich: Benziger Verlag, 1998).

Joly, R. *Le vocabulaire chrétien de l'amour est-il original? Φιλεῖν et Ἀγαπᾶν dans le grec antique* (Bruxelles: Presses Universitaires de Bruxelles, 1968).

Kreinecker, C. M. *2. Thessaloniker* (Papyrologische Kommentare zum Neuen Testament, 3; Göttingen: Vandenhoeck & Ruprecht, 2010).

Lampe, G. W. H. (ed.) *A Patristic Greek Lexicon* (Oxford: Clarendon, 1961).

Lee, J. A. L. 'The Vocabulary of the Septuagint and Documentary Evidence', in E. Bons and J. Joosten (eds.), *Die Sprache der Septuaginta* (Handbuch zur Septuaginta, 3; Gütersloh: Gütersloher Verlagshaus, 2016), 98–118.

Légasse, S. *Les épîtres de Paul aux Thessaloniciens* (Lectio Divina Commentaires, 7; Paris: Cerf, 1999).

Liddell, H. G., and R. Scott (eds.) *A Greek-English Lexicon: With a Revised Supplement* (9th edn; Oxford: Clarendon, 1996).

Malherbe, A. J. *The Letters to the Thessalonians: A New Translation with Introduction and Commentary* (The Anchor Bible, 32B; New York, NY: Doubleday, 2000).

Morgan, T. *Roman Faith and Christian Faith: Pistis and Fides in the Early Roman Empire and Early Churches* (Oxford: Oxford University Press, 2015).

Moulton, J. H. and G. Milligan *The Vocabulary of the Greek Testament illustrated from the Papyri and other Non-literary Sources* (London: Hodder and Stoughton, 1929).

Richard, E. J. *First and Second Thessalonians* (Sacra Pagina, 11; Collegeville: The Liturgical, 1995).

Rigaux, B.	*Saint Paul: Les épitres aux Thessaloniciens* (Paris: Lecoffre, 1956).
Robert, L. and J. Robert	'Décret de Colophon pour un chresmologue de Smyrne appelé à diriger l'oracle de Claros', *Bulletin de correspondance hellénique* 116.1 (1992), 279–91.
Schreiber, S.	*Der erste Brief an die Thessalonicher* (Ökumenischer Taschenbuchkommentar zum Neuen Testament, 13.1; Gütersloh: Gütersloher Verlagshaus, 2014).
Söding, T.	*Die Trias Glaube, Hoffnung, Liebe Bei Paulus: Eine Exegetische Studie* (Stuttgarter Bibelstudien, 150; Stuttgart: Katholisches Bibelwerk, 1992).
Spicq, C.	*Theological Lexicon of the New Testament* (3 vols.; Peabody, MA: Hendrickson, 1994).
Steimle, C.	*Religion im römischen Thessaloniki: Sakraltopographie, Kult und Gesellschaft, 168 v. Chr.–324 n. Chr.* (Studien und Texte zu Antike und Christentum, 47; Tübingen: Mohr Siebeck, 2008).
Strubbe, J. H. M.	'Epigrams and Consolation Decrees for Deceased Youths', *L'antiquité classique* 67 (1998), 45–75.
Swinn, S. P.	'Ἀγαπᾶν in the Septuagint', in T. Muraoka (ed.), *Melbourne Symposium on Septuagint Lexicography* (Septuagint and Cognate Studies, 28; Atlanta, GA: Scholars, 1990), 49–81.
Veyne, P.	*Le pain et le cirque: Sociologie historique d'un pluralisme politique* (Paris: Seuil, 1976).
Weiß, W.	'Glaube—Liebe—Hoffnung: Zu der Trias bei Paulus', *Zeitschrift für die neutestamentliche Wissenschaft* 84 (1993), 196–217.
Wischmeyer, O.	'Vorkommen und Bedeutung von Agape in der außerchristlichen Antike', *Zeitschrift für die neutestamentliche Wissenschaft und die Kunde der älteren Kirche* 69 (1978), 212–38.
Wissowa, G. et al. (eds.)	*Paulys Realencyclopädie der classischen Altertumswissenschaft* (Stuttgart: J. B. Metzler, 1894–1978).

GRACE AFTER PAUL

Virtues in New Testament Letters and Corresponding Names
on Early Christian Sepulchral Epitaphs in *ICG*

Cilliers Breytenbach

Abstract

This essay explores the nature of those virtues that the writers of the New Testament commend, their occurrence in Christian funerary epitaphs in *Inscriptiones Christianae Graecae* from the third to the sixth centuries AD, and offers an explanation for the occurrence of these particular virtues as personal names among Christians of Late Antiquity.

Sometimes the information on Christian funerary epitaphs is very terse, revealing nothing but the name of the interred person. Therefore, the onomastic study of inscriptions is important. In some cases, Christian name-giving adapts the local tradition of name giving. Apart from the tradition to name children after their grandparents, parents started to name their children after the figures in the Bible: Peter, John, Mary, Paul, Andrew, Thomas, Susanna. They also named them after—especially the local—Christian martyrs. As from the fourth century onward, specific Christian names like Anastasia/os, Pistos, Kyriakos and Kyriake become popular. For Lycaonia and Attica, this has been discussed.[1]

There is, however, another interesting aspect. Christian inscrip-

---

1   Breytenbach and Zimmermann, *Lycaonia*, 399–418; Breytenbach and Tzavella, *Attica*, 245–248, 258–260.

tions collected, translated and published in *ICG*² reveal a high incidence of names derived from adjectives and nouns denoting abstract entities. Generally, there are many examples that personal names were derived from adjectives and nouns, some of them denoting commendable behaviour or virtues. In fact, many Latin cognomina were derived from adjectives.³ Since classical times, Greeks have used adjectives and nouns as personal names too and since imperial times there was a notable increase in this tendency.⁴ Like other Greek-speaking people from Antiquity, Christians also used adjectives and nouns to name their children.⁵ In particular, they tend to use words denoting the behaviour required in the exhortations in the letters of the New Testament. Many of these virtues commended by especially Paul and the author of the Pastoral Epistles, overlap with what the Cynic philosopher Musonius Rufus (30 – *c.* AD 100) calls the law of Zeus, the common father of all humans and all gods: 'His command and law is that man be just and honest, beneficent, temperate, high-minded, superior to pain, superior to pleasure, free of all envy and all malice; to put it briefly, the law of Zeus bids man be good.'⁶ Against this background this essay explores the nature of those virtues that the writers of the New Testament commend,⁷ and their occurrence in Christian funerary epitaphs in *ICG*

---

2   See the newest version at https://icg.uni-kiel.de. Since the database covers mainland Greece and central Asia-Minor the names listed are representative but not complete. Monuments from coastal areas of Asia Minor and the Agean Islands still have to be integrated.
3   See Kajanto, *Cognomina*.
4   see LGPN 1–5b at http://clas-lgpn2.classics.ox.ac.uk/name.
5   E.g. Ἀγαθος, Ἀγάπη, Ἀδήσιτος, Ἀδόλιος, Ἀνικητία, Ἀνίκητος, Ἀνέγκλητος, Ἐπαγάθη, Εὐτροπία, Εὐφράσιος, Σωφρονία and Σωφρόνιος (For references see Breytenbach and Tzavella, *Attica*, 257–258; Breytenbach and Zimmermann, *Lycaonia*, 412–413). Typically Christian: Ἀκάκιος (ICG 1360, 3277, 3279, 4247), Εὐσταθία and Εὐστάθιος (ICG 1268, 1571, 1823, 2039, 2294, 2318, 2377, 2522, 2606, 2989, 3331, 3349, 3952, 4068, 4087, 4183).
6   Musonius Rufus, *Dissertatonium*, 16.84–88 (trans. Lutz): πρόσταγμά τε γὰρ ἐκείνου καὶ νόμος ἐστὶ τὸν ἄνθρωπον εἶναι δίκαιον, χρηστόν, εὐεργετικόν, σώφρονα, μεγαλόφρονα, κρείττω πόνων, κρείττω ἡδονῶν, φθόνου παντὸς καὶ ἐπιβουλῆς ἁπάσης καθαρόν· ἵνα δὲ συντεμὼν εἴπω, ἀγαθὸν εἶναι κελεύει τὸν ἄνθρωπον ὁ νόμος ὁ τοῦ Διός.
7   To identify the adjectives or nouns, I used section 88 of Louw and Nida's *Lexicon*.

from central Asia-Minor and mainland Greece from the third to the sixth centuries AD. The use of most of these adjectives and nouns date back to the beginnings of the written Greek language. Some of those expressing requirements set for clergy in the Pastoral Epistles were already used as names in pre-Christian times. Some of these names are not attested for Christians.[8] Neither did all virtues make it to personal names.[9] In the following, we focus on those virtues that were also used as personal names in early Christian epitaphs in *ICG* and offer an explanation for the occurrence of this particular group of names among Christians of Late Antiquity.

1. κόσμιος → Κοσμία and Κόσμιος

1 Tim. 3:2 expects that a ἐπίσκοπος should be orderly, well behaved (κόσμιος).[10] 1 Tim. 2:9 the author uses the same adjective instructing the women to clothe themselves in an orderly dress (ἐν καταστολῇ κοσμίῳ ... κοσμεῖν). For Musonius Rufus κόσμιος, like πρᾶος/πραΰς, is an attribute for a real philosopher. Someone, man or woman, has become superlatively well ordered (κοσμιώτατος), if the person is free from unlawful love, other pleasures and desires, does not live a lavish and extravagant life and can control all emotions.[11] κόσμια, in close connection with prudence or self-control (σώφρων), qualify behavior attributed to many Christian women from the third and fourth centu-

---

8   E.g. Ἀκέραιος (see Rom 16:19; Phil 2:15), Ἄμεμπτος (see Phil 2:15; 1 Thess 3:13), Ἄμωμος (see Eph 1:4; 5:27; Col 1:22; Jude 24), Ἀμώμητος (see Phil 2:15; 2 Pet 3:14), Ἄπλα/ος (see ἁπλότης in Rom. 12:8; 2 Cor 1:12; 2 Cor 8:2; 9:11,13; 11:3; Eph. 6:5; Col. 3:22), Ἀσπιλία (see James 1:27; 2 Pet 3:14), and Ἄφθορος (see Titus 2:7).

9   As far as I could check, οἰκτιρμός, μακροθυμία, and ταπεινοφροσύνη were not elevated to personal names; cf. LGPN. This also applies to ἀμώμητος, ἀνεπίληπτος, ἀνυπόκριτος, ἀφελότης, εἰλικρίνεια, εἰλικρινής, νηφάλεος, οἰκτίρμων, πολύσπλαγχνος, and ταπεινός.

10 On the background of the adjective, which has ist place in the rhetorical tradition, see Spicq, *Lexicon*, 2.330–335. Musonius Rufus, *Dissertatonium*, 16.70 associates orderly and friendly behaviour. References to ancient authors follow the canon of the *TLG*, see Pentelia, *Thesaurus* [http://stephanus.tlg.uci.edu/canon.php].

11 Musonius Rufus, *Dissertatonium*, 16.70; 3.25–33.

ries onward.¹² In fact, Κοσμία and Κοσμίος were old Greek names, and from the third century onward, Christian parents gave them to their children too.¹³

2. σωφροσύνη and σώφρων → Σωφροσύνιη, Σωφρόνη or Σωφρονία, and Σωφρόνιος or Σωφρόνις

As in other texts, a form of σωφρονέω, in 1 Timothy 2:9 the noun σωφροσύνη, follows κοσμία.¹⁴ For Philo of Alexandria (*c.* 15 BC – *c.* AD 50) to be σώφρων and κόσμιος belong together; to be prudent and orderly is what was expected from a woman.¹⁵ The author of 1 Timothy 2:9 requires that women should wear appropriate clothes with respect (αἰδώς) and with restraint (σωφροσύνη). The noun αἰδώς denotes the regard and respect for others and the respect one gains through orderly behaviour.¹⁶ For Musonius Rufus philosophy teaches one to have respect.¹⁷ σωφροσύνη designates 'soundness of mind, prudence, discretion', more specifically 'moderation in sensual desires, self-control, temperance'.¹⁸ It is a key term in philosophical texts and according to the Stoics, followed by Philo, one of the four virtues. It controls choices with respect to the appetite and passions.¹⁹ Musonius Rufus underlines that every human being needs σωφροσύνη, not to talk about it,

---

12 See ICG 2465, 2557, 2577, 2706, 3393, 3716, 3860, 3881, 4082, and 4135.
13 LGPN, s.v. See the married Christian women from 3rd c. Apollonia (ICG 1136) and 5th c. Thebes in Thessaly (3821) as well as two presbyters from 4th c. Laodicea Combusta (23 and 232).
14 See Philo, *Spec.*, 1.102. Musonius Rufus, *Dissertatonium*, 18b.17; Claudius Aelianus, *Varia historia* 13.27. See also Spicq, *Lexicon*, 2. 332 and his valuable treatment of σωφρονέω κτλ., 3.359–365.
15 Philo, *Spec.*, 1.102; Ios., 1.50; Nicolaus, *Fragmenta*, 6.59; 101.76. Musonius Rufus, *Dissertatonium*, 2.25.
16 LSJ, s.v. Musonius Rufus, *Dissertatonium*, 8.50–53. The name Αἰδοῖος is attested only twice and pre Christian.
17 Musonius Rufus, *Dissertatonium*, 8.47.
18 LSJ, s.v. See also Malherbe, *Virtus*, 467–472.
19 Philo *Leg.*, 1.63: εἰσὶ (sc. ἀρετάς) δὲ τὸν ἀριθμὸν τέτταρες, φρόνησις σωφροσύνη ἀνδρεία δικαιοσύνη. See also Musonius Rufus, *Dissertatonium*, 18b.18; 6.45; 9.123; 12.15: ὡς μετά γε σωφροσύνης οὔτ' ἂν ἑταίρᾳ πλησιάζειν ὑπομείνειέ τις, οὔτ' ἂν ἐλευθέρᾳ γάμου χωρὶς οὔτε μὰ Δία θεραπαίνῃ τῇ αὑτοῦ.

but to be moderate in real life and to exercise self-control.[20] 'In general, of all creatures on earth man alone resembles God and has the same virtues that He has, since we can imagine nothing even in the gods better than prudence, justice, courage, and temperance'.[21] Enhanced by popular philosophy and the exhortations in the New Testament, believers cherished the virtue of self-restraint. From the third to the sixth century, women and men are praised on Christian epitaphs for their σωφροσύνη,[22] and a presbyter from third century Gdanmaa gave the Greek name Σωφροσύνιη to his daughter.[23]

The adjective conveys the same meaning as the noun σωφροσύνη, which is discussed above. 4 Maccabees 3:17 puts it well: 'For the temperate mind can conquer the compulsions of the passions and quench the flames of frenzied desires'.[24] Men and women can become prudent, albeit not without great effort.[25] The ἐπίσκοπος should be σώφρων (1 Tim. 3:2). Here the adjective can have the nuance of 'in control of himself'. Musonius Rufus writes that he who reigns (the king) himself must be in control of himself in order to demand self-control from his subjects.[26] For an overseer would be thus also essential to always act with self-control. In 2:9 the nuance 'chaste, temperate' fits the context better.[27] Some Christian women were called by the Greek names

---

20 Musonius Rufus, *Dissertatonium*, 4.22: ἀποφαίνει τὴν σωφροσύνην ἀναγκαιοτάτην οὖσαν ἀνθρώπῳ παντί. Also 5.24–28; 8.44–45.
21 Musonius Rufus, *Dissertatonium*, 17.20–23 (trans. Lutz): ἐπεὶ μηδ' ἐν θεοῖς μηδὲν ὑπονοῆσαι κρεῖττον ἔχομεν φρονήσεως καὶ δικαιοσύνης, ἔτι δὲ ἀνδρείας καὶ σωφροσύνης. See also Fragment 24.2.
22 ICG 17, 60, 215, 278, 564, 1174, 1175, 1269, 1360, 1498, 2025, 2103, 2881, 3389, 3716, and 4181.
23 ICG 60. According to LGPN, s.v., the Greek names Σωφρονίων, Σωφροσύνα, and Σωφροσύνη occur relatively seldom. The latter until Late Antiquity. Σώφρων was used from 500 BC until AD 400.
24 4 Macc. 3:17 (trans. NETS): δυνατὸς γὰρ ὁ σώφρων νοῦς νικῆσαι τὰς τῶν παθῶν ἀνάγκας καὶ σβέσαι τὰς τῶν οἴστρων φλεγμονάς.
25 Musonius Rufus, *Dissertatonium*, 4.78; 7.41.
26 Musonius Rufus, *Dissertatonium*, 8.44. This applies always for everyone; see id. 5.27; 6.9.
27 LSJ s.v. σώφρων: 'esp. having control over the sensual desires, temperate, self-controlled, chaste'. See Musonius Rufus, *Dissertatonium*, 3.25: ἀλλὰ δεῖ δὴ καὶ σώφρονα εἶναι τὴν γυναῖκα.

Σωφρόνη or Σωφρονία, the men by Σωφρόνιος or Σωφρόνις.[28] A fifth century inscription found in the central section of the nave of the basilica in Sithonia in Macedonia mentions that the mosaic was laid under the most holy bishop Sophronios.[29]

3. φιλόξενος → Φιλόξενος

The ἐπίσκοπος should also be hospitable (φιλόξενος) and Paul instructs the Romans to strive for hospitality (φιλοξενία).[30] For Philo, Abraham's φιλόξενον is a paragon of a greater virtue, his θεοσέβεια.[31] Epictetus (*c.* AD 50–125) places τὸ φιλόξενον on the same level as τὸ αἰδῆμον (modesty), πιστός (trustworthiness) and κόσμιον (orderliness). If one loses these, one comes to one's fall.[32] Christians praised those who kept to the rules of hospitality,[33] and used the very popular and old Greek name Φιλόξενος.[34]

4. ἄμαχος → Ἀμάχιος

Ordinary believers and the overseer (Tit. 3:2; 1 Tim. 3:3) should also be disinclined to fight (ἄμαχος). Menogenes Eustates from early third-century Apamea claims to have lived without strife; the Christian use of the Greek name Ἀμάχιος is attested once.[35] Preferring Εἰρήνη[36] and Εἰρηναῖος,[37] Christians increased the use of the latter well known names.

---

28   Women ICG 60, 69 (?), 251, 360, 366, 1094, 1207; men 83, 1265 and 1270.
29   See Ogereau, *Macedonia*, on ICG 4451.
30   1 Tim. 3:4; Rom. 12:13.
31   Philo, *Abr.*, 114.
32   Epictetus, *Dissertationes*, 1.28.24.
33   ICG 60, 4100 (perhaps Christian, see line 9).
34   ICG 2174, 3181, 3549 (f.).
35   See ICG 1571 and MAMA III 224.
36   ICG 10, 93, 192, 2113, 4095.
37   ICG 30, 119, 565, 734, 1517, 1923, 2393, 3592, 3704, and Breytenbach and Zimmermann, *Lycaonia*, 417.

5. σεμνότητος and σεμνός → Σέμνη and Σέμνος

According to 1 Timothy 3:4,8, the ἐπίσκοπος should manage his household and keep his children submissive with all dignity (μετὰ πάσης σεμνότητος) and deacons must be respectable (σεμνός).[38] For Musonius Rufus a man has dignity and self-command (σεμνὸν καὶ σώφρονα) when he reigns over lust and greed, lives frugally, has a sense of shame, can control his tongue, has discipline, order, and courtesy, and behaves orderly and appropriate.[39] On their tombstones some Christians were praised for living their life in dignity,[40] women were called most dignified (σεμνοτάτη);[41] presbyters, priests and female deacons were kept in dignified memory and women praised as august because of feeding the poor.[42] Since early imperial times both Σέμνος and Σέμνη were used as personal names,[43] but it is attested only in the sixth century AD for Christians.[44]

6. ἀνέγκλητος → Ἀνένκλητος

Deacons (1 Tim. 3:10) should also be blameless, irreproachable (ἀνέγκλητος). Derived by negation of the law term ἐγκαλέω ('to prosecute, take proceedings against') the adjective means 'giving no ground for dispute'.[45] The Greek name Ἀνέγκλητος is broadly attested since early imperial times, especially in Asia Minor.[46] Christians in Lycaonia wrote the name Ἀνένκλητος, *inter alia* referring to a presbyter in Laodicea Combusta and to a priest in Gdanmaa.[47] Probably

---

38 See 1 Tim. 3:4 and 8.
39 Musonius Rufus, *Dissertatonium*, 8.45-50. See also 44-50.
40 ICG 3304, 4140, 4269, 4404.
41 ICG 312, 320, 648, 767, 1050, 1137, 1230, 1360, 2451, 2494, 2558. This could be an indication for nobility, but it is also generally used as a feminie virtue ; see Breytenbach and Zimmermann, *Lycaonia*, 134, 447, 495, 660.
42 ICG 145, 1502, 229, 81.
43 LGPN, s.v.
44 See IGLrom 141 in Popescu, *Inscripțiile grecești*..
45 LSJ, s.v. Plato, *Leg.* v 737a.b. The legal connotations are not always essential; see Longinus, *Subl.*, 33.1.
46 LGPN, 1-3a, 4-5.
47 Written Ἀνένκλητος. See ICG 161 (Tyriaeum), 148, 432, 594, 525 (Laodicea) and 350 (Gdanmaa).

the Pauline message that nobody can prosecute the faithful in Christ (Rom. 8:33; Col. 1:22) broadened to the use of the adjective as a name for Christians.

7. ἀγνός → Ἁγνη

To be pure (ἀγνός) is a Christian virtue.[48] Paul regards purity (ἁγνότης) as commendable (2 Cor. 6:6). In line with the morality of contemporary Greek writing Judaism,[49] Titus 3:5 advocates the purity of women.[50] Christian epitaphs reveal that in the light of biblical tradition, chastity of women was highly regarded.[51] Ἁγνη, a customary epithet of Aphrodite in Delos and of other deities, is attested since imperial times as personal name, and even became the name of two Christians, a woman married to a Lycaonian Paul and a deaconess from Macedonia.[52]

8. ἡσύχιος → Ἡσυχία/η and Ἡσύχιος

If we move to 1 Peter, the letter commends chaste behaviour (ἀγνὴ ἀναστροφή) and, alluding to Isaiah 66:2 LXX, a gentle (πραΰς) and quiet (ἡσύχιος) spirit (3:2 and 4) for Christian women.[53] Ἡσυχία/η is an old Greek name, but the use of the masculine Ἡσύχιος starts in imperial and reaches into Byzantine times. On epitaphs, it is used for Christian women and men.[54]

---

48 See Phil. 4:8; 2 Cor. 11:2; 1 Tim. 5:22; 1 Pet. 3:2; 1 John 3:3.
49 See the final words of the mother who witnessed the martyrdom of her seven sons in 4 Macc. 18:7–9a: 'I was a pure virgin and did not step outside my father's house, but I kept watch over the built rib. 8 No seducer or corrupter on a desert plain corrupted me, nor did the seducer, the snake of deceit, defile the purity of my virginity. 9 At the time of my maturity I remained with my husband'. (trans. nets).
50 Tit. 2:5. Derived from ἀγνός, 2 Cor. 6:6 is the earliest occurrence of the word in the TLG.
51 ICG 1531, 1597.16, 1689D.29, 3609.
52 ICG 565, 3642.
53 The adjective occurs once more in Ps. Sol. 12:5: φυλάξαι κύριος ψυχὴν ἡσύχιον μισοῦσαν ἀδίκους, καὶ κατευθύναι κύριος ἄνδρα ποιοῦντα εἰρήνην ἐν οἴκῳ.
54 Women ICG 407, 1906. Men ICG 446, 498, 2712, 3881.

9. Negations → Ἀκάκιος, Ἀδόλιος, Ἀφθόνιος and Ἀφθόνις/Ἀπτόνις

There is more to learn from 1 Peter. In 2:1, the author instructs the faithful to lay aside all moral vice (κακία), deceit (δόλος), envy (φθόνος). Ἄδολος is lacking from the LXX, ἄφθονος occurs only twice.[55] The ἀκακία (innocence) motif, however, has its place in Jewish wisdom literature: 'Because mercy and truth the Lord God loves, favor and glory he will bestow. The Lord will not withhold good things from those who walk in innocence'.[56] In the course of time, the negation of these vices return in names of Christians. Believers should not be bad, as the name of the temperate Ἀκάκιος from the upper Tembris region or a martyr from Thesus expresses.[57] The faithful should be honest (1 Pet. 2:2), without deceit (ἄδολος), as Ἀδόλιος the name of a sixth-century Athenian Christian articulates.[58] Lycaonian Christians frequently used Ἀφθόνιος and Ἀφθόνις/Ἀπτόνις.[59] The names show that their parents denounced jealousy.[60]

10. χρηστότης

We return to Paul and the Pauline tradition. He presupposes (Rom. 2:4; 11:22) the goodness (χρηστότης) of God and Ephesians 2:7

---

55 ἄφθονος in 3 Macc. 5:2 and 4 Macc. 3:10.
56 Ps. 83:12 (trans. NETS). See also Pss. 7:9; 25:1, 11; 36:37; 40:13; 77:72; 100:2; Job 2:3; 4:6; 27:5; 31:6; Ps. Sol. 4:23; 8:23
57 ICG 1360, 3277, also in 3279. The name Ἀκάκιος is used widely from the 3rd c. onward (LGPN, s.v.).
58 ICG 2013. According to LGPN 5a Ἄδολος is also atteted in Cios in the 4th c. BC. The name Ἀδόλιος occurs twice, from the 3rd c. AD onward; see LGPN 4 and 5b.
59 ICG 97, 182 (?), 251, 283, 554, 1271, 1494. Ἄφθονος is only attested twice and only since imperial times. The older more frequently used Greek name is Ἀφθόνητος (see LGPN, s.v. and for Christian use ICG 3498 [Corinth]).
60 See the Christian poem from Docimium in Phrygia (ICG 1581) on φθόνος: 'Jealousy is the worst thing, but it brings the greatest benefit; it causes those who are jealous to rot away, punishing their bad deed. O jealous person, why are you jealous? You do nothing more than rot yourself. It is God who provides everything unstintingly to all those who put their hope in him. But you, I say, jealous man, can provide nothing even if you want to, and your jealousy achieves nothing. So, you are throttled by your evil conduct. God utterly detests evil and jealous men' (Translation, Mitchell, *Phrygia*).

and Titus 3:4 the kindness of Christ. Paul (2 Cor. 6:6), and the Deuteropauline Colossians (Col. 3:12) appeal to their addressees to practice goodness. As God's chosen ones, sanctified and loved by him, the baptised Colossians have to lay of the vices of former life and (Col. 3:12) have to clothe themselves with gut-affecting compassion (σπλάγχνα οἰκτιρμοῦ), kindness (χρηστότης), humility (ταπεινοφροσύνη), meekness (πραότης), and patience (μακροθυμία).[61] Such behaviour leads to reciprocal forgiveness among the addressees. The noun χρηστότης has its firm place within Stoic ethics. For Chrysippus (3rd c. BC) χρηστότης is the skill to do good (εὐποιητική) out of free will.[62] In works of Philo and Musonius Rufus, it is mentioned with other virtues like φιλανθρωπία, τὸ εὐεργετικὸν εἶναι and τὸ κηδεμονικὸν εἶναι etc.[63] χρηστότης and καλοκἀγαθία mark the required ἦθος for men and women.[64] Although χρηστότης also did not make it to a personal name, χρῆστος (useful, good) was a personal name, widely attested from early imperial times until the third century AD.[65] From Old Testament and Jewish tradition (Pss. 106:1; 136:1; 144:9; Wis. 15:1; Dan. 3:89) Christians knew that God is good (χρηστός in Luke 6:35; Rom. 2:4; *ICG* 1008) and believers should strive for goodness and to be kind, not only toward each other (Eph. 4:32; 1 Peter 2:3), but toward everybody (Luke 6:35). However, due to the closeness to the Lord Jesus's cognomen χριστός, use of the name Χρῆστος declines as from the fourth century onwards and seems absent among Christian

---

61 See note 9 above.
62 Chrysippus, *Fragmenta moralia* 273.4: χρηστότης δὲ ἕξις ἑκουσίως εὐποιητική. See also 264.28.
63 See Philo, Sacr. 1.27: συνείποντο δὲ αὐτῇ εὐσέβεια ὁσιότης ἀλήθεια θέμις ἁγιστεία εὐορκία δικαιοσύνη ἰσότης εὐσυνθεσία κοινωνία ἐχεθυμία σωφροσύνη κοσμιότης ἐγκράτεια πραότης ὀλιγοδεΐα εὐκολία αἰδὼς ἀπραγμοσύνη ἀνδρεία γεννaιότης εὐβουλία προμήθεια φρόνησις προσοχὴ διόρθωσις εὐθυμία χρηστότης ἡμερότης ἡπιότης φιλανθρωπία μεγαλοφροσύνη μακαριότης ἀγαθότης.·Philo, *Legat.* 1.73; *Spec.* 2.141: ἡμερότητα, κοινωνίαν, χρηστότητα, μεγαλόνοιαν, εὐφημίαν, εὔκλειαν. Musonius Rufus, *Dissertatonium*, 14.35-37: ἀρετὴ δὲ φιλανθρωπία καὶ χρηστότης καὶ δικαιοσύνη ἐστὶ καὶ τὸ εὐεργετικὸν εἶναι καὶ τὸ κηδεμονικὸν εἶναι τοῦ πέλας·. καλοκἀγαθία,
64 Musonius Rufus, *Dissertatonium*, 4.99.
65 LGPN, s.v.

epitaphs.⁶⁶ Theonymic naming, giving a child the exact name of a god, was uncommon among the Greeks. They would rather call their children Apollonios or Dionysios than Apollon or Dionysos.⁶⁷ In the same vein, believers did not use χριστός as personal name, but rather composita like Χριστόδουλος, Χριστοφόρος and Χριστοφορία.⁶⁸

11. πραΰς → Πραΰλιος and Πραΰλος

To explore πραΰς, a wider approach is needed. Paul urges the Corinthians by the gentleness (πραΰτης) and mildness (ἐπιείκεια) of the Christ (2 Cor. 10:1). Plutarch also combines the two adjectives.⁶⁹ Πραΰνω can be glossed by 'to make soft, mild, or gentle, soothe, calm'.⁷⁰ The adjective (πραΰς or πρᾶος) is used in the lxx⁷¹ and occurs in Matthew 5:5; 11:29; 21:5 and 1 Peter 3:4 and means 'mild, soft, gentle, meek'.⁷² The derived noun ἡ πραΰτης, 'the quality of not being overly impressed by a sense of one's self-importance, gentleness, humility, courtesy, considerateness, meekness',⁷³ is attested since Aesop, used by Plato and Aristotle⁷⁴ and in the lxx⁷⁵ and occurs in the NT.⁷⁶

If we focus our attention on the virtue πραΰς or πρᾶος among Christians, it must be remembered, that others were also praised for

---

66 It is absent from ig II/III² v, IV² II, IV² III and iankara II.
67 See Parker, 'Theophoric Names', 57.
68 Χριστόδουλος (ICG 94, 2579, 3105, 3566; BCH 18 (1894) 24, no. 19; IG XII v 712,62: [Κ](ύρι)ε βοήθει | τῷ δού[λῳ] | σου Χρισ[το]|[δο]ύ[λου]) or Χριστοφόρος (ICG 1315, 3281; seg 30.1625, 34.1362, 35.1451, 40.1313, 42.1193) and Χριστοφορία (seg 8.865).
69 Plutarch, *Caes.* 57; *Per.* 39; *Sert.* 25.
70 LSJ, s.v.
71 Num. 12:3; Pss. 24:9; 33:3; 36:11; 75:10; 146:6; 149:4; Job 24:4; 36:15; Sir. 10:14; Joel 4:11; Zeph. 3:12; Zech. 9:9; Isa. 26:6; and Dan. 4:19.
72 LSJ, s.v.
73 BDAG, s.v. See also Spicq; *Lexicon*, 3.161–162.
74 Cf. IG XII.7 240, 397, 401405. The following uses shed light on the background in the NT (according to Spicq, 3.161–162): Pindar, *Pyth.* 3.71; 4.136; Thucydides 4.1083; Aristophanes, *Pax* 934, 998; Euripides, *Bacc* 436; Isocrates, *Antid.* 20; Demosthenes, *C. Tim.* 170, 218; Aristotle, *Ath. Pol.* 22.4; Polyb. 1.72.2–3.
75 Plato, *Symp.* 197d; Aristotle, *E.N.* 1125b; Esth. 5:1; Pss. 44:5; 89:10; 131:1; Sir. 3:17; 4:8; 10:28; 36:23; 45:4.
76 1 Cor. 4:21; 2 Cor. 10:1; Gal. 5:23; 6:1; Eph. 4:2; Col. 3:12; 1 Tim. 6:11; 2 Tim. 2:25; Tit. 3:2; Jas 1:21; 3:13, and 1 Pet. 3:15.

it.[77] Two fourth – fifth century inscriptions re-used in the caravanserai Zazadin Han close to ancient Iconium lauds Apollinaris and Gregorios, both priests of the great God, who, because of their meekness, found heavenly renown.[78] Another priest of God, Aniketos from Altınekin, was the mildest of all (πράυστρς πάντων).[79] A Christian veterinary surgeon named Komas from fifth-century Kisamos on Crete is called a truly mild and (ἀληθῶς πρᾶος) and quiet (κἠσύχιος) man (ἀνήρ), he stopped seeking mercy before God. Leontios from ad 607/8 in Madaba was the most mild priest.[80]

The more common names derived from the adjective πραΰς or πρᾶος were Πραΰλιος and Πραΰλος.[81] The latter is attested from Hellenistic until imperial times. More interesting for us is Πραΰλιος, which was in use in western Asia Minor from imperial times until the Byzantine period. An inscription from third-century Lydia shows that the name Πραΰλιος was also used by non-Christians.[82] However, there are several Christians with this name, the most prominent the Bishop of Jerusalem in the early fifth century.[83] Amongst others, it was also the name of the anointed holy (bishop?) Πραΰλιος, the patron of a village on an estate, who was buried ten miles north-west of Philadelphia in Lydia in ad 515,[84] and of a presbyter from Milet.[85]

---

77 Cf. CIG 2788.22–23 (= IAph 12.22) for Aelius Aurelius Ammianus Paulinus from Aphrodisia.
78 ICG 480.1–3: ἐνθάδε κῖτε ἀνὴρ, ἱερεὺς μεγάλοι|ο θεοῖο, | ὃς ἔνεκεν πραότητος ἐπ|ουράνιον κλέος ἦρεν. Cf. also ICG 481.
79 ICG 603.4.
80 IC II VIII 8; ICSyr 21,2 145.
81 According to the current evidence in LGPN, the names Πρᾶος and Πραούλα are attested once, the name Πράοχος was more often (30x) used in pre-Christian Delphi. Before the rise of Christianity Πράυχος is attested 4 times. There are single attestations of the names Πραΰλα (pre Christian), Πραΰλιον, Πραϋλίς, Πραΰλις (Christian), Πράϋλλα, Πραΰλλας, Πραϋλλίς, Πράϋλλος, Πραΰχα, and Πραϋχίων.
82 Malay, 'Greek and Latin Inscriptions', 336.7.
83 Theodoretus, Historia ecclesiastica, 342.3; 349.5; Epistulae, 110.10; Marcus Diaconus, Vita Porphyrii episcopi Gazensis, 10.3; 12.8 and 15; 14.15{2806.001}
84 TAM V,3 1882.1–2: ☧ ἀνελήμφθη ὁ ἅγι[ο]ς Πραΰλι[ος]| ὁ κοινωνὸς ὁ κατὰ τόπον ☧.
85 ICG 1741.

12. ἐπιεικής

We finally turn to ἐπιεικής. In this case, Christian attestations of the name Ἐπιείκης, which is attested in the fifth century BC, are lacking.[86] The word expresses the ability to be flexible and tolerant and stems from a Greek background. It is used in the lxx. Psalm 85:5 praises the Lord as χρηστὸς καὶ ἐπιεικὴς καὶ πολυέλεος, he is reasonable and forgiving (*Ps. Sol.* 5:12).[87] In his prayer added to the Greek versions of Daniel, Azariah appeals to the fairness and abundant mercy of God.[88] In the same vein Paul appeals to the Corinthians διὰ τῆς πραΰτητος καὶ ἐπιεικείας τοῦ Χριστοῦ (2 Cor. 10:1). The motif is neither specific Old Testament nor Jewish. Because of acts of ἐπιεικής and πραότης after the civil wars, Plutarch (*c.* AD 45 – before AD 125) regards Caesar as ἀνέγκλητος.[89] 1 Timothy 3:3 requires that the ἐπίσκοπος should be reasonable, fair (ἐπιεικής), and using ἐπιεικές as noun, Paul calls on the Philippians (4:5) that all humans should get to know their fairness.[90] According to an early Christian epitaph from Karaman towards the Isaurian border, Tabeis had put up a gravestone for his 'reasonable and pure' brother Tarasis, but Christian attestations of the name Ἐπιείκης, which is attested in the fifth century BC, are lacking.91

13. Conclusion

Most of the words designating virtues that were also used as personal names, were not part of the reception history of the vocabulary of the Hebrew Bible transmitted via the lxx. 4 Maccabees teaches us that

---

86 lpgn attests two occurrences of the a very old and rare pre-Christian Greek name Ἐπιείκης, six of Ἥπιος and three of Ἡπία/η and one of Διδακτικός. In spite of 1 Tim. 3:3, 2 Tim. 2:24 and Tit. 3:2, these names are not attested for Christians.
87 With the exception of the comparative in the additions to Esther (3:13b; 8:12i), the translators of the lxx did not use ἐπιεικής elsewhere. For ἐπιείκεια see 2 Macc. 2:22; 10:4; 3 Macc. 3:15; 7:6; Wis. 2:19; 12:18
88 Pr. Azar. 3:42: ἀλλὰ ποίησον μεθ' ἡμῶν κατὰ τὴν ἐπιείκειάν σου καὶ κατὰ τὸ πλῆθος τοῦ ἐλέους σου. See also Dan. 4:27 lxx.
89 Plutarch, *Caes.* 57.4.
90 BDAG, s.v.
91 1 Tim. See note 86 above.

for Greek-writing early Judaism, the Torah teaches the people those virtues propagated by popular philosophy. The adjectives ἄμαχος, φιλόξενος and ἄδολος do not occur in the lxx; κόσμιος, σώφρων, σεμνός, ἀνέγκλητος, ἁγνός, and ἄφθονος,[92] as well as the nouns σωφροσύνη and σεμνότης,[93] are restricted to those parts of the lxx written in Greek. On the other hand, χρηστότης, χρηστός, πραΰς, πραότης and ἐπιεικής have a stronger occurrence in the lxx, especially in the Psalms.[94] This also applies to ταπεινοφροσύνη, μακροθυμία, οἰκτιρμός, οἰκτίρμων, πολύσπλαγχνος, and ταπεινός. Like the former, they are rooted in the lxx, and were used to designate God or Christ as saviours of unjust humans. However, with the exception of χρηστός and derivatives of πραΰς, they were not used as personal names, and none of them for Christians.[95] It thus seems as if those adjectives and nouns that advanced to personal names, were those who were firmly rooted as common virtues from the Greek philosophical tradition.[96]

The First Letter of Peter calls upon their addressees to live their lives virtuously. To put it in the words of 1 Peter 3:4: 'let your adornment be the inner self with the lasting beauty of a gentle and quiet spirit, which is very precious in God's sight'. The Pastoral Epistles set standards for overseers and deacons: An overseer must be above reproach, the husband of one wife, temperate, prudent, respectable, hospitable, able to teach, not addicted to wine or pugnacious, but gentle, uncontentious, free from the love of money. He must be one who manages his own household well, keeping his children under control with all dignity. Many of these virtues re-emerge as proper names on

---

92 κόσμιος in the sense of the orderly arrangement of parables by the Eccelsiast (Eccl. 12:9); σώφρων only in 4 Macc. that writes about the temperate mind (ὁ σώφρων νοῦς in 1:35; 2:16, 18, 23; 3:17,19; 15,10) keeping passion in control with Joseph as an example (2:2). With the exception of Proverbs (6:8; 8:6; 15:26), the adjective σεμνός is retricted to 2 and 4 Maccabees (2 Macc. 6:11.28; 8:15; 4 Macc. 5:36; 7:15;17:5), ἀνέγκλητος to 3 Maccabees (5:31), ἁγνός to occurs more often (2 Macc. 13:8; 4 Macc. 5:37; 18:7–8, 23; Pss. 11:7; 18:10; Prov. 15:26; 19:13; 20:9; 21:8), ἄφθονος in 3 Macc. 5:2 and 4 Macc. 3:10.
93 For σωφροσύνη see Add.Esth. 3:13c; 4 Macc. 1:3, 6, 18, 30–31; 5:23; Wis. 8:7; for σεμνότης 3 Macc. 3:12.
94 See the treatment above.
95 See note 9 above.
96 For more detail on those traditions, see Malherbe, *Virtus*.

the funerary epitaphs of Christians in central Asia Minor and mainland Greece from the third to the fifth centuries. On the one hand, this is because since imperial times there was a growing tendency to use adjectives and nouns designating those virtues propagated especially by Stoic and Cynic philosophers for personal names. On the other hand, since moral exhortation in the letters of the New Testament urged believers to live their lives according to the same virtues, they played an important role in evaluating the life of believers in the light of the apostolic tradition. Parents gave their children names expressing such virtues in the expectation that their offspring might live according to these virtues. Without strife, deceit or jealousy they should live orderly, self-controlled, respectable, dignified lives quietly and blamelessly, marked by purity, kindness, mildness and fairness. These virtues were part of the ethos of the Greek-speaking world and their impact on emerging Christianity was enhanced by the exhortation in the letters claiming the authority of Paul and Peter. Together these two factors explain the occurrence of the names expressing virtues among the Christians of Late Antiquity.

Prof. Dr. Cilliers Breytenbach
University Professor emeritus, Humboldt University of Berlin
Professor Extraordinary, Stellenbosch University

Bibliography

Breytenbach, C., and C. Zimmermann *Early Christianity in Lycaonia and Adjacent Areas* (ECAM 2/ AJC 101: Leiden: Brill, 2017).

Breytenbach, C., and E. Tzavella *Early Christianity in Attica, Athens and Adjacent areas* (ECG 1/ AJC 114: Leiden: Brill, 2022).

Breytenbach, C., and C. Zimmermann *Inscriptiones Christiane Graecae*, online at https://icg.uni-kiel.de (ICG)

Kajanto, I. *The Latin Cognomina* (Helsinki: Societas scientiarum Fennica, 1965).

LPGN *The Lexicon of Greek Personal Names*, on-line at https://www.lgpn.ox.ac.uk/home

Liddell, H.G.R., R.A. Scott, and H.S. Jones *Greek-English Lexicon* (9th ed., Oxford, 1996). (LSJ)

Louw, J.P., and E.A. Nida *Greek-English Lexicon of the New Testament: Based on Semantic Domains* (New York: United Bible Societies, 1996).

Lutz, C. E. 'Musonius Rufus. "The Roman Socrates"', *Yale Classical Studies* X (1947) 3–147.

Malherbe, A.J. 'The *Virtus Feminarum* in 1 Timothy 2:9–15 (2007)', in C. R. Holladay, J. T. Fitzgerald, G. E. Sterling, and J. W. Thompson (eds.), *Light from the Gentiles: Hellenistic Philosophy and Early Christianity: Collected Essays, 1959–2012, by Abraham J. Malherbe* (NovT Supp. 150; Leiden: Brill, 2014), 459–477.

Malay, H. *Greek and Latin Inscriptions in the Manisa Museum* (Ergänzungsbände zu den Tituli Asiae Minoris 19; Vienna: Österreichische Akademie der Wissenschaften, 1994).

Mitchell, S. *The Christians of Phrygia. from Rome to the Turkish Conquest* (ECAM 4/AJEC; Leiden: Brill, 2023).

Ogereau, J. M. *Early Christianity in Macedonia. From Paul to the Late Sixth Century* (ECG 2/ AJEC, Leiden: Brill, 2023).

Pantelia, M. C. *Thesaurus Linguae Graecae: A Bibliographic Guide to the Canon of Greek Authors and Works* (University of California Press, 2022).

Parker, R.	'Theophoric Names and the History of Greek Religion', in S. Hornblower and E. Matthews (eds.), *Greek Personal Names: Their Value as Evidence* (Proceedings of the British Academy 104; Oxford: University Press, 2000), 53–82.
Pietersma, A., and B.G. Wright	*A New English Translation Of The Septuagint And The Other Greek Translations Traditionally Included Under That Title* (Oxford: University Press, 2007). (NETS)
Popescu, E.	*Inscripțiile grecești și latine din sec. IV-XIII descoperite în România* (Bucharest: Editura Academiei Republicii Socialiste Romania, 1976).
Spicq, C.	*Theological lexicon of the New Testament* (Peabody, Mass.: Hendricks, 1994).

Antioch, Rome, and 1 Peter

Rosalinde Kearsley

Abstract

There are no significant textual problems in the five chapters of 1 Peter, and early Christian sources are unanimous in accepting the letter's self-attribution to the apostle Peter, yet modern scholarship is far from unified with respect to its authorship, date, and its audience.

A fresh paradigm with the aim of providing an interpretation which balances the historical and sociological character of the letter is proposed here. Some fundamental assumptions underlie the discussion, namely that 1 Peter is an authentic work of the apostle Peter as stated in 1:1, and that it was written before his death in Rome c. 64/65. The proposals concern the provenance and date of the letter as well the social circumstances of the readers. It is hoped that, through discussion of these fundamental questions surrounding 1 Peter from new perspectives, a convincing interpretation of the letter in its socio-historical context will emerge.

The textual reliability of 1 Peter is not disputed. The letter is found complete in P^{72} and, together with the sections of the letter found in a multiplicity of corroborating manuscripts, there is now generally considered sufficient evidence for 1 Peter as a single rather than composite document.[1] There is also patristic testimony of notable size to

---

[1] It is a pleasure to contribute to this volume in honour of Jim with whom I have shared many common research interests at Macquarie University, notably the history and epigraphy of Asia Minor under Roman government and the study of early Christian groups within the Roman empire.
Elliott, *1 Peter*, 39–40.

1 Peter when allusions as well as specific quotations and references to the letter by name are included. The unanimous view of the early church is that Peter the apostle was its author as stated in 1:1.[2] Yet the fact that the text of 1 Peter contains no information that can be indisputably linked to a datable historical event or period has allowed doubts about Peter's authorship to arise and alternative chronologies for the letter to be explored.

Up to the present time, scholarly commentators remain divided in their opinions about the authorship and date of 1 Peter.[3] A decision made regarding the authorship of 1 Peter is integrally linked to the date assigned it. Petrine authorship usually means a composition date before c. 64/65 given the general agreement that Peter's death in Rome occurred then. A decision against Petrine authorship in favour of pseudonymity opens up the chronological possibilities. It has frequently led to the proposal of a much later date, towards the end of the first century.[4] Consequences flow from this primary decision on authorship and date, particularly the reconstruction of the provenance of the letter and the circumstances of the letter's readers.[5]

Whereas acceptance of Petrine authorship involves a straightforward relationship with the text due to the self-identification of the apostle in 1:1, the view of pseudonymity must be justified by arguments from silence. Among those who support pseudonymity there is a lack of consensus on the reasons underpinning their decision. Five main issues have been used to challenge Petrine authorship over the decades: the quality of the Greek; dependence on the Pauline corpus; links to the life of Jesus; church organisation of the readers' communities; the source of suffering within the communities.[6] The lack of consistency between proponents of pseudonymity in the weight given any one of these over the others is evident. A clear example of the interpretative division is found between those who are persuaded by the attri-

---

2 Elliott, 1 Peter, 148-49.
3 Jobes, 1 Peter, 19; Williams, Persecution, 30-34; Rodgers, 1 Peter, 1-6; Edwards, 1 Peter, 19-20.
4 Elliott, 1 Peter, 138.
5 Achtemeier, 1 Peter, 42-43, 49-50, 63-64.
6 Jobes, 1 Peter, 6-14.

bution of 1 Peter to a Petrine circle following John Elliott's thesis and those who deny it as a possibility, such as David Horrell.[7]

The commentators who challenge Petrine authorship are currently greater in number than those who support it. Despite this majority, it is surely the case that the pseudonymous interpretation of 1 Peter will only be confirmed when discussions are characterised by some consensus on the reasons for it.[8] Meanwhile, since the solution for the outstanding questions of 1 Peter's authorship and date is still elusive, there remains scope to attempt a new approach. It is hoped that the discussion below will bring a fresh perspective to bear on the debate even if, in this case also, certainty cannot be demonstrated. It is offered in response to the encouragement of Raymond Brown and John Meier for others to join them in exploring the relationship of Antioch and Rome in the earliest stages of Jewish Christianity.[9]

Provenance. Rome or Antioch?

The most frequent provenance attributed to 1 Peter is the city of Rome. However, the scholarly consensus that 'Babylon' in 5:13 is not the Mesopotamian city has led interpreters to default towards identifying Babylon as code for Rome.[10] Further investigation as to whether or not 'Babylon' might refer to an existing church elsewhere,[11] has not been carried out. The fact that Peter died in Rome has also been accepted as an anchor for the provenance of 1 Peter. However, such a link becomes irrelevant if the letter was written before Peter reached Rome in c. 56/57. Then, an alternative to Rome must be sought and Antioch, the great centre of the earliest Christian groups of the apostolic mission in Syria, is the natural place to consider because of Peter's

---

7   Elliott, 'Peter', 253-54; Horrell, 'Product', 30-32.
8   Cf. Michaels, *1 Peter*, lxvi-vii.
9   Brown and Meier, *Antioch & Rome*, 213.
10 Elliott, *1 Peter*, 131-4, 137; Grudem, *1 Peter*, 34-36. Since the report of Papias contained in Eusebius (*HE* 2.15.2) attributes Peter's letter to Rome based on the anachronistic interpretation of Babylon it is has no independent value: cf. Horrell, 'Product', 49.
11 Cf. Witherington, *Hellenized Christians*, 248.

well-documented connections with that city also.¹²

The Jewish population in Antioch included a large number of Babylonian Jews from the time of its Hellenistic foundation. A second Jewish group of significant size arrived in Antioch from Babylon in the years 9–6 B.C.¹³ The Jewish community flourished as an integral component of Antioch and grew markedly in size, prosperity, and diversity during the first half of the first century.¹⁴ Of the various synagogue communities postulated for Antioch,¹⁵ the one closest to the agricultural plain of Antioch is likely to have been that joined by the settlers from Babylon in the Herodian period.¹⁶

Among the farming settlers on the plain there was a conservative tendency towards long-term possession, exemplified in one case by a Jewish family who maintained occupancy over four generations and in another case by a village preserving the memory of Hellenistic settlers in its name κώμη Θρακῶν, village of Thracians.¹⁷ Strong historical memory denoted by identity markers is a characteristic of antiquity and Antioch was no exception.¹⁸ Therefore, Antioch's synagogue on the plain, because of a historical link with the waves of immigrant

12   Cf. Meeks and Wilken, *Jews and Christians*, 1–2.
13   Brooten, 'The Jews', 30; Downey, *History*, 189; Downey, *Ancient Antioch*, 87–88.
14   Downey, *History*, 163–71; Brown and Meier, *Antioch & Rome*, 31. Satellite imagery has revealed the density of farms and small towns on the alluvial plain of Antioch: De Giorgi, *Ancient Antioch*, 80–81. There was continuous population there from the Hellenistic into the early Roman period.
15   Kraeling, 'The Jewish Community', 143; Meeks and Wilken, *Jews and Christians*, 8–9.
16   Downey, *History*, 87–88. See De Giorgi, *Ancient Antioch*, 64 on the symbiotic relationship between those in the χώρα of Antioch and the city itself in a.d. I, and Kraeling, 'The Jewish Community', 145 for the relationship of Herod with the Jewish community in Antioch. Manaen was a leader in the church there (cf. Acts 13:1). As his *syntrophos*, Manaen would have had an ongoing and affectionate relationship with Herod Antipas: Meeks and Wilken, *Jews and Christians*, 15.
17   De Giorgi, *Ancient Antioch*, 81–82. Ethnics were important in death as well. Burials at Jaffa name one man as a Babylonian and another as a Cappadocian: Williams, *The Jews*, 77, III. 46–47.
18   Downey, *Ancient Antioch*, 75, 82–83; Downey, *History*, 171; Meeks and Wilken, *Jews and Christians*, 9; De Giorgi, *Ancient Antioch*, 38, 172. In Rome: Rutgers, 'Roman Policy', 131–32.

Babylonians, may have borne their name.[19] Certainly, in Rome, the multiple synagogues were identified from each other starting in Augustan times by reference to their membership, location, or even patron.[20]

The existence of a tradition that used ethnics as identity markers is attested within the NT also.[21] The fact that sites later connected with the Christians lie in the same district of Antioch is an indirect indication that such a link is not entirely without support given the evidence from Rome.[22] A Christian group within this district of Antioch and still within such a synagogue community would have been dubbed with its nickname.[23] Therefore, the possibility exists that 'Babylon' in 5:13 is actually a reference to a church named 'Babylon' worshipping Jesus in the synagogue of the Babylonians in Antioch and not a coded reference to Rome.[24]

The possibility is strengthened when, as will be demonstrated below, Peter can only be found in company with Mark and Silvanus in Antioch independently of 1 Peter 5:12–13. In addition, the familiarity of Peter, Silas, and Mark with events in Antioch makes a suitable context for interpreting the conjunction between Acts 11:26 and 1 Peter 4:16 in recording the epithet Χριστιανόι for Jesus-followers.[25]

The movements of Peter, Silvanus, and Mark

Peter left Jerusalem in 44 because he had been targeted and persecuted by Agrippa I (Acts 12:17). There is uncertainty about where he

---

19 Cf. Meeks and Wilken, *Jews and Christians*, 8–9.
20 Richardson, 'Augustan Era', 19–20, 29; Schürer, *History*, 95–98.
21 Those who heard Peter's speech (Acts 2:1–11) were κατοικοῦντες (2:5) and so are unlikely to be fresh pilgrim visitors to Jerusalem: Trebilco, *Jewish Communities*, 25. The fact that they are, nevertheless, described by their geographical origin is yet one more insight into the memory of origin and its importance; cf. also Nicolaus of Antioch (Acts 6:5); Aquila of Pontus (Acts 18:2).
22 Downey, *History*, Pl. 11; Kraeling, 'The Jewish Community', 145; cf. Légasse, 'Paul's Pre-Christian Career', 387–88; Lampe, *From Paul*, 19–23; Jewett, *Romans*, 69–70.
23 See Williams, *Jews*, 73, III. 26 for the Babylonian synagogue in Sepphoris.
24 Cf. Brown and Meier, *Antioch & Rome*, 32; Lampe, *From Paul*, 38–39, 42; Barclay, *Jews*, 283 n. 2.
25 Meeks and Wilken, *Jews and Christians*, 15–16.

went then and what he did because Acts falls almost silent about those details as Luke shifts his focus to Paul and his mission to the gentiles.[26] Peter's speech at the Council in Jerusalem is given before Barnabas and Paul addressed the assembly (Acts 15:7–13), but there is no information about where he was before attending that gathering, or where he went immediately afterwards.[27] Nevertheless, it is surely important to note as a possible indication of where he went, and with whom, that Peter's position at the Council was in harmony with the delegates from Antioch.

It is Paul who provides the information that from this point, if not before, Peter joined the Christians in Antioch (Gal. 2:11).[28] This was apparently in the late 40s after the Council in Jerusalem,[29] and was shortly before he and Silas set off on a trip together (Acts 15:40). Thus, the tradition which held that Peter became leader of the church in Antioch may be genuine.[30] During such a period of leadership presbuteros 'elder' (1 Pet. 5:1) would be a fitting designation for him as an apostle and former leader of the Jerusalem Church.[31] Despite assumptions that Peter was an elder in Rome,[32] there is nothing in the title intrinsically that links it to that city or which denotes a particular stage of church development in the first century.[33] Therefore, 5:1 does not contribute to clarifying the provenance or the date of 1 Peter. As already acknowledged by both Elliott and Horrell, the best opportunity to determine these aspects of the letter lies in establishing when the three men associated with 1 Peter by name were together in one

26 Bauckham, 'James', 434, 439.
27 As Peter was present at the Council he must have returned to Jerusalem for the occasion since he had a large stake in the outcome. The fact that it was James who spoke as leader of the church shows that Peter was not there permanently anymore: cf. Bauckham, 'James', 462–63.
28 There is no indication from the verb ἦλθεν that Peter made only a visit to Antioch, contra Meeks and Wilken, Jews and Christians, 17.
29 The relative dating for the dispute involves some difficulty in synchronizing Gal. 2:11 and Acts 15:6–21 but this is the most probable conclusion: Gibson, Peter, 218; Brown and Meier, Antioch & Rome, 36–39.
30 Downey, History, 281–84; cf. Elliott, 1 Peter, 131.
31 Downey, History, 584–86.
32 Cf. Barnett, 'Paul in Rome', 202.
33 Jobes, 1 Peter, 302–3; contra Brown and Meier, Antioch & Rome, 139 n. 292.

place.[34] It remains, then, to turn to Silvanus and Mark and discover where they were in the months after the Council in Jerusalem.

With respect to Silvanus, generally accepted to be Silas,[35] he journeyed to Antioch as the messenger of the Jerusalem Council's decision and bearer of its letter. While there, he taught and encouraged the church for some time (Acts 15:22–32). Paul chose him as his companion for the planned visit to the churches he and Barnabas had founded in Asia Minor.[36] His choice of Silas coincided with a dispute between himself and Barnabas (Acts 15:36–40). Thus, a considerable amount is known about Silas's activity in Antioch after the Council. By contrast, there is no evidence at all that he was ever in Rome, unless 1 Peter is permitted to provide its own testimony.[37]

Peter describes Silvanus in 1 Peter 5:12 in a manner which suggests he viewed him as a reliable person who, by being the messenger for Peter, was his collaborator.[38] Even though Silas's role may only have involved him delivering Peter's letter as far as the church in Troas, since that was where he and Paul paused before crossing to Macedonia (Acts 16:8–11), his standing as a leader in the Jerusalem church would certainly have made him a trustworthy representative of Peter's authority. Perhaps, Paul's intended trip and his selection of Silas to join him was the impetus for Peter to write his letter. His own standing as head of the Jerusalem church's missionary venture towards Jews accorded him this authority (Gal. 2:9).[39] Silas's role in the letter's delivery, likewise, showed that it was connected with the leaders in Jerusalem. These two

---

34 Elliott, 'Peter', 256–57; Horrell, 'Product', 46–47.
35 Brown and Meier, *Antioch & Rome*, 135; Witherington, *Hellenized Christians*, 245 n. 593.
36 The *app. crit.* of the Greek text indicates some manuscripts included an extra verse, 15:34, stating that only Judas returned to Jerusalem but the testimony for it is not the majority. The difference is not a crucial one for the present argument because if Silas did leave Antioch for Jerusalem with Judas to report on the letter's reception, his absence was temporary (Acts 15:40).
37 Corinth is the furthest west that Silvanus is documented (Acts 18:5; 2 Cor. 1:19).
38 The translation of 1 Pet. 5:12 should read: '*Through Silvanus, the faithful brother to you, as I deem it, I have written briefly …*,' with the implication being: 'I know my letter and its message will arrive safely through him'.
39 Bauckham, 'James', 439.

facts meant the usual procedure, that a general letter to the diaspora was issued by the Jerusalem church,[40] was fulfilled despite Peter's forced physical absence from the city at the time.

Mark, the third member of the trio referred to by name in 1 Peter, was also in Antioch after the Council. His association with Antioch was already extensive in terms of years and involvement. This was due chiefly, it appears, to the initiative of Barnabas his relative (Col. 4:10; Acts 12:25; 13:5, 13; 15:37–39) and Mark may have returned to Antioch after the Council with Barnabas. Or, perhaps, he was there beforehand. He is not mentioned in Acts 12:12–17 when Peter visits the house of Mark's mother's after escaping from imprisonment by Agrippa, nor is he named as a participant at the Council. However, his presence in Antioch after the Council when the delegates had returned is guaranteed by Acts 15:37–39. While it is Barnabas to whom Mark was related, it does seem that he also had a close relationship with Peter in some way given Peter's description of him as ὁ υἱός μου in 1 Peter 5:13.[41]

The clear evidence for Mark's presence in Antioch with Peter and Silas is significant for the question of the provenance of 1 Peter because the three men are not found together in Rome. Although Peter probably arrived in Rome c. 56,[42] there is no evidence that Mark arrived with him then or was there before him.[43] Mark was still in the East c. 64/65.[44] Thus, like Silvanus, Mark is not attested in Rome independently of Peter's letter.

It is for this reason that the time when Peter, Silas, and Mark were together in Antioch in the late 40s is so far the best clue available to when and where 1 Peter might have been written.[45] It also means that

---

40 Bauckham, 'James', 423–25.
41 Horrell, 'Product', 48 stresses this as a weakness in Mark's connection with Peter but does not take account of their joint time in Antioch.
42 Barnett, 'Paul in Rome', 202.
43 The Pauline prison letters in which Mark is mentioned (Phlm. 3:23; Col. 4:10) were probably written in Ephesus rather than Caesarea or Rome: Barnett, *Paul*, 216–17; Freed, *The Apostle Paul*, 144; White, 'Imprisonment', 550–56.
44 2 Tim. 4:11–13; cf. Barnett, 'Paul in Rome', 206.
45 Cf. Jobes, *1 Peter*, 36–37; contra Elliott, 'Peter', 263, who proposes that, apart from Rome, it was Jerusalem where the three men were together. He acknowledges, however, that Mark's presence in Jerusalem has to be presumed.

the identification of Babylon in 1 Peter 5:13 as a church in Antioch should be seriously considered. Thirdly, there are significant implications for the dating of the letter.

Chronology—relative and absolute

According to a chronological framework formed by Peter's escape from gaol and the death of Agrippa I in 44;[46] the date of the Council in Jerusalem c. 47–48,[47] and the residence of Paul and Silas in Corinth when Gallio was Proconsul of Achaea in mid-51 to mid-52,[48] an estimate for Peter's presence in Antioch together with Silas and Mark belongs sometime between the years 48–50:

Table 1

44	Peter	Jerusalem	Persecution by Herod (Herod's death)	Acts 12:1–23
Early/mid-40s	Antioch church	Antioch	Disputes with visiting Jewish Christians over requirements for gentiles in church	Gal. 2:1–5; Acts 15:1
Mid-40s	Peter	Away from Jerusalem	Departs from Jerusalem; travelling in Judaea as missionary	Acts 12:17–18; cf. Acts 9:32; 10:44–48
c. 47–48	Peter	Jerusalem	Visit to Jerusalem for the Council	Acts 15:6–11
c. 48–49	Peter Silvanus Mark	Antioch	**Peter:** Criticised by Paul.	Gal. 2:11–14
			Silvanus: Bearer of letter from James; chosen as travelling companion of Paul.	Acts 15:22; Acts 15:40
			Mark: Travelling companion of Barnabas	Acts 15:39
51–52	Silas	Corinth	**Silas:** Teaching and encouraging with Paul	Acts 18:5; 2 Cor. 1:19

46 Gibson, *Peter*, 266; Gill, 'Roman Policy', 19.
47 Barnett, 'Paul in Rome', 203.
48 Gibson, *Peter*, 217.

The period 48–49 falls within the years of Claudius' rule. This is reflected in 1 Peter by the naming of Galatia and Cappadocia separately (1:1) consistent with the Roman provincial system at that time.[49] The Roman geo-political structure of the mid-first century is also reflected in the prominence accorded a client king by Peter in 2:13 and 17. Claudius endorsed several client kings as rulers within the empire's East.[50] Included among these were members of the Herodian family in Judaea. Claudius and Agrippa I had a close friendship in the early 40s and a similar relationship existed between Claudius and Agrippa II later in the same decade.[51] At the time 1 Peter was written, Agrippa II was in Rome successfully championing the cause of Judaean Jews before Claudius against the accusations of Samaritans and the Roman procurator, Ventidius Cumanus (48–c. 52).[52] Agrippa's action would have been well known among those in the Jewish diaspora as well as those in Judaea and it would have been a sufficient cause for Peter to call on his readers to honour him.[53]

Claudius had already proved his friendly attitude towards the Jewish people in general when he issued a world-wide decree confirming their privileges in 41.[54] He was honoured by communities in Syria and Asia Minor.[55] The Jews there were generally untroubled by impe-

---

49 Vespasian combined them into one province named Galatia in 72: Mitchell, *Anatolia* vol. 1, 63.
50 Osgood, *Claudius Caesar*, 114; Sullivan, 'Dynasts', 928.
51 Josephus, *AntJ* 20.137–38. Schwartz, *Agrippa I*, 91–93.
52 Gill, 'Roman Policy', 21, 26.
53 For 'king' rather than 'emperor', see Witherington, *Hellenized Christians*, 141. Peter has not employed either *Sebastos* or Caesar which are the commonly-used terms for the emperor in inscriptions and the NT during the Julio-Claudian period: cf. Price, *Rituals and Power*, 2 n. 1; Börker, and Merkelbach (eds.), *Die Inschriften*, nos 402; 459; Mark 12:16–17; Acts 25:11–12, 25. Rule by the Herodians rather than Roman procurators was extremely important to Jewish political sentiment: cf. Gibson, *Peter*, 169–73.
54 Josephus, *AntJ* 19.286–91. Schürer, *History*, 77; Williams, *Jews*, 163–68; Trebilco, *Jewish Communities*, 10–11.
55 Cf. Downey, *Ancient Antioch*, 90; Ricl, *Inschriften*, no. 16; Mitchell and French (eds.), *Inscriptions of Ankara*, 151–52 no. 3; Horsley, 'Five Inscriptions', 299–300 no. 5.

rial intervention during his reign.⁵⁶ Peter's instruction that his readers submit to and honour the authorities (2:13-14,17) was a practical one for them everywhere in their local situations because Roman authorities were amenable to provincials living according to their own customs as long as there was no public disorder.⁵⁷ Moreover, civic-minded behaviour was a long-standing aspect of the Jewish theological tradition and practice,⁵⁸ but Peter's teaching at this point is particularly related to the way he envisages his readers having a submissive attitude in all situations of life. Everything is viewed from a theological perspective in Peter's letter. Thus it is only a small step for him to move from specific advice on behaviour for household-slaves (2:18-20) to a broad application of the servant theology for all his readers regardless of their status (2:21-25).

Circulation of the letter

1 Peter indicates that the gospel had been brought to the regions where his readers lived in advance of his letter (1:12). The means by which the gospel travelled there is not documented. However, the many who heard Peter's Pentecost speech probably communicated the news to their widespread families and friends (cf. Col. 1:7). The existence of routes crossing Anatolia opened up the possibilities for inland distribution.⁵⁹ The constant coastal trade between Judaea and Syria with Asia Minor offered a

---

56 Jobes, *1 Peter*, 176. Claudius' expulsion of Jews from Rome in the forties was caused by local rather than empire-wide circumstances. The same was true of the trouble between Greeks and Jews in Alexandria that forced his intervention: Schürer, *History*, 77-78. Gibson, *Peter*, 182-86 argues for a less favourable attitude of Claudius towards the Jews but his view that Claudius' punitive actions against Jews in Alexandria and Rome during the 40s were world-wide rather than localised is not convincing.
57 Rutgers, 'Roman Policy', 105-106, 111; Barclay, *Jews*, 275-80. Williams, *Persecution*, 277, seeks to establish that the Christians had an illegal standing in the eyes of the Romans when 1 Peter was written. However, his argument rests on a date after the Neronic persecution. By contrast, it is clear from the ruling of Gallio in Corinth that under Claudius this was not the case: Winter, 'Gallio's Ruling', 222.
58 Cf. Winter, *Seek*, 15-17.
59 Cf. Hemer, '1 Peter', 239-43; Thompson and Wilson, 'Route', 240-42.

ready avenue for circulation also.[60] The reverse procedure would probably have been the means that made Peter aware, in general terms, of his readers' situations.[61] Communications by Christian networks across great distances are frequently referred to in the NT.[62]

Troas's location and its regional importance made it an ideal centre for the dissemination of Peter's letter to the provinces he nominates. Troas was a flourishing city at the turn of the era. Its position made it a strategic nodal point for routes to many destinations by land and sea.[63] It is attested as a pivotal city for Christian travellers and a church existed there already in the 40s (Acts 16:8–12; 20:5–6; cf. 2 Tim. 4:13).[64] Once the letter had reached the church in Troas by the hand of Silas, there would have been many opportunities for its circulation to other Christian groups in the province of Asia, and Christian communities further away in Bithynia, Pontus, Galatia, and Cappadocia. Paul's comments about a door opening to him at Troas (2 Cor. 2:12) and Ephesus being a door to Asia (1 Cor. 16:8–9) are indications of the wide-ranging Christian networks extending from large cities within Asia Minor such as these. The fact that 1 Peter was written to communities living in geographical separation from each other would not have hindered its distribution.[65]

Peter's readers

The letter does not indicate Peter was acquainted with any of the inhabitants or that he knew exactly how they became believers. Neither does he know the details of problems the groups faced individually (1:6). Crucially, however, the scattered locations of the communities, the fact that their unhappy circumstances could be addressed in com-

---

60 Cf. Judge, 'Origin', 443–45.
61 Peter evangelised in Samaria and in the coastal areas of Phoenicia and Israel, including the Roman capital Caesarea (Acts: 8.25; 9:32–10:48).
62 Acts 11:27–28; Rom. 1:8; 16:4; 1 Cor. 1:11; 2 Cor. 9:2; Eph. 6:21–22; Phil. 4:21–22; Col. 1:3–4, 7–8.
63 Ricl, ed., *Inschriften*, 15; Hemer, 'Alexandria Troas', 87, 90–92.
64 Hemer, *Alexandria Troas*, 95.
65 The area was vast. In the words of Elliott: '129,000 square miles' (*1 Peter*, 84).

mon by Peter, and the deeply Jewish ethos of his letter are all features which suggest the readers of 1 Peter were Christians who were part of the Jewish diaspora in Asia Minor, Jews predominantly with among them, no doubt, some God-fearers.[66] It is the diaspora that offers the closest parallel for the communities' ubiquity and widespread distribution in Roman Asia Minor, as well as their shared cultural and religious experiences.[67] The encyclical character of 1 Peter is understandable when the communities of the diaspora are understood as his readership. Peter was the apostle to the Jews (Gal. 2:7–8). He identifies his readers initially as the ἐκλεκτοῖς παρεπιδήμοις διασπορᾶς (1:1; in paraphrase, 'those called by God as aliens among the Jews who are scattered'). The nature of their calling is explained immediately in the language of Jewish ritual as one of sacrifice (1:2).

Peter's use of both παρεπίδημος and πάροικος later in the letter (2:11) is not a tautological repetition as some have supposed.[68] The terms παρεπίδημος and πάροικος do overlap in some respects but in the context of the letter's theology they have separate applications. The readers are both παρεπιδήμοι *and* πάροικοι. Peter makes intentional use of both terms to acknowledge two different situations in which his readers find themselves. His repeated use of words with the παροικ- stem in his letter (1:17; 2:11) constitutes an unexceptional description of the Jewish diaspora. Παροικία, πάροικος are relatively frequent in extra-biblical material to denote inhabitants of an ancient city who live as resident foreigners in a long-term association with its citizens but without possessing all the rights and privileges of those who are full

---

66 Barclay, *Jews*, 14–15; Trebilco, *Jewish Communities*, 13; Rajak, 'The Jewish Community', 346–48. The introduction of Noah by Peter (1 Pet. 3:20), might have arisen from his knowledge that this would be a point of contact with his readers because of its popularity among the diaspora of Asia Minor. The account of Noah and the flood was adopted as early as late I b.c. by Phrygian Apamea under the Jewish influence when it became known as Apamea Κιβωτός: Mitchell, *Anatolia* Vol. 2, 33–35; Trebilco, *Jewish Communities*, 176.
67 Schürer, *History*, 17–38. First-century commentators, both gentile and Jewish, register the extent of the Jewish diaspora: Strabo (*apud* Josephus, AntJ 14.115); Philo, *Leg.*, 281–82. Trebilco, *Jewish Communities*, 188 notes the significant diversity between Jews regionally but stresses that significant features of Jewish identity and faith were maintained.
68 Cf. Green, *1 Peter*, 67.

citizens.⁶⁹ The use of πάροικος and its cognates with reference to his very widely scattered readers is one further indication that Peter had diaspora Jews in mind.⁷⁰ They were παροίκοι with respect to the Graeco-Roman cities and towns.⁷¹ Such an existence was characteristic of the many Jewish communities in the diaspora of Asia Minor and other regions during the early Roman empire.⁷²

By contrast, neither παρεπίδημος nor its cognate forms are commonly found in either historical sources from Asia Minor or the NT.⁷³ It is from the letter that the meaning of παρεπίδημος must be discerned.⁷⁴ For this, it is important to note that in 1:1 the datives, ἐκλεκτοῖς παρεπιδήμοις, belong together grammatically. This clarifies that παρεπίδημος is a term with theological significance in 1 Peter because it is a category to which only the chosen ones, the ἐκλεκτόι, belong. Translation of the phrase, ἐκλεκτοῖς παρεπιδήμοις διασπορᾶς as 'chosen aliens of the diaspora' signifies, in advance of the more descriptive sections later in the letter, that far from being a category of privilege and prosperity, the status of a παρεπίδημος in 1 Peter involves social rejection and personal suffering. In line with the aim of this discussion to present a new perspective on the context as well as the provenance and date of 1 Peter, the following describes three aspects of the letter indicating the Christians were people who were still worshipping in the synagogues.

69 Cf. Ricl, *Inschriften*, 15; Kearsley, 'A Civic Benefactor', 234–36 *ll*. 17, 37, 44; 238.
70 Elliott, *1 Peter*, 478.
71 Williams, *Persecution*, 69–74.
72 Williams, *Jews*, 107.
73 In the rare documentary attestation at Priene the term is used for Hellenistic visiting judges: Blümel and Merkelbach (eds.), *Die Inschriften*, no. 67; 69; 119. The word more commonly juxtaposed with πάροικοι for the civic category 'foreigner' is ξένοι: cf. Kearsley, 'A Civic Benefactor', 234–36 *ll*. 17, 37, 44. The same pairing occurs in Eph. 2:19.
74 Παρεπίδημος occurs more than once in the LXX with the meaning 'alien', a person of a different ethnicity, culture, and religious commitment. In Gen. 23:4, it describes Abraham in a situation which, though not paralleling that of Peter's readers, does express the vulnerability engendered by a lack of belonging. Heb. 11:13 is the only place apart from 1 Peter where παρεπίδημος occurs in the NT (Achtemeier, *1 Peter*, 173–74).

Intimation of conflict within synagogues and chronological context

a) The framing of Peter's message. Peter's response to the news of the Christians' suffering initially is to affirm the deep and everlasting relationship they have with God because of the resurrection of Jesus and to assure them of God's protection (1:3–5). From the beginning of the letter, Peter's emphasis on God the Father and his causative actions through Jesus for the eternal salvation of his readers is clear. He consistently maintains this perspective as the theological position of the letter (cf. 1:20–21; 2:4; 3:18–22; 4:10–11,14,19; 5:6–7). He is aiming to assure those Jews who have embraced the gospel that, as believers in Jesus, they are still within the will of the God that they have traditionally worshipped as synagogue Jews. Their situation is fraught with difficulty and challenges to their faith. They are within the diaspora but living as outsiders within it because of their belief in Jesus.

Peter's reference to the prophets (1:10–12), his description of Jesus as the sacrificial lamb (1:19), and the characterisation of his readers as the 'new Israel' (2:5) are to demonstrate to the readers that they stand in a spiritual relationship to God which is distinct from historical Judaism. His numerous allusions to the OT and quotations from the LXX in 1:10–25 are not introduced as proof-texts, however. They are included as a continuing affirmation of the unique spiritual standing of the 'elect aliens'. This is particularly illustrated by his inclusion of the stumbling stone (2:6–8). This metaphor is used by both Jesus (Matt. 21:42–45) and Paul (Rom. 9:32–33) in similar contexts.

Peter organises the OT citations in a series of contrasts. He employs contrast so consistently because of its relevance to the situation of his readers. By this, he repeatedly makes his point about the change from the old religion to the new faith into which his readers have entered (1:14–18).[75] Their break with the past and their adoption of the new beliefs and manner of life needs to be absolute even though their social context remains the same. Peter has not just appropriated the language of Israel by the thoroughness with which he couches his teaching in

---

75 Jobes, *1 Peter*, 113.

metaphors and citations from the OT. He reinterprets the Scriptures for his readers so that they will not doubt that Moses and the Law have been replaced with Christ and Grace.[76] This long section of the letter confirms that Peter is writing to a Jewish audience which is very familiar with the Jewish interpretation of the OT Scriptures. His teaching on living by hope rather than the ancestral ways (1:8–9) and in imitation of Jesus' humility (1:21–23), is followed by the prophetic message containing assurance of a good relationship with God (2:25), a passage which clearly points to the need to remember that their salvation lies in embracing Jesus (cf. 5:4).[77] The subliminal message from Peter's distinctive use of the OT is undoubtedly his desire to provide positive assurance to the Christians that the synagogue's Scriptures were confirming their discipleship of Jesus.[78]

b) The life of the Christians. The NT documents of the apostolic age speak of the opposition to the gospel in synagogues and of the suffering inflicted on Christians as a result.[79] This, too, is the suffering of Peter's readers. It is the followers of Moses even more than society at large who are causing deep and persistent grief for them (5:8–9; cf. 2 Cor. 11:28). Obedience to the gospel faith within Judaism meant not living any longer according to the ancestral Mosaic Code with its futility for salvation (1:18–21). The freedom of living under grace caused offence to, and condemnation from, synagogue associates. This is the reason Peter refers to the testing of their faith (1:7). Peter expresses the contrast between Judaism and the gospel he wishes to convey with clarity in 2:4: the believers are despised by humanity but chosen as precious by God. The ἐκλεκτόι belong to God and have a new and precious spiritual heritage as a result. It is as ἐκλεκτόι that the readers now stand in relation to their diaspora Jewish synagogue communities. They are being maligned and persecuted as παρεπιδήμοι for not cohering to the group norms.

Nowhere in his letter does Peter minimize the difficulty of living

---

76 Green, *1 Peter*, 55.
77 Ezek. 34:5–10.
78 Cf. P. Walker, 'A First-Century Sermon', 239.
79 Acts 18:12–17; 2 Cor. 11:24–26; cf. Trebilco, *Jewish Communities*, 20–27.

for Christ in the diaspora communities.[80] He stresses that it will require self-discipline and energy (1:13). He calls the readers to extend the impact of their new relationship with God through Christ to all aspects of their lives, starting with themselves (2:1-2). They have choices to make in living the right way. Peter presents the way of a faithful life as one of enduring obediently, and even of welcoming suffering (4:13-14). In this context, Peter urges the believers to keep behaving admirably in the public eye. He writes to them to keep behaving admirably ἐν τοῖς ἔθνεσις (2:12). The phrase 'among the nations' does not have an exclusive reference to gentiles.[81] The reference to the nations in 4:3 as well as 2:12 allows the possibility that Jews are included as well as the local population.[82] Peter describes the abusers as ignorant and foolish people who should be silenced by the Christians good conduct (2:15).[83] Nevertheless, the possibility remains that a Christian may have to face a formal hearing to explain their new faith as Jesus had prophesied (Matt. 10:17-22; Mark 13:9; Luke 12:11, 21:12-19; John 16:1-2). He charges his readers not to be intimidated by such a prospect (1 Pet. 3:14-16). It was members of the synagogues who were the chief opponents of the new teaching and who perpetrated the most virulent and persistent action against Christians in the Apostolic period (Acts 7:54-60, 14:19; 22:19-20). Peter's words of guidance and comfort reflect Jesus' earlier advice on the same topic (Luke 21:12-19).

Peter draws a contrast between a self-indulgent life and a life lived according to the will of God involving an attitude which is internally developed and established (4:1-2). He illustrates the behaviour he condemns by a list of vices. The assumption is often made, especially, by those who interpret Peter's readers as gentiles,[84] that Jews would not have undertaken such activities. However, in fact, the Jewish communities of Asia Minor were deeply Hellenised and their life-style was similar in many ways to that of the gentiles. They participated in a

---

80 His letter contains the greatest number of words denoting suffering in the NT: Witherington, *Hellenized Christians*, 40.
81 Witherington, *Hellenized Christians*, 140.
82 Elliott, *1 Peter*, 466-67.
83 Cf. Williams, *Jews*, 33-38.
84 Cf. Edwards, *1 Peter*, 172.

range of diverse aspects of Graeco-Roman culture, including civic activities, religious observations, and economic occupations.[85] Festival gatherings with free food, banqueting, drinking and sacrificing were all part of the normal way of life in a Graeco-Roman city. Such activities were usually associated with the local cultic calendar and the celebrations were a valued expression of generosity by civic benefactors.[86] The *paroikoi*, the civic category which includes Jews, was among those who took part in such social gatherings.[87] There is nothing in the list of vices which inherently defines the ethnicity of Peter's readers. On both occasions (2:12; 4:3), Peter is simply referring to society outside the Christian groups, both gentiles and Jews.[88]

c) **Judgement and the vindication of the Christians.** Peter identifies the abusers as blasphemers (4:4). No doubt the Christians were suffering sporadic local attacks outside their synagogues because of cultural differences (1:6),[89] but that is not Peter's point in 4:4. The lexical combination of ξενίζονται (take offence) and βλασφημοῦντες (blaspheming) indicates that Peter's view of the situation focuses, not on gentiles as the offenders, but on those who should know better, that is God's people in the synagogues. The connection between the blaspheming of the abusers and divine judgement shows that Peter has used βλασφημοῦντες in its particular sense of speaking ill of God. His statement that they stumble because they were destined to so (2:9) makes it far less likely that he is alleging that gentiles were blaspheming in their ignorance than that he is referring to Jewish people who refused to recognise the Messiah.[90]

Peter draws a link between the Christians' changed behaviour and the abuse they are suffering. The verb ξενίζονται (4:4) recalls their state of alienation. It is because those who have become Christians are no

---

85 Williams, *Jews*, 114-16; Rajak, 'Benefactors', 383-84; Trebilco, *Jewish Communities*, 173-83; Harland, 'Acculturation', 227-35.
86 Donelson, *I & II Peter*, 121-22; Edwards, *1 Peter*, 171.
87 Kearsley, *A Civic Benefactor*, 233-39.
88 Grudem, *1 Peter*, 123.
89 Barclay, *Jews in the Mediterranean Diaspora*, 262-74.
90 Cf. Acts 26:11; Rom. 2:17-24; 11:7-10.

longer taking part in the synagogue communities' social and religious activities, as they used to, that is causing offence.[91] The blasphemers will ultimately have to explain their actions when standing before God (4:5). At that time, it will become clear that the Christians have not been shamed despite the constant attempts by their opponents to achieve it (4:16). On the contrary, the faithful sufferers will be vindicated and it will be the unbelievers who will be put to shame (3:16).

A consciousness of the end times and the final judgement has guided Peter's appeals to his readers to ensure their salvation through enduring obedience (1:3–5; 2:12; 3:21–22). In Chapter 4 he adopts a new note of urgency saying the end of all things is near (4:7; πάντων δὲ τὸ τέλος ἤγγικεν). He also explains the implications of Christ's redemptive action, particularly emphasizing the weight and relevance of the coming Judgement for those who refuse to accept the claims of Jesus. It is the knowledge of their reward and justification, Peter underlines, which will sustain the readers in their suffering.

The One who judges at the final judgement in 1 Peter is God (1:17; 4:5).[92] Peter's emphasis on God, characteristic of the entire letter, is particularly significant in Chapter 4 for highlighting the two contrasting theologies which he is setting before his Jewish readers, the Old Covenant and its replacement, the New Covenant. At Sinai, God had provided for a place where he would dwell among the people of Israel (Exod. 25:8–9). By the epithet οἶκος τοῦ θεοῦ ('household of God') in 4:17 Peter identifies the Christians metaphorically as those among whom God now dwells (cf. 2:5).[93] The impassable spiritual chasm now existing between unbelieving Jews and the Christians has impressed itself upon him to such an extent that he asks the question: τί τὸ τέλος τῶν ἀπειθούντων τῷ τοῦ θεοῦ εὐαγγελίῳ; (4:17; 'What is the end of those who do not believe the good news of God?'). His question is striking because of the general lack of such rhetorical flourishes in his letter. By it, Peter refers to the condemnation awaiting unbelieving Jews with an anguish similar to that of Paul (Rom. 9:1–3).

---

91 For the translation, see Elliott, *1 Peter*, 725-26; Donelson, *I & II Peter*, 119.
92 Christ is often described as Judge in the NT: Donelson, *I & II Peter*, 123.
93 Elliott, *1 Peter*, 414-16; Achtemeier, *1 Peter*, 315-16.

Conclusion

The history and archaeology of Antioch has been re-examined with a view to explaining Peter's reference to the church in Babylon in literal rather than metaphorical terms. A connection between Antioch's pre-Christian Jewish community and the emerging church has been proposed. Antioch's involvement with the apostles and the Jerusalem church has also been discussed with a special focus on establishing the movements of Peter, Silvanus, and Mark and on defining the period when the three men were all in the one place at the same time. From this, it has been concluded that 1 Peter was written in Syrian Antioch rather than Rome. The period when Peter had the opportunity to write the letter has been identified as c. 48–49 on the basis of a chronological framework derived from both Roman rule and from the NT's account of activity within and between the churches in Antioch and Jerusalem.

The ethnicity of the readers of Peter's letter has been characterised as predominantly Jewish on the basis that the long-standing Jewish diaspora synagogue communities in Asia Minor were the context in which the readers responded to the gospel initially. The suffering that characterises their lives according to Peter's letter has been shown to arise from their continuing membership of these same communities after they became Christians and from the resentment of fellow Jews due to the readers' changed beliefs and behaviour. The suffering of Peter's readers in Pontus, Galatia, Cappadocia, Asia, and Bithynia is viewed as the outworking of Jesus' prophecy that division and suffering of this kind would be caused by belief in himself as the Son of God. The earliest Christian groups in Jerusalem were persecuted as they worshipped at the temple and within synagogue communities. 1 Peter has been found to portray similar trials experienced by the first generation of churches in Asia Minor. As a result, in terms of the outline proposed by Meier and Brown, the letter belongs now in the first stage of Christian development at Antioch rather than the second stage in Rome.[94]

Peter wrote his pastoral letter encouraging the Christians to stand firm in their faith after he heard news of their painful experiences

---

94 Meier and Brown, *Antioch & Rome*, 28, 128.

within their diaspora communities. He speaks mostly of θεός rather than Jesus because this is familiar language to the Christians as synagogue members. Nevertheless, he repeatedly reminds his readers of the fact that Jesus is God's agent for their salvation and he repeatedly draws contrasts between the old way of Judaism and the new faith. His readers' background and current context necessitated the saturation of his text with citations and allusions to the Jewish Scriptures. He repeatedly shows how familiar Scriptures actually point to Jesus when correctly understood. Far from denying the Scriptures which his readers were hearing every Sabbath in the synagogues he seeks to establish a new understanding of them. Peter does not tell the readers to separate themselves from the synagogue. His repeated message to the readers is to be true to the Word of God following the example of the prophets. He urges them to do good and to embrace the suffering that comes their way in imitation of Jesus.

The accusations causing the Christians to suffer are not described in detail by Peter. He does, however, describe the vast difference between Jews who believe and those who are spiritually blind because they fail to recognise Jesus as Messiah. The tenor of their attacks against the Christians leads Peter to label them 'blasphemers' and the ultimate division he identifies between them and the Christians is one with eternal significance marked by the final Judgement. Peter's expression of heartfelt dismay for those whose unbelief will condemn them at that time is the point in his letter when Peter reveals the depth of his pain at the ongoing opposition to the gospel by those to whom, as apostle to the Jews, he was devoted.

Rosalinde Kearsley
Macquarie University

Bibliography

Achtemeier, P. J.   *1 Peter* (Minneapolis, MN: Augsburg Fortress, 1996).

Barclay, J. M. G.   *Jews in the Mediterranean Diaspora* (Edinburgh: T&T Clark, 1996).

Barnett, P. W.   *Paul: Missionary of Jesus. After Jesus,* vol. 2 (Grand Rapids, MI: Eerdmans, 2008).

Barnett, P. W.   'Paul in Rome', in C. S. Sweatman and C. B. Kvidahl (eds.), *Treasures Old and New. Essays in Honor of Donald A. Hagner* (Wilmore, KY: Glossa House, 2017), 202–11.

Bauckham, R.   'James and the Jerusalem Church', in R. Bauckham (ed.), *The Book of Acts in Its First Century Setting* Vol. 4 (Grand Rapids, MI: Eerdmans, 1995), 415–80.

Blümel, W. and R. Merkelbach (eds.)   *Inschriften griechischer Städte aus Kleinasien. Die Inschriften von Priene* (Habelt: Bonn, 2014).

Börker, C. and R. Merkelbach (eds.)   *Inschriften griechischer Städte aus Kleinasien. Die Inschriften von Ephesos* Vol. II (Habelt: Bonn, 1979).

Brooten, B. J.   'The Jews of Ancient Antioch', in C. Kondoleon (ed.), *Antioch. The Lost City* (Princeton, NJ: Princeton University Press, 2006), 3–11.

Brown, R. E. and J. P. Meier   *Antioch & Rome. New Testament Cradles of Catholic Christianity* (London: Geoffrey Chapman, 1983).

De Giorgi, A. U.   *Ancient Antioch from the Seleucid Era to the Islamic Conquest* (Cambridge: CUP, 2016).

Donelson, P.   *I & II Peter and Jude. A Commentary* (Louisville, KY: Westminster John Knox, 2010).

Downey, G.   *A History of Antioch in Syria from Seleucus to the Arab Conquest* (Princeton, NJ: Princeton University Press, 1961).

Downey, G.   *Ancient Antioch* (Princeton, NJ: Princeton University Press, 1963).

Edwards, D. R.   *1 Peter* (Grand Rapids, MI: Zondervan, 2017).

Elliott, J. H.   *1 Peter. A New Translation with Introduction and Commentary* (New York, NY: Doubleday, 2000).

Elliott, J. H.   'Peter, Silvanus and Mark in I Peter and Acts:

	Sociological-Exegetical Perspectives on a Petrine Group in Rome', in W. Haubeck and M. Bachmann (eds.), *Wort in der Zeit. Neutestamentliche Studien. Festgabe für Karl Heinrich Rengstorf zum 75. Geburtstag* (Leiden: Brill, 1980), 250–67.
Freed, E.	*The Apostle Paul and His Letters* (London: Routledge, 2014).
Gibson, J. J.	*Peter Between Jerusalem and Antioch* (Tübingen: Mohr Siebeck, 2013).
Gill, D. W. J.	'Acts and Roman Policy in Judaea', in R. Bauckham (ed.), *The Book of Acts in its Palestinian Setting* Vol. 4 (Grand Rapids, MI: Eerdmans, 1995), 16–26.
Green, J. B.	*1 Peter* (Grand Rapids, MI: Eerdmans, 2007).
Grudem, W.	*1 Peter* (London: IVP, 1988).
Harland, P. A.	'Acculturation and Identity in the Diaspora: A Jewish Family and "Pagan" Guilds at Hierapolis', *JJS* 57 (2006), 222–44.
Hemer, C. J.	'Alexandria Troas', *TynBul* 26 (1975), 79–112.
Hemer, C. J.	'The Address of 1 Peter', *ExpT* 89 (1977–78), 239–43.
Horrell, D. G.	'The Product of a Petrine Circle? A Reassessment of the Origin and Character of 1 Peter', *JSNT* 86 (2002), 29–60.
Horsley, G. H. R.	'Five Inscriptions from Turkey', in M. Nollé, P. M. Rothenhoefer, G. Smied-Kowarzik, H. Schwarz, and H. C. von Morsch (eds.), *PANEGYRIKOI LOGOI. Festschrift für Johannes Nollé zum 65. Gerburtstag* (Bonn: Habelt, 2019), 291–300.
Jewett, R.	*Romans. A Commentary* (Augsburg: Fortress, 2007).
Jobes, K.	*1 Peter* (Grand Rapids, MI: Baker Academic, 2005).
Judge, E. A.	'The Origin of the Church at Rome: A New Solution?', in J. R. Harrison (ed.), *The First Christians in the Roman World: Augustan and New Testament Essays* (Tübingen: Mohr Siebeck, 2008), 445–49.
Kearsley, R. A.	'A Civic Benefactor of the First Century in Asia Minor', in S. R. Llewelyn (ed.), *New Documents Illustrating Early Christianity* vol. 7 (North Ryde: Macquarie University, 1994), 233–41.
Kraeling, C. H.	'The Jewish Community at Antioch', *JBL* 51 (1932), 130–60.
Lampe, P.	*From Paul to Valentinus. Christians at Rome in the First Two Centuries* (Minneapolis, MN: Fortress, 2003).

Légasse, S. 'Paul's Pre-Christian Career according to Acts', in R. Bauckham (ed.), *The Book of Acts in Its Palestinian Setting* vol. 4 (Grand Rapids, MI: Eerdmans, 1995), 365–90.

Meeks, W.A. and R. L. Wilken *Jews and Christians in Antioch in the First Four Centuries of the Common Era* (Missoula, MO: Scholars, 1978).

Michaels, J. R. *1 Peter* (Grand Rapids, MI: Zondervan, 1988).

Mitchell, S. *Anatolia. Land, Men, and Gods* Vols 1—2 (Oxford: OUP, 1993).

Mitchell, S. and D. French (eds.) *The Greek and Latin Inscriptions of Ankara (Ancyra)* vol. I (Munich: C. H. Beck, 2012).

Osgood, J. *Claudius Caesar. Image and Power in the Early Roman Empire* (Cambridge: CUP, 2011).

Price, S. R. F. *Rituals and Power. The Roman Imperial Cult in Asia Minor* (Cambridge: CUP, 1984).

Rajak, T. 'Benefactors in the Greco-Jewish Diaspora', in T. Rajak, *Studies in Cultural and Social Interaction* (Leiden: Brill, 2001), 373–91.

Rajak, T. 'The Jewish Community and Its Boundaries', in T. Rajak, *Studies in Cultural and Social Interaction* (Leiden: Brill, 2001), 335–54.

Richardson, P. 'Augustan Era Synagogues in Rome', in K. P. Donfried and P. Richardson (eds.), *Judaism and Christianity in First-Century Rome* (Grand Rapids, MI: Eerdmans, 1998), 17–29.

Ricl, M. (ed.) *Inschriften von Alexandreia Troas. Inschriften griechischer Städte aus Kleinasien* (Bonn: Habelt, 1997).

Rodgers, P. R. (ed.) *1 Peter. A Collaborative Commentary* (Eugene, OR: Wipf and Stock, 2017).

Rutgers, L. V. 'Roman Policy toward the Jews: Expulsions from the City of Rome during the First Century C.E.', in K. P. Donfried and P. Richardson (eds.), *Judaism and Christianity in First-Century Rome* (Grand Rapids, MI: Eerdmans, 1998), 56–74.

Schürer, E. *The History of the Jewish People in the Age of Jesus* Christ vol. III pt. I (rev. English ed.; Edinburgh: T&T Clark, 1986).

Schwartz, D. R. *Agrippa I. The Last King of Judaea* (Tübingen: Mohr Siebeck, 1990).

Sullivan, R.D.   'Dynasts in Pontus', in H. Temporini (ed.), *Aufstieg und Niedergang der römischen Welt* vol 7 II (Berlin: De Gruyter, 1980), 913–30.

Thompson, G. L., and M. Wilson   'The Route of Paul's Second Journey in Asia Minor', *TynBul* 67 (2016), 217–46.

Trebilco, P. R.   *Jewish Communities in Asia Minor* (Cambridge: CUP, 1991).

Walker, P.   'A First-Century Sermon', in P. J. Williams, A. D. Clarke, P. M. Head, and D. Instone-Brewer (eds.), *The New Testament in Its First Century Setting. Essays on Context and Background in Honour of B. W. Winter on His 65th Birthday* (Grand Rapids, MI: Eerdmans, 2004), 231–49.

White, J.   'The Imprisonment That Could Have Happened (And the Letters Paul Could Have Written There): A Response to Ben Witherington', *JETS* 61 (2018), 549–58.

Williams, M. (ed.)   *The Jews among the Greeks and Romans. A Diasporan Sourcebook* (Baltimore, MD: Johns Hopkins University Press, 1998).

Williams, T.   *Persecution in 1 Peter. Differentiating and Contextualizing Early Christian Suffering* (Leiden: Brill, 2012).

Winter, B. W.   'Gallio's Ruling on the Legal Status of Early Christianity (Acts 18:14–15)', *TynBul* 50 (1999), 213–24.

Winter, B. W.   *Seek the Welfare of the City* (Grand Rapids, MI: Eerdmans, 1994).

Witherington, B., III   *Letters and Homilies for Hellenized Christians vol. II. A Socio-Rhetorical Commentary on 1–2 Peter* (Downers Grove, IL: IVP Academic, 2006).

Alexander and the High Priest

Guy MacLean Rogers

Abstract

Josephus' dramatic account of Alexander's encounter with the high priest Jaddus and his offering sacrifice at the Jerusalem temple in July 332 BC is problematic in terms of chronology, archaeological evidence, and plausibility. Alexander's punitive mission against the Samaritans, however, is supported by literary and archaeological evidence. If Alexander granted privileges to the Jews at all, they were limited, but Josephus' readers would be pleased to read that Alexander favoured the Jews over the Samaritans.

While Alexander III of Macedon and his pan-Hellenic army were besieging the city of Tyre between January and July of 332 B.C.E. the Macedonian king reportedly sent a letter to Jaddus (or Jaddua), the high priest of the Jews. In the letter Alexander asked for an alliance, provision for his army, and as many gifts as previously had been given by the Tyrians to the Persian King Darius III. Alexander promised friendship in return.[1]

Jaddus responded that he had made an oath to Darius not to take up arms against him. As long as Darius was alive, the high priest would not violate his pledge. Alexander replied that when he had taken Tyre, he would march against the high priest and through him teach all what people it was to whom they must keep their oaths.[2]

A nearby governor, however, wagered that Darius's days were num-

---

1   Josephus, *Antiquities* 11.317.
2   *Antiquities* 11.318-9; *Yom.* 69a.

bered. Sanaballat or Sanballat (probably III), the governor of the Persian province of Samaria, located just to the north of Judah/Yehud, abandoned Darius, and made his way to Alexander at Tyre. Sanballat brought with him eight thousand followers.³ These eight thousand presumably comprised Sanballat's army.

Sanballat told Alexander that his son-in-law Manasseh was the brother of Jaddus, and that there were many with him who wished to build a temple in the land of Samaria subject to him. It was to Alexander's advantage, Sanballat stated, that the power of the Jews should be divided. In case of a revolution, he told the Macedonian King, they should not be of one mind and act together, giving trouble to the kings, as they had done to the (earlier) Assyrian rulers. After Alexander granted his request, Sanballat devoted himself to building the temple on Mount Gerizim, overlooking the biblical city of Shechem, and made his son-in-law Manasseh high priest of the shrine.⁴

Following the capture of Tyre in July of 332 Alexander marched southward and besieged the emporium city of Gaza. Gaza was captured after a siege lasting at most three months (September to November of 332).⁵ Alexander then made his way to Jerusalem (according to Josephus).

The high priest Jaddus feared Alexander because he had declined Alexander's offer of an alliance. But Jaddus had been reassured by a dream. In the dream God had told the high priest to open up the gates of Jerusalem and to go out and meet the Macedonians. So Jaddus, dressed in a robe of hyacinth-blue and gold, and wearing a gold-enplated mitre with God's name inscribed upon it, climbed up Mt Scopus to greet the king. Priests clothed in white linen and the cit-

---

3   The province was named after the city of Samaria built by Omri after he purchased the hill from Shemer according to 1 Kgs 16:24; see Briant, *History*, 714. The total of 8,000 soldiers may sound like an exaggeration but surveys of both northern and southern Samaria indicate that the province had a much larger population than Yehud at the time; see Grabbe, *History*, 34, 156.
4   *Antiquities* 11.321–24.
5   Rogers, *Alexander*, 85.

izens of Jerusalem accompanied the high priest.[6]

The Phoenicians and Chaldeans who escorted Alexander expected the young Macedonian king to allow them to plunder Jerusalem and to put the high priest to death, we are told. Instead Alexander greeted Jaddus and prostrated himself before the Jew. Alexander's general Parmenio asked the king why he, before whom everyone else bowed, prostrated himself before the high priest of the Jews.

Alexander explained to Parmenio that he did not prostrate before the priest but before the high priest's God. Josephus then provides an explanation for why Alexander, who not only was a king, with his own pretensions of divine descent, but also an active and inquisitive polytheist, bowed down before the God of the Jews.[7]

Before he crossed over to Asia, while he was in Dium in Macedon, Alexander too had a dream. In the dream the high priest Jaddus, wearing the robes of the high priesthood, had appeared and urged the king to cross over to Asia with confidence, saying that he (the high priest) would lead his army and give to Alexander the empire of the Persians. Having seen no one else in such vestments before, and seeing the priest now dressed up in the robes of his office, Alexander told Parmenio that he recalled the vision of his dream and the priest's promise. He now believed he had made the expedition under divine guidance. He would defeat Darius and destroy the power of the Persians and carry out all the things he had in mind.[8]

Alexander then took Jaddus by the hand and entered Jerusalem. The twenty-four year old king went up to the Temple and sacrificed as directed by the high priest. When the book of Daniel was shown to him, in which it was predicted that one of the Hellenes would destroy

---

6   *Antiquities* 11.325–29. In the version of the story related later in the *Babylonian Talmud Yom.* 69a, Alexander met the high priest Simeon who had gone out to meet him in Antipatris (Aphek). Simeon had walked all night to meet Alexander to persuade him not to destroy the Temple, as he was advised to do by the Cutheans (another name for the Samaritans).

7   In the *Babylonian Talmud Yom.* 69a, Alexander said that he bowed down before the Jew because it was his image which won for him in all his battles. For a comprehensive and persuasive religious portrait of Alexander see Naiden, *Alexander*.

8   *Antiquities* 11.330–35.

the empire of the Persians, he believed that he was the king indicated. Afterward he invited the people to ask for any gifts they might desire.

When the high priest made his requests the next day, Alexander granted the Jews the right to observe their ancestral laws and in the seventh year to be exempt from tribute. He also gave the Jews in Babylon and Media the right to have their own laws, though he had not yet conquered either. After he promised the Jews that while serving in his army they would be allowed to observe their ancestral customs, many Jews accepted service with him.[9]

The Samaritans met with Alexander shortly after he departed from Jerusalem.[10] They asked him to come to their city, to visit their temple, and for remission of their tribute in the seventh year. Alexander promised to visit their city another time, Josephus writes. After they denied that they were Jews, he told them that he had given those privileges (of remission of tribute) to the Jews. He did, however, order soldiers who had been sent to him by Sanballat to accompany him to Egypt, where they received allotments of land.[11]

Alexander and the Jews

Stories about Alexander's preferential treatment of the Jews and relations with the Samaritans may have originated during the fourth century B.C.E., and may have been passed down from the fourth century B.C.E. until the time that Josephus completed his massive, twenty book, c. 60,000 line *Archaeologica* or *Antiquities* (as the title is commonly translated by scholars writing in English), probably between September of 93 and September of 94 C.E..[12] But it is not possible to identify a specific source or sources for the story of Alexander's encounter with

---

9   *Antiquities* 11.336–39.
10 For the contested origins of the Samaritans as descendants of the colonists who reportedly had been sent to occupy the land of Israel by Shalmanezer V and/or Sargon II and intermarried with Jews there see 2 *Kgs* 17:24–41; for general works on the Samaritans and the question of their origins see Pummer *Samaritans*; *Samaritans in Josephus*; Kartveit, *Samaritans*; Dušek, *Inscriptions*, 74–81; and Vermes, *Herod*, 6.
11 *Antiquities* 11.340–45.
12 Rogers, *Freedom*, 473.

the high priest of the Jews that Josephus based his account upon.[13]

No matter where Josephus got his information from, there are problems of chronology, archaeological evidence, and plausibility with Josephus's account of Alexander's interactions with the Jews of Judaea and the Samaritans.[14] To begin with the question of chronology, in Josephus's account of Alexander's relations with Sanballat and the Samaritans the Macedonian king granted them the right to build their temple when he was besieging Tyre during the first half of 332 B.C.E. and then was invited to visit the temple only a few months later, after the capture of Gaza, by November of the same year.

Archaeological evidence on Mount Gerizim, however, shows conclusively that the building of the original Samaritan Temple on Mount Gerizim should be dated to the reign of Sanballat I, at least a century before Alexander's arrival in the region.[15] Even if Josephus did not simply get the chronology of the building of the Samaritan temple wrong by 100 years, at most what Alexander could have done in 332 B.C.E. was to authorise some kind or work or expansion of the pre-existing Samaritan temple. He could not have been invited to visit a structure that was authorised and then completed from the ground up between January and November of 332.[16]

More importantly for the question of whether Alexander engaged directly with the high priest of the Jews, no source that can be traced back to Alexander's lifetime or the period just after it reports a meeting between Alexander and the high priest of the Jews. Nowhere do any of the contemporary or near-contemporary sources for Alexander's campaigns in the Middle and Near East, including Callisthenes, Anaximenes, Alexander's land-surveyors, Eumenes of Cardia and Diodotus of

---

13 Shahar, 'Jews', 406 n.5.
14 Among the most influential contributions to the debate about Alexander's alleged interactions with Jaddus, the Jews, and the Samaritans in 332 B.C.E. see Grabbe, 'Josephus', 231–46; Cohen, 'Alexander', 41–68; Kasher, 'Thoughts', 153–57; Shahar, 'Jews', 403–26.
15 Bull, 'Excavation', 58–72; Magen, 'Dating', 157–211.
16 Mor, 'Samaritan History', 7, argues that the temple was built hastily to realise the Samaritans' goals before the period of uncertainty (about who would end up ruling the region) ended. That seems unlikely; note that Josephus has Sanballat with Alexander at Tyre at the time. See also Schäfer, History, 4.

Erythrae (the purported authors of the so-called *Royal Diaries*), Onesicritus, Nearchus, Ptolemy, Aristobulus, Chares, Cleitarchus, Ephippus and Nicobule, Polycleitus, Medius, or Hieronymus, who are quoted in the later works of Diodorus Siculus, Strabo, Curtius Rufus, Plutarch, Arrian, or Justin, report a meeting between the young king and the high priest. Neither are we able to identify a specific Jewish source for the story of the meeting before the time of Josephus (and subsequently found in the Babylonian Talmud and the Scroll of Fasting (*Meg.*).[17] We therefore do not know whether Alexander granted to the Jews of Jerusalem, or Babylon, or Media the right to observe their own laws, remitted the tribute of the Jews during the seventh year, or enlisted Jews to serve in his army at that time.

We do know, however, that Alexander cannot have been shown a copy of the finished book of Daniel, since the complete, edited version of the book at any rate was not put together until the third or early second century B.C.E., long after Alexander's death in Babylon in early June of 323 B.C.E.[18] Thus, all that can be supported, based upon evidence that can be dated back to the last quarter of the fourth century B.C.E., is that after the capture of Tyre Alexander made his way southward down to Gaza.

In his *Historiae Alexandri Magni* (which made extensive use of the now lost, earlier works of Cleitarchus and Ptolemy) Curtius Rufus reports that Alexander ordered Hephaestion to skirt the coast of Phoenicia with his fleet, and Alexander came with his full army to the city of Gaza.[19] From Curtius's statement it can be inferred plausibly that Alexander's army marched along the coast as it made its way southward. A trip by Alexander up into the Judaean hills to Jerusalem to confront the high priest of the Jews would have been a departure from the army's coastal route, if the plan was for the fleet and the army to stay in at least periodic contact during Alexander's southward pro-

---

17 Josephus, *Antiquities* 11.326–339 ; *Yom.* 69a; *Meg.* (21 Kislev); and despite the ingenious reconstructions of Cohen, 'Alexander', 66–68.
18 Collins, *Daniel*, 34; Satlow, *Bible*, 130–32.
19 Curtius Rufus 4.5.10. While the siege was in progress Alexander sent for the siege engines that he had used to capture Tyre earlier in the year and the machines were brought by sea.

gression toward Egypt. In any case we know that after the capture of Gaza Alexander marched on to Pelusium in the eastern delta of the Nile River a week later.[20]

Therefore the dramatic meeting between Alexander and the high priest cannot be verified to have occurred. Rather the story probably comprises one of three separate and independent narrative strands in the most famous section of the second half of Josephus's *Antiquities*.[21] The function or purpose of the meeting story in the *Antiquities* and the anecdote about Alexander bowing down before the god probably was to glorify the Jews by demonstrating that Alexander honoured Jerusalem, the Temple, and the high priest, and to add the famous Alexander's name to the list of 'pagans' who acknowledged God's supremacy.[22]

But is it also true that Alexander had no provable interactions with the Samaritans while he was in the region from late 332 into the spring of 331?

Curtius Rufus reports that while Alexander was in Egypt he learned that the Samaritans had burned alive Andromachus. Andromachus was a Macedonian and had been the naval commander (*nauarchos*) of the Cypriot fleet that blockaded the northern harbour of Tyre in 332 B.C.E. Afterwards Parmenio apparently had appointed Andromachus as governor of Coele-Syria, or perhaps a not-precisely defined part of it, but including Samaria.[23] In doing so Parmenio, undoubtedly authorised by Alexander, at least undermined the authority of Sanballat's line in Samaria. The result was a revolt of at least some Samaritans that led to Andromachus's murder.[24]

In response to the killing of his governor Alexander marched northwards as fast as possible to avenge Andromachus's murder, and when Alexander arrived, those who had murdered Andromachus were

---

20 Arrian 2.26.1–27.7; Diodorus Siculus 17.48.1; Rogers, *Alexander*, 85–86; for further analysis of the reasons why the encounter story was propagated during and after the Hellenistic period see Shahar, 'Jews', 417–19.
21 Cohen, 'Alexander', 41–2.
22 Cohen, 'Alexander', 49, 54.
23 Arrian, Anabasis 2.20.10; Curtius Rufus 4.8.10; 4.5.9; Mohr, 'Samaritan History', 9–11; Kasher, 'Thoughts', 153–57.
24 Mor, 'Samaritan History', 9.

handed over to him.[25] Alexander appointed Memnon to replace Andromachus and executed those who had burned Andromachus alive.[26] The Samaritans were removed from Samaria, which was subsequently settled by Macedonian military veterans.[27]

At least some of the Samaritans, however, survived the Macedonian attack and escaped to a cave (of Abu Shinjeh) in the Wadi Daliyeh (c. 14 km north of Jericho), bringing with them supplies and written records, including registers of slave sales. The Macedonians, however, tracked the Samaritans down and more than 200 of the unfortunate refugees were suffocated after Alexander's men lit a fire at the entrances of the cave.[28] A survey of sites in northern Samaria during the Hellenistic period shows a marked decline in the number of sites occupied after Alexander's conquest.[29]

Curtius's literary account and the material evidence from Wadi Daliyeh support the idea that there was a bloody conflict between Alexander and the Samaritans, just as Josephus reports. Unfortunately we do not know all of the details. However, it is tempting to connect the evidence for the conflict with the story Josephus tells about Alexander denying to the Samaritans the privileges that he granted to the Jews, and then the appointment of a new governor by Parmenio. Whatever happened between Alexander and the Samaritans was not to the benefit at least of the line of Samaritan governors. Murdering Alexander's governor was not an act likely to endear the Samaritans to Alexander. Jaddus's God forgave repentant individuals and nations for their sins, Alexander rarely.

Many Jews named their sons Alexander in honour of the great king after 332. But there is no unambiguous contemporary evidence that

---

25 Curtius Rufus 4.8.10.
26 Curtius Rufus 4.8.11.
27 Eusebius, Παντοδαπὴ ἱστορία 2.114; Hieronymus (Jerome), *Chronicon* 123; Syncellus, *Chronographia* I 496.
28 Cross, 'Discovery', 110-26; 'Papyri', 45-69; 'The Papyri', 17-29; Lapp and Lapp, *Discoveries*; Cross, 'SAMARIA PAPYRUS', 7-17; 'Report', 17-26; Mor, 'Samaritan History', 10; Gropp, 'Language', 169-87; 'Sanballat', 823-25.
29 Zertal, 'Northern Samaria', 164-66; for a summarising survey see Grabbe, *History*, 33.

Alexander granted to the Jews of the former Persian province independence. Even if Josephus is right, and Alexander granted the Jews the right to observe their ancestral laws—despite never meeting Jaddus himself—there is no indication that the political or constitutional status of the Jews of the former Persian province of Yehud changed much, at least at first. At most the Yehudites enjoyed internal, but not external, autonomy and were subject to tribute for six out of every seven years.

While Alexander was still alive their status may have similar to that of other non-Hellenic peoples Alexander had gained mastery over on his campaign route from the coast of Asia Minor to Egypt, such as the Lydians.[30] Because Josephus was most concerned with highlighting the differences between the way Alexander dealt with the Jews and the Samaritans, the larger and far more significant point about Alexander's conquest of the region and its consequences for the Jews living there has been distorted and obscured.

It would have pleased Jews who read Josephus's works to be reminded that Alexander supposedly had bowed down before their God and given them the right to observe their ancestral laws. That pleasure, however, must have been tempered among later Jews who knew their own history by the knowledge that at least some of Alexander's successors most certainly did not concede the right of the Jews of the former Persian province to follow their laws, and that the Jews of the former Persian province would not be free from paying tribute to one or another of the Macedonian successor dynasts for almost 170 years after Alexander passed through the region. Alexander's encounter with Jaddus—whether real, or much more plausibly, invented or at least embellished to promote an ethno-nationalist agenda—was the high point of relations between Jews and Macedonians, especially for Jews, such as Josephus, who never wavered in the belief that there was no such thing as a good Samaritan.

Guy MacLean Rogers
Wellesley College

30   Arrian 1.17.7–8.

Bibliography

Briant, P.	*From Cyrus to Alexander: A History of the Persian Empire* (University Park, Pa.: Eisenbrauns, 2002 [French: 1996]).
Bull, R.	'The Excavation of Tell er-Ras on Mt. Gerizim', *The Biblical Archaeologist* 31, 2 (1968), 58–72.
Cohen, S.	'Alexander the Great and Jaddus the High Priest according to Josephus', *Association for Jewish Studies Review* Volumes 7/8 (1982/1983), 41–68.
Collins, J. J.	*Daniel: With an Introduction to Apocalyptic Literature* (The Forms of Old Testament Literature, 20; Grand Rapids, Mich.: Eerdmans, 1984).
Cook, E. (ed.)	*Sopher Mahir: Northwest Semitic Studies Presented to Stanislav Segert* (Santa Monica, Calif.: 1990).
Cross, F.	'A Report on the Samaria Papyri', in J. A. Emerton (ed.), *Congress Volume: Jerusalem, 1986* (Vetus Testamentum Supplements, 40; Leiden: Brill, 1988), 17–26.
Cross, F.	'Papyri of the Fourth Century B.C. from Daliyeh', in D. Freedman, and J. Greenfield (eds.), *New Directions in Biblical Archaeology* (1969), 45–69.
Cross, F.	'SAMARIA PAPYRUS 1: AN ARAMAIC SLAVE CONVEYANCE OF 335 B.C.E. FOUND IN THE WÂDÎ ED-DÂLIYEH', *Eretz-Israel* 18 (1985), 7–17.
Cross, F.	'The Discovery of the Samaria Papyri', *The Biblical Archaeologist* 26 (1963), 110–26.
Cross, F.	'The Papyri and their Historical Implications', in P. W. Lapp and N. L. Lapp (eds.), *Discoveries in the Wadi ed-Daliyeh* (Cambridge, Mass.: American Schools of Oriental Research, 1974), 17–29.
Crown, A. D. (ed.)	*The Samaritans* (Tübingen: Mohr Siebeck, 1989).
Dušek, J.	*Aramaic and Hebrew Inscriptions from Mt. Gerizim and Samaria between Antiochus III and Antiochus IV Epiphanes* (Culture and History of the Ancient Near East, 54; Leiden: Brill, 2012).
Emerton J. A. (ed.)	*Congress Volume: Jerusalem, 1986* (Vetus Testamentum Supplements, 40; Leiden: Brill, 1988).

Grabbe, L.	*A History of the Jews and Judaism in the Second Temple Period, Vol.1: Yehud, the Persian Province of Judah* (Library of Second Temple Studies; Dallas, Tex.: T&T Clark, 2004).

Grabbe, L.	'Josephus and the Reconstruction of the Judaean Restoration', *Journal of Biblical Literature* 106 (1987), 231–46.

Grabbe, L. and O. Lipschits (eds.)	*Judah Between East and West: The Transition from Persian to Greek Rule* (Dallas, Tex.: T&T Clark, 2011).

Gropp, D.	'Sanballat', in L. Schiffman, and J. VanderKam (eds.) *Encyclopedia of the Dead Sea Scrolls* (2000), 823–35.

Gropp, D.	'The Language of the Samaria Papyri: A Preliminary Study', in E. Cook (ed.), *Sopher Mahir: Northwest Semitic Studies Presented to Stanislav Segert* (Santa Monica, Calif.: 1990), 169–87.

Kartveit, M.	*The Origin of the Samaritans* (Vetus Testamentum Supplements, 128: Leiden: Brill, 2009).

Kasher, A.	'Further Revised Thoughts on Josephus' Report of Alexander's Campaign to Palestine (AJ XI 304–347)', in L. Grabbe and O. Lipschits (eds.), *Judah Between East and West: The Transition from Persian to Greek Rule* (Dallas, Tex.: T&T Clark, 2011), 153–57.

Lapp, P. W., and N. L. Lapp (eds.)	*Discoveries in the Wadi ed-Daliyeh* (Cambridge, Mass.: American Schools of Oriental Research, 1974).

Lipschits, O., G. Knoppers, and R. Albertz (eds.)	*Judah and the Judeans in the Fourth Century B.C.E.* (University Park, Pa.: Eisenbrauns, 2007).

Magen, Y.	'The Dating of the First Phase of the Samaritan Temple on Mount Gerizim in Light of the Archaeological Evidence', in O. Lipschits, G. Knoppers, and R. Albertz (eds.), *Judah and the Judeans in the Fourth Century B.C.E.* (University Park, Pa.: Eisenbrauns, 2007), 157–211.

Moore, K. R. (ed.)	*Brill's Companion to the Reception of Alexander the Great* (Leiden: Brill, 2018).

Mor, M.	'Samaritan History: The Persian, Hellenistic and Hasmonean Period', in A. D. Crown (ed.), *The Samaritans* (Tübingen: Mohr Siebeck, 1989), 9–11.

Naiden, F. S.   *Soldier, Priest, and God: A Life of Alexander the Great* (New York, N.Y.: Oxford University Press, 2019).

Pummer, R.   *The Samaritans* (Leiden: E. J. Brill, 1987).

Pummer, R.   *The Samaritans in Flavius Josephus* (Tübingen: Mohr Siebeck, 2009).

Rogers, G. M.   *Alexander: The Ambiguity of Greatness* (New York, N.Y.: Random House, 2004).

Rogers, G.M.   *For the Freedom of Zion: The Great Revolt of Jews against Romans, 66–74 CE* (New Haven, Conn.: Yale University Press, 2021).

Satlow, M.   *How the Bible became Holy* (New Haven, Conn.: Yale University Press, 2014).

Schäfer, P.   *The History of the Jews in the Greco-Roman World* (2nd edn; Abingdon, Routledge: 2003).

Schiffman, L., and J. VanderKam (eds.)   *Encyclopedia of the Dead Sea Scrolls* (New Haven, Conn.: Yale University Press, 2000).

Shahar, M.   'Jews, Samaritans and Alexander: Facts and Fictions in Jewish Stories on the Meeting of Alexander and the High Priest', in K. Moore (ed.), *Brill's Companion to the Reception of Alexander the Great* (Leiden: Brill, 2018), 403–26.

Tropper, A.   *A Legend Reinvented: Simeon the Righteous in Rabbinic Literature* (Leiden: Brill, 2013).

Vermes, G.   *The True Herod* (Dallas, Tex.: T&T Clark, 2014).

Zertal, A.   'Survey of Northern Samaria', in E. M. Meyers (ed.), *The Oxford Encyclopedia of Archaeology in the Near East* Vol. 4 (New York, N.Y.: Oxford University Press, 1997), 164–66.

Reading the Shepherd of Hermas with Roman Eyes:
Urbanity, Self, and Emergent Neighbourhood Religion in the Imperial Capital

Harry O. Maier

Abstract

This essay investigates the Shepherd of Hermas as an instance of emergent urban religion in first century Rome. With the help of sociological tools of modern urban geography it situates the work in the crowded streets and insulae of the Roman capital. The work respatialises and retemporalises the city by locating its audience in a series of visions through which Hermas exhorts wealthier members to live in greater solidarity with poorer members. Hermas uses an apocalypse genre to create an imagined community centred on economic and spiritual symbiotic relationships of richer and poorer listeners. The essay deploys the urban geographical notion of aspirational space to show the way in which Hermas as a religious entrepreneur promoted mutually beneficial neighbourhood relationships. The essay concludes with a treatment of the self and community in the Shepherd as it relates to the idea of the porous, partible, and dividual self. Gifts of the rich to the poor create networks of identity and self, distributed across a variety of neighbourhood relationships.

The scholarly guild owes a great debt of gratitude to James Harrison for his pioneering readings of the corpus of Paul's letters in its Roman imperial context. His ground-breaking work has alerted us to the importance of attending to imperial ideology and propaganda as well as the material and lived realities of the Roman Empire in treating the Pauline corpus and the New Testament in general. This essay is offered as a token of deep appreciation to Professor Harrison for his contributions to the field of New Testament and Early Christian studies. If imitation is the sincerest form of flattery, it has been written in the same spirit of Professor Harrison's, namely to promote engagement of early Christianity in its imperial and material contexts. It considers the Shepherd of Hermas in the light of its urban location in the imperial capital. In what follows, after a brief introduction to the writing, I will discuss the Shepherd of Hermas as it relates to urbanity, the promotion of the city as an aspirational space, and, with the help of cross-cultural anthropological discussion of dividuality, Hermas's understanding of the self as divisible and partible. My chief thesis is that Hermas's concern with the poor and the cementing of relations between people of differing economic power presents us with a picture of an urban religion seeking to practise a new form of sociality. This portrait gains relief when placed in the context of the crowded neighbourhoods of the imperial capital.

Hermas, a Roman freedman, wrote the Shepherd in Rome sometime during the late first and early second century C.E., perhaps over several decades.[1] The work comprises a series of revelations Hermas received in the form of visions, commandments, and parables, which together exhort local Christ followers more faithfully to conduct their religious practices. Scholars have traditionally criticised the work for its long, rambling, and monotonous contents. It was however one of the most widely read works in the early church, attested by the numerous manuscripts from across the Mediterranean Basin that preserve its contents, frequent quotation, as well as its early translation into several languages. Hermas's revelations focus on the failures of Christ believers to obey God's commandments, most those committed after baptism. Hermas anticipates an imminent final judgement and offers his audience a chance to repent of their misdeeds before it is too late. Earlier historians examined the Shepherd of Hermas as a moment

---

1 For theories of authorship and dating, Maier, *Social Setting*, 55.

in an unfolding theological tradition of penitential theology, as an early Christian solution to the problem of post-baptismal sin. Carolyn Osiek in her ground-breaking *Rich and Poor in the Shepherd of Hermas* as well as her Hermeneia commentary challenged this reading by showing that whatever Hermas had to say about the challenge of post-baptismal sin, it was not with a view to offering an abstract solution to a theological problem, but rather with reference to the real economic challenges of rich and poor Christ followers co-existing within the same Roman community.[2] Osiek has drawn attention to ways Hermas's revelations admonish Jesus followers who pursue their economic interests at the expense of allegiance to their Christ assembly. In one vision, for example, he sees the assembly personified as a worn out, old woman (Vis. 3.11.1–4); her loss of the vitality of youth symbolises a church that has turned away from its earlier life of obedience to God's commandments and the pursuit of a communal ethics of solidarity. Osiek's insights gain fuller relief when read against the backdrop of Roman urban realities and with a view to neighbourhood identity, specifically as that identity relates to emergent lived urban and neighbourhood Christ religion in Rome. This is the approach this essay advances, offered in the same spirit as James Harrison's work, with a focus on the lived imperial realities of Christ religion in its ancient contexts.

Hermas and Neighbourhood Urbanity

The modern social urban geographer Talja Blockland describes a neighbourhood as 'a geographically circumscribed, built environment that people use practically and symbolically'.[3] This definition serves well for a material reading of the Shepherd as a text addressed to urban dwellers. Rome was the most densely populated city of the Roman Empire with a concentration of people that at least equals that of the

---

2   Osiek, *Rich and Poor*; *Shepherd*.
3   Blokland, *Urban Bonds*, 213.

most crowded cities of the modern world.[4] Once one left the main thoroughfares of the city, one found oneself in a warren of crowded streets. Alan Kaiser in an extensive study of four Roman cities, measuring the frequency of roads, their length, number of intersections, and the distance from primary streets, has furnished a picture of Italian cities with two types of streets.[5] Primary thoroughfares with avenues wide enough for two carts to pass were main arteries that united districts and were the chief means for pedestrians to reach marketplaces, gymnasia, plazas, baths, theatres, and other civic structures. These furnished what Kaiser describes as nodes for people who were able to escape the impoverished conditions of their urban dwelling-places which in any case lacked basic amenities to congregate and take care of basic needs. Secondary passageways by contrast divided up neighbourhood living quarters. Once off the primary avenues, the city was carved up by a labyrinth of narrower side streets. These constituted the pathways for local activities. They inhibited access by people who did not work in the area and offered privacy as well as promoting daily face-to-face relations with neighbours. In Rome, once off the primary thoroughfares, side streets were unmarked. This meant that knowledge of neighbourhoods and their residents and access to services such as water and shops was based on personal knowledge, a reality that helped establish a local identity. Neighbourhood location was also created through the clustering of different ethnicities in different regions of the city, a demographic reality that has been confirmed by Peter Lampe in his analysis of the location of Jews in the capital and by extension the first Christ followers, as well as by Philip Harland in his investigation of ethnic associations.[6] This would have been further magnified by the clustering of occupations in various quarters where neighbourhood

---

4   The population of imperial Rome is notoriously difficult to estimate, but all guesses result in high densities; for an analysis, Storey, 'Population', 966–78, who estimates that a population of 750,000 in Augustan Rome had a density of 54,112 per sq. km.; according to the World Population Review, Manila, the most densely populated city in 2021, had one of 46,356 per sq. km. (https://worldpopulationreview.com/world-city-rankings/population-density-by-city).
5   Kaiser, *Roman Urban Streets*, 99–201.
6   Lampe, *Paul*; Harland, *Dynamics*, 199–216.

identity was magnified by the meetings of trades associations as well as neighbourhood celebrations such as, in the capital, the compitalia and other recurring religious celebrations.[7]

As their immediate urban surroundings were the primary sources for face-to-face contact for typical Roman urban dwellers, social ties were reinforced through the existence of face-block neighbourhoods, a phrase used by urban geographers to describe the organisation of facing residences on opposite sides of the street and people living in proximity to one another.[8] Unlike modern cities where rich and poor live separately from one another in different areas, in Rome they dwelt alongside each other in the same face-block neighbourhoods. In the capital, such neighbourhoods were constituted by six- to eight-storey apartment blocks or insulae, each of which could house several hundred people. Densely populated insulae assured that residents were on constant view and made modern distinctions between the private and the public impossible. It also meant that residents not only defined themselves by their urban location, but also by the social relations that face-block neighbourhoods helped to create. People of varying economic status lived in the same apartment blocks, with wealthier residents occupying lower-level floors and the poor crowded into one- or two-bedroom units on the higher levels.

It is in this urban situation of face-block neighbourhoods that we should place Hermas's concerns with the relation between rich and poor Christ followers. Taken as evidence of an emerging city religion, the Shepherd of Hermas may be analysed as an expression of urbanity. Susanna Rau defines urbanity as

> a city-related phenomenon that materializes, takes spatial and temporal form. Taking spatial form means urbanity can emerge out of spatial practices and that these practices [can] also be translated into spatial structures. Taking tem-

---

7   For clustering of trades, MacMullen, *Roman Social Relations*, 69–74. For the compitalia and the role of compital shrines in defining urban quarters, Flower, *Lares*; Lott, *Neighborhoods*.
8   American Planning Association, *Neighborhoods*, 409; Suttles, *Social Construction*, 55– 6; Carmon, 'Neighborhood', 10488.

poral form means urbanity can emerge out of temporal practices and that the practices can also be translated into temporal structures.[9]

How did the Shepherd of Hermas materialise the urban space and time of Roman neighbourhoods and how did such spatio-temporal materialisation result in a particular kind of urban imagination and practice? To pose the question of urbanity invites us to conceive of Hermas's concerns in the recurring neighbourhood life situation of Rome. Hermas's visions, mandates, and similitudes repeatedly take us—as Osiek has shown—to those who because of their pursuit of economic interests neglect the poor. But more critically, they take us to neighbourhood practices and place those practices in a particular spatio-temporal formulation. The material aspects of Roman neighbourhoods gain relief when considered in the light of recent economic analysis of the urban demography of typical Roman cities. They were not only crowded but were also marked by squalor and poverty. Steven Friesen and Walter Scheidel's picture of the imperial economy suggests a setting where as much as sixty percent of urban dwellers lived at or just above subsistence.[10] If we add to their statistical analysis, the low life expectancy of urban dwellers due to communicable illness as well as—in the spring—malaria and premature death compounded by low nutrition, then we can imagine Roman face-block neighbourhoods marked by desperate social conditions.[11]

Hermas's Imagined Community of Urban Aspiration

This is the backdrop for a material reading of Hermas's visions, mandates, and parables. Hermas spatio-temporalises the city by placing its social relations into a series of revelations that locate his audience in a series of divine visions and instructions. Those revelations locate his more well-to-do listeners in a set of spatio-temporal narratives in which they are represented as facing an immanent judgement for their

---

9   Rau, 'Urbanity', 1.
10 Scheidel and Friesen, 'Size,' 61–91.
11 Scheidel, 'Physical Well-being', 321–33.

lack of solidarity with the poor. As his messages unfold, he repeatedly returns to the pursuit of business interests as undermining communal solidarity. In Vision 3 and Similitude 9, for example, Hermas sees a vision of a tower being constructed from various kinds of stones quarried from different mountains that represent different kinds of people. As the stones are incorporated into the building, they reveal different qualities which results in their ultimate rejection or incorporation. In one vision, he sees round stones cut into square shapes. Hermas learns that these represent people who, when persecution comes, deny the Lord because 'of their riches and their business affairs' and who cannot be useful for the building until their wealth is cut away (Vis. 3.6.5; Sim. 9.30.4). In other revelations he learns that those occupied with many businesses are preoccupied with their economic interests and not with the members of the community (Sim. 4.5; 8.8.1; 9.20.2).

Hermas promotes neighbourhood solidarity and integration through revelations that invite their audience to imagine their neighbourhood relations as creating a set of social bonds between people of varying economic means. The contemporary urban theorist Benedict Anderson has coined the phrase 'imagined communities' to describe the ways in which different groups come to self-identify with one another through a shared set of activities.[12] Anderson describes imagined communities as the means by which a set of 'we' experiences are created and nurtured, through which actors imagine themselves belonging to one another and not to other groups. He developed the phrase to investigate the origin and spread of nationalism, but Talja Blokland has used it for an analysis of neighbourhood identity. Imagined communities, she remarks, 'are *imagined* but are not imaginary'. They are created by a shared sense of doing things with one another whereby a common set of symbols arise, and a symbolic universe is produced and reproduced.'[13] In doing so, a sense of the local is manufactured, comprised of locally bounded and overlapping social ties. These concepts are useful for the kind of spatio-temporal investi-

---

12   Anderson, *Imagined Communities*, 5–7.
13   Blokland, *Urban Bonds*, 63, also citing Jenkins, *Social Identity*, 107.

gation of the Shepherd of Hermas and urbanity presented here. If neighbourhoods are bounded areas that people use practically and come to interpret symbolically, then we can see the role that Hermas plays as a religious entrepreneur who uses the genre of an apocalypse to create an imagined community that is to be sustained through certain kinds of urban behaviour and patterns of belonging. For Hermas, the nurturing of neighbourhood ties through solidarity between richer and poorer assembly members creates an imagined community. Hermas uses the genre of an apocalypse to remap the neigbourhoods where his emerging Christ religion is being practised and to put those with and without means in relation with one another. To put it differently, he uses revelations to make neighbours visible to one another in a new way. Apocalypse is in the service of a new urbanity that respatialises and retemporalises Hermas's listeners.

Tim Burnell and Daniel Gog, building on Arhun Appadurai, in their study of contemporary Asian cities, speak of urban space as marked by intersecting geographies of aspiration.[14] Appadurai speaks of 'navigational capacity' as the relative possibilities of rich and poor to realise a future. Aspiration is not a phenomenon that actors practise in isolation from one another, but rather unfolds in shared social networks and cultural traditions. The notion of shared cultural tradition is critical for a social reading of Hermas. His visions create from these conditions aspirational spaces for the realisation of new forms of community building that ruptures lines that might otherwise exist between people of similar interests (for example in trades associations or clustered along ethnic or socio-economic lines) and creates new ones of people of unlike interests. Hermas's second parable furnishes an excellent example. As he walks through the country, Hermas sees a fruit-bearing vine growing on an elm tree and notices that without the vine, the tree would be fruitless. His revelatory guide the shepherd points out to Hermas that if the vine's produce ripened on the ground, it would bear little fruit and would rot. As it is, by growing on a tree it produces a rich harvest. He turns this into an object lesson concerning

---

14 Burnell and Goh, 'Urban Aspirations', 1–3. Appadurai, 'Capacity', 59–84.

the religiously symbiotic relationship between rich and poor Christ followers.

'Listen,' he said. 'The rich have much wealth, but are poor in the things of the Lord, being distracted by their wealth, and they have very little confession and prayer with the Lord, and what they do have is small and weak and has no power above. So, whenever the rich go up to the poor and supply them their needs, they believe that what they do for the poor will be able to find a reward from God, because the poor are rich in intercession and confession, and their intercession has great power with God. The rich, therefore, unhesitatingly provide the poor with everything. And the poor, being provided for by the rich, pray for them, thanking God for those who share with them. And the rich in turn are all the more zealous on behalf of the poor, in order that they may lack nothing in their life, for the rich know that the intercession of the poor is acceptable and rich before God. They both, then, complete their work: the poor work with prayer, in which they are rich, which they received from the Lord; this they return to the Lord who supplies them with it. And the rich likewise unhesitatingly share with the poor the wealth that they received from the Lord. And this work is great and acceptable to God, because the rich understand about their wealth and work for the poor by using the gifts of the Lord, and correctly fulfill their ministry. So, as far as people are concerned, the elm does not seem to bear fruit, and they neither know nor realize that if a drought comes the elm, which has water, nourishes the vine, and the vine, having a constant supply of water, bears double the fruit, both for itself and for the elm. So also, the poor, by appealing to the Lord on behalf of the rich, complement their wealth, and again, the rich, by providing for the needs of the poor, complement their souls. So, then, both become partners in the righteous work. Therefore, the one who does these things will not be abandoned by God but will be enrolled in the books of the living. Blessed are the rich who also understand that they have been made rich by the Lord, for the one who comprehends this will be able to do some good work' (Sim. 2.1–10).[15]

Hermas scholarship has not fully enough contextualised this passage. As an urban exhortation, its recurring life situation is not an abstract illustration, but points toward the daily lived realities of those with relatively more means living cheek by jowl with the impoverished. Once we place this passage within a context of a face-block neighbourhood, where Roman urban dwellers lived in full view of one another and came to recognise one another even if they had no other social relations other than by way of visibility, we can see the creation of urban networks of 'navigational capacity'.

On this account, the face-block neighbourhood becomes the means toward an imagined community of mutually beneficial shared practices that unfold within a geographically circumscribed network of overlapping social relations and that thereby creates a 'we' out of groups who otherwise might have limited social intercourse with one another. In this view, benefactions and prayer complement one another

---

15 Περιπατοῦντός μου εἰς τὸν ἀγρὸν καὶ κατανοοῦντος πτελέαν καὶ ἄμπελον, καὶ διακρίνοντος περὶ αὐτῶν καὶ τῶν καρπῶν αὐτῶν, φανεροῦταί μοι ὁ ποιμὴν καὶ λέγει· Τί σὺ ἐν ἑαυτῷ ζητεῖς; Περὶ τῆς πτελέας καὶ τῆς ἀμπέλου συζητῶ, φημί, κύριε, ὅτι εὐπρεπέσταταί εἰσιν ἀλλήλαις. Ταῦτα τὰ δύο δένδρα, φησίν, εἰς τύπον κεῖνται τοῖς δούλοις τοῦ θεοῦ. Ἤθελον, φημί, κύριε, γνῶναι τὸν τύπον τῶν δένδρων τούτων ὧν λέγεις. Βλέπεις, φησί, τὴν πτελέαν καὶ τὴν ἄμπελον; Βλέπω, φημί, κύριε. Ἡ ἄμπελος, φησίν, αὕτη καρπὸν φέρει, ἡ δὲ πτελέα ξύλον ἄκαρπόν ἐστιν· ἀλλ' ἡ ἄμπελος αὕτη, ἐὰν μὴ ἀναβῇ ἐπὶ τὴν πτελέαν, οὐ δύναται καρποφορῆσαι πολὺ ἐρριμμένη χαμαί, καὶ ὃν φέρει καρπόν, σεσηπότα φέρει μὴ κρεμαμένη ἐπὶ τῆς πτελέας. ὅταν οὖν ἐπιρριφῇ ἡ ἄμπελος ἐπὶ τὴν πτελέαν, καὶ παρ' ἑαυτῆς φέρει καρπὸν καὶ παρὰ τῆς πτελέας. βλέπεις οὖν ὅτι καὶ ἡ πτελέα πολὺν καρπὸν δίδωσιν, οὐκ ἐλάσσονα τῆς ἀμπέλου, μᾶλλον δὲ καὶ πλείονα. Πῶς, φημί, κύριε, πλείονα; Ὅτι, φησίν, ἡ ἄμπελος κρεμαμένη ἐπὶ τὴν πτελέαν τὸν καρπὸν πολὺν καὶ καλὸν δίδωσιν, ἐρριμμένη δὲ χαμαὶ σαπρὸν καὶ ὀλίγον φέρει. αὕτη οὖν ἡ παραβολὴ εἰς τοὺς δούλους τοῦ θεοῦ κεῖται, εἰς πτωχὸν καὶ πλούσιον. παρὰ τοῖς ἀνθρώποις οὖν ἡ πτελέα δοκεῖ καρπὸν μὴ φέρειν, καὶ οὐκ οἴδασιν οὐδὲ νοοῦσιν ὅτι, ἐὰν ἀβροχία γένηται, ἡ πτελέα ὕδωρ ἔχουσα τρέφει τὴν ἄμπελον, καὶ ἡ ἄμπελος ἀδιάλειπτον ἔχουσα τὸ ὕδωρ διπλοῦν τὸν καρπὸν δίδωσι, καὶ ὑπὲρ ἑαυτῆς καὶ ὑπὲρ τῆς πτελέας. οὕτω καὶ οἱ πένητες ἐντυγχάνοντες πρὸς τὸν κύριον ὑπὲρ τῶν πλουσίων πληροφοροῦσι τὸν πλοῦτον αὐτῶν, καὶ πάλιν οἱ πλούσιοι χορηγοῦντες τοῖς πένησι τὰ δέοντα πληροφοροῦσι τὰς ψυχὰς αὐτῶν.

to create social cohesion. This insight gains greater power if Richard Last's interpretation of the phrase 'church in the household of X' is correct, namely that 'household' here may refer to a block of residences that together form a unit, of the sort for example one would have found in the urban insulae that comprised Roman streets and districts.[16] Last's analysis builds on Andrew Wallace-Hadrill's account of 'households' and 'housefuls' in the capital, where people who lived at lower economic levels intersected in various ways with those of more means, offering them services, honouring them as patrons, or living in close proximity to their erstwhile masters as clients. In Last's analysis, the phrase 'house church' implies a dispersed set of social relations that extends beyond the traditional scholarly model of a group gathered in a single dwelling of a Christ assembly patron.[17]

Porous Selves and Neighbourhood Relations in the Shepherd of Hermas

The importance for a social consideration of the neighbourhood as a bounded unit used practically and symbolically gains further strength when we consider Hermas's model of the self and the relation of the self to others. It is to the issue of the partible and dividual self that we now turn. Charles Taylor distinguishes between the modern 'buffered self' of modernity and the 'porous self' of pre-modernity.[18] The buffered self describes an individual that exists as an entity unto itself. The porous self, by contrast, expresses a concept of the individual not as bounded, but created from social relations as well as forces and powers that penetrate individuals or communities. We can see evidence of the porous self in Hermas's representations of himself in relation to other than human powers. In Similitude 9.15.2 he encounters twelve virgins with whom he spends a night in prayer and then learns that they bear the names of various virtues (Faith, Self-Control, Power, Patience, Sincerity, Innocence, Purity, Cheerfulness, Truth, Understanding,

---

16 Last, 'Neighborhood', 399–425.
17 Wallace-Hadrill, 'Domus and Insulae', 3–18.
18 Taylor, *Secular Age*, 27–41.

Harmony, and Love). In Similitude 10.3 he learns that the virgins have been sent to live with him and that he must keep his house clean so that they do not leave it. The household includes Hermas's self; these spirits not only live *with* Hermas they possess and constitute him by taking up residence *in* him.

The cultural anthropologist Mary Strathern in her study of Melanesian culture use the terms 'partible self' and 'dividuality' to describe a model of the self in which individuals are not 'buffered' or bounded as they are in modern western models, but rather where they are 'porous,' namely capable of being divided into different kinds of relations.[19] Of special interest in her analysis is the way that gift giving creates networks of relations that serve to constitute identities in plural ways. She deploys the term dividuation as a reference to persons 'frequently constructed as the plural and composite site of relationships that produce them.'[20] The dividual is both single agent and cause of effects but is also multiple. 'The singular must also be seen with respect to the two forms out of which unity is composed—the multiple or composite person and the dividual. Here what is taken for granted are the multiple external relations in which a person is embedded...'.[21] This means that when a person acts as an in/dividual s/he also is acting as a plurality: 'a person in the form of a dividual, is potentially one of a pair [in taken-for-granted relationships], or may know him or herself as a composite microcosm, potentially bounded as a unit'.[22] The self as porous then is an entity that comes into being through interpenetrating assemblages of human actors and other than human animate and inanimate phenomena. Selves are not individual—that is incapable of being divided—but rather outcomes of relations; they are embedded in social webs.

This concept of dividuality is particularly useful for a study of the self in Hermas as partitive, or a composite of social relations, supernatural powers, spaces, and material objects.

---

19 Strathern, *Gift*.
20 Strathern, *Gift*, 13.
21 Strathern, *Gift*, 275.
22 Strathern, *Gift*, 275.

For Hermas, the networks which embed the self include human and more than human actors as well as the material objects people give themselves over to. Hermas's vision of a tower under construction made up of differing kinds of stones quarried from different mountains expresses this porous notion of the self as an assemblage. As indicated above, in Vision 3 and Similitude 9 he sees a vision of a tower under construction and near completion. In the ninth parable the various stones built into a white tower are tested by the shepherd for their soundness for construction (Sim. 9.9.8). Some of them are black or reveal cracks when the the shepherd tests them, whereupon they are removed from the tower. Again, the image becomes an extended allegory for differing kinds of Christ followers that are members of the Christ assembly; those removed from the tower are those who have failed to live according to the shepherd's commandments.

The ideal tower is a single white edifice constructed as though from one stone (9.4.1–8). Here we find an image of a symbolically constructed neigbhbourhood of Christ believers that together form an interlacing community, but it also describes a self that a composite of a certain set of relations. In Similitude 1 he exhorts the wealthier members to use their money not to buy fields, but rather widows, and orphans: 'So instead of fields, buy souls that are in distress, as anyone is able, and visit widows and orphans, and do not neglect them; and spend your wealth and all your possessions, which you received from God, on fields and houses of this kind' (Sim. 1.8). Later in Similitude 5.4.7, where the shepherd instructs Hermas about fasting, he links the practice to social solidarity:

> And this is what you must do: when you have completed what has been written, you must taste nothing except bread and water on that day on which you fast. Then you must estimate the cost of the food you would have eaten on that day on which you intend to fast, and give it to a widow or an orphan or someone in need. In this way you will become humble-minded, so that as a result of your humble-mindedness the one who receives may satisfy his own soul and pray to the Lord on your behalf.

Here again we can see the way in which the assembly becomes an urban aspirational space and where the self extends across neighbourhood relations into a network of symbiotic relationships. Those with means give to widows and orphans, and orphans and widows pray for them. In the context of lived neighbourhood relationships dividuals are dispersed into an assemblage of neighbourhood identities in which social networks become a means to express sociality and to the construction of selves. Gift-giving in the form of food or other offerings creates bonds by which selves mutually construct each other. Further bonds are constituted by the habitation of spirits both within selves and in the domestic settings in which people find themselves. We might say that the insula becomes a living assembly through which people, social relations, and other than human actors circulate. This creates a dynamic notion of dividuals and partible or porous selves and neighbourhoods that co-constitute one another.

And so…

James Harrison's work has invited an imperial reading of ancient Christ religion. In doing so, he has of course published his work in a scientific and rigorously exegetical and social-historical form. But he has also invited us to consider these topics for the ways in which they challenge us to read ancient texts in relation to contemporary life. In a world of glaring social inequities where the buffered self can live in happy isolation not only from people a continent away but even from neighbours next door, the social-historical analysis he has promoted has timely relevance. My hope is that the analysis of the Shepherd of Hermas offered with the same set of socio-historical interests that has shaped Professor Harrison's work also will find relevance by asking us how we conceive of self and neighbour. Not many of us can imagine ourselves possessed by spirits. We do however know as western consumers what it is to be consumed by greed, envy, and covetousness and to be captured by the desire to own the latest popular thing. Indeed, a global economy banks on us having insatiable desires. It seeks opportunities to commodify the world as a means toward profit and enjoyment. The present environmental apocalypse is one of the products of this way of seeing and using the world in the pursuit of individual identity separate from neighbour. The Shepherd of Hermas belongs to another time and era, but its call to an understanding of self and community that is constituted by life-giving relationships is as timely as it was two millennia ago. Indeed, the threat of an imminent apocalypse makes it an urgent one.

Harry O. Maier
Vancouver School of Theology

Bibliography

American Planning Association *Neighborhoods: Planning and Urban Design Standards* (Oxford: John Wiley, 2006).

Anderson, B. R. *Imagined Communities: Reflections on the Origin and Spread of Nationalism* (London: Verso, 1991).

Appadurai, A. 'The Capacity to Aspire: Culture and the Terms of Recognition', in V. Rao and M. Walton (eds.), *Culture and Public Action* (Stanford, CT: Stanford University Press, 2004), 59–84.

Blokland, T. *Urban Bonds* (Cambridge: Polity, 2003).

Burnell, T. and P. S. Goh 'Urban Aspirations and Asian Cosmopolitanisms', *Geoforum* 43 (2012), 1–3.

Carmon, N. 'Neighborhood: general,' in N. J. Smelser and P.B. Baltes (eds.), *International Encyclopedia of the Social and Behavioral Sciences* (Amsterdam: Elsevier, 2001), 10488–494.

Flower, H. *The Dancing Lares and the Serpent in the Garden: Religion at the Roman Street Corner* (Princeton, NJ: Princeton University Press, 2017).

Harland, P. *Dynamics of Identity in the World of the Early Christians* (London: T.&T. Clark, 2009).

Jenkins, R. *Social Identity* (London: Routledge, 1996).

Kaiser, A. *Roman Urban Street Networks* (London: Routledge, 2011).

Lampe, P. *From Paul to Valentinus: Christians at Rome in the First Two Centuries* (trans. Michael Steinhauser; Minneapolis, MN: Fortress, 2003).

Last, R. 'The Neighborhood (*vicus*) of the Corinthian *Ekklesia*: Beyond Family-Based Descriptions of the First Urban Christ-Believers', *Journal for the Study of the New Testament* 38 (2016), 399–425.

Lott, J. B. *The Neighborhoods of Augustan Rome* (Oxford: Oxford University Press, 2004).

MacMullen, R. *Roman Social Relations 50 B.C. to A.D. 284* (New Haven, CT: Yale University Press, 1974).

Maier, H. O.	*The Social Setting of the Ministry as Reflected in the Writings of Hermas, Clement and Ignatius* (Studies in Christianity and Judaism/ Études sur le chirstianisme et le judaïsme 12; Waterloo, ONT: Wilfred Laurier University Press, 2002).
Osiek, C.	*Rich and Poor in the Shepherd of Hermas: An exegetical-Social Investigation* (Washington, DC: Catholic Biblical Association of America, 1983).
Osiek, C.	*The Shepherd of Hermas: A Commentary* (Hermeneia; Minneapolis, MN: Fortress, 1999).
Rau, S.	'Urbanity (urbanitas, Urbanität, urbanite, urbanità, urbanidad…) – An Essay', in S. Rau and J. Rüpke (eds.), *Religion and Urbanity Online* (Berlin, Boston: De Gruyter, 2020). <https://www.degruyter.com/database/URBREL/entry/urbrel.11276000/html>.
Scheidel, W.	'Physical Well-Being', in W. Scheidel (ed.), *The Cambridge Companion to the Roman Economy* (Cambridge: Cambridge University Press, 2012), 321–33.
Scheidel, W. and S. J. Friesen	'The Size of the Economy and the Distribution of Income in the Roman Empire', *Journal of Roman Studies* 99 (2009), 61–91.
Storey, G. R.	'The Population of Ancient Rome', *Antiquity* 71 (1997), 966–78.
Strathern, M.	*The Gender of the Gift: Problems with Women and Problems with Society in Melanesia* (Berkeley: University of California Press, 1988).
Suttles, G. D.	*The Social Construction of Communities* (Chicago: University of Chicago Press, 1972).
Taylor, C.	*A Secular Age* (Cambridge, MA: Belknap, 2018).
Wallace-Hadrill, A.	'Domus and Insulae in Rome: Families and Housefuls', in D. Balch and C. Osiek (eds.), *Early Christian Families in Context: An Interdisciplinary Dialogue* (Grand Rapids, MI: Eerdmans, 2003), 3–18.

The Literal Meaning of the Most Common Epistolary Greeting
— and How Seriously We Should Take It

Peter Arzt-Grabner

Abstract
Soon after its introduction in the early fourth century B.C.E., the infinitive χαίρειν became the most usual opening greeting of Greek private letters, but soon thereafter the isolated infinitive was no longer understood syntactically and its literal meaning began to fade. In modern epistolography, it is often assumed that the semantic meaning of expressions or phrases fades considerably in the case of their formulaic use, or is by no means to be taken literally. Some examples from letters preserved on papyrus and potsherds suggest, however, that such a view should not be generally accepted.

1. An Awkward Stroke of Ink

Hardly any other short horizontal stroke of ink above a single Greek character has provoked a more heated and prolonged discussion among papyrologists than the one above the first letter of the simple epistolary greeting χαίρειν in P.Oxy. 42.3057.2,[1] a papyrus letter that was edited by Peter J. Parsons in 1974. Especially the combination of ὁμόνοιαν καὶ φιλαλλη⟨λ⟩ίαν in lines 15–16 ('concord and mutual affection') and 'the curious overlined χ̄ in line 2' made the editor argue that a 'Christian context would be possible'.[2] Parsons' reference made others suggest that the horizontal stroke over the χ of χαίρειν 'is probably

---

1 A digital image is available at <http://www.papyrology.ox.ac.uk/POxy/> [accessed 14 January 2022] (search for '3057').
2 P. J. Parsons in P.Oxy. 42, p. 146.

the sign of a *nomen sacrum*, that of Christ'.³ If this were true, P.Oxy. 42.3057 would be the oldest Christian papyrus letter so far, because it is dated to the first or second century C.E. Apart from the fact that this early period would represent an absolute peculiarity for a Christian letter, the interpretation of the χ̄ as a *nomen sacrum* for Christ can be easily replaced by a simpler and more conclusive explanation, thus invalidating the most essential argument for the Christian origin of the letter. Regarding the superlinear stroke above the χ, P. J. Parsons himself asked in his first edition of the papyrus: 'Did the writer intend χ(αίρειν), and then decide to complete the word?'⁴ Which means: Did the writer intend to abbreviate the opening greeting χαίρειν by writing only the initial character (i.e., χ) and marking the abbreviation with a superlinear horizontal stroke, but immediately afterwards chose to add the remaining characters of χαίρειν, so that the recipient of the letter could read the full form of the greeting, albeit still provided with the superlinear stroke (i.e., χ̄αίρειν)? A look at the images of numerous letters written on papyrus or potsherds during the first or second century C.E. proves that Parsons' idea is very likely.

2. Abbreviated Opening Greetings

The most common type of abbreviation is the omission of one or more final letters of a word, even all letters after the first as in the case

---

3   Ramelli, 'A New Reading', 127; following Montevecchi, 'Τὴν ἐπιστολήν', 189–194. For the entire discussion and for other editions of this papyrus letter (some with corrections to the first edition) or commentaries on it, see especially also: Arzt-Grabner, *Philemon*, 61–63; Blumell, 'Is P.Oxy. XLII 3057 the Earliest Christian Letter?'; Cadwallader, 'Tertius', 388 n. 81; Chouliara-Raïos, 'P.Oxy. XLII 3057'; Hemer, 'Ammonius'; Llewelyn, 'Ammonios'; Minehart, 'P.Oxy. XLII 3057'; Parsons, 'The Earliest Christian Letter'; Stanton, 'The Proposed Earliest Christian Letter'; Wipszycka, 'Les papyrus', 1310–1312.
4   See Parsons in P.Oxy. 42, p. 145 (note on line 2). By using the phrase 'crossed letter' in line 3, Ammonios most probably refers to a sealed letter that he had previously received from Apollonios. After a letter had been folded, the address was written on the back, and then a string of papyrus was wrapped around the folded papyrus. Sometimes a real seal was used to seal it, but in most cases, the sender of a letter placed an X-shaped 'cross' of ink or the sign ⨳ across this string, and when the string was taken off (or if it had been taken off), the broken lines became (or were) visible (i.e., ⨯ or ⨳).

of χ(αίρειν). In many instances the omission is indicated by a special marker, whereby the use of a straight horizontal stroke above the letter as here above the χ is only one of several options.[5] The only preserved contemporary example in a papyrus letter that I could find seems to be the x̄ at the end of line 8 of P.Oxy. 45.3240 (ca. 88/89 C.E.),[6] where it serves as the opening greeting of an official letter from the *praefectus Aegypti* Mettius Rufus to Hestiaios, the *strategos* of the Oxyrhynchite nome. Examples preserved on ostraca are, however, numerous. Among the letter senders from Didymoi, a Roman fort in Egypt's Eastern Desert, is a certain Iulius, who lived during the late first and early second centuries C.E. and was himself probably illiterate since his letters are written by two different hands. Yet both writers employed by Iulius obviously liked to abbreviate the χαίρειν in the respective way.[7] Several other letter authors from Didymoi used the same abbreviation,[8] as also did several writers of ostracon letters from Krokodilo.[9] From Mons Claudianus, we have O.Claud. 1.148.3 (ca. 100–120 C.E.) and 2.364.2 (II C.E.).[10]

Two observations suggest that such abbreviations are not due to a lack of space on the writing surface, which on potsherds is usually small anyway. First, ostraca such as O.Claud. 1.148 (ca. 100–120 C.E.) prove

---

5   Cf. Gonis, 'Abbreviations', 171–174.
6   Digital image at <http://www.papyrology.ox.ac.uk/POxy/> [accessed 14 January 2022] (search for '3240'). The χ is the last completely preserved letter of the line, and a slightly faded stroke is visible above it, but to the right of it, where the margin of the papyrus is damaged, further traces of ink can be seen which leave the abbreviation marker uncertain.
7   Scribe 1 in O.Did. 320.2, 322.2 and 323.2; scribe 2 in O.Did. 317.1, 318.2, 319.2 and probably also 324.2. For digital images see <https://www.ifao.egnet.net/bases/publications/fifao67/> [accessed 14 January 2022] (enter the number of the ostracon in the field to the left of 'n° ostracon [1–479]', e.g., '320' for O.Did. 320).
8   See O.Did. 361.2; 428.2; 134.2; 437.1; 383.25; 385.3; 389.2; 427.2.
9   See O.Krok. 2.152.4; 156.2; 160.3; 184.1; 192.3; 203.2; 206.1; 331.2 (all 98–117 C.E.); 186.3 (98–138 C.E.). For digital images see <https://www.ifao.egnet.net/bases/publications/fifao81/> [accessed 14 January 2022] (enter the number of the ostracon in the field to the left of 'n° ostracon [152–334]').
10 Digital images of O.Claud. are available at <https://www.nakala.fr> [accessed 14 January 2022] (search for 'O.Claud.' followed by the number of the ostracon).

that this is at least not generally the case, for the entire line 3 of this letter is merely occupied by a nicely centred χ̄, while the scribe has left several centimetres blank to the left and right of it. And second, several other abbreviation markers are found not only in ostracon letters, but also in a number of papyrus letters.

One of these options which comes close to the horizontal stroke is a small loop, sometimes open to the right, but always extended to a curved or straight horizontal line and written above the χ. Two examples of this marker are preserved in P.Genova 1.10.v.3 (55 C.E.), the official papyrus letter of the Emperor Nero to the city of the Alexandrians (image on Tavola VII), and in BGU 2.597.2 (5 December 75 C.E.),[11] the letter from Chairemon to his 'brother' Apollonios with various instructions, probably concerning the management of a rural estate.

Another frequently used marker is the sinusoid, which may have 'initially represented the ligature alpha plus iota written increasingly cursively'[12] and which is preserved, for example, in line 1 of the papyrus letter P.Oslo 3.155 (II C.E.; image on Plate XI) and in 156.2 (II C.E.).[13] The latter is the opening greeting of a papyrus letter from Ammonios to the teacher Theon about the teacher's salary being paid in victuals; here we have another perfect example of how the abbreviated form is not a matter of lack of space, for line 2 consists of nothing but this abbreviation, nicely centred. Something similar applies to the ostracon letter O.Claud. 1.171 (ca. 100–120 C.E.; cf. line 3) or to the already mentioned papyrus letter BGU 2.597, where line 2 consists only of the well-centred opening greeting πλεῖστα χ(αίρειν) καὶ ὑγ(ιαίνειν).[14]

Actually, it should not be seen as a big difference whether the

---

11 Digital image at <https://berlpap.smb.museum/01860/> [accessed 14 January 2022].
12 Gonis, 'Abbreviations', 174.
13 Digital image at <https://ub-baser.uio.no/opes/record/28> [accessed 14 January 2022].
14 Another example for the abbreviation of the opening greeting in the form of a single χ is attested in P.Haun. 2.24.2 (I–II C.E.), a papyrus letter from Chrysas to Ptolemaios requesting permission to fetch dung (image on Plate V); due to damage, however, it is no longer possible to determine with which sign above the χ the abbreviation was marked.

abbreviation line is completely straight or slightly curved and a bit moved to the right as in the case of P.Giss. 1.12.2 (ca. 113–120 C.E.).[15] In this letter, the clerk Chairemon begs the *strategos* Apollonios, who is still in charge of the family's weaving workshop during his time in office, to send him a certain pattern. The same marker is preserved in line 2 of another letter from the Archive of Apollonios (TM Arch 19),[16] P.Giss. 1.22,[17] which was sent by Eudaimonis to her son, the said Apollonios, but most probably written by a secretary.[18]

Based on the overall record on abbreviations, N. Gonis has observed that the 'documents in which abbreviation is rife are predominantly those produced on a massive scale and bound to repeat the same words, such as tax accounts and receipts.'[19] It is therefore no wonder that abbreviated greetings also appear in numerous receipts and similar documents preserved on potsherds.[20] P.Oxy. 41.2970 (13 Oct 62 C.E.)[21] is a receipt of produce in wine which was written on papyrus and preserves the χ̄ in line 2.

A further selected papyrus document preserving the χ̄ is P.Sarap. 11 (1 Mar 128 C.E.), a deed of sale for a cow (cf. line 4).[22] In P.Sarap. 15 (20 Feb 104 C.E.), a contract of loan, the single χ is used without a

---

15 Digital image at <https://papyri.uni-leipzig.de/receive/GiePapyri_schrift_00002810> [accessed 14 January 2022].
16 TM Arch = <https://www.trismegistos.org/arch/> [accessed 14 January 2022].
17 Digital image at <https://papyri.uni-leipzig.de/receive/GiePapyri_schrift_00003150> [accessed 14 January 2022].
18 On this archive, and in particular on Eudaimonis, see most recently Arzt-Grabner, 'Two Weavers', 26–31 (in particular on P.Giss. 1.22 see p. 29).
19 Gonis, 'Abbreviations', 171.
20 See O.Berenike 2.138.2 (ca. 24 April–24 June 66 C.E.); 139.2 (12 July 66 C.E.); 140.4 (27 January–25 February 68 C.E.), 154.2; 155.2; 158.3; 159.2; 162.2; 167.2; 169.2; 173.1; 174.1; 175.2; 182.2; 183.2 (all ca. 50–75 C.E.; images available at <https://papyri.info/ddbdp/o.berenike;2;138> etc.); O.Cair. 117.2 (7 July 77 C.E.; image on Tav. XXX); O.Brux. 3.2 (23 April 115 C.E.; digital image at <http://www.globalegyptianmuseum.org/detail.aspx?id=84>); O.Wilck. 35.3 (18 April 89 C.E.; digital image at <https://berlpap.smb.museum/00671/>) [all accessed 14 January 2022].
21 Digital image at <http://www.papyrology.ox.ac.uk/POxy/> [accessed 14 January 2022] (search for '2970').
22 Digital image at <https://www.bl.uk/manuscripts/FullDisplay.aspx?ref=Papyrus_839> [accessed 14 January 2022].

marker (cf. line 3).[23] A curved line as a marker is used, for example, in orders for payment on papyrus.[24] A χ with a partly damaged supralinear stroke is visible at the end of line 3 of P.Oxy. 41.2956 (28 Oct or 27 Dec 148 C.E.), an official letter from the *strategos* Aelius Aphrodisios to *sitologoi* with an order for a grant of seed.[25]

3. The Scribe of P.Oxy. 42.3057

Looking at the entire record, it is reasonable to assume that most of the abbreviated greetings were written by professional or at least experienced scribes since receipts, deeds, and orders for payment were usually written by such. The same is true for letters and documents originating from the Roman administration, the Roman army, or from business life. Above all, these contexts have in common that the respective scribes are accustomed to using abbreviations extensively, as they often have to write or copy identical texts over and over again in the course of their work.

As far as P.Oxy. 42.3057 is concerned, I would like to draw two conclusions from this evidence: First, since the elegant and even handwriting certainly indicates that this was written by a professional scribe, who probably even mentions himself by name in line 29,[26] it is reason-

---

23   Digital image at <http://www.rzuser.uni-heidelberg.de/~gv0/Papyri/VBP_II/040/VBP_II_40.html> [accessed 14 January 2022].
24   See, e.g., P.Lond. 3.1213a.3 (p. 121) and b.2 (p. 122) (both 16 Dec 65 C.E.); 1214a.3 (p. 122) (5 Jan 66 C.E.); in P.Lond. 3.1215.2 (p. 122), the χαίρειν is written in full, perhaps due to a different scribe. Digital images at <http://www.bl.uk/manuscripts/FullDisplay.aspx?ref=Papyrus_1213>; <..._1214>; <..._1215>; [all accessed 14 January 2022].
25   Digital image at <http://www.papyrology.ox.ac.uk/POxy/> [accessed 14 January 2022] (search for '2956').
26   As already suggested by John Rea (cf. P.Oxy. 42, p. 146) and in light of P.Oxy. 49.3505.24–25. P. J. Parsons (in P.Oxy. 42, p. 146) assumes that 'Leonas' is a proper name. Its meaning 'lion' could also 'be a self-characterisation by (or second name of) the author of the letter, given its content about overcoming adversity' (Cadwallader, 'Tertius', 388 n. 81), but in this case the author's second name or nickname would be inserted quite abruptly, which could have been avoided by adding ἐγώ or by inserting ὡς ('as') in front of 'Leonas' (similar to Paul of Tarsus in Phlm. 9), which would then translate as 'I greet you as Leonas/Lion'.

able to conclude that this scribe was well acquainted with the use of abbreviations and at first actually abbreviated the opening greeting χαίρειν simply by χ̄. That this scribe could have been a member of the Roman administration is possible, but in the absence of further evidence, speculative. Secondly, since the opening greeting was eventually written in full (i.e., the χ̄ was completed to χ̄αίρειν), we have here a clear indication that an abbreviated greeting was considered inappropriate in letters as personal and in such style as this one. Although we cannot verify whether the author of P.Oxy. 42.3057 necessarily understood the χαίρειν in its literal sense, namely as a direct invitation to the addressee to rejoice, we can at least recognise that it was important to him that this formulaic greeting was written in full. But how is the question of the meaning and intention of this formula to be approached?

4. History and Development of the Opening Greeting χαίρειν

SEG 26.845 (second half VI or ca. 500 B.C.E.), a lead tablet from Berezan, one of the earliest Greek colonies in the northern Black Sea region, is so far considered the earliest Greek private letter containing an opening formula which starts with the vocative of the recipient's name followed by a clause with the verb ἐπιστέλλω: ὦ Πρωταγόρη, ὁ πατήρ τοι ἐπιστέλλε ('Oh Protagoras, your father "sends" to you').[27] The Greek term ἐπιστέλλω is significant for the earliest opening formulas of letters, and already hints at the general function and intention of a letter: in the literal sense of the Greek term ἐπιστολή, a 'letter' is a written message by a certain sender to a certain recipient which is sent by the former to the latter with a specific request or instruction.

Syll.[3] 3.1259, a lead tablet incised during the early fourth century B.C.E., probably preserves the earliest extant letter in which the verb ἐπιστέλλω is combined with the Greek infinitive χαίρειν, thus urging the addressees to rejoice in receiving the letter. From that stage onwards, a letter (ἐπιστολή) is sent to the addressee to make him or her

---

27 A similar example is SEG 61.614 (V B.C.E.) from Hermonassa/Black Sea.

rejoice in receiving a message from a relative, friend, or another person. Obviously not very much later on, the verb ἐπιστέλλω is regarded as self-evident and thus dropped from the opening formula of a letter,[28] and the absolute infinitive χαίρειν at the beginning of a written text becomes a marker by which this text can be identified as a letter. One of the earliest examples is attested on a squarish fragment of an amphora from Sinope, SEG 59.814 (375–325 B.C.E.).[29] It was found in Chersonesus Taurica and mentions the recipient, a certain Timosthenes, in the dative at the beginning, followed in line 2 only by χαίρεν (read χαίρειν). The letter sender is not mentioned on this sherd, contrary to the lead letter SEG 43.488 (ca. 350–325 B.C.E.) from Torone/Macedonia and SEG 65.631 (second half IV B.C.E.), a letter preserved on a fragment of an amphora wall from the settlement of Vyshesteblievskaya-3/Black Sea.

From that time onwards, a letter's opening greeting is very rarely omitted, and χαίρειν remains the most common. In some letters we can still find a reason for such an omission, as for example in O.Krok. 2.208 (98–117 C.E.), where the explanation is obviously the sender's anger against the woman Secunda. The shipmaster Horion, on the other hand, inserted in his letter to Ploution the greeting πολλὰ χαίρειν, which had been initially omitted, between lines 1 and 2 of P.Oxy. 40.2926 (III C.E.). And a certain Areios, who opened the letter P.Ryl. 2.245 (III C.E.) by naming only himself as the sender of the letter, even added the name of his recipient and the formula πλεῖσ[τ]α χαίρε[ιν] only to the closing greeting in lines 24–26.

While examples such as these clearly show that a non-existent opening greeting of a letter could indeed be missed and thus provoke reflection on the reasons behind it, they do not prove that the literal meaning and function of χαίρειν, namely as an appeal to the addressee to rejoice in the receipt of the letter, was actually still understood. There is good reason to assume that in the course of time the isolated infinitive χαίρειν became a simple phrase, was no longer understood

---

28 The verb ἐπιστέλλω is used, more or less frequently, in the simple sense of 'to write (by letter)'; cf., e.g., P.Warr. 20.2 (late III/early IV C.E.).
29 Cf. Ceccarelli, *Ancient Greek Letter Writing*, 346 no. 21.

syntactically, and that its literal meaning also began to fade. During the first and second centuries C.E., for example, even grammarians such as Dionysius of Alexandria and Apollonios Dyskolos were no longer able to solve the questions arising from the special syntax appropriately.[30] And in modern epistolography, it is usually assumed that the semantic meaning of expressions or phrases fades considerably in the case of their formulaic use, or is by no means to be taken literally. Some examples suggest, however, that such a view should not be generally accepted.

5. Special Examples Regarding the Original Meaning and Function of χαίρειν

That χαίρειν had not completely lost its original meaning even in Hellenistic and Roman times, is demonstrated, for example, by the papyrus letter P.Fouad 75, which was authored by a certain Thaubas on 15 October 64 C.E. and afterwards sent to her father. Originally, Thaubas herself or her scribe started the letter with the words: Θαυβᾶς Πομπηίωι τῶι πατρὶ πλεῖστα | χαίρειν (lines 1–2 with BL 4:32: 'Thaubas to Pompeios, her father, very many greetings'; literally '... to rejoice very much'). Immediately afterwards, Thaubas asks her father: 'After you have received my letter, you will do well to come here at once, for your poor daughter Herennia has died' (lines 3–6). As Thaubas further informs her father, Herennia had already endured a miscarriage. She had given birth to a dead eight-month-old baby and survived for four days, but then she died (lines 6–11). Indeed, such sad news cannot be combined with a serious invitation to rejoice over it, which suggests that πλεῖστα χαίρειν is not to be taken seriously here at all, but is to be understood as a mere formula without the literal meaning. A. Bataille, the first editor of this papyrus letter, however, has already recognised in 1939 that πλεῖστα at the end of the first line is barely legible, and therefore assumed that Taubas herself (or her scribe on her instructions) subsequently erased the word. R. Coles, A. Geissen and L. Koenen, however, argued in 1973: 'The ink at the end

---

30 See Koskenniemi, *Studien*, 41–42, 157.

of l.1 is faded, but it is highly improbable that Thaubas in her letter to her father washed out the πλεῖστα. Since the very top right corner of the papyrus looks affected too, the "deletion" of πλεῖστα is rather due to natural causes, so that τῶι πατρὶ πλεῖστα | χαίρειν has to be retained'.[31] A closer look at the digital image of the papyrus, now accessible online,[32] seems to me to confirm Bataille's interpretation. As can be clearly seen, the ink at the word πλεῖστα is very much faded, but this is only the case in exactly this area of the papyrus, while the surrounding text is clearly legible. As for the upper right corner of the papyrus, possible damage there is nowhere near as severe as in the upper left corner; but there the ink is still clearly legible. This rather suggests to me that there was no later natural damage in the area of and around πλεῖστα, but that the superlative had already been abraded or washed out by Thaubas herself or by her scribe. It is therefore plausible that Thaubas still had a notion of the original meaning of πλεῖστα χαίρειν (literally 'to rejoice very much') and finally considered the superlative inappropriate in the context of the sad news to her father.

In my view, some special versions of the opening greetings πολλὰ χαίρειν and πλεῖστα χαίρειν can also contribute something to the question of the meaning and function of χαίρειν. BGU 1.93 (II–III c.e.) is a letter from a certain Ptolemaios to his father Abous. Line 2, edited as πατρὶ πλ(εῖστα) χαίρειν, is indented from both sides, and πλεῖστα is abbreviated as π with λ written above it.[33] It is quite possible that the scribe first wrote only πατρὶ χαίρειν, because this too would have been beautifully designed, and when the second line of a letter contains only the last two words of the opening greeting, we often find a space between these words. This would have enabled the writer to insert the abbreviation for πλεῖστα at a later stage, and thus to intensify the χαίρειν very consciously. However, it is of course also possible that he wrote everything as it stands right from the start. BGU 2.597.2 (5

---

31 Coles, Geissen and Koenen, 'Some Corrections', 239.
32 At <http://ipap.csad.ox.ac.uk/Fouad.html> [accessed 14 January 2022] (select no. 75).
33 See the digital image at <https://berlpap.smb.museum/01894/> [accessed 14 January 2022].

December 75 C.E.), on the other hand, has πλεῖστα written in full, followed by χ(αίρειν) καὶ ὑγ(ιαίνειν).³⁴ Did the scribe thereby emphasise the πλεῖστα? P.Mich. 8.473.1 (early II C.E.) may be considered a similar case, since a single χ at the end of the line stands for χαίρειν, preceded by a fully written out πλεῖστα.³⁵ There are several other examples like these³⁶ and some more examples with a single χ for χ(αίρειν) preceded by πολλά written in full.³⁷ Other letter writers obviously did not put any emphasis on differentiation: O.Did. 406.2 (before 115–140 C.E.), for example, has both parts of the greeting formula abbreviated: πλ(εῖστα) χ(αίρειν),³⁸ which is similarly true for O.Claud. 2.293.1 (142/143 C.E.) preserving πολ(λὰ) χα(ίρειν).

When letter writers do not prefer a single formula but vary their opening greetings, this may indicate deliberate differentiation and thus emphasis. This can be observed particularly well by looking at ostraca or papyri, which contain several letters by the same author on one artefact. The ostracon O.Claud. 2.259 (125–175 C.E.), for instance, preserves three very short letters from a certain Titianos, who opens each of them by using a different greeting: πολλὰ χαίρε(ν) for the first letter (cf. line 2), πλεῖστα χαίρειν for the second (cf. line 6), but χαίρειν alone for the third (cf. line 11). At the same time, the two addressees of the first letter are addressed without any epithet, whereas the recipient of the second letter is addressed as φίλτατος ('most beloved'), as are the four addressees of the third letter. This cannot be a coincidence and

---

34 See the digital image at <https://berlpap.smb.museum/01860/> [accessed 14 January 2022].
35 A digital image is available at <http://ipap.csad.ox.ac.uk/4DLink4/4DACTION/IPAPwebquery?vPub=P.Mich.&vVol=8&vNum=473> [accessed 14 January 2022].
36 Cf. BGU 4.1141.1; 16.2621.1; 2648.1; 2650.2; 2656.2; CPR 7.55.1; O.Amst. 32.2; O.Berenike 3.461.2; O.Claud. 1.163.2; 2.276.2; O.Did. 325.2; 361.2; 367.2; O.Krok. 2.160.2-3; 183.2; 217.1-2; 231.1; 277.2; P.Bon. 43.2; P.Gen. 12.74.1; P.Graux 2.10.1; P.Oxy. 7.1061.1-2; 12.1481.1; P.Worp. 16.1; SB 6.1017.9.2; 20.14330.2-3; 22.15380.2; 15452.2; 26.16608.2-3.
37 Cf. O.Claud. 2.224.2; 225.3; 226.6; 228.3-4; 229.3; 237.3; 238.2; 243.2; P.Giss. 1.22.2; 23.3.
38 Similarly O.Krok. 2.280.2 (118–130 C.E.): πλεῖ(στα) χ(αίρειν).

was definitely not caused by the limited space on the ostracon.[39] Variations are deliberate, and the writer must have had something in mind here.

Papyrus BGU 3.775 (III C.E.) preserves two letters that were probably authored by one and the same person, a certain Horion (cf. line 13); sure enough, they were written by the same scribe. The first letter is introduced with the greeting formula πολλὰ χαίρειν (line 1), while the second letter sharply rebukes the addressee Castreses by beginning with πολλά σε μέμ|φομε (read μέμφομαι) in lines 13–14. The difference could not be expressed more clearly, and we must not overlook the fact that both addressees could easily see it right before their eyes, since a blank space was left between the two letters and the opposing messages could easily be seen in line 1 of each letter.

Papyrus P.Leid.Inst. 42 (II C.E.) contains two private letters, the first from Heras to his sister Taphes, the second presumably by Taphes, who placed her reply on the same papyrus sheet below the first letter and addressed it to Heras. Both letters appear to have been written by the same scribe, albeit with different pens, suggesting that the scribe in both cases was the letter carrier, whose spelling is extremely phonetic. It is noteworthy that the opening greeting in Taphes' reply is πλεῖστα χαίρειν (lines 21–22: 'very many greetings') and not only a copy of her brother's opening greeting which is πολλὰ χαίρειν (line 2: 'many greetings'). Most likely, Taphes chose her even friendlier greeting on purpose.

6. Conclusion

Despite the general tendency that the literal meaning and original function of phrases or sentences usually fades when they are used formulaically, it should not be overlooked that, depending on the situation, a letter writer may still very well clarify them and even reinforce their expression.

In this sense, I can testify that Jim Harrison's usual 'Cheers' at the end of his emails always comes across to me as an expression of his

---

39 Digital image available via <https://www.nakala.fr> [accessed 14 January 2022] (search for "O.Claud. 259").

great cordiality, and further that it is also meant quite literally when I wish him χρόνια πολλά and *ad multos annos* and close these lines with the extended formula: ἐρρῶσθαί σε εὔχομαι διὰ βίου εὐτυχοῦντα καὶ εὐδοξοῦντα καὶ εὖ διάγοντα μεθ' ὧν ἡδέως διάγεις.

Peter Arzt-Grabner
Associate Professor of Papyrology
University of Salzburg

Bibliography

Arzt-Grabner, P. 'Two Weavers Writing Letters: Paul of Tarsus and Apollonios of Hermopolis', in M. Rescio, C. Facchini, C. Gianotto, and E. Lupieri (eds.), *Non uno itinere: Ebraismi, Cristianesimi, Modernità: Studi in onore di Mauro Pesce in occasione del suo ottantesimo compleanno* (Humanitas, 76 Suppl. 1; Brescia: Morcelliana, 2021), 24–31.

Arzt-Grabner, P. *Philemon* (Papyrologische Kommentare zum Neuen Testament, 1; Göttingen: Vandenhoeck & Ruprecht, 2003).

Blumell, L. H. 'Is *P.Oxy.* XLII 3057 the Earliest Christian Letter?', in Th. J. Kraus and T. Nicklas (eds.), *Early Christian Manuscripts: Examples of Applied Method and Approach* (TENTS, 5; Leiden: Brill, 2010), 97–113.

Cadwallader, A. H. 'Tertius in the Margins: A Critical Appraisal of the Secretary Hypothesis', *NTS* 64 (2018), 378–396.

Ceccarelli, P. *Ancient Greek Letter Writing: A Cultural History (600 BC – 150 BC)* (Oxford: Oxford University Press, 2013).

Chouliara-Raïos, H. '*P.Oxy.* XLII 3057: ē archaioterē christianikē epistolē', *Bella: Epistēmonikē epetērida* 4 (2007), 687–732.

Coles, R., A. Geissen, and L. Koenen 'Some Corrections and Notes to P. Fouad', *ZPE* 11 (1973), 235–239, Tafel XVII.

Gonis, N. 'Abbreviations and Symbols', in R. S. Bagnall (ed.), *The Oxford Handbook of Papyrology* (Oxford: Oxford University Press, 2009), 170–178.

Hemer, C. J. 'Ammonius to Apollonius, Greeting', *BurH* 12 (1976), 84–91.

Koskenniemi, H. *Studien zur Idee und Phraseologie des griechischen Briefes bis 400 n.Chr* (Suomalaisen Tiedeakatemian Toimituksia, B/102,2; Helsinki: Suomalainen Tiedeakatemia, 1956).

Llewelyn, St. R. 'Ammonios to Apollonios (*P. Oxy.* XLII 3057): The Earliest Christian Letter on Papyrus?', in St. R. Llewelyn, *New Documents Illustrating Early Christianity*, vol. 6: *A Review of the Greek Inscriptions and Papyri Published in 1980–81*, with the collaboration of R. A. Kearsley (Sydney: Macquarie University, 1992), 169–177.

Minehart, M.	'P.Oxy. XLII 3057: Letter of Ammonius: The [Mis]identification of an Oxyrhynchus Papyrus [as the Earliest Christian Letter]', in P. Schubert (ed.), *Actes du 26e Congrès international de papyrologie, Genève, 16–21 août 2010* (Recherches et rencontres, 30; Genf: Librairie Droz, 2012), 543–548.
Montevecchi, O.	'Τὴν ἐπιστολὴν κεχιασμένην: P. Oxy XLII 3057', *Aeg* 80 (2000), 189–194.
Parsons, P. J.	'The Earliest Christian Letter?', in R. Pintaudi (ed.), *Miscellanea Papyrologica* (Papyrologica Florentina, 7; Firenze: Edizioni Gonnelli, 1980), 289, image: Tav. XII.
Ramelli, I. L. E.	'A New Reading of One of the Earliest Christian Letters Outside the New Testament and the Dangers of Early Christian Communities in Egypt', *Nova Tellvs* 28 (2010), 125–159.
Stanton, G. R.	'The Proposed Earliest Christian Letter on Papyrus and the Origin of the Term Philallelia', *ZPE* 54 (1984), 49–63.
Wipszycka, E.	'Les papyrus documentaires concernant l'Église d'avant le tournant constantinien: Un bilan des vingt dernières années', in I. Andorlini et al. (eds.), *Atti del XXII Congresso Internazionale di Papirologia (Firenze, 23–29 agosto 1998)*, vol. 2 (Firenze: Istituto Papirologico 'G. Vitelli', 2001), 1307–1330.

Christian Women in Oxyrhynchus and Environs (2nd – 6th Century C.E.)

Peter Lampe

Abstract

Papyri bring to light the life of Christian women from the second to sixth centuries CE in the Nile Delta. They reveal two female ecclesiastical officeholders, some women eager to read, independent and unmarried female 'nuns' ('apotactic' religious women), and widows receiving charity from the church. Others suffered from the traumatic effects of their childhood or marriage, or turned to a Christian form of magic to alleviate sufferings they endured in their lives.

James Harrison, wonderful colleague and magnificent scholar, has greatly enriched our knowledge about Early Christianity by masterfully handling all genres of ancient sources available to classical historians and exegetes of ancient texts. This little papyrological piece comes as modest token of my appreciation.

The following papyri take us on a visit to Christian women in the late Roman/early Byzantine Nile delta, who often speak for themselves. In some cases, we get surprisingly close to them, being invited to peek into their houses, seeing their hardships, fights, traumata, and illnesses, yet also sharing their enjoyments, for example, when looking over their shoulders and reading books with them. We also witness the self-determination and independence of several women. The methodological problem when looking at the colourful life reflected in the papyri is, of course, the conundrum of how to proceed from anecdotic evidence to wider-ranging insights. If we are lucky, using induction, we might discover traces of individual lives that share common denominators. However, when working with ancient sources, particularly papyri, we never know how representative of a whole population the samples of documents we hold in our hands are.

Six topics will be touched upon:

- Female Officeholders
- Women Eager to Read
- Independent Women – Apotactic 'Nuns'
- Widows Receiving Charity
- Marriages: From Abuse to Affection
- Magic and Paganism.

Officeholders

In the Egyptian papyri and mummy tablets, hardly any women are documented as ecclesiastical officeholders (contrary to literary sources; see n. 4 and 8, below). The two we encounter are of Egyptian provenance, but we cannot specify their hometown.

1. A female Christian 'teacher' is evidenced twice in SB 14.11532,[1] a fragmentary private letter of unknown Egyptian origin dating to the first quarter of the fourth century.[2] It was sent from one Christian household to another: from Phoibammon and his household to the teacher Philoxenos and his people in Alexandria(?). The fragment does not convey why the female teacher ('Lady teacher' Κυρία ἡ διδάσκαλος) and the addressee Philoxenos are called teachers, nor does it clarify how she relates to the two households. Maybe she got a copy of the letter, being greeted by the sender (see the accusative), which would explain her second mentioning on the margin. The function (title?) διδάσκαλος is indiscriminately used for both genders. Therefore, it is unlikely that this female teacher 'only' taught women (Titus 2:3–5) or children (like second-century Grapte in Herm. *Vis.* 2.4.3). It is possible that these two teachers taught entire congregations as in 1 Corinthians

---

1 Tibiletti, *Le lettere*, 32.
2 For the date, see Broux and Clarysse, 'Name', 347–62, here 352.

12 and 14 as well as 11:5.³

The unanswerable question arises whether the rare female 'teacher' taught an unorthodox congregation, maybe a Montanist one.⁴

The beginning is lost -- -- -- -- -- -- -- -- -- --
to you a new (letter?) in Alexandri[a...]
ναι σοι καινη ἐν Ἀλεξανδρεί[ᾳ - ca.16 -]
my K(yrio)s brother Jul[i]anus (acc.) [...]
ἀδελφὸν κ(ύριό)ν μου Ἰουλ[ι]ανὸν πι [- ca.16 -]
and if you⁵ wish [...]
καὶ ἐὰν θέλετε μ[..]ον ομου[- ca.16 -]
what good we can. The [...]
μεν ὃ δυνάμεθα καλόν· τὸν [- ca.16 -]
Lady/Kyria the teacher (acc.). The K[yrios?...] (acc.)
Κυρίαν τὴν διδάσκαλον· τὸν κ [- ca.16 -]
(a male person; masc. acc.) who also wrote a letter to me [...]
τὸν γράψαντά μοι καὶ ἐπιστολὴν [- ca.16 -]

---

3   1 Cor. 12:29 (διδάσκαλος); in 11:5 and 14:31 ('all') both genders, prophetesses and prophets, enable 'learning' (μανθάνω); 12:8; 14:1,3f,6,26 ('each one' implying both genders). Was the Christian community, in which the papyrus' female teacher lived, familiar with 1 Cor.? The ending of the papyrus letter alludes to 2 Cor. 13:13 after all.
4   For a further interpretation of the papyrus, see Eisen, Amtsträgerinnen, 87–93. Holding that this woman taught in the "catholic" church, Eisen (92 in the German version) helpfully points out the parallel of Theodora and Synkletike, the teaching Egyptian "Wüstenmütter" ("desert mothers"), in the Apophthegma Patrum 5 and 12 (5th cent., with a nucleus probably dating from about 400 CE; see also PsAthan., Vita Synkl., esp. 22; 56 and 103). Female Christian teachers, non-ordained non-clerics teaching the catechumens, seem to have been a wider spread phenomenon in Egypt, if the Canones Hippolyti (Egypt, 4th cent.), esp. 12; 17–19, can be read as inclusive language. The Canones Hippolyti never state that women should not teach in the church. The balanced ratio of 3 women/3 men (50%) in our papyrus is typical of Christian papyri and uncharacteristic of literary texts (Naldini, Cristianesimo, 45f).
5   You = Philoxenos and his people, line I and 9.

the Kyr(ia) Xenike, the Kyr(ia) Arsinoe (acc.), and [...]
κυρ(ίαν) Ξενικὴν, κυρ(ίαν) Ἀρσινόην καὶ π [- ca.16 - ἀ-]
of (tru)th(?) the august,[6] free K(yrios?) [...]
ληθείας τὸν σέβας [...] ἐλεύθερον κ [- ca.16 -]
Philoxenos and your people (acc.). M[y?] K(yrio)s [...]
Φιλόξενον καὶ τοὺς σοὺς. ὁ κ(ύριο)ς μ [- ca.16 -]
The good Phoibammon and the entire ho(usehold gree)t
ὁ καλὸς Φοιβάμμων καὶ πᾶσα ἡ ο[ἰκία προσαγορεύου-]
you (pl.). The grace of our K(yrio)s Je(sus) [Ch(ristos) be with all of
    you; cf. 2 Cor. 13:13].
σιν ὑμᾶς. ἡ χάρις τοῦ κ(υρίο)υ ἡμῶν Ἰη(σοῦ) [Χρ(ιστοῦ) μετὰ
    πάντων ὑμῶν].

On the left margin:
Kyria, the teacher (acc.)
[Κυρ]ίαν τὴν διδάσκ(αλον)
Verso:
[Deliver to the] tea(cher) Philoxenos, best of all people.
[ἀπόδος τῷ] παναρίστῳ Φιλοξένῳ διδ(ασκάλῳ)

.τ....ολο( )
    vac. ?
[-ca.?- πρ]άγματος

A well-known antipode to this text is proudly presented by the Gospel of Thomas, where a blatantly misogynic bias in favour of men, the 'living spirits' 'worthy of the Life' and to 'enter the Kingdom', is displayed. The Egyptian Nag Ham. Codex II 99.18–26 (late third cent.?) reads:

> Simon Peter said to them: 'Let Mary go away from us, for women are not worthy of the Life.' Jesus said: 'Behold, I shall impel her to make her male, so that she herself may become

---

6 σέβας = reverential awe or the object of it. A neuter noun, here in an attributive position.

a living spirit, being like you males. For any woman who makes herself male shall enter the Kingdom of Heaven.'[7]

2. A second female ecclesiastical officeholder is evidenced by a Christian label ("tablette")[8] on an Egyptian mummy in the Louvre Museum, dating from the second/third century. The label reads '(Mummy of) Artemidora (genitive), of Mikkalos (father), of the mother/μητ(ρὸς) Paniskiaine, a female ecclesiastical elder/πρεσβ(υτέρας). She fell asleep in the Lord/ ἐκοιμήθη ἐν κ(υρί)ῳ.'[9] Did πρεσβύτερα indicate age, as Barratte and Boyaval (see n.8, above) suspected? No, as elsewhere,[10] instead of using unspecific categories such as 'old' or 'young', it was easy

---

7   In the *Martyrdom of Perpetua and Felicitas* 10.15, the transgender shift is not misogynic but rather a solution for a female honour/shame problem (nakedness in public); it disappears as soon as Perpetua becomes a man like other fighters in the arena: In a vision anticipating her fight in the amphitheater, Perpetua realises that her 'clothes were stripped off, and (suddenly) I became a man' (ἐξεδύθην καὶ ἐγενήθην ἄρρην/*expoliata sum, et facta sum masculus*). Of course, one can also interpret the metamorphosis as gaining strength and courage before the martyrdom; then clichés of male 'advantages', regarding physis and virtue, would be in the background. The two interpretations do not exclude one another. For gender transformations in early Christian writings, see further Mader, 'Frühchristliche Theologinnen', 240–54, esp. 247 and 251 (with further lit.); Petersen, 'Maria Magdalena', 117–40.

8   Thus not a proper papyrus. Published in Barratte and Boyaval, 'Catalogue', 264 no. 1115; see also Horsley, *New Documents*, 240, referring to no. 6, as well as Eisen (see note 4, above) 125–128. On the basis also of epigraphical evidence, Eisen (128) holds that in Greece, Asia Minor and Egypt "catholic" Christian presbyteresses lead congregations until the 4th century on a wider scale, when first attempts (Synod of Laodicea Can.11; Epiphanius) surfaced to abolish or downgrade this office. Yet, still in the 5th century, the—possibly Egyptian—*Testamentum Domini* 1.35 and 2.19 knows Christian presbyteresses, but by now ranks them under the higher clerics (i.e., bishops, male presbyters, male deacons; above subdeacons, readers and diaconesses), no longer leading congregations.

9   Horsley, *New Documents*, 240, assumes that Artemidora herself was a *presbytera*, not just the mother. This is the most probable solution. In papyri, the parents are most often named before the profession (see below, e.g. P.Lond. 5.1711.5f; 5.1712; P. Oxy. 44.3203.1).

10   There is a plethora of examples, just four: 'Julia Saturnina, 45 years of age, wonderful wife, excellent physician' (*ILS* 7802), 'Hapate, short-hand writer of Greek, she lived for 25 years' (*ILS* 7760), 'Luria Privata, actress in mimes, lived 19 years' (*ILS* 5215; 19 is not even a rounded number), 'Sarapion ... age of 55' (SB 14.1193).

for families and their morticians to indicate the exact age.[11] In view of the immediately following ἐκοιμήθη ἐν κυρίῳ it is more likely that πρεσβύτερα designates 'a female elder in the Church'.[12]

Women Eager to Read

According to the short letter P.Oxy. 63.4365 (fourth cent.), written on the back of a cut-down petition, two sisters are exchanging religious books:

To my dearest lady sister in the Lord, greeting. Lend the Ezra, because I lent you the Little Genesis (i.e. the Book of Jubilees).[13] Farewell in God.[14]

τῇ κυρίᾳ μου φιλτάτῃ ἀδελ-
φῇ ἐν κ(υρί)ῳ χαίρειν.
χρῆσον τὸν Ἔσδραν,
ἐπεὶ ἔχρησά σοι τὴν
λεπτὴν Γένεσιν.
ἔρρωσο ἡμεῖν ἐν θ(ε)ῷ.

The short note shows both affection between the two sisters and fervour for learning. It also illustrates that reading of Biblical books (canonical or not), also by women, was not necessarily guided by clergy but private. The next papyrus shows this as well.

Female learning also seems to be reflected in P.Lips. 1.43 (fourth cent.), possibly from Hermopolis Magna. A Christian 'ever-virgin', Thaésis, a single female living a religious life without immediate family duties,

---

11 The same applies if anyone wanted to read πρεσβ as πρεσβ(ῦτις) (Titus 2:3). Some, albeit late, evidence of πρεσβῦτις, however, even denotes an ecclesiastical office; see in Tabbernee, *Montanist*, 69f.
12 Thus Horsley, *New Documents*, 240.
13 *Little Genesis* is Jubilees: 'Ὡς δὲ ἐν τοῖς Ἰωβηλαίοις εὑρίσκεται, τῇ καὶ λεπτῇ Γενέσει καλουμένῃ (Epiphanius, *Pan.* 2.76.16).
14 The ἡμεῖν may be a dativus commodi: 'be strong in God for us', that is, 'It is in our interest that you thrive in God'.

appears to like books. She is accused of having stolen several books from an estate:

Pharmouthi 18 in the entrance of the catholic

Φαρμοῦθι ιη ἐν τῷ πυλῶνι τῆς κ[αθ]ολι-

church, which is under Plousianos, the most respected

κῆς ἐκκλησίας τῆς ὑπὸ Πλουσιανὸν ἐπιδιμώ-

bishop. When arbitration was held

τατον (1. ἐπιτιμώτατον) ἐπίσκοπον. διέτης (1. διαίτης) γενομένης μετα-

between Thaesis, the ever-virgin, and the

ξὺ Θαήσιος ἀειπαρθ[ένο]υ καὶ τῶν κλη-

heirs of Besarion, the arbitrament

ρο[ν]όμων Βησαρίωνος [τὸ διαιτ]ητικὸ[ν π]ροσ-

was delivered by the same bishop Plousianos

εδόθη ὑπὸ τοῦ α(ὐτοῦ) ἐπισκόπου Πλουσιανοῦ

after he had arbitrated in the presence of Dioskorides, son of Hymnion,

διετήσαντος (1. διαιτήσαντος) παρ[όντων] Διοσκ[ο]ρ[ίδου] Ὑμνίω-

a town councillor, and E[...], alias

νος βουλ(ευτοῦ) καὶ Ε[. . . . . τοῦ] καὶ

Herakleios, son of Eith[...., and of..(a name)]

[Ἡ]ρακλείου Εἰθ[. . . καὶ . . .].ου

[...(a name)], a deacon (genitive), so that/saying that: Either the heirs

[(a name)]του διακό[ν]ου ὥστε ἢ τοὺς κληρο[νό]μους

of Besarion are to produce witnesses who

[Βησ]αρίωνος π[α]ρενεγκεῖν μάρτυρας τ[οὺ]ς

expose/disgrace Thaesis regarding the removal

ἐλλέγχοντας Θαῆσιν περὶ ἀφαιρέσε[ω]ς

of Christian books as being done by her,

βιβλίων χρε[ιστ]ια\νι/κῶν ὡς [γ]ενομένης ὑ[π'] αὐ-

and she is to bring these back,

τῆς καὶ ταῦτ[α] αὐτὴν εἰσενεγκεῖν

or she is to swear an oath about not having done

ἢ αὐτὴν ὅρκο[ν διδ]όναι περὶ τοῦ μηδ[ε]μίαν

any removal to her advantage (medium), and in this way all

ἀφαίρησιν (1. ἀφαίρεσιν) πεποιῆσθαι καὶ [ο]ὕτω πάντα

the things left at the house are to (be divided) into two

τὰ ἐπὶ τῆς οἰκείας καταλιφθέντα (1. καταλειφθέντα) εἰς δύο
parts, and Thaesis, on the one hand, is to have for herself one part,
μέρη καὶ τ[ὴ]ν μὲν Θαῆσιν ἓν μέρος
the heirs, on the other, the other
ἕξασθαι, τούς δὲ κληρονόμους τὸ ἕτερον
part. And this is to happen by the thirtieth
μ[έ]ρος, τοῦτο δὲ γενέσθαι εἴσω τριακάδος
of the same Pharmouthi.
τοῦ αὐτοῦ Φαρμοῦθι.

Several items are of interest. (1) Thaesis is characterised by the epithet 'ever-virgin' (ἀειπαρθένος), instead of a patronymic. In 163/4 C.E., in Oxyrhynchus, the patronymic also was dropped from the name of a pagan 'sacred virgin' (ἱερά παρθένος) (P.Merton 2.73); she had left her natural family serving at a temple for Athena, Isis, and other gods, being charged with the task of organising processions. In Christian circles, 'ever-virgin' (ἀειπαρθένος) also was the epithet of Mary, e.g. in an amulet invoking her (P. Bon. 1.9, probably also fourth cent.; for later times, see SB 1.4665: 656 C.E.). (2) As an unmarried woman, devoted to a religious life,[15] Thaesis is interested in reading Christian books. Did she even steal some? This is the conflict described: A man named Besarion died and left an entire household to his heirs, among them Thaesis, because she inherited one part of the estate while two or more other heirs inherited the other.[16]

Before all heirs can divide up the goods of the estate, Thaesis, however, seemed to have been eager to have a look at several of Besarion's

---

15 Thaesis was not a 'nun' in the sense of 'member of a convent' with communal property, rules and certain hierarchies and dependencies. Thaesis used her right to inherit material property, and no official of a convent was involved in the arbitration. She appears to have lived independently in the city.
16 The more adequate translation of κληρονόμοι in the papyrus would be 'co-heirs'. Otherwise, the scenario of dividing the estate between Thaesis and the group of κληρονόμοι who voiced allegations against her would make no sense. There is no hint of any distinctions between bequest (for Thaesis) and inheritance (for the κληρονόμοι). The text does not necessarily say that Thaesis gets half of the estate, while the others get the other half, as Rowlandson (ed.), *Women and Society*, 78, assumes.

Christian books. In any case, the other heirs accused her of having taken these books. The most likely scenario is that these books were missing in Besarion's house; otherwise, the allegation would have had no basis. However, if Thaesis had taken the books home, the question would have been whether she deliberately had intended to withhold them from the inheritance that was about to be divided—this would be stealing—or whether she simply wanted to look at them before they got distributed among the heirs. Did she have selfish intentions? (3) The local bishop settled the conflict, arbitrating in the vestibule of his 'catholic'[17] church while three respectable witnesses were present. The parent of the first one was a city councillor, thus a *decurio*; the father of a third one a deacon.[18] The papyrus documents the growing role of church officials as arbitrators, appearing to be the oldest source evidencing an *episcopalis audientia*.[19] (4) The bishop wisely decided: (a) The accusing heirs need to procure witnesses who saw Thaesis take the books or have the books in her possession—and then she has to return them. No punishment is envisioned. Not even a search of her home is planned. (b) The alternative is that Thaesis swears that she did not take the books for her advantage (the middle voice ἀφαίρησιν πεποιῆσθαι in l. 16 is crucial),[20] which would be stealing. (c) A third alternative—in case Thaesis refused to swear—was not verbalised by the four arbitrating authorities. Apparently, it was implied that such a refusal equalled a confession. The bishop's arbitrament—especially the mildness in the first ruling: no punishment and no search are planned—seems to show the esteem and respect for this 'ever-virgin', with the churches of that time increasingly valuing women who lived a religious, unmarried life.

17 In the fifth century, the *Historia Monachorum in Aegypto* 5 brags that Oxyrhynchus virtually had no heretics and pagans. Monks had moved into the former pagan temples and public buildings.
18 The name preceding διάκονος seems to have a masculine ending. Otherwise, διάκονος is generic, encompassing both genders. Cf. e.g. Rom. 16:1 and the deaconess P.Oxy. 1162.3 (fourth cent. c.e.).
19 For this institution and its history, see, e.g., Loening, *Geschichte*, 260f, 289f.
20 In the ACJ, πεποιῆσθαι could be passive too. However, the question of Thaesis' intent, which appears to be crucial in the case—more crucial than previously seen—would be swept under the rug by a passive translation.

Other Independent Women—Apotactic 'Nuns'

In the fifth century, the hagiographic *Historia Monachorum in Aegypto* (5.1–30) hyperbolically praised allegedly '20,000 virgins' (δισμυρίας δὲ παρθένους 5.27) in Oxyrhynchus. Their hospitality (φιλοξενία) and agape were supposed to be overwhelming. They were nuns living in convents—contrary to Thaesis (see n.15, above), contrary also to two apotactic nuns (μοναχαὶ ἀποτακτικαί) in P.Oxy. 44.3203, who owned real estate in Oxyrhynchus as personal property and rented out parts of it. The letter from July 400 C.E is addressed to both of them; they are sisters:

'To Aureliae Theodora and Tayris whose father is Silvanus, of the illustrious and most illustrious city of the Oxyrhynchites" (Αὐρηλίαις Θεῳδώρ[ᾳ καὶ] Ταῦριν (l. Ταύρι) ἐκ πατρὸς Σιλβανοῦ [ἀ]πὸ τῆς λαμπρᾶς καὶ λαμπροτάτης ['Ο]ξυρυγχιτῶν πόλεως μοναχαῖς ἀποτακτικαῖς). The sender, a Jew,[21] is called Aurelius, Jose son of Judas, of the same city (παρὰ Αὐρηλίου Ἰωσὴ Ἰούδα Ἰουδαίως (l. Ἰουδαίου) ἀπὸ τῆς αὐτῆς πόλεως). In their property in the Calvary Camp quarter of Oxyrhynchus he leases one ground floor room, i.e., a dining hall (ἐξέδραν / τὸ συμπόσιον), and a cellar in the basement with all appurtenances (ἐπίπεδον τόπον ἕνα ἐξέτραν (l. ἐξέδραν) κα[ὶ] [τ]ὴ[ν] ἐν τῷ καταγείῳ καμάραν μία[ν] [σὺν] χρηστηρίοις πᾶσιν) for an annual price of 12 million denarii, which was a considerable income to support the sisters.[22] Did he plan to offer festivities in this ground floor hall, open a restaurant? The cellar and its equipment would have been useful for such a project. He seems well-to-do but appears to be analphabetic or less versed in legal matters than the writer, dictating the letter to a cer-

---

21 For an extensive list of Oxyrhynchus papyri with this epithet, see Blumell and Wayment (ed.), *Christian Oxyrhynchus*, 457. For a Jewish quarter in Oxyrhynchus in the 1st and 2nd centuries c.e., see P.Oxy. 2.335.8: ἐν Ὀξ(υρύγχων) πόλ(ει) ἐπ' ἀμφόδ(ου) Ἰουδαϊκ(ῆς); 1.100.9: Ἰουδαικῆς λοιπῶν ψειλῶν (l. l. ψιλῶν) τόπων. Both papyri document real estate sales.
22 In *Diocletian's Edict on Maximum Prices*, price ceilings were set for about 1200 items. 120 Mio *denarii communes* could have bought 819,000 litres of ordinary wine (0.546 l / 8 denarii, II.1.10; numbering following Lauffer), or 80 first-class male lions from Africa (XXXIV.1), or 80 pounds of purple-dyed silk (royal purple from rock snails; XXIV.1). Even with inflation continuing to rise, 12 Mio denarii were a considerable annual income for the sisters.

tain Aurelius Elias, who signs at the end (ἔγραψα ὑπὲρ αὐτο͂υ/ γράμματα μὴ εἰδ[ότος/"I wrote the piece of writing for him because he does not know"). As sisters, the nuns apparently had inherited the house, making good money from their personal property. Yet, their lifestyle was apotactic (μοναχαὶ ἀποτακτικαί), meaning they were anchorites,[23] living in seclusion either outside the city or rather in the city,[24] e.g., in their own town house, which appears to have been a spacious *insula*. In any case, they did not live in a community of a convent where property was communal and self-determination restricted.

Regarding religious women like the ones discussed, we have been used to focus on asceticism or chastity, triggered by terms such as *virgo* and παρθένος, which, however, say less about sex life, or the absence of it, than social role, with these terms simply denoting unmarried females.

The two sisters as μοναχαὶ ἀποτακτικαί and Thaesis as ἀειπαρθένος illustrate that their unmarried lifestyle was a socially accepted model that gave women a chance to live a self-determined and self-paced life without the dependency on men; in the case of Thaesis, even the patronymic was dropped.[25] They also were independent from monasterial authorities. The term μοναχή/'nun',[26] of course, literally means 'unique, solitary'. The apotactic lifestyle allowed for individuality and independence to handle one's own economic affairs by oneself and to own personal property,[27] as is well illustrated in the two papyri discussed. This lifestyle model was open to rather well-to-do women, who had some economic means at their disposal. However, it also was open to women *working* for their own income, as the following example may show.

---

23 See ἀποτακτήρ in P.Oxy. 10.1311, fifth cent. c.e. This hermit also lived from personal money he made on his own by selling olive oil.
24 Like Thaesis probably. See note 15, above.
25 The freedom provided by this model seems to have been mirrored in the rather wide range of terms denoting the model: μοναχαὶ ἀποτακτικαί or (ἀει) παρθένος and with patronymic or without. There wasn't any fixed terminology yet. Correspondingly, there seemed to have been a certain freedom to shape this lifestyle model individually. For Thaesis being independent from a convent, see above n.15.
26 This meaning of the term emerges in the papyri in the fourth cent. c.e. See Judge, 'Fourth-Century Monasticism', 613–20.
27 Cf. further Elm, 'Virgins of God', 235–38.

How traumatising family life could be so that a woman decided to become a self-determined nun is shown in P.Lond. 5.1731.1–20 (C.E. 585; from Syene). The papyrus, a legal paper, was dictated by a nun (μοναχή) in this town, Aurelia Tsone, who talks in the first person. It is addressed to her mother and represents an official receipt for money received and complaint against the mother about Tsone's bad childhood. The text is wordy, the grammar wanting, and the author tries too hard to fabricate 'fancy' subordinate clauses (e.g. lengthy but clumsy participle and infinitive constructions), betraying a lack of education but a will to cover up this flaw. Tsone dictated the legal document to a man named Marcus (last line: δι' ἐμοῦ Μάρκου Ἄπα Δίου ἐγράφη), but this does not automatically suggest analphabetism. Possibly this Marcus, more versed than she in legal matters, helped her to set up the document, creating many formulations on his own after Tsone had told him the entire story. Then the verdict about poor grammar and style does not strike Tsone but Marcus.

At the outset, Aurelia Tsone emphasises that she, as a nun, handles business affairs by herself without a husband as her guardian and kyrios (line 8: ἄνευ κυρίου αὐτη (l. αὐτης) ἀνδρὸς χρηματίζουσα). She complains that her parents got divorced—these were the workings of Satan (κατὰ διαβουλικὴν (l. διαβολικὴν) καὶ σατανικὴν ἐνέργειαν)[28]—while she was still young (ἔτι νέας οὔσης). For his child, the father gave his ex-wife four coins of gold. 'After my reaching the legal age, I proceeded against you (the mother), accusing you over the same four coins, and saying that these had been given to you for the necessary maintenance of me from childhood' (δοθῆναι περὶ τῆς ἐκ παιδιώθην (l. παιδιόθεν) ἀναγκαίας μου τροφῆς). However, the mother did not raise the child; the father did: 'I was maintained by my father, after I had been thrown out by you and you joined with another man' (διὰ τὸ οὖν τραφῆναί με ὑπὸ τοῦ πατρός μου ἐκβληθεισαν (l. ἔκβλητον) δὲ ὑπὸ σοῦ γενομενης καί <σε> κολλᾶσθαι ἑτέρῳ ἀνδρί). The mother, however, at that time resisted returning the coins, pretending that they were for the daugh-

---

28 Blaming an evil demon for failure of marriages and divorce was not unique: cf. e.g. P.Lond. 5.1712 (569 C.E., Antinoopolis).

ter's 'dowry' (προίξ). 'After many claims, counter-claims and opinions, it was later decided that I should receive the same four coins', the transfer of which the nun acknowledges by sending this document. Several witnesses sign the sad story.

Rowlandson (79; see n.16, above) subsumes the document under 'monasticism'. However, Tsone hardly was a nun living in a convent. None of the witnesses signing the document at the end are monastic authorities.[29] On the contrary, three belong to the clergy of local churches in town—a presbyter of Syene (πρεσβ[ύτερος] Συήνης), an archdeacon of St. Mary's church in Syene (ἀρχιδιάκο[νος] τῆς ἁγίας Μαρίας Συήνης), and a deacon of the Ecclesia of Syene (διάκο[νος] ἐκκλ[ησίας] Συήνης). The other five witnesses belong to the military stationed in town: a centurio (κεντυρ[ίων] ἀριθμ[οῦ] Συήνης),[30] an *actuarius* (ἀκτουαρης ἀριθμοῦ Συήνης), that is, an official of the troops at Syene, most probably charged with the distribution of provision and money to the military, and three soldiers (στρα[τιώτης] ἀριθμοῦ Συήνης). These five witnesses confirm that the military at that time was the most important stabilising societal force, with its members acting as esteemed and trustworthy witnesses even in everyday matters of civil law.

After all, it is highly probable that Tsone—like Thaesis and the two sisters Theodora and Tayris—also was one of the city-dwelling, independent μοναχαί. At least in 585 C.E., she had financial means, four gold coins. The most common gold coin at that time was the stable early-Byzantine *solidus*. Tsone could have bought a herd of twelve donkeys for four *solidi*; one generation later, a casual labourer at Alexandria in the early seventh century had to work ninety-two days for this kind of money, a construction worker at Jerusalem in the sixth century eighty days. Four *solidi* also could have bought fish for 560 days, half a

---

29 If not female conventual authorities, the Oxyrhynchus bishop could have signed as witness, with him being the authority overseeing convents and monasteries (see, e.g., SB 4.7449 below: the bishop is expected to discipline a monk).

30 ἀριθμός in the sixth century (*CIG* 5187, *BGU* 673) has the meaning of 'unit of troops' = numerus.

pound per day.³¹ Not a huge fortune but a convenient extra income.

It is unknown what else was bequeathed to her by her father whom she kept in high esteem (ὁ μακάριός μου πατὴρ Μηνᾶς line 9) and who apparently was not poor, nor do we know what else she possessed. If she was not working for her own income, it is at least possible that, in all these three cases of independent nuns, a parent, specifically a father,³² had been in the background from whom they inherited some wealth.³³

Widows Receiving Charity

Another kind of 'independent' women were Christian widows without family. A number of them became dependent on the ecclesiastical aid organisation. The churches had become increasingly efficient in distributing relief via specialised officers, as the reused papyrus P.Wisc. 2.64 from Oxyrhynchus, from January 480 C.E., illustrates. 'The holy church' (through a presbyter³⁴ or another authority) orders³⁵ a certain Petros, steward (οἰ[κονόμῳ]) of the local church of St Kosmas, to hand over one cloak, and only one, to the widow Sophia (Σοφίᾳ χήρᾳ)— one of the coats Petros had 'for good use' (ἀφ' [ὧν] ἔχεις ἱματίων εἰς καλὴν χρείαν). Apparently, this Petros administered a collection of donated second-hand coats. As the order strictly limits the support to only one coat, one wonders whether some of the widows had become

31 Cf. Mango, *Byzantium*, 40.
32 Thaesis: Besarion, her father?—The sisters: their father Silvanus.—Tsone: her *makarios* father Menas who raised her after the mother deserted her.
33 Thaesis: a significant portion of an estate.—The sisters: probably the large town house.—Tsone: probably more than just the four gold coins.
34 Thus P.Oxy. 16.1951 (485 C.E.): ἡ ἁγία ἐκλης[ία] δ[ι'] ἐμοῦ Γρηγορίου πρεσ[βυτέρου].
35 For other instructions given by the church, see, e.g., P.Oxy. 6.993 (late Dec. 478/early Jan. 479 or late Dec. 493/early Jan. 494 C.E.): wine for a plasterer on the occasion of the Tubi feast—which is more than emergency relief; 16.1951: on the occasion of the same feast, 'the holy church through me, the presbyter Gregorios', gives an order to a wine manager to hand out wine to a craftsman specialised in beds and dinner couches. The same in 16.1950 (487 C.E.): wine on the occasion of the same feast. Like temples organised public feedings on the occasion of festivals, the church, on the occasion of the Τῦβι feast, made analogous donations beyond emergency relief. Τῦβι was the month of January in which Epiphany was celebrated.

known for begging for more than they needed. Widows like Sophia in January 480 were freezing; the church—not a family—supported her.

Wine also was donated to widows according to P. Oxy. 16.1954 (late fifth cent. C.E., Oxyrhynchus). Wine, consumed in moderation, was a basic food, healthier than bacteria-loaded water. Here it was handed out to a group of widows of the church of St Michael's in Oxyrhynchus. 'To Victor wineseller: Give to the widows of Michael only one double-jar of wine'[36]—only one.

Marriages: From Abuse to Affection

Trauma of family life—the background of Tsone's life as an independent religious woman—is vividly illustrated by another case in P.Oxy. 6.903 (fourth cent.), a case of a toxic marriage between two well-to-do partners, each having their own possessions and property. On this reused papyrus from Oxyrhynchus a Christian wife, with an irregular uncial hand, notes all the abuses her husband committed in his household against her and other household members. It is a strong indictment against him, with even his mother and God called upon as witnesses. The wife apparently plans to sue her husband, with this document functioning as preparation (not unlike an affidavit).

The common denominator of all abuses the wife lists is that the man is paranoid about the household members stealing his possessions. He seems obsessed with greed and mistrust, which leads to verbal and physical violence, even sadistic violence. (1) He hides his keys from the wife, but not from his slaves whom he seems to trust more than his wife, she complains. He insults his wife. (2) This leads to a mediation by his own brothers and the bishop. A marriage deed is drawn up, and he swears to stop this behaviour. (3) However, he again hides the keys

---

36 Nothing is mentioned about the Epiphany feast, contrary to the examples of the previous note where wine was handed out for merriment on the occasion of the celebration of Epiphany, not just as food aid.

from her. (4) After she went out to church 'on a Sabbath',[37] he did not let her back in the house, questioning her, 'Why did you go to the church?' We do not know whether he himself is still pagan, or whether he suspects her of carrying away some of his possessions or of complaining about him to clergy (see n.37, above). He abuses her verbally, apparently steaming with wrath ('terms of abuse to my face, and through his nose'). (5) Owning and managing land property and possessions in her own right, including slaves, she owes the State 100 *artabae* of corn. Taking away and locking up her books containing her bookkeeping, the husband claims that *he* paid for these dues, and not his wife, and that his wife should repay him, although he never paid anything for these 100 *artabae*. She refuses, and he asks his slaves to find allies who can lock up his wife for not paying the alleged debt she has with him. (6) The husband's assistant Choous also owes the State but cannot pay the dues. Choous therefore is incarcerated. A certain Euthalamus pays for his bail, which, however, turns out to be 'insufficient'. Therefore, the wife comes up with additional money to complete the bail. The husband hates this, apparently suspecting his wife of having stolen the bail money from him; Choous was *his* assistant, after all, not hers. Therefore, when meeting his wife again in Antinoopolis—they both go their own ways—he threatens her with taking away all ornaments that she carries. (7) He repeatedly pesters his wife with the request to 'throw out' his slave Anilla, whom he suspects of stealing. Although the husband owns this slave, the wife seems to have de facto

---

37 Saturday church services were not uncommon in the fourth/fifth centuries, in addition to Sunday worship. Cf. Sokrates, *H.E.* 5.22, and above all The coptic *Vita of Apa Aphou* (24–26), bishop of Oxyrhynchus around 400 C.E.: On the Sabbath/Saturday evenings, in church, this Oxrhynchus bishop and 'the people' celebrated 'their services and their prayers and their psalms. He presided over them in the holy liturgy. And he used to lead them until the sixth hour of the Lord's Day' (24; ed. Blumell–Wayment, *Christian Oxyrhynchus* [see n.21, above], 652). Before the liturgical night starting Saturday evenings, he spent his Saturdays 'among those in need or *badly treated*; he used to meet their needs and continued to bear their petitions until the ninth hour' when worship began (25f; ed. Blumell–Wayment, *Christian Oxyrhynchus*, 654). As this Oxyrhynchus bishop from around 400 C.E. was used also to receive people on Saturdays who were 'badly treated' it is possible that the abused wife, a few decades earlier, went to see clergy to complain about her husband and get advice.

authority over her in the household, which would explain why the wife is requested to send Anilla away. The wife herself marvels about the husband's behaviour: He 'wanted to get me involved, and on this pretext to take away whatever I possess myself' (to make up for what the slave Anilla allegedly stole; by throwing out Anilla, the wife would agree that Anilla is a thief. This seems to have been the husband's wicked reasoning, although the papyrus does not spell it out). (8) The worst is still to come: He locks up his slaves, her slaves, her foster daughters, his agent, and the agent's son in his cellars for seven days. He insults and tortures his slaves and her slave Zoe, beating them almost to death to find out what the wife had stolen from him. However, even under pressure they replied: 'Nothing'. He strips her foster daughters naked and hurts them with fire, pressuring them to give him all they have that belongs to the wife. However, they reply: 'She has nothing with us'. The scene shows a sadistically violent psychopath with a tendency toward sexual perversion who, in his delusion of being surrounded by thieves, found a pretext to rage in his pathology for seven days. (9) Finally, the husband threatens to take a mistress. (10) The wife not only quotes her mother-in-law as witness but also God, who 'knows this'.

P. Oxy. 6.903 (fourth cent., Oxyrhynchus):
Concerning all the violent insults uttered by him against me.
    περὶ πάντων ὧν εἶπεν κατ' ἐμοῦ ὕβρεων.
He locked up his own slaves and
    ἐνέκλεισεν τοὺς ἑ[α]υτοῦ δούλους καὶ τοὺς
mine together with my foster daughters and the agent and his (the agent's)
    ἐμοῦ ἅμα των (l. ταῖς) τροφιμ[ω]ν (l. τροφίμ[αι]ς) μου καὶ τὸν προνοητὴν καὶ τὸν
son for seven whole days in his cellars.
    υἱὸν αὐτοῦ ἐπὶ ὅλας ἑ[πτ]ὰ ἡμέρας εἰς τὰ κατάγαια αὐτοῦ,
Having insulted his slaves and my slave Zoe,
    τοὺς μὲν δούλους αὐτ[οῦ κ]αὶ τὴν ἐμὴν δούλην Ζωὴν ὑβρίσας
(and almost) having killed them with blows, he also applied fire to my foster

ἀποκτίνας (l. ἀποκτείνας) αὐτοὺς τῶν π[λ]ηγῶν, καὶ πῦρ
 προσήνεγ'κεν ταῖς τρο-
daughters, after having stripped them totally naked, which the laws do
 not do (= permit). And
φίμαις μου γυμνώσας αὐ[τὰ]ς παντελῶς ἃ οὐ πο\ιο/ῦσι οἱ νόμοι, καὶ
when he said to the same foster daughters, 'Give up all that is hers',
 they also spoke,
λέγων τοῖς (l. ταῖς) αὐτοῖς (l. αὐταῖς) τροφίμοις (l. τροφίμ[αι]ς)
 ὅτι δότε πάντα τὰ αὐτῆς, καὶ εἶπαν
'She has nothing with us'; but to the slaves when they were being
 beaten he said:
ὅτι οὐδὲν ἔχει παρ' ἡμῶν, τοῖς δὲ δούλοις λέγων μαστιγ'γομενοι
 (l. μαστιγουμένοις) ὅτι
'What did she take from my house?' They then under torture said:
 'Nothing
τὶ ἦρκεν ἐκ τῆς οἰκίας μου; βασανιζόμενοι οὖν εἶπαν ὅτι οὐδὲν
of yours has she taken, but all your property is safe.'
 τῶν σῶν ἦρκεν ἀλλὰ σῶά ἐστιν πάντα τὰ σά.
Zoilus then went to see him because he also had locked up his foster
 son,
ἀπήντησεν δὲ αὐτῷ Ζω[ίλ]ος ὅτι καὶ τὸν τρόφιμον αὐτοῦ ἐνέ-
and he said to him, 'Did you come because of your foster son or
 because of the
κλισεν (l. ἐνέκλεισεν), καὶ εἶπεν αὐτῷ ὅτ[ι] διὰ τὸν τρόφιμόν σου
 ἦλθας ἢ διὰ τὴν
such-like (woman) to talk about her?'
 τοίαν ἦλθας λαλῆσαι ἐπάνω αὐτῆς;
And he swore in the presence of the bishops and of his own brothers,
 καὶ ὤμοσεν ἐπὶ παρουσίᾳ τῶν ἐπισκόπων καὶ τῶν ἀδελφῶν αὐτοῦ
'From now on I will certainly not hide all my keys from her, and I
 hold it together,
ὅτι ἀπεντεῦθεν οὐ μὴ κρύψω αὐτη (l. αὐτὴν) πάσας μου τὰς κλεῖς
 καὶ ἐπέχω
 —and he trusted his slaves and did not trust me (this bitter
 interjection is squeezed between the lines) —

—καὶ τοῖς δούλοις αὐτοῦ ἐπίστευσεν κἀμοὶ (l. καὶ ἐμοὶ) οὐκ
 ἐπίστευσεν —
and I do (will) not insult her from now on.' And a marriage deed was
 made, and after
οὔτε ὑβρίζω αὐτὴν ἀπεντεῦθεν. καὶ γαμικὸν γέγονεν, καὶ μετὰ
these articles of agreement and the oaths, he again hid the keys from
 me—
τὰς συνθήκας ταύτας καὶ τοὺς ὅρκους ἔκρυψεν πάλιν ἐμὲ τὰς κλεῖς
from me! And when I had gone out to the church on a Sabbath he
 had
εἰς ἐμέ. καὶ ἀπελθοῦσα [εἰ]ς τὸ κυριακὸν ἐν σαμβάθῳ (l. σαββάτῳ)
 καὶ ἐποίησεν
his outside doors shut on me, saying, 'Why did you go out
τὰς ἔξω θύρας αὐτοῦ ἐνκλισθῆναι (l. ἐγκλεισθῆναι) ἐπάνω μου
 λέγων ὅτι διὰ τί ἀπῆλ-
to the church?' and saying many licentious things/vulgar abuses to my
 face,
θας εἰς τὸ κυριακόν; καὶ πολλὰ ἀσελγήματα λέγων εἰς πρόσωπόν
and through his nose. And about 100 artabae of corn due to the State
 on
μου καὶ διὰ τῆς ῥινὸς αὐτο[ῦ], καὶ περὶ σίτου (ἀρτάβας) ρ τοῦ
 δημοσίου τοῦ
my account: Although he had given/paid nothing, not a single artaba,
 he then locked up
ὀνόματός μου μηδὲν δεδωκὼς μηδὲ ἀρτάβ[ην] μίαν. ἐνέκλεισεν δὲ
the books, after he had gotten hold of them, (saying) 'Pay the price of
 the hundred artaba'
τοὺς τόμους κρατήσας αὐτ[ο]ὺς ὅτι δότε τὴν τιμὴν τῶν [ἀρταβῶν]
 ρ, μηδὲν
although he had paid nothing, as I stated before. And he said to his
 slaves, 'Provide
δεδω[κὼς] ὡς προεῖπον. καὶ εἶπεν τοῖς δούλοις αὐτοῦ ὅτι δότε
 συμμά-
allies so that they also lock up her.' And Choous, his assistant, was
 taken
χους ἵνα καὶ αὐτὴν ἐνκλείσωσι. καὶ ἐκρατήθη Χωοῦς ὁ βοηθὸς αὐτοῦ

into prison, and Euthalamus gave security for him, and it was not
satisfactory.
: εἰς τὸ δημόσιον καὶ παρέσχεν αὐτῷ Εὐθάλαμος ἐνέχυρον καὶ οὐκ
ἠρκέσθη.
So I also took a little other (amount) and gave it for the said Choous.
However, I met
: ἦρκα κἀγὼ ἄλλο μικρὸν καὶ παρέσχον τῷ αὐτῷ Χωοῦτι. ἀπαντησας
(l. ἀπήντησα) δὲ
him at Antinoopolis having what is for my bath (probably a bag
with its contents), with which (incongruent numerus) I have
(part of my)
: αὐτῷ εἰς Ἀντινόου ἔχουσα τὸ πρὸς βαλανῖόν (l. βαλανεῖόν) μου
μεθ' ὧν ἔχω κοσμαρι-
little ornaments, and he told me, 'If you have anything with you I
(will) take them (sic) because of what you have given to
: δίων, καὶ εἶπέν μοι ὅτι εἴ τι ἔχεις μετ' ἐσοῦ αἴρω αὐτὰ δι' ὅ δέδωκες
(l. δέδωκας) τῷ
my assistant Choous as security because of his dues to the State.'
: βοηθῷ μου Χωοῦτι ἐνέχυρον διὰ τὰ δημόσια αὐτοῦ. μαρτυρήσαι
(l. μαρτυρήσει) δὲ
To all this his mother will bear witness. And about his slave Anilla
: περὶ τούτων πάντων ἡ μήτηρ αὐτοῦ. καὶ περὶ Ἀνίλλας τῆς δούλης
he kept vexing my soul both in Antinoopolis and here:
: αὐτοῦ ἔμεινεν θλίβων τὴν ψυχήν μου καὶ ἐν τῇ Ἀντινόου καὶ
ἐνταῦθα
'Throw out this slave because she herself knows how much she pro-
cured for herself,' probably
: ὅτι ἔκβαλε τὴν δούλην ταύτην ἐπειδὴ αὐτὴ οἶδεν ὅσα κέκτηται,
ἴσως
wanting to involve me and on this pretext, if I have anything, to take
(it) away. And I
: θέλων μοι (l. με) καταπλέξαι \καὶ/ ταύτῃ τῇ προφάσει ἆραι εἴ τι
ἔχω· κἀγὼ οὐκ
refused to throw her out. And he kept saying, 'After a month
: ἠνεσχόμην ἐκβαλεῖν αὐτήν. καὶ ἔμεινεν λέγων ὅτι μετὰ μηναν
(l. μῆνα)

I take a mistress for myself.' God, however, knows this.
λαμβάνω πολιτ\ικ/ὴν ἐμαυτῷ. ταῦτα δὲ οἶδεν ὁ θ[εός].

The misery of this wife was not unparalleled. In Pap. Oxy. 1.129 (sixth cent., Oxyrhynchus), a Christian father, named John,[38] under whose *patria potestas*[39] his daughter Euphemia still lives, even after her marriage, is upset about the son-in-law's unspeakable[40] 'lawless deeds',[41] which threaten the 'security' (ἀσφάλεια) of his daughter and do not let her 'lead a peaceful and quiet life' (εἰρηνικὸν καὶ ἡσύχιον βίον διάξαι). In this document, written by a municipal official concerned with justice, and signed by the father, the alarmed father takes formal action and dissolves the marriage. It is an official deed of divorce, a *repudium* (διαλύσεως ῥεπούδιον, συναφίας (l. συναφείας) ῥεπούδιον).[42] The father says that the unacceptable behaviour of the husband 'came to his ears' (εἰς ἀκοὰς ἐμὰς ἦλθεν). It stands to reason that the daughter herself instructed him about what was going on in her home and that she supported his action that protected her interests.[43] The official document shows that the early Byzantine society held up certain standards for the treatment of married women.

A similar case, this time not involving a father but a matron mother and her daughter in a village near Oxyrhynchus, both strong-willed women, can be found in the Oxyrhynchus papyrus SB 4.7449 (second half of the fifth cent. C.E.) showing female self-determination. A monk (μονάζων), cousin of this daughter (her guardian?), tries to push her into an arranged marriage with another relative. However, the daughter resists the bullying monk and the suitor (θυγάτηρ ἐκείνῳ οὐ βούλεται συνάπτεσθαι), and the mother sides with her, supporting her.

---

38 The document ends with a drawn cross.
39 πατὴρ Εὐφημίας τῆς ἐμῆς ὑπεξουσίου θυγατρός.
40 οὐ δέον ἐστὶν ταῦτα ἐγ (l. ἐν) γράμμασιν ἐντεθῆναι.
41 ἔκθεσμα πράγματά τινα.
42 The son-in-law is a γαμβρός, that is, connected by marriage, and not just by engagement, as is suggested in the Duke Databank of Documentary Papyry (https://papyri.info/ddbdp/p.oxy;1;129).
43 A contrary case is P.Oxy. 2.237 (coll.VI.4–VIII.7), where a father tries to dissolve his daughter's marriage against her will (Oxyrhynchus, 186 C.E., pagan).

Thereupon the monk starts mobbing the mother, even ruining her clothes. Taking action, the mother approaches the Oxyrhynchus bishop asking him to stop the monk. Clergy again is called in for mediation. Unfortunately, no other papyrus tells us the rest of the story.

P.Oxy. 50.3581 again shows a reckless husband, again mediation by *presbyteroi*, again contractual sanctions (two ounces of gold in case the reckless behaviour continues), and finally divorce. Again, it is the woman who takes initiative by writing down the problems, here in a petition to an officer in charge of the peace in Oxyrhynchus (fourth/fifth cent. C.E.), trying to open a trial in court and receive the said two ounces of gold from him as well as compensation for the damages he left behind; she also suggests criminal charges and punishment. Earlier she already sent a deed of divorce to him via the city's *tabularius* 'in accordance with imperial law' (κατὰ τὸν βασιλικὸν νόμον).

The case is a rare example of a woman unilaterally dissolving the marriage, with most known divorce cases of this time period being based on mutual consent.[44] As an orphan[45] without support from a parent and as survivor of marital terror—the long list of reckless behaviours and crimes is appalling[46]—the woman impresses, as she keeps resisting and fighting, willing to bring her difficult private life

---

44 See, e.g., P.Lond. 5.1712 (blaming a demon for the marriage failure made it easier for the divorcing partners, an oarsman and his wife Kyra, also to agree on many additional things connected with the divorce, e.g., that the unborn child was to be raised by the father if he paid for the childbirth; they even claim to be 'reconciled with one another'); further Rowlandson, *Women and Society*, 209. A unilateral *repudium* issued by a Christian woman of the 2nd cent. is found in Justin, Apol. 2.2.6.

45 καταφρονήσας τῆς ὀρφανίας μου.

46 Abduction; repeated rape; in response to the *repudium*, 'punishing' rape—possibly even gang rape with 'lawless men'—during several days while she was involuntarily locked up in his house (συνπαραλαβὼν μεθ' ἑαυτοῦ πλῆθος ἀνδρῶν ἀτάκτων ἀφήρπασέν με καὶ κατέκλεισεν ἐπὶ τῆς οἰκείας αὐτοῦ ἐπὶ <οὐκ(?)> ὀλίγας ἡμέρας), she emerged pregnant from this torture; stealing; repeatedly leaving her in precarious financial situations; almost killing her (ὕβρεις καὶ ζημίας ὑπέστην ἄχρις οὗ συνχωρήσουσίν (l. συγχωρήσωσίν) μοι τὸ ζῆν); threats to stir up malice (φθόνος) against her; infidelity; verbal abuse. Especially after her divorce letter the criminal side of his behaviour intensified, which probably is to be interpreted as revenge for the unilaterality of the divorce.

with all its personal details into open court.⁴⁷

To end this section on a more peaceful note, P. Lond. 5.1711/ P.Cair.Masp. 3.67310 (= the draft of the first papyrus; 566–573 C.E., Antinoopolis) is a marriage contract written up by a husband, Horouonchis, a soldier of the troops stationed in Antinoopolis and gatekeeper *(ostiarius)* of the city.⁴⁸ He and his bride Scholastikia aim for a marriage 'of mutual love' (φιλάλληλος), with him—in polite early Byzantine manner—respectfully addressing her as Your Nobility and Your Propriety (τῇ σῇ εὐ[γενείᾳ], τ]ῇ σῇ κοσμιότητι).

The contract lists positive behaviours the couple intends to display in their marital life and allows glimpses at the expectations women of elevated social status faced when defining their role. The values displayed—besides procreation and 'holy' virginity⁴⁹ of the bride—are 'support' of the wife by the husband (διαθρέψαι σε), including clothing for her 'in likeness to all those of my class and in proportion to the wealth available to me, as far as my modest means will allow'⁵⁰ and a gift of six gold coins, imperial *solidi*,⁵¹ for her to have as personal property. He vows to respect her ('no contempt in any way'),⁵² not to divorce her (except for adultery),⁵³ not to invite people into their home

---

47 Since the document is a petition for money, it may well be that some of the details were exaggerated, as Rowlandson, *Women and Society*, 209, suspects. However, the woman also petitions for a trial in court and therefore could not afford to make things up in this official document.
48 [στρατ]ι̣[ώτ]η[ς ἀριθμοῦ Ἀντι(νόου) καὶ ὀστιάριος ἀπὸ τ[ῆ]ς αὐτῆς πόλεως.
49 Τὴν σὴν σεμνὴν...παρθένειαν. The groom happily established it after having discovered it: εὑρὼν διηκόρευσα (1. διηγόρευσα).
50 ἐνδιδύσκειν καθ' ὁμοιότητα πάντων [τῶν σ]υνμετρίων μο(υ) καὶ τὸν προσόντα μοι πόρον κατὰ τὸν δυνατὸν τρόπον [τῆς ἐμῆς μετ]ριότητος.
51 For their buying power, see above; e.g., fish for 2 years and 2 months (840 days), half a pound per day.
52 ἐν μηδένι καταφρονῆσαί σο(υ).
53 Matt. 5:32. However, at least three male free and trustworthy witnesses are needed to establish such 'physical misbehaviour'" (σωματικῆς ἀταξίας).

for drinking parties if she does not like it,⁵⁴ and never to leave her marriage bed or to commit other 'indiscipline or licentiousness'⁵⁵—provided(!) the wife is 'obedient' to him (ὑπακουούσης) and shows for him 'all goodwill and sincere loving affection (πᾶσαν εὔνοιαν καὶ εἰλικρινῆ στοργήν) in all fine and useful deeds and words'.⁵⁶ She is expected to be 'subject to me (ὑποταττομέ[νης] μοι)⁵⁷ in all ways just as it befits all women of nobility to display toward their well-to-do and most beloved husbands'⁵⁸ and to avoid 'outrage/insult' (ὕβρις), 'fickleness' (ἀψικορία), or 'disdain' (καταφρόνησις), to be a 'full-time housekeeper and husband-loving' (φίλανδρος), 'in keeping with the good and prudent character/devotion/goodwill (ἀγαθῇ καὶ σώφρονι προαιρέσει) that will be displayed to you by me'.⁵⁹ As a military man, he appears rather self-confident.

However, if either one in the marriage does not keep his or her part of the deal, he or she will be sanctioned with a payment of eighteen solidi to the other.

54 This is a sort of add-on to the text—apparently upon the wife's request, after she had read his draft as basis for discussion. She also does not like to waste her time with 'inconsequential/inconsequent/inconsistent' (ἀνακόλουθος) visitors. And the husband has to write down again that he will not take other women beside her—although he had already vowed to stay faithful to her. These are interesting glimpses at her fears and concerns. These also include the husband being driven by 'fear, deceit, physical violence, fraud, and compulsion', which he in the add-ons vows to avoid (μὴ φόβῳ, μὴ δόλῳ, μὴ βίᾳ καὶ ἀπάτῃ, μήτε ἀνάγκῃ συνελαυνόμενος).
55 μηδαμῶς ἀποστῆναί με τῆς σῆς [κοίτης μη]δ᾽ ἑτέρας δραμεῖν ἀταξίας ἢ ἀσελγίας (l. ἀσελγείας).
56 ὑπακουούσης μοι καὶ φυλαττούσης μοι πᾶσαν εὔνοιαν καὶ εἰλικρινῆ στοργὴν ἐν πᾶσι καλοῖς καὶ ὀφελίμοις (l. ὠφελίμοις) ἔργοι[ς] τε κ[αὶ λόγοι]ς.
57 Cf. Clement of Alexandria (c. 200): Women 'are destined for pregnancy and housekeeping', although they are equal to men regarding the soul, virtues, self-control, and ability to become perfect Christians as well as martyrs (*Stromata* 4.8.58.2–60.1).
58 ὑποταττομέ[νης] μοι τρόποις ἅπασιν ἅτε δὴ ἀνήκει ἀπάσαι[ς εὐγενεστάταις γυναιξὶν] ἐνδείκνυσθα[ι] ε[ἰ]ς τρ[ὺ]ς ἐξαυτῶν εὐμοίρους καὶ φιλαιτάτους ἄνδ]ρας.
59 ἀκολού[θως] τῇ παρ᾽ ἐμ[οῦ δε]ιχθησομένῃ σοι ἀγαθῇ καὶ σώφρονι προαιρέσει.

Magic and Paganism

Christianity did not uproot paganism entirely, as numerous papyri document. Christian amulets were popular, such as an amulet invoking the 'ever-virgin' and 'holy god-bearing' Mary (P.Bon. 1.9; unknown origin, probably fourth cent.) or Christian love charms (e.g. SB 14.11534; third/fourth cent., unknown Egyptian origin, Christian names).[60]

Palladius (*Historia Lausiaca* 17.6–9; c. 420 C.E.) in his Egyptian desert narrates that a love-crazed man ordered a love-charm from a magician to make a Christian married freeborn woman fall in love with him—or at least to make the husband throw her out, so that he could take advantage of her misery. The magician allegedly achieved the latter, at least partially—and here the legend starts: The magician created the illusion that the wife changed into an animal, and when the husband came home he saw her lying on his bed naked[61]—but as a mare. It got worse, for three days she didn't eat bread—nor hay, with the husband fearing she would die. So, he took her to hermits who lived with St Makarios in the desert. Luckily the Christian holy man could release her from the equine spell. However, he admonished the wife to attend communion regularly, explaining, 'These things happened to you because for five weeks you had not attended the myster-

---

60   For more material, see De Bruyn and Dijkstra, 'Greek Amulets and Formularies', 163–216; Jones, *New Testament Texts*. Often these amulets contain Psalm verses, the Lord's Prayer, or the incipits of the Gospels (see, e.g., *PSI* 6.719). However, not all texts categorised as amulets today were magic. P. Oxy. 76.5073 (c. 300 C.E., containing Mark 1:1), e.g., often was identified as an amulet because it has no fold marks and the citation from Isaiah in Mark 1:1, 'I send my angel before your face', taken out of Mark's context, sounds like a comforting assurance for the readers and therefore could qualify as magically protective text. However, missing fold marks and a therefore possibly rolled-up papyrus do not automatically imply that it was worn around the neck. More importantly, the first line introducing Mark 1:1, 'Know well the beginning of the Gospel and see', sounds more like a teacher's homework assignment (in catechesis?) to read the beginning of Mark's book thoroughly or even memorise it. Was the paper a memory aid in the pocket (or on the wall) of a catechumen? See further Naldini, *Il Cristianesimo in Egitto*, 155; De Troyer and Arzt-Grabner, 'Ancient Jewish and Christian Amulets', 5–46.

61   Later in the story: Καὶ εὐλογήσας ὕδωρ καὶ ἀπὸ κορυφῆς ἐπιχέας αὐτῇ γυμνῇ ἐπηύξατο while she still looked like a horse for those who were not as holy as Makarios who only saw a naked lady (17.9.3).

ies.' Thus—and this is the point of the story—in popular Christian opinion, regular communion and worship had apotropaic power immunising against spells.

P.Oxy. 8.1151 (fifth cent.?, Oxyrhynchus) was folded, with a cord tied around it. It most probably was worn around the neck as a Christian amulet against pagan magic that had caused recurring 'fevers and every kind of chill' in a woman named Joannia. As is expected in an amulet, in her prayer to God Joannia talks about herself in the third person. (1) The papyrus starts with a *spell* addressed directly to the wicked spirit as an exorcism. 'Flee, hateful spirit! Christ pursues (διώκει) you, the Son of God and the Holy Spirit have overtaken you' (προέλαβέν σε).

(2) Only after the spell, *prayers* follow, first to God ('deliver from all evil your servant Joannia') and then to Christ, containing Biblical and liturgical reminiscences. The healing of John 5:2–9 is alluded to ('O God of the pool at the Sheep Gate'), and the quotation of the incipit of the Gospel of John (1:1,3; not v.2) recalls the divine creative power through the Word (δι' αὐτοῦ). Christ accordingly is characterised as 'healing every sickness and every infirmity'. She prays, 'O Lord Christ, Son and Word of the living God, heal and watch over your servant Joannia too' (ἴασαι καὶ ἐπίσκεψαι καὶ τὴν δούλην σου). The 'too' is of interest. The Biblical reminiscences commit God/Christ to their own Biblical words (in the sense of: What you did there, please, also do it to me).

(3) To further support her prayer, Joannia calls attention to *interceding prayers* (εὐχ[αῖ]ς) of Mary, the archangels, and all saints, particularly John, the 'glorious apostle, evangelist and theologian', who is listed first among the saints mentioned by name. John's Gospel seems to be Joannia's favourite Biblical book, as the two references to John 1 and 5 already indicated.[62]

(4) However, Joannia not only relies on prayers, that is, on the

---

62 Interceding or vicarious prayers also on P.Lond. 6.1926 (unknown Egyptian origin, mid-fourth cent.): A sick lady, Valeria, implores an anchorite to pray for healing from her breathlessness, as she believes that 'ascetics and devotees' pray more effectively. To keep the man busy she also asks for prayers for her two daughters and her husband, who, together with the entire household, sends greetings. She in turn vows to pray for 'the honoured father'.

healing power of the Creator God (John 1:3). She also appears to rely on magical energy inherent in some *matter* carried on her feverish body. The material presence of written-down holy Biblical and liturgical words, of four crosses drawn on the papyrus, of a spell penned in ink and of written invocations of the Trinity—this material presence around the neck suggests that she also hoped for a healing effect of magically charged matter—which is a signature feature of amulets. It stands to reason that she attributed healing energy to the Biblical text bits themselves: for her, written down in ink on the papyrus, they probably infused healing power to the object around the neck. Today's science knows that placebos generate real positive effects.[63] To criticize this woman for mixing Christian and magical practices would be hasty. In part, Christian contact relicts of martyrs' bones replaced the amulets in late antiquity[64] without, however, replacing them entirely.

(5) The last sentence also has a magical touch, showing that apotropaic power was attributed to the divine name itself, because it 'frightens' adversary spirits: 'O Lord God, in my interest (middle voice) I (finally Joannia talks in the first person) have invoked your name that is awesome, super glorious and causes fear to the enemies. Amen' (τὸ ὄνομά σου ἐπικαλεσά[μ]ην τὸ θαυμαστὸν καὶ ὑπερένδοξον καὶ φοβερὸν τοῖς ὑπεναντίοις. ἀμήν. †).

P.Oxy. 6.924 (fourth cent.) presents a prayer—again in the third person—of a woman named Aría to ward off all kinds of fever chills from her. The prayer expresses confidence: 'This you graciously will do completely according to your will (ταῦτα εὐ[μενῶ]ς πράξεις ὅλως κατὰ τὸ θέλημά σου) and according to her faith (πίστιν), because she is a servant of the living God.' Thus, the text commits God to God's graciousness and kindness, but it also commits Aría herself to faithfulness to God (as a kind of bargaining chip?). At the end 'Abrasax', a holy name of the Basilidians, can be read, which frequently occurs in Christian magic papyri but also in ecclesiastical writings referencing ideas consid-

---

63 See e.g. Kaptchuk and Miller, 'Placebo Effects', 1–9.
64 See, e.g., Lampe, 'Traces'.

ered 'gnostic'.[65] The papyrus therefore was probably carried on the body to protect against illness. Was it a charm of a Basilidian woman?[66]

At the end, it may be appropriate to commemorate two courageous and steadfast Alexandrian women who, on the eve of the so-called Decian 'persecution' (249/250 C.E.), resisted the pressure to become contaminated with pagan cult and lost their lives: *Quinta*, who was forced to worship at a pagan temple, and the πρεσβῦτις *Apollonia*, a παρθένος (possibly an apotactic nun like the παρθένος Thaesis above), who was pushed to say 'impieties' (τὰ τῆς ἀσεβείας κηρύγματα).[67]

Conclusion

Although some women we encountered were eager to read and exchange books, only one female Christian διδάσκαλος surfaces in the Egyptian papyri (more appear to be evidenced in literary sources). The one πρεσβύτερα in the papyri and mummy tablets, most likely leading a congregation, was paralleled by other presbyteresses in the literary sources. They were not necessarily Montanists. However, they were contrasted by people holding that women needed to become male to be complete and equal to men. Yet, even when women, in their femininity, were considered equal, within their marriages they nonetheless faced the expectation to be housekeepers and subordinated to their husbands.

However, several women lived independently from men as unmarried females, protected by a religious aura: they lived as autactic religious women, μοναχαί/'solitaires without children and husbands,

---

65 E.g. Hippol. *Haer.* 7.26.6 ('the great Archon of these [the Basilidians] is Abrasax'); Epiph. *Pan.* 1.264.1 (Abrasax is a 'holy name' according to the Basilidians, because its numeric value is 365, the number of heavens in the Basilidian system).
66 Thus Grenfell and Hunt (ed.), *The Oyrhynchus Papyri VI*, 289f (nr. 924).
67 Letter of Dionysios of Alexandria, quoted in Eusebius *H.E.* 6.41.1–7. Another female martyr of the Diocletian persecution in Alexandria may have been a Thekla (see the Coptic legendary *Martyrdom of Paese and Thekla* (9th-cent. manuscript; ed. Reymond–Barns). πρεσβῦτις means "aged" and not "elder", pace Eisen 123 (see note 4, above), where the equation πρεσβῦτις = πρεσβυτερίδας is erroneous.

dropping their patronymic, and showing no interest in joining a convent. Those we met were probably city-dwelling and had their own belongings, making their own money, for example by renting out some of their real estate property. The μοναχαὶ ἀποτακτικαί represented a socially accepted model, even respected by clergy, that gave females who wanted to remain single a chance to live a self-determined and self-paced life without dependency on men. The apotactic lifestyle allowed for individuality and freedom to handle one's own, legal, and economic affairs by oneself.

The model was open to more or less well-to-do women who had their own means of financial support. Nuns in convents, on the other hand, even when poor, could count on support by the communal possessions of the convent, trading this support for dependencies on authorities and conventual rules. The difference between conventual nuns and autotactic religious women may need further large-scale exploration of sources. The apotactic model also was open, of course, for women *working* for their income. Future research may evidence them more clearly.

In one case, a traumatic childhood in a broken family led a woman to become an autotactic μοναχή. Difficult family situations abounded—from grave, even criminal, abuse by husbands to infidelity to an abandoning mother to divorce. Several times marriage contracts and contractual sanctions attempted to reign in reckless husbands or women asked for clerical mediation in conflicts. The abused women took things into their own hands by writing down the problems and looking for solutions. Those who silently suffered are not reflected in the papyri.

We read an authentic *repudium*, drawn up by a father of a wife who still lived under his *patria potestas*. But we also witnessed the *repudium* drawn up by a brave and self-determined wife against the husband's will, a rare case of unilateral divorce whereas most divorces were consensual. This woman makes an impression, as she kept resisting and fighting, willing to bring the details of her difficult private life into open court. Two other strong-willed and self-determined women, daughter and mother, resisted an arranged marriage the daughter detested, fighting bullying male relatives.

On a positive note, married women could have their own possessions, manage their own landed property, own slaves, and raise foster children besides their own offspring. The early Byzantine society and its officials held up certain standards for the treatment of wives, and the example of a marriage contract—to which the bride had contributed—voiced positive marriage values—resolutions such as mutual affection and mutual emotional support and benevolence as well as mutual responsibilities, including material support and care by the husband, not just female subordination and housekeeping.

When marriage ended by death life could become dire. Widows without supporting families became dependent on the charity system of the churches. We met a widow freezing in January who received a coat from a church charity manager. Others received portions of wine, a basic food, from their church.

We stood at the beds of fever-chilled women who used amulets to ward off evil spirits causing illness. Regular attendance at communion also was believed to have apotropaic effects. Other women, however, withstood the temptation to use magic practices or become contaminated by pagan cult. In this resistance the bravest even lost their lives as martyrs.

Thus, a diversity of female lives was mirrored in the sources. However, we gained only few insights into women's belief systems. Yes, a woman we met went to church even on Saturdays, and, as we saw, women were expected to attend communion regularly. A woman could be praised as 'most pious and law-loving'.[68] Women studied Jewish/Christian books beyond the borderlines of our known canon(s), they trusted clergy when asking them to mediate in personal conflict situations,[69] they prayed and some relied on magically charged amulets, but we have no testimonies similar, for example, to the logia of the Montanist prophetesses.[70] What did the mentioned female Christian

---

68 IGA 5.48, March 409, a woman's Christian tombstone in Alexandria.
69 Future research may want to investigate how often *men* were inclined to ask clergy to mediate in conflicts.
70 For these and their deep involvement with Biblical traditions, see especially Mader, *Montanistische Orakel*.

διδάσκαλος teach?

The apotropaic use of amulets and of Biblical texts such as John 1 demonstrated a need for protection and thus the insecurity of the lives and times. Above all, the personal human aspects were in the foreground, timeless suffering, hopes, angers, and affections.

Peter Lampe
University of Heidelberg

Bibliography

Barratte, F and B. Boyaval   'Catalogue des étiquettes de momies du musée du Louvre, IV', *Cahiers de Recherches de l'Institut de Papyrologie et d'Égyptologie de Lille* 5 (1979), 237–339.

Blumell. L. H. and T. A. Wayment (ed.)   *Christian Oxyrhynchus: Texts, Documents, and Sources* (Waco, TX: Baylor University Press, 2015).

Broux, Y and W. Clarysse   'Would You Name Your Child after a Celebrity? Arsinoe, Berenike, Kleopatra, Laodike and Stratonike in the Greco-Roman East', *Zeitschrift für Papyrologie und Epigraphik* 200 (2016), 347–62.

Eisen, U. E.   *Amtsträgerinnen im frühen Christentum: Epigraphische und literarische Studien* (FKD 61; Göttingen: Vandenhoeck & Ruprecht, 1996); ET: *Women Officeholders in Early Christianity: Epigraphical and Literary Studies* (Collegeville: Liturgical Press, 2000).

Elm, S.   *'Virgins of God': The Making of Asceticism in Late Antiquity* (Oxford: Clarendon, 1994).

De Bruyn, T. S. and J. H. F. Dijkstra   'Greek Amulets and Formularies from Egypt Containing Christian Elements: A Checklist of Papyri, Parchments, Ostraka, and Tablets', *The Bulletin of the American Society of Papyrologists* 48 (2011), 163–216.

De Troyer, K. and P. Arzt-Grabner   'Ancient Jewish and Christian Amulets and How Magical They Are', *BN.NF* 176 (2018), 5–46.

Grenfell, B. P. and A. S. Hunt (eds.)   *The Oxyrhynchus Papyri VI* (London: Egypt Exploration Fund, 1908).

Horsley, G. H. R.   *New Documents Illustrating Early Christianity, 4: A Review of the Greek Inscriptions and Papyri Published in 1979* (North Ryde, NSW: Macquarie University Ancient History Documentary Research Centre, 1987).

Jones, B. C.   *New Testament Texts on Greek Amulets from Late Antiquity* (Library of NT Studies 554; London/New York: Bloomsbury T&T Clark, 2016).

Judge, E. A.	'Fourth-Century Monasticism in the Papyri', in R. S. Bagnall (ed.), *Proceedings of the XVI International Congress of Papyrology* (American Studies in Papyrology 23; Chico, CA: Scholars, 1981), 613–20.
Kaptchuk, T. J. and F. G. Miller	'Placebo Effects in Medicine', *The New England Journal of Medicine* 373 (July, 2015), 1–9. <http://programinplacebostudies.org/wp-content/uploads/2015/07/PerspectivesNEJM-KaptchukMiller.pdf> [accessed July 2022].
Lampe, Peter	'Traces of Peter Veneration in Roman Archaeology', in H. K. Bond/L. W. Hurtado (ed.), *Peter in Early Christianity* (Grand Rapids, MI/Cambridge, UK: Eerdmans, 2015) 273–317 (http://doi.org/10.11588/heidok.00025161).
Loening, E.	*Geschichte des deutschen Kirchenrechts I* (Reprinted; Berlin: de Gruyter, 2014).
Mader, H. E.	'Frühchristliche Theologinnen im Profil: Maximillas und Quintillas Visionen für die Kirche', in O. Lehtipuu and S. Petersen (eds.), *Antike christliche Apokryphen: Marginalisierte Texte des frühen Christentums* (Die Bibel und die Frauen 3; Stuttgart: Kohlhammer, 2020), 240–54.
Mader, H. E.	*Montanistische Orakel und kirchliche Opposition: Der frühe Streit zwischen den phrygischen »neuen Propheten« und dem Autor der vorepiphanischen Quelle als biblische Wirkungsgeschichte des 2. Jh. n. Chr.* (Göttingen: Vandenhoeck & Ruprecht, 2012).
Mango, C.	*Byzantium: The Empire of New Rome* (Collingdale, PA: Diane, 2006).
Naldini, M.	*Il Cristianesimo in Egitto: Lettere private nei papiri dei secoli II-IV* (Florence: Le Monnier, 1968).
Petersen, S.	'Maria. Magdalena wird männlich, oder: Antike Geschlechtertransformationen', in C. Gerber, S. Petersen, and W. Weiße (eds.), *Unbeschreiblich weiblich? Neue Fragen zur Geschlechterdifferenz in den Religionen* (Theol. Frauenforschung in Europa 26; Münster: LIT, 2011), 117–40.
Rowlandson, J. et al. (eds.)	*Women and Society in Greek and Roman Egypt: A Sourcebook* (Cambridge: Cambridge University Press, 1998).

Tabbernee, W.   *Montanist Inscriptions and Testimonia: Epigraphic Sources Illustrating the History of Montanism* (North American Patristic(s) Society Patristic Monograph Series 16; Macon, GA: Mercer University Press, 1997).

Tibiletti, G.   *Le lettere private nei papiri graeci des III e IV secolo d. C.: Tra paganesimo e cristianesima* (Milano: Vita e Pensiero, 1979).

Raised in Pieces:
Resurrection and Disability in the Ezekiel Cycle of the Dura-Europos Synagogue

Isaac T. Soon

Abstract

This chapter asks what the depiction of Ezekiel 37 on the walls of the Dura synagogue can tell us about conceptions of resurrection and disability among the Jewish community at Dura. Bodily resurrection is a common theme among ancient Jewish literature, and while text is a useful medium for conveying conceptions of revivification and life after death, it is not the only medium available. Ancient iconography and visual media can convey aesthetic and physical aspects of resurrection otherwise absent in ancient literature. This study argues that not only does the portrayal of The Vision of Dry Bones at Dura depict eschatological resurrection, but that disability is an integral part of understanding the process and dynamics of revivification in the mural.

1. Introduction

In 1932, excavations at Dura-Europos, a small Roman garrison on the banks of the Euphrates river, uncovered a synagogue on the southwestern wall to the city. In the third century, Roman backfilling of the synagogue with sand in preparation for Sasanian incursions froze the building in time, as the city was abandoned in 256 C.E. once the Neo-Persian army sacked the city and deported its inhabitants.

The wall paintings from this synagogue at Dura-Europos preserve some of the most exquisite Jewish art from the ancient Near Eastern world. The frescoes feature a variety of scenes from the Hebrew Bible, as many as fifty-eight different episodes.¹ Among others, there is the ark of the covenant in the temple of Dagon, the sustaining of the Israelite camp by waters in the wilderness, Esther and Mordecai, the drawing of Moses out of the waters in Egypt, the anointing of David by Samuel, and the crossing of the Reed Sea. One of the largest set of images, spanning at least twenty-five feet across, is the Ezekiel cycle that portrays the Valley of Dry Bones episode from Ezekiel 37 and the beheading of the prophet.

This short chapter asks what the depiction of Ezekiel 37 on the walls of the Dura synagogue has to tell us about conceptions of resurrection and disability among the Jewish community at Dura. Bodily resurrection is a common theme among ancient Jewish literature, and while text is a useful medium for conveying conceptions of revivification and life after death, it is not the only medium available. Ancient iconography and visual media can convey aesthetic and physical aspects of resurrection otherwise absent in ancient literature. It is a pleasure to offer this chapter as a tribute to Jim Harrison, who has spent his career demonstrating the immense exegetical and historical value of putting the textual and the archaeological, word and image, in conversation with one another.

2. Ezekiel 37 at the Synagogue in Dura-Europos

On the north wall of the synagogue (NC 1) we find two panels dedicated to the events in Ezekiel 37 (Section A and B), depicting three scenes in total. Scholars are virtually unanimous that this cycle concerns Ezekiel 37, but M. H. Ben-Shammi once argued that the cycles instead depicted haggadic traditions about events after the destruction of the first temple.² The first scene depicts the prophet Ezekiel dressed in Parthian trousers and a flared jacket interacting with a hand that

---

1 Rutgers, 'Diaspora Synagogues', 80. Many thanks to Camille Leon Angelo, Lisa Brody, Jennifer Baird, Sari Fein, Sarah Porter, and Yonatan Miller for help with finding resources for this article.
2 Ben-Shammai, 'Destruction', 93–97. The many correspondences between Ezekiel 37 and the fresco (the assembling of bodies, infusing of breath/spirit, the reformulation of the tribes of Israel) show otherwise.

appears from the heavens, the divine hand of God. The divine hand first holds Ezekiel by the hair and drops him on a plain (cf. Ezek. 37:1). Based on the Talmudic connection between Ezekiel 37 and Daniel 3:1 (בקעת דורא, 'plain/valley of Dura') in b. Sanh. 92b, some interpreters have suggested that the Jews of Dura understood 'the valley' of dry bones to be the location of their very city, and thus why the scene takes up such an enormous amount of wall space.[3]

The prophet is in multiple different positions in the artist's attempt to portray progression across a static two-dimensional image. That multiple scenes are collapsed and amalgamated together is not common to the Dura synagogue. For example, the Elijah cycle on the opposite wall clearly demarcates each scene through 'regular bands of divisions'.[4] As Goodenough remarks, the Ezekiel cycle is only one of three that have this continuous visual depiction, the two others being the exposure of Moses on the river Nile and the exodus from Egypt. Although the scenes could in theory be read from left to right or right to left, the progression from left to right coheres with the progression in Ezekiel 37 and is the approached accepted by the vast majority of scholars.[5]

As Ezekiel interacts with God the embroidery on his jacket evolves, first appearing on the flared section of his jacket below the waistline and then on the arm lengths and then finally on the part of the jacket across his breast.[6] Kraeling notes that the designs initially covered more of Ezekiel's tunic but later faded, and that such designs had an analogy with the depiction of Esther's husband Ahasuerus also at Dura.[7] There may be a connection to Ezekiel 16:10 where God describes clothing

---

3 André Grabar, 'Le Thème Religieux', 152–54; Riesenfeld, *Resurrection*, 30. Whether or not the Dura community knew of these rabbinic traditions is impossible to know, but if they did it would make sense why they portrayed this event in their city's synagogue.
4 Goodenough, *Symbolism*, 179.
5 For an example of scholarship that reads the account from right to left, see Rajak, 'Dura-Europos Synagogue', 151; 'Synagogue Paintings', 106.
6 Wischner-Bernstein once made the implausible suggestion that these three parallel depictions of Ezekiel were three different men, Judah, Benjamin, and Levi, despite the fact that they look virtually the same other than the difference in embroidery. Wischnitzer-Bernstein, 'Resurrection', 48.
7 Kraeling, *Synagogue*, 182 n. 694.

Jerusalem with embroidered cloth.

At Ezekiel's feet are numerous severed hands, feet, and heads on the ground. Beside Ezekiel is a mountain that has been split in two. Attempts to definitively classify this mountain have been unconvincing, but a relatively common interpretation is that it is the Mount of Olives.[8] There are pieces of a building on the mountain but no one has been able to identify firmly what it might be.[9] On one side of the mountain, a dark chasm appears to be spitting out more body parts (heads, arms, and feet). On the other side, the bodies of three men/youths lie on their backs.

In the next section, Ezekiel stands near to the bodies of the three men that have now been removed from the mountain. Three winged spirits hover over the bodies, while a fourth cups her hands around the head of one of the lifeless bodies, presumably about to breathe life into the man's body.[10] These have been identified as depictions of Psyche-figures, like the goddess of the soul. See for example the mosaics of 'Psyche and Cupid-Eros' from Smandağı (Hatay Archaeological Museum) and 'Eros and Psyche' at Pompeii from the House of Terenzio Neo, both of which depict Psyche with the same shape of butterfly/moth-type wings, a common feature of Psyche portrayals.[11]

In the final scene Ezekiel presents a host of ten now living persons, often understood as the ten lost tribes of Israel.[12] All of them, including the prophet, are clothed in robes and are wearing sandals. The living persons are in three rows (3, 3, 4) and three of the four in the front row

---

8   E.g. Bossu, 'Une Prophétie', 518.
9   Cf. Goodenough, *Symbolism*, 183; Kraeling, *Synagogue*, 191; Kraeling, 'Meaning', 13.
10 For a discussion about whether they are about the enter the bodies or breathe into the bodies see Kraeling, *Synagogue*, 186–7.
11 Moon, 'Nudity and Narrative', 608. Landsberger argues that these are not in fact Psyches but Jewish angels and the artist adapted what was a common image for spirits but understood it from a Jewish cosmological point of view. Landsberger, 'Origin', 249.
12 Wischnitzer-Bernstein, 'Resurrection', 47; Block, *Ezekiel*, 391. Kraeling is hesitant to limit it to the ten tribes because of what he views as Ezekiel's emphasis on the unity of Israel and Judah. Kraeling, 'Meaning', 17. Goodenough suggests that the ten raised men are symbolic of ten pillars of the inner shrine of the temple depicted on the western wall adjacent to the Ezekiel cycle. Goodenough, *Symbolism*, 194.

have scrolls tucked into their robes. Next to the prophet lie left-over body parts, arms, legs, and a head.

One of the key problems of the presentation of Ezekiel 37 at the Dura Synagogue is the portrayal of the reformulation of the bodies. Goodenough surmises, 'The "bones" have perplexed all commentators, for they are already covered with sinews, flesh, and skin, so that they could not have "rattled", as they do in the biblical text when Ezekiel prophesies to them'.[13] It is, however, first important to note that it is not the bones that rattle in Ezekiel 37:7 but the ground itself, for the text implies an earthquake (רעש; cf. OG: σεισμός). Secondly, despite Goodenough's close observation of many details of the text he does not notice the pieces of rib bones at the base of the mountain in the initial scene.[14] Four pieces of rib (evident by their curvature and length) lie at the base of the mountain, possibly an allusion to the formulation of Eve in Genesis 2:21.[15] So there is a progression from bones to enfleshed body parts just as in Ezekiel 37:7-8.[16]

Goodenough argues that the omission of bones from the scene can be found in early Christian art, and he cites two parallels. One is from a third to fourth century C.E glass disc or plate found in Cologne now housed at the British Museum (S.317), and numerous Roman Christian sarcophagi that supposedly portray the Ezekiel scene.[17] For the sarcophagi, Goodenough refers to Vatican inv. 31450, Vatican inv.

---

13 Goodenough, *Symbolism*, 181. See also Kraeling, 'Meaning', 12.
14 These were identified as early as Kraeling, 'Meaning', 13 and recognised by his younger brother, although Kraeling assigned it to a different section: Kraeling, *Synagogue* (Reprint), 192 n.752.
15 Philonenko, 'De Qoumrân', 6.
16 Kraeling is confused as to why the bones appear in what he designates a middle portion of the piece (adhering to a strict left to right reading of the frescoes). Kraeling, *Synagogue* (reprint), 192 n.752. But it may be that the action is multi-directional in Section A, Ezekiel's placement in the valley and call by God to speak to the bones coincides with the mountain opening up and the bones coming out and then becoming enfleshed; the action for Ezekiel moves from left to right, while the transformation of bones to body parts moves from right to left.
17 An image can be found online at: https://www.britishmuseum.org/collection/object/H_S-317. Goodenough, *Symbolism*, 181-82. A similar comparison has been done by Kuniya, 'Iconographical Study', 67-86, although despite my best efforts I have not been able to access it.

63130, and something similar to Vatican inv. 31537.[18] None of the sarcophagi images refers to Ezekiel, however, and more likely depict Jesus raising either the widow's son or Lazarus (see also Vatican inv. 63149). The glass disc from Cologne, however, does look very similar to the depiction of body parts in the Dura Ezekiel cycle even though it is also possible that it is a depiction of Moses striking the rock in the wilderness (cf. Exod. 17:1–7; Num. 20:1–13) or perhaps even the closing of the sea upon the Egyptian armies. There is a head, two legs, and possibly two hands (the glass is damaged and faded terribly, so it is difficult to tell). While the artist for the glass was limited by space—the depiction of Ezekiel only occupies one eighth of a part of the whole piece—the artist of the Dura synagogue did not have the same spatial limitations.

3. The Valley of Dry Bones as a Representation of Eschatological Resurrection

Apart from a few exceptions, Hebrew Bible scholars understand the initial historical meaning of the Valley of Dry Bones in Ezekiel 37:1–14 to be concerned about the restoration of the nation of Israel after the exile in the sixth century B.C.E.[19] By the Second Temple period, however, Ezekiel 37 could readily be understood by ancient Jewish readers to be concerned about eschatological resurrection of the dead, for example, fragments from the Qumran Scrolls like 4QPseudo-Ezekiel (e.g., 4Q386 and 4Q388).[20] Scholarship on this passage often uses the language of 'resurrection' alongside 'revivification' to speak about humans who were dead coming back to life.[21]

---

18   For the latter image see the image that Goodenough refers to in Giuseppe Wilpert, *I Sarcofagi*, CXII.
19   For exceptional views, see Höffken, 'Beobachtungen', 305–17; Bartelmus, 'Ez 37,1–14', 366–89.
20   Dimant, 'Resurrection', 532; Schöpflin, 'Revivification', 82.
21   In this essay, I limit our understanding of resurrection to this plain sense and not to other extensions of resurrection such as the glorification and or translation of human corporeal bodies into heavenly *pneuma* as in the early Jesus movement (e.g., Paul in 1 Corinthians 15:35–50). On this see Engberg-Pedersen, *Cosmology*, 8–74; Thiessen, *Paul*, 135–54.

The close connection that the Ezekiel cycle at Dura has with the scriptural text complicates the interpretation of revivified bodies. The understanding of the initial textual significance of Ezekiel 37 to be about historic Israel obscures what the Dura images might convey about late antique Jewish beliefs about bodily resurrection. Thus, interpreters have had to choose between either a historical explanation or an eschatological one.[22] Given the association between Ezekiel 37 and resurrection in 4QPseudo-Ezekiel, Daniel 12:1–2, and LXX Isaiah in the late second temple period, we are not forced, however, to choose only one option.[23] The Valley of Dry Bones at Dura can concern both the historical restoration of the nation of Israel as well as current beliefs about coming eschatological resurrection.[24] As Tessa Rajak notes, the revivification in this scene 'can scarcely fail to have a personal significance over and above any possible symbolic meaning'.[25] In other words, the initial symbolic meaning of the synagogue depiction of Ezekiel 37 does not cancel out the eschatological one.

A puzzling feature of the final scene of the dry bones episode also points to the legitimacy of an eschatological reading of the fresco. Among the ten men revived by the hand of God and Ezekiel are remaining body parts, four legs, two hands, and a head.[26] If the cycle were only about the national restoration of Israel, why are there bodies left unrevived? Surely this cannot be representative of Judah or Benjamin.[27] Instead, the presence of dismembered limbs suggests that what the artist has in mind is the eschatological resurrection of the

22 As noted by Bossu, 'Une Prophétie', 509–13.
23 The LXX translator for Isa. 26:19 and 1QIsa^a understands the resurrection of the dead to be a future occurrence, signally an eschatological expectation of future revivification. Blenkinsopp, *Isaiah 1–39*, 370; Dimant (ed.), *Qumran*, 36.
24 So Riesenfeld, *Resurrection*, 28–9; Bossu, 'Une Prophétie', 513.
25 Rajak, 'Synagogue Paintings', 106.
26 Assuming a normal body, the number of limbs corresponds to more than a single corpse as suggested by Grabar, 'Le Thème Religieux', 153.
27 Goodenough, *Symbolism*, 194.

righteous but not the resurrection of the wicked.[28]

One has to ask, if the Ezekiel panels are not concerned with the mechanics of actual bodily resurrection instead of merely the symbolic resurrection of the Israelite nation, then why has the artist expanded and changed the details of physical re-assemblage? If it was merely about following the textual *Vorlage*—and its symbolic meaning—then the artist could simply have connected bones with bones to make skeletons (Ezek. 37:7), added sinews and flesh (37:8), and finally breath (37:10). Instead, there are bones, as noted above, but the majority of the 'bones' are dismembered limbs and heads that somehow are joined together and become bodies. What is strange, however, is that among the body parts there are only hands and feet and heads. There are no torsos, despite there being rib cage bones and eventually 'whole' bodies (more on this below). Are we to assume the limbs coughed up from the open mountain (cf. the 'graves' in Ezek. 37:12) join to these rib bones and then sinew, flesh, and skin are added? Or is something else the case? There is something happening here that betrays an intentional and particular understanding of the mechanics of bodily resurrection, so much so that it alters Ezekiel 37's conception of the reformulation and revivification of human bodies. It is to the transformation of these bodies that we now turn.

4. The Elimination of Disability in Resurrection

What do the mechanics of bodily resurrection depicted on the Dura synagogue walls tell us about what this particular ancient Jewish community believed about disability and resurrected bodies? Disability is a cultural phenomena that is a product of de-normalising people with

---

28 Bossu, 'Une Prophétie', 520. Kraeling suggests that these *disjecta membra* are 'a device of the artist intended to remind us that those restored to their homeland are brought up out of their graves, according to Ezek. 37:12-13, and thus to make sure that the scene is understood as a continuation of those that have gone before'. Kraeling, *Synagogue*, 193. He denies, however, that this depiction is meant to 'distinguish between the resurrection of the righteous and the eternal death of the wicked', but this cannot be excluded and is not mutually exclusive from his interpretation that the cycle emphasises bodily continuity between the bodies that died at the bodies that are raised.

bodies that differ from aesthetic and/or functional ideals and norms established by a particular society. The discourse of disability is not alien to ancient Jewish discussions of resurrection. As Jon Levenson has pointed out, one problem that the rabbis in the Talmud tried to resolve was the issue of whether those with disabilities (e.g. those with blindness, people with mobility impairments, those with speech impairments) will be resurrected in the same condition.[29] The scriptural discrepancy arises from Jeremiah 31:8 and Isaiah 35:6, the former which suggests disabilities are retained in the eschaton and the latter which suggests that disabilities are removed/healed.[30] The theological problem is bodily consistency. If humans with disabilities are resurrected without disabilities then they are not raised as the same person but if they are raised with disabilities then why does a text like Isaiah 35:6 expect them to be healed?[31]

This discussion about disability and resurrection may seem irrelevant to the Ezekiel images at the Dura synagogue because disability is not pictured explicitly. Putting aside the problematic assumption that all disabilities are visible, we are not able to tell if any of the key characters represented have a particular disability or not. Ezekiel, the Psyche, and the ten raised men all appear to be nondisabled. Just because impairment is not imaged, however, does not mean that the discourse of disability is absent.

Since the telic nature of the scene is toward resurrected bodies it is fair to understand the bodies of the ten raised men to be in some sense an ideal form. Whereas they were dead before they are now alive, and this aliveness as opposed to deadness is an ideal as well. There are some other aspects of these idealised bodies to note. The first is that, as Wischnitzer-Berstein points out, there are only men who are raised.[32] Resurrected bodies are male bodies. The second is that unlike the re-formed corpses lying on the ground which await the wind of the Psyches the ten raised men have 'breath' in them. Their eyes are open,

29 Levenson, *Resurrection*, 225.
30 See the discussion in b. Sanh. 91b.
31 Löwinger, 'Die Auferstehung', 77.
32 Wischnitzer-Bernstein, 'Resurrection', 50.

they can see, and presumably they can worship God, as suggested by their raised hands upward.[33] The other important feature is that these are unmutilated persons, that is, in contrast to the body parts strewn across the valley both at their feet and at the feet of Ezekiel their bodies are assembled. In context of the trajectory toward resurrection, the Valley of Dry Bones depicts the elimination of fragmentation, mutilation, dismemberment, and presents a resurrected human as one with two hands, two feet, head, body, and even clothing. This movement from the fragmented to the put-together, the naked to the clothed and thus the 'barbaric' to the 'civilised', denotes the momentum toward resurrected bodies as the human ideal and the elimination of disability from such bodies. The Ezekiel cycle at Dura depicts human disability as absent from the final stage of resurrection.

At the same time, although it is not explicitly a part of the end goal, disability is very much a part of the resurrection process in the Ezekiel mural. The artist chooses orphan body parts and human heads as key transition points for persons on the way to a resurrection. So although disabilities appear to be non-existent or eliminated from resurrected bodies, disability is nevertheless an integral part of the stages of revivification. Its function in the Ezekiel scenes of the Dura Europos synagogue is to show the liminality of the corpses. Death and disability are synonymous.

For the unrighteous who remain unresurrected—a situation alluded to by the remaining head and limbs at the feet of the ten men—they persist both in death and a state of disrepair. From the perspective of the resurrected person as ideal, their bodies remain fragmented, mutilated, and dismembered—disconnected from the visual

---

33 Bossu, 'Une Prophétie', 522–23. This is how the Rabbi Eliezer as portrayed in the Talmud understands the resurrected people of Ezekiel 37 (b. Sanh. 92b). Levenson argues that this shows the rabbis understood Ezekiel's historical portrayal of the resurrection in the Valley of Dry Bones as temporary. Levenson, *Resurrection*, 163. If the vision is symbolic of Israel's restoration, however, but the bodies are only revived temporarily does not this anticipate the fall and death of Israel again? Unless Levenson thinks Ezekiel's initial vision is about God's continual restoration of Israel despite death and not a one-time event, this interpretation is inconsistent.

depiction of wholeness, from breath, and thus life as well. While the righteous humans who are assembled only experience the disability as a temporary liminal period, the unrighteous in their disabled and dismembered state exist in perpetual liminality.

Is such a state existence at all? The Dura synagogue mural presents a perplexing contradiction. There is one other figure in the Dura Ezekiel cycle that is both living and dismembered. The right hand of God appears five times in the cycle, four times in Section A and once in Section B. It is evident that these are depictions of God's right hand because the artist differentiates between the palm side of the right hand by emphasising the thumb line, and when they emphasise the backside of the hand, fingernails are present. Two out of the five times, God's hand extends beyond the border of the piece and looks attached to a further body. This mirrors the depiction of the hand of God elsewhere in the Dura synagogue, for example in the images of Moses and the burning bush, the exodus and the crossing of the Reed Sea, as well as Elijah's revivification of the widow's son—all of which are miraculous events. But in the other three instances of the Ezekiel cycle, God's hand is dismembered from the rest of his body, and the artist has drawn a clear line demarcating the end of God's forearms and wrist. In these instances, his hand looks exactly like the dismembered hands in the Valley, save for the fact that they are larger in size and are in a higher position in the sky. Should we assume that for the artist and their Jewish audience at the time, they would have understood the hand of God being connected to a further body?[34] It is true that in the synagogue depiction of the Akedah (the binding of Isaac), the hand of God is also dismembered and the sleeves of the Lord's clothing can be seen. But in the Ezekiel cycle, the presence of divine dismembered hands alongside human hands may be an intentional contrast between the two. One as life-giving and the other as lifeless. Even so, by depicting God in an analogous fashion to the body parts of disabled persons, the artist cannot prevent the possible interpretation that although the

---

34 On the body of God in ancient Israelite and ancient Jewish thought see Sommer, *The Bodies of God*; Bockmuehl, "'The Form of God'", 1–23.

limbs at Ezekiel's feet are a transient disabled stage on the way to a resurrected existence, they also can suggest that in this visual plane the God of Israel exists in a dismembered fashion and is himself disabled.

Isaac T. Soon
Crandall University

Bibliography

Bartelmus, R.	'Ez 37,1–14, die Verform *Weqatal* und die Anfänge der Auferstehungshoffnung', *ZAW* 97 (1984), 366–89.
Ben-Shammai, M. H.	'The Legends of the Destruction of the Temple Among the Paintings of the Dura Synagogue (Hebrew)', *Bulletin of the Jewish Palestine Exploration Society* 9.4 (1962), 93–97.
Blenkinsopp, J.	*Isaiah 1–39: A New Translation with Introduction and Commentary* (AB 19; New Haven, CT: Yale University Press, 2000).
Block, D. I.	*The Book of Ezekiel: Chapters 25–48* (NICOT; Grand Rapids, MI: Eerdmans, 1998).
Bockmuehl, M.	'"The Form of God" (Phil. 2:6): Variations on a Theme of Jewish Mysticism', *Journal of Theological Studies* 48.1 (1997), 1–23.
Bossu, N.	'Une Prophétie Historique Devient Eschatologique: L'Oracle Des Ossements Desséchés (Ez 37,1–14) dans la Synagogue de Dura-Europos', *Etudes Bibliques* 77 (2018), 508–28.
Dimant, D.	'Resurrection, Restoration, and Time-Curtailing in Qumran, Early Judaism, and Christianity', *Revue de Qumran* 19.4 (2000), 527–48.
Dimant, D. (ed.)	*Qumran Cave 4 XXI Biblical Texts, Part 4: Pseudo-Prophetic Texts* (DJD; Oxford: Oxford University Press, 2001).
Engberg-Pedersen, T.	*Cosmology and Self in the Apostle Paul: The Material Spirit* (Oxford: Oxford University Press, 2010).
Goodenough, E. R.	*Symbolism in the Dura Synagogue* (Jewish Symbols in the Greco-Roman Period, Volume 10; New York, NY: Bollingen, 1964).
Grabar, A.	'Le Thème Religieux Des Fresques de la Synagogue de Doura (245–256 Après J.-C.)', *Revue de l'Histoire Des Religions* 123 (1941), 143–92.
Höffken, P.	'Beobachtungen zu Ezechiel XXXVII 1–10', *VT* 31 (1981), 305–17.
Kraeling, C. H.	*The Synagogue: Excavations at Dura-Europos, Final Report VIII, Part 1* (Brooklyn, NY: Ktav Publishing House, 1979).

Kraeling, C. H.   *The Synagogue* (Reprint, with new foreword and indices; New Haven, CT: Yale University Press, 1979).

Kraeling, E. G.   'The Meaning of the Ezekiel Panel in the Synagogue at Dura', *Bulletin of the American Schools of Oriental Research* 78 (1940), 12–18.

Kuniya, N.   'An Iconographical Study on the So-Called "Ezekiel Panel" of the Synagogue Excavated at Dura-Europos' (Japanese), *Bijutsu-Shi: Journal of the Japan Art History Society* 9.3 (1960), 67–86.

Landsberger, F.   'The Origin of the Winged Angel in Jewish Art', *Hebrew Union College Annual* 20 (1947), 227–54.

Levenson, J. D.   *Resurrection and the Restoration of Israel: The Ultimate Victory of the God of Life* (New Haven, CT: Yale University Press, 2006).

Löwinger, A.   'Die Auferstehung in der Jüdischen Tradition', *Mitteilungen Zur Jüdischen Volkskunde* 25 (1923), 23–122.

Moon, W. G.   'Nudity and Narrative: Observations on the Frescoes from the Dura Synagogue', *Journal of the American Academy of Religion* 60.4 (1992), 587–658.

Philonenko, M.   'De Qoumrân à Doura-Europos: La Vision Des Ossements Desséchés (Ezéchiel 37, 1–4)', *Revue d'Histoire et de Philosophie Religieuses* 74.1 (1994), 1–12.

Rajak, T.   'The Dura-Europos Synagogue: Images of a Competitive Community', in L. R. Brody and G. L. Hoffman (eds.), *Dura-Europos: Crosswords of Antiquity*, (Boston, MA: McMullen Museum of Art, 2011), 141–54.

Rajak, T.   'The Synagogue Paintings of Dura-Europos: Triumphalism and Competition', in S. J. Pearce (ed.), *The Image and Its Prohibition in Jewish Antiquity* (Oxford: Journal of Jewish Studies, 2013), 89–109.

Riesenfeld, H.   *The Resurrection in Ezekiel 37 and in the Dura-Europos Paintings* (Uppsala Universitets Arsskrift; Uppsala: Almqvist and Wiksells, 1948).

Rutgers, L. V.   'Diaspora Synagogues: Synagogue Archaeology in the Greco-Roman World', in S. Fine (ed.), *Sacred Realm: The Emergency of the Synagogue in the Ancient World* (Oxford: Oxford University Press, 1996), 67–95.

Schöpflin, K.	'The Revivification of the Dry Bones: Ezekiel 37:1–14', in T. Nicklas, F. V. Reiterer, J. Verheyden, and H. Braun (eds.), *Yearbook 2009: The Human Body in Death and Resurrection* (Berlin: De Gruyter, 2009), 67–85.
Sommer, B. D.	*The Bodies of God and the World of Ancient Israel* (Cambridge: Cambridge University Press, 2009).
Thiessen, M.	*Paul and the Gentile Problem* (Oxford: Oxford University Press, 2016).
Wilpert, G.	*I Sarcofagi Cristiani Antichi. Volume Primo: Tavole* (Rome: Pontificio instituto di archaeologia cristiana, 1929).
Wischnitzer-Bernstein, R.	'The Conception of the Resurrection in the Ezekiel Panel of the Dura Synagogue', *JBL* 60.1 (1941), 43–55.

The Language of Grace

Neil Ormerod

Abstract
This chapter examines the shifting contexts of the language of grace from the New Testament, to Augustine, Aquinas and Luther. Each was responding to a different social and cultural context, according to the needs of the time. However, these shifts can lead to a certain incommensurability which requires careful attention to these contexts if we are to do justice to their thought. It also raised the question of how of contemporary context is itself a new one requiring faithful yet creative ways to speak of grace to the current generation.

1. My context

The language of grace, and disputes over its meaning, have shaped the experience of western Christianity. There is the language of grace in Paul, dealing with the radical and unprecedented revelation of grace in the person of Jesus Christ, writing in the context of Jewish law and Roman empire; the language of grace in Augustine, in disputation with Pelagius and Julian of Eclanum over the radical priority of grace in salvation; the language of grace in Aquinas in the Middle Ages drawing on metaphysical categories to develop a 'scientific' account of grace and its relationship to a metaphysically conceived notion of human 'nature'; and the language of grace in Luther, returning to the radical existential perspective of Augustine, of the interior struggles of grace and the inadequacy of the law to save us. Augustine, Aquinas, and Luther all draw on the same sources but bring to those sources different questions and concerns, responding to different exigencies of their eras.

For myself, I remember as a theological student reading Ernst Käsemann's *Commentary on Romans* with its powerful dialectic of grace versus the works of the law, reflecting his strong Lutheran commitments.[1] Later as a budding theologian I worked my way through Edward Schillebeeckx's monumental work, *Christ, the Christian Experience in the World*, where he argued that the Reformation debates had misread Paul; that the key issue was not grace versus law, but whether God's graciousness was revealed through the gift of the Torah or through the person of Jesus.[2] I also read through the then-recent Lutheran-Catholic dialogue, dealing with the shifting ecclesial and theological perspectives on grace.[3] Now that I am comfortable with these shifts, James (Jim) Harrison reminds us that at least for the readers of Paul's Letter to the Romans, Paul is juxtaposing the grace of Christ with the 'Augustan age of grace' in the Roman empire.[4] Yet another new and challenging perspective has been added.

As primarily a systematic theologian, I do not have the skills needed to analyse historical texts or read ancient languages—in this I happily concede to my friend Jim. My skills lie in the organisation of concepts and their interrelationships, hopefully without losing the grounding of those concepts in lived Christian experience. It is a skill not so frequently in demand in our present age with its stronger focus on the key historical documents of the Christian tradition. But I hope to bring what I would call a more global perspective, more forest than trees, in considering the key epochs identified above. In the end it is an apologia for the place of systematic theology as a necessary part of our theological culture as we face the challenges of our present age.

2. The New Testament writings

Increasingly when I consider the New Testament as a whole, the question that arises for me is, What is it that produced such a massive outpouring of love? Every Epistle, every Gospel reflects a falling in love without bounds in relation to Jesus. The documents witness a massive

---

1 Käsemann, *Commentary on Romans*.
2 Schillebeeckx, *Christ*.
3 *Justification by Faith: Lutherans and Catholics in Dialogue Vii* (Augsburg Publishing House, 1985).
4 Harrison, *Reading Romans*.

communal religious conversion focused on him, a love response to a love first given, 'while we were yet sinners' (Rom. 8:5). According to Bernard Lonergan, religious conversion is 'being grasped by ultimate concern. It is otherworldly falling in love. It is total and permanent self-surrender without conditions, qualifications, reservations'.[5] That Jesus is the focus of such an unrestrained love it most evident in the language of 'excess' of Philippians 2:6–11 (NRSV):

> [6] who, though he was in the form of God,
>   did not regard equality with God
>   as something to be exploited,
> [7] but emptied himself,
>   taking the form of a slave,
>   being born in human likeness.
> And being found in human form,
> [8] he humbled himself
>   and became obedient to the point of death—
>   even death on a cross.
>
> [9] Therefore God also highly exalted him
>   and gave him the name
>   that is above every name,
> [10] so that at the name of Jesus
>   every knee should bend,
>   in heaven and on earth and under the earth,
> [11] and every tongue should confess
>   that Jesus Christ is Lord,
>   to the glory of God the Father.

No title, no claim is too much to apply to him. Jesus is: the Son of David (Rom. 1:3); the new Moses who delivers the Sermon on the Mount (Matt. 5–8); the Son of God (Matt. 16:16); the Son of Man, the apocalyptic figure of the Book of Daniel (Matt. 25:31); the prophet of the end times (Matt. 13:57); the high priest who abolishes all sacrifices (Heb. 7:27); the second Adam (Rom. 5:12–21); the Christ/Messiah; the incarnate word of God (John 1:1,14), on whom God's spirit rests

---

5   Lonergan, *Method*, 226.

(John 1:32), and so on.

Paul in particular also uses the language of grace in relation to Jesus: as the 'grace of Christ/Lord Jesus Christ' (Rom. 5:15, 2 Cor. 8:9, 13:14, Gal. 6:18 etc.), usually as a blessing at the end of his letters. Jesus himself is grace or gift from God, the unique entry of God's love into human history, the Son who is above all the angels (Heb. 1:3). Grace then becomes a larger notion to capture the graciousness of God, in forgiveness, mercy, compassion, a free gift of love 'while we were yet sinners' manifest through Jesus and given to all who believe. This grace justifies us, makes us right in the eyes of God: 'are now justified by his grace as a gift, through the redemption that is in Christ Jesus' (Rom. 3:24). Still grace is not just the person of Jesus, but the manifestation of the power of his work in the lives of believers: 'We have gifts that differ according to the grace given to us' (Rom. 12:6). These gifts become linked to the presence or work of the Holy Spirit (1 Cor. 12), who is poured into the hearts of believers as the 'love of God' (Rom. 5:5). The language of grace has a trinitarian dimension.[6]

In overview, the language of grace in the New Testament has two distinct poles: the first being the person and work of Jesus, who through his death and resurrection raises a fallen humanity to new life; and the second increasingly associated with the work of the Holy Spirit as agent of transformation in the lives of believers giving the gifts and fruits of the Spirit in their daily living. As historical debates unfold, the focus of the language of grace will be more on the latter aspect.

3. Augustine and grace

The proximate cause of the explosion of religious conversion in the New Testament was the person and work of Jesus Christ and the outpouring of his Spirit into the life of the Christian community. That created the context for best understanding these documents. When we come to the time of Augustine of Hippo this proximate cause recedes more into the background to be replace by the promixate cause of a

---

[6] On the trinitarian dimensions of the supernatural see Neil Ormerod, 'Grace, Nature and the Theorem of the Supernatural'.

polemic debate between Augustine and Pelagius and his disciple Julian of Eclanum.[7] This dispute shaped forever the direction of Western theology on grace, original sin, and salvation, in a way not found in the Orthodox tradition.

It was *The Confessions* which set Augustine and Pelagius on a collision course. In it Augustine wrote, 'Give what you command, and then command whatever you will' (Book 10:40), asserting the priority of God's grace in meeting the requirements of the moral law.[8] Pelagius took offence at this, seeing it as undermining moral effort and responsibility. Augustine on the other hand had a strong sense of our solidarity in sinfulness which undermined our freedom, leaving us *non posse non peccare*, not able not to sin. In some sense Pelagius can be depicted as a forerunner of modern individualistic self-determination, while Pelagius depicted Augustine as locked into a Manichean pessimism and powerlessness in the face of evil.[9]

What emerged from this debate is the importance of clarifying the nature of human freedom and indeed the very notion of human nature itself. Indeed Alasdair MacIntrye credits Augustine with the invention/discovery of the very notion of the will itself as an independent faculty: 'For both Plato and Aristotle reason is independently motivating; it has its own ends and it inclines those who possess it towards them ... For Augustine intellect itself needs to be moved to activity by the will. It is will which guides attention in one direction rather than another.'[10] This requires a shift away from the biblical text *per se* to the reality the text refers to which may in fact be analysed using non-sciptural approaches such as philosophy. To speak about grace is to speak about it in relation to freedom, and as the discussion about freedom becomes more technical, so too must the language around grace.

Still Augustine did not have the luxury of working out a full-blown account of grace and freedom. He was engaged in a heated polemic

---

7 For a discussion of the debates, one sympathetic to the more humanistic position of Julian, see Brown, *Augustine of Hippo*.
8 Augustine, *The Confessions*, 263.
9 For an enlightening discussion of the tensions involved see Duffy, 'Original Sin'.
10 MacIntyre, *Whose Justice? Which Rationality?*, 156.

debate with his opponents, developing his arguments and terminology 'on the run' so to speak. So rather than a stable notion of human nature there was prelapsarian, postlapsarian, and redeemed human nature. Similarly he multipled the categories of grace: sanctifying, operative, cooperative, habitual, sufficient, prevenient, healing, persevering, as needed for his argument.

Overall then Augustine's language on grace marks a first step towards a more technical form of theological reflection, interrogating the notion of human freedom and correlative human nature, drawing on both philosophical traditions and his own interiority. However, it remains an incomplete turn to more systematic meaning simply because the primary exigence for his writings was rhetorical not technical. He leaves future theology with a rich vocabulary begging further clarifications and systematisations and suffering from various ambiguities.

4. Aquinas and the context of the Middle Ages

The writings of Aquinas, on the other hand, arise in a very different context. Aquinas, like Augustine, was steeped in the Scriptures, writing commentaries on various Old and New Testament books. He was also immersed in the work of the Fathers, most prominently his master Augustine, then being collated into thematic collections. Finally he was being exposed, through his teacher Albert the Great, to the recently recovered philosophical writings of Aristotle whom Aquinas referred to as 'the Philosopher'.[11] And all this was taking place, not under the urgent need to confront heresy, but to educate a generation of preachers and teachers in sound doctrine of the Church.[12] There were of course medieval disputations, but their purpose was more to refine arguments, to hone academic skills than to defeat heresy. And all this was taking place within the newly founded institution of the medieval university. What emerged from this is a major shift from descriptive and rhetorical expression to the development of a truly explanatory theology.

One way to explain the significance of this is to note the difference

---

11   In a similar way, he refers to St Paul as 'the Apostle'.
12   For an account of the context of Aquinas see Mongeau, *Embracing Wisdom*.

between 'going faster' and 'acceleration', or 'feeling hot' and 'it's 35 degrees celsius'. The first of these statements provides a descriptive account in relation to the speaker. The second depends on measuring things in terms of relations to other things, for example the second derivative of distance against time, or the height of a column of mercury in a tube. The second pair of statements allows for the emergence of a 'scientific' or explanatory account, in the first case, Newtonian mechanics; in the second, thermodynamics. An explanatory account allows for the development of a total system which can be expanded to address not just this or that situation, but a total perspective to address a wide range of problems. This is what begins to happen in the medieval university, and particularly in the writings of Aquinas.

When it comes to the language of grace we may miss the shift because we continue to use the same word, 'grace' in both the descriptive and explanatory contexts. But the meaning has shifted from that of commonsense meaning to theoretic meaning which allows and indeed demands a greater control of meaning. And this control of meaning allows for some resolution of the tensions present in the inherited tradition, dominated by Augustine.

The key step here predates Aquinas and was made by Phillip Chancellor (ca.1160–1236) who posited 'the theory of two orders, entitatively disproportionate: not only was there the familiar series of grace, faith, charity, and merit, but also nature, reason, and the natural love of God'.[13] The distinction made it possible simply '(1) to discuss the nature of grace without discussing liberty, (2) to discuss the nature of liberty without discussing grace, and (3) to work out the relations between grace and liberty'.[14] The impact of this is very evident when we ask about the meaning of human nature. As noted above, for Augustine human nature was a pliable term which shifted in terms of its place in salvation history. Now human nature becomes metaphysically stable, the same before and after the Fall, not subject to substantial change because if it were so to change we would cease to be human. This is the human

---

13 Lonergan, *Grace and Freedom*, 17.
14 Lonergan, *Method*, 289.

nature then that Jesus shares with us, like us in all things but sin (Heb. 4:15). This distinction between grace and nature provides Aquinas with a key element of the architechtonics of his *Summa Theologiae*.

Now is not the place to go into all the ways in which this distinction assists Aquinas in the systematisation of Christian belief, but I will indicate one important aspect. For Augustine the necessity of grace lay in the sinfulness of human beings who were not able not to sin without healing grace. Aquinas, however, has a stronger stance, and indeed posits two grounds for the necessity of grace. As with Augustine, grace heals the distortions of human nature brought about through sin; but grace also elevates human nature to attain what it would otherwise not be able to attain from its own resources. Grace belongs to an ontologically higher level of being, a participation in the divine life, which no finite being can attain of its own effort. This is a much stronger position from which to reject Pelagianism than was available to the more descriptive stance of Augustine.

Aquinas's theology was a major systematic achievement, one which we can still benefit from in reading him today. However, it is a form of technical language, not readily accessible without effort and training. There is a gap between this type of work and the communicative task of translating this into the everyday language of a believer. And when the technical language becomes rote, without an effort to properly understand it, communication to the body of the faithful becomes mere jargon, a form of obfuscation rather than illumination.

5. The existential return in Luther

Luther again presents us with a very different context for the language of grace. The Catholic Church was caught in a cycle of moral and intellectual decline. Morally the papacy was corrupt and the church practice of selling indulgences was indefensible. Intellectually the high scholasticism of Aquinas was in a cycle of decline into nominalism, and failed to provide a language to engage the heart. On the other hand there was a growing 'middle class' of people, religiously serious, literate, and yearning for a richer religious life that extolled marriage and family life. The 'two-tier' Christianity of the Middle Ages, the split between the religious virtuosi and the 'common folk', was breaking down as scandals involving priests, monks, and nuns made clear how religiously ordinary many of them were.[15]

What we witness at this time was the emergence of the importance of the individual and a corresponding loosening of the bonds of communal life. The strongly communal religiosity of Catholicism, particularly in rural settings, was less effective in maintaining religious life in an increasingly urban setting. The rise of the individual was captured in three major figures of the era: Martin Luther, Ignatius of Loyola, and René Descartes. Each of these figures expressed a 'turn to the subject': Luther and Ignatius in the religious realm, Descartes in the philosophical realm. Significantly Augustine, himself a master on the interior life, was a key influence upon Luther and Descartes. The appeal to interior experience decentres the locus of authority from the communally accepted authority of religious leaders, to one's own experience and judgement. Notably each of these figures fell foul of religious authorities, with Ignatius only escaping condemnation by swearing loyalty to Catholic Church teaching.

The key question then for Luther was one of personal salvation. Given the breakdown of a more communal participation in salvation, mediated by the Church and sacrament, how can I be assured of salvation? Neither the sacramental system of Catholicism nor the metaphysical theology of Aquinas could satisfactorily address this existential question; Luther returns to the more existentially and interiorly relevant language of Augustine to articulate his own interior struggle and its resolution in the doctrines of salvation by faith alone, grace alone, and Scipture alone. Writing of his own breakthrough experience, Luther wrote:

> At last, by the mercy of God, meditating day and night, I gave heed to the context of the words: 'In it the righteousness of God is revealed … He who through faith is righteous shall live.' I began to understand that the righ-

---

15 On the whole shift in religious sentiment away from the previous 'two-tier' form of Christian life at the time see Taylor, *A Secular Age*.

> teousness of God is that by which the righteous lives by a gift of God, that is, by faith. And this is the meaning: the righteousness of God is revealed by the gospel, that is, the passive righteousness with which the merciful God justifies us by faith ... Here I felt that I was altogether born again and had entered paradise through open gates.[16]

As a Catholic theologian I do not agree with many of Luther's formulations, but I do appreciate the magnitude of the task he faced. It was a time of massive social and cultural upheaval, the breakdown of Christendom, and the inadequacy of the received theological approach to address these problems. Luther's problem was both intellectual and communicative, to find a new language that expressed Christian faith for a new age in a coherent fashion, and communicated this new understanding in an existentially effective way. The Catholic response to Luther in the Council of Trent basically reiterated the metaphysical language of Aquinas. To that extent the two were speaking at cross purposes, adopting different theological idioms, making real comparison difficult if not impossible.[17] The more recent Luther-Catholic Dialogue and subsequent Joint Declaration on Justification illustrates the care needed to identify where both agreement is possible and the significance of possible disagreement between the two traditions.

6. Conclusion

Our present context is not that of Paul, Augustine, Aquinas, or Luther. Our present culture is not concerned with heresies, nor anxious about personal salvation, nor thrilled by the intellectual coherence of Christian belief. Rather as Taylor would argue we are more locked in an immanent frame, struggling to identify even the possibility of transcendence.[18] Still it is a culture that has developed rich interest in the interior life, in depth psychology (Freud, Jung), psychological thera-

---

16 Quoted in Duffy, *The Dynamics of Grace*, 186.
17 See the piece by Cardinal Avery Dulles on this point, Dulles, 'Two Languages of Salvation'.
18 Taylor, *A Secular Age*.

pies, and movements such as 'mindfulness' with roots in Buddhism. At times this fascination with inwardness can feed into narcissism and individualism devoid of interpersonal connectivity. Rather than anxiety about salvation, our culture seeks out authenticity and shuns inauthenticity. But it struggles with those who 'authentically' embody the inauthenticity of the surrounding culture.[19] The shift to interiority has also highlighted the difference between the inner psychologies of victims and their perpetrators, so any meaningful communication of the language of grace must be attuned to the fact that grace has different meanings for victims (healing) and for their perpetrators (repentance).[20] And perhaps most importantly of all our culture struggles with the very notion of God. Whereas all those we have considered lived in a culture that took the notion of God (or gods) for granted, now we live in 'a society where belief in God is unchallenged and indeed, unproblematic, to one in which it is understood to be one option among others, and frequently not the easiest to embrace'.[21] All this creates enormous difficulties for theologians seeking to communicate the reality of God's graciousness in a way which is faithful to the tradition while being creatively engaged with the contemporary realities.

Neil Ormerod
Sydney College of Divinity

---

19 We see this in the way people will often refer to Donald Trump as 'authentic' despite his constant lying and distortions of the truth.
20 As literature around sexual abuse make clear, victims are often haunted by feelings of guilt, for which forgiveness is simply inappropriate. What is needed is healing of trauma, which can truly be mediated by the experience of God's love. Too often victims have been met with condemnation which only adds to their trauma.
21 Taylor, *A Secular Age*, 3.

Bibliography

Augustine	*The Confessions* (trans. by Maria Boulding; New York, NY: Vintage Books, 1998).
Brown, P.	*Augustine of Hippo* (Berkeley, CA: University of California Press, 1967).
Duffy, S.	*The Dynamics of Grace: Perspectives in Theological Anthropology* (Collegeville, MN: Liturgical Press, 1993).
Duffy, S.	'Original Sin: Our Hearts of Darkness Revisited', *Theological Studies* 49 (1988), 597–622.
Dulles, A.	'Two Languages of Salvation: The Lutheran-Catholic Joint Declaration', *First Things* 98, (December 1999), 25–30.
Harrison, J. R.	*Reading Romans with Roman Eyes: Studies on the Social Perspective of Paul* (Lanham, MD: Lexington/Fortress, 2020).
	Justification by Faith: Lutherans and Catholics in Dialogue Vii (Augsburg Publishing House, 1985).
Käsemann, E.	*Commentary on Romans* (Translated by Geoffrey W. Bromiley. GrandRapids, MI: Eerdmans 1994).
Lonergan, B. J. F.	*Grace and Freedom: Operative Grace in the Thought of St. Thomas Aquinas* (Collected Works of Bernard Lonergan. Edited by F. E. Crowe and R. M. Doran; Toronto: University of Toronto Press, 2000).
Lonergan, B. J. F.	*Method in Theology* (Collected Works of Bernard Lonergan. Edited by R. M. Doran and J. D. Dadosky; Toronto: University of Toronto Press, 2017).
MacIntyre, A.	*Whose Justice? Which Rationality?* (Notre Dame, IN.: University of Notre Dame Press, 1988).
Mongeau, G.	*Embracing Wisdom: The Summa Theologiae as Spiritual Pedagogy* (Toronto: PIMS, 2015).
Ormerod, N.	'Grace, Nature and the Theorem of the Supernatural—a Trinitarian Perspective', *Louvain Studies* 42, no. 1 (2019), 26–42.
Schillebeeckx, E.	*Christ, the Christian Experience in the Modern World* (trans. J. Bowden; London: S.C.M. Press, 1980).
Taylor, C.	*A Secular Age* (Cambridge, MA: Belknap Press, 2007).

On Finding One's Way in Ancient History

E. A. Judge

Abstract

Conceived in Classical Greek, the two mutually exclusive ways of knowing, historia and philosophia, proceeded respectively through empirical experience, or theoretical logic. For Paul, the knowledge of the gospel came through demonstration. Select aspects of Paul's demonstration were then picked up by thinkers of the modern era and their associated movements. Galen lauded the rational approach, rather than empiricism, which he recognised as the approach of the Jew or Christian. Through his indebtedness to Aristotle, Augustine sustained a rationalistic approach, although moving thought beyond apathy to the personal. But the empirical science of Bacon and his Puritan successors owes a debt to Genesis as the world became an artefact and ceased to be eternal, and thus an empiricist approach to knowledge opened up the universe for scientific inquiry.[1]

There are two ways of understanding anything, both conceived in Classical Greek, *historia* and *philosophia*. These were not reduced to curriculum subjects until the seventeenth century, after symbolism had been rejected as a way of interpreting mythical texts. The abstract ideal of the philosophically experimental categories must face the historical documentation of what had actually happened. Philosophy defines and classifies the general truth of what is necessarily the case, as

---

1 Judge's original, briefer essay for this volume was expanded by reference to his published work, by James Dalziel and Peter Bolt, who give advance apologies for any infelicities introduced!

with mathematics, but history looks for the reality of a particular person's experience.

The authenticity of this early discovery by James Harrison soon found its way to the now highly productive exploration of the social setting of the Pauline churches. Harrison has himself written of having 'lost [his] way' across his first two years (1971, 1972) at Macquarie. Though he had 'enjoyed' Philosophy it could not 'earn' [him] a living. He had been 'disillusioned' with English Literature and was 'barely tolerating' Modern History, with its 'melée of social movements and ideologies'. This must however have qualified him to enrol for 1973 in a 200-level unit: 'The Roman nobility'. The alternative qualification for that (through 'Augustan Rome') he only took in the second half of 1973, having already in February, during the first two weeks of 'The Roman nobility', 'decided [his] future career would be teaching ancient history in some form or another'. This 'transformative experience' arose as the new unit 'plunged us from the beginning into the methodology of history'.[2]

1. History or Philosophy?

Neither 'science' nor 'religion' was known to ancient Athens. These Latin words only acquired their modern Western sense in the seventeenth century, as the religious revolution triggered our scientific one as described in the works of Peter Harrison.

History and philosophy are the two intellectual methods developed by the Greeks, seeking 'understanding' (*episteme*). They can be seen as mutually exclusive.

An 'arbitrator' (Homer's *histor*) tests things: 'I saw' (*eidon*) and so 'I know' (*oida*). These three Greek words are from the same stem. They constitute enquiry, testing for knowledge, i.e. (from Latin) 'science'—that which has been empirically found out.

A 'philosopher' defines and classifies things theoretically, by logic, yielding necessary truth, that which must be the case, as with mathe-

---

2   Citations from James R. Harrison in the 'Preface' to Judge, *First Christians*, ix.

matics. It was to Greeks axiomatic that 'rationality' (*logos*) was the very principle of the universe itself (Blyth):

> Pythagoras (sixth century B.C.): the four-fold nature (*tetractys*) of it all.
>
> Parmenides: since the universe cannot be wrong, there can be no change.
>
> Empedocles: change is an illusion, it is only rotation.
>
> Plato: we see only the shadow of eternal ideas until the soul escapes its bodily cave.
>
> Aristotle (fourth century B.C.): logical categories express the fixity of the eternal universe.
>
> Diogenes: to a Cynic, absolute self-sufficiency (*autarky*) defies any convention.
>
> Epicurus: everything is random, requiring 'imperturbability' (*ataraxia*).
>
> Chrysippus (third century B.C.): everything comes round again for ever, requiring Stoic 'apathy'.

By contrast, the 'open universe' provided an alternative to everything coming round again:

> The experimental method only came into its own once the eternity of the universe was rejected. It was not Greece, but Genesis, that has created modern science. By downgrading the universe to a temporary artefact, made and run by its creator, devout experimentalists gradually opened it up.[3]

2. Paul's *apodeixis* for the 21st Century

For Aristotle, 'logic is the science of necessary truth', with the syllogism being 'that *logos* in which from stated premises the conclusion follows

---

3   Judge, 'The religion of the secularists', 315.

"of necessity" (*Prior Analytics* 24b 19–20)'. This logical necessity is the 'demonstration' (*apodeixis*) the philosopher required.[4]

Although sharing the same concern for 'demonstration', the apostle Paul confronted the world of the philosopher with the gospel of Christ, which worked *experimentally* (1 Cor. 2:4; compare 1 Thess. 1:5; 2:13):

> Paul himself had also hinted at the intellectual revolution. He has a word (*logos*) that upstages philosophy. It carried its own proof, the "demonstration" (*apodeixis*), delivered not by rationality but by spiritual experience of God's influence.[5]

His letters chronicle this 'demonstration' at work:

> 'After three years I went up to Jerusalem to "interview" (*historesai*) Cephas' (Gal. 1:18).

> 'My *logos* and my "message" (*kerygma*) were not in the persuasion of *sophia*, but in the "demonstration" (*apodeixis*) of spirit and power' (1 Cor. 2:4).

> 'You remember me in everything and maintain the "traditions" (*paradoseis*) even as I have delivered them to you' (1 Cor. 11:2).

> 'So "authenticate" (*dokimazete*) yourselves ... unless indeed you are "inauthentic" (*adokimoi*)' (2 Cor. 13:5).

> 'Endurance produces "authenticity" (*dokime*), and authenticity hope' (Rom. 5:4).

> 'I have learned to be "self-sufficient" (*autarkes*) in what I am' (Phil. 4:11).

> 'See that no one shall be "confiscating" (*syllagogon*) you according to the tradition (*paradoseis*) of men, according to the "elements" (*stoicheia*) of the cosmos' (Col. 2:8).

---

4 Judge, 'Experimental Proof', 107.
5 Judge, 'The Paradox of Private Faith', 189.

'Avoid the antitheses of the falsely named "knowledge" (*gnosis*)' (1 Tim. 6:20).

With God's place in the world 'decisively tied to the experimental method', the apostle was opening a pathway in the first-century towards his abiding legacy:

> The intellectual shift [from the ancient to the modern world] is the legacy not of Athens, but of Jerusalem. Genesis has led us beyond logic to the empirical testing for truth that has delivered the developmental world of modern science.[6]

The developmental pathways behind major themes in the contemporary world can be traced back to aspects of Paul's thought, commending itself across a range of human experience.

Gal. 3:28	Neither Jew nor Greek	Neither bond nor free	Nor male and female
Pauline *koine*	*agape*	*oikodome*	*dokime*
abstract categories	race	class	gender
19th c.	Darwin	Marx	Freud
20th c.	Fascism	Communism	Psychoanalysis
21st c.	Globalisation	Human rights	Cognitive science

3. Galen's *Apodeixis* Until the 18th Century (Only in the 19th Overturned by Microbiology)

Some of Paul's contemporaries, like the Stoic philosopher Seneca, were impressed by the Jews' awareness of 'the origin and meaning of their rites' (from a lost work cited by Augustine, *City of God* 6.11). In the

---

6   Judge, 'The Secular Jerusalem of the West', 162–163. The table that follows can be further supplemented by the more extensive tabular contrasts between 'Athens' and 'Jerusalem' on pp.163, 165, 167.

school of Chrysippus and therefore no doubt holding to the fixed cycle of the universe, Seneca admires the Jews for 'the purposefulness of their tradition [, which] implies some sense of its historical mission'.[7]

If searching for an intellectual explanation for his seeming envy of the Jews' historical tenacity, Seneca could have turned to his older contemporary, Philo. Despite being a Platonist, this 1st c. Alexandrian had affirmed the Scriptural doctrine of creation, over against the universe that had neither beginning nor end.

> There are some people who, having more admiration for the cosmos than for its maker, declared the former both ungenerated and eternal, while falsely and impurely attributing to God much idleness. (*On the Creation of the Cosmos*, 1.2.7; Runia).

But more than a millennium and a half of speculative argument assuming such an 'ungenerated and eternal' universe would block the opening up of the universe to the 'experimental history' displayed so impressively in the Jews' historical mission, and hence to modern science.[8]

In discussing the question of God amongst the philosophical schools, Justin appealed to the Israelite prophets, whose truth was now clearly demonstrated in their predictions of

> future events, which are now happening. [...] They alone saw the truth [...] for they did not argue from deductive logic (*apodeixis*) since as witnesses of the truth they were more trustworthy than all such logic. (*Dialogue with Trypho* 7.1–2).

Galen, the medical polymath and philosopher, 'offered an academic critique of those who followed Justin, even winning over some of them to his deductive syllogisms (cf. Eusebius, *History of the Church* 5.28.13–14)'.[9] Despite being impressed by Christian behaviour, which sometimes corresponded to that of true philosophers, Galen felt that,

---

7   Judge, 'Experimental Proof', 114.
8   Judge, 'Experimental Proof', 115.
9   Judge, 'Experimental Proof', 116.

intellectually, the Christians were using the wrong method.

> I learned from Aristotle [...] to add some adequate reason, if not a cogent demonstration (*apodeixis*). [...] Thus one would not, at the very start, as if one had come into the school (*diatribe*) of Moses and Christ, hear about laws that have not been demonstrated (*apodeixis*) [...] he (Galen's medical rival) did not consider it necessary to guide us by any logical method but adopted an empirical method of teaching.
>
> (Galen, *On the Difference Between the Pulses*, 2.4; tr. Walzer; cf. Stern, vol. 2, 306–315).

From roughly the same time as Justin and Galen, Celsus produced a full-scale repudiation of the biblical corpus, recoiling 'from its grotesque historical exaggeration of the human predicament as the key to cosmic reality'.[10] He was nevertheless impressed with some Christians who were 'moderate, reasonable and intelligent people who readily interpret allegorically' (Origen, *Contra Celsum* 1.27).

> The Greek literary principle of analogy had required an ancient text to be read symbolically. So the "male and female" of Gen. 1:27 did not refer to Adam and Eve, but to the masculine spirit (hot and dry) and the feminine soul (cool and moist). Only when it was taken as literally true that the world was itself an artifact, having been made and set on its course by God, could empiricism begin to take it apart to see how it worked.[11]

Himself a practitioner of 'the allegorical interpretation of traditional texts [enabling] civilized people to find moral meaning in the all-too-human behavior, e.g. of the gods in Homer', Origen 'opened his response to Celsus by asserting, for the first time in recorded thought, the right to defy the law':[12]

---

10 Judge, 'Experimental Proof', 117.
11 Judge, 'Where is the Truth in History?', 176.
12 Judge, 'Experimental Proof', 117.

> (Celsus) harps on the commonlaw, saying this is infringed by Christians through their associations [... but] judged by the test of truth [...] it is not contrary to reason to form associations against the law. (Origen, *Contra Celsum* 1.1).

Celsus had himself clearly grasped the 'truth' behind why the Christians acted against custom:

> They say, "God shows and proclaims everything to us beforehand, and he has even deserted the whole *kosmos* and the motions of the heavens [...] to give attention to us alone". (Origen, *Contra Celsum* 4.23).

In other words, Celsus recognised that the Christian gospel had brought with it a 'challenge to the perfect cosmos of the philosophers by the test of human experience'. But nevertheless, the Greek philosophy epitomised by the logical syllogism that Galen inherited from Aristotle, continued to block intellectual progress for centuries to come, for it:

> locked the world into a false construction of its reality. This was only broken when the biblical doctrine of creation was taken in its literal sense, meaning that the world was not eternal, but was itself an artifact, not designed to last forever.[13]

Although attracted by some elements of the Empiricists, his rivals in medicine, Galen remained a dogmatician. Although attracted to the 'philosophical' lifestyle of the Christians, the great second century physician saw them as enslaved to the empirical approach to which he was opposed. But despite abiding attempts to use symbolic readings to apply the Bible to the present, as the Greeks applied their heroic tales of the past told by Homer, 'it was the church and its sanctification of the experiential message of the Bible, which nevertheless developed the intellectual conditions that created modern science'.[14]

---

13   Judge, 'Paul and Greek Philosophy', 63.
14   Judge, 'Paul and Greek Philosophy', 63.

> No amount of symbolic interpretation could take away the ineradicable historicity of the crucifixion. When the literal sense of creation as an act of God was fully grasped, and the *kosmos* was seen as an object that had been created, the way was open for the empirical method to be applied to the study of it. The world could be probed and tested, and taken apart. This happened in jerky stages, sometimes against the bans of the Roman church as guardian of established truth.[15]

In the history of medicine, Galen brought the next great phase after the Hippocratic medicine that preceded him. But it was not dogmatic medicine or the philosophy of logical necessity that advanced things further to the medicine of today.

> The experimental method, falsifying speculative theory by practical tests, is ultimately the legacy of the Christianization of Greek thought. The progressive exploding of the doctrine of the four elements, ending with empirical microbiology, opened the way to modern medicine.[16]

4. Augustine's Monastic Soul from the 4th Century

The massive new interpretation of Augustine by Lane Fox shows vividly how he fell under the spell of the *Categories* of Aristotle as mediated through the Neoplatonic tradition. He would have had available to him the introduction to the *Categories* by Porphyry, the disciple of Plotinus (Mortley). Porphyry also formulated the elementary digest of Aristotelian logic that was later to regulate the formal study even of Christian thought' as the churches 'reluctantly undertook sponsorship of public education'.[17] Already by Porphyry's day, 'philosophical his-

---

15 Judge, 'Paul and Greek Philosophy', 63.
16 Judge, 'Paul and Greek Philosophy', 63. After 'the splendid rear-guard action' of the eighteenth-century Enlightenment, the discovery of microbes put a brake on the human tendency to reduce everything down to a simple order; Judge, 'The Religion of the Secularists', 244–245.
17 Judge, 'Experimental Proof', 118.

tory' had provided the various philosophical schools with 'their written pedigree in the form of verbatim citations from the words of their founder or of later heads'. Through applying this practice to 'ecclesiastical history', Eusebius gained credit for 'the modern standard of verbatim source documentation in history'.[18]

> Thus, as the theologians developed their legacy guided by the philosophical standard of logical definition, the historians of philosophy passed over to the churches the principle of eyewitness testimony to what had actually been said.[19]

The early fourth century (A.D. 311) was also when 'the Roman state itself formally conceded the independent principle of Origen. It was now made legitimate to live and behave differently from one's own ancestors'.[20] A century later, Augustine, a bishop converted from neo-platonic principles, 'laid out the classic Christian synthesis: one must live in two cities at once, loyal to civil Rome as God had ordained, but also to "the City of God" itself whose hour was soon to come'.[21]

Augustine was also captivated by the monastic discipline of Evagrius Ponticus:

> 'The kingdom of heaven is apathy of soul accompanied by true knowledge (*gnosis*) of beings (*ta onta*)'
> (*Logos Praktikos*, 2; tr. Adapted from Sinkewicz; edited by Guillaumont).

However, contemplating the Trinitarian relations at the heart of all being, he moved beyond apathy by turning 'his very candid introspective powers onto the analysis of the heart' to great impact.

> He distinguished varous triadic facets of the human psyche: the three in one of memory, intelligence, will; of reason, freedom, self-consciousness; of mind, knowledge, love. With the Godhead he settled for eternity, truth, and

---

18 Judge, 'Experimental Proof', 118.
19 Judge, 'Experimental Proof', 118.
20 Judge, 'Experimental Proof', 118.
21 Judge, 'Experimental Proof', 119.

love. Love indeed is not only the bond between God and man, but the key to our life in society; not, however, self-love, which is pride, the root of all sin, but the love of the other in which we find our true identity.[22]

This was counter to classical ethics, whose focus was on 'the practice of the virtues, that is, the good qualities we possess, rather than our response to others'. Classical ethics was 'a subset of the fixed universe', and so 'Stoics therefore trained their students in apathy, the dispassionate protective against contact, courtesy rather than care'.[23] But, first through the 'retrospective disclosure of motives and emotions' begun by Paul, and then 'carried to an extreme by Augustine', in the contemporary West 'everyone is now engrossed with the personal life'.[24] Once again, this is due not to Athens but Jerusalem, for 'open-hearted emotions are our culture's legacy from the passion of Christ'.[25]

5. The Puritan Creation of Science from the 17th Century

In the seventeenth century the long dominant philosophical understanding of the world was dislodged by that of history, thus creating modern science. 'The decades between Bacon's death in 1626 and the Restoration in 1660 witnesses a remarkable combination of Puritan millenarianism and Baconian science'.[26] In particular,

> the natural philosophers who followed Francis Bacon under the Puritan Commonwealth, and went on to found "the Royal Society" for natural knowledge (sc. "physics" in Greek), abandoned the allegorical interpretation of Genesis. The creation was demystified, and the text taken in matter-of-fact terms. The physical world could now be opened by experimental testing. [...] If our culture credits "Greek science" with founding the modern world, it is

---

22 Judge, 'The Religion of the Secularists', 247.
23 Judge, 'The Religion of the Secularists', 247.
24 Judge, 'The Biblical Shape of Modern Culture', 158.
25 Judge, 'The Religion of the Secularists', 247.
26 Harrison, 'The Bible', 636.

upending the reality of what happened. Modern science became possible only when the straitjacket of philosophical logic was put aside for the experimental method. That method was clarified when history set rhetoric aside for the testing of documented eyewitnesses. "History" was for the first time made a curriculum subject in 1622, with the creation of the Camden chair at Oxford.[27]

But our Western languages embed both 'philosophy' and 'history', incoherently. This problem has its origins long before the seventeenth century:

> The peculiar paradox of the West [is] that we live intellectually in both Athens and Jerusalem. But there is no easy amalgam or seamless web as ancient historians often claim. The initiative is decisively with Jerusalem. The progressive developments seen by Darwin and Marx could not have been imagined in the serene cosmos of Athens. But churches and most other institutions cultivate such moderation. Thanks to Jesus, we never tire of mocking their hypocrisy and inconsistency. Contemporary secularism, however, is in serious danger of misunderstanding its own credentials.[28]

Contradictions also exist in the relationship of church and state:

> The churches themselves are relieved to have stepped back beyond the long shadow of Constantine. Are we then back with the bracing confrontations of the third century? Hardly, since our whole cultural tradition has been fundamentally transformed through the interaction of church and state. The modern world can no longer choose between Athens and Jerusalem. It depends too much on both of them. Their very contradictions maintain the ferment of the West.[29]

---

27 Judge, 'Experimental Proof', 119-120.
28 Judge, 'The Religion of the Secularists', 319.
29 Judge, 'The beginning of religious history', 395.

Behind that ferment the voice of the apostle might still be heard.

> Only in our lifetime has empirical science at last delivered a universe that actually began, and is no longer locked down in a "steady state" of logical fixity, but is opening up. If not quite its prophet, Paul may surely be claimed as a pioneer of the developmental world as we now take it to be.[30]

Keen for 'experimental proof' (*apodeixis*), 'he was neither a philosopher nor a student of the natural world. With the psalmist (Ps. 102:25–26) he knew it was all an artifact of God, who would get rid of it like a worn-out garment'. In his 'own catastrophic life crisis (his personal "big bang")' he was confronted 'with what he now sees as the penultimate turning point in the world history of God's making'.[31] Documented in his letters 'with their intensely introspective heart-searching, still unmatched for its intellectual integrity', Paul 'projects it as it were onto the cosmos as a whole'—to the later offence of Celsus. Sin entered the cosmos, and 'the whole creation is groaning under the pangs of child-birth "until now" (Rom. 8:22). We must not be captivated (*sylagogon*) by philosophical tradition, subject to the "elements" (*stoicheia*) of the cosmos, rather than to Christ'.[32]

6. On Finding One's Way as a *Discipulus*

Current history remains profoundly influenced by ancient history, and finding one's way in the latter assists finding one's way in the former. This is not only a matter of Rome, but also of Jerusalem. Finding one's way as a *discipulus* remains surprising both then and now:

> What also can it mean to be sent to all the nations to "make students" (*matheteusate*) of them, "teaching" (*didaskontes*) them "to observe all the directions I gave you" (Matt. 28:19–20), if there are to be no teachers? Jesus himself is often called in the Gospels the "teacher" (*didaskalos*),

---

30   Judge, 'Experimental Proof', 121.
31   Judge, 'Experimental Proof', 120.
32   Judge, 'Experimental Proof', 120.

while those who "followed" him are the "students" (*mathetai*, Latin *discipuli*). In Acts, however, the "students" upon whom "teaching" had been enjoined turn out to be "emissaries" (*apostoloi* 1:2). Moreover they are not called "teachers," but "witnesses" (*martyres*, 1:8) [...] In the epistles the term "students" has disappeared. Whatever can have happened to the international teaching mission?[33]

[With Jesus] there was no academy or museum in which the new learning might be transmitted across the centuries. What made it different was the call to 'follow': abandon security in a personal commitment to the one who would lead them into the kingdom.[34]

E.A. Judge
Emeritus Professor of History,
Macquarie University

---

33   Judge, 'Higher Education', 94.
34   Judge, 'The Religion of the Secularists', 301.

Bibliography

Blyth, D.	*Aristotle's Ever-turning World in* Physics *8: Analysis and Commentary* (Leiden: Brill, 2016).
Christian, D.	*Big History: Between Nothing and Everything* (New York, NY: McGraw Hill, 2014).
Guillaumont, A.	*Evagrius Ponticus* (Paris: Éditions du Cerf, 1952).
Harrison, J. R.	*Reading Romans with Roman Eyes: Studies on the Social Perspective of Paul* (Lanham, MD: Lexington, 2020).
Harrison, P.	*'Religion' and the Religions in the English Enlightenment* (Cambridge: Cambridge University Press, 1990).
Harrison, P.	*The Bible, Protestantism and the Rise of Natural Science* (Cambridge: Cambridge University Press, 1998).
Harrison, P.	*The Fall of Man and the Foundation of Science* (Cambridge: Cambridge University Press, 2007).
Harrison, P.	*The Cambridge Companion to Science and Religion* (Cambridge: Cambridge University Press, 2010).
Harrison, P.	*Wrestling with Nature: From Omens to Science* (Chicago, IL: Chicago University Press, 2011).
Harrison, P.	*The Territories of Science and Religion* (Chicago, IL: Chicago University Press, 2015).
Harrison, P.	'The Bible and the Emerging "Scientific" World-view', in Euan Cameron (ed.), *The New Cambridge History of the Bible*, vol. 3 (Cambridge: Cambridge University Press 2016), 620–40.
Johnston, I. and G. H. R. Horsley	*Galen: Method of Medicine*, vol. 1 (Cambridge, MA: Harvard University Press, 2011), ix-cxxxix.
Judge E. A.	'The beginning of religious history', *Journal of Religious History* 15.4 (1989), 394–412.
Judge, E. A.	*Social Distinctives of the Christians in the First Century: Pivotal Essays* (Peabody, MA: Hendrikson, 2008).
Judge, E. A.	*The First Christians in the Roman World: Augustan and New Testament Essays* (Tübingen: Mohr Siebeck, 2008).
Judge, E. A.	*Jerusalem and Athens: Cultural Transformation in Late Antiquity* (Tübingen: Mohr Siebeck, 2010).

Judge, E. A.	'The religion of the secularists', *Journal of Religious History* 38.1 (2014), 307–19.
Judge, E. A.	*Engaging Rome and Jerusalem: Historical Essays for our Time* (Melbourne: Scholarly, 2014).
Judge, E. A.	'Paul and Greek Philosophy', in E. A. Judge, *Paul and the Conflict of Cultures: The Legacy of his Thought Today* (Eugene, OR: Cascade, 2019), 53–64.
Judge E. A.	'Higher Education and the Pauline Churches', *Paul and the Conflict of Cultures: The Legacy of His Thought Today* (James R. Harrison ed.; Eugene, OR: Cascade Books, 2019), 94–105.
Judge, E. A.	'Experimental Proof in Paul', in E. A. Judge, *Paul and the Conflict of Cultures: The Legacy of his Thought Today* (Eugene, OR: Cascade, 2019), 106–121.
Judge, E.A.	'The Biblical Shape of Modern Culture', in E. A. Judge, *Paul and the Conflict of Cultures: The Legacy of his Thought Today* (Eugene, OR: Cascade, 2019), 143–158.
Judge, E.A.	'The Secular Jerusalem of the West', in E. A. Judge, *Paul and the Conflict of Cultures: The Legacy of his Thought Today* (Eugene, OR: Cascade, 2019), 159–170.
Judge, E. A.	'Where is the Truth in History? How Does the Discipline of History Relate to "the Faith of the Gospel" (Phil. 1:27)?', in E. A. Judge, *Paul and the Conflict of Cultures: The Legacy of his Thought Today* (Eugene, OR: Cascade, 2019), 171–182.
Judge, E.A.	'The Paradox of Private Faith and Public Reality', in E. A. Judge, *Paul and the Conflict of Cultures: The Legacy of his Thought Today* (Eugene, OR: Cascade, 2019), 183–202.
Judge, E. A.	'The Religion of the Secularists', in E. A. Judge, *Paul and the Conflict of Cultures: The Legacy of his Thought Today* (Eugene, OR: Cascade, 2019), 236–249.
Judge, E. A.	*On this Rock: When Culture Disrupted the Roman Community* (Eugene, OR: Cascade Books, 2020).
Judge, E. A.	*The Failure of Augustus: Essays on the Interpretation of a Paradox* (Newcastle upon Tyne: Cambridge Scholars, 2019; paperback edition with corrections and index included, 2021).
Judge, E. A.	*Out Here Down Under: Turning History Inside Out* (pending).

Judge, E. A.	*Paul did not mean to found a New Religion: The Case of Egypt* (projected).
Lane Fox, R.	*Augustine: Conversions to Confessions* (London: Penguin, 2015).
Mortley, R. J.	*Plotinus, Self and the World* (Cambridge: Cambridge University Press, 2013).
Oslington, P.	*The Oxford Handbook of Christianity and Economics* (New York, NY: Oxford University Press, 2014).
Runia, D. T.	*Philo: On the Creation of the Cosmos according to Moses* (Leiden: Brill, 2001).
Sorabji, R.	*John Philoponus Against Aristotle on the Eternity of the World* (London: Bloomsbury, 1987).
Sorabji, R.	*Philoponus and the Rejection of Aristotelian Science* (London: Duckworth, 1987).
Stephens, M. B.	'Destroying the Destroyers of the Earth: The Meaning and Function of New Creation in the Book of Revelation' (Diss. Macquarie, 2009).
Stern, M.	*Greek and Latin Authors on Jews and Judaism* (Jerusalem: Israel Academy of Sciences and Humanities, 1974).
Stroumsa, G. G.	*Barbarian Philosophy: The Religious Revolution in Early Christianity* (Tübingen: Mohr Siebeck, 1999).
Stroumsa, G. G.	*The End of Sacrifice: Religious Transformations in Late Antiquity* (Chicago, IL: University of Chicago Press, 2009).
Stroumsa, G. G.	*The Scriptural Universe of Ancient Christianity* (Cambridge, MA: Harvard University Press, 2016).
Walzer, R.	*Galen on Jews and Christians* (London: Oxford University Press, 1949).

Publications of James R. Harrison, BA, Dip Ed, MA, PhD (Macquarie), FAHA.

2022 (and forthcoming)

Edited (with E. R. Richards), *Ancient Literature for New Testament Study vol. 10: Inscriptions, Graffiti, Documentary Papyri, Ostraca, Coin Legends* (Grand Rapids, MI: Zondervan, forthcoming).

Edited (with L. L. Welborn), *The First Urban Churches 7: Thessalonica (Thessalonike)* (Atlanta, GA: SBL Press, forthcoming).

Edited (with L. L. Welborn), *The First Urban Churches 8: Lycaonia and Galatia* (Atlanta, GA: SBL Press: forthcoming).

Edited (with L. L. Welborn), *The First Urban Churches 9: Jerusalem and Caesarea* (Atlanta, GA: SBL Press, forthcoming).

'Early Christians and Their Cultural Contexts', in B. W. Longenecker and D. E. Wilhite (eds.), *Cambridge History of Early Christianity* (Cambridge: Cambridge University of Press, forthcoming).

'Letter as Gift', in E.-M. Becker, U. Egelhaaf-Gaiser, and A. Fürst (eds.), *Handbuch Brief Bd. 1: Antike* (Berlin: Walter de Gruyter, forthcoming).

'Living Astutely in Neronian Rome: Paul, Seneca, and Musonius Rufus', in D. Briones, J. Dodson, and A. W. Pitts (eds.), *Reading Paul Among the Philosophers* (Grand Rapids, MI: Zondervan, forthcoming).

'Sayings of the Seven Sages', in W. Wilson (ed.), *The Library of Wisdom: An Encyclopedia of Ancient Sayings Collections* (Atlanta, GA: SBL Press, forthcoming).

'The Politics of Oneness Among Romans', in S. C. Barton and A. J. Byers (eds.), *One God, One People: Oneness, Unity, and Christian Origins* (Atlanta, GA: SBL Press, forthcoming).

2021

Edited (with P. G. Bolt), *The Impact of Jesus of Nazareth. Historical, Theological, and Pastoral Perspectives vol. 2: Social and Pastoral Studies* (CGAR Series, 2; Macquarie Park, NSW: SCD Press, 2021).

'Reactions to Roman Officialdom to Christ and His Followers in the Early First Century AD: A Case-Study of Pontius Pilate', in P.G. Bolt and J.R. Harrison (eds), *The Impact of Jesus of Nazareth: Historical, Theological, and Pastoral Perspectives Volume 2: Social and Pastoral Studies* (CGAR Series, 2; Macquarie Park, NSW: SCD Press, 2021), 27–81.

'The City of Rome from the Late Republic to the Julio-Claudian Period: An Epigraphic and Archaeological Portrait', in J. R. Harrison and L. L. Wellborn (eds.), *The First Urban Churches 6: Rome and Ostia* (WGRW, 18; Atlanta, GA: SBL Press, 2021), 1–66.

'Ostia, Harbor Port of Rome: An Epigraphic and Archaeological Portrait', in J. R. Harrison and L. L. Wellborn (eds.), *The First Urban Churches 6: Rome and Ostia* (WGRW, 18; Atlanta, GA: SBL Press, 2021), 67–136.

'Romans 1:2–4 and Imperial "Adoption" Methodology: Paul's Alternative Narrative to Julio-Claudian Sonship and Apotheosis', in J. R. Harrison and L. L. Wellborn (eds.), *The First Urban Churches 6: Rome and Ostia* (WGRW, 18; Atlanta, GA: SBL Press, 2021), 357–425.

'Social Stratification and Poverty Studies in First-Century Roman Palestine: An Evaluation of Recent Research on the Economic Context of the First Disciples', in Peter G. Bolt (ed.), *The Future of Gospels and Acts Research* (CGAR Series, 3; Macquarie Park, NSW: SCD Press, 2021), 1–49.

(With P. Harrison), 'TEE in Historical Context', in D. Burke, R. Brown, and Q. Julius (eds.), *TEE for the 21st Century: Tools to Equip and Empower God's People for His Mission* (Carlisle, UK: Langham Global Library, 2021), 99–123.

2020

Reading Romans with Roman Eyes: Studies on the Social Perspective of Romans (Paul in Critical Contexts Series; Minneapolis, MN: Fortress/Lexington, 2020).

Edited (with P. G. Bolt), *Justice, Mercy and Wellbeing. Interdisciplinary Perspectives* (Eugene, OR: Pickwick [Wipf & Stock], 2020).

Edited (with L. L. Welborn), *The First Urban Churches 6: Rome and Ostia* (WGRW, 18; Atlanta: SBL Press, 2020).

Edited (with P. G. Bolt), *The Impact of Jesus of Nazareth. Historical, Theological, and Pastoral Perspectives vol. 1. Historical and Theological Studies* (CGAR Series, 1; Macquarie Park, NSW: SCD Press, 2020).

'Introduction—Finding Well-Being in an Unjust and Unmerciful World', in P. G. Bolt and J. R. Harrison (eds.), *Justice, Mercy, And Well-Being. Interdisciplinary Perspectives* (Eugene, OR: Pickwick [Wipf & Stock], 2020), 1–30.

'The "Clemency" of Nero and Paul's Language of "Mercy" in Romans—Paul's Reconfiguration of Imperial Values in Mid-Fifties Rome', in P. G. Bolt and J. R. Harrison (eds.), *Justice, Mercy, And Well-Being. Interdisciplinary Perspectives* (Eugene, OR: Pickwick [Wipf & Stock], 2020), 193–220.

'The Polis and the Revitalisation of Its Indigenous Gods in the Second Sophistic: Ionian, Phrygian and Lydian Perspectives', in U. E. Eisen and H. Mader *Talking God in Society: Multidisciplinary (Re)constructions of Ancient (Con)texts, vol. 1: Theories and Applications* (Göttingen: Vandenhoeck & Ruprecht, 2020), 621–39.

'Two approaches to Ageing in Antiquity: Comparing Cicero's *De Senectute* and Paul's Intergenerational Relationships in Philemon and 1 Timothy', in S. Smith, E. Blair, and C. Kleemann (eds.), *Embracing Life and Gathering Wisdom: Theological, Pastoral, and Clinical Insights into Human Flourishing at the End of Life* (Occasional Series, 2; Macquarie Park, NSW: SCD Press), 247–74.

2019

Paul and the Ancient Celebrity Circuit: The Cross and Moral Transformation (WUNT, 430; Tübingen: Mohr Siebeck, 2019).

Edited, E. A. Judge, *Paul and the Conflict of Cultures: The Legacy of His Thought Today* (Eugene, OR: Cascade, 2019).

Edited (with P. G. Bolt), *Romans and the Legacy of St Paul. Historical, Theological, and Social Perspectives* (Occasional Series, 1; Macquarie Park, NSW: SCD Press, 2019).

Edited (with L. L. Welborn), *The First Urban Churches. 5: Colossae, Hierapolis, and Laodicea* (WGRW, 16; Atlanta, GA: SBL Press, 2019).

'Judging the Legacy of Paul', in E. A. Judge, *Paul and the Conflict of Cultures: The Legacy of His Thought Today* (Eugene, OR: Cascade Books, 2019), 3–48.

(with A. H. Cadwallader) 'Perspectives on the Lycus Valley: An Inscriptional, Archaeological, Numismatic, and Iconographic Approach', in J. R. Harrison & L. L. Welborn (eds.), *The First Urban Churches. 5: Colossae, Hierapolis, and Laodicea* (WGRW, 16; Atlanta, GA: SBL Press, 2019), 3–70.

'Romans and the Western Intellectual Tradition: From Church to Society and Back Again', in P. G. Bolt and J. R. Harrison (eds.), *Romans and the Legacy of St Paul. Historical, Theological, and Social Perspectives* (Occasional Series, 1; Macquarie Park, NSW: SCD Press, 2019), 3–15.

'Paul's Legacy in Romans and the Confession Inscriptions of Asia Minor: The Difficulty of Moving Beyond Divine Justice to Mercy in Antiquity', in P. G. Bolt and J. R. Harrison (eds.), *Romans and the Legacy of St Paul. Historical, Theological, and Social Perspectives* (Occasional Series, 1; Macquarie Park, NSW: SCD Press, 2019), 337–88.

(with P.G. Bolt and P. Laughlin) 'The Legacy of Paul's Epistle to the Romans: From Augustine to Agamben', in P. G. Bolt and J. R. Harrison (eds.), *Romans and the Legacy of St Paul. Historical, Theological, and Social Perspectives* (Occasional Series, 1; Macquarie Park, NSW: SCD Press, 2019), 455–518.

'The Inscriptions and Oracular Prophecy in the Eastern Mediterranean Basin: Assessing the Book of Revelation in Its Graeco-Roman Revelatory Context', in J. R. Harrison and L. L. Welborn (eds.), *The First Urban Churches. 5: Colossae, Hierapolis, and Laodicea* (WGRW, 16; Atlanta, GA: SBL Press, 2019), 363–415.

'The Rhetoric of "Consolation" in 2 Corinthians 1:3–11/7:4–13 in the Context of the Jewish and Graeco-Roman Consolatory Literature', in S. E. Porter and C. D. Land (eds.), *Paul and Scripture* (Pauline Studies, 10; Leiden: Brill, 2019), 233–62.

2018

Edited (with L. L. Welborn), *The First Urban Churches* 4: *Roman Philippi* (WGRW, 13; Atlanta, GA: SBL Press, 2018).

Edited (with L. L. Welborn), *The First Urban Churches* 3: *Ephesus* (WGRW, 9; Atlanta, GA: SBL Press, 2018).

'An Epigraphic Portrait of Ephesus and Its Villages', in J. R. Harrison and L. L. Welborn (eds.), *The First Urban Churches* 3: *Ephesus* (WGRW, 9; Atlanta, GA: SBL Press, 2018), 1–67.

'Ephesian Cultic Officials, Their Benefactors, and the Quest for Civic Virtue: Paul's Alternative Quest for Status in the Epistle to the Ephesians', in J. R. Harrison and L. L. Welborn (eds.), *The First Urban Churches* 3: *Ephesus* (WGRW, 9; Atlanta, GA: SBL Press, 2018), 253–331.

'Excavating the Urban and Country Life of Roman Philippi and Its Territory', in J. R. Harrison and L. L. Welborn (eds.), *The First Urban Churches* 4: *Roman Philippi* (WGRW, 13; Atlanta, GA: SBL Press, 2018), 1–61.

'From Rome to the Colony of Philippi: Roman Boasting in Philippians 3:4–6 in Its Latin West and Philippian Epigraphic Context', in J. R. Harrison and L. L. Welborn (eds.), *The First Urban Churches* 4: *Roman Philippi* (WGRW, 13; Atlanta, GA: SBL Press, 2018), 307–70.

'The Apostle Paul and the Spiral of Roman Violence', in N. Elliott and W. H. Kelber (eds.), *Bridges in New Testament Interpretation* (Minneapolis, MN: Fortress, 2018), 119–47.

'The Historical Jesus as "Social Critic": An Investigation of Luke 6:27–36', *Journal of Gospels and Acts Research* 2 (2018), 53–74.

2017

Paul's Language of Grace in Its Graeco-Roman Context (Tübingen: Mohr Siebeck, 2003; Reprint, Eugene, OR: Wipf and Stock, 2017). [with new 'Introduction' to the Second Edition]

Edited (with D. Costache and D. Cronshaw), *Well-being, Personal Wholeness and the Social Fabric* (Cambridge: Cambridge Scholars Press, 2017).

'Beneficence to the Poor in Luke's Gospel in Its Mediterranean Context: A Visual and Documentary Approach', *Australian Biblical Review* 65 (2017), 30–46.

'Introducing Well-being, Personal Wholeness and the Australian Social Fabric: Ancient and Modern Perspectives', in D. Costache, D. Cronshaw, and J. R. Harrison (eds.), *Well-being, Personal Wholeness and the Social Fabric* (Cambridge: Cambridge Scholars Press, 2017), 2–30.

'"Laughter is the Best Medicine": St Paul, Well-being, and Roman Humour', in D. Costache, D. Cronshaw, and J. R. Harrison (eds.), *Well-being, Personal Wholeness and the Social Fabric* (Cambridge: Cambridge Scholars Press, 2017), 209–40.

'Jesus and the Grace of the Cross: Luke 23:34a and the Politics of "Forgiveness" in Antiquity', *Journal of Gospels and Acts Research* 1 (2017), 42–67.

'The Persecution of Christians from Nero to Hadrian', in M. Harding and A. Nobbs (eds.), *Into All the World: Emergent Christianity in Its Jewish and Greco-Roman Context* (Grand Rapids, MI: Eerdmans, 2017), 266–300.

Review of C. M. Hays, *Renouncing Everything: Money and Discipleship in Luke* (New York/Mahwah, NJ: Paulist, 2016) in *Journal of Gospels and Acts Research* 1 (2017), 93–6.

2016

Edited (with L. L. Welborn), *The First Urban Churches* 2: *Roman Corinth* (WGRW, 8; Atlanta, GA: SBL Press, 2016).

'Excavating the Urban Life of Roman Corinth', in J. R. Harrison and L. L. Welborn (eds.), *The First Urban Churches 2: Roman Corinth* (WGRW, 8; Atlanta, GA: SBL Press, 2016), 1–45.

'Paul and Empire II: Negotiating the Seduction of Imperial "Peace and Security" in Galatians, Thessalonians and Philippians', in A. Winn (ed.), *New Testament and Empire* (Atlanta: SBL Press, 2016), 165–84.

'Paul and the *agōnothetai* at Corinth: Engaging the Civic Values of Antiquity' in J. R. Harrison and L. L. Welborn (eds.), *The First Urban Churches* 2: *Roman Corinth* (WGRW, 8; Atlanta, GA: SBL Press, 2016), 271–326.

'Sponsors of *Paideia*: Ephesian Benefactors, Civic Virtue and the New Testament', *Early Christianity* 7.3 (2016), 346–67.

'The Erasure of Honour: Paul and the Politics of Dishonour', *Tyndale Bulletin* 66.2 (2016), 161–84.

'The Seven Sages, The Delphic Canon and Ethical Education in Antiquity', in M. R. Hauge and A. W. Pitts (eds.), *Ancient Education and Early Christianity* (London/New York: Bloomsbury T&T Clark, 2016), 71–86.

'Who Is the "Lord of Grace"? Jesus' Parables in Imperial Context', in A. Weissenrieder (ed.), *Borders: Terms, Ideologies and Performances* (Tübingen: Mohr Siebeck, 2016), 383–417.

2015

Edited (with L. Ball), *Learning and Teaching Theology: Some Ways Ahead* (Northcote: Morning Star, 2014; reprinted, Eugene, OR: Wipf and Stock, 2015).

Edited (with L. L. Welborn), *The First Urban Churches, 1: Methodological Foundations* (WGRW, 7; Atlanta, GA: SBL Press, 2015).

Edited (with Y. Debergue), *Teaching Theology in a Technological Age* (Cambridge; Cambridge Scholars Press, 2015).

'Developing Personal Resilience in a Dangerous Virtual World: Historical, Social Biblical and Theological Perspectives', in J. R. Harrison and Y. Debergue (eds.), *Teaching Theology in a Technological Age* (Cambridge; Cambridge Scholars Press, 2015), 86–112.

'Paul and Ancient Civic Ethics: Redefining the Canon of Honour in the Graeco-Roman World', in C. Breytenbach (ed.), *Paul's Graeco-Roman Context* (Leuven: Peeters, 2015), 75–118.

'The First Urban Churches: Introduction', in J. R. Harrison and L. L. Welborn (eds.), *The First Urban Churches* 1: *Methodological Foundations* (WGRW Supp, 7; Atlanta, GA: SBL Press, 2015), 1–40.

'Tracking God's Digital Footprint', in J. R. Harrison and Y. Debergue (eds.), *Teaching Theology in a Technological Age* (Cambridge: Cambridge Scholars Press, 2015), 3–13.

'Urban Portraits of the "Barbarians" on the Fringes of the Roman Empire: The Archaeological, Numismatic, Epigraphic, and Iconographic Evidence', in J. R. Harrison and L. L. Welborn (eds.), *The First Urban Churches* 1: *Methodological Foundations* (WGRW Supp, 7; Atlanta, GA: SBL Press, 2015), 277–317.

2014

Edited (with L. Ball), *Learning and Teaching Theology: Some Ways Ahead* (Northcote: Morning Star, 2014).

'Paul and the Ancient Gymnasium: Research Paradigms for "Academic Citizens" of the New World', in L. Ball and J. R. Harrison (eds.), *Learning and Teaching Theology: Some Ways Ahead* (Northcote: Morning Star Publications, 2014), 33–48.

Review of A. J. Harrill, *Paul the Apostle: His Life and Legacy in Their Roman Context* (New York: Cambridge University Press, 2012) in *Review of Biblical Literature* 01/2014 (online).

Review of H. V. A. Kuma, *The Centrality of Αἷμα (Blood) in the Theology of the Epistle to the Hebrews: An Exegetical and Philological Study* (Lewiston / Queenstown/ Lampeter: Edwin Mellen, 2012) in *Review of Biblical Literature* 04/2014 (online).

2013

'Augustan Rome and the Body of Christ: A Comparison of the Social Vision of the *Res Gestae* and Paul's Letter to the Romans', *Harvard Theological Review* 106.1 (2013), 1–36.

'Modern Scholarship and the "Nature" Miracles: A Defence of Their Historicity and Affirmation of Jesus' Deity', *Reformed Theological Review* 72.2 (2013), 86–102.

'Paul among the Romans', in M. Harding and A. Nobbs (eds.), *All Things to All Cultures: Paul among Jews, Greeks and Romans* (Grand Rapids, MI: Eerdmans, 2013), 143–76.

'Paul's "Indebtedness" to the Barbarian (Rom 1:14) in Latin West Perspective', *Novum Testamentum* 55.4 (2013), 311–48.

'The Imitation of the Great Man in Antiquity: Paul's Inversion of a Cultural Icon', in S. E. Porter and A. W. Pitts (eds.), *Christian Origins and Greco-Roman Culture: Social and Literary Contexts for the New Testament* (TENTS, 9; Leiden: Brill, 2013), 213–54.

'The Politics of Family Beneficence: Paul's "Parenthood" in First-Century Context (2 Cor 12:14–16)', in R. Beiringer, M. S. Ibita, and T. A. Vollmer (eds.), *Theologizing in the Corinthian Conflict: Studies in Exegesis and Theology of 2 Corinthians* (Leuven: Peeters, 2013), 399–426.

2012

Edited (with S. R. Llewelyn), *New Documents Illustrating Early Christianity vol. 10* (Grand Rapids, MI: Eerdmans, 2012).

'Overcoming the "Strong Man"', in J. R. Harrison and S. R. Llewelyn (eds.), *New Documents Illustrating Early Christianity vol. 10* (Grand Rapids, MI: Eerdmans, 2012), 10–15.

'All Grades of Angels', in J. R. Harrison and S. R. Llewelyn (eds.), *New Documents Illustrating Early Christianity vol. 10* (Grand Rapids, MI: Eerdmans, 2012), 16–19.

'Livia as Hekate', in J. R. Harrison and S. R. Llewelyn (eds.), *New Documents Illustrating Early Christianity vol. 10* (Grand Rapids, MI: Eerdmans, 2012), 26–30.

'Family Honour of a Priestess of Artemis', in J. R. Harrison and S. R. Llewelyn (eds.), *New Documents Illustrating Early Christianity vol. 10* (Grand Rapids, MI: Eerdmans, 2012), 31–38.

'Artemis Triumphs over a Sorcerer's Evil Art', in J. R. Harrison and S. R. Llewelyn (eds.), *New Documents Illustrating Early Christianity vol. 10* (Grand Rapids, MI: Eerdmans, 2012), 39–49.

'A "worthy" neopoios Thanks Artemis', in J. R. Harrison and S. R. Llewelyn (eds.), *New Documents Illustrating Early Christianity vol. 10* (Grand Rapids, MI: Eerdmans, 2012), 50–56.

'The "Grace" of Augustus Paves a Street at Ephesus', in J. R. Harrison and S. R. Llewelyn (eds.), *New Documents Illustrating Early Christianity vol. 10* (Grand Rapids, MI: Eerdmans, 2012), 61–66.

'Diplomacy over Tiberius' Accession', in J. R. Harrison and S. R. Llewelyn (eds.), *New Documents Illustrating Early Christianity vol. 10* (Grand Rapids, MI: Eerdmans, 2012), 67–80.

'Every Dog Has Its Day', in J. R. Harrison and S. R. Llewelyn (eds.), *New Documents Illustrating Early Christianity vol. 10* (Grand Rapids, MI: Eerdmans, 2012), 136–45.

'Paul and the Social Relations of Death at Rome (Rom 5:14, 17, 21)', in S. E. Porter and C. D. Land (eds.), *Paul and His Social Relations* (Pauline Studies 7; Leiden: Brill, 2012), 85–123.

'Humility', in M. Gilmour (ed.), *Dictionary of the Bible and Western Culture* (Sheffield: Sheffield Phoenix, 2012), 203–204.

'Poor, Poverty', in M. Gilmour (ed.), *The Dictionary of the Bible and Western Culture* (Sheffield: Sheffield Phoenix, 2012), 406–407.

'Simon the Zealot', in M. Gilmour (ed.), *The Dictionary of the Bible and Western Culture* (Sheffield Phoenix, 2012), 498–99.

'Third Heaven', in M. Gilmour (ed.), *The Dictionary of the Bible and Western Culture* (Sheffield: Sheffield Phoenix, 2012), 542.

Review of B. W. Longenecker (ed.) *Remember the Poor: Paul, Poverty, and the Greco-Roman World* (Grand Rapids, MI: Eerdmans, 2010) in *Biblical Theology Review* 42 (2012), 108–109.

Review of the SBL 2011 Consultation 'Polis and Ekklesia', in *Henoch* 34/1 (2012), 196–98.

2011

Paul and the Imperial Authorities at Thessalonica and Rome: A Study in the Conflict of Ideology (WUNT, 273; Tübingen: Mohr Siebeck, 2011).

'"More Than Conquerors" (Rom 8:37), Paul's Gospel and the Augustan Triumphal Arches of the Greek East and Latin West', *Buried History* 47 (2011), 3–21.

Review of C. N. Toney, *Paul's inclusive Ethic: Resolving Community Conflicts and Promoting Mission in Romans 14–15* (Tübingen: Mohr Siebeck, 2008), in *Review of Biblical Literature* 10/03/11 (online).

2010

'The Social Context', in M. Harding and A. Nobbs (eds.), *The Content and Setting of the Gospel Tradition* (Grand Rapids, MI: Eerdmans, 2010), 105–26.

'The Brothers as the "Glory of Christ" (2 Cor 8:23), Paul's *Doxa* Terminology in Its Ancient Benefaction Context', *Novum Testamentum* 52 (2010), 156–88.

2009

'Paul and the Roman Ideal of Glory in the Epistle to the Romans', in U. Schnelle (ed.), *The Epistle to the Romans* (Leuven: Leuven University Press, 2009), 323–63.

2008

Edited, E. A. Judge, *The First Christians in the Roman World: Augustan and New Testament Essays* (Tübingen: Mohr Siebeck, 2008).

'Preface' and 'Introduction' in E. A. Judge, *The First Christians in the Roman World* (Tübingen: Mohr Siebeck, 2008), ix–xiii, 1–31.

'Paul and the Gymnasiarchs: Two Approaches to Pastoral Formation in Antiquity', in S. E. Porter (ed.), *Paul: Jew, Greek, and Roman* (Pauline Studies 5; Leiden: Brill, 2008), 141–78.

2007

'Paul and the Athletic Ideal in Antiquity: A Case Study in Wrestling with Word and Image', in S. E. Porter (ed.), *Paul's World: Pauline Studies vol. IV* (Leiden: Brill, 2007), 81–109.

2006

'Paul, Theologian of Electing Grace', in S. E. Porter (ed.), *Paul the Theologian* (Pauline Studies 3; Leiden: Brill, 2006), 77–108.

'Paul Goes to Rome', in B. J. Beitzel (ed.), *Biblica: The Bible Atlas* (Sydney: Global Books, 2006), 478–83.

'The Third Journey of Paul', in B. J. Beitzel (ed.), *Biblica: The Bible Atlas* (Sydney, NSW: Global Books, 2006), 484–89.

2005

Review of J. A. Glancy, *Slavery in Early Christianity* (Oxford: Oxford University Press, 2002) in *International Journal of the Classical Tradition* 11.3 (2005), 471–73.

2004

'Why Did Josephus and Paul Refuse to Circumcise?', *Pacifica* 17.2 (2004), 137–58.

'In Quest of the Third Heaven: Paul and His Apocalyptic Imitators', *Vigiliae Christianae* 58.1 (2004), 24–55.

2003

Paul's Language of Grace in Its Graeco-Roman Context (WUNT II, 172; Tübingen: Mohr Siebeck, 2003).

'"The Fading Crown": Divine Honour and the Early Christians', *Journal of Theological Studies* 54.2 (2003), 493-529.

2002

'A Share in All the Sacrifices', in S. R. Llewelyn (ed.), *New Documents Illustrating Early Christianity vol. 9* (Grand Rapids, MI: Eerdmans, 2002), 1-3.

'Saviour of the People', in S. R. Llewelyn (ed.), *New Documents Illustrating Early Christianity vol. 9* (Grand Rapids, MI: Eerdmans, 2002), 4-5.

'Benefactor of the People', in S. R. Llewelyn (ed.), *New Documents Illustrating Early Christianity vol. 9* (Grand Rapids, MI: Eerdmans, 2002), 6.

'Times of Necessity', in S. R. Llewelyn (ed.), *New Documents Illustrating Early Christianity vol. 9* (Grand Rapids, MI: Eerdmans, 2002), 7-8.

'Excels Ancestral Honours', in S. R. Llewelyn (ed.), *New Documents Illustrating Early Christianity vol. 9* (Grand Rapids, MI: Eerdmans, 2002), 20-1.

'Paul and the Imperial Gospel at Thessaloniki', *Journal for the Study of the New Testament*, 25.1 (2002), 71-96.

1999

'Paul, Eschatology and the Augustan Age of Grace', *Tyndale Bulletin* 50.1 (1999), 79-91.

'Paul and the Cultic Associations', *Reformed Theological Review* 58.1 (1999), 31-47.

1997

'Benefaction Ideology and Christian Responsibility for Widows', in S. R. Llewelyn (ed.), *New Documents Illustrating Early Christianity vol. 8* (Grand Rapids, MI: Eerdmans, 1997), 106-16.

1989

Review of A. J. Podlecki's *Plutarch Life of Pericles: A Companion to the Penguin Translation* (Bristol: Bristol Classical Press, 1987), in *Ancient History: Resources for Teachers* 19.2 (1989), 108-110.

Online Bibliographies

'Virtues and Vices: The New Testament in Its Graeco-Roman Context', *Oxford Online Bibliographies.*

www.ingramcontent.com/pod-product-compliance
Lightning Source LLC
Chambersburg PA
CBHW072042110526
44590CB00018B/3005